AF845855

The ECONOMICS of COMMUNIST EASTERN EUROPE

The ECONOMICS of COMMUNIST EASTERN EUROPE

NICOLAS SPULBER

Associate Professor of Economics
Indiana University

GREENWOOD PRESS, PUBLISHERS
WESTPORT, CONNECTICUT

Library of Congress Cataloging in Publication Data

Spulber, Nicolas.
The economics of Communist Eastern Europe.

Reprint of the ed. published by Technology Press of Massachusetts Institute of Technology, Cambridge, in series: Technology Press books in the social sciences.
Bibliography: p.
Includes index.
1. Europe, Eastern--Economic conditions.
I. Title.
[HC244.S6 1976] 330.9'43 76-13904
ISBN 0-8371-8609-9

Copyright © 1957
by
The Massachusetts Institute of Technology

All Rights Reserved

This book or any part thereof must not be reproduced in any form without the written permission of the publisher.

Originally published in 1957 by The Technology Press of Massachusetts Institute of Technology, Cambridge, Mass., and John Wiley & Sons, Inc., New York

Reprinted with the permission of The MIT Press

Reprinted in 1976 by Greenwood Press, a division of Williamhouse-Regency Inc.

Library of Congress Catalog Card Number 76-13904

ISBN 0-8371-8609-9

Printed in the United States of America

FOREWORD

The analysis of recent history is a perilous exercise. Today's headlines inevitably set the framework against which we interpret the events of the last five or ten years. A new headline tomorrow, while it cannot alter the hard facts as to what occurred where and when, may radically alter our appraisal of the significance of those facts.

This book is one of a series of studies launched by the Center for International Studies in 1952 when the Communist world was still ruled by the will of Josef Stalin. At that time it looked as though the patterns of social, economic, and political control which the Russians had established over the Eastern European countries might last for some decades and might even be extended, if things went badly, to other countries still in the Free World. We felt that there was needed a description of those patterns which would be as detailed and objective as careful scholarly research could make it.

As work on the studies has progressed, we have been confronted by a series of headlines each of which has changed our conception of why we were doing the study. Stalin died, and his immediate heirs soon gave evidence, both within the Soviet Union and in their policies in the satellites, that they had a somewhat different conception of tactics if not of strategy. Malenkov's "new course" brought with it a shift of emphasis in economic planning. His subsequent unusually gentle fall from grace raised speculation as to what the Khrushchev era might bring. The shattering events in Poland and Hungary in the fall of 1956 made plain that for the satellites the postwar decade was a transition not to a new long period of subjugated stability but to still more radical changes whose full consequences have not unfolded themselves as I write this.

We were very fortunate in being able to persuade Nicolas Spulber to undertake this examination of the economies of the Eastern European countries during the postwar period. He had done a great deal of work on this subject before he joined the Center staff in 1952, and has spent a good deal of time on it since his departure to accept a post at Indiana University in 1954. His conception of his task was fortunately one well designed to withstand the shock of rapidly changing events.

He has not only assembled and presented in orderly fashion every scrap of quantitative information he could find relating to the East European economies since 1945 but also kept his material under review and revision up to the completion of his manuscript in the spring of 1957. The result is more than a handbook of factual information on which others could reliably depend in making their own evaluations; for he has explored the implications of the policies of autonomy and integration in the Soviet orbit, the mechanisms and the propects of trade, and, perhaps most significantly, the limitations of the Soviet model of growth.

As Professor Spulber has stressed in his introduction, the bulk of the data contained in the book's 138 tables is derived of necessity from official sources; and he discusses his reasons for believing that in spite of the absence of conclusive checks the official data can be used, with appropriate reservations, to portray structural change in these economies. His arguments seem to me to carry weight, but the reader will have to make his own judgments on this question.

World War II and the years which have followed have brought fundamental changes in the economies of the Eastern European countries which will leave their mark on whatever history has in store for these nations. Whether Communist economic policy, Soviet style, persists, or the tendencies apparent in Poland toward a more liberal consumer-oriented and market-directed economy gather force and momentum, future changes can be appraised only in the light of a detailed picture of what has already happened in these countries. Professor Spulber has drawn such a picture for us and thus provided an indispensable point of departure for all subsequent studies of the economies of contemporary Eastern Europe.

MAX F. MILLIKAN

Cambridge, Massachusetts
March 16, 1957

PREFACE

The basic research for this book has been carried on over a number of years. The preliminary draft of this study was completed during the two years extending from the summer of 1952 to the summer of 1954, when I was associated with the Center for International Studies, Massachusetts Institute of Technology. The manuscript was brought up to date and revised for publication throughout 1955, 1956, and 1957.

For the completion of this book and for its publication in its present form, I am deeply indebted to Professors Max F. Millikan and Everett Hagen and to Mr. Richard W. Hatch.

Professor Millikan, the director of the Center for International Studies, manifested a kind understanding of the difficulties connected with the preparation and completion of the work and throughout extended his moral support.

Professor Hagen subjected the entire draft to a critical examination and made numerous comments and suggestions which were invaluable to the completion of the book.

Mr. Hatch patiently edited the manuscript and gave it a great deal of time, energy, and thought. Whenever necessary, he eliminated, so far as possible, obscurities of language and form.

Thanks are also due to Professor George B. Baldwin and to Messrs. Andrew Brimmer and Agit Biswas, as well as to others from the Center, for their helpful advice and suggestions during the preparation of the manuscript. I am grateful to Professor Norman J. G. Pounds, of Indiana University, for having prepared the two maps of Eastern Europe.

Mrs. Ruth Hollis, Miss Ann Gilligan, and Miss Dee Winn did arduous and competent secretarial work during the two years of the preparation of the preliminary draft.

An indirect, but valuable, contribution to the revision of the study was made by the Graduate Faculty of Indiana University, whose research grants enabled me to carry on some of the research needed in this respect in 1955 and 1956.

Thanks are also due to the publishers who have kindly granted permission for quotation from copyrighted materials: Harper and Brothers: *Let's Do Business with Russia,* Stela K. Margold; Radio Free Europe: *Satellite Agriculture in Crisis,* from a study by Nicolas Spulber included in the text; and, *Economic Treaties and Agreements of the Soviet Bloc in Eastern Europe, 1945–1951;* The Royal Institute of International Affairs: *Soviet Trade with Eastern Europe 1945–1949,* Margaret Dewar; and, "Agricultural Surplus Population in Eastern and South Eastern Europe," Dr. P. N. Rosenstein-Rodan (unpublished paper); Simon and Schuster: *Tito,* Vladimir Dedijer; *World Politics:* "East European Developments in Social Economic Structure," George Kemény.

As usual, all errors are the sole responsibility of the author.

NICOLAS SPULBER

Bloomington, Indiana
July 22, 1957

CONTENTS

CHAPTER

CHARTS AND MAPS

CHART

TABLES

TABLE

TABLE

TABLE

TABLE

INTRODUCTION

This book proposes to study the structural changes in the economies of Eastern Europe after World War II, their performance under Communist planning, and their prospective development. The focus is on the economic aspects of these problems; the concomitant changes on the political scene are taken for granted.

The changes undergone by this region and the complex relations that have developed between it and Soviet Russia are of obvious importance for understanding the pattern of socioeconomic displacements that can be expected to occur under the conditions of any extension of the Soviet sphere. Conversely, they are illuminative of certain developments which have occurred in Soviet Russia itself. Viewed through the prismatic refractions of six countries with dissimilar traditions and different levels of development and resources, certain accepted assumptions (derived, for instance, from the Soviet process of growth) can be retested and examined from new angles.

The term Eastern Europe is taken here as embracing the following countries: Czechoslovakia, Poland, Hungary, Romania, Bulgaria, and Yugoslavia, i.e., the countries that have reshaped their economy (like Soviet Russia) on the basis of large-scale nationalization of production and distribution and of over-all planning. The term Eastern Europe is a compromise between geographic and political realities. Geographically there is no reason why the term should not include other countries, e.g., Greece or Albania. On the other hand, although, from the point of view of the economic changes mentioned, Greece must be excluded, there is no reason why the term should not include Albania and perhaps even Eastern Germany. We have, however, for a variety of reasons, excluded these two countries also. Up to the middle of 1948 small Albania was tied closely, almost as a satellite, to the Yugoslav economy; afterwards it developed in isolation for one or two years. East Germany was handled as a Soviet colony up to the turn of 1949, when it started to enter quite slowly as an "autonomous unit" into the economic circuit of the region. Both these countries thus had a specific evolution remote from that of the entire group on which we are focusing. Finally, it should be added that, despite the fact that for Yugoslavia centralized planning since 1950 has started to mean something different from what it meant in other countries of the area, its inclusion in this study appeared indispensable. This is so not only because these changes present interesting variations in the same framework (i.e., that of a largely nationalized economy) but also because the Yugoslav displacements have left lasting imprints on the area as a whole.

There have been analyses of the postwar evolutions in Eastern Europe based on the summary and scattered data reported in the Soviet press.[1] However, there is an abundance of data and statistics from East European sources which is usually overlooked. It is essentially from the latter that this study has been constructed. Up to early 1949 most of these countries published complete and detailed statistics and information on the changes occurring in their economies. After the deepening of the break with the West and the parting of Yugoslavia from the Soviet orbit (in 1948), the data released became scarce and less and less complete, a condition which prevailed until the middle of 1953 when information started again to be released from official sources in quite significant amounts and in usable form. These data illuminate up to a certain point some of the areas obscured by lack of information during the 1949–53 period.

Although East European statistics continue to exhibit many of their traditional methodological differences, they are becoming more uniform as more and more data are collected, processed, and published according to the Russian system. Before 1949 the national differences had, of course, been greater. Up to that date the economic information and statistics for countries like Czechoslovakia, Poland, Bulgaria, and Hungary represented a solid and detailed coverage in many fields. The Romanian data presented many deficiencies and were often incomplete. The Yugoslavs have built an impressive body of information and statistics mostly since 1950, which compensates for the almost total lack of data for the period before their break with the Soviet orbit. The differences in methods and coverage are evidently one of the biggest obstacles in the way of any attempt at achieving a uniform and complete tabulation for each topic for the region as a whole.

Since 1949 much information has been made available, in increased amounts, as in Soviet Russia, through official pronouncements, often

[1] Typical of these is the book by Margaret Dewar, *Soviet Trade with Eastern Europe 1945–1949,* Royal Institute of International Affairs, London, 1951.

contradictory in detail and lacking precision either in their formulation or in the explanation of the units counted. It is difficult to chart some areas of inquiry, as certain data are still withheld and the nexus between series of statistics is broken. As considerable data are embodied in political speeches or political publications, there is quite often a problem of sifting, comparing, and discarding a great deal of superfluous and disconnected material. The continuous shaping of the data according to Russian patterns is accompanied by the typical shortcomings and peculiarities of Russian statistical methods and reporting, which often tend to be combined, for the worse, with the ingrained national shortcomings. Thus, for instance, the almost built-in system of upwardly biased reporting of all the planned performances, characteristic of Soviet Russia, has also become a distinctive trait of East European statistics since 1949. Equally common is the method of expressing performances as percentage increases, when the absolute data for the base year are lacking. Romania, for instance, has carried this practice learned from the Russians almost to perfection. Finally (and this is a problem familiar to all students of Soviet Russia's economy), there is no way of checking on the spot the exact significance of most of the claimed performances.

On the other hand, the handling of these data undoubtedly presents certain specific facilities which do not exist in the case of Soviet Russia's statistics: (1) for Eastern Europe, there are better checks on the general reliability of the present-day information, given the solid coverage up to the middle of 1948. (2) Certain data on the postwar changes, published by persons who directly participated in these events as late as 1948/49, illuminate many aspects which official data tend more or less to obscure.[2] The question still remains, for Eastern Europe as for Russia, whether, in spite of these checks and the close basis of comparison, any valid use of the official data can be made.

It is the author's feeling that this question should be answered in the affirmative. These statistics can and should be used. It is not the writer's intention to repeat here some of the arguments presented with reference to Soviet Russia refuting the often repeated contention that we might be confronted in the case of those economies with a double set of data: one produced for the outside world and another set kept in storage by the policy makers of these countries for their own

[2] Thus, for instance, the excellent book of George Kemény, *Economic Planning in Hungary, 1947–49*, Royal Institute of International Affairs, London, 1952, presents a penetrating analysis of Hungary under planning up to 1949, based on personal experience.

use. To our mind the data released are the *frame of reference* of the East European policy makers and economists themselves, and represent (notwithstanding their obvious shortcomings, often exasperating lack of precision, and defective methodology) the only possible bases for coherent research in this field.[3] It should be added that at various decisive historical turning points substantial data are released that tend to place in a clear perspective many trends willingly obscured previously. Quite often official statements correct the past defective reporting and overestimated accomplishments. Certain planned targets of various of these countries, although sometimes great in relation to the past, appear quite modest not only by Western standards but even when compared to the other countries of the orbit itself. Moreover, the constant regional and functional comparison of this set of six countries, underlining implicitly the range of possible development of each of the national units considered, and in each economic sector, has the advantage of furnishing a supplementary step-by-step check on the consistency of the data released and their inner connections. The positive existence of this consistency *as between countries* reinforces in our mind the argument of those who think that this type of material, including that of the Soviet Union, can and should be used, subject to the qualifications of prudence and constant checking of the data from a multiplicity of angles. This is not an empty generalization; certain official measurements, such as the index numbers of industrial production, as well as the data on the net material product, are very imperfect and must be handled with the utmost circumspection.[4]

This being so, it has been argued that, after all, the official data deserves to be treated only as the raw material for new computations if one wants to achieve accuracy and comparability with the Western data. While recognizing the validity of this argument, the author has, however, considered that an adequate goal was first to explore all the implications contained in the official data such as they are and to combine the elements available into uniform tabulations for the area as a whole. Notwithstanding their deficiencies, these data do illustrate both the concrete deviations from the planned patterns of development, and the differences arising in development among the various

[3] See the exhaustive presentation of the elements of this discussion in Professor Abram Bergson's Introduction to his book, *Soviet National Income and Product in 1937,* Columbia University Press, New York, 1953, pp. 6–9.

[4] See below, Introductory Note to Section III, pp. 272 ff., and to Chapter 12, pp. 469 ff.

countries and regions of the area. The author looks upon his study only as a point of departure: new analyses should follow on each and every problem considered, and should evolve finally indicators comparable to those of the West.

Two basic periods can be distinguished in the post-World War II evolution of the area considered. The first extends up to the early part of 1949; the second starts in 1949 and continues to this day.

During the first period these economies presented a "complicated interweaving of various types of social-economic structures—socialism, private economy, capitalism and partly state capitalism, petty-commodity economy, and in some countries even a patriarchal economy."[5] Large state sectors in banking and industry, but also capitalist undertakings in industry and trade, joint state and private companies in wholesale and in the foreign trade business, small producers in the crafts lines and in the countryside—those were the different types of ownership combining in the body economic in varying degrees from one country to the next. Trade with the West was at the time more important for certain of these countries than the trade among themselves and with the Soviet Union. Planning was undertaken, as in the Soviet Union up to 1928, more by sectors than on an "all-round" basis.

All these forms of property and economic relations were brutally overturned in 1948/49. The large-scale extension of nationalization in all the spheres outside agriculture, the beginning of a collectivization drive in the latter, and the launching of long-term plans of development substantially eradicated many structural and organizational differences existing among those countries during the first period. Planning started to be, as in the Soviet Union after 1928, on an "all-round" basis, affecting every aspect of economic life.

Trade with the West began to decline sharply, and later increased only spasmodically in certain years and with certain countries, while trade within the Soviet orbit started to become decisive for each of the countries of the area. In this second period various phases can be distinguished. The first phase extended from 1948–49 to the middle of 1953 and can be broadly defined as the phase of the first long-term plan. The second phase extended from 1953 to 1955 and can be defined as the phase of the "new course." The third phase, opened at

[5] Hilary Minc, "Concerning the Basis of Planning in the People's Democracy," in *FLP*, Nov. 18, 1949.

the beginning of 1956, introduced a new quinquennium, scheduled to last up to the end of 1960. This third phase was, however, cut short toward the end of 1956, at least for some countries of the area.

The beginning of both the basic periods and the specific phases within each period is marked by a convergence of events of a political or economic nature. Thus the end of the first period and beginning of the second, 1948–49, coincides with the deepening of the break with the West, started in 1947–48 and the drifting away of Yugoslavia in the middle of 1948. Within the satellite bloc the end of the first period is marked by the extension of nationalization to all the spheres of activity of these economies, and by the launching of long-range planning in each of the countries considered; the progressive entrance of East Germany into the economic circuit of the region as an "autonomous" unit; and the broadening of the trade among these countries and with the Soviet Union. The end of the first phase of the second period, and the beginning of a "new course" in 1953, appear also as the product of a convergence of events: e.g., the death of Stalin, the first open revolt in East Germany, the agricultural crisis in the Soviet Union and in the area as a whole. It is marked by the revision of the long-range targets of the plans inaugurated previously, a reappraisal of the agricultural policy, a new allocation of resources with a view toward increasing consumption, and an implicit slowing of the previous rate of growth of the economy. The end of this phase in 1954–55 corresponds also to political changes: e.g., the shifts in the top hierarchy of the Soviet Union, namely, the replacement of Georgi Malenkov by Nikita Khrushchev at the summit of the Soviet "apparatus."

No sooner had the second plans of development begun than they were thrown out of gear by the upheavals in Poland and Hungary in the autumn of 1956. The broad Hungarian revolt of October–November 1956—the first mass revolt since the extension of the Soviet bloc to the West—suddenly placed in jeopardy the Communist control in that country and the planning and trade in the area as a whole.

Although the impact of all the political factors is clearly of tremendous significance, its analysis falls outside the stated scope of this work. The focus will here be kept only on the economic factors that distinguished one period, or one phase, from the next.

Two main topics are related in this work to the two basic periods 1944–45 to 1948–49 and 1948–49 to the present. The first concerns the process of nationalization and structural reorganization of the various spheres of the economy and is considered in Chapters 3 to 7, inclusive; the second deals with the process of planning and the performance of these countries under planning and is discussed in Chapters 8 to 11, inclusive.

The choice of a given pace in the application of various economic policies as well as the method and the results obtained in the conditions prevailing in Eastern Europe are quite indicative of the changes and patterns of evolution of Soviet Russia itself: in a sense, Eastern Europe is a testing ground of the cardinal Soviet model of planning and reveals, in the context of six economies with varying economic potentials and different resource bases, flaws in the structure of this model not so readily observable in the context of the Soviet economy itself.

As already indicated, this study is functional and considers systematically, in the framework of each topic, the entire set of six countries. From the point of view of the level of development (as measured by a series of indicators), these countries may be arranged in the following three groups: (1) Czechoslovakia (an industrial country); (2) Poland and Hungary (agricultural and raw-material producers with substantial processing facilities); (3) then, in descending order, Romania, Yugoslavia, and Bulgaria (agricultural and raw-material producers with only small processing facilities).

On the other hand, certain "circumstantial" factors, such as the participation of these countries on the side of the Allies or on the side of the Axis powers in World War II, had lasting economic consequences during the entire postwar period both in the political and in the economic sphere. Thus, as a result of the war alignment, certain countries had to pay reparations, witnessed an increased development in their economies of the Soviet position, and had to adopt a different pace in the process of nationalization and hence in planning, whereas other countries of the area (the former allied countries) could from the beginning conduct large-scale nationalizations, anticipate eventual reparations, and have more leeway as far as the Soviet Union was concerned. From this point of view, it is convenient to resort for certain subjects to a different grouping from the strictly economic one suggested above. Thus, we have treated Czechoslovakia, Poland, and Yugoslavia (i.e., the group of former allies) as one group, and Hungary, Romania, and Bulgaria (i.e., the group of ex-enemy countries) as another.

Finally, at times, when, for instance, it appeared useful to assess the contribution of the region as such to the Soviet potential, we either placed Yugoslavia after all the other countries or simply excluded it from certain regional computations. The utilization of one or the other of these three types of grouping explains the varying arrangements to be observed in certain tables throughout the text.

A few remarks now, on the reference apparatus. Each reference is given in full at its first appearance either in tables or in the footnotes, and is repeated only in a shortened form thereafter. In order to simplify somewhat the bulky body of references employed, a series of abbreviations has been established for the periodicals most frequently used. These abbreviations are utilized throughout the text, even when the periodicals concerned enter into a reference that is given for the first time. A complete list of the abbreviations and of the publications quoted, together with translations, appears in the list of "Publications Cited." (The sources in Russian and Bulgarian are transliterated following the system used by the Library of Congress, with certain modifications. For Serbian, the Croatian system is used. The languages with Latin alphabets are not transliterated.) In addition, there will be found there a comprehensive list of "Other Periodicals Used," which includes the name, translation (if necessary), and place of publication of titles found most useful in research in this field. Finally, there is an extensive bibliography of "Selected Publications," which serve both as documentation and as source material for students of this subject.

SECTION I

PRELIMINARY DATA

INTRODUCTORY NOTE TO SECTION I

This section sets forth the basic economic characteristics of Eastern Europe and an "inventory" of the social strata present in the region at two historic moments: on the eve of the war (i.e., 1938–39), and immediately after World War II (i.e., 1945–46), at the opening of the postwar period. Only in relation to these data can the successive economic (and social) displacements that occurred in the region be registered and measured.

So far as the prewar economic characteristics are concerned, Chapter 1 presents a series of indicators of the occupational structure of the population, the development of agriculture, industry and its branches, regional differentiations, and foreign trade. Data are also given on ownership in agriculture and industry and on the relative economic importance of the state.

In Chapter 2 we focus on a specific group of factors conditioned either by the war itself or by the armistices and the peace treaties that followed the war. Our analysis considers in turn: (*a*) the impact of territorial changes on planned resource allocation; (*b*) the impact of the population shifts on the total population and its occupational structure; (*c*) the over-all pattern of development in the region at the liberation period, as reflected in its total labor-force distribution. In the second place, the lasting postwar consequences of the military alignments of the war period are noted, as well as the heavy impact of the settlement concerning the former German assets and the reparations obligations imposed on the ex-enemy countries: Hungary, Romania, and Bulgaria.

CHAPTER

1

MATERIAL AND HUMAN RESOURCES OF PREWAR EASTERN EUROPE

AREA AND POPULATION

The six countries to be considered extended before the war over an area of more than 1,250,000 square kilometers and had a combined population of around 100 million. Except in Czechoslovakia, the majority of the population was dependent on agriculture for its income: this majority ranged from 50-plus to 60 per cent for Poland and Hungary, to over 70 per cent for Romania, Yugoslavia, and Bulgaria (see Table 1).

A rapidly expanding population,[1] a high density per acre of farm land, an acute shortage of agricultural equipment, and a relatively low number of livestock combined to discourage intensive methods of cultivation. Surplus agricultural population and low productivity per capita and per hectare were characteristic of the area.

The figures on the occupational structure of the labor force presented in Table 2 suggest a basic classification of the countries considered in three main categories: (1) with less than 30 per cent of the labor force engaged in agriculture and with up to 40 per cent in mining and industry—Czechoslovakia; (2) with 50 to around 60 per cent in agriculture and 20 per cent in industry—Poland and Hungary; (3) with 75 to 80 per cent in agriculture and less than 10 per cent in mining and industry—Romania, Yugoslavia, and Bulgaria.

[1] The population increases in Eastern Europe were on the average about 3 times as rapid as in Western and Northern Europe.

TABLE 1. AREA AND POPULATION

Country	Area (1,000 sq. km.) 1	Population (in millions) 2	Increase in population, 1932–37 (%) 3	Characteristic Importance of Agriculture: Population depending on agriculture (%) 4	Average yield of wheat, 1934–38 (metric quintals per ha.[a]) 5	Hectares[a] per tractor, 1938 6
Czechoslovakia	140	15.2	[b]	33	17	1,027
Poland	389	34.5	5.8	60	14	12,540
Hungary	93	8.9	3.0	52	14	841 [c]
Romania	295	19.2	6.0	72	10	6,618
Yugoslavia	248	15.0	7.7	76	11	3,570 [d]
Bulgaria	103	6.2	6.2	73	12	1,387 [e]

[a] 1 hectare = 2.471 acres.
[b] Not available.
[c] 1935.
[d] 1939.
[e] 1934.

Sources:
1, 2: *UNDY, 1949–1950,* UN, New York, 1950, pp. 92 ff.
3: *Europe's Trade: A Study of the Trade of European Countries with Each Other and with the Rest of the World,* League of Nations, Geneva, 1941, p. 50.
4, 5: Active and passive population: *FAOY, 1949.* Vol. I, *Production,* UN, FAO, Washington, 1950, p. 24.
6: *ESE in 1949,* UN, ECE, Geneva, 1950, p. 293.

RESOURCES AND FOREIGN TRADE

In spite of the concentration of the population in agriculture, the region's exportable surpluses of grain, dairy products, and meats were relatively modest.

As for raw materials, several of these countries depended on imports for coal, iron ore, pig iron, steel, and a variety of metals. This was by and large true of Czechoslovakia (for ores and metals), as well as Hungary and Romania. Several of these countries had surpluses of timber, coal (Poland), oil (Romania), and, in smaller amounts, of a variety of ores (Yugoslavia). Since the area was the only European source of grain and oil outside the Soviet Union its exports of these commodities were important during the interwar period and even more so during

TABLE 2. OCCUPATIONAL DISTRIBUTION OF EMPLOYED LABOR FORCE

Country	Ratios of Total Employment to Total Population	Principal Occupational Structure, percentages					
		Total active	In agriculture	Mining and industry	Commerce and credit	State administration	Other actives [a]
Czechoslovakia	44.38	100	25.59	38.25	9.23	5.28	21.65
Poland	47.01	100	64.99	18.55	6.50	3.16	6.80
Hungary	46.03	100	50.80	23.04	7.43	2.94	15.79
Romania	57.91	100	79.96	9.06	2.87	2.37	5.74
Yugoslavia	47.95	100	76.29	9.94	4.16	3.12	6.12
Bulgaria	56.48	100	79.95	8.00	3.09	2.84	6.49

[a] Includes army, domestic service, other professions.

Sources: (Certain adjustments had to be made for some countries in order to insure the comparability of the data.)

C: *Annuaire statistique de la République Tchécoslovaque* (Statistical Yearbook of the Czechoslovak Republic), *1934*, State Statistical Office, Orbis, Prague, 1935, p. 12.

P: For total active population outside agriculture: *Drugi Powszechny Spis Ludności, Dec. 9, 1931* (Second General Census, 1931), *Statystyka Polski* (Statistics of Poland), Series C Z-62, Warsaw, p. 65; for active population in agriculture: *FAOY, 1949,* Vol. I, *Production, op. cit.*, p. 211.

H: *Annuaire statistique hongrois 1938* (Hungarian Statistical Yearbook), Office central royal hongrois de statistique (Royal Hungarian Central Statistical Office), Budapest, 1940, p. 18.

R: For total active population outside agriculture: *Anuarul Statistic al României 1939 și 1940* (Statistical Yearbook of Romania), Institutul Central de Statistică (Central Statistical Institute), Bucharest, 1940, p. 346; for active population in agriculture: *UNDY, 1949–1950, op. cit.*

Y: *Statistički Godišnjak Kraljevine Jugoslavije—Annuaire statistique 1936* (Statistical Yearbook of the Kingdom of Yugoslavia), Statistique générale de l'état (Central Statistical Office), Belgrade, 1937, p. 32.

B: *Statisticheski Godishnik' Na Tzarstvo Bălgariia 1939—Annuaire statistique du royaume de Bulgarie* (Statistical Yearbook of the Kingdom of Bulgaria), Statistique Generale de l'état (Central Statistical Office), Sofia, 1940, p. 42.

the war. It is interesting to note both the strong similarity as far as certain import and export surpluses are concerned between the area and the USSR (e.g., for grain or livestock produce) and the clear possibility of interchanges between them (see Table 3). However, this sort of trade remained negligible, given the respective *global* trade patterns and, above all, a complexity of political motives.

Except in Czechoslovakia, which inherited the largest part of the industry of the former Austro-Hungarian Empire, the industrial base was

TABLE 3. FOREIGN TRADE—TRADE AND RESOURCES (1935) [a]

Commodities	Czechoslovakia	Poland	Hungary	Romania	Yugoslavia	Bulgaria	USSR
Wheat	−95	69	331	252	30	35	704
Rye	−1	414	21	9	2	2	43
Barley	46	285	−7	177	5	2	588
Oats	6	90		17	6		156
Maize	−122		−247	635	388	5	10
Potatoes	−6.9	28.3	56.3	1.1	0.2	1.2	
Tobacco	−11.6	−8.2	8.4	−0.1	6.1	24.3	2.2
Meat							
Beef and veal	0.2	6.1	0.7	1.1	1.4	1.0	−4.4
Mutton		0.7	0.4	0.2	0.1		
Pork	−1.5	27.5	13.7	1.6	6.3		2.0
Milk		0.1			0.5		
Butter	−1.3	5.7	2.5	0.1	0.2	0.1	29.2
Cheese	−0.4	0.2	0.3		2.0	1.9	−0.2
Cotton	−76	−66	−22.5	−6.0	−14.9	−6.3	−44
Wool	−16.7	−18.5	−0.8	−0.5	−3.2	−1.0	−32
Flax	−16.8	13.5	3.0		7.4		59.1
Hemp	−3.6	0.5	1.4	−1.4	10		−20
Rubber	−11.4	−4.4	−1.9	−0.8	−2.0	−0.1	
Sawed softwood	317	1291	−522	1220	771		5161
Coal (millions of tons)	0.1	8.8	−0.2		−0.2		2.2
Lignite (millions of tons)	1.7		0.2		0.07		
Petroleum: crude			−165	335	−88	−18	206

Gasoline		42	−1	1952	−2	−5	658
Kerosene	−45	29		1167	−11	−21	417
Heavy oils	−164	29		3044		−21	1740
Lubricating oils	−18	17	−4		−3	−6	279
Benzol	5.3	13	0.1				3.3
Iron ore: crude (millions of tons)	−0.47	−0.24		0.013	0.18	−5.7	0.16
Pig iron and ferroalloys	−4.7	6.1	−66	−6.9			324
Steel (ingots and castings)	3.0	−30	62	−94	−9.4		
Copper ore: crude					0.2		
Metal	−21.6[b]	−11.9	−8.3	−5.1[b]	−35.7	−0.7	−32.2
Lead ore: crude		−9			75		
Metal	−10.0[b]	1.9[b]	−6.1[b]		6.8	−1.1[b]	−30.8
Zinc ore: crude	−2.7	−64		5.2	89		
Metal	−8.8[b]	65.6[b]	−5.0[b]	−5.0[b]	1.3[b]	−1.0[b]	−1.5
Tin: metal	−1.3	−0.9	−0.5	−0.3	−0.3	−0.2	−7.4
Aluminum: bauxite	−0.4	−2.2	22.9		172		
Metal		−1.2	−0.2	−0.2	−0.2		−0.6
Chrome ore: crude	−8				21		11
Magnesium (tons)							−320
Magnesite: crude	70.8	−2.2	−11.7	−0.1	22.8	−0.1	32.7
Pyrites	−139	−33	−40		63		
Manganese ore: crude	−55	−63					645
Phosphates: natural	−113	−50	−27		−11		386
Superphosphates	−0.2	21.0					
Basic slag	−28	−12					28

[a] Export surplus (+). Import surplus (−). Unless otherwise specified, in thousand metric tons.
[b] Including scrap.

Source: Raw Materials and Foodstuffs, League of Nations, Geneva, 1939, II.A.24. Excerpts from Table III ("Raw Materials. Net Imports and Exports in 1935"), pp. 48 ff.

small, and lack of capital combined with the absence of effective demand prevented rapid industrial growth.

The commodity structure of the foreign trade of most of the countries considered clearly reflects their low level of development and explains the geographic orientation of their trade. Except for Czechoslovakia, the exports of these countries consisted of foodstuffs, raw materials, and slightly processed goods, and their imports of manufactured goods, raw materials, and semimanufactured goods in advanced stages of processing. Czechoslovakia alone was a large exporter and importer of manufactured goods (see Table 4).

TABLE 4. FOREIGN TRADE—STRUCTURE OF TRADE (1938)

Class of Commodities	Czechoslovakia	Poland	Hungary	Romania	Yugoslavia	Bulgaria
Percentages of the Value of Total Exports						
Manufactured goods	71.8	6.4	13.0	1.9	0.8	2.0
Raw materials and semimanufactured goods	19.8	65.1	31.7	64.3	49.5	66.6
Foodstuffs and live animals	8.4	28.5	55.3	33.8	49.7 [a]	31.4
Total	100.0	100.0	100.0	100.0	100.0	100.0
Percentages of the Value of Total Imports						
Manufactured goods	29.6	28.4	30.2	68.3	44.8	68.0
Raw materials and semimanufactured goods	57.5	54.1	61.5	27.3	50.1	31.5
Foodstuffs and live animals	12.9	17.5	8.3	4.5 [a]	5.1 [a]	0.5 [a]
Total	100.0	100.0	100.0	100.0	100.0	100.0

[a] Foodstuffs only.

Sources:

C: *Zahraniční Obchod* (Foreign Trade of the Czechoslovak Republic), Vol. 177, 1946, and Vol. 179, 1947; Prague, 1948.

P: *Concise Statistical Yearbook of Poland*, September 1939–June 1941, Polish Ministry of Information, Glasgow, 1941.

H: *Magyarország 1939 évi. Külkereskedelmi Forgalma* (Foreign Trade of Hungary in 1939), Budapest, 1940.

R: *Anuarul Statistic al României 1939 şi 1940*, *op. cit.*

Y: *Statistički Godišnjak Kraljevine Jugoslavije—Annuaire statistique 1938–39*, Belgrade, 1939; *Statistika Spoljne Trgovine za 1939* (Statistics of Foreign Trade in 1939), Belgrade, 1940.

B: *Statisticheski Godishnik' Na Tzarstvo Bălgariia*, *op. cit.* *Statistikata Na Vănshnata Tărgoviia* (Statistics of Foreign Trade), Sofia, 1938.

The foreign trade of the region as a whole was basically geared to the industrialized countries of Europe. In 1938 around 60 per cent of the Polish imports and from 75 to over 80 per cent of the imports of the other East European countries (except Czechoslovakia) came from the industrialized countries of Western and Central Europe. Symmetrically, from 70 to 80 per cent of their exports were directed toward the Western countries. The inter-East and South-East European trade constituted from 10 to 15 per cent of their total trade. Czechoslovakia had a wider distribution of trade: around 45 per cent of her trade was with the highly industrialized countries of Europe, 30 per cent with the rest of Europe, around 10 per cent with the European overseas territories, and the balance with the rest of the world. As already stated, for the region as a whole the interchanges with the Soviet Union were negligible or extremely small (at their prewar peak they involved about 1.5 per cent of the Czechoslovak and Polish trade).

It should be noted that the trade with the region represented no more than 10 to 15 per cent of the foreign trade of Western Europe in the mid-1930's (the largest trade of the West being carried on among the industrialized countries themselves and with the other continents). In the late thirties the strong economic drive of Germany in this region converted Eastern and South-Eastern Europe into a supplier of up to 35 per cent of the German imports and an outlet for up to 34 per cent of her exports.

Industry: Gainfully Employed, Plants, Power Available

The tabulations of the number of industrial workers, of industrial plants, and of available power point up the very uneven development of the countries of the area.

Out of a total 3.3 million gainfully employed in larger-scale industry (i.e., in establishments with over 5 gainfully employed), Czechoslovakia alone had 1.2 million, or 37 per cent of the total, that is, a labor force equal to that of Poland and Hungary combined. These two countries in turn had a significantly larger industrial labor force than any of the last three countries of the region (see Table 5). The labor force was equally distributed between "producer-" and "consumer-goods" industries in Czechoslovakia, Hungary, and Romania; it was more heavily concentrated in the consumer-goods industries in Poland, Yugoslavia, and Bulgaria. If we were to take into consideration the small-scale industries with less than 5 workers, the concentration in the consumer-

TABLE 5. THE INDUSTRY AND ITS BRANCHES—IMPORTANCE OF DIFFERENT BRANCHES OF INDUSTRY IN TOTAL INDUSTRIAL EMPLOYMENT IN EACH COUNTRY

(in thousands of gainfully employed)

Industries	Czecho-slovakia	Po-land	Hun-gary	Ro-mania	Yugo-slavia	Bul-garia
Mining	83	94	44	69	58	11
Metal and Metalwork	367	156	127	51		6
Chemicals	52	50	22	28	12	4
Saw mills	33	10	14	20	54 [a]	2
Stone, clay	28	[b]	15	[b]	[b]	2
Paper	27	20	8	10	5	1
Electricity	17	30	10 [a]	10	7	2
Food-processing	93	97	62	38	40	33
Textile	242	173	69	74	61	32
Clothing	51	16	17	6 [a]	33	[b]
Leather	54	10	16	13	6	1
Woodwork	46	72	10	43	22	4
Glass, ceramics	101	84	45	6	[b]	4
Printing	24	14	10	5	3	1
Total	1218	826	469	373	301	103

[a] Estimate.
[b] Not available.

Sources:

C: *První Československý Plán* (The First Czechoslovak Plan), Ministry of Information, Prague, 1946; "Zaměstnanost v Průmyslu" (Employment in Industry), in *Statisticky Zpravodaj*, IX, 7–8 (1946), pp. 235–238; *Statistical Digest of the Czechoslovak Republic in 1948*, State Statistical Office, Prague, 1948.

P: (Computed from) *Statistical Yearbook of Poland 1948*, Central Statistical Office, Warsaw, 1949, p. 60.

H: *Annuaire statistique hongrois 1938, op. cit.;* the Hungarian figures refer to employment capacity and not to actual employment.

R: *Anuarul Statistic al României 1939 şi 1940, op. cit.; Breviarul Statistic al României* (Statistical Digest of Romania), I, II, Bucharest, 1940 (data for 1938). For electricity: *Intreprinderile Particulare Industriale, Comerciale şi de Transport. Rezultatele Provizorii ale Inventarului din Octomvrie 1947* (Private Industrial, Commercial, and Transportation Enterprises. Provisional Results of Census of October 1947), in *Statistica Industrială* (Census of Manufacturers), I, 1, Institutul Central de Statistică (Central Institute of Statistics), Bucharest, 1947, p. 52.

B: *Statisticheski Godishnik' 1939, op. cit.;* also; F. N. Petrov, editor, *Balkanskie Strany* (The Balkan Countries), Gosudarstvennyi Nauchnyi Institut "Sovetskaia Entsiklopediia" (State Scientific Institute "The Soviet Encyclopedia"), OGIZ, Moscow, 1946, p. 316.

Y: Milorad Milovanovitch, *Jugoslav Post-War Reconstruction Papers*, Office of Reconstruction and Economic Affairs, Government of Yugoslavia, New York, 1943.

TABLE 6. THE INDUSTRY AND ITS BRANCHES—NUMBER OF INDUSTRIAL ESTABLISHMENTS BY SIZE-GROUPS [a]

Industry Groups by Number of Persons Employed	Number of Establishments				
	Czechoslovakia [b]	Poland [b]	Hungary [b]	Romania [b]	Bulgaria [b]
10– 20 persons	8,455	4,202	2,028 [c]	1,483	503 [d]
20– 50 persons	7,088	3,411	897	1,253	388 [d]
50– 100 persons	2,950	1,321	404	500	218 [e]
100– 200 persons	1,845 [f]	726	484 (100–500)	297	119 [e]
200– 500 persons	631 [f]	460		244	86 [e]
500–1,000 persons	325	185	105 (500 and over)	101 (500 and over)	[g]
1,000 and over	124	147			[g]
Total	21,418	10,452	3,918	3,878	1,314

[a] No statistics are available of the workers employed by size-groups of firms in Yugoslavia. The census figures show, however, by industries, the numbers of independent owners, of employees, and of various types of manual workers. Of the 15 odd groups into which the 1931 census classifies industry, in only 9 are there more than 5 workers to 1 owner. In these 9 categories, 1,605 employers employ 44,020. The grouping of these 44,020 is as follows: large enterprises, 77 employers and 24,067 workers, 313 each; medium-sized enterprises, 1,528 employers and 19,953 workers, 13 each. Small enterprises are found in those industries in which the census lists from 3 to 5 workers per employer. Cf. John Morris: *Yugoslavia*, St. Botolph Co., London, 1948, pp. 26–27.

[b] 1930 for Czechoslovakia, Poland, and Romania; 1935–37 for Hungary, and 1934 for Bulgaria.

[c] This figure also comprises some industries with less than 10 workers.

[d] Data for 1939.

[e] Data for 1940.

[f] These industry groups are 100–250 and 250–500 for Czechoslovakia.

[g] Not available.

Sources:

C: *Annuaire statistique de la République Tchécoslovaque 1935*, Prague, 1936, p. 72.

P: Alfred Switgall, *La Pologne industrielle* (Industrial Poland), thesis, Montpellier, 1934, pp. 98–99.

H: *Annuaire statistique hongrois 1937*, Budapest, 1938, p. 140. (In the figures for Hungary presented in this table, we have included the mines and the blast furnaces as computed from pp. 124 and 127, *ibid.*)

R: *Anuarul Statistic al României 1939 şi 1940*, *op. cit.*, p. 347. The first group (10–20 employed) was computed as a residual from the figure given for the whole industry, p. 478, *ibid.*

B: *Statisticheski Godishnik' 1939*, op. cit., p. 387; *Spisanie i Izvestiia*, Glavnata Direktsia Na Statistikata, *Revue et bulletin de la Direction générale de la statistique* (Review and Bulletin of the Central Bureau of Statistics), Sofia, 1945, No. 3–4, pp. 171 and 175.

TABLE 7. THE INDUSTRY AND ITS BRANCHES—HORSEPOWER [a] IN PRINCIPAL INDUSTRIES AND ELECTRIC GENERATING CAPACITY

(in thousands)

Industries	Czecho-slovakia	Po-land	Hun-gary	Ro-mania	Bul-garia
Metal and metalwork	740	649	297	152	10
Textile	424	333	122	79	41
Food-processing	510	512	258	137	96
Stone, glass, ceramics	229	168	78	4	18
Wood and timber	217	135	26	64	10
Paper and printing	187	170	39	53	12
Chemicals	82	429	71	183	5
Leather	26	23	29	13	4
Electric generating capacity (in thousands of kilowatts) [b]	1,642	1,483 [c]	794	510	80

[a] Horsepower in use, 1930: total of: (1) hp of motors developing energy and serving for directing operating machines; (2) hp of operating electromotors; (3) hp transmitted by other sources to direct operating machines.

[b] 1933.

[c] 1935.

Sources (for horsepower in industry):

C: *Annuaire statistique 1934, op. cit.*, p. 71.

P: *Concise Statistical Yearbook of Poland*, Bureau of Statistics, Warsaw, 1938, p. 113.

H: *Annuaire statistique hongrois 1938, op. cit.*, p. 337.

R: *Anuarul Statistic al României 1939 şi 1940*, op. cit., pp. 478–479.

B: *Statisticheski Godishnik na Tzarstvo Bălgariia 1937*, Sofia, 1938, pp. 284–285.

(For electric generating capacity):

Statistical Yearbook of the World Power Conference, No. 1, 1933 and 1934, published by the Central Office, WPC, London, 1936, Tables 16A and 17.

goods industries would normally appear far greater in all the countries considered except Czechoslovakia.

Of a total of some 43,500 industrial plants with over 10 gainfully employed,[2] 21,500 were located in Czechoslovakia; 10,500 in Poland; 3,900 in Hungary; 3,850 in Romania; 2,500 in Yugoslavia; and some 1,300 in Bulgaria. As can be deduced from Table 6, a rather significant concentration of employment is to be noted, except in Bulgaria, in the industrial establishments with more than 200 gainfully employed. Thus the nationalization of even the largest 5 to 10 per cent of the establishments would immediately bring into the "state sector" the majority of the labor force and would involve around 1,000 firms in

[2] The data for Yugoslavia are derived from La Yugoslavie économique (The Economy of Yugoslavia) Office of Foreign Trade, Belgrade, 1935, pp. 113 ff.

Czechoslovakia, 800 in Poland, 500 in Hungary, and around 400 in Romania.

The analysis of the distribution of power available in the region reveals again the foremost place occupied by Czechoslovakia, which accounts for only 11 per cent of the area and 15 per cent of the population. Not only was its total generating capacity substantially larger than that of any other country of the area, but in certain key branches, e.g., metals, textiles, it was nearly equal to that of Poland and Romania combined—two countries covering 54 per cent of the area of the region and accounting for 54 per cent of its population.

The quite limited significance of the industrial equipment and output of the area, as related to those of the rest of Europe, is, however, indicated by the fact that only 8 per cent of the total European industrial equipment and 8 per cent of the European industrial output were to be imputed in 1938 to Eastern Europe. In turn, from this latter total, a third is to be imputed to Czechoslovakia.

Agriculture: Importance of Subsistence Units

The data on the structure of land ownership in the 1930's reveal the importance in the area of holdings under 5 hectares—holdings which hardly produced for the market (see Table 8).

Of a total of some 13 million holdings, about 9.2 million or almost three quarters of the total holdings of the area were small or "dwarf" peasant holdings.[3] About 2.3 million farms were between 5 and 10 hectares. Some 1.2 million holdings were between 10 and 50 hectares. The relatively small number of peasant holdings between 10 and 50 hectares to a large degree explains the possibility of their subsequent isolation.[4]

The country-by-country comparison indicates that the small and "dwarf" holdings varied in relative importance from 60 per cent of the total number of holdings in Bulgaria to 85 per cent in Hungary, and from 15 per cent of the farm land acreage in Czechoslovakia and Poland to some 30 per cent in Romania, Yugoslavia, and Bulgaria. On the other hand, the large holdings and the domains (50 hectares and up)

[3] The "dwarf" peasant holdings embrace the farms with less than 2 or 3 hectares, whose output is generally insufficient for the sustenance of a family.

[4] In the postwar period this group was "sliced" into various subgroups of "kulaks" (the Russian term for "rich peasants") by adding to the extension of land tenure such complementary criteria as number of persons employed on these lands, number of livestock and agricultural machinery owned, etc.

TABLE 8. STRUCTURE OF OWNERSHIP IN AGRICULTURE—ABSOLUTE NUMBER OF HOLDINGS IN THE AREA

(in thousands)

Holdings (ha.)		Czechoslovakia	Poland	Hungary	Romania	Yugoslavia	Bulgaria	Total	%
Small	Up to 5	1,168	2,211	1,388	2,460	1,344	599	9,170	71.4
Medium	5–10	258	696 [a]	144	560	407	232	2,297	18.0
Large	10–20	147	349 [a]	60	180	174	81	991	7.7
	20–50	58	76	28	55	49	12	278	2.2
Large and domains	Over 50	16	30	12	25	6	[b]	89	0.7
Total		1,647	3,362	1,632	3,280	1,980	924	12,825	100.0

[a] The estimates are based on one datum available for these two successive groups of holdings.
[b] Not available.

Sources:
C: *Annuaire statistique de la République Tchécoslovaque 1934, op. cit.*, p. 44.
P: *Concise Statistical Yearbook of Poland 1930, op. cit.*, p. 13.
H: *GT*, I, 13 (December 1947), p. 696.
R: *Anuarul Statistic al României 1939 şi 1940, op. cit.*, p. 403.
B: *MI*, 1947, p. 25.
Y: *Statistički Godišnjak Kraljevine Jugoslavije 1936, op. cit.*, pp. 88–89.

represented about 1 per cent of the number of holdings and areas varying from 1.6 per cent of the farm land in Bulgaria to around 45 per cent in Czechoslovakia, Poland, and Hungary (see Table 9).

TABLE 9. STRUCTURE OF OWNERSHIP IN AGRICULTURE—AGRICULTURAL HOLDINGS AND ACREAGE; PERCENTAGE DISTRIBUTION

Groups of Agricultural Holdings According to Size of Property[a]

Holdings (ha.)	Czecho-slovakia	Po-land	Hun-gary[b]	Ro-mania[c]	Yugo-slavia	Bul-garia
1. Under 2 ha.	44.2	34.0	72.5	52.1	33.8	27.1
2. 2–5 ha.	26.6	30.7	12.5	22.8	34.0	36.1
3. 5–10 ha.	15.7	32.0 (rows 3–4)	8.8	17.1	20.5	26.2
4. 10–20 ha.	8.9		5.4 (rows 4–5)	5.5	8.8	9.2
5. 20–50 ha.	3.6	2.3		1.7	2.5	1.4
6. 50–100 ha.	0.5	0.4	0.3	0.4	0.3	[d]
7. 100–500 ha.	0.4	0.6 (rows 7–8)	0.5	0.3	0.1	
8. 500 plus	0.1			0.1	0.0	
Total	100.0	100.0	100.0	100.0	100.0	100.0

Respective Share in the Total Farm Land Acreage[e]

Holdings (ha.)	Czecho-slovakia	Po-land	Hun-gary	Ro-mania	Yugo-slavia	Bul-garia
1. Under 2 ha.	4.8	3.5	10.1	12.7	6.5	5.3
2. 2–5 ha.	11.4	11.3	9.2	15.3	21.5	24.7
3. 5–10 ha.	14.1	30.8 (rows 3–4)	12.6	20.0	27.0	36.8
4. 10–20 ha.	15.9		20.0 (rows 4–5)	12.0	22.3	24.4
5. 20–50 ha.	8.2	7.1		7.8	13.0	7.2
6. 50–100 ha.	4.0	2.5	5.0	4.5	3.2	1.6 (rows 6–7)
7. 100–150 ha.	11.2	44.8 (rows 7–8)	43.1 (rows 7–8)	10.6	2.8	
8. 500 plus	30.0			17.1	3.7	
Total	100.0	100.0	100.0	100.0	100.0	100.0

[a] Data for 1930–31, except for Poland (figures of the 1921 census), Bulgaria (data for 1934), and Hungary (1935).

[b] Hungary: divisions are 0–2.8 ha.; 2.8–5.7 ha.; 5.7–11.4 ha.; 11.4–28.7 ha.; 28.7–57.5 ha.; 57.5–115.0 ha.; and from 115 ha. up.

[c] Romania: the first group consists of holdings under 3 ha.; the second from 3 to 5 ha.

[d] Less than 1%, i.e., 0.06%.

[e] The figures for Yugoslavia refer only to land excluding pasture land.

Sources: As in Table 8.

A clear graphical representation of both the inequality in the distribution of land by size-groups of holdings and the large differences that existed in this respect among the various countries of the area can be obtained by plotting a series of Lorenz curves. If we show along the abscissa the percentage distribution of holdings and along the ordinate the percentage distribution of farm land acreage, we obtain the group of curves shown in Chart 1. The deeper the curve, the sharper the inequality—the larger the number of holdings with a

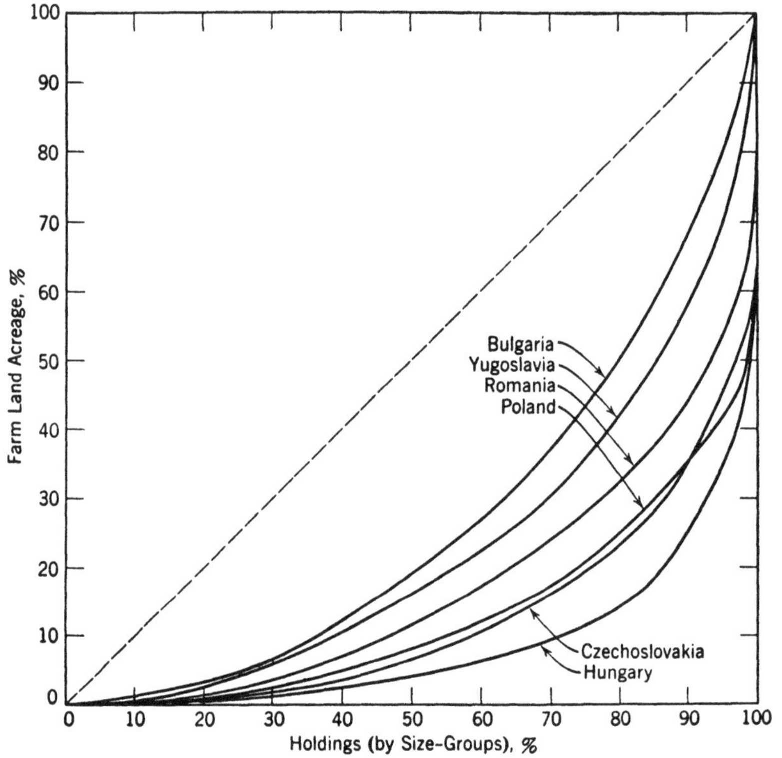

CHART 1. SIZE-GROUPS OF HOLDINGS AND SHARE IN FARM LAND ACREAGE, PREWAR

small share of the farm land acreage. For Bulgaria the curve shows the least deviation from the theoretical line of equality (the diagonal), and for Hungary, the country with large domains, the curve presents the sharpest deviation.

"PRODUCTIVITY" AND "ACCUMULATION" MARGINS

There were large differences in *productivity* (i.e., output per unit of labor) and hence in per capita income in these countries (see Table 10).

TABLE 10. "PRODUCTIVITY" IN INDUSTRY AND AGRICULTURE [a]

(in dollars of 1938 purchasing power)

Countries	Net Value of Industrial Output per Person Engaged in 1938: Excluding small-scale industry	Including small-scale industry	Net Value of Agricultural Output 1934–38: Per person engaged	Per hectare
Czechoslovakia	550	450	200	67
Poland	500	400	130	52
Hungary	430	340	150	43
Romania	430	290	80	27
Bulgaria	320	300	110	45

[a] The figures refer to the net value of output after deducting depreciation. Industry comprises manufacturing and handicrafts, mining, and power production. Building and construction are not included.

The estimates relating to the productivity of labor in agriculture are merely approximations.

Source: ESE in 1948, UN, ECE, Geneva, 1949, p. 225.

The estimated net value of output per person engaged in industry as a whole (including small-scale industry) was much larger in Czechoslovakia than in the other countries; in agriculture the Czechoslovak output per person seems to have been more than double the output per person engaged in Romania. Here, too, a three-way classification seems appropriate: (1) net value of output per person of $450 in industry and $200 in agriculture–Czechoslovakia; (2) net value of output per person between $350 and $400 in industry and around $150 in agriculture–Poland and Hungary; (3) net value of output per person of around $300 in industry and $100 in agriculture–Romania and Bulgaria.

The percentage of income saved in most of these countries was low, capital markets were ill developed, and interest rates were high. Investment needs were met mainly by government investment or provision of funds, by specific extensions of bank activities, or by the inflow of foreign capital.

STATE INTERVENTION, THE BANKS, AND FOREIGN CAPITAL

The confused state of property claims at the breakup of the Austro-Hungarian Empire, at the end of the First World War, had led to large-scale state assumption of ownership. Subsequently, private investment atrophied in most of these countries, and governments expanded their sphere of operation. In Poland, for instance, besides owning the transport system (a feature current all over Europe) the state owned also 100 per cent of the chemical industry, 70 per cent of the steel industry, 50 per cent of the metal production, and so on. The state ownership and participation were multiple; they ranged from forests and fisheries to all kinds of monopolies, to metallurgical enterprises and even more unexpected undertakings such as health resorts.[5] Outside this large field of control, the state ran various banks with the aim of supplementing the usual financial institutions "in such fields where initiative or private action have proved themselves insufficient." [6]

The private banks themselves purchased large numbers of shares of privately operated enterprises. The principle of specialization of banks was disregarded—a practice common in Central Europe. The local banks bought and sold shares, were active in the import-export business, and loaned capital at very high rates. The strong dependence of the local industries on the banks (Verbankung, as the Germans call it) can be readily seen from the following examples.

In Czechoslovakia one of the four great banks of Prague, the Živnostenská Banka, was the principal shareholder in the sugar industry (in 3 major enterprises), in the coal, iron and steel, and machinery industries (in 17 enterprises), in chemicals (in 5 enterprises), in paper (in 4 enterprises), in textiles (in 7 enterprises), in ceramics (in 5 enterprises), in food-processing and breweries (in 7 enterprises), in navigation and insurance (in 6 enterprises).[7] In Hungary the General Bank of Hungarian Credit controlled 9 mines and brick-making factories, 6 metallurgical enterprises and construction workshops (among the most important in Central Europe), 3 transport societies, 3 food-processing in-

[5] The percentage distribution of the capital values of public properties in Romania reveals that the three main headings in the total were: railways (47%); forests (29%); and lands and farms (11%). The rest constituted ownership of fisheries, ports, post-telegraph and telephone systems, state monopolies, state metallurgical enterprises, and some health resorts. Cf. Virgil Madgearu, *Rumania's New Economic Policy*, King & Son, Orchard House, London, 1930, p. 15.

[6] The Polish Bank of the National Economy, a bank controlled by the state, became in fact in the 1930's the principal credit institution of Poland. See Casimir Grzegorzek, *Le Rôle économique de la Banque de l'Économie Nationale en Pologne* (The Economic Role of the National Economic Bank in Poland), thesis, Paris, 1935; also, I. Goldberg, *Les Banques polonaises dépendants de l'état* (The Polish Banks Dependent on the State), thesis, Nancy, 1935.

[7] Milos Ivan Bergmann, *Kreditbanken in der Tschechoslowakei* (Credit Banks in Czechoslovakia), thesis, Frankfort-am-Main, 1932, pp. 88–94 and 148–155.

dustries, 10 textile enterprises, and so on.[8] In Yugoslavia the First Croatian Savings Bank controlled 2 woodwork enterprises, 1 paper business, 7 flour mills (including the central flour-mill holding Narodna), 3 construction firms, and 9 other enterprises ranging from coal and textiles to cement and electricity.[9]

Finally, the limited amount of domestic saving, the multiple recourse of these governments to the foreign-capital market, and the recourse of the banks and industries to foreign loans and investments increased enormously the activity of foreign capital in this region as a whole. It is interesting to note that a change in the structure of foreign investments always corresponded to changes in the system of political alliances: thus the German participations were taken over by the Western Allies between the two world wars; during the Second World War German capital bought or simply floated a significant amount of these shares and enlarged tremendously its sphere of financial operations in the area.

Between the two world wars, foreign capital owned some 80 per cent of the capital and reserves, held some 80 per cent of the deposits, and received some 80 per cent of the profits of the local banks.[10] Actually, many of these banks were simple "intermediaries between foreign capital and the local market."[11] Foreign investment in mining and industry was also heavy in the entire area except in Czechoslovakia. To cite some typical examples, it varied in Poland from 7 per cent in the sugar industry to 87 per cent in petroleum mining, and encompassed such industries as chemicals, textiles, and electricity. In Yugoslavia virtually the entire capital invested in the metal mines was foreign: this was true for the copper mines at Bor (French concessions) and lead at Trepca (English concessions), the largest enterprises in Yugoslavia, as well as for bauxite, pyrites, chromium, manganese, etc.[12]

[8] For the participation of this and other important Hungarian banks, see Paul Lénárd, *La Crise industrielle et l'intervention de l'état en Hongrie-Étude économique et juridique* (The Industrial Crisis and the Intervention of the State in Hungary—an Economic and Juridical Study), thesis, Lyons, 1935, pp. 78 ff.

[9] Vladimir Košak, *Die bankmässige Finanzierung der Jugoslawischen Industrie* (Financing by the Banks of the Yugoslav Industry), Bechhold Verlag, Frankfort-am-Main, 1938, pp. 101 ff.

[10] Constantin V. Colocotronis, *L'Organisation bancaire des pays balkaniques et les capitaux étrangers* (Banking Organization of the Balkans and Foreign Capital), thesis, Recueil Sirey, Paris, 1934, pp. 70–71, 136–137, 176–178, *passim*.

[11] Cf. Košak, op. cit., p. 42.

[12] See Mirko Lamer, "Die Wandlungen der ausländischen Kapitalanlagen auf dem Balkan" (Change in Foreign Investments in the Balkans), *Weltwirtschaftliches Archiv* (Achives of World Economy), Vol. 48, November 1938. For Poland see L. Wellisz,

If from the point of view of ownership of their capital the industries were divided into three groups: (*a*) directly dependent on foreign capital; (*b*) dependent on foreign and local capital; (*c*) dependent on local capital, it would be evident that most of the large enterprises were in the first group, whereas all the small industries, close to agriculture, were in the third category.

THE STATE MACHINE

To understand the subsequent expansion of the state interventions and the development of the state economic organs, a careful assessment of the role of the prewar state "apparatus" is required.

Employment by the government, as is seen from Table 2 above, varied before the war from 2 to 5 per cent of total employment. Power was concentrated in the senior officials of the state administration proper (excluding state enterprises and monopolies), a total of around 250,000 persons in the region as a whole (see Table 11). Among these officials, the key posts in the Ministries of the Interior involved a personnel in each country varying between 4,000 and 11,000 persons, including all the cadres of the intelligence, police, "gendarmes," and related forces; the lower personnel of the security forces numbered between 10,000 to 30,000 persons in each of the countries considered.

The combined cadres of the Ministries of Interior, Justice, and War (i.e., senior officials, judges, officers) varied from 10,000 to 30,000 persons, each group consisting of some ten different salary classifications.

The whole state administration proper comprised personnel varying from 40,000 to 170,000 persons in the lower echelons. The noncommissioned officers for the group numbered about 10,000 to 20,000 men in the countries considered.[13] The service ranks, important in Czechoslovakia, Poland, and Romania, do not appear in the tables.

Foreign Capital in Poland, George Allen, London, 1938. For Yugoslavia: Slobodan Čurčin, *Pénétration des capitaux étrangers en Yugoslavie* (Penetration of Foreign Capital in Yugoslavia), Pierre Bossuet, Paris, 1935; also, Dr. Božidar Jurković, *Das ausländische Kapital im ehemaligen Jugoslavien* (The Foreign Capital in Former Yugoslavia), W. Kohlhammer Verlag, Stuttgart, Berlin, 1941.

[13] The above figures changed appreciably with the expansion of the armies in all the countries considered in the late 1930's. Thus in Czechoslovakia, the officers and noncommissioned officers in the army amounted to around 19,000 persons in 1933, and to around 57,000 in 1935.

TABLE 11. THE STATE MACHINE—STATE ADMINISTRATION PROPER [a]

(in thousands)

	Czecho-slovakia	Po-land	Hun-gary	Ro-mania	Yugo-slavia	Bul-garia [b]
I. State administration proper						
A. Senior officials, including:	42.6	75.0	22.2	71.2	37.7	
Top central administration	0.5	[c]	0.4	[c]	0.5	(0.6)
Ministry of Interior	6.9	7.0	4.9	11.8	3.5	(10.5)
Ministry of Justice	5.6	15.0	3.9	10.1	6.4	(3.4)
Ministry of War	9.5	25.0	2.9	17.6	12.3	(9.5)
B. Lower-category employees	58.2	97.0	45.1	67.6	77.0	
Total state administration proper	100.8	172.0	67.3	134.9	114.7	35.8
II. Teachers	75.0	77.0	8.6 [d]	67.6	35.4	27.2
III. State enterprises and monopolies [e]	169.5	192.0	41.9	45.5	58.6	34.7
Grand total for state administration	345.3	441.0	117.8	248.0	208.7	97.7

[a] Data for Czechoslovakia, Poland, and Romania, 1934–35 budgets. Data for Hungary, Yugoslavia, and Bulgaria, 1937–38.

[b] The figures in parentheses include lower-category employees.

[c] Nil.

[d] Hungary had a great number of private teachers in parochial schools.

[e] Data covering the "administrative monopolies," including the postal service, railroads, etc.

Sources:

C: *Annuaire statistique 1934*, op. cit., pp. 256–257.

P: *Concise Statistical Yearbook of Poland 1934*, *op. cit.*, pp. 210–211.

H: *Annuaire statistique hongrois 1936*, Budapest, 1937, pp. 336–337.

R: *Anuarul Statistic al României*, *1939 şi 1940*, *op. cit.*, p. 25.

Y: *Statistički Godišnjak 1936*, *op. cit.*, pp. 506–507.

B: *Statisticheski Godishnik' 1937*, *op. cit.*, pp. 612–613.

CONCLUDING REMARKS

The basic characteristics of the prewar socioeconomic structure of the region may now be defined as follows:

The countries may be classified in three groups: (1) industrial coun-

Table 12. The State Machine—Police and "Gendarmes" (around 1930)

	Czecho-slovakia	Po-land	Hun-gary	Bul-garia
State police				
Officers	745	863	745	503
Policemen	6,171	27,835		
Plainclothesmen	976	2,379	8,194	
"Gendarmes"				17,490
Officers	33		588	
Noncommissioned officers	11,740		11,412	

Sources: As in Table 11.

tries—Czechoslovakia; (2) agricultural countries with significant processing facilities—Poland and Hungary; (3) agricultural and raw-material producing countries—Romania, Bulgaria, and Yugoslavia.

The structure of ownership in agriculture reveals the decisive importance of farms not producing for the market and the relatively small number of medium and large peasant holdings in each of the countries considered; the aspect of land tenure underlines the possibility of "slicing" and isolating, economically and politically, successive small strata of landowners.

In industry the pattern of employment and the size of factories point toward a significant concentration in a number of large industries (large according to East European standards).

The value of industrial output contributed by the region to the rest of Europe was quite limited; in agricultural products, though the share was proportionately three times as large, the exports of the region remained relatively modest; the trade of the area with Western Europe amounted to about 15 per cent of the West European foreign trade; in the late 1930's the trade with Germany accounted for over 30 per cent of the foreign trade of that country; however, the strategic location of the region made its contribution in grains and raw materials important.

CHAPTER 2

DISPLACEMENTS BROUGHT ABOUT BY THE WAR AND "LIBERATION"

Effects of the Displacement of Boundaries

Following the armistice decisions or other agreements reached by the Soviet Union with each of the East European countries, mostly in the closing months of the war, the Soviet Union obtained from Poland the territories east of the Curzon Line; from Czechoslovakia the South Carpathian Ukraine; from Romania North Bukovina and Bessarabia. These territories, except Transcarpathia, first secured by the Soviet Union at the opening of World War II in 1939–40 on the basis of the 1939 Stalin-Hitler pact, had been lost in the course of the war. After recapturing them the Soviet Union "compensated" Poland by turning over to her 21 per cent of the prewar German territory, comprising most of Prussia and the Oder-Neisse region. Romania was "compensated" with a slice of her own territory, Northern Transylvania, taken by Hungary in 1941 and occupied in late 1944 by Soviet and Romanian troops. In addition to these basic boundary changes made at the end of World War II, two small adjustments are to be recorded: the loss by Romania to Bulgaria of about 2.64 per cent of her prewar territory, and minor gains obtained by Yugoslavia in the West. The results of these changes are summarized in Table 13.

As can be seen from columns 3 and 4, only Hungary returned to its prewar territorial status, losing the various acquisitions of the war period. Leaving Poland aside for the moment, Czechoslovakia and Romania lost respectively up to 9 and 20 per cent of their prewar territories, and Yugoslavia and Bulgaria obtained slices of land equal, respectively, to over 3 and over 7 per cent of their prewar territory.

TABLE 13. AREA AND POPULATION, 1947,[a] COMPARED TO PREWAR

Country	Area (1,000 sq. km.)	% of Total Area of the Region	Gain (+) Loss (−) (1,000 sq. km.)	Gain and Loss of Prewar Area of Each Country (%)	Population (in millions)	% of Total Population in Area	Gain (+) Loss (−) (in millions)
	1	2	3	4	5	6	7
Czechoslovakia	127.8	11.2	−12.6	−8.9	12.2	14.7	−3.0
Poland	311.7	27.4	−194.8 +118.5	−50.2 +30.5	23.8	28.4	−10.7
Hungary	93.1	8.2	None	None	9.1 [b]	10.9	+0.2
Romania	237.3	20.9	−58.1	−17.0 −2.6	15.8 [b]	18.9	−3.4
Yugoslavia	256.8	22.6	+8.8	+3.5	15.6 [b]	18.7	+0.6
Bulgaria	110.8	9.7	+7.7	+7.4	7.0 [b]	8.4	+0.8

[a] This series was chosen in preference to 1945 or 1946 since it is at the close of the period of expulsion of the German population, notably from Czechoslovakia and Poland.
[b] Estimated on the basis of census data of 1948 and subsequent years.

Sources:
C: *Statistical Digest of Czechoslovak Republic in 1948, op. cit.*, p. 11, for columns 1 and 5.
P: *Statistical Yearbook of Poland 1948, op. cit.*, p. 16, for columns 1 and 5.
For all countries, all other columns, same sources as in Table 1, Chapter 1, above.

Finally, there were dramatic changes in Poland: it lost to the Soviet Union over half its prewar territory but acquired a former German area equal to over 30 per cent of prewar Poland. Thus a new entity with a new structure of natural resources, agricultural land, and industrial installations emerged in Eastern Europe.

Considering the whole area conceded to the Soviet Union, it may be noted that the easternmost territories of prewar Poland, Czechoslovakia, and Romania were the least developed regions of these countries. Less than 10 per cent of her industry was in the eastern half of Poland.[1] Transcarpathia contained only a small percentage of the productive capacity of Czechoslovakia, except for the wood industry. North Bukovina and Bessarabia combined did not represent over 7 per cent of Romanian capacity and output. Except for the Polish region of Boryslaw-Drohobycz, moreover, the region as a whole lacked important mineral resources. Territorial changes were therefore most significant in relation to agricultural resources. Leaving Poland for the moment, we find that Czechoslovakia lost a significant

[1] According to prewar Polish statistics, the territorial repartition by provinces of the gainfully employed in industry was the following for the seven provinces forming by and large the territories ceded to the USSR: Vilno—0.6% of the total gainfully employed in mining and industry in Poland; Novogrodek—0.4%; Polesie—0.5%; Wolhynia—1.2%; Lwów—4.2%; Stanisławów—1.8%; Tarnopol—0.8%, that is, for the entire lost territory, 9.5% (of which almost half was concentrated in the Lwów region).

CHART 2. DISPLACEMENT OF FRONTIERS IN EASTERN EUROPE AFTER WORLD WAR II

amount of land devoted to the raising of corn, wheat, and coarse grains. Romania lost over 25 per cent of her bread-grain area and 50 per cent of her potato-raising area. On the other hand, the relatively light transfer of territory from Romania to Bulgaria looms quite large in Bulgaria's increases of land for all types of grain (see Table 14).

TABLE 14. LAND UTILIZATION [a]

Commodity	Czechoslovakia	Poland			Romania	Bulgaria
	Losses	Gains from Germany	Losses to USSR	Gains or losses	Losses	Gains
Wheat	−3.8	20.1	−42.9	−22.8	−26.7	8.0
Rye	−2.7	24.1	−31.4	−7.3	−57.4	35.6
Barley	−0.5	29.6	−42.9	−13.3	−46.2	29.0
Oats	−3.8	28.0	−41.2	−13.2	−12.7	16.0
Maize	−10.6	[b]	[b]	[b]	−24.2	17.4
Potatoes	[b]	28.1	−33.0	−4.9	−53.5	6.0
Sugar-beets	[b]	85.4	−12.3	+73.1	−27.8	[b]

[a] Gain or loss following boundary displacements after World War II in percentage of respective prewar area. Gain +, loss −.
[b] Not available.
Source: FAOY, op. cit., pp. 236 ff. (Figures for Poland are computed.)

Turning to the figures for Poland, we observe a notable loss in the wheat, rye, barley, oats, and potato-raising areas, and an increase only in the sugar-beet area. Although the area extending from the easternmost regions of Poland to the easternmost regions of prewar Germany is basically uniform in agricultural potential, appreciable variations in crop yield were registered in prewar years from East to West because of the difference in technical development. In the eastern provinces lost by Poland to the Soviet Union the yields per hectare in wheat and coarse grain were on the average 7 to 8 quintals per hectare as compared with 11 to 13 in Central Poland, around 15 in Western Poland, and 17 to 22 in the Oder-Neisse region; the yield in potatoes varied from 100 to 110 quintals per hectare in the East to 165 to 175 in the districts near Germany.[2]

As the only country which acquired land in the West, Poland gained some of the richest mineral-endowed land of Europe, the Oder-Neisse region increasing tremendously its resources in coal, lignite, ferrous and non-ferrous metals, clay, quartz, etc., as well as a highly developed industrial area.

The Balance Sheet of Resources

In completing an inventory of resources at the end of the war for the region as a whole, important account has to be taken of war destruction. In the group of ex-enemy countries, Hungary, Romania, and Bulgaria, the heaviest losses by far were incurred by Hungary, which suffered wide destruction in the summer and fall of 1944 and large-scale plundering of her national wealth during the combined reign of the Fascist Arrow Cross and of the Nazis.[3]

In the group of Allied countries, Czechoslovakia, Poland, and Yugoslavia, the greatest destruction was incurred by Yugoslavia, which suffered war, partisan guerrilla battles, and dismemberment, and by Poland, which was for a prolonged period a major battleground. Yugoslavia, with a worn-out, badly damaged, and inefficient industry, had to reconstruct a ruined and exhausted land. As a result of the acquisition of land in the West, Poland was partially compensated for her losses and increased her industrial potential. Despite the fact that the buildings, machinery, and power economy of the Oder-Neisse region were heavily damaged, they supplied Poland with a large industrial base both for her reconstruction and for her subsequent development.

As can be seen from Table 15, the shift from East to West, although it did not appreciably increase the total number of Polish plants (em-

[2] See "Long-Term Tendencies of European Agriculture," in *Economic Bulletin for Europe,* United Nations Economic Commission for Europe, Vol. III, No. 2, Geneva (Oct. 1951), p. 36.

[3] It is worth noting that, in a speech at the Paris Peace Conference concerning the draft peace treaty with Hungary, the representative of the USSR, F. T. Gusev, stated almost in the same breath the tremendous destruction of Hungary as a reason why the Western countries should not insist on the restitution of their former property, and the right of the USSR to request for herself large reparations. Cf. *Pravda* (Truth), Oct. 14, 1946 (speech of Oct. 12, 1946).

TABLE 15. POLAND: 1945–46. INDUSTRIAL PLANTS EMPLOYING 5 AND MORE WORKERS, AND POWER OF INSTALLED MACHINES, AS COMPARED TO 1936–37

Industries	Industrial Plants						Power of Installed Machines (in hp)		
	Total number of plants employing 5 and more workers			Of which plants employing 20 and more workers					
	1 1937	2 August 1946	3 + or −	4 December 1937	5 August 1946	6 + or −	7 1936	8 1945	9 + or −
Total	24,362	24,671	309	4,998	7,125	2,127	1,378,452	1,527,173	148,721
Metal and metalwork	1,964	2,985	1,021	957	1,191	234	283,272	339,080	55,808
Textile	2,384	987	−1,397	770	707	−63	175,482	161,563	−13,919
Foodstuffs and kindred	9,342	12,095	2,753	682	1,627	945	376,119	478,100	101,981
Stone, glass, and ceramics	2,053	1,261	−792	712	776	64	93,915	117,498	23,583
Wood and timber	2,581	2,370	−211	646	738	92	109,402	99,571	−9,831
Paper, printing, and allied	971	865	−106	339	451	112	90,564	98,079	7,515
Chemicals	992	813	−179	302	472	170	238,972	224,708	−14,264
Leather	474	223	−251	111	177	66	10,726	8,574	−2,152

Sources:

Industrial plants: *Statistical Yearbook of Poland, 1947*, Central Statistical Office, Warsaw, 1947, p. 79.

Power of machines: *Spis Zakładów Przemysłowych, 1945* (List of Industrial Enterprises), Statystyka Polski (Statistics of Poland), Seria D, Issue No. 3, Central Statistical Office, Warsaw, 1947, p. xi.

ploying 5 and more workers), changed substantially: (*a*) the number of plants with more than 20 employees (which increased from 4,998 to 7,125, or an increase of over 42 per cent above prewar); [4] (*b*) the power available in the economy (increase of installed capacity from 1.3 million horsepower to 1.5 million horsepower, or a 10.8 per cent increase over prewar); (*c*) the general structure of industry, thanks to an appreciable increase in the size of producers' goods industries (the metal and metal-working machinery plants, for instance, increased in number by 24.4 per cent and in power of installed machines by 19.6 per cent as compared to prewar). It should be noted that the distribution of labor and power in Table 10 is based on a still chaotic stage in the postwar reconstruction of the country.[5] The inventory of resources does not reveal the full potentialities of the region, but obviously repair of plant, introduction of machines, and restoration of the power economy were bound to be more rapidly rewarding in this country than the start from the very limited and inefficient prewar basis in the other East European countries (except Czechoslovakia).

Population Changes

In the course of the war, combat casualties, the flight of certain minority populations, and the wholesale expulsion of people notably from Prussia, the Oder-Neisse region, and the Sudetenland changed appreciably the structure of population of both Poland and Czechoslovakia. In Poland the urban population was largely dispersed, and the Jewish minorities dispersed or exterminated. After the war the shifts in population continued: according to official Polish figures, between 1944 and the end of 1947, 1.5 million Poles were repatriated in Poland from the territories ceded to the Soviet Union, and over 500,000 Ukrainians were transferred from Poland to the Soviet Union. During the same period 2.2 million Germans were transferred from

[4] A discrepancy exists here, because of the coverage, between the figures of Switgall (in our Table 6) and these figures. Switgall gives 6,250, as compared to 4,998 in Table 15. It should, however, be noted that these two figures refer, respectively, to 1930 and 1937.

[5] This balance sheet is as of the end of 1945, beginning of 1946. It must be noted that, immediately after the war, a Soviet-Polish agreement attributed to Russia 25 per cent of the industrial installation in the newly acquired Polish territories, representing a value of 6 per cent of the estimated wealth of these territories. According to H. Minc, the dismantlement of these installations was ended in August 1945. Cf. Minc's speech in Wroclaw in August 1945 in *Przegląd Górniczy* (Mining Review) (October 1945), p. 230.

Poland to Germany; this "organized transfer" followed the flight and "unorganized expulsion" of over 4 million Germans from Prussia and the Oder-Neisse region.[6] The western territories of Poland, which before the war had a population of 8.2 million, counted in 1947 an almost entirely new population of 5 million settlers, constituted as follows: 1 million autochthonous Poles; 2.5 million originating from old Poland (peasant settlers); the rest transferees from Eastern Poland incorporated into the Soviet Union.[7] As compared to prewar, postwar Poland presented in 1946 the population structure by urban and rural divisions shown in Table 16.

TABLE 16. POLAND: CHANGES IN URBAN AND RURAL POPULATION, 1946, COMPARED TO PREWAR

(in millions)

	Total Population		Urban		Rural	
Territory	1931–33	1946	1931–33	1946	1931–33	1946
Poland total	30.0	23.9	11.0	7.5	18.9	16.1
Former Polish territory	21.8	18.8	7.4	5.7	14.3	13.1
Former German territory	8.2	4.8	3.6	1.8	4.6	3.0

Source: Statistical Yearbook of Poland 1947, op. cit., p. 12.

The total population in 1946 was 79.6 per cent of prewar, i.e., 86.2 per cent of prewar in the former Polish territory, and 58.5 per cent in the former German territory. The uban population had a substantially greater drop: it was 68.1 per cent of the prewar level [8] (77 per cent in the former Polish territory and 50 per cent in the new area), whereas the rural population fell to 85.1 per cent (91.6 per cent of pre-

[6] The figures given above are from the *Statistical Yearbook of Poland 1948*, op. cit., pp. 27–28. According to the figures supplied by the U.S. High Commissioner for Germany, as of September 1950, the number of expellees from the former German territories east of the Oder-Neisse amounted to 4.7 millions, to which should be added around 350,000 ethnic Germans expelled from Central Poland. Cf. "Assimilation of Displaced Persons," in *Report on Germany*, Fifth Quarterly Report, October–December 1950, Office of the U.S. High Commissioner for Germany, Frankfort-am-Main, p. 58.

[7] Eugene M. Kulischer, "Population Changes behind the Iron Curtain," in the *Annals of the American Academy of Political and Social Sciences*, Vol. 271, September 1950, p. 107.

[8] Account has to be taken here of the extermination of some 2 million Jews of prewar Poland.

war in the former Polish territory and 65.2 per cent in the new areas). The expulsion of the German population created an acute shortage of skilled workers; in order to fill the gap, Polish émigrés in France and Belgium were invited to return.

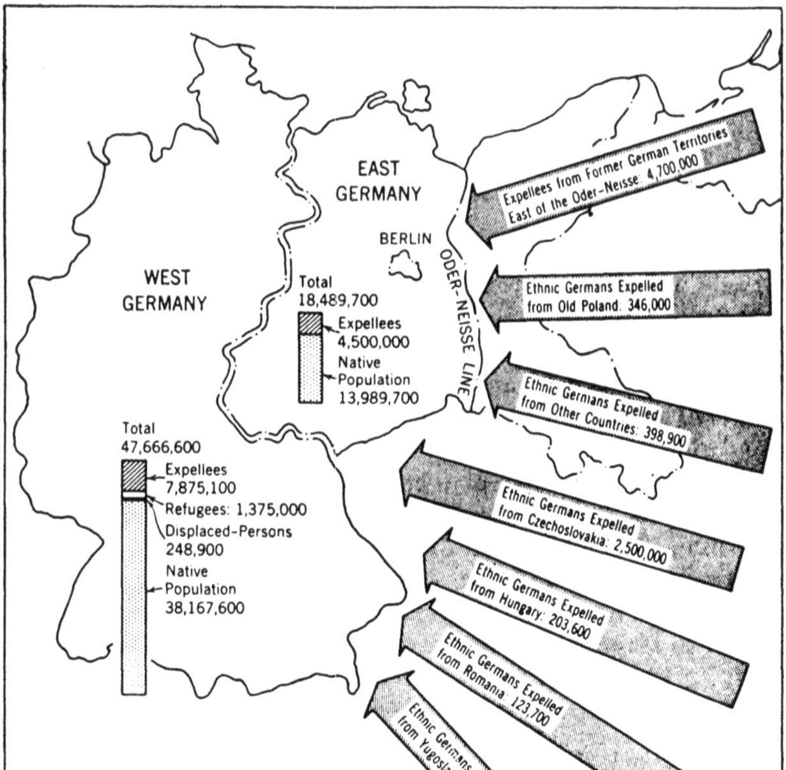

After U. S. High Commissioner, *Report on Germany, 1950*

CHART 3. POPULATION MOVEMENTS IN CENTRAL AND EASTERN EUROPE (STATUS AS OF SEPTEMBER 1950)

In Czechoslovakia the expulsion of the Sudeten Germans (about 2.5 million persons) and of other minority groups had an immediate and very strong impact on the population structure of the country. The general population changes by provinces are reflected in Table 17.

TABLE 17. CZECHOSLOVAKIA: POPULATION BALANCE SHEET, 1937–47

Provinces	Bohemia	Moravia and Silesia	Slovakia	Total State
Area (in sq. km.)	52,062	26,808	48,953	127,823
Population as evaluated on Dec. 31, 1937	7,251,000	3,644,000	3,536,000	14,431,000
Population as of May 22, 1947	5,626,566	3,135,765	3,402,300	12,164,631
Total reduction	−1,624,434	−508,235	−133,700	−2,266,369
Of which natural growth	229,236	259,031	250,322	738,589
Balance sheet of migration	−1,853,670	−767,266	−384,022	−3,004,958

Source: SZ, XI, 1, January 1948, p. 5.

War losses and expulsions reduced the population of Bohemia, for instance, compared to 1937, by 25.5 per cent (contrasting with a loss of 21.0 per cent in Moravia and Silesia and 10.8 per cent in Slovakia).

The impact on the labor force in the Czech territories (Bohemia, Moravia, and Silesia) was very heavy. The total labor force of these territories had fallen in 1947 to 3.4 million (or 39.2 per cent of the population of the region) as compared to 4.5 million in 1930 (or 42.4 per cent of the population of the region at that time). The changes in each of the economic units are shown in Table 18. The agricultural labor force had decreased substantially. All the productive professions exhibited a sharp drop, whereas only the number of state employees and non-productive categories of the population showed an appreciable increase. As the source of Table 18 states, "the

TABLE 18. CZECHOSLOVAKIA: CHANGES IN THE LABOR FORCE IN 1947 COMPARED TO 1930[a]

Category	% Increase +, Decrease −
Agriculture, forestry, fishing	−37.8
Mining	−22.1
Industry, handicrafts	−24.6
Commerce and credit	−24.3
Transportation	−8.7
Administration, public service	+31.9
Professions	−31.3
Domestic help, personal service	−39.8
Non-specified	+37.8
Total	−24.1

[a] "Czech territories" only.

Source: SZ, XI, 7/8 (July–August 1948), pp. 261–267.

basic reasons for those changes are [first] the transfer of the Germans and only in the second place the changes in the age structure of the population and the economic reorganization of the state."

Besides the Germans who fled or were expelled from Eastern Europe as a whole (not only materially decreasing the German population in the area[9] but also opening up new possibilities of redistribution of land in Poland and Czechoslovakia), other minorities were moved. Ukrainians were transferred to the Soviet Union; Hungarians were expelled from Czechoslovakia, which in turn received some Slovaks from Hungary; Poles, Czechoslovaks, and many Romanians were repatriated from the Soviet Union. The Turkish minority was expelled from Bulgaria. These minority changes did not involve, however, any group as large as the Germans.

The Employment Pattern in the Region

War losses, territorial displacements, and population shifts brought about some notable changes in the pattern of employment in the region as a whole. Except perhaps for Romania, where the relative percentage of total population depending on agriculture showed an increase,[10] significant drops in this percentage were registered in four of the other countries and especially in Poland.[11] However, in spite of these changes, the characteristic prewar pattern of the region has not been fundamentally modified. In the first category, industrial Czechoslovakia is still alone, with less than 30 per cent of her total population dependent on agriculture; in the second category, we again

[9] The flight and unorganized expulsion of Germans from Eastern Europe involved, between 1944 and 1947, some 4.8 million, the majority of whom were expelled from Poland. To this should be added the organized transfer between 1945 and 1947 ot 2.4 million from Czechoslovakia, 2.9 million from Poland, and some 240,000 from Hungary. In 1948 it was estimated that the number of Germans remaining in East European countries was around 100,000 to 150,000, except for Romania where 250,000 remained. Cf. note 8, above.

[10] Cf. Dr. A. Golopenţia and P. Onică, "Recensământul Agricol din Republica Populară Română, la 25 Ianuarie, 1948, Rezultate Provizorii" (Agricultural Census of RPR, Jan. 1948, Provisional Results), in *PE* No. 3, March 1948.

[11] It has been estimated for 1949 that the percentage of the Polish population dependent on agriculture represented about 52 per cent of the total population. However, it would be erroneous to compare this percentage to that of prewar (61 per cent dependent on agriculture), as these data refer to two distinct territories. It should be noted that in the old Polish lands which are still part of the present Polish state this percentage was approximately 52 per cent before the war, whereas in the Western territories, previously German, it varied between 54 per cent in East Prussia to as little as 34 per cent in Lower Silesia (see below, Chapter 10).

find both Poland and Hungary with around 50 per cent of their population dependent on agriculture; finally, in the last category we can place the other three countries with over 70 per cent of their population dependent on agriculture.

As far as employment in industry is concerned, the advance of Poland appears more striking when compared, on the one hand, with the slow recovery in Hungary and, on the other hand, with the diminishing of the labor force in Czechoslovakia. As can be seen from Table 19, in 1946 Poland had a factory labor force of over 930,000 as

TABLE 19. CZECHOSLOVAKIA, POLAND, HUNGARY: IMPORTANCE OF DIFFERENT BRANCHES OF INDUSTRY IN TOTAL INDUSTRIAL EMPLOYMENT IN EACH COUNTRY, 1945–46 [a]

Industries	Czechoslovakia, March 1946	Poland (1946): Total (average within a year)	Poland (1946): Of which in "recovered territories"		Hungary, June 1945
Mining	119	201	64	31.8%	[b]
Metal and metalwork	313	106	34	17.0	62
Chemicals	52	66	15	22.7	13
Sawmills	22	35	11	28.5	[b]
Stone, clay	44	30	8	26.7	6
Paper	24	23	8	34.8	3
Electricity	28	29	9	30.7	8
Food-processing	84	117	26	22.2	24
Textile	191	181	42	23.2	28
Clothing	64 (Clothing and Leather)	44	11	25.0	4
Leather		8	1	12.5	4
Woodwork	40	27	8	29.6	4
Glass, ceramics	24	50	14	28.0	6
Printing	20	15	3	20.0	6
Total industry	1,025	932	254	27.3	168

[a] In thousands of gainfully employed.
[b] Not available.

Sources: (Figures apply to "manufacturing" industries, i.e., industrial plants with more than 5 workers.)
C: *SZ*, IX, 7–8 (July–August 1946), pp. 235–238.
P: *Statistical Yearbook of Poland 1948*, *op. cit.*, pp. 58–60.
H: *GT*, II, 8 (June 1948), p. 448.

compared to over 1 million in Czechoslovakia and between 170,000 (1945) and slightly over 200,000 (1946) in Hungary. A large proportion of the new Polish labor force was already concentrated in the newly acquired territories (up to 30 per cent in producers' goods industries, with a large emphasis on mining, and up to 27 per cent in the consumers' goods industries, especially in textile and food-processing). The basic structural pattern in the region is nevertheless again noticeable if we compare the ratio of employment in industry to total population. This ratio was, for the period considered: 8.4 in Czechoslovakia; 3.9 in the new Poland; and only 1.8 in the slowly recovering Hungary. Before the war the ratios were: 8.0 in Czechoslovakia; 2.4 in Poland; 3.3 in Hungary at the level of actual employment. War damage pushed Hungary back to the Romanian-Yugoslav level, whereas the boundary shift accentuated on the other hand the semi-industrial and semiagricultural characteristics of Poland, as compared to the characteristics of industrial Czechoslovakia.

The German Assets

We turn now to the second subject of this chapter, the postwar economic obligations arising from the wartime economic, military, and political alignments.

The principle of reparations from enemy countries was inserted in all the armistices concluded by the Soviet Union with the former satellites of the Reich (Hungary, Romania, Bulgaria). For Germany it was incorporated both in the Yalta protocol and in the subsequent Potsdam agreement which provided for Soviet recovery of reparations claims against Germany by: (1) levies on the current production and dismantling in her own occupation zone; (2) taking over of German assets located in the ex-enemy countries of the Balkan-Danubian area; (3) delivery of 25 per cent of the equipment dismantled as superfluous to peacetime production in West Germany, two-fifths of this to be percentage-free, the other three-fifths remaining to be compensated for by Soviet exports of foodstuffs and coal.

Provisions for the disposition of German assets in the former satellite countries were embodied in the Paris Peace Treaty with these countries in 1947.[12] Moreover, the peace treaty with Italy transferred to the Soviet Union Italian assets in these countries.[13] Finally, each of

[12] Articles 28 of the Hungarian Treaty, 26 of the Romanian Treaty, and 24 of the Bulgarian. Cf. U.S. Department of State, *Treaties and Other International Acts Series,* Government Printing Office, Washington, 1947; 1649, Treaty of Peace with Romania;. 1650, Treaty of Peace with Bulgaria; 1651, Treaty of Peace with Hungary (Paris, Feb. 10, 1947).

[13] Article 24 of the Italian Peace Treaty. *Ibid.,* 1648, Treaty of Peace with Italy.

the former satellites agreed to waive claims against Germany and its nationals arising out of contracts or any other obligations between September 1, 1939, and May 8, 1945.[14]

The disposition of the German assets and the exchanges involved in the delivery of reparations from the West have had a great and enduring impact in this area. The first served as a basis for the subsequent multiple development of the so-called "joint partnerships"—Soviet-Hungarian, Soviet-Romanian mixed companies; the second served as a justification for a special agreement on Polish coal.

In order to grasp the importance for the satellites of the transfer of the ex-enemy assets to the Soviet Union let us recall briefly the position and scope of the German economic penetration in the area. Concomitantly with the war expansion of the Reich, German capital increased tremendously its sphere of activity in the Balkan-Danubian area. The annexation of Austria, the occupation and dismemberment of Czechoslovakia, Poland, and Yugoslavia, and the occupation of the Western countries opened for German capital innumerable opportunities for economic and financial penetration of the European economy as a whole. In Eastern Europe two big German banks, the Deutsche Bank and the Dresdner Bank, acted virtually as the "economic branch of the Wehrmacht" in the exploitation of the resources of the region.[15] The multiple ties between Balkan-Danubian and Central European banks, as well as the phenomenon of Verbankung, already described, gave the Reich a growing control over the banking, industrial, and commercial structures of both the occupied and "Allied" Danubian countries.

With the penetration of Austria, the Deutsche Bank took hold of the Kreditanstalt, the largest Austrian bank, and still the most important bank in Eastern Europe. The Dresdner, for its part, formed the Länderbank-Wien through the merger of Mercurbank with the subsidiary of the French Banque des pays de l'Europe centrale, and later with the Czechoslovak Živnostenská Banka, and used it as a "spearhead for its Balkan activities." After the dismemberment of Czechoslovakia the Deutsche Bank acquired the Böhmische Bank, the Dresdner taking the Živnostenská. In Poland the main organ of German financial penetration was the Dresdner Bank, which established its subsidiaries

[14] Articles 30 of the Hungarian, 28 of the Romanian, and 26 of the Bulgarian Treaties. *Ibid.*, 1649, 1650, 1651.

[15] For data concerning the activities of the two German banks, see U.S. Military Government of Germany, Finance Division, *Dresdner and Deutsche Banks: Special Report to the Military Governor*, Frankfort-am-Main, June 1947 (mimeo.).

in the main cities and formed, immediately after the Polish defeat, two financial institutions which played a nefarious role during the occupation: the Ost-Bank of Poznan and the Kommerzialbank of Kraków. The two main German banks, moreover, worked in close cooperation with the Haupt-Treuhandstelle Ost (H.T.O.–Chief Trustee Office East), responsible for the confiscation, administration, and liquidation of Polish property. The conquest of the West gave Germany the general control over the famous "Société générale de Belgique," the largest holder of Franco-Belgian banking and industrial participations in Czechoslovakia, Luxembourg, Romania, and Yugoslavia.[16] The biggest share of the Société générale holdings and sphere of operation was taken over by the Deutsche Bank and transferred to the Kreditanstalt. The latter operated in Yugoslavia through two separate banks, one for Croatia (Bankverein für Kroatia) and one for Serbia (Bankverein A.G.–Belgrade).

In the satellite countries the two great German banks were extremely active. The Dresdner Bank took the upper hand in Hungary, where it acquired the Zipser Bank, as well as participating in the Hungarian Allgemeine Kreditanstalt previously held by the French. The Deutsche Bank took the upper hand in Romania, where it acquired the Banca Commerciala Română (COMRO), previously held by the Société générale de Belgique and by the Banque de l'union parisienne, the third largest Romanian bank. Other significant participations of the German banks were acquired in Romania in the Banca Hrissoveloni, Banca de Credit Român, and Banca Românească. In Bulgaria, where extensive German penetration had started long before the war, the Deutsche Bank enjoyed a strong position through its subsidiary, the Deutsch-Bulgarische Kreditbank-Sofia.

In addition to the operation of banks and bank holdings through the ramifications of the control of the two big German banks, the Reich created "interlocked" companies, financed partly by German and partly by satellite capital, which compelled local industries to join German cartels and established in the satellite countries numerous subordinate companies of various German business concerns. Thus

[16] In a special address to German bank leaders, Hermann Göring declared on Aug. 17, 1940:

> I take special interest in a most intensive penetration of the Dutch and Belgian economies by German capital on the broadest possible basis, even before the end of the war. . . . Furthermore, I want you to promote with all means the acquisition of dominating economic positions in third countries from French, Dutch, Belgian, Danish, or Norwegian ownership, by the German economy, and this already during the period of war. [*Ibid.*, p. 21.]

the Hermann Göring Werke acquired industrial property and interests in a score of enterprises ranging from mining, foundries, and armament factories in Czechoslovakia and Poland to metal and metal-working factories in the satellite countries. In Hungary the Deutsche Mineralöl took a share in the bauxite and petroleum exploitation; chemical, optical, and other types of plants were established throughout the country. In Romania the Germans took shares in a dozen petroleum companies and acquired large interests in the key metallurgical concern Reşiţa, and in the metal-working factories Malaxa (which accounted between them for more than 90 per cent of Romanian steel production, 90 per cent of coke, and 100 per cent of locomotive manufacturing).[17] In that country the German penetration became probably as great as in any of the occupied countries "where a policy of outright confiscation has not been general." [18] Last, Germany secured participation in mining and industry in Bulgaria through the acquisition of shares previously held by the West and belonging notably to the French portfolio of the (Yugoslav) Bor mines, various holdings in zinc, lead, and other types of undertaking.

Denouncing the "German legal make-up of their looting," responsible Russians affirmed during the war that after the defeat of Germany "all property grabbed by German financial capital in the occupied countries would be returned to these countries." [19] Moreover, the "foreign trade of Germany" was expressly denounced as "outright looting, effected thanks to every kind of tricky device." [20] However, at the end of the war only the Allied countries, Czechoslovakia, Poland, and Yugoslavia, recovered the "German assets"; in the ex-enemy countries Russia requested, obtained, and kept these assets in spite of the overt knowledge that they were largely based on loot "dressed up in legal

[17] The complicated competition between Germans and Romanians for the control of Malaxa is sketched in the U.S. War Department pamphlet, No. 31–135, *Organization of the Iron and Steel Industry of Enemy Europe,* March 1945, U.S. Government Printing Office, Washington, 1945.

[18] Cf. *Occupied Europe,* Royal Institute of International Affairs, London, 1944. See also *The Penetration of German Capital in Europe,* Inter-Allied Information Committee, H.M. Stationery Office, London, 1943.

[19] E. Varga, "Kontsentratsiia i Tsentralizatsiia Proizvodztva i Kapitala vo Vremia Voiny" (Concentration and Centralization of Production and Capital during the War), *Mirovoe Khoziaistvo i Mirovaia Politika* (World Economy and World Politics), No. 7–8, 1944, pp. 9–17.

[20] D. D. Mishustin, "Kak Gitlerovskaia Germaniia grabit Okupirovannye Strany" (How Hitlerite Germany Plunders the Occupied Countries), *Bolshevik,* No. 18, September 1941, pp. 34–40.

proceedings."[21] Furthermore, Russia made additional profits on the so-called "foreign trade of Germany" by compelling the former satellites to sign waivers of their claims on Germany from September 1, 1939 (i.e., before the actual entrance of these countries into the war), to May 8, 1945 (i.e., long after Hungary and Romania had left the side of Germany and had joined the Allies against her).[22]

Restitutions and Reparations

Outside the stated dispositions of German reparations and the Italian treaty but directly affecting the former German satellites, the Armistice agreements, and subsequently the peace treaties, required Hungary to deliver over a period of six years 300 million gold dollars' worth of reparations to the Soviet Union, Czechoslovakia, and Yugoslavia ($200 million worth of goods of all types, ranging from agricultural to metallurgical products, to the Soviet Union; $50 million to Czechoslovakia; $50 million to Yugoslavia). Romania had to send 300 million gold dollars' worth of reparations to the Soviet Union alone, half in oil products, half in agricultural and industrial goods; and Bulgaria, 75 million gold dollars' worth ($25 million to Yugoslavia, and $50 million to Greece). The substantial Soviet demands for reparations were alleviated by extending the initial period of delivery (from 6 to 8 years), changing the initial composition of the quantity of goods requested, increasing the price of goods delivered, and, finally, in mid-1948, by halving the balance. Hungary and Romania, which had direct parts in the invasion of the Soviet Union, were also compelled both to restore

[21] The main laws and decrees taken by the countries concerned in this matter were: *Czechoslovakia*—the decrees of May 21, 1945, concerning the confiscation of the agrarian wealth of the Germans and Hungarians and the decree of Oct. 25, 1945, concerning the confiscation of the enemy properties; *Poland*—the laws of Jan. 3, 1946, and the decree of Mar. 8, 1946; *Yugoslavia*—decision of the Yugoslav Assembly, Nov. 21, 1944, and the law of July 31, 1946. See *Deutsches Vermögen im Ausland, internationale Vereinbärungen und ausländische Gesetzgebung* (German Properties Abroad—International Agreements and Foreign Laws), Bundesministerium der Justiz, Verlag des Bundeseinzeiger (publ. by Federal Ministry of Justice), Köln, 1951, pp. 269, 329, 431.

[22] At the Paris Peace Conference, G. Tatarescu, the Minister of Foreign Affairs of Romania at the time, stated:

> . . . Most unjust of all is the clause provided by Article 28, which obliges Romania to renounce all her active claims on Germany, even those proceeded from the period of neutrality. Obliged to renounce these claims, Romania is still held to pay debts to Germany. . . . Moreover, Romania considers unjust . . . the demand to restitute gold received from Germany in payment of grain or oil removed from Romania. . . ." Cf. *RR,* II, 3–4, 1947, p. 32.

installations and objects removed from Soviet territory and to supply commodities to replace those consumed by their troops in the zone of occupation during the war. In fact, this request translated itself into a very heavy mortgage on Romanian and Hungarian current production and resources, whereas no account whatsoever was taken by the Soviet Union of the costs of feeding large Soviet armies incurred by those countries in the period from 1944 to 1945 (when these countries participated in the war with Germany) and after their "liberation."

Thus at the end of the war, and for the first time in its history, the Soviet Union, without having invested anything in those countries, became a large holder of foreign assets in the ex-enemy countries of Eastern Europe. This fact strongly affected the pace of nationalization in the region and the pattern of trade and trade settlements, and it played a decisive role in shaping the integration of the area into the Soviet orbit. The character of these developments will be examined in subsequent chapters.

Concluding Remarks

The impact of the "circumstantial factors," territorial changes, population shifts, economic clauses of the peace treaties, can be summarized as follows:

The boundary changes brought about the emergence in Eastern Europe of what can be called a new entity—postwar Poland, with a substantially changed structure of resources, agricultural potentialities, and industrial installations. The boundary displacements significantly modified also the agricultural resources of Czechoslovakia and Romania.

The wholesale displacements of various national groups opened up large possibilities of "interior colonization" in Poland and Czechoslovakia, and brought about substantial changes in the structure of their populations; however, these changes did not modify completely the fundamental structural pattern of development of the region apparent in prewar times.

After five years of concentrated German exploitation of their industrial machinery, after war destruction and dismantlings, all these countries were left with largely obsolete and inefficient economies, a fact even more significant since each of them, except Czechoslovakia and the new western Poland, had a prewar industry of modest proportions and efficiency. The heaviest losses were those of Yugoslavia,

Hungary, and Poland; the latter, however, in the final analysis, increased her industrial potential and resources through her bodily shift to the West.

Finally, the ex-enemy countries entered the postwar "liberation" period burdened by innumerable Soviet economic mortgages. This factor was bound to play a multiple role in their subsequent development.

SECTION II

THE NATIONALIZATION OF THE ECONOMY

INTRODUCTORY NOTE TO SECTION II

This section studies the process of the restriction and then the elimination by the state of private ownership, control, and initiative in the East European economies. *Pari passu,* the study sketches the main characteristics of the reorganization of these economies, both in the period preceding and in that following the launching of all-round planning. The process of the extension of the sphere of the state is currently described as "nationalization." Actually, the term *statification,* patterned on the French term *étatisation,* designates more accurately the process in question, since the process includes extension of the power of the state. However, to avoid obscurity, the term nationalization is used here.

The process of nationalization in any given sector of an economy affects, obviously, not only this sector but the economy as a whole. It would therefore be logical to follow for every measure taken (let us say in the industrial sphere) the immediate and multiple effects that occur in the other sectors. Furthermore, in order to have a complete picture of the dynamics of nationalization in each of its phases, it would be necessary to show step by step how each nationalization measure in the diverse sectors of the economy combined with other such measures at any given moment. For the sake of clarity, however, it seems preferable to follow the process of nationalization separately in each sector through to its completion, and to reconstruct only subsequently the over-all picture at various decisive time periods.

We intend to follow this unfolding process in turn in the manufacturing sphere (Chapter 3), in the financial system (Chapter 4), and in the distribution channels (Chapter 5). This study of the reshaping of the economy outside agriculture is completed by an analysis of the specific positions that have been held by the Soviet Union in these economies under the form of either pure Soviet companies or so-called "joint partnerships" with some of these states (Chapter 6). The last chapter of the section (Chapter 7) turns finally to agriculture and to the two cycles of reorganization of it. It details first the extent and character of the agricultural land reforms and analyzes, second, the process of socialization of agriculture, which took the form of the extension of the state farms and of the "producers' cooperatives."

Because the nationalization process presented different characteristics in the former Allied countries (Czechoslovakia, Poland, Yugoslavia) and in the group of ex-enemy countries (Hungary, Romania, Bulgaria), and because, moreover, considerable lags developed between them, we shall study the two groups separately.

CHAPTER 3

PROCESS OF NATIONALIZATION AND STRUCTURAL REORGANIZATION IN INDUSTRY AND CRAFTS

Industry and Crafts

In the course of the analysis of nationalization in the manufacturing sphere, several distinctions are implied and hence some preliminary explanations are in order. Following the Marxian concept, the official literature distinguishes between producers' goods industries and consumers' goods industries according to the *destination* of their output. *Ex definitione,* some uncertainties are bound to arise from this type of classification. For instance, certain industries produce both for producers and consumers, e.g., coal-mining. Here the problem is solved by considering the destination of the larger share of the output. By established statistical custom, certain industries are grouped together, e.g., stone, clay, and ceramics, and no elements are available for dividing the total between producers and consumers. Furthermore, since producers' goods industries embrace both mining and manufacturing, an indicated increase of the share of the producers' goods industries in total industrial output implies either an increase in the mining output, or growth of the heavy industry, or both, leaving us again on very uncertain ground.

The groupings are hence broadly defined, and no attempt has been made here to create a rigorous classification of producers' goods industries by the recomputation of the data available. Throughout the study we have considered basic industries and consumers' goods industries as rather broad frameworks of reference.

A second important distinction is made currently in Eastern Europe between industries of national and of local interest. Here again the distinction is not quite precise; it seems to be applied not always as a function of, say, size of the plant or even of the output but rather of the location and source of raw materials. The industries of local interest generally comprise some of the small industries close to agriculture or to the village, such as small flour mills, vegetable-oil factories, limestone quarries, small brick kilns, and so on, using only locally available resources. Obviously the less developed a given country is, the greater the economic importance of these industries of local interest. Here again the distinction between the two groups is not always made in a clear-cut way, and one or another East European country will include a given type of industry in one of the two groups and another in the other. As distinct from industries, the crafts form a group in which the East European regions have tried to delimit as sharply as possible the functions of *new production, repair work,* and *services.* Generally the producing units of any significance, ranging from metallurgical workshops to shoemaking or woodworking, have been assimilated into "manufacturing" and have tended to be absorbed in the state sphere. The border cases between manufacturing and crafts, e.g., building trades, or paper and chemical craft enterprises, have also been taken into the state sphere. The term crafts has thus tended to apply more and more only to small food-processing trades (confectioners, bakers, butchers, etc.), to repair work (shoe repair, small tailor shops, etc.), or to personal-services outfits (barbers, launderers, etc.).

By its nature, the broader line between manufacturing sphere and crafts on the one hand and trade and crafts on the other has frequently been a very fuzzy one. Often the distinction between crafts and private retail trade (the first supposedly to be encouraged and the second restricted) has seemed to be so blurred that the nationalization process has avowedly nationalized, as small retail outfits, certain shops which have been subsequently re-established as crafts.

The sphere of nationalization has tended to expand steadily. At the beginning of the nationalization process, small-scale production was considered as encompassing even part of the local industries, crafts, and domestic manufacture. After the annihilation of the capitalist sector in industry, the sphere of small-scale production has shrunk continuously.

Our analysis of the process of nationalization will attempt to take into consideration not only the changes in industry proper but also those in the quite important sectors of local industry and crafts that gravitate around the central manufacturing core.

Nationalization and Structural Reorganization of Industry and Crafts in the Former Allied Group—Czechoslovakia

Before the war the economic importance of the entrepreneurial classes was large only in Czechoslovakia; it was extremely limited in Yugoslavia. The Nazi occupation, accompanied by large-scale physical liquidations and confiscation of property, and civil war almost annihilated these strata in Poland and in Yugoslavia. Only in Czechoslovakia did the democratic political parties upon liberation regain an effective role in the life of the country. In Poland the "bourgeois" parties were reconstituted, but they could not regain effective power in the sharply changed setting of a country shifted bodily 150 miles to the West. In Yugoslavia the victory of Tito resulted in the complete liquidation of the previous political formations. Thus it is understandable that the economic and political resistance to nationalization was bound to be of decreasing significance from Czechoslovakia to Yugoslavia. In this general framework, the "discontinuity" in the nationalization process in Czechoslovakia can basically be attributed to the resistance encountered in the various sectors of the economy. In Poland, and even more so in Yugoslavia, the rhythm of the nationalization process can be considered as a function both of the difficulties inherent in any process implying such large-scale transfers of ownership and of the deliberate volitional action of the ruling Communist group. Each case thus has some distinct features which deserve study in their own right.

Nationalization in Czechoslovakia passed through two stages, the first beginning in October 1945, under the slogan of "national concord," and the second at the time of the Communist coup d'état of February 1948.

The 1945 nationalization measures were defined in a series of presidential decrees which ended a period of virtual chaos. Having been preceded by various confiscations of ex-enemy property or of collaborationist-owned undertakings, they appeared to set a more or less definite limit to the multiple and, as it were, almost limitless growth of the public sector. Applying such criteria as "national interest" or "bigness" of given enterprises (either in number of employees or in capacity of production), the decrees transferred to the state all the mines of the country; all power plants which did not serve non-nationalized industries; iron and steel works and rolling mills; all non-ferrous metal works except those which were economically independent and not included in a combine or trust; foundries with more than 400 employees; engineering works, electrotechnical, optical, and precision works with more than 500 workers; armament and munitions plants; chemical industries with a specified equipment and with more than 150 employees; various categories of glass industries; stone, clay, and ceramic undertakings with over 150 employees; brick-making enterprises with over 200 employees; pulp and paper manufactures with over 300 employees; silk enterprises with over 150 workers; saw mills and mills producing semi-manufactured wood products with over 300 employees; fiber-spinning mills with over 400 employees; fiber-weaving mills with 500 workers; plants for textile printing with over 200 employees; clothing factories with over 500 employees; tanning and leather manufactures with over 400 employees; all phonograph-recording enterprises; sugar factories and refineries; alcohol distilleries and beverage breweries with specified capacities; and chocolate and oleomargarine plants with over 500 employees. Nationalization was applied to "building and equipment and auxiliary installations, stock of raw materials, patents and trade marks, checks and deposits, etc." The periods adopted in establishing the number of employees for determining nationalization were those extending from January 1938 to January 1940 (for most of the consumers' goods industries) and from January 1942 to January 1944 (for the basic industries), i.e., the peak employment periods for these branches.

The varying limits set by the nationalization decrees for different industries suggest at times some arbitrariness but at other times painstaking intraparty transactions. It is in fact known that many dispositions represented hard-bargained compromises.[1] The ensemble of these

[1] For the "behind-the-doors" negotiations, this note, sent on the morrow of the 1945 nationalization by the *Manchester Guardian's* Prague correspondent, is vivid:

> . . . The principle of nationalization was accepted by all four Czech Government parties in April this year in the so-called Košice programme. The working out of its details, however, entailed a considerable amount of hard work as well as some fairly tough political argument behind the closed doors of the Coalition Government's offices, and throughout October the Cabinet has been in almost constant session. . . . It is clear that the Communists and Social Democrats have been working pretty closely together and that together they have succceeded in enlarging the scope of the play beyond what was originally envisaged at Košice. On the other hand, the less radical parties seem to have succeeded in saving the cooperatives, which play a very important part in Czech social and political life, especially in the agricultural industry. A fierce battle seems to have been fought over the sugar industry—one of the staple industries—and at one stage the "sugar barons" were being denounced by works councils in various refineries for bringing pressure on their members to demand that refineries should be turned into cooperatives rather than nationalized. . . . [Cf. *Manchester Guardian,* Manchester, England, Oct. 30, 1945.]

provisions was deemed to establish enduring limits between the national and the private sectors. As Clement Gottwald, Secretary of the Communist Party, specified at the time:

> Through the nationalization of key industries of the economy we are bringing an important element of stabilization in the sense that we are establishing fixed limits between the nationalized and the private sectors. That is why we have decided to proceed not by steps, but by one stroke. We wish to make, as the saying goes, *tabula rasa:* we wish that everybody know what he can do. We are reserving a large part, and in some branches, a decisive part, to private initiative.[2]

The nationalization laws of 1945 brought into the state sector around 57.7 per cent of the total industrial labor force. As can be seen from Table 20, column 1, the nationalized sector included between 50 and 100 per cent of the gainfully employed in the "basic" industries (except saw mills) and between 15 and 50 per cent of those employed in consumers' goods industries (except for printing). If we compare column 1 of Table 20 and column 1 of Table 21, some significant aspects of the concentration of the Czechoslovak industries are immediately apparent. Nationalization of only 17 per cent of the total number of technical units [3] brought into the state sector 57.7 per cent of the gainfully employed. On the average, except for power plants and mining, in the producers' goods industries the percentage of the nationalized technical units varied between 10 and 25 per cent. In the consumers' goods industries, except for textile and glass, it was below 10 per cent. As columns 1 and 2, Table 22, reveal, the nationalization process as such moved along parallel lines in the Czech territories (Bohemia, Moravia, and Silesia) and in Slovakia.

Once nationalization was carried out, the immediate results of efforts to keep a "fixed line" between the state and private sectors began to be blurred by such factors as the absorption of former enemy and collaborationist undertakings by the state, the closing down of certain units in either the state or private sectors, the reorganization of certain industries and the increase in their employment, and so on. As can

[2] Demonstration of Oct. 25, 1945. Cf. *RP,* Oct. 26, 1945.

[3] "Local unit" (or "technical unit") in Czech statistics means any *undertaking* or *part of an undertaking* in separate premises which carries on one or more kinds of production in the same branch of industry. An establishment in which coexist two kinds of production pertaining to two different branches of industry is considered as divided into two parts, each of which is counted as a local unit of the relevant branch of industry. Cf. "Nationalization of the Czechoslovak Industry," in *Statistical Bulletin of Czechoslovakia,* III, 7 (September 1948), p. 120.

TABLE 20. CZECHOSLOVAKIA: THE NATIONALIZED SECTOR—IN PERCENTAGES OF TOTAL EMPLOYMENT IN EACH BRANCH, 1946–49

Industries	1st Quarter, 1946	Average, 1947	Jan. 1, 1948	Jan. 1, 1949
	1	2	3	4
Mining	100.0	100.0	100.0	100.0
Metal	66.6	76.5	74.5	95.4
Chemical	70.6	77.5	78.5	93.9
Saw mills	12.9	17.6	16.9	60.9
Stone, clay	53.9	58.2	59.6	83.7
Paper	53.2	61.5	63.2	92.8
Power plants	93.9	99.0	99.1	99.4
Food-processing	27.0	26.5	29.2	66.7
Textile	49.2	58.0	60.1	93.4
Clothing	17.4	26.3	24.8	82.9
Hides and leather	54.0	58.8	59.1	94.2
Wood-working	20.5	27.3	27.4	71.7
Glass	59.1	70.0	69.3	90.1
Printing	2.7	2.8	3.3	54.8
Total industry	57.7	63.7	63.9	89.2

Sources:

1: Computed from *Průmyslové Zprávy, Státního Úřadu Statistického, Republica Československá* (Industrial Reports of the State Statistical Office of Czechoslovakia), Series A, No. 3–5, II, 17–19, Prague, 1947, pp. 108 (A-24) ff.

2: *Ibid.*, Series A, No. 1–2, II, 7–8, p. 52 (A-12).

3, 4: *Československý Průmysl* (Czechoslovak Industry), publ. by Central Union of Czechoslovak Industry, Prague, 1948, p. 17.

be seen from column 2, Tables 20 and 21, the nationalized sector grew methodically through 1947. By January 1948, i.e., before the unfolding of the second nationalization process, the percentage of the labor force gainfully employed in the state sector rose to 63.9 per cent as against 57.7 per cent in 1946, revealing anything but stable relations among the sectors of the economy.

The February Communist coup d'état tremendously enlarged the boundaries of the state sector in the industrial sphere. Column 4, Table 20, shows that in January 1949 the state sector absorbed, on the basis of nationalization measures, 89.2 per cent of the gainfully employed. In the producers' goods industries the percentage of extension of the state sector varied between 92 and 100 per cent (except for saw mills, and stone and clay), and in the consumers' goods industries this percentage rose to between 70 and 90 per cent (except for printing). On the average, these increases entailed the absorption of over 72 per cent of the technical units. The pace during 1948 appears parallel

TABLE 21. CZECHOSLOVAKIA: THE NATIONALIZED SECTOR—IN PERCENTAGES OF THE TOTAL NUMBER OF TECHNICAL UNITS (PLANTS), 1946–49

Industries	1946	1947	1948	1949
	1	2	3	4
Mining	100.0	99.3	100.0	100.0
Metal	21.3	43.0	71.3	73.2
Chemical	24.7	33.9	70.0	74.3
Saw mills	10.3	15.7	61.9	
Stone, clay	22.8	25.8	56.0	66.3
Paper	18.1	44.4	81.2	84.2
Power plants	81.3	77.3	97.1	98.2
Food-processing	9.1	21.6	80.7	84.8
Textile	22.8	39.8	71.4	63.2 (Textile and Clothing)
Clothing	3.5	15.8	49.6	
Hides and leather	5.8	28.5	68.1	69.9
Wood-working	4.7	18.3	56.0	69.5
Glass	11.5	19.2	49.6	50.7
Printing	3.3	10.7	42.2	49.1
Total industry	17.4	29.4	68.5	72.7

Sources:
1: *Průmyslové Zprávy, op. cit.*
2: *Ibid.*, Series G, No. 4–6, XXX, 15–17, Prague, 1949, pp. 117 (G-31) ff.
3: *SZ*, XI, 7–8 (July–August 1948), p. 282.
4: *Ibid.*, XII, 5–6 (May–June 1949), p. 186.

again in the Czech and Slovak territories (columns 3 and 4, Table 22).

If the film of nationalization is slowly unfolded, some notable aspects of the process of elimination of the private sector become clear. The figures given thus far have covered the enterprises that had fallen directly under the scope of the nationalization decrees. In fact, the private sector was smaller than these figures suggest: account must be taken of the enterprises already owned by the state before the nationalization, the former ex-enemy and collaborationist enterprises confiscated or placed under custody until the determination of their status, the enterprises belonging to local authorities, and the share of cooperatives. As Table 23 indicates, employment in the nationalized sector increased from 61 to 64 per cent of total industrial employment between November 1947 and May 1948. The confiscated industries rapidly increased their share from 13 per cent to 27.8 per cent between February and May 1948. By 1949 almost all these "confiscated" undertakings were drawn into the nationalized sector. The private sector, which employed 22 per cent of industrial workers in November 1947 and 20 per cent in February 1948, had dwindled by three quarters three

TABLE 22. CZECHOSLOVAKIA: NATIONALIZATION IN THE CZECH TERRITORIES (BOHEMIA, MORAVIA, AND SILESIA), AND IN SLOVAKIA IN 1946 AND 1948 [a]

Industries [b]	1946 (yearly average) Czech territories 1	1946 (yearly average) Slovakia 2	1948 (yearly average) Czech territories 3	1948 (yearly average) Slovakia 4
Mining	100.0	100.0	100.0	98.3
Metal	72.4	81.2	87.9	90.5
Chemicals	72.9	82.2	84.2	89.4
Saw mills	18.6	18.5	28.7	41.4
Stone, clay, and ceramics	57.2	55.0	66.8	70.8
Paper	45.5	94.7	73.8	98.2
Electricity	96.6	95.3	98.4	99.4
Food-processing	33.0	20.3	46.9	48.2
Textile	52.4	71.8	77.4	85.7
Clothing	24.5	36.3	52.2	52.9
Leather	56.5	64.1	75.4	73.8
Wood-working	22.4	35.8	47.1	56.5
Glass	64.4	82.0	80.0	84.5
Printing	2.6	4.5	31.2	6.8
Total industry [b]	61.5	62.9	75.8	75.6

[a] As percentages of total industrial employment in each branch in the respective region.

[b] Because of coverage in the sources, the producers' goods industries include ceramics. This is at variance with the grouping in Tables 6 (Chapter 1) and 18 (Chapter 2).

Sources:

1946: Computed from *Průmyslové Zprávy*, *op. cit.*, pp. 110 (A-26) ff.

1948: *Ibid.*, Series G, No. 4–6, XXX, 15–17, pp. 117 (G-31) ff.

months later. Finally, by 1949, when the process of over-all nationalization in manufacturing was virtually completed, the share of the private sector was only 3.6 per cent of total employment. An interesting feature revealed in the same table is the striking decrease of the cooperative enterprises' share, which fell from 2.5 per cent of the total employed in 1947 to 1.4 per cent at the end of the process. Thus, in the dynamics of nationalization, the cooperatives, the so-called "defensive weapon in the fight against the capitalists," played only a marginal role.

The pressure of the combination of nationalization, confiscations, and encroachments of other sectors on the private sector at the peak of the second nationalization drive is illustrated in Table 24. As appears in column 9 (upper part of the table), the actual number of gain-

TABLE 23. CZECHOSLOVAKIA: LEGAL STATUS OF ENTERPRISES AND PERCENTAGE DISTRIBUTION OF PERSONS EMPLOYED IN INDUSTRY—1947–49

Status of Enterprises	Percentage Distribution of Persons Employed			
	XI, 1947	II, 1948	V, 1948	I, 1949
Nationalized	61.0	63.0	64.4	89.4
Confiscated	13.0	12.8	27.8	3.8
State-owned	1.1	1.3	1.3	1.3
Run by local	0.4	0.4	0.5	0.5
Cooperative	2.5	2.1	0.9	1.4
Private-owned	22.0	20.4	5.1	3.6
Total	100.0	100.0	100.0	100.0

Sources: *SZ*, XII, 5–6 (May–June 1949), p. 185.

TABLE 24. CZECHOSLOVAKIA: EMPLOYMENT AND TECHNICAL UNITS IN INDUSTRY AS OF MAY 1, 1948 [a]

Status of Enterprises	Groups by Number of Gainfully Employed								
	0 [b]	1–5	6–10	11–20	21–50	51–100	101–250	251–	Total
	1	2	3	4	5	6	7	8	9
	Gainfully Employed (in thousands)								
Nationalized		1.0	1.6	3.8	16.0	35.7	102.6	747.7	907.7
Confiscated		4.3	9.2	20.9	63.9	89.6	123.8	80.0	391.7
State-owned		0.1	0.2	0.9	2.5	2.5	3.2	9.1	18.5
Local authorities		0.3	0.6	0.9	1.8	0.8	0.4	1.4	6.2
Cooperatives		0.8	0.6	1.4	3.7	3.1	2.8	0.8	13.2
Private		5.7	9.3	21.7	31.1	0.7	1.2	2.6	72.3
Total		12.2	21.5	49.6	119.0	132.4	234.0	841.6	1,409.6
	Local Units								
Nationalized	165	306	200	250	469	492	619	828	3,329
Confiscated	286	1,377	1,185	1,370	1,906	1,269	831	186	8,410
State-owned	40	26	25	64	73	34	23	21	306
Local authorities	32	137	70	60	57	13	3	3	375
Cooperatives	183	324	77	96	115	46	19	2	862
Private	438	1,992	1,185	1,433	1,038	8	9	5	6,108
Total	1,144	4,162	2,742	3,273	3,658	1,862	1,504	1,045	19,390

[a] By size of establishment according to employment and by status of enterprise.
[b] The employees in these units worked only part-time and were included in the other groups.
Source: SZ, XI, 7–8 (July–August 1948), p. 281.

fully employed in the private sector amounted then to around 72,000 persons out of a total 1,409,000 gainfully employed.[4] At that time there were in the private sector of manufacturing 15,000 persons working in small enterprises employing up to 10 persons (columns 2 + 3); 52,000 in the group of medium-sized enterprises (columns 4 + 5); and 4,500 in the group of enterprises with over 50 persons (columns 6 + 7 + 8). In the medium range forming the core of enterprises left in private hands we find 2,471 enterprises, as compared to a total of 5,931, or nearly 42 per cent. In the range over 50, only 22 enterprises, of which but 5 had more than 251 employees, were still in private hands. The nationalization drive inflicted the sharpest blows not on the medium and upper range, as might have been expected, but on the extremes, i.e., on the *small* enterprises and on the *big* ones; thus the process liquidated the "inefficient" small producers and absorbed the large units, but left in private hands the enterprises in the medium range.[5]

The over-all nationalization of the industrial sector was thus achieved in Czechoslovakia after about two years of uneasy coexistence with a private sector accounting for no more than one-fifth of total manufacturing employment. This state of affairs in the foremost country of the Allied group, where the "bourgeois" resistance was initially the strongest and where it was finally overcome by a coup d'état, strongly suggests that no prolonged coexistence was conceivable between a very large state sector and an even highly controlled marginal private economy.

Having followed the process of nationalization in industry, the discussion turns now to the process of dislodgment of private owners in the *handicraft* field. "Craft" production was conceived as comprising in Czechoslovakia both certain undertakings usually considered as industries of local interest (e.g., milling, brewing, food-canning, etc.) and large workshops of dozens of hands[6] often classified as manufacture in the other East European countries. Significant differences in classification of craft establishments existed between the Czech lands (i.e., Bohemia, Moravia, and Silesia) and Slovakia.[7] According to an ex-

[4] This figure is slightly larger than the average for the whole of 1948.

[5] "Social-Economic Structure of Czechoslovak Industry on the Threshold of the Five-Year Plan," *SZ*, XII, 5–6 (May–June 1949), p. 184.

[6] Radovan Šimáček, *Czechoslovak Economy in a Nutshell*, Press Dept., Czechoslovak Ministry of Foreign Trade, Prague, 1948, p. 42.

[7] A number of trades in Slovakia came under the head of crafts, whereas in the Czech provinces they were classified as industries, e.g., printing establishments, or as commerce, e.g., building contractors. Cf. *Statistical Digest of the Czechoslovak Republic in 1948, op. cit.*, p. 64.

haustive inquiry made at the close of 1946 in the Czech territories, there were at the time in that part of the country 177,119 workshops (i.e., technical units) with a total of some 565,000 gainfully employed. The most important branches listed comprised: metal-working—some 27,000 technical units and 104,000 gainfully employed; [8] clothing and fashion—31,300 technical units and 98,000 gainfully employed; food-processing—29,300 technical units and 89,000 gainfully employed; and building trades—15,000 firms and 81,500 gainfully employed.[9] According to figures gathered in December 1947 there were at that time in Slovakia 50,207 craftsman undertakings with a total of over 54,000 journeymen and apprentices. Food and provisions led with over 8,500 workshops, followed by leather-working—7,600; metal-working—6,700; clothing—6,500; wood-working—5,700; and building trades—5,100.

The large-scale nationalization measures opened the way for vast structural changes affecting both production and the organization of industry as a whole. Medium and small establishments were combined to make larger units; production was ended in some establishments and concentrated in others; the industrial machine was revamped from top to bottom and made dependent on the commanding (political) center.

Immediately after the first stage of nationalization the 2,586 largest enterprises in the country were reorganized into some 220 national corporations grouped in eleven sectors under central managements placed under the supervision of the Ministry of Industry. In addition some 125 food-processing industries, organized under the same pattern, were placed under the supervision of the Ministry of Provision. The three-layer structure (base works, national industrial corporations, central managements) was modified in Slovakia by the insertion of a regional administration between the national corporations and the central managements. In the framework of the regional organization each national enterprise possessing its own capital was to have a certain autonomy and was to be administered as a "private" enterprise. The state did not assume the responsibility for any eventual losses. Part of its profits (after the coverage of a given percentage for reserves and other funds) was to be turned over to the state.[10]

[8] These and the following figures are rounded for the purpose of simplification.

[9] Excluding master carpenters, master masons, and architects, who were included in the statistics of the building trades.

[10] *L'Évolution économique de la Tchécoslovaquie* (Economic Evolution of Czechslovakia), Notes et études documentaires (Notes and Documentary Studies), No. 1426, La Documentation Française (French Documentation), Paris, Jan. 26, 1951, pp. 12–13; also, "Nationalization of the Czechoslovak Industry," in *Statistical Bulletin of Czechoslovakia*, III, 7 (September 1948), pp. 120–121.

After the February coup a total of 2,919 new enterprises came under the control of the Ministry of Industry. The Ministry of Provision took control over some 650 enterprises, the Ministry of Technics, 900 enterprises (mostly building), and the Ministry of Information, 250 firms (polygraphic enterprises.[11]

The data available for 1948 and 1949 point toward a substantial drop in the total employment in crafts.[12] By 1948 there were in Czechoslovakia 220,100 workshops with a total employment of over 570,000. By mid-1949 the number of workshops had fallen to 202,000, and the number of gainfully employed to 488,000. As can be seen from the lower part of Table 25, throughout this process the share of

TABLE 25. CZECHOSLOVAKIA: DEVELOPMENT OF HANDICRAFTS, 1946–49

	No. of Workshops	Gainfully Employed
1946–47	227,326	669,207
1948	220,100	570,803
1949 [a]	202,700	488,520
	Czech Territory	
1946	177,119	564,800
1948	179,300	465,200
1949 [b]	169,900	431,200

[a] Mid-1949.
[b] March 1949.

Sources:
1946–47: R. Šimáček, *op. cit.*, p. 42.
1948: *SZ*, XII, 11 (November 1949), p. 413.
1949: *Ibid.*, XIII, 1 (January 1950), p. 16, and XIII, 7 (July 1950), p. 240.

the Czech territory has continued to remain overwhelming. The previous allowance for private crafts with a large number of employees has been substantially modified: e.g., in mid-1949, out of a total 488,520 gainfully employed, 272,774 were wage earners employed in some 200,000 workshops.

By then, the policy of systematic restriction of private ownership to small producers brought about a relatively rapid increase of the state sector in crafts and a clear-cut differentiation between the larger producing workshops and the smaller ones. By 1950 it was indicated

[11] "Reorganization of Czechoslovak Industry," in *Bulletin of the National Bank of Czechoslovakia*, May 1949, pp. 95–97.

[12] These figures must be considered with much caution, given (*a*) the differences in classification mentioned above between the Czech lands and Slovakia, and (*b*) a redefinition of the crafts categories in 1949.

that nationalized shops accounted for 14.3 per cent of total handicraft production, the "capitalist sector" for 58.8 per cent, and small-scale private production for 26.9 per cent.[13] In the "border cases" between industry and crafts such as the building industry, the public sector, which had produced but 7 per cent of the output before February 1948, increased its share to 75 per cent by the end of the year, and in 1949 to 93 per cent.[14]

The basic organizational structure of industry was modified as follows: the scope of basic plants was broadened so as to embrace a few branch works and workshops. The entire industry was divided into 249 corporations under the Ministry of Industry, 191 corporations under the Ministry of Provision, and two other corporations, one each under the Ministries of Technics and Information. The centralization of decision-making was strengthened by placing the central managements in the above-mentioned ministries, where they assumed thenceforth the former function of the ministerial production departments. In certain cases (e.g., metal industry) this centralization did not, however, prevent the splitting of the central managements into two or three units in order to achieve a higher specialization by branches (e.g., metal-working and engineering) (see Chart 4).[15]

In 1951–52 the central managements themselves were abolished and their tasks transferred directly to specific ministries (in Slovakia, commissionnaireships) of mining, light industry, heavy industry, etc., the object being to secure "the greatest possible simplification, economy, and resilience of the administrative apparatus." [16]

Substantial changes occurred also in the control of local industry and crafts after the February coup. Small plants of local interest were transferred to the administration of the local authorities. These plants, producing mainly objects of daily and household use from local materials and residual materials from the state sector, were first placed under the Ministry of Interior, on which the local authorities depended. Subsequently, because of the crisis in the supply of con-

[13] See Introduction by N. Tiapkin to *Pervyi Piatiletnii Plan Razvitiia Narodnogo Khoziaistva Chekhoslovakii.* (First Five-year Plan of Development of the Czechoslovak People's Republic), Izdatel'stvo Inostrannoi Literatury (Foreign Literature Publishing House), Moscow, 1950, p. 9.

[14] Jaromír Dolanský, *Three Years of Planning in the Czechoslovak People's Republic,* Orbis, Prague, 1949, p. 9.

[15] See, in *Adresář Československého Průmyslu, 1949* (Directory of the Czechoslovak Industry for 1949), Orbis, Prague, 1949, p. 12, a list of the national corporations and central managements.

[16] *CEB,* No. 233, Oct. 15, 1951, pp. 13–14.

sumer goods apparent in 1953, the supervision of the enterprises was placed under a new Ministry of Local Economy.[17]

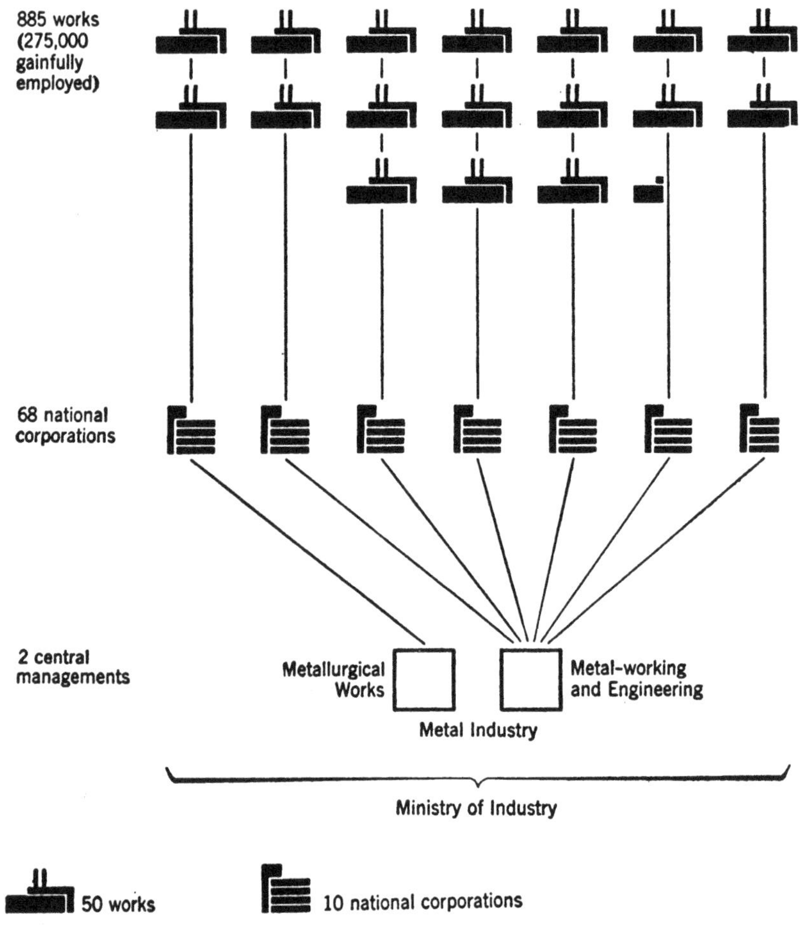

CHART 4. ORGANIZATIONAL SCHEME OF AN INDUSTRY (THE METAL INDUSTRY, CZECHOSLOVAKIA, 1949)

In the fields of crafts the most important structural changes occurred after 1949. State intervention followed essentially the lines already stated: (1) establishment of a consolidated list of crafts, sharply separating production and distribution, to effect better control and integration of craft production within the framework of the long-

[17] "Plans for Local Industry," in *Prague News Letter,* IX, 24 (Dec. 5, 1953).

term plan; (2) enlargement of the state sector, mainly in the sphere of the larger craft enterprises; (3) development of cooperatives.

Poland

Considering the structure of postwar Poland—half being its own prewar but now devastated territories and the other half former German land from which the Germans had fled or been expelled—it is easy to visualize the inevitable enormous extension of state ownership, even in the closing days of the war. Thus the decree of January 3, 1946, the only Polish nationalization law, sanctioned a process well under way. By the provisions of this law the state was to take over (besides the industrial, mining, and transportation undertakings of the Germans, the former Danzig administration, and their nationals) the mines, the petroleum industry, the power, gas, and water works in public service, all synthetic fuel industries, foundries for ferrous and non-ferrous metals, armament industries, cokeries, sugar factories, industrial distilleries and alcohol refineries, breweries, yeast factories, flour mills of a given capacity, cold-storage installations, and printing establishments, as well as any other industrial undertaking "capable of employing more than 50 workers per shift."

Article 3 of the law contained, moreover, a general clause which in fact extended the state's prerogatives for the nationalization of industries far beyond the enormous field already specified since it provided that a decree of the Council of Ministers would be sufficient to effect the nationalization of any type of enterprise not included in the categories mentioned by the law.[18] The decree of January 3, 1946, provided also for the possibility that the cooperatives might absorb a number of the undertakings turned over to state ownership. At the time the cooperatives included only a small section of the economy and were limited mostly to establishments such as commercial mills, yeast factories, confectionery factories, fruit-preserving plants, distilleries, and bakeries.[19]

At the same time the Polish regime, which expressed the desire to preserve a "substantial" sector of the economy in private hands, adopted a special law designed to "encourage private initiative."

[18] See the detailed analysis of the law by Alfred Kraus (Vice-President, Trib. of Kraków): "La Nationalisation de l'industrie en Pologne" (The Nationalization of Industry in Poland), *Droit social* (Social Right), X, 3 (March 1947), pp. 131–141.

[19] *Quarterly Review of the Bank Gospodarstwa Krajowego* (National Economic Bank), XV, 5 (December 1946), p. 7.

Article 2, paragraph 4, of this law specified that "newly created private enterprises would not be transferred to the state, even if they were capable of employing more than 50 workers per shift"; Article 3 of the same law assured the owners of private enterprises ". . . of the liberty to develop these undertakings" and of state "assistance as far as their economic activity was concerned within the framework of the national economic plan." [20] Thus, perhaps more than any other "people's democracy," Poland insisted on "specific characteristics of development" combining "three growing interwoven forms of property": state, cooperative, and private.[21]

According to the data available for 1946, in industrial plants with more than 5 workers the three sectors mentioned above included, respectively: (1) the state sector (and local authorities), 32.5 per cent of the number of plants and 84.3 per cent of the gainfully employed; (2) the cooperative sector, 10.2 per cent of the number of plants and 5.2 per cent of the gainfully employed; (3) the private sector, 57.3 per cent of the number of plants and 10.5 per cent of the gainfully employed.[22]

The state sector included the whole of mining and metal manufacture of the country and embraced over 80 per cent of the workers in other basic manufacturing fields. In the consumers' goods branches, the state took over from 65 to 90 per cent (and even up to 98 per cent in textiles) of the gainfully employed (see Table 26). The cooperatives and the private sector included a significant portion of the food-processing industries. In these industries the cooperative portion was 16.3 per cent of the total employment in plants with 5 and more workers, as against an average of 10.2 per cent of the gainfully employed in industry, including plants with less than 5 workers. The private sector amounted to 17.8 per cent of the total

[20] *Les Nationalisations en Europe orientale* (Nationalizations in Eastern Europe), Notes et études Documentaires (Notes and Documentary Studies), No. 1592, La Documentation Française (French Documentation), Paris, March 1952.

[21] "The Three-Year Investment Plan will introduce new characteristics in Poland's economic structure which will be divided into three fundamental sectors—public, private and cooperative. In the private sector, the State will exert its influence by issuing political and economic instructions, and by a policy of regulating prices and investment." Cf. Hilary Minc, "The Polish Three-Year Plan," speech of Sept. 21, 1946, to the National Assembly; English translation in *Changing Epoch* Series, No. 2, Birch Books, London, 1947, p. 31.

[22] Cf. *Statistical Yearbook of Poland 1948, op. cit.,* p. 61. These figures are for the end of 1946 and are slightly different from the accounts for mid-1946 presented in Table 26.

Table 26. Poland: The State Sector in Industry in 1946 as Percentage of the Total Gainfully Employed in the Respective Branch in Industrial Plants with 5 and More Workers

Industry	% of Total Employed in Respective Industry
Mining and liquid fuel	100.0
Metallurgical	100.0
Electrotechnical	83.3
Precision and optical	80.0
Chemical	80.5
Saw mills	81.5
Stone, quarries, cement	81.4
Paper	84.6
Power plants	82.0
Food	63.2
Textile	98.4
Clothing	78.7
Leather	88.8
Woodworking	66.5
Glass and ceramics	82.3

Source: Computed from *Statistical Yearbook of Poland 1948*, *op. cit.*, pp. 61–66.

employment in plants with 5 and more workers, as against a share of 10.5 per cent of the total employment in industry.

The process of reducing the private sector can be readily inferred from the following data. According to official accounts, the private sector in mid-1946 controlled 9,700 manufacturing plants with 5 to 20 workers, or double the number of this type of plant held by the state, and some 950 plants with more than 20 workers, or one-sixth of this type of plant held by the state (see Table 27). At the beginning of that year Polish planners gave assurances that the private sector was going to hold "40 per cent of the industry in its hands," but the reference remained relatively accurate only so far as the percentage distribution of the number of plants was concerned, not in relation to the effective importance of this sector.[23] The evolution of the three sectors in industry (i.e., including industrial plants with less than 5 workers) points clearly toward the rapidly decreasing importance, in both absolute and relative terms, of the private sector and to the rather sluggish development of cooperatives relative to the growth of the state sector.

[23] Actually Hilary Minc was speaking, at the beginning of 1946, of the persistence of a private sector employing "40 per cent of the industrial gainfully employed." Cf. *Życie Warszawy* (Warsaw Life), No. 3, Jan. 3, 1946.

TABLE 27. POLAND: LEGAL STATUS OF INDUSTRIAL PLANTS WITH 5 AND MORE WORKERS AS OF AUGUST 1946

Branches	Number of Plants								Total Percentage Distribution of Plants with 5 and More Workers			
	With 5–20 workers				With 20 and over							
	State	Coop-erative	Pri-vate [a]	Other [a]	State	Coop-erative	Pri-vate [a]	Other [a]	State	Coop-erative	Pri-vate [a]	Other [a]
	1	2	3	4	5	6	7	8	9	10	11	12
Mining and liquid fuel					396				100.0			
Metal and metallurgical	296	47	1,108	118	767	32	198	17	41.2	3.1	50.5	5.2
Electrotechnical	28	4	103	4	113	4	22	2	50.4	2.9	44.6	2.1
Chemical	79	4	185	7	304	15	58	4	58.4	2.9	37.0	1.7
Wood and timber	570	63	938	61	612	22	95	9	49.8	3.6	43.6	3.0
Stone, glass, ceramics	120	43	304	18	682	25	68	1	63.6	5.4	29.5	1.5
Paper	21	3	124	2	117	2	27		46.6	1.7	51.0	0.7
Power plants [b]	170	1	6		402	5	7		96.8	1.0	2.2	0.0
Food-processing	3,320	803	5,771	570	910	318	346	53	35.0	9.3	50.5	5.2
Textile	68	12	111	89	688	3	16		76.6	1.5	12.9	9.0
Clothing	34	36	842	18	162	18	39	4	17.0	4.7	76.4	1.9
Leather	10	3	28	5	171	2	4		81.2	2.3	14.3	2.2
Printing	80	19	155	7	230	1	60	14	54.8	3.5	38.0	3.7
Total	4,796	1,038	9,675	899	5,554	447	940	104	44.1	6.3	45.3	4.3

[a] Including one-person firms, public (firms) partnerships, joint-stock limited companies, etc. In another legal status have been included establishments belonging to political parties, social organizations, ecclesiastical and scientific institutions, etc., and establishments of an unknown legal status. (There were no data concerning some counties in the newly acquired territories.)

[b] Including gas and water.

Source: Statistical Yearbook of Poland 1947, op. cit., p. 76.

TABLE 28. POLAND: EVOLUTION OF THE "THREE SECTORS" IN INDUSTRY PROPER, 1947–49 [a]

Sectors	Employment 1947	Employment 1948	Employment 1949 [c]	Percentages [b] 1947	Percentages [b] 1948	Percentages [b] 1949 [c]
1. Public sector [d]	1,349,297	1,305,880	1,436,880	86.8	87.4	89.3
2. Cooperatives	64,028	82,587	98,058	4.1	5.5	6.1
3. Private	141,308	105,942	73,765	9.1	7.1	4.6
Total	1,554,633	1,494,409	1,608,703	100.0	100.0	100.0

[a] Total employment and percentage distribution by sectors.
[b] Rounded percentages.
[c] March 1949.
[d] State and local authorities.

Sources: Total employment in *industry proper* has been derived for 1947 by deducting total employment in crafts (cf. *Statistical Yearbook of Poland 1948*, op. cit., pp. 57, 68). Total employment in 1948 has been obtained by the same procedure [cf. *Rocznik Statystyczny 1949* (Statistical Yearbook 1949), Główny Urząd Statystyczny Polskiej Rzeczypospolitej Ludowej (Central Statistical Office of the Polish People's Republic), Warsaw, 1950, pp. 38, 42]. These figures are smaller than those given in the last-mentioned source for employment in these years in industries engaged in "material production" (a term which obviously includes also certain workshops). From total employment obtained, the employment in the state sector has been derived as a residual, the employment in the private sector and cooperatives being supplied in the last-mentioned source, p. 33.

For 1949, cf. *Rocznik Statystyczny 1949, op. cit.*, p. 38.

As can be seen from Table 28, the relative share of the private sector in total industrial employment fell from 9.1 per cent in 1947 to 7.1 per cent in 1948 and to 4.6 per cent in 1949; in absolute terms, it fell from some 141,300 gainfully employed in 1947 to 73,700 in 1949.

Official data for 1954 still claim the existence in Poland of some 5,008 of private manufacturing enterprises with a total of 10,664 gainfully employed. Actually the term "manufacturing plant" is applied to very small enterprises with no more than 1 to 3 workers. Many of these enterprises, producing small electrical appliances, construction materials, toys, brushes, and so forth, are typical "border cases" between industry and crafts, and some of them have been previously classified in the latter group. The liquidation of the private industry is illustrated by the following figures: this industry accounted in 1949 for 5.5 per cent of the gross value of industrial production; it accounted in 1954 for only 0.6 per cent of that value.[24]

[24] Cf. *Rocznik Statystyczny 1955*, Warsaw, 1956, pp. 69, 98.

A modern building industry was founded and developed by the state through extensive reorganizations in a few years. By 1949 the state sector accounted for 82.1 per cent of the total building construction; a few years later nearly all building construction was carried out by state enterprises.[25] In fact, by 1948 the Polish planners had discarded their previous theories on the "three sectors of development" and were saying that Poland was, after all, a socialist state; that capitalist influence had to be eliminated first and foremost in industry; and that planning under the conditions prevailing in the "people's democracies" "could not be different from planning in the Soviet Union." [26] From then on there was constantly increased pressure to curtail private industry.

While manufacturing of any importance was being concentrated in the hands of the state, and local industries were coming progressively under the control of cooperatives and local authorities, the private sector gained increased importance in handicrafts. In effect, the official data available show, up to 1948, an increase in both the number of workshops and the gainfully employed in crafts (see Table 29). However, this was an increase only of units with an average employment of 2 or less persons per workshop. As of 1948 the most important craft branches were: clothing (some 61,000 workshops and over 100,000 gainfully employed); food-processing (32,000 units and close to 75,000 gainfully employed); wood-working (16,000 workshops and 34,000 gainfully employed); and building trades (over 11,000 units and 43,000 gainfully employed). Except for the latter group, where the number per unit is close to double the average, the average number of gainfully employed per unit was 2.

The share of private handicrafts in total production dwindled sharply from 1949 on. Although no comprehensive data are available on the extension of nationalization in crafts, the over-all results are quite clear. By 1953 there were only some 82,000 workshops left, with some 124,000 gainfully employed. The emphasis placed since 1953 on the "positive role" of private handicrafts has not brought about, thus far, new and significant developments in this field (see Table 29).

[25] Stefan Jędrychowski, "Economic Development and Growth of National Income in Poland," in *FLP*, May 1, 1953. According to the *Rocznik Statystyczny 1955*, there were in 1954 some 1,427 gainfully employed in the private building companies as against 704,912 gainfully employed in the nationalized building companies. Cf. *Rocznik 1955*, *op. cit.*, p. 142.

[26] Cf. Hilary Minc, "Concerning the Basis of Planning in the People's Democracies," *op. cit.*

TABLE 29. POLAND: DEVELOPMENT OF HANDICRAFTS, 1946–54

Year	No. of Workshops	Gainfully Employed
1946	113,113	183,426
1947	151,872	227,162
1948	178,581	383,837
1953	82,611	123,865
1954	87,882	133,184

Sources:

1946: *Statystyka Zakładów Premysłowych i Rzemieśluiczyck, 1946*, Statystyka Polski, Seria D (Statistics of Industry and Crafts, 1946, Polish Statistical Series D), Central Statistical Office, Warsaw, 1948.

1947–48: *Rocznik Statystyczny 1949, op. cit.*, pp. 33 and 38.

1953–54: *Rocznik Statystyczny 1955, op. cit.*, p. 98.

The pattern of structural reorganization of Polish industry, generally very similar to the Czechoslovak pattern, presents some distinct features.

In the early phase of nationalization, the large and medium-sized state industrial establishments (as well as the small establishments combined whenever possible into larger producing units) were organized into a three-layer pyramid: (1) base works, (2) branch unions, (3) central administration boards. The branches were basically similar to the Czech "national corporations." The central administration boards, totaling 14, controlled all industry except the food-processing lines and operated under the authority of the Ministry of Industry and Trade. They also controlled the "centrales of supply" and the "centrales of sales," charged, respectively, with the supply of the given industry and with the distribution of its products. The food-processing industries were under certain specific boards; the monopolies (alcohol, tobacco, etc.) were under the Ministry of Finance; small industries closely related to agriculture were connected with the Ministry of Agriculture and Land Reform. By the close of 1946 the central administration boards became commercialized state enterprises endowed with their own legal and financial status.[27]

At the close of 1950 the entire organization of industry was revamped. The central administration boards, now largely diversified,[28] were

[27] Cf. "Organization of Industry in Poland," in *Quarterly Review of the Bank Gospodarstwa Krajowego,* XV, 5, December 1946, pp. 1–7.

[28] An idea of the continuous diversification of these boards, owing to a diversification in production, can be obtained from the following table from Stefan Wiktorowicz, "Przemysł Panstwowy" (State Industry), in *Kultura* (Culture), Numer Krajowy

decommercialized and reconverted into departments in ministries. The centrales of sales, removed from the control of the boards after 1948, passed under the direct control of the ministries, following a general pattern evolved by the Soviet Union and extending progressively to the entire area.[29]

Various structural arrangements of local industries have been adopted in Poland. In the early period of nationalization they functioned under the direction of local authorities and under the supervision of the Ministry of Industry and Trade. Subsequently some of them were transferred to provincial authorities, and others were placed directly under a newly created Ministry of Small-Scale Production and Handicrafts. As in Czechoslovakia, these are industries producing mostly goods for household use and having either a local base of raw materials or using residual materials from large-scale state manufacturing.[30]

During the reconstruction period handicrafts in Poland were organized into guilds, membership in which was made compulsory. The guilds, organized into provincial handicraft Chambers, were grouped in a Union of Chambers of Crafts. The actual control of both supply and output in this sector was vested in the state-controlled Central

(Special Issue on Poland), Vol. II, 1952, p. 158.

POLAND: CENTRAL BOARDS DEPENDING ON THE MINISTRIES OF INDUSTRY

1947		1949		1951 (Jan.)
Ministries of:		Ministries of:		
Trade	16	Heavy industry	4	20
Reconstruction	2	Mines	3	4
		Light industry	7	10
		Agriculture and consumables	5	7
		Chemical industry	—	5
		Building	2	2
		City construction and colonization		1
	18		21	49

[29] R. P. Rochlin, *Die Wirtschaft Polens von 1945 bis 1952* (The Polish Economy from 1945 to 1952), Deutsches Institut für Wirtschaftsforschung (German Institute for Economic Research), new series, No. 20, Duncker and Humblot, Berlin, 1953, p. 55.

[30] Hilary Minc, "Sześcioletni Plan Rozwoju Gospodarczego i Budowy Podstaw Socjalizmu w Polsce" (The Six-year Plan of Economic Development and the Construction of the Basis of Socialism in Poland), *Nowe Drogi*, IV 22, 1950, p. 6; also, Adam Fonar, "Nowa Organizacja Państwowego PrzemysłuTerènowego" (New Organization of the State Local Industry), in *Zycie Gospodarcze* (Economic Life), April 16, 1951, pp. 460 ff.

Handicraft Establishment for Supply and Sale, dependent for supplies on residual materials from the state enterprises and for sales on the state distribution channels.[31]

YUGOSLAVIA

In the last phase of Yugoslavia's liberation from the Nazis Yugoslav industry was placed under the management of the state on the basis of a decree of November 24, 1944, which provided for the confiscation of property of ex-enemies, collaborationists, and war profiteers. The constitution of January 1946 contained the formula that "all mineral wealth, sources of power, and communications are public property." The Parliament adopted on December 5, 1946, a detailed nationalization law transferring to the state all the undertakings in 42 specified branches of industries of "national importance." Thus all the mines, power plants, metal and metal-working industries, most of the chemical plants, cement factories, and food-processing industries of any significance were nationalized. The limits of the national sector were very loosely defined. In 1948, after the first year of the Five-Year Plan, it was officially stated that it was "impossible to count upon private enterprises for the fulfillment of the Plan," and consequently in April of that year nationalization was extended to all enterprises of "local interest."

The main developments of the nationalization process are summarized in the following figures taken from an official statement of Boris Kidrič.[32] In 1945–46, 55 per cent of Yugoslav industry was nationalized and 27 per cent was sequestered by the state, "which, for all practical purposes, meant the same as nationalization." In 1946–47 the state sector "already held the whole of industry on the federal and republican levels and 70 per cent of the local industries." Finally, in 1948, the whole of industry, including that of local interest, was transferred to the state.

Although nationalization of industry was extended to include even the village-type industries of local interest, *most* crafts remained under

[31] *Quarterly Review of the Bank Gospodarstwa Krajowego,* XV, 1, March 1948, p. 14. See also Władysław Kowalczyk, "Prywatny Przemysł, Handel i Rzemiosło" (Private Industry, Trade, and Crafts), in *Kultura,* Numer Krajowy, Vol. II, 1952, pp. 212 ff.

[32] Boris Kidrič, *On the Construction of Socialist Economy in the FPRY,* speech delivered at the Fifth Congress of the CPY, publ. by the Office of Information of the FPRY, Belgrade, 1948, pp. 7–8.

private ownership. The main reasons for this situation were expressed as follows in the 1947 Five-Year Plan, the first all-round plan of development adopted in the region:

> . . . The opinion that handicrafts have had their day still subsists, that handicrafts are no longer necessary when powerful industries are being built, that, falling as they do within the private economic sector, they hinder the proper development of social, i.e., socialist production. . . . This is completely erroneous. We need the handicrafts and they are useful to us. In many branches, our industry will not, for a long time to come, satisfy all the needs of our peoples, and some branches cannot as yet be replaced by industry at all. . . . Not to neglect and eliminate handicrafts but to incorporate them in our general economic plan, to give them assistance, to organize them into producers' cooperatives that they may serve the general economic development of our country as usefully as possible—such is our policy regarding handicrafts and all should abide by it.[33]

Before the war there were in Yugoslavia some 156,000 craft workshops with 296,000 gainfully employed. Metallurgical workshops and repair shops, wood-working, leather, textile, and food-processing each accounted for around 20,000 units, the rest consisting of building, personal services, printing, etc.[34] According to the data available for 1946 there were at that time in Yugoslavia a total of 150,000 workshops with as many owners and 75,000 workers, or a total of 225,000 gainfully employed in crafts (see Table 30).

By 1951 the total number of workshops decreased, but that of gainfully employed rose to a total of over 278,000. Since then there has been a marked recovery in the fields of private crafts. According to the data for 1954, out of a total of 157,000 workshops, some 142,000 establishments were in the private sector and counted some 192 workers and close to 50,000 apprentices. Notwithstanding this recovery the number of gainfully employed per unit is still under 2. In contrast the number of gainfully employed per unit in the socialist sector is over 9. The most important private crafts continued to be metal workshops, wood-processing crafts, and textiles.[35]

In the early postwar period the nationalized Yugoslav industry was immediately organized on the centralized patterns outlined above for

[33] *Five-Year Plan of the Federal People's Republic of Yugoslavia,* Jugoslovenska Knjiga (Yugoslav Book), Belgrade, 1947, pp. 11–12.

[34] *Statistički Godišnjak 1938–1939,* op. cit., pp. 192–193.

[35] Following a different classification adopted since 1955, the total number of workshops for 1954 is given as 217,352, instead of 157,000 as in Table 30. See: *Statistički Godišnjak FRNJ 1956* (Statistical Yearbook of the FPRY 1956), Belgrade, 1956, p. 157. For consistency we used the pre-1955 classification.

TABLE 30. YUGOSLAVIA: DEVELOPMENT OF HANDICRAFTS, 1946–54

	Number of Workshops		Number of Artisans [a]	
	Total	In Socialist Sector	Total	In Socialist Sector
1946	150,000	746 [b]	225,000	[c]
1951	115,682	10,346	278,757	114,324
1954	157,076	15,163	377,360	135,299

[a] Including private owners.
[b] Data for 1947.
[c] Not available.

Sources:

1946 total: *Yugoslavie: Articles et documents* (Yugoslavia: Articles and Documents), No. 670, La Documentation Française (French Documentation), Paris, 1946.

State: Edward Kardelj, *On People's Democracy in Yugoslavia*, Yugoslav Information Center, New York, 1949, p. 75.

1951 and 1954: *Statistički Godišnjak FNRJ 1956*, *op. cit.*, p. 155.

Czechoslovakia and Poland, i.e., base works, national corporations, and directorates. After the 1948 break with the Kremlin, the Yugoslavs gradually evolved a new system of organization, the main characteristic of which is a marked decentralization of control and, hence, a more systematic reliance on the "intermediate" echelons. The underlying idea of the reform is the preparation of conditions for the "withering away" of the state and the prevention of the development of a bureaucracy with "vested interests." [36]

The reorganization started around 1950 [37] with the transfer of enterprises producing consumers' goods such as textiles and shoes from federal authority to that of the people's republics. Subsequently a whole series of industries were similarly transferred: coal, chemicals, glass, paper, food-processing, tobacco, cement, printing, federal agricultural enterprises, etc. There were left under federal control the oil industry, metallurgy, and machine construction (i.e., key producers' goods industries), and building and transport.

The organizational setup of industry took the following shape:

[36] M. Pešković and M. Čečez, "Nacionalizacija u FNRJ i Istočno-Evropskim Zemljama" (Nationalization in Yugoslavia and in the East European Countries), in *Ekonomist* (Economist), II, 5–6, 1950, pp. 55 ff.

[37] See mainly Dr. Nikola Balog, "Neka pitanja u vezi reorganizacije saveznih i republičkih privrednoupravnih organa" (Some Questions in Connection with the Reorganization of Federal and Republican Economic-Administrative Organs), in *Ekonomist*, III, 3 (1950), pp. 3–18.

basic plants, "associations of enterprises," and general directories. The type of association of enterprises determines the nature of the respective General Directory. The association can consist either of establishments producing the same type of goods or of establishments with common commercial interests. The General Directories were established as independent government organs, the head of a General Directory being a member of either the republican or federal government, and holding the rank of Minister. The structure was thus tied either to the respective people's republic government or to the federal government, usually to the former, only those industries for which absolute national unity was considered necessary being tied to the federal government. The Directors-Ministers were members of the governmental councils, which, together with certain ministers, formed the Economic Council of a given republic (see Chart 5).

The Council performed both controlling and managerial functions. At the federal level, in the Federal Economic Council, were the Directors-Ministers of certain specific industries (e.g., machine construction, building industry) and federal Ministers of Finance, Labor, etc. The role of the *federal* council was defined as aiming to "coordinate and control—not to manage."

This organizational setup, although permitting decentralization of control and some leeway at the republican levels, remains top-heavy and its modification appears to be in the making.

Local industry was to be managed and controlled both at the local and the republican level (see Chart 5).

Nationalization and Structural Reorganization of Industry and Crafts in the Ex-Enemy Group—Hungary

In the ex-enemy countries, Hungary, Romania, and Bulgaria, the dynamics of nationalization followed a different path, mainly because of three sets of factors of unequal impact: (1) In contrast to conditions in the former Allied countries, the social structures were better preserved in these countries (especially in Romania and Bulgaria); (2) multiple Soviet mortgages were placed on these economies, and a certain period of adjustment and "sifting" was necessary before the expansion of the state sector proper could occur; (3) up to the end of 1946 these countries tried to make a legal return to the international scene and did not feel entirely free in their movements, even after the signature of the 1947 peace treaty.

Whereas in 1945 the nationalization process was in full swing in

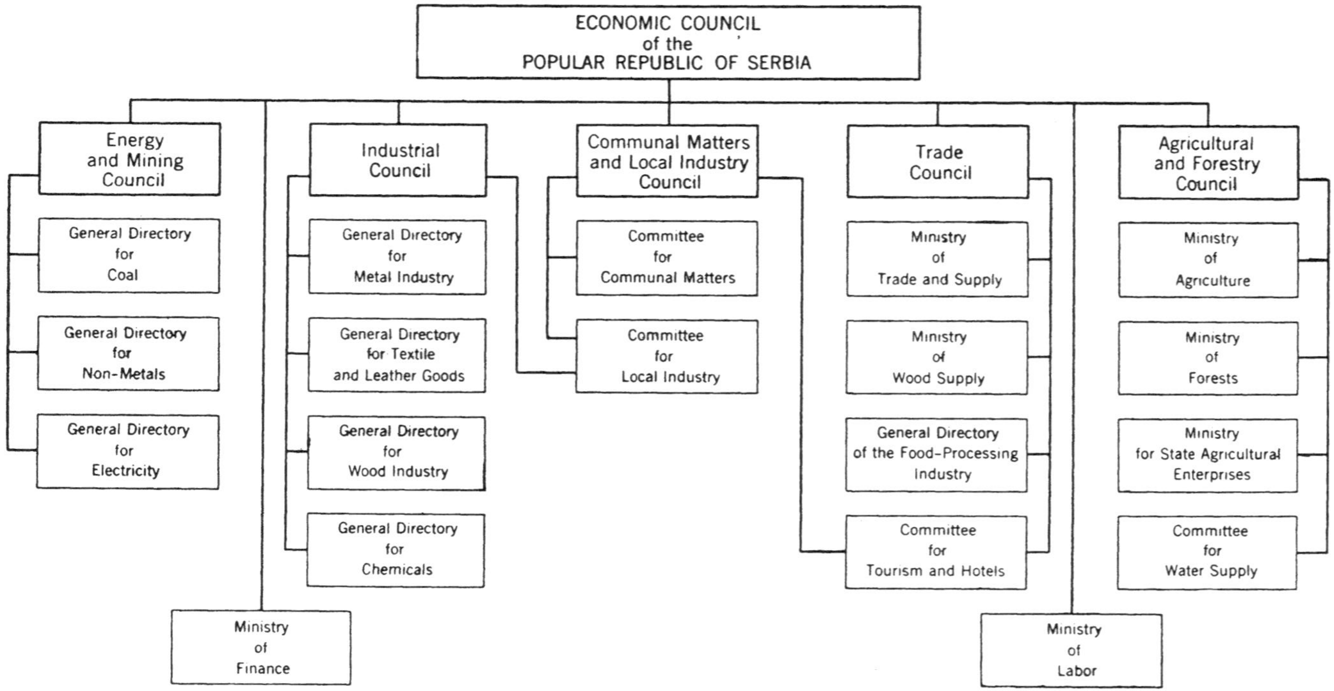

After N. Balog

CHART 5. ECONOMIC COUNCIL AND INDUSTRIAL DIRECTORATES AT THE LEVEL OF A REPUBLIC (SERBIA, YUGOSLAVIA, 1950)

the former Allied countries, the only nationalization measures taken in Hungary at that time were those affecting the coal mines and the large power plants (decree of December 20, 1945). However, in addition to the German ownerships, which were placed provisionally under state control (before being turned over to the Soviet Union or changed into joint Soviet-Hungarian partnerships), the state at the end of 1946 took possession of the largest concerns forming the backbone of Hungarian heavy industry (Rimamurany, Ganz, and Manfred-Weiss). In mid-1947, given the prewar or war-acquired state ownerships and the nationalizations mentioned above, the state sector contained a total of some 32 per cent of the employment in manufacture. In the consumers' goods branches the share of the private sector remained far more significant (see Table 31).

By the end of 1947, after the nationalization of banks, the state share increased to between 40 and 50 per cent of the total employment in industry, leaving some 50 to 60 per cent in the private sector.[38]

Confident that the process of nationalization was going to slow down, the private sector and the foreign companies invested substantially at that time in mining, industry, and in the economy as a whole.[39] However, by early 1948 the break with the West brought about a complete transformation in the political and economic climate of the country.

In March 1948 a decision of the Council of Ministers, followed by the adoption of a nationalization law (March 16) concerning all the undertakings with over 100 employees, doubled the share of the state sector of total employment in manufacture (see Table 31). At this time the state share in mining as a whole increased to 93.3 per cent, with coal-mining nationalized up to 98.6 per cent and manganese and iron ore up to 100 per cent, whereas no nationalization had yet taken place in oil production.[40] In manufacturing the state shares ranged from 65 per cent in the paper industry and 68.2 per cent in the chemical industry to 73.7 per cent in the food industry and up to 100 per

[38] See Chapter 4, the section on nationalization and structural modification of the banking system in the ex-enemy group.

[39] Private investment in mining and industry amounted to 10.3 per cent of the total investment, foreign investment, to 9.3 per cent. The Soviet and Soviet joint-company investments represented only 3.5 per cent of the total. Cf. *GT*, II, 13 (November 1948), p. 886.

[40] Oil production was still entirely in American hands (Standard Oil); the Soviet-Hungarian Oil Corporation (Maszovol) was at the time engaged in exploration and research only.

TABLE 31. HUNGARY: THE NATIONALIZED SECTORS IN MANUFACTURE, 1947 AND 1948 EMPLOYMENT AND PERCENTAGES

By Industries (1947)

Industries	State	Private and other [a]
	Percentages of total employment	
Mining	90.6 [b]	9.4 [b]
Steel and metal	74.2	25.8
Machinery	57.8	42.2
Chemical	3.6	96.4
Stone, clay, and ceramics	3.4	96.6
Paper	[c]	100.0
Power plants	14.2	85.8
Food-processing	17.9	82.1
Textile	1.5	98.5
Clothing	[c]	100.0
Hides and leather	[c]	100.0
Lumber	9.1	90.9
Printing	11.4	88.6
Other consumer industries [d]	[c]	100.0

By Systems of Ownership (1948)

	Absolute figures (workers, average)	Percentages	
State sector	285,680	77.0	
Private and other, of which:	98,320	23.0	
Cooperative and municipal ownership			1.2
Soviet ownership			3.6
Owned by Western citizens			5.5
Private small-scale			12.7
Total	384,000	100.0	

[a] "Other" includes plants withdrawn from the private sector and turned over to the Soviet Union as German assets.
[b] Figures for coal-mining only.
[c] Not available.
[d] Including rubber, feather, bristle, and hair manufacturing.

Sources:
for 1947: *GT*, I, 6 (May 1947), pp. 245–246.
for 1948: *HB*, No. 26, May 10, 1948.

cent in the basic industries (e.g., 92.5 per cent in the iron and steel industry, 100 per cent in the paper mills).[41]

Less than two years later, on the eve of launching the first five-year plan, December 29, 1949, the state sector absorbed "all the enterprises where the total number of employees has been 10 or more since September, 1949," and all foreign concerns except those "whose ownership is based upon the treaties and laws in force which were passed on January 20, 1945," i.e., the undertakings acquired by the Soviet Union.

[41] Cf. *HB,* No. 26, May 10, 1948.

TABLE 32. HUNGARY: DEVELOPMENT OF HANDICRAFTS, 1948–55

Year [a]	Members of Artisan Cooperatives [b]	Independent Artisans
1948	[c]	180,087
1951	26,527	120,383
1952	53,559	75,602
1953	76,791	46,199
1954	92,141	103,922
1955	95,364	94,158

[a] Data as of end of year, except for independent artisans: 1951, January; 1952 and 1953, February; 1954, March.

[b] Data for productive members of industrial cooperatives only.

[c] None.

Source: Magyar Statisztikai Zsebkőnyv, 1956 (Hungarian Statistical Handbook 1956), Kozgazdásagi eś Jogi Kőnyvkiadó (Economic and Legal Book Publishers), Budapest, 1956, pp. 79–80.

The new nationalization absorbed some 30,000 gainfully employed in the private sector and 21,000 in the foreign-owned concerns.[42] The state sector attained roughly 90.5 per cent of the total employment in manufacturing as against 4.7 per cent in the private sector, 3.6 per cent in the Soviet-owned group, and 1.2 per cent in cooperative and municipal ownership. Thus, after a lull extending from 1946 to March 1948 during which it continued to play a substantial role in manufacture, the private sector was rapidly liquidated by two sweeping measures.

In the fields of *"industries of local interest"* and of *crafts,* usually grouped together in the Hungarian statistics, a marked development had been registered through the war and the postwar years up to 1948. From a total of some 156,000 small industries and workshops with approximately 170,000 gainfully employed in 1930 the number of shops increased to 178,000 and that of gainfully employed to 260,000 in 1948. As in the prewar period, 15–20 per cent of the total were one-man shops; 30 per cent had 2–5 gainfully employed; 30 per cent had 6–10; and 20 per cent had over 10. The most important groups were clothing (50,000 shops and close to 40,000 gainfully employed); metalwork and small mechanical workshops (30,700 shops and 34,700 gainfully employed); building trades (16,700 units and 39,000 gainfully employed); food-processing (23,000 units and 28,700 gainfully em-

[42] "The Hungarian People's Republic Centralizes All Means of Large-Scale Production in Its Own Hands," in *HB,* No. 67, Jan. 15, 1950, pp. 1 ff.

ployed); and personal services (30,000 technical units with 32,000 gainfully employed).[43]

For 1948 through 1955, data on handicrafts only, excluding small industries, indicated that the number of working artisans had fallen to a total of 123,000 in 1953, as against 180,000 in 1948. The nationalization processes in other fields (e.g., trade)[44] converged to bring about a sharp drop in the privately operated crafts, especially in the villages.[45] The number of gainfully employed in the privately owned and operated crafts fell to 46,000 and the contribution of the private artisans to the national product fell to less than 1 per cent.[46] The pace of liquidation of handicrafts was finally described as having been "too fast,"[47] and the pressures against the private artisans were diminished. By the end of 1955, the number of artisans again reached the 1948 level.

The reorganization of industry progressed from 1946 on, in spite of the then "limited" scope of nationalization. This reorganization assumed a variety of forms up to the nationalization wave of 1948, however. From 1946 to 1948 the nationalized coal mines were centrally directed by a National Council of Mines and an Executive Committee of the Coal Mines. The latter was in charge of managing a company called "Hungarian State Coal Mines, Ltd." (MASZ), which operated as a commercial company but whose shares were exclusively owned by the state. A similar company was formed for the power plants (the AVIRT). All the nationalized enterprises in the bauxite and aluminum fields were grouped provisionally into a state corporation for bauxite and aluminum (ALBART). Heavy industry was placed under the management of the Central Office of Heavy Industry (NIK) with

[43] Cf. for prewar: Alexander Farkasfalvi, "La Statistique de la petite industrie en Hongrie" (Statistics of Small Industry in Hungary), in *Journal de la Société hongroise de statistique* (Journal of the Hungarian Statistical Society), XIII, 3, 1935, pp. 268 ff.; for postwar: *GT*, III, 4–5 (April–May 1949), pp. 209 ff., and *ibid.*, No. 6 (June 1949), pp. 265 ff., and No. 7 (July 1949), p. 322.

[44] See Chapter 5.

[45] As stated by Mátyás Rákosi during the 1953 "new course" reversal: "Whole villages and city districts have remained without a cobbler, tailor, locksmith, plumber, electrician, and other craftsmen. . . . If anyone wanted to have a broken window replaced, or a farm implement repaired, he would have to travel 20 to 30 miles to the county seat." (*SN*, July 12, 1953).

[46] Third Congress of the Hungarian People's Party, *New Hungary*, Supplement, Vol. 4, No. 6, Budapest, June–July 1954, p. 60.

[47] *Magyar Nemzet* (Hungarian Nation), Nov. 19, 1953.

a four-member directing council, one member of which was in the Ministry of Industry.[48]

After the March 1948 nationalization the industry was organized along the familiar three-layer pattern: base works, industrial centers, and directorates. The base works were appreciably reshuffled,[49] and newly set up "industrial centers," coordinators of the activities of groups of nationalized enterprises, started to play in fact the role of national corporations, although in principle the legal entity of the individual firm was left unchanged. Industrial directorates, i.e., production departments of ministries, topped the entire structure.[50] The former Central Office of Heavy Industry, the "Hungarian Coal Mines," etc., were transformed into industrial directorates. Thus the entire industrial reorganization was streamlined on the familiar and strongly centralized pattern of Soviet organization.

The small enterprises with up to 10 workers lived until 1948 on the margin of the economy, carrying on their business "under a controlled but not a planned economy." [51] After the 1949 nationalization the integration of the local industries and crafts into the planned economy was rapidly effected through the transfer of the local industries to the local authorities and through both nationalization and extension of cooperatives in the crafts (essentially in their production lines).

Romania

Romania officially adopted its nationalization law in June 1948. Up to the middle of 1947 the private sector had developed under

[48] "L'Industrie hongroise depuis la fin de la guerre" (Hungarian Industry since the End of the War), in *EC*, IV, 3 (May–June 1949), p. 37.

[49] The following is a concrete example of this reshuffling occurring at the time in order to achieve "uniform processes of production" on a large scale:

> . . . it was necessary to reorganize rationally the various factories and to divide production in such a way that they should specialize in their production in the most convenient lines for them. This was already feasible in the first year of the plan when, for instance, on the basis of capital investment the production of agricultural machinery of Mavag [the state plant for wagons and machinery] has been transferred to the plant Hoffer-Schrantz, and Mavag concentrated on the production of transport equipment. In the same time the mass output of small agricultural machines was entrusted to the plant Emag [first Hungarian plant of agricultural machinery]. In the interests of profitability of production in the other plants of industry the same type of reorganization occurred between enterprises. Cf. Zoltán Vas, *A hároméves terv befejezése—népünk győzelme* (The Completion of the Three-Year Plan—A Victory of Our People), Budapest, 1950, p. 5.

[50] "The Role of Industrial Directorates and Industrial Centers in a Planned Economy," in *HB*, No. 41, Oct. 25, 1948, pp. 4–6.

[51] George Kemény, *Economic Planning in Hungary 1947–49, op. cit.*, p. 40.

conditions which, in the circumstances, might be considered as "favorable" and had even managed to grow in certain respects.

According to the provisional results of the "stock-taking of private industrial, commercial, and transport enterprises" of October 14, 1947, there were in Romania at the time a total of some 35,500 private industrial enterprises of which about 1,100 were in mining and 34,400 in processing industries. Of the latter, more than half (52.6 per cent) were in the food industry; of the balance, most were in the timber industries (13.8 per cent), textile industries (11.2 per cent), metallurgical industry (7.2 per cent), and chemical industry (4 per cent). In that census the term "industrial enterprises" was used in a broad sense, covering a substantial number of the so-called industries of "local interest."

Out of the grand total of 35,500 industrial undertakings registered, only some 4,200 enterprises (or over 4,500 including the mines) employed over 10 persons. Less than 5,000 had over 20 horsepower, and only 2,300 employed 10 persons and had over 20 horsepower.[52] Compared to the prewar period, the increase in the number of enterprises with over 10 workers (4,224 in 1947 against 3,878 in 1939) was mostly localized in the lower layer of enterprises employing between 10 and 20 workers.[53] In all the private industrial enterprises with over 10 workers employment had increased, as compared to prewar, from 370,000 in 1939 to 460,000 in 1947, more than 24 per cent.

The balance of some 31,300 private industrial enterprises with less than 10 workers was composed of small town industries and industries of local interest. Although they were 87.3 per cent of the total registered industries, they accounted for less than 20 per cent of the gainfully employed and for 38 per cent of the available motor power.

After the uneasy lull which lasted until the beginning of 1947 various economic measures such as the monetary refunding of August 15, 1947,[54] and the stock-taking of October 1947 laid the groundwork for nationalization. On June 11, 1948, a sweeping nationalization law almost entirely wiped out private industry. The law detailed seventy-

[52] *Intreprinderile Particulare Industriale, Comerciale şi de Transport, op. cit.,* pp. 2–3. (Our figures are rounded for simplification purposes.)

[53] Mircea Biji, "Intreprinderile industriale particulare având peste 10 persoane ocupate sau forţa motrică peste 20 H.P., pe ramuri şi grupe de personal" (Private Industrial Enterprises with More than 10 Employees or More than 20 H.P., Classified by Branches of Industry and Number of Employees). Reprinted from *PE,* No. 2–3, March–April, 1948, p. 17.

[54] See below, Chapter 4, the data on the monetary refunding.

seven categories of enterprise and applied five main criteria for nationalization: (1) national economic importance (for subsoil riches and transportation, etc.); (2) regional or even circumstantial importance, e.g., flour mills, soap manufacturers, large bakeries—important in a period of rationing; (3) number of gainfully employed, e.g., over 100 for the metallurgical industries; (4) number of horsepower (over 50 in the wood-working industries, over 30 in printing shops, over 10 in the footwear industry), or a given productive capacity, e.g., number of looms; (5) or simply the nominal designation of given enterprises either in the text of the bill or in its twenty-eight annexed lists.[55]

Even though the groundwork for nationalization had already been prepared by various measures, the law seems to have been written in haste. It included provisions of the following type: enterprises nominally designated would be validly transferred to the state "even if their name or address is partially inaccurate," or "if they have changed their name or address," the new directors would be empowered to sign validly in their new capacity, even before their specific nomination appeared in the Official Gazette, etc.[56] The only undertakings and capital of significance left outside the scope of nationalization were "the enterprises, or the part of their capital, of a United Nations state having acquired this ownership in execution of the peace treaty, or of certain reparation obligations resulting from the war," i.e., the enterprises, installations, and shares of the Soviet Union alone.

The rapid extension of nationalization in industry may be gaged by the following data: in 1949 the state sector "commanded up to 85 per cent of the total industrial production"; by 1952 this percentage rose to 95 per cent; by 1955 it was stated that the socialist sector in industry "now represents nearly 100 per cent." [57]

Nationalization from the outset affected not only the sector of "industry proper" but also a substantial number of the industries of local

[55] The nominal designations cover 687 key firms, i.e., 20 metal and 120 metalworking undertakings, 25 oil concerns, 10 railroad companies. For text in English, see *Nationalization of Industrial, Banking, Insurance, Mining and Transport Enterprises,* Ministry of Arts and Information, Bucharest, 1948.

[56] Serban Voinea, *La Socialisation* (Socialization), Presses universitaires de France (University Presses of France), Paris, 1950, p. 180.

[57] Cf. *RN,* June 19, 1949; AIB, III, 20, May 24, 1952; and Gh. Gheorghiu-Dej, *Raportul de Activitate al Comitetului Central al Partidului Muncitoresc Romîn la Congresul al II-lea al Partidului* (Report on the Activity of the Central Committee of the Rumanian Workers' Party to the Second Party Congress), Editura de Stat pentru literatura Politică (State Publishing House for Political Literature), Bucharest, 1955.

interest and a number of craft shops (e.g., automobile repair shops, soap manufacturers of any size, mechanized bakeries). According to the prewar data, small industries and workshops employing up to 20 workers totaled about 102,700 establishments with some 210,000 gainfully employed. A limited number of large workshops, some 700 units, had over 20 gainfully employed and a total employment of 57,000. Of those employing up to 20 workers the overwhelming majority of shops and gainfully employed were typically small workshops with 1 to 5 workers, a total of 98,000 units with 172,000 gainfully employed.[58] Data based on the 1941 census give for the handicraft field (excluding food-processing) a total of 72,500 establishments with 153,-500 gainfully employed. The most important groups of crafts listed were: clothing (30,900 units and over 68,000 gainfully employed), metalworking and repair shops (17,000 units and close to 34,000 gainfully employed), building trades, printing, etc.[59] It can be assumed that a large number of establishments, though deprived of credits, supplies of raw materials, and auxiliary materials, and prevented from hiring apprentices, continued to remain in private hands after the 1948 nationalization. However, the nationalization measures in the related fields (e.g., trade) constantly restricted their sphere of operation. The official data indicate that at the beginning of 1956, there were in the country some 131,000 artisans organized into 637 cooperatives. This corresponds to the total number of artisans, since organization in cooperatives is compulsory.[60] The figure indicates a significant drop in the number of artisans as compared to 1939 and 1941.

No significant deviations from the pattern sketched above for Czechoslovakia or Poland were apparent in the reorganization of industry in Romania. The nationalization law contained only two indications of future structural reorganization: "The nationalized industries shall be administered by those ministries in whose sphere they operate"; the flour mills, bakeries, vegetable-oil factories, and slaughterhouses for which no directors have been appointed by a ministry were transferred to the "authority of organs of local mayoralties." [61] Thus, practically from the outset, the pyramid of basic plants, national corporations, and directorates was closely tied to the respective ministries, and most of the industries of local interest were placed under local authorities. It

[58] Data computed from *Anuarul Statistic 1939 şi 1940, op. cit.*

[59] Cf. *CS*, No. 16, Jan. 15, 1947, p. 5.

[60] Cf. *SC*, March 21, 1956.

[61] Serban Voinea, *op. cit.*, p. 179.

became apparent during the 1953 crisis that the new setup brought about the rapid withering away of the industries of local interest.[62]

Bulgaria

Bulgaria was the first of the ex-enemy countries to nationalize its industry. The nationalization law adopted December 24, 1947, specified in its introduction that Bulgarian industries had developed up to that point as "a consumers' goods industry on the basis of means handed out by the State and by the collectivity." For this reason, the law stated, the industries' status and structure had become a "handicap for their large reconstruction" and they "belonged to the people." The nationalization measure covered 5,500 industrial enterprises with a stated employment of 125,000. Of the total number, 2,000 may be called manufacturing establishments[63] if one stretches the term. The balance of 3,500 units were essentially small industries of local interest and certain workshops. The small industries, with 13,000 gainfully employed, included flour mills (1,756 units), carding establishments (557), vegetable-oil factories (414), undertakings producing building materials, etc.

The state sector, which had produced only 6 per cent of the gross value of output in manufacture before nationalization, produced 85.3 per cent of this output in 1948, and together with the cooperatives 92.9 per cent. Subsequently the cooperatives increased their share (10.7 per cent of total industrial output compared to 87.9 per cent for the state in 1953), but this expansion was due mostly to the organization of the crafts fields.[64]

Before the war Bulgaria had some 70,000 craft workshops with a total of 135,000 gainfully employed. After the war the number of

[62] "One of the major shortcomings [in the work of the people's councils] is that they did not give sufficient attention to the development of local industry, that they did not in due measure utilise the local resources at their disposal, did not always display concern for steadily raising the living standards of the working people. They did not devote sufficient attention to production of foodstuffs, household goods and to their quality and did not take into account the requirements of the consumers. Nor did the people's councils help adequately to provide industry with raw materials and the workers with foodstuffs." D. Coliu, "Eve of Elections to Local People's Councils in Rumania," in *FLP,* Nov. 27, 1953.

[63] "Vătreshen Pregled, Bălgarskoto Stopanstvo, ot Septemvri 1947 do Septemvri 1948" (Interior Outlook of the Bulgarian Economy, September 1947 to September 1948), *PK,* No. 2, 1948, pp. 78–79.

[64] Vălko Chervenkov, "Report of the Central Committee to the Sixth Party Congress," *FLP,* March 5, 1954.

shops and gainfully employed increased to 100,000 and 191,000, respectively, the average employment per unit remaining, however, less than 2 gainfully employed per unit. In 1946 the most important crafts were the traditional clothing shops (13,000 units and 28,000 gainfully employed), leather-working (12,000 units and 25,000 gainfully employed), food-processing (18,000 units and 27,000 gainfully employed), metal-working (close to 18,000 units and 30,000 gainfully employed), wood-working (13,000 units and 24,000 gainfully employed), building trades (9,000 units and 20,000 gainfully employed), personal services, printing, etc.

After the 1947 nationalizations the craft cooperatives increased in both number and membership whereas the private crafts declined substantially. In 1946 there were 570 artisans' cooperatives with 15,000 members; by 1948 there were 1,050 with 44,000 members. By 1951 there were 1,100 cooperatives and 1,200 artisan sectors dependent on other cooperatives accounting for 70,000 members, i.e., over one-half the total number of artisans,[65] figures which explain how and why the share of the private craftsmen, which in 1948 was 19 per cent of the production of local industry, had fallen by 1951 to 1 per cent of this production.[66] Having first "restricted" and then "dislodged" the private craftsmen, and having prevented the training of private apprentices, the Bulgarian government found it difficult to resuscitate a large private-crafts stratum in order to cope with the consumers' goods shortages as they appeared in the open after the 1953 crisis.[67]

Immediately after nationalization the manufacturing sector as a whole underwent widespread amalgamations and structural changes. The 2,022 "large" and "medium" industrial establishments under the authority of the Ministry of Industry were consolidated. The available equipment was concentrated, and duplications of production were

[65] Data up to 1948 from E. B. Valev, *Bolgariia: Ekonomiko-Geograficheskoe Opisanie* (Bulgaria, Economic-Geographic Survey), Gôsudarstvennoe Izdatel'stvo Geograficheskoi Literatury (State Publishing House of Geographic Literature), Moscow, 1949, p. 180; after 1948, E. B. Valev, *Narodnaia Respublika Bolgariia* (People's Republic of Bulgaria), Voennoe Izdatel'stvo, Voennogo Ministerstva Soiuza SSSR (Military Publishing House of the War Ministry of the USSR), Moscow, 1952, p. 89.

[66] Dr. Ivan Matov, "Social and Economic Changes in Bulgaria," *Free Bulgaria,* VI, 12 (June 10, 1951), p. 186.

[67] Early in 1954 a decree of the Council of Ministers instructed various administrative organs (both at the ministerial and at the local level) as well as the Central of Cooperatives and the Central Union of Craftsmen Cooperatives "to help the craftsmen activities, especially in places where the public sector network is insufficient and where the need is felt by the population for consumers' goods and craft services." *RD,* Feb. 2, 1954.

avoided as far as possible. The number of enterprises was reduced to 1,264, and they were grouped into twenty industrial concerns, all under the Ministry of Industry.[68] Thus nationalization effected a centralized three-level structural organization in manufacture. The other 3,500 small enterprises were placed under the control of the Ministry of Communal Economy and Public Works and, at the local level, under the management of the local people's councils. A total of some 230 undertakings passed under the control of the Ministry of Agriculture.

As in the other countries of the area, in the field of crafts the state apparatus insured a privileged role to the Central Union of Craftsmen Cooperatives, which, as already stated, in Bulgaria in 1953 controlled a major part of the crafts output.

Summary on Area Trends and Concluding Remarks

Nationalization in the sphere of *industry proper* (i.e., excluding local industry and handicrafts) can be considered as virtually completed in the area as a whole by the end of 1949.

In the former Allied countries, where large postwar nationalization had been nourished mostly by taking over the numerous and extensive ex-enemy assets, up to the beginning of 1948 the private sector continued to decline in importance. In 1946 it controlled slightly over 25 per cent of the total industrial employment in Czechoslovakia, 11 per cent in Poland, and some 8 per cent in Yugoslavia. In 1948 the disparity among these countries narrowed sharply. In Poland the share fell to 7 per cent, in Czechoslovakia to 4 per cent; in Yugoslavia

[68] Of the 2,022 enterprises, 1,388 of the largest were combined in 623 new establishments, which represented the core of Bulgarian manufacture. The following table shows the numbers of the largest enterprises before and after reorganization.

Enterprise	Before	After
Cotton textile	331	96
Wool textile	185	69
Rubber	63	26
Food-processing	130	100
Wood-working	214	86
Paper	35	28
Construction materials	122	60
Machine building	106	50
Metal-working	115	61
Chemicals	87	47
Total	1,388	623

Source: E. B. Valev, *Bolgariia, op. cit.*, p. 180.

the private sector in manufacture was completely liquidated. In 1949 the share of the private sector in manufacture fell in Poland to some 5 per cent of the total of gainfully employed in this sphere.

In the ex-enemy countries nationalization developed rapidly from the end of 1947 (Bulgaria) to the end of 1948 (Romania and Hungary). At the beginning of 1949 only the last two countries still had a private sector accounting for around 15 per cent of the employment in manufacture. In that period the share of the socialized sector in the value of gross output of manufacture ranged from a low of 85 per cent in Romania to 92 per cent in Hungary, 93 per cent in Bulgaria, 94 per cent in Czechoslovakia and Poland, and 100 per cent in Yugoslavia.[69] From the end of 1949 on, the "residual" private share was completely annihilated.

Up to 1948–49 local industry and handicraft thrived generally on the margin of the planned economy in spite of a maze of "controls." After the 1948–49 extensions of nationalization the transfer of industries of local interest to the local authorities and the extension of cooperatives into crafts brought about a marked decline both in their output and in their employment in the area as a whole. Up to the 1953 turning point, the stated objectives in the craft lines were to watch carefully the workshops that might engage in industrial production and to check their "isolated" development, i.e., to limit their sphere of activity, to prevent them from taking apprentices, and to compel them to join the cooperatives so that planned control over craft production could be enforced.

The nationalization of industry did not encounter any effective resistance except in Czechoslovakia. The other countries, well absorbed into the orbit, lived after the liberation in a kind of "unreal" framework. Small national units heavily mortgaged by Soviet Russia (whose "lines of communication" extended over to Berlin) could hardly cling to the previous economic and political equilibriums. Actually, except in Czechoslovakia, nationalization cannot be considered a lever for political change. In all these countries the nationalization processes unfolded either after or coevally with the liquidation of all political opposition. Thus these measures served basically as *economic levers* [70]

[69] M. Pešković and M. Čečez, *op. cit.*, p. 72.

[70] A precise idea of what "economic lever" means in this context is furnished by the following quotation from Hilary Minc:

The pivot of such planned development of the productive forces is the industry which has become the property of the State. This industry constitutes the leading position of the State and together with other State sectors in the hands of State for setting the stage for planning in general and for the rapid liquidation of the capitalist forces in the economy as a whole.

The early Czechoslovak and Polish assurances of the survival of an "important private sector" appear today as deceiving, but it would be perhaps erroneous to attribute the deception uniquely to the general changes in the political climate rather than to the internal dynamics of nationalization. In fact, it might be argued that once such large sectors of nationalized and confiscated property are established (sectors engulfing from 75 to 85 per cent of the gainfully employed in the key industrial sphere) these sectors tend necessarily to expand and to crush the private property that originally escapes their "interference" and coordination. The attempts of a three-phased development, so much stressed in 1946 in Poland, did not and perhaps could not gain much vitality. Not only did the manufacturing cooperatives wind up with diminishing importance in the area as a whole and small manufacture disappeared into the nationalized sector, but finally even large sectors of the crafts were chewed up in increasing proportions.

After mid-1953, and again since the fall of 1956, stressing of the "positive role" of handicrafts and of private enterprise has brought about a certain reanimation in the crafts lines and in the very small-scale privately owned industries. In certain countries the number of independent craftsmen is scheduled by 1960 to reach, and even surpass, the prewar level. Even after these developments occur, the share of crafts in the total national product will not amount to more than 1 or 2 per cent.

The changes in the interior climate and in international relations mirror themselves quite clearly in certain aspects of the nationalization processes. When nationalization was effected in Czechoslovakia in 1945 the nationalized enterprises were organized as independent juridical persons with the state as owner—"as in any other enterprise [but] with the difference that this time the state is to be the *exclusive* owner." [71] This was established in order to draw a clear line between

(transport, banking, monopoly of foreign trade, and the leading State and cooperative positions in wholesale and retail trade) makes possible, on the basis of planned direction, to direct the development of the national economy as a whole. ["Concerning the Basis of Planning in the People's Democracies," *op. cit.*]

[71] Here is an early comment on this juridical framework which reflects certain illusions about its efficacy:

From the point of view of law, the national enterprises have the position of independent moral persons. The state is the owner, somewhat as if it were the owner of all the shares of a normal company. There are no shares and they are not necessary because there are no participants in the capital. Participation in the capital

the *nationalized property* and the state. In Poland such questions were viewed at the time as being of secondary importance, and the legal problem concerning the framework of industry as a whole, once it was nationalized, was left open.[72] During the second wave of nationalization no distinct line was traced in the area as a whole between the nationalized sectors as such and the state machine. Only subsequently, and this time in the framework of centralized planning, were the state enterprises treated and managed financially as autonomous units,[73] i.e., as were the public corporations in the early period of Czechoslovak nationalization.

The highly centralized forms of organization of industry which emerged after the completion of the indicated nationalization processes should be viewed only as transitional forms. Since the completion of the first long-term plans, clear-cut tendencies toward decentralization have appeared in the area as a whole. Larger responsibilities at the district and province level, and in some countries a reanimation of the "workers' councils" in the base-works, might in the long run bring the presently divergent types of organization of industry existing in Yugoslavia and in the Soviet bloc closer together.

The evolution of compensation for nationalized property is also characteristic of the changes of climate. In theory, all the nationalization laws established the principle of compensation for enterprises transferred to the state (except, of course, ex-enemy property or that of "collaborationists"). For the *nationals,* compensation was to be made by the treasury in the form of state bonds, money payments, or special evidences of obligation issued by funds created *ad hoc.* (Actually, with the political changes in some countries, usually no indemnity whatso-

by a person other than the state is not possible in the national enterprises. That doesn't exclude, however, an eventual agreement between national enterprises and foreign ones, in view of a collaboration in which the contributions would be assured by both parties by contract. [Cf. M. Miloslav Trnec, "Le Problème de la nationalisation de l'industrie en Tchécoslovaquie" (The Problem of Nationalization of Industry in Czechoslovakia), in *Droit social,* IX, 4 (April 1946), p. 146.]

[72] The law of Jan. 3, 1946, simply regulated in a very general way the problem of nationalization of the enterprises by attributing property to the state, to autonomous administrations, to cooperatives, to political or social organizations. The industry was organized by branches under the direction of central committees, which were working in the name of and for the account of the state in the service of various given ministries. Cf. Dr. Alfred Kraus, "La Nationalisation de l'industrie en Pologne," *loc. cit.*

[73] This type of arrangement, in the conditions of centralized planning, constitutes the basis of what the Russians call the "khozraschet" system (economic-calculation system).

ever was paid.[74]) No special procedure was established for the dispossessed *foreign owners.* Some foreign companies succeeded in concluding compensation agreements, but generally the foreign governments concerned took this problem into their own hands and tried to negotiate directly with the East European countries, a series of agreements being concluded by Great Britain, France, Switzerland, and others. In such instances compensation did not conform to any previously established juridical disposition. Whenever an East European country urgently needed commercial goods from a Western country the property of whose nationals had been expropriated, the Western country could tie the negotiations for the commercial agreement to the problem of compensation of the dispossessed owners. Thus the "strategic embargo" of the Soviet sphere became somewhat of an indirect lever for securing compensation for expropriated owners.[75]

The pace of nationalization in manufacturing appears far more rapid in Eastern Europe than in the Soviet Union. In the Soviet Union in 1928, i.e., at the end of the first decade after the revolution, the state sector controlled 82.4 per cent of the total industrial production.[76] In Eastern Europe, as we have seen, this percentage was attained in the former Allied countries during the first nationalization wave and in

[74] In Hungary some former small owners received certain compensation. According to Hungarian sources over 8 million forints were handed out as compensation to nationals. Cf. *Bulletin Économique,* Bureau hongrois de presse et de documentation (Economic Bulletin, Hungarian Bureau of Press and Documentation), No. 14, Mar. 1, 1950.

[75] France was particularly skillful in negotiating certain compensation agreements. She signed such agreements with Poland, Czechoslovakia, Hungary, and Yugoslavia. The agreement with Poland foresaw the deliveries of coal over fifteen years, starting in 1951; the agreement with Czechoslovakia foresaw the payment of a flat indemnity, etc. Cf. *Les Nationalisations en Europe orientale,* op. cit., pp. 11–12.

This same embargo was cited on certain occasions as proof that it was "criminal" to sign such agreements with the capitalist powers. One of the basic accusations brought in November 1952 at the Prague trial of R. Slansky and his associates against "the criminal activities in the Ministry of Foreign Trade of E. Lobl, R. Margolius, and L. Frejka" was their participation in the establishment of three compensation agreements concerning the nationalization of British assets and especially of some assets belonging to Unilever at Usti-nad-Labem. See *Documents sur l'évolution récente de la République Populaire de Tchécoslovaquie* (Documents on the Recent Evolution of the Czechoslovak People's Republic), Notes et études documentaires (Notes and Documentary Studies), No. 1792, La Documentation Française (French Documentation), Paris, October 14, 1953, p. 17.

[76] *Mirovoe Khoziaistvo i Mirovaia Politika* (World Economy and World Politics), No. 10, 1937, quoted by C. Bettelheim, *La Planification soviétique* (Soviet Planning), 2nd ed., Rivière et cie., Paris, 1945.

the other countries during the second nationalization wave, and the process was carried even further in the industrial sphere in less than five years. The explanation lies simply in the fact that these countries did not pass through periods of war communism and blockade but encountered a different set of "historical conditions." [77]

[77] Cf. B. Kidrič, "On the Construction of Socialist Economy in the FPRY," *op. cit.*, p. 7.

CHAPTER 4

PROCESS OF NATIONALIZATION AND STRUCTURAL REORGANIZATION IN BANKING, INSURANCE, AND FINANCE

BANKS AND FORMS OF BANK ACTIVITY

The concept of nationalization of the central bank had acquired in some capitalist countries a sort of legitimacy long before the unfolding of nationalization of the bank system in Eastern Europe. However, as has been pointed out on many occasions, the transfer of central bank ownership to the state can often be "more a symbol than a change of substance." What actually matters "more than the nationalizations are the general relations between the central bank and the State and their respective roles in determining the monetary and credit policies." [1] In the capitalist economy these relations are based in principle on the concept of the autonomy of the banking organism, an autonomy which is called upon to express itself according to given rules and given limitations. Conversely, in a planned economy of the Soviet type the concept of bank autonomy is meaningless. The banking system is only "a wheel moved by the motor of the State engine." [2] On the movement of this motor depend the intended pace and movement of the banking system as a whole, the activities of which are not a function of bank authorities but a function of state economic policy and planning.

In broaching the problem of nationalization in the financial field, evidently we have to consider not only nationalization of the banking

[1] Miroslav A. Kriz, "Central Banks and the State Today," in *American Economic Review*, XXXVIII, 4 (September 1948), p. 580.

[2] "New Banking Systems," in *Review of Polish Law*, II, 1 (April 1948), p. 13.

and insurance business as such, as we would any other business, but also what is called in the present East European financial parlance the "nationalization of forms of bank activity" such as the new structures of credit and of interest, monetary manipulations, and so on.

The adjustment between the flow of money and the flow of goods and services from the planned and "semiplanned" sectors of the economy [3] is evidently a complex and continuous process in which a series of levers are called into play. In pursuing the study of nationalization of forms of bank activity, certain incursions in other domains might appear inevitable: we shall try, however, to limit these incursions to the utmost, keeping in mind particularly the fact that the overall problems of *financing* will also be discussed in the chapter on planning.

NATIONALIZATION AND STRUCTURAL MODIFICATION OF THE BANKING SYSTEM IN THE FORMER ALLIED GROUP—CZECHOSLOVAKIA

In the former Allied countries (Czechoslovakia, Poland, and Yugoslavia) the nationalization of the banking system was accomplished so to speak "automatically" through the very process of liberation. There was no private ownership in these countries except of secondary institutions such as financial cooperatives. From the outset, either specific nationalization measures or the simple state privilege of granting concessions for the carrying on of business precluded the resurgence of private banking. The "higher" phase of the nationalization process (i.e., the structural changes of the banking system and the completion of the "nationalization of forms of bank activity") did not develop at the same pace in the three countries.

In Czechoslovakia the nationalization decrees affecting banks and insurance companies were promulgated in October 1945. They provided that bank and insurance company shares be "expropriated at the current price fixed in the balance sheet" and that the dispositions relative to the operation, tax assessment, etc., of the other nationalized enterprises be equally applicable to banks and insurance companies.[4] Apparently the decrees provoked some resistance in the political coalition running the country, but this resistance was neither systematic nor effective.[5]

[3] Notably goods coming from agriculture.

[4] The decrees applied nominally to "commercial banks." As there was no distinction in Czechoslovakia between commercial and savings banks, etc., the decree embraced in fact all banking business, except the cooperative banks.

[5] In his report to the first meeting of the Communist Information Bureau (Comin-

In the perspective of the first two-year plan of reconstruction (launched in October 1946), two main organizations in the banking and insurance fields, the Central Banking Board and the Insurance Advisory Board, received the task of insuring "the harmonious *cooperation* of the national and privately owned sectors in carrying out the plan." In practice, as with the industrial concerns, each bank and insurance company retained substantially its traditional sphere of operation.

The structural changes, i.e., extensive amalgamations and progressive limitation of the sphere of operation of the various banks, were effected by stages after the February coup. The first measures were taken in March 1948. The National Bank of Czechoslovakia received then, besides the right of issue, the direction of the entire monetary market through the control of credits and foreign trade.[6] All commercial operations were thereafter channeled through two banks: the Živnostenská Bank, "commercial bank" for the Czech territories, and the Tatra Bank, "commercial bank" for Slovakia.[7] A new institution, the Investment Bank (successor mainly to the mortgage banks, etc.), assumed the direction of long-term investments as distinct from the short-term credit operations left in the domain of the "commercial banks." [8] Besides these main organs of the banking apparatus, there were the Postal Savings Bank (organized as a national enterprise) and the People's Banking Center (established as a financial institution for cooperatives, in which were merged, without previous liquidation of their affairs, the credit and savings cooperative societies),[9] both of which assumed the tasks of concentrating individual savings and facilitating the financing of small-scale enterprises.

Similarly, the insurance companies, which had been first incorporated into five national-enterprise insurance companies, were merged

form) the Secretary-General of the Czechoslovak Communist Party at the time, Rudolph Slánský (purged in 1951), declared in connection with this problem:

In October, 1945, the decrees on the nationalization of heavy industry and the financial system became law. Nationalization provoked a bitter struggle. Nationalization was opposed by some people who argued that it should not be carried out all at once, but by degrees. . . . The National Socialists were in general against the nationalization of banks.

Our Party, supported by the masses, and above all with the help of the United Trade Unions, was able to ensure that nationalization be carried out in one move. The nationalization covered all the banks, all the so-called insurance societies, all basic and heavy industries. . . . [Cf. R. Slánský, "Report at the Conference of Nine Communist Parties in Poland," in *FLP*, Dec. 15, 1947.]

6 Law of March 11, 1948.

7 Law of March 25, 1948.

8 Law of July 20, 1948.

9 Law of July 20, 1948.

in a single national enterprise, the Czechoslovak Insurance Company at Prague. In October 1948 obligatory insurances, formerly distributed among several insurance institutions, were concentrated in a single body, the National Insurance Institute of Prague.[10] Subsequently, the Czechoslovak Insurance Company was converted into the State Insurance Institute, affiliated with the Ministry of Finance.[11]

By January 1949 a series of new measures further strengthened the principle of "bank control" over the economic life of the country, i.e., the principle of making the banking system "the central bookkeeping and control department of all production and trade." [12] All business connections, claims, and liabilities of the nationalized enterprises were concentrated exclusively with the commercial banks, which at the same time were required to transfer outstanding investment credits to the Investment Bank. Accounts with other banks, including the National Bank of Czechoslovakia, were prohibited. Henceforth, nationalized enterprises requesting short-term credit were required to present their budgets for revenue and expenditure, and, if requesting investment credits, their investment budgets. These budgets had to be in accord with the provision of the over-all plan. Alongside the "credit control," periodic bank inspection in the nationalized sector was instituted.[13]

In 1950, in the process of over-all planning, the whole banking system was again revamped. A new Czechoslovak State Bank carried on all operations connected with money issue, payments, short-term credit, and deposits, and took over the rights and obligations of the National Bank of Czechoslovakia, the two "commercial banks" (Živnostenská and Tatra Banks), and the Postal Savings Bank. Not included in this new bank were the Investment Bank for the channeling and administration of long-term credits and the People's Banking Center, on which the small savings and banking cooperatives continued to depend.[14] Finally, at the end of 1952, the people's savings banks lost their semi-cooperative character and became state savings banks, and the Invest-

[10] Dr. J. Hoffman, "Organisační Změny v čs. peněžinctví pojišťovnictví v letech, 1945–48" (Changes in the Organization of the Financial and Insurance Systems, 1945–48), *SZ*, XII, 1 (January 1948), p. 8.

[11] Law of December 11, 1952. Cf. *CEB*, No. 262, Jan. 1, 1953.

[12] Jaromír Dolanský, *Three Years of Planning in the Czechoslovak People's Democracy*, op. cit., p. 32.

[13] *Hospodář (Economist)*, Dec. 16, 1948. Cf. *International Financial News Survey*, I, 29, International Monetary Fund, Washington, Jan. 13, 1949.

[14] The National Bank of Czechoslovakia, which had been the country's bank of issue since 1926, thus ceased to exist on July 1, 1950. Cf. *Hospodář*, June 29, 1950, and *International Financial News Survey*, July 14, 1950.

ment Bank abandoned the status of "national enterprise" and became a state bank. The object of the reform was to create "out of the whole banking system, a (state) compact body." [15]

Thus, as compared to the first period (1945–48), the period after

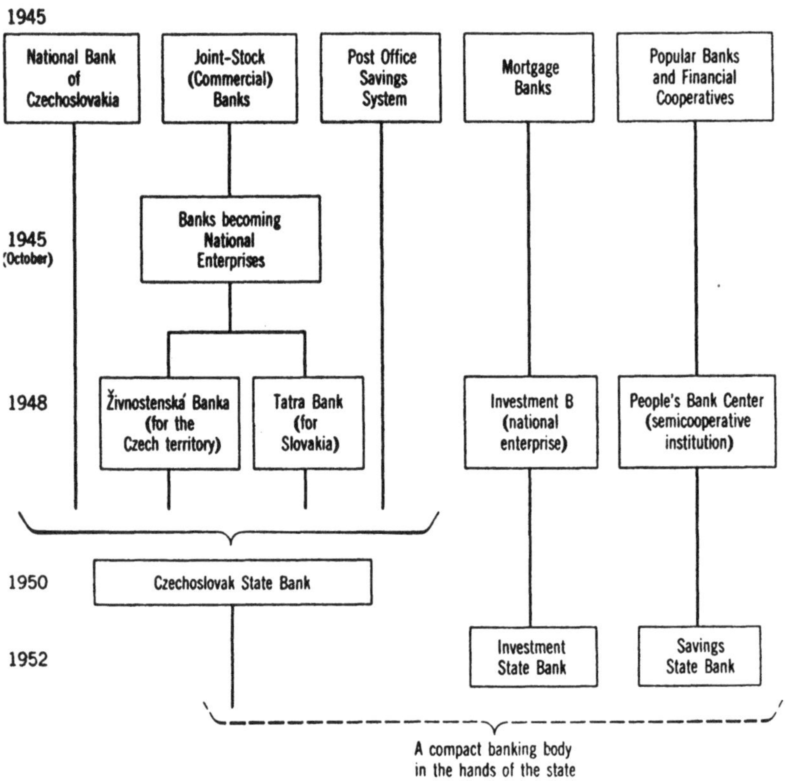

CHART 6. STRUCTURAL REORGANIZATION OF THE BANKING SYSTEM (CZECHOSLOVAKIA, 1945–52)

1948 was characterized by the tremendous expansion of the sphere of the central bank, in which were ultimately concentrated practically all the operations related to money and credit except for the long-term credits. Henceforth all transactions other than wage payments, retail sales, and construction transactions were to represent *transfers* from one deposit to another of the State Bank. Wage payments and retail sales (through the state network, from crafts, and from the villages)

[15] Law of Dec. 11, 1952. Cf. *CEB*, No. 262, Jan. 1, 1953.

became the channels for the circulation of cash. All main construction transactions were to be covered by the funds made available to the enterprises, on the basis of the plan for capital construction, through the Investment Bank.[16] (See Chart 6.)

POLAND

In Poland a series of decrees and "amendments" to the prewar Bank Law [17] reserved to the Council of Ministers the right to decide about the liquidation of banking concerns and credit institutions, the withdrawal of standing concessions, and the permanent control over the whole credit system. As a result of these provisions, "banking houses and money exchanges received no concessions to carry on business, [and] joint-stock banks, with only a few exceptions, passed into liquidation." [18] Having thus insured a free hand for the state in the banking field, the new regime created a group of banks which were from the outset "the special instruments of the financial and economic policy of the State," [19] a policy which looked to the concurrent economic development of the state, cooperative, and private sectors.

The right of issue was entrusted to a new National Bank of Poland, created early in 1945 "in place of the Bank of Poland evacuated abroad in 1939." The other new banks were specialized either by particular types of enterprises or by sectors. The credit operations connected with the state enterprises were to be performed by the National Economic Bank; the economic operations connected with the agrarian reform, by the State Land Bank; the financial operations connected with municipalities, by two municipal banks; the operations connected with cooperatives, by a specialized bank. Two special banks were "entrusted with the financing of the private sector." As stated in the *Review of Polish Law,* the state, cooperative, and privately oriented banks "notwithstanding their legal form, assumed the feature of an auxiliary organ in the State fiscal apparatus," their legal form being relevant

[16] For comparison with the Soviet model, see Edward Ames, "Banking in the Soviet Union," *Federal Reserve Bulletin,* Board of Governors, Federal Reserve System, Washington, April 1952.

[17] In principle, the prewar Bank Law of March 17, 1938, remained in force after the liberation, many of the new banking features being established on the basis of "amendments" to this law. Cf. "New Banking System," in *Review of Polish Law, op. cit.,* p. 13.

[18] *Loc. cit.*

[19] "The Monetary and Credit System in Poland," in *Quarterly Review of the Bank Gospodarstwa Krajowego,* XII, 2–3, March–June 1946, p. 2.

"only as the source of revenue, the kind of turnover and the purpose for which the profits are designed." [20] In the perspective of long-term planning and virtual liquidation of the "private sector" excluding agriculture, the banking and insurance systems underwent extensive "structural" reorganization. Thus far, except for the National Bank of Poland, the state banking objectives had been carried on through the "prewar legal forms [of banks]"; henceforth the banking process was to be carried out through banks "fully adapted to the practice of a planned economy." [21]

From October 1948 on, the National Bank of Poland was placed at the apex of the new banking system—henceforth to be the bank of issue, bank of banks, and supplier of the short-term credits for nationalized enterprises. A newly created Investment Bank, replacing the National Economic Bank, became the executor of banking functions of the state investment plan (except in agriculture). A newly created joint-stock bank, Bank of Foreign Trade, took over the financing of foreign trade operations. The State Land Bank assumed further the supply of both short- and long-term credits to this part of the economy. One municipal bank, one bank for the "private sector" (handicraft, small-scale industry, and trade), and one central savings institution (General Savings Bank) remained in operation.

The small cooperative credit establishments were attached, according to their location or sphere of operation (rural cooperatives, workers' cooperatives, town credit societies) to one of the above-mentioned institutions. All other national and foreign "inactive" banks were liquidated.[22] Furthermore there was liquidated the whole "ballast of an enormous number of prewar and occupation accounts" which had been carried on by the previous type of bank and which were "obstructing current credit operations." [23]

In the insurance field the only institutions licensed after the liberation were those included in the state sector, leaving to the Postal Savings Bank and to the cooperative sectors just a few insurance lines. At the beginning of 1947 two main insurance companies were functioning in Poland: one for all types of insurance (General Mutual Insurance

[20] "New Banking System in Poland," in *Review of Polish Law, op. cit.*, p. 18.

[21] "The Polish Banking Reform," in *Quarterly Review of the Bank Gospodarstwa Krajowego*, XVII, 4, December 1948, pp. 1 ff.

[22] This concerned the liquidation of 78 "inactive" banking enterprises including stock banks, banking houses, and exchange offices, as well as five companies of long-term mortgage credit. *Ibid.*, p. 5.

[23] *Loc. cit.*

Company) and one for reinsurance (Vesta). Every other national or foreign private insurance institution had been officially liquidated. After the 1948 banking reform all the insurance business was taken over by a consolidated General Insurance Institution, the central organization of all insurances, Vesta continuing to conduct reinsurance operations.[24]

Subsequently the collection of savings of the population was entrusted exclusively to a Common Savings Bank. Furthermore, the National Bank began to serve as the clearing house for trade and trade settlements with foreign countries, leaving some minor operations in the hands of the Commercial Bank of Warsaw, the only prewar joint stock bank to be incorporated into the new Polish banking system.[25]

YUGOSLAVIA

As in Czechoslovakia and Poland, the banking and insurance systems fell into the hands of the new Yugoslav regime through the very process of liberation.[26] On the one hand, a large number of banks which had German capital, or which had "collaborated with the enemy," passed, so to speak, "automatically" into state ownership. On the other hand, a law concerning the organization of the credit system established the principle of revision of licenses for all banks and simultaneously determined the procedure of liquidation for those banks "which did not receive licenses." As no private banks received licenses, the rule of revision (just as in Poland) insured the maintenance of the state as the sole operator of banks.[27] In the early postwar period there were created the new central National Bank of the Federal People's Republic of Yugoslavia, established both as bank of issue and as credit regulator; the Agricultural Mortgage Bank, for long-term credits; and a series of banks oriented either toward a given branch of the economy or toward a specified field. Among the latter were the Industrial Bank, for supplying short-term credits to industry; Cooperative and Agricultural Bank, for short-term credits to agriculture; Craftsmen Bank, for credit

[24] "Insurance Reform in Poland," in *Review of Polish Law*, III, 1 (6) (April 1949), *op. cit.*, pp. 1–7.

[25] Juliusz K. Serafin, "Pieniądz i Bankowość" (Money and Banking), in *Kultura*, Numer Krajowy, Vol. I, Paris, 1952, pp. 279 ff; and *A Survey of Poland*, Supplement to *The Statist*, Vol. CLXIV, No. 4107, London, November 24, 1956, p. 11.

[26] For Yugoslavia see Djordje Milević, et al., *Razvoj privrednog sistema FNRJ* (Development of the Economic System of the FPRY), Znanje (Knowledge), Belgrade, 1954, pp. 247 ff.

[27] Law of October 1945.

to craftsmen; Yugoslav Export and Credit Bank; the Postal Savings Bank and the local communal banks for the centralization of individual savings; and, finally, six Economic Banks of the National Republics (one in each republic) were established for regional short-term credit.[28] The insurance business was merged from the outset in one state institution, DOZ;[29] since 1947 DOZ has controlled all insurance except social security.

In the perspective of a five-year plan of both reconstruction and development (launched in April 1947), Yugoslavia envisaged earlier than the other East European countries the discarding of "prewar banking forms" and the structural revamping of its postwar banking system. Accordingly, following an ordinance of August 25, 1946, all the banks were amalgamated into two main banks: (*a*) the National Bank of the FPRY, which, aside from the right of issue, centralized henceforth all the short-term credit, thus also acquiring the right of supervision and control over the production plans of all the state enterprises; and (*b*) the Investment Bank (successor to the Agricultural Mortgage Bank), which channeled long-term credit.[30] A third phase of reorganization of the banking system started in August 1948 and extended up to early 1952. In August 1948 the state created six banks, one for each republic, whose purpose was to serve as special investment banks for the collective farms and agricultural cooperatives. At the same time there was also created the Municipal Bank whose object was to give an impetus to the local economy and to municipal activity. A fourth phase of reorganization was started in 1952. All the banks were then absorbed into the National Bank of the FPRY which thus became the unique banking institution of the country. In the mobile conditions of the Yugoslav economy where bank experimenting has been impressive[31] a

[28] *Finansije* (Finance), I, 4 (April 1946).

[29] See Dr. Miloš Vučković, *Uloga i organizacija banaka i kredita u FNRJ* (The Role and Organization of Banking and Credit in FPRY), Rad, Belgrade, 1953.

[30] *Ibid.;* also, G. J. Conrad, *Die Wirtschaft Jugoslaviens* (The Economy of Yugoslavia), Deutsches Institut für Wirtschaftsforschung (German Institute for Economic Research), new series, No. 17, Duncker and Humblot, Berlin, 1952.

[31] Thus, for instance, after the fusion of all the credit established in the National Bank of the FPRY (October 1946–March 1947), the commercial drafts were abolished and replaced by a system of so-called "automatic payment." According to this system the seller had to send to the office of the National Bank where he had his account the order of payment accompanied by the invoice and bill of lading. Without waiting for the acceptance of the buyer, the National Bank used to credit the seller at the charge of the buyer. The system was given up in May 1951, as it proved itself "negative" because of the lack of control of the buyer over the quality and assortment of the goods delivered. Cf. Dr. Kosta Vasiljević, "Pitanje organizacije

fifth phase of reorganization of the banking system is under way. Co-operative Savings Banks had already been established by 1954. New credit institutions are now organized for long-term investments, for agriculture, and for economic bodies of local character.[32]

In summary, in these three countries the banking business (except for secondary country-type banks and financial cooperatives) has been taken over completely by the state. For a certain period, extending to late 1946 or early 1947 in Yugoslavia, to mid-1948 in Czechoslovakia, and to late 1948 in Poland, the states continued to use what can be called the "prewar type of banking institution." In a second period, during which over-all planning was done and extensive liquidation of the private sector (except in agriculture) was carried out, these prewar "bank-molds" were finally cast away. They were replaced by a new banking structure, the distinct features of which were the disproportionate expansion of the central bank and the sharp distinction between short-term ("working capital") and long-term (investment) credits as criteria for determination of banking institutions (see Chart 6).

Nationalization and Structural Modification of the Banking System in the Ex-Enemy Group—Hungary

The armistice agreements with Hungary, Romania, and Bulgaria did not *immediately* have a direct effect on the economic structure of these countries. In banking as in industry private business survived until the end of 1947, but in a shrinking framework.

In Hungary, after the liberation of the territory from the Nazis and the Arrow Cross troops (September 1944–March 1945), the bank of issue, the Bank of Hungary, passed under the supervision and control of the provisional government but remained in private hands. As the runaway monetary inflation of 1945 to July 1946 rapidly wiped out the liquid resources of the joint-stock banks and savings banks, they became strongly dependent on the rediscount facilities of the National Bank, which was then placed in the position of exercising effective control over the total quantity and circulation of money. However, in spite of this dependence which preceded various amalgamations, the banks apparently improved their capital strength after the monetary

plaćanja u privredi" (The Question of the Organization of Payments in the Economy), *Ekonomist*, No. 3–4, 1951, pp. 47 ff.

[32] *Ekonomska Politika* (Political Economy), Feb. 23, 1956.

reform, because of their large portfolios of industrial shares (Verbankung) and the rise in the share prices after the stabilization.[33]

The continued existence of a governmental coalition, the special international position of Hungary, and the apparently slow pace in the nationalization process encouraged Ernest Czejkey, President of the National Bank of Hungary at the time, to express early in 1947 the desire that "the autonomy of the National Bank of Hungary, which has been reduced to the limit, would be not further restricted, but gradually restored.[34] Almost immediately on the heels of this statement, however, developments turned in the opposite direction.[35] In the perspective of the Three-Year Plan, a revamped political coalition approved the introduction of state controls into the banking business. By the end of the year, in order to "insure productive use and adequate circulation of capital mobilized under the Three-Year Plan," the state nationalized the Hungarian shares of the bank of issue and the leading banking institutions of the country.[36] As these banks controlled over 80 per cent of the banking business and had a considerable influence in industry,[37] state control over the economy as a whole was thus tremendously increased.

From April 1948 on, after the liquidation of any effectively organized political opposition,[38] an extensive structural reorganization of the

[33] Francis Rona, "Hungary's Banks before Nationalisation," *The Banker,* July 1947, pp. 23 ff.

[34] Cf. "Minutes" of the meeting in *Reports to the 21st Annual Meeting of the General Assembly of the National Bank of Hungary, March 27, 1947,* National Bank of Hungary, Budapest, 1947, p. xxxi.

[35] George Kemény, *Economic Planning in Hungary, 1947–49, op. cit.,* p. 22.

[36] "Report of the Board of Directors of the National Bank of Hungary on the Course of Business in 1947," in *Reports to the 22nd Ordinary Annual Meeting of the General Assembly of the National Bank of Hungary, March 1948,* National Bank of Hungary, Budapest, 1948, p. xxi. The shares of the National Bank of Hungary became state property by the Act of Dec. 4, 1947, those of the other banks, by the Act of Dec. 31, 1947.

[37] According to different sources, this enlarged the public sector in industry to 35 or 50 per cent. Cf. Kemény, *op. cit.,* p. 22, and V. A. Sotnikov, Introduction to *Planirovanie Narodnogo Khoziaistvo Vengrii, Sbornik Materialov* (Planning of Hungarian People's Economy, Collection of Materials), Izdatel'stvo Inostrannoi Literatury (Publishing House of Foreign Literature), Moscow, 1950, p. 10. Sotnikov refers to 264 enterprises controlled by these banks.

[38] Although from the early months of 1947 on the banking leaders warned against the extension of the state sphere in the banking business, the warning did not reach the political scene. First the Smallholders Party was forced (in May 1947) to purge its leaders; then the Social Democrats "purged" themselves in March 1948. The rump parties accepted afterwards the extension of state control

bank and credit system was effected. Along lines already familiar in the other East European countries, the entire current banking business was transferred to the National Bank. This central institution became not only the bank of issue but also the exclusive source of credit for the economy as a whole, i.e., for the state enterprises as well as for those still in private hands. All monetary transactions of the industrial corporations had to be recorded and supervised by the National Bank by means of a single-account system, no accounts other than those with the National Bank being permitted.[39] Moreover, the National Bank extended its direct control over the operation of the new bank of Foreign Trade (into which was "converted" the former leading Hungarian Bank of Pest) and over the National Savings Institution. The Institution, at first operated as a section of the National Bank, was subsequently established as a separate institution which absorbed the savings banks, including the important Postal Savings Bank, and was entrusted with the task of acting as a bank for small-scale and retail trade. Outside the National Bank and its two annexes, all the financial administration of capital expenditure was henceforth entrusted to a new Investment Bank (into which was "converted" the leading Hungarian General Credit Bank). Also integrated into the state banking system but independent of the above-mentioned organizations, the National Credit Institute of Cooperative Societies, a long-established center for cooperative credit, assumed, in addition to its traditional functions, the functions of a bank for the peasantry and the small producers.[40]

The sweeping nationalization law of March 1948 assured the state of commanding positions in the insurance field, since the Hungarian companies were more important by far than the foreign companies nationalized later, in 1949.[41]

Compared to the former Allied countries, the truly distinctive feature of the Hungarian banking system after the nationalization and consolidation process of 1948–49 was the survival outside this supercen-

over the "banking monopolies," thus handing over to the Communists the whole of the "commanding heights" of the economy.

[39] "Report of the Board of Directors of the National Bank of Hungary on the Business Year 1948," in *Reports to the 23rd Ordinary Annual Meeting of the General Assembly of the National Bank of Hungary*, March 21, 1949, National Bank of Hungary, Budapest, 1949, pp. xxv–xxviii.

[40] *Ibid.*

[41] According to Hungarian figures released in July 1948, 96 per cent of the insurance policies outstanding in 1946 and over 80 per cent of the insured value were carried out at that time by the Hungarian companies, the rest being conducted by foreign companies. Cf. *GT*, II, 9 (July 1948), p. 611.

tralized system of an "independent" Soviet-owned bank enjoying, as Kemény correctly puts it, "*de facto* extra-territoriality." [42] The Soviet Bank (the previously Austrian-owned Bank of Commerce and Industry) played for nearly a decade the role of banker for various Russian enterprises and manager of Hungarian foreign trade operations related to the Soviet Union. Together with the Soviet positions in the insurance field, and even in the "nationalized" National Bank of Hungary itself,[43] the Soviet Bank remained an untouchable alien stronghold in the new Hungarian economy up to the end of 1954.[44]

ROMANIA

A similar evolution took place in the banking and insurance fields in Romania. The National Bank of Romania, largely owned by a group of private shareholders, was nationalized in December 1946.[45] In accordance with the nationalization law, besides assuming the role of "defender of the national monetary unit," the National Bank was made the "directing organ of all State and private credit institutions.[46]

[42] Kemény, *op. cit.*, p. 59.

[43] The new manager of the nationalized National Bank of Hungary, Francis Jeszensky, declared in a flight of oratory at the meeting of the General Assembly of the Bank in March 1949:

> At the present meeting, delegates of the Ministry of Finance represent the State as the principal shareholder, not as in the past when the representatives and toll-takers of capitalism, such as bankers, factory owners and private shareholders, attended the General meeting. No! Today it is the representatives of the Ministry of Finance who are present, workers themselves in the service of the people. In addition, in view of the fact that it controls a few shares, we have also representatives of the greatest nation of working people, the socialist Soviet Union. [Cf. "Minutes" of the meeting, in *Reports to the 23rd Ordinary Annual Meeting . . . , op. cit.*, p. xliv.]

The text, which at this point records "Applause!," does not attempt to explain why the "greatest nation of working people" adhered so strongly to the positions it inherited from the former (Nazi) "toll-takers of capitalism."

[44] See below, Chapter 6.

[45] Cf. Law of Nationalization, *Monitorul Oficial* (Official Gazette), Dec. 28, 1946, i.e., after the consolidation of Communist control in the first postwar parliament elected in Romania. The measure took effect on Jan. 1, 1947.

[46] Actually the object of the nationalization was to effect a complete redirection of the system of credit:

> "The nationalization of the National Bank of Romania has the object of eliminating the past errors concerning the credit policy. . . . The institute, of course, has not directed the credits towards the basic industries or towards those for which the raw materials are available in the country, but has channeled them towards the economic activities which produced important profits . . ." [Cf. Rapport au conseil des ministres concernant la gestion de l'année 1946 (Report to the Council of Ministers on the Business Year 1946), *Rapports du Conseil d'administration et du Conseil des*

Since the National Bank of Romania was the largest and the permanent shareholder in such institutions as the National Industrial Credit, the National Company of Agricultural Credit, the Mortgage Bank, the Tradesman's Credit Bank, and the National Cooperative Institute, nationalization enlarged tremendously the sphere of direct state control in the banking field and in the economy.[47] In July 1947 the National Bank was given the power to control the utilization of credits extended by all the banking institutions, a step which for all practical purposes ended their independence. The nationalization law passed a year later, in June 1948, nationalized all the banking business as well as the insurance companies.[48]

After nationalization a governmental decree dissolved most financial institutions except the National Bank of Romania, the National Industrial Credit, the State Savings Bank, the People's Banks, and the Soviet-Romanian (Sovrom) Bank, created in 1945. Following the familiar pattern, the National Bank of Romania became the institution of issue, the source of short-term credit, and the center of all financial transactions between state enterprises. The National Industrial Credit became the channel for long-term capital.[49] The Soviet-Romanian Bank, just as the Soviet Bank in Hungary, enjoyed *de facto* extraterritoriality. It acted as the central organ for the management and financing of the Soviet holdings in Romania until its dissolution in 1954.[50]

Bulgaria

Finally, in Bulgaria, since the National Bank had been from its formation (1879) a state bank, the central banking institution could be operated from the outset according to the objectives of the government and its Ministry of Finance. Thus the National Bank could be instructed, in the perspective of the Two-Year Plan (launched in April 1947), to "guarantee bank loans sufficient to finance the construction work anticipated." [51] The government had already proceeded

censeurs (Reports of the Council of Administration and of the Council of Censors), Banque Nationale de' Roumanie (National Bank of Romania), LXVI, Bucharest, 1947, p. 7.]

47 Professor G. Mladenatz, "Reform of the National Bank of Romania," *RR*, No. 4–5 (August–September 1946).

48 Law of June 11, 1948.

49 Decree of August 13, 1948.

50 See below, Appendix 2, Chapter 6, the official documents relating to the formation of the Sovrombank.

51 See Ivan Paliiski, Governor of the National Bank of Bulgaria, "Novi Sotsialis-

(1946) to nationalize the insurance companies.[52] In December 1947, simultaneously with the over-all nationalization of industry, the banking system was nationalized and remodeled on the same pattern as that of the other countries. Two institutions, the National Bank of Bulgaria and a newly created Bank of Investment, became the main organizations of the banking system. The National Bank of Bulgaria, besides holding the right of issue, handled payments and short-term credit; the Bank of Investment, basically the successor to the Mortgage Bank, took over the administration of long-term capital.[53] The credit cooperatives were empowered to continue banking operations only under special authorization of the National Bank of Bulgaria.[54] Thus, in the ex-enemy countries, Bulgaria preceded Hungary and Romania in the process of nationalization and reshaping of its banking system. The banking measures taken in Bulgaria after the combined nationalization-reshaping act of December 1947 very substantially increased the control of the National Bank of Bulgaria over the nationalized sector but left untouched the banking structure as it had emerged at the end of 1947.[55]

Summarizing for the whole area:

Generally, up to the end of 1947 the banking system, either completely nationalized (as in the former Allied countries) or only "indirectly" controlled through the National Bank and its agencies, functioned on the basis of an accepted coexistence of three economic sectors: state, cooperative, and private. However, this "acceptance" was never a static one; the state continued, by various means (such as credit policies and monetary manipulations which we shall discuss below), to enlarge its own sphere of operation.

At the end of 1947 in some countries and early in 1948 in others the nationalization of the banking system (maintaining its pace with the nationalization of industry) gained momentum.[56] As a direct result of

ticheski Merki v Bankovata Sistema" (New Socialist Measures in the Banking System), *PK,* No. 5, 1950, pp. 5 ff.

52 June 27, 1946.

53 Law of December 26, 1947.

54 Lazar Ralchev, "Activnosta na Bankite na Zemedelskite Svetovni Cooperativi" (The Activity of the Banking Agencies of the Agricultural Universal Cooperatives), *PK,* 3, 1948, p. 13.

55 See Ivan Paliiski, *op. cit.*

56 It is precisely in the "indissoluble connection between nationalization of banks and nationalization of industry and of other strongholds of the socioeconomic setting" that the Soviet economists see the distinctive feature between the nationalization of banks in Eastern Europe "and the nationalization of the institute of issue

the over-all nationalization process the banking system was revamped in the whole area by the close of 1948, and in each country centered around one or two main institutions: the National Bank and the Investment Bank.

From this point on, the banking system was adapted to over-all planning, the underlying principles of the reorganization being: (1) the banking system passes as a monopoly into the hands of the state; (2) a sharp distinction is made between short-term capital (in Marxian terms "circulating capital," i.e., working capital) and long-term capital ("fixed capital," i.e., investment); (3) as a function of this distinction, the National Bank (or Central Bank) becomes not only the issuing institution but also the "central bookkeeping unit of the economy" for intraenterprise payments and for short-term capital and an element of control and supervision of each plan; the Investment Bank (sometimes just a separate section of the National Bank itself) takes over the channeling, consistent with the plans, of the long-term capital available.[57]

As distinct from developments in the other countries, in Hungary and Romania a Soviet Bank remained outside the centralized banking system up to the end of 1954. Because of their autonomous position these banks played an "independent and decisive role" which will be analyzed in a later chapter.[58]

Keeping in mind this combined evolution, let us now survey briefly the activities of the banking system in the monetary field, in the channeling of credits (short-term and long-term capital), and in the bringing about of new price-wage equilibriums.

and of some commercial banks in the West" (in France, for instance). Cf. A. Alekseev, "Finansy Stran Narodnoi Democratii na Sluzhbe Stroitel'stva Sotsialisma" (The Finances of the Countries of the People's Democracies in the Service of the Construction of Socialism), in *Bolshevik,* No. 13, Moscow, 1950, p. 39.

[57] As K. Gottwald put it in the speech preceding the 1948 bank reorganization in Czechoslovakia:

> Banking must be reorganized according to the requirements of planned economy. The chief idea underlying the measures to be taken will be the concentration of all capital assets and their centralized distribution into two channels: towards investment and production. . . . Measures such as these will facilitate and simplify the control of taxation, prices, wages, as well as the control of the speed of turnover of goods and of the efficiency and economic operation of the national enterprises. [Cf. *Statement of Policy of Mr. Gottwald's Government,* Orbis, Prague, 1946.]

[58] See below, Chapter 6.

The Liquidation of the Occupation Currencies in the Former Allied Group

In the study of the liquidation of the monetary heritage of the occupation period close attention must be given to: (*a*) the mechanism of refunding old monetary units in circulation; (*b*) the social implications of these operations; (*c*) the general results achieved over a period extending through 1948, when new monetary measures were called into play.

During the process of liberation from the Nazi occupation and the reassembling of the dismembered territories of their countries the new (provisional) governments of Czechoslovakia, Poland, and Yugoslavia were faced with complete chaos in the monetary field.

In Czechoslovakia four currencies had been in circulation during the occupation: the Czech Koruna (legal tender in the "Protectorat" of Bohemia-Moravia), the Slovak Koruna (established by the Tiso government of Slovakia), the Hungarian pengö in the southern part of Slovakia, and the Reichsmark. Finally, in their rapid passage through the country, the Russians had introduced also a certain quantity of rubles. The amount of the currencies in circulation attained in 1945 a total of 122 billion Korunas (Kčs), i.e., over 17 times the 1938 amount (7 billion).

In Poland two basic monetary systems were in existence during the closing days of the Nazi regime. One consisted of the notes issued by the Bank of Issue in Poland (Bank Emisyjny w Polsce) created by the Germans for the so-called General Government of Poland; the other represented the currency notes issued by the Reichsbank in either the annexed areas or in the German territories proper which were subsequently absorbed by Poland (such as Prussia and Silesia). Finally, here also Russian troops introduced during their advance and especially in the sectors occupied by them in the Oder-Neisse region an appreciable amount of rubles.

In Yugoslavia the situation was probably even more confused. There had been in circulation during the various occupations of that dismembered country: dinars (issued in Serbia by the Nedič government), Kunas (issued in Croatia by the Pavelić government), and a number of occupation currencies such as Reichsmarks, Italian lire, Albanian francs, Hungarian pengös, and Bulgarian leva. To these should also be added all types of promissory notes issued by the Slovene fascists, the occupying forces, and the Partisans themselves. The money in circulation represented in 1945 a total of 292 billion dinars, or over 42 times the prewar amount (6.9 billion).

In each of these countries the process of monetary reunification and reorganization included drastic deflationary measures in order to bring somewhat into equilibrium the volume of money and the fantastically low supply of commodities forthcoming from the shattered, damaged, or totally disorganized production systems. Complicating elements in the process of readjustment were the different value of various types of money in a country and the varying degrees of inflation.[59] Furthermore, in some regions the monetary system had broken down completely and the economy had reverted to barter trading.

Financial reunification was achieved in Czechoslovakia by successive steps: First, Reichsmarks were recalled in the former "Protectorat," then in the former Sudetenland; then the pengö was taken out of circulation; finally Czech and (stamped) Slovak Korunas, which were left as legal tender up to October 19, 1945, were exchanged for a new Czechoslovak Koruna (Kčs). From November 1, circulation of the old currencies was forbidden, and they were blocked in a banking account in the name of the depositor; similarly, bank deposits, foreign assets, etc., were blocked. Bank notes not declared before the fifteenth of that month were confiscated for the benefit of the treasury. Each person was authorized to receive out of his blocked account a maximum of 500 new Kčs. After November 1, wages and salaries were paid in the new currency. The immediate result of these measures was the lowering of the amount of money in circulation from 122 billion Kčs to 25 billion, the blocked accounts amounting to some 250 billion Kčs.

In Poland, in the wake of the Russian advance, the Polish Committee of National Liberation (the so-called Lublin Committee) decided in October 1944 to convert the currencies in circulation into a new zloty to be issued by a bank created *ad hoc*, the National Bank of Poland.[60] It is interesting to note that Poland adopted sharply differentiated rates and quotas of conversion according to the province and the type of currency involved. The occupation zloty (circulating in the area of the so-called Polish General Government) was converted at par, and the conversion quota was at the same time fixed at 500 zloty per person over 18 years of age; in the province of Bialystock,

[59] Thus, for instance, on the basis 1938 = 100, prices in 1945 were at the index 170 in the "Protectorat" of Bohemia-Moravia and 240 in Slovakia; salaries were, respectively, at 150 and 200. Cf. *L'Évolution économique de la Tchécoslovaquie, op. cit.,* p. 13.

[60] Decrees of October 23, 1944, January 6, and February 5, 1945.

Reichsmarks could be converted only in quotas of 300 Reichsmarks at the rate of 1 zloty equals 1 RM; this quota was raised to 500 zloty in the remaining provinces (recovered later), but the conversion rate was then changed to 2 RM to 1 zloty. Remaining quantities of notes of the bank of issue in Poland were liable to be put into deposit accounts, payment of which required special permits from the Minister of Finance. The monetary circulation was thus appreciably reduced by the end of 1945.

In Yugoslavia the conversion of occupation currencies was effected on April 10, 1945. A new ("federal") dinar replaced the currencies on the basis of a widely differentiated rate adjusted in principle to the respective depreciation of the currencies but in practice strongly underevaluating the Croatian Kuna.[61] Bank deposits created after April 1941 were automatically reduced according to the new rates. Each person was entitled to receive up to 5,000 new dinars, except for the big enterprises (already run by the state). Sums over 5,000 dinars were blocked. By the end of the conversion, when the money in circulation had fallen to the low level of 6 billion dinars, severe economic pressure made it necessary to increase the circulation to 18 billion dinars, a total 16 times less than before the conversion (see Chart, 7, p. 118).

The "surgical" liquidation of the occupation monies, the limited quota of money distributed per person, and the blocking of accounts over this quota gave the new regime a free hand for monetary "satiation" of the economy according to their own objectives. As a Polish source puts it, "there arose, in a certain sense, a *moneyless state* in both the productive and consumptive domains of the economy."[62] Concomitantly with the launching of the new currency, prices and wages were established in given relationships; in Czechoslovakia, for instance, wages and prices were adjusted at a level of around 300 (1938 = 100), with an especially marked improvement for the lower wages. Various systems of control (allocation of scarce materials, rationing, etc.) were put into operation.

In order to maintain economic stability and to avoid either extended deflation or the reappearance of inflationary pressures, combined efforts were made to: (1) relate the financial plans to the materials avail-

[61] *Les récentes expériences monétaires à l'étranger* (Recent Foreign Monetary Experiences), Notes et études documentaires (Notes and Documentary Studies), No. 604. La Documentation Française (French Documentation), Paris, Sept. 15, 1946, p. 8.

[62] "The Monetary and Credit System in Poland," *op. cit.*, p. 2.

able and the profitability of enterprises; (2) survey the increases in the volume of credit extended; (3) severely control the freeing of blocked accounts; (4) finally, "mop up" the new money accumulating outside the "controlled" public sector.

If we survey the period through 1948, these efforts appear to have had very different results in the various countries. Only little by little did these countries succeed in limiting the amount of money in circulation to a sum that would not imperil the stability of prices.

Thus in Poland the monetary issues for treasury purposes, which at first increased rapidly, did not start to slow down until about 1947, and only at that time was some order brought about in the system of expansion of bank credit.[63]

In order to finance state investment and check inflationary pressures, the blocked accounts, instead of being restored fully to former owners, were turned either immediately or progressively into a financial source for the state. In Yugoslavia these accounts were liquidated early in 1945. They were "freed" after deducting for the "State's Fund of Reconstruction" sums varying from 5 to 30 per cent for the industrial enterprises; 8 to 50 per cent for the commercial undertakings; and 10 to 70 per cent for private persons, conditional upon the amount involved and the social position of the owner.[64] In Poland the blocked accounts of occupation zloty were unfrozen "in fact very rarely, and then only for the corporate bodies." [65] In Czechoslovakia the system of unfreezing the blocked accounts changed at various times. A special tax on capital was established in 1946, ranging between 5 and 30 per cent when applying to "regular" wealth, and up to 100 per cent when applying to "war profiteering." The blocked accounts were used to establish the social stratification of their owners and as a basis for assessing taxes. The balance after tax deduction was supposed to be gradually freed by fixed amounts.[66] Actually, a very large number of accounts passed under the management of a "Fund of Monetary Liqui-

[63] Thus a considerable part of the liabilities of the National Economic Bank, the bank of investment, were indebtedness to the National Bank of Poland. At the end of 1945–46, the methods of refinancing started, to be revised "with the result that the participation of refinancing means in the form of credits in standing account with the National Bank of Poland may substantially diminish in the next financial year." Cf. "National Economic Bank Activity in 1945–46," in *Quarterly Review of the Bank Gospodarstwa Krajowego,* XIV, 3, September 1947, p. 5.

[64] *Les récentes expériences monétaires à l'étranger, op. cit.,* p. 9.

[65] "The Monetary and Credit System in Poland," *loc. cit.*

[66] *Statement of Policy of Mr. Gottwald's Government, op. cit.*

dation" (1947) and ultimately found their way into the hands of the state.[67]

The expanding financial requests of the state and the limited amount of goods available generated new and constantly increasing inflationary pressures.

In Czechoslovakia continuous budgetary deficits, lack of foreign credits, an increase in income greater than that in the production of consumers' goods, and a low rate of saving built up strong inflationary pressures, notoriously more severe than the official price index suggests. Thus, on the basis of 1938 = 100, the indices of currency circulation rose from 254 in 1945 to 908 at the end of 1948. The official retail price indices for the same period rose from 185 to 323. The government campaign to lower prices, started in April 1947, had but a passing effect. According to a computation published by the Czechoslovak National Statistical Office, on the basis of official prices equaling 100, the indices of black market prices for all consumables rose from 255 in September 1946 to 305 in September 1947, and to 629 in September 1948.[68]

In Poland the inflationary pressures were even more severe. On the basis of 1938 = 100, the indices of currency circulation rose from 1,878 at the end of 1945 to 12,440 at the end of 1948; the official retail price indices rose from 7,950 in 1945 to 13,300 in 1948.

Only in Yugoslavia was the increase of money in circulation quite moderate. Thus, on the basis of 1938 = 100, this index rose from

[67] The last data available on the blocked accounts are for 1947 (IV); at that time they amounted to 223 billion Kčs as compared to a total of 250 billion Kčs as of January 1946 (hence they had fallen by 11%). Cf. Dr. Gruzín, "Oběživo a Vklady" (Currency Circulation and Deposits), in *SZ*, XII, 1 (January 1949), p. 11. In spite of this evidence, the massive increase of money in circulation and the depreciation of the currency were later attributed to the "sabotage of the reactionary elements" who allegedly unfroze the blocked accounts in favor of the capitalists. Cf. Z. V. Atlas, *Ukreplenie Denezhnykh Sistem SSSR, Stran Narodnoi Demokratii—Infliatsia v Stranakh Kapitalizma* (The Strengthening of the Monetary System of the USSR and People's Democracies—Inflation in the Capitalist Countries), Gosfinizdat, Moscow, 1951, p. 83; also, J. S. Lavruhin, *Narodno-Demokraticheskaia Chekhoslovakiia na putsi k Sotsialismu* (The Czechoslovak People's Democracy on the Road to Socialism), publ. by *Pravda*, 1950, p. 11.

[68] Cf. *RZ*, "Ceny v černém obchodě v září 1948" (Black Market Prices in September 1948), in *SZ*, XI, 12 (December 1948), p. 427. Hence the real value of cash holdings, i.e., the ratios of indices of currency circulation and retail prices, would be, at the official price index, 161 (in 1946) and 281 (in 1948); with the black market prices the real value of cash holdings would stand at 63 (in 1946) and 44 (in 1948), a declining trend.

231 in 1945 to 509 at the end of 1948. Early in 1945 and 1946, aside from the UNRRA supplies thinly spread over the country as a whole, only a small flow of commodities was available either from agriculture or from the nationalized consumers' goods sector. Therefore, the early "equilibrium" attained in this domain was achieved, so to speak, between a very low level of income and a very low level of supply.[69] By the end of 1948 quite substantial increases in prices were registered. As compared with a 217 per cent increase since 1945 of the currency in circulation, in the same period prices in the free market rose 3 times (potatoes), 4 to 5 times (flour, milk, eggs), or even 7 times (butter).[70]

Yugoslavia seems to have kept the inflationary pressures in check, whereas in Poland and Czechoslovakia highly inflated currencies, unstable prices, and deteriorating wages were more than obvious at the end of the period under review.

The First Monetary Refundings in the Ex-Enemy Group

Of the ex-enemy countries Hungary and Romania had very different monetary problems from those described above. Having been under Soviet occupation in the latter part of the war, they had to cope with the financial problems arising from the obligations of continuing the war (this time on the side of the Allies), providing for the needs of the occupying forces, paying heavy reparations, and putting their shattered economies in motion again.

In Hungary the state revenues, as against the requirements of both reconstruction and reparations, had declined in early 1945 to an insignificant figure. The destruction of assessable objects, the dislocation of economic life, and the disorganization of tax collection accounted

[69] "Commodities other than food only began to come on the market in the spring and summer of 1946, and that in the towns. The sections of the population who have so far benefited from the redistribution of purchasing power are in the main the urban workers and the peasants of the south. The latter have been guaranteed at least a minimum subsistence diet, by UNRRA in 1945 and by the harvests of 1946 and 1947; and have benefited substantially from the first releases of household utensils and small tools (plowshares, hammers, saws, axes, etc.). The peasantry of the more prosperous north and west have so far received little benefit, and are not likely to do so until the output of light industry is higher." Cf. John Morris, *Yugoslavia, op. cit.*, p. 82.

[70] These figures on prices were computed on the basis of data published by the Romanian review, *PE,* May 1949, and quoted by G. J. Conrad, *op. cit.,* p. 29.

for the fact that revenue, in the second half of 1945, covered only 7 per cent of expenditures.[71] The reparations obligations were so severe and pressing that the government had to resort to the issue of treasury bills, which in turn required the use of the resources of the Central Bank. Inflation accelerated from month to month and, finally, from day to day—almost from hour to hour. Parallel with the issue of treasury bills, the bank's bill portfolio increased rapidly as did the notes in circulation. Compared to these demands of the state, the credits extended to the enterprises for production appeared insignificant. Thus, in the discount portfolio of the Bank, the latter represented 2.8 per cent as against 97.2 per cent for the state. The note circulation (including 9.1 billion pengös which had been taken to the West) increased from 20.2 billion at the end of 1944 to 21.2 billion by the end of May 1945, and then to 265.4 billion by the end of that year, or over 12 times in 8 months. The rapid acceleration in pace of postwar inflation from April 1945 on (i.e., after the expulsion of the Nazis) can be seen from Table 33. On a quarterly basis (taking the last month of the preceding quarter as 100), the increases in 1945 and 1946 were 104 (I); 124 (II); 290 (III); 1,826 (IV); 4,442 (I, 1946); 185×10^6 (II, 1946). Taking the currency circulation of the preceding year as 100, compared to an index of 253 in 1944, the index stood in 1945 at 6,876 and for the seven months of 1946 up to the monetary reform at $6{,}143 \times 10^{15}$.

With the expansion of the note circulation during the last month of 1945, the rise in prices became more and more rapid. At first the government did not intervene. After price controls had been introduced, prices still continued to rise more than 6 times as fast as currency. Wages and salaries had to be constantly readjusted. In order to slow down the inflation, the government ordered a 75 per cent bank levy at the end of 1945, a measure which, however, apart from inducing a decline in prices which lasted a few days, proved ineffective. On January 1, 1946, the government introduced the tax-pengö (a unit of calculation intended to prevent the depreciation of tax payments), the value of which was fixed from day to day. The tax-pengö was then employed in credit transactions, and the Central Bank accepted for discount only bills of exchange drawn in tax-pengös. By May 1946 the Treasury began to issue state notes in tax-pengös which finally

[71] For the data on Hungarian inflation, the basic source of reference is the "Report of the Board of Directors of the National Bank of Hungary on the Course of Business in the Years 1944, 1945, and 1946," in *Reports to the 21st Qrdinary Annual Meeting . . . , op. cit.*, pp. ix–xix.

TABLE 33. HUNGARY: MONTHLY, QUARTERLY, AND YEARLY PACE OF THE INFLATIONARY MOVEMENT,[a] 1944–46 (VII)

End of	1944	1945			1946		
	Year	Month	Quarter[b]	Year	Month	Quarter[b]	I–VII
January		100			215		
February		104	104		318	4,442	
March		100			649		
April		99			1,276		$6,143 \times 10^{15}$
May		103	124		15,112	185×10^{6}	
June	253	119		6,876	9,657,340		
July		112			789,150		
August		149	290				
September		171					
October		250					
November		332	1,826				
December		215					

[a] Preceding month, or final month of preceding quarter, or preceding December = 100.
[b] Rounded figures.

Source: (Computed from) "Assets and Liabilities as in the Years 1944, 1945, 1946 (VII). Annex to the Annual Report for the Incomplete Business Year 1946," in *Reports to the 21st Ordinary Annual Meeting . . . , op. cit.*, Supplements 4 and 5, pp. 34–36.

entered into circulation as means of payment along with the ordinary bank notes. At the end of that month the value of notes in circulation was 3.2 million times as great as in April 1945, and the index of the cost of living was 128 million times as great. Then and in the following month of June the flight from the national money became general, and even the tax-pengö notes became useless as a means of payment.[72] "Business was done partly in gold and dollars, but principally by exchange of goods, and, as the inflation progressed, the country showed signs of sinking back into a primitive state of barter." [73]

The basic conditions for a return to stability were: increase in production, reduction of the reparations burden, and reorganization of

[72] Prof. Atlas notes that an almost similar situation existed in the USSR in 1922–23: a bank currency circulating within narrow limits for the needs of commodity exchanges (but not for the open expenses of the state) and, along with it, a depreciating currency. In Hungary the tax-pengö circulated also for state purchases outside the banking system, which could be the reason for its depreciation. Cf. Z. V. Atlas, *op. cit.*, pp. 96–101.

[73] "Report of the Board of Directors of the National Bank of Hungary on the Course of Business in the Years 1944, 1945, and 1946," *op. cit.*

public expenditures. In order to help Hungary attain stability, the United States agreed to return to the Hungarian Bank its gold reserves, valued at 32 million dollars, which had been in American custody. The Soviet Union, following the example of Yugloslavia, extended the period of reparations deliveries from 6 to 8 years, agreed to a progressive scale of payments, and finally took over, in the Hungarian reparations account, the shares of the Romanian Petroşani coal mines which were owned by Hungary. As a result, reparations for 1946 were reduced from the original 51.4 million dollars to 27.5 millions, and for 1947 from 53.2 to 29.3 millions.[74] Hence, the state budget could be reduced. Under these conditions there was launched on August 1, 1946, a new currency, the forint (or the florin). Since its content was defined as 1 kilogram of fine gold equal to 13,210 forints, the new monetary unit was equal to 400,000 quadrillion pengös or 200,000 million tax-pengös. Simultaneously with the stabilization, state control over the central bank was further increased.

Stopping the Hungarian hyperinflation was thus due largely to the return by the United States of the gold reserves (which instilled confidence in the new monetary unit) and to the reduction by the Soviet Union of her own reparations claims. The success of the stabilization by the end of 1948 appears quite remarkable. Notes in circulation rose from 968 million forints to 2,816 millions between August 1946 and the end of 1948; or, on the basis of 1938 = 100, the index of currency in circulation rose from 106 in August 1946 to 307 at the end of 1948. Yet substantial progress was achieved during the same period in the field of industrial production. Prices which had risen steadily, though at varying paces since the stabilization, reached their peak in May 1948 and then began again to fall. The index of retail prices, on the basis of 1938 = 100, rose from 416 at the end of 1946 to 498 at the end of 1947 but fell to 450 at the end of 1948.[75] The decrease in the cost of living during 1948, in its turn, brought about an increase in real wages which, on the average, were now higher than before the war.[76]

As in Hungary, in Romania after the expulsion of the Nazis a new and powerful inflationary movement started to develop as a result of the heavy burden of Soviet occupation, the continuation of the war, and the payment of reparations.

[74] See below, Chapter 6.

[75] *ESE in 1948, op. cit.*, p. 32.

[76] "Report of the Board of Directors of the National Bank of Hungary on the Business Year 1948," *op. cit.*, p. xx.

From 1939 to the end of August 1944 (the period of preparation for the war, 1939–41, and the period of the war carried on beside the Axis powers, 1941–44, up to the expulsion of the Nazis), the bank notes in circulation increased from 39 billion lei to 228 billion lei. On the basis of 1939 = 100, the index of the currency in circulation in August 1944 stood, therefore, at 584. From September 1944 to May 1945 (from the armistice until the end of the war on the side of the Allies), the currency in circulation rose to 560 billion lei, or from the index 584 to 1,437.[77] From June 1945 on, the country had to make increased reparations deliveries and recover from the destruction brought about by the war. Lack of raw materials and the deficient harvests of 1945 and 1946 contributed to make these tasks more and more difficult. By the end of 1945 the bill portfolio of the National Bank had increased 4 times over 1944. By the same token, its structure changed also. According to the reports of the Bank, priority was now given to the financing arising from the armistice obligations, followed in order of importance by the financing of the reconstruction of the petroleum industry, now a joint Soviet-Romanian business,[78] the exports to the USSR, the reconstruction and transformation of the metallurgical industry (now heavily controlled by the Soviet Union),[79] and, last, by other sectors of the economy.[80]

As the state stepped up its demands, inflation was accelerated, although it did not reach the degree of that in Hungary. From May 1945 to August 15, 1947, the currency in circulation increased from 560.6 billion lei to 48,451 billion lei, or from an index of 1,437 to one of 124,233. The progressive acceleration can readily be seen in the following figures: in 1944 the circulation of currency doubled as

[77] After the armistice and with their arrival in Romania, the Russians also put Soviet lei and rubles into circulation, along with the Romanian national currency. The situation created by the simultaneous circulation of three currencies produced confusion and encouraged speculation. The National Bank of Romania negotiated for and obtained the right to exchange rubles and Soviet lei, leaving the national lei as the only currency to circulate in the country. Because of military events the monetary unification could not be carried out in Transylvania before early in 1945 when the currencies in circulation in this province were exchanged for 39 billion lei. Cf. Rapport à l'Assemblée Generale des Actionnaires (Report to the General Assembly of Shareholders), *Rapports du Conseil d'administration et du Conseil des censeurs* (Reports of the Council of Administration and of the Council of Censors), Banque Nationale de Roumanie (National Bank of Romania), Feb. 18, 1945, Vol. LXIV, Bucharest, 1945, p. 6.

[78] See below, Chapter 6.

[79] See below, Chapter 6.

[80] *Rapports* . . . , (as in Note 77, above).

compared to the preceding year; in 1945 it increased almost 3½ times over 1944; in 1946 it increased 5 times over 1945; in the seven and one-half months preceding the monetary refunding of August 15, 1947, it had increased 8 times over 1946 (see Table 34). The cost of living index, on the base 1938 = 100, increased to 145 in 1940;[81] to 8,419 in 1945; to 46,120 at the end of 1946; and to 514,664 in July 1947.[82]

TABLE 34. ROMANIA: MONTHLY, QUARTERLY, AND YEARLY PACE OF THE INFLATIONARY MOVEMENT,[a] 1944 (VI)–1947 (VIII)

End of	1944	1945			1946			1947		
	Year	Month	Quarter	Year	Month	Quarter	Year	Month	Quarter	I–VIII
January		104			104			105		
February		108	123		107	128		110	136	
March		109			115			118		
April		110			118			132		
May		120	148		108	147		172	331	792
June	223	113		340	116		504	145		
July		113			113			146		
August		110	140		117	160		120		
September		112			121					
October		110			120					
November		108	133		121	168				
December		112			116					

[a] Preceding month, or final month of preceding quarter, or preceding December = 100.

Sources: Up to July 1945: (Computed from) ***Bulletin d'information et de documentation*** (Bulletin of Information and Documentation), Banque Nationale de Roumanie (National Bank of Romania), XVII year, No. 4–6, April–June 1945, p. 41. From July 1945 to August 1947: *Ibid.*, XIX year, No. 7–9, July–September 1947, p. 124.

The launching of a new currency and the monetary refunding undertaken on August 15, 1947, were conceived "not as a monetary conclusion of the process of economic recovery of the country, but rather as a means in order to achieve this recovery."[83] On that day, the money in circulation was ordered to be exchanged at the rate of 20,000 lei for 1 new "stabilized" leu (defined as representing 6.6 mg. of metal 9⁄10 gold,

[81] *CS,* No. 19, January 31, 1948.

[82] Costin Kiritzesco, "La Réforme monetaire roumaine de 1947" (The Romanian Monetary Reform of 1947), in *Bulletin d'information et de documentation,* National Bank of Romania, XIX, 7–9, July–September 1947, p. 128.

[83] *Ibid.,* p. 122.

or equal to 66 per cent of the 1929 Romanian leu). The quotas of old lei to be exchanged were fixed, per social category, as follows: 5 million old lei (250 new lei) per peasant family (or 7.5 million old lei—325 new lei—for peasants having fulfilled the crop delivery quotas); 3 million (150 new lei) per worker, employee, pensioner, war widow, and war orphan; 1.5 million (75 new lei) per person without profession and per soldier. Corporations received a quota equal to their payroll for June. Commercial undertakings were excluded from the process of conversion. Public institutions were allowed to change all the sums in their possession, the diplomatic missions a sum equal to that at their disposal in the preceding month.

By allowing the exchange of only a small part of the old currency either by blocking the other lei in the banks or by canceling them in the hands of their possessors, the amount exchanged was limited to about 27,550 billion lei, only 57 per cent of the total in circulation on August 14, 1947. This amount was exchanged for 1.3 billion new lei, distributed through the mechanism of the quotas unequally between the holders of old lei and the state. A second package of 550 million new lei was put into circulation for the purchase of gold and foreign currencies (the private holding of which was henceforth forbidden).

The low ceilings set on the sums admitted to conversion destroyed a large part of the value of the previous currency reserves and deposits.[84] The exclusion of the commercial undertakings from the conversion, supposedly aimed at forcing them to "disgorge their stocks," represented one of the major steps in the process of "dislodgment" of the private entrepreneurs and businessmen from the economy.[85] Finally,

[84] Except for the small savings deposits unfrozen a year later. Cf. *RR*, III, 11 (September 1948), p. 66.

[85] Actually, a few days before the "stabilization," control groups carried out an inventory of merchandise in all the enterprises. Once the inventory had been completed and the merchandise catalogued, the merchandise was blocked and put at the disposal of a state organization called the National Institute of Cooperation (INCOP). INCOP "purchased" this merchandise for the value of some tens of billions of lei with checks drawn on the National Bank. The day after the issue of the INCOP checks, August 15, the government enacted the monetary reform and canceled the National Bank's debts, therefore also the checks in question. The acute shortage of lei led employers to "credit" their own businesses; thus they divested themselves of everything at their disposal in order to operate the business which had now become a burden. Therefore, it can be assumed that, if the nationalization had occurred immediately after liberation from the Nazis, on August 23, 1944, the businessmen would have lost perhaps only their businesses; by subjecting them to the gamut of the INCOP checks, the stabilization, the blocking of accounts, and only lastly the nationalization, their economic weakening was absolute.

the relationship between prices and wages was redefined in the "stabilized" currency by allowing a certain increase in basic wages.[86]

No sooner had the enormous capital levy of August 15, 1947, been undertaken than the Communist regime started to circulate large quantities of the new currency. By the end of 1947 the amount of currency in circulation had increased from the 1.5 billion distributed at the beginning of the reform to between 24 and 28 billion, in addition to a very substantial rise in scrip.[87] As the money in circulation continued to increase in the face of the low supply of consumables, prices of consumables began to rise appreciably. The prolonged scarcity of industrial goods having prevented a return flow of money from the countryside, substantial reserves of new currency started to be built up in the villages. As we shall see below, in the analysis of the period following 1949, this was subsequently construed as proof of the "sabotage activity" of the Minister of Finance, Vasile Luca, and as justification for new monetary refunding.

The third ex-enemy country, Bulgaria, was in an exceptional position. As stated before, she had to pay reparations to Yugoslavia and Greece but not to the Soviet Union, which became the sole successor to the German assets in Bulgaria.[88] At the end of the collaboration with Germany and after the brief Soviet military intervention of 1944, the currency in circulation in Bulgaria amounted to 48 billion leva (to which should be added some 14.8 billion in 3 per cent special bonds circulating as means of payment equal to the currency). This total compares to the 2.8 billion leva in circulation in 1938. The continuation of the war (this time against Germany), the Soviet occupation, and the payment of reparations [89] further inflated the volume of currency in circulation to around 73 billion by the end of 1945, in spite of a successful loan of 20 billion leva oversubscribed at the beginning of that year. By the end of 1946 various confiscations brought into the

[86] See below, Chapter 10.

[87] Costin Kiritzesco, *op. cit.*, p. 125, gives for Dec. 20, 1947, a total of 24.5 billion in circulation. Prof. Z. V. Atlas, *op. cit.*, p. 94, gives for 1947 the figure of 28 billion lei.

[88] See above, Chapter 2, pp. 35–36 and 39.

[89] It is interesting to note that Prof. Atlas remarked unhappily that Bulgaria was "compelled to pay reparations to Greece and to Titoite Yugoslavia in the conditions of the complete disorganization of her economy." However, no note of distress was recorded by that Soviet author for Hungary and Romania who were compelled in the same situation to assume even heavier obligations towards the Soviet Union. Cf. Z. V. Atlas, *op. cit.*, p. 86.

hands of the state some 4.5 billion leva, and the volume of currency and bonds in circulation fell slightly.

On March 7, 1947, the government decided to withdraw from circulation the 3 per cent bonds in question and to exchange the old currency for new leva at the ratio of 1 to 1, i.e., without any depreciation, but to block all sums above 2,000 leva per person. At the end of the operation the total in circulation was reduced from 75.9 billion (44.4 in bank notes and 31.5 billion in bonds) to around 30 to 35 billion leva.[90] The Minister of Finance gave assurances at the time that all undertakings "whether private, State or cooperative, would be provided with all the necessary funds during the period of emergency."

Bulgarian currency refunding was closer to the Czechoslovak pattern than to the type of monetary manipulations that took place in the other East European countries. The refunding did not have lasting consequences in this country. The official index of wholesale prices, which stood at 550 in 1945 (1939 = 100) and at 627 at the beginning of 1947, was at 687 in June of that year. The official cost of living index, which stood at 570 in 1945 (1939 = 100) and 636 at the beginning of 1947, rose to 703 in mid-1947. However, it may be noted that the cost of living was considerably higher before the monetary refunding if one takes into consideration the black market,[91] and the fact that the black market receded for a while after the monetary reform.

Examining the currency situation through 1948 in Bulgaria, it should be noted that inflationary pressures, nourished partly by the substantial unfreezing of blocked accounts after nationalization and also by the bidding up for the scarce consumables available, favored increases in prices here also (especially of agricultural commodities) and a substantial depreciation of real wages.

In summary, as Chart 7 clearly illustrates, whereas the former Allied countries could liquidate the war inflation in 1945 and make a "fresh start" at the opening of the postwar period, in the ex-enemy countries the war inflation was topped by a postwar inflation which finally reached a fantastic peak in the different countries in 1946 or 1947. In

[90] All the figures on currency circulation up to the reform are from *MI*, No. 2–3, 1947, p. 54. The series has been discontinued since the refunding. The estimate that the circulation had dropped to 30–35 billion leva was made by Georgi Dimitrov in "1947 Balance Sheet," in *Free Bulgaria*, III, 2 (Jan. 15, 1948).

[91] Cf. Prof. Dinko Toshev, "The Cost of Living," in *Free Bulgaria*, II, 23 (Dec. 15, 1947).

Hungary and Romania the main factor in the acceleration of this inflation was the heavy obligation of reparations payments to the Soviet Union.

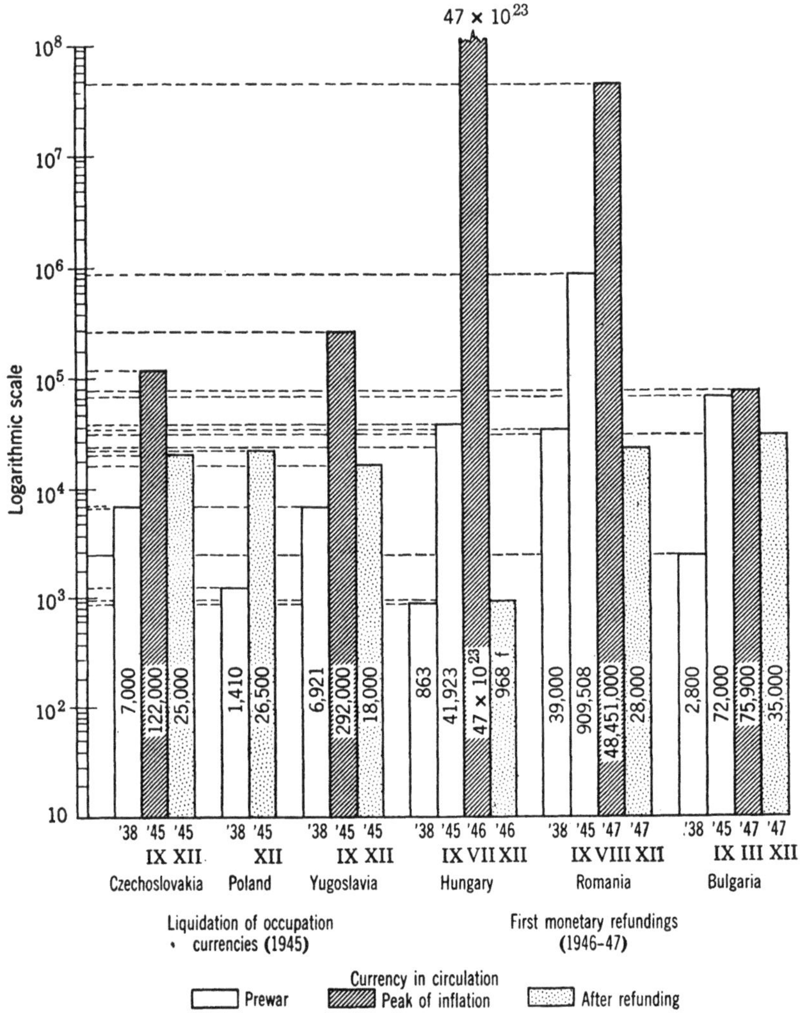

CHART 7. LIQUIDATION OF OCCUPATION CURRENCIES AND FIRST MONETARY REFUNDINGS

Thus two "waves" of currency manipulation can be observed in the area. The first, in 1945, was aimed at liquidation of the effects of the war period and took place in the former Allied countries; the second, in 1946 or 1947, was intended mainly to liquidate the first consequences of the reparations and took place in the ex-enemy countries.

As stated above, after liquidation of the occupation currencies new inflationary pressures started to build up in both Poland and Czechoslovakia. In the ex-enemy countries also the 1946 and 1947 currency refunding did not have an enduring effect. The continuation of a high level of government spending and the low level of supplies rapidly made the purchasing power of the new currencies and the general structure of prices extremely unstable. New and drastic measures were to be called into play in order to effectuate again the transfer of liquidities to the state, this time mostly from the agrarian sector.

Before passing to this second period, let us examine briefly the credit policies between 1945 and 1948, which, along with the monetary manipulations, played a decisive role in the process of "dislodgment of the capitalists" from the economy.

Credit Policies and Interest Rates for the "Dislodgment" of Capitalist Elements

The early concentration of the entire banking business in the hands of the state in Czechoslovakia, Poland, and Yugoslavia permitted a systematic utilization of the banking machinery as an instrument for the "dislodgment" of capitalist elements. As a Soviet writer remarks,

> After the liquidation of the occupation currencies . . . the second task lying before these countries was the utilization of money as one of the most powerful instruments in the fight against the capitalist elements and . . . for the social reorganization of the economy.[92]

First Yugoslavia and Poland (from 1945 on), then Czechoslovakia (because of the special political conditions in this country), and finally the ex-enemy countries (around 1947 and 1948) perfected the utilization of money and bank channels as an instrument for the "restriction and dislodgment of urban and rural capitalists." The basic procedure was a combination of a policy of "starving out" the private sector in working capital and high cost for the eventual small credits extended.

The use of the banking machinery of Poland for this purpose is reflected in the changing distribution of bank loans (both short- and long-term) among state, cooperative, and private enterprises. In 1945 state enterprises already held 73 per cent of bank credit. By the end of 1948 their share had risen to 86 per cent. The share of the cooperative

[92] A. Alekseev, *op. cit.*, p. 41.

sector fell from 21 per cent in 1945 to around 13 per cent in 1948. The share of the private sector thus became extremely limited during the years under review.[93] In Yugoslavia, as early as 1946, the total bank credit was distributed as follows: 90.2 per cent to the nationalized sector; 7.9 per cent to the cooperative sector; 1.9 per cent to the private sector.[94] In Hungary in 1948 the central banking institution distributed its credits as follows: 70 per cent to state undertakings; 26 per cent to cooperatives; 4 per cent to the private sector.[95] In the following period the direct destruction of the private sector in the economy, except for agriculture, further reduced its participation in the credits extended.

This lopsided distribution did not correspond to the respective roles of these sectors in the economy. The sources of capital for these sectors in the period considered were, in order of importance: (1) the state budgets; (2) the large resources of the nationalized enterprises obtained chiefly from the liquidation of stocks; (3) UNRRA deliveries of investment goods (for the Allied countries); and (4) bank credits.

From the outset the state budgets included certain amounts for investment purposes. The sale of stocks of ready-made articles and half-finished products represented "important sources of financing" and "was largely responsible for the removal [i.e., the rehabilitation] of war devastations in the producing establishments of many enterprises." [96] Investment goods arriving with UNRRA (or utilization of the proceeds from the sale of other UNRRA products) made an appreciable contribution to the financing of the state sector.[97] Bank credit played a decisive role in 1945,[98] but its share in financing investment outlays decreased year by year. Thus in Poland, whereas in 1946 and 1947 bank credit financed nearly two-thirds of these outlays, in

[93] See *Statistical Yearbook of Poland 1948, op. cit.*, p. 145.

[94] Obren Blagojević, Budget Debate Speech, March 1947: *Changing Epoch Series*, No. 1, London, 1947, p. 75.

[95] *Reports to the 23rd Ordinary Annual Meeting . . . , op. cit.* p. xxvi.

[96] "Investment Financing in Poland," in *Quarterly Review of the Bank Gospodarstwa Krajowego,* XVII, 3, September 1948, pp. 1–5.

[97] Thus for instance, the source quoted above on Poland (note 96) states:

> Investment goods arriving within the UNRRA deliveries, although not constituting a large percentage of the total material bulk, made—nevertheless—their contribution towards quickening the pace of the country's reconstruction. . . .
>
> Receipts obtained from the distribution of UNRRA deliveries were disbursed—under the banks' supervision—to cover investment costs for the development of science, education, culture and arts, of labour and social welfare, as well as of health. . . .

[98] In the first postwar period, a current phenomenon was the financing of investments with short-term credits designated to increase working capital. *Ibid.*, p. 2.

1948 it financed slightly more than half. In this sense the state sector's share in the capital availabilities was far larger than the percentage distribution of bank credits would suggest.

A good illustration of the type of "credit channeling" that operated in these economies during that period can be obtained from the quite complete figures available for Poland and Hungary. The distinction in Poland between banks according to the sectors of the economy is very helpful for the purpose. According to the official data, nearly half the credits put at the disposal of the state sector by the specific state banks went to industry and one quarter to state trade. Agriculture as a whole, essentially dependent on the state Land Bank, obtained less than 10 per cent. In the cooperative and private sectors the largest percentages of the credit distributed went to trade. In spite of the often advertised help to the "small artisans," the volume of credit channeled into handicrafts was conspicuously low.[99]

The available breakdown of bank credit by branches in Hungary in 1948 reveals a similar pattern: 41 per cent of the total bank credit went to industry and mining, 31 per cent to agriculture (including 18 per cent for the state bulk purchase of crops), 22 per cent to commerce, and the remaining 6 per cent was put to other purposes (building transport, handicrafts, etc.).[100]

Thus, in the period of "dislodgment" of the capitalist elements from the various economic branches (1945–49), the private sector, totally deprived of long-term capital, received a constantly decreasing amount of short-term (working) capital. Most of this went to the trading branches, whereas private industry and handicrafts were left entirely to their own diminishing resources.

The systematic channeling of credit by sectors and by character of economic activity was reinforced by a widely differentiated rate of interest. Typical from this point of view is the example of Hungary. In 1946, after the monetary reform and with a very tight money supply, interest rates ranged up to 36 per cent in Budapest and even more in the provinces. In 1948, after the extensive nationalization of industry and banks, the whole structure of interest rates was lowered, but the difference in rates according to economic sectors was sharply delineated.

Thus the state banks charged 5 per cent on loans to cooperatives engaged in collective production; 7 per cent on loans to nationalized

[99] Cf. *Statistical Yearbook of Poland 1947, op. cit.*, p. 124; *ibid.*, 1948, p. 195; *Rocznik 1949, op. cit.*, p. 170.

[100] Cf. *Report to the 23rd Ordinary Annual Meeting . . . , op. cit.*

companies; 12 per cent on loans to private industrial enterprises; and 18 per cent on loans to merchants.[101]

After extensive liquidations of the private property in the non-agricultural sectors, interest rates were lowered in the entire area. The interest rates for short-term credits thereafter ranged between 1 and 5 per cent (according to the destination of the credit),[102] and interest rates for long-term capital (i.e., for investment), now determined centrally, generally became token rates of 1 per cent for coverage of the cost of bank administration of the credits.

THE NEW METHODS OF FINANCIAL ADJUSTMENT AND "ACCUMULATION"

A new period opened for the area at the end of 1948. Nationalization of manufacturing, banking, insurance, and substantial parts of the distribution apparatus [103] completed, new over-all long-term plans were now put into operation. As the state sector had absorbed large sections of the economy (except in agriculture), the dynamics of nationalization in the financial sphere changed both in character and in aims. Now these aims became to prevent capital concentration outside the state sectors; to transfer to the state any substantial accumulation of liquid funds over and above given wages, savings, or personal property; and to increase the excess of state revenues over expenditures for current purposes, maintaining, however, the purchasing power of the currency and the balance between established prices and wages.[104]

In order to prevent the formation of surplus purchasing power, the East European countries have specific means at their command. They

[101] *Ibid.*

[102] In Yugoslavia where this process was accomplished earlier, the rates of interest, differentiated according to the branch of economy, production, and distribution, ranged from 2 to 6 per cent in 1947. In 1953 they were differentiated as follows: 1 per cent for state enterprises and cooperatives; 2 per cent for seasonal credits; 3 per cent for credits to all other institutions; 5 per cent for short-term credits. Cf. Dr. Miloš Vučković, *op. cit.*, pp. 31 ff.

[103] See below, Chapter 5.

[104] The basic problems of this period of development are, for these economies: to reduce the share of consumption in the national income at a moment when industrialization implies an increase in consumption (owing to urbanization); to maintain the balance between prices and wages in spite of a "lopsided" development of heavy industry relative to the consumers' goods industry (a development which implies a limited supply of consumers' goods).

can determine the monetary demand, e.g., through the determination of wages, and they can determine both the supply and the prices of various commodities.

However, these "determinations" are not rigorous. The wage bill for each individual factory is related to output, but there is a tendency to increase the number of employees in order to fulfill the targets set.[105] Furthermore, overfulfillment of the plan, which occurs usually in the heavy goods industry, results in creation of more income than had been planned, and hence in increased inflationary tendencies. In order to prevent these inflationary pressures, increases in employment have to be kept in check, and the norms, i.e., the basis for the establishment of piece rates, have to be revised frequently. In addition to its use for this purpose, methodic revision of norms represents an essential means of systematic transfer to the state of the results of increases in productivity. As the chief Polish planner, Hilary Minc, remarked:

> We must do away with the erroneous conception that increase in productivity must always be accompanied by an equal or even superior increase in wages. This was the case during the Three-Year Plan when the gains in real wages were faster than those in productivity. . . . On the contrary, we cannot and will not follow such a policy during the Six-Year Plan. That would be an effective contradiction to the fundamental laws of socialist accumulation. These laws imply that increases in wages should progress more slowly than the increase in productivity because this is the only means of achieving a decrease in cost and an increased accumulation for investment. . . .[106]

Only in a *secondary* and limited way does the "reduction of cost" lead to a "progressive reduction of prices of the consumer goods which are in large demand," and hence to an increase in real wages. First and foremost, the revision of norms serves to increase the "accumulation fund," the fund for further investment. The methodical revision of norms has in effect become one of the current features of planning in the area; frequent recourse to it has been necessitated by the increased ratio of output of capital goods to the output of consumers' goods.[107]

[105] Employment has tended here to increase faster than output. See below, Chapter 8, on planning.

[106] H. Minc, "Sześcioletni Plan Rozwoju Gospodarczego i Budowy Podstaw Socjalizmu w Polsce," *op. cit.*

[107] Along with various structural changes, the Yugoslavs devised a different solution. After Jan. 1, 1952, when new planning and budget systems were introduced in that country, the wages and salaries were defined as consisting of two parts: a *fixed* part (financed by a special fund established under the plan and guaranteed by the state) and a *variable* part (dependent on the results of the work of the enterprise

In order to absorb an excess purchasing power already created, two groups of measures are at the disposition of these economies, fiscal measures and various systems of pricing goods.

After 1948–49 the fiscal system was revamped on the Soviet pattern. The so-called turnover tax, essentially a sales tax on foodstuffs and consumer goods,[108] became henceforth the main instrument of absorption of purchasing power [109] as well as the main source of revenue for each state budget, as can be seen from Table 35.

The turnover tax, which represents between 50 and 60 per cent of the state revenues in budgets whose scope has been tremendously increased, became far more important than all the other sources of revenue, in all the countries of the area, excepting Yugoslavia.[110]

and financed from profits). If, however, an enterprise, for reasons beyond its control, does not gain any profits, the state guarantees the wages of its workers in order to avoid wage discrepancies. See *Les Nouvelles Yugoslavs* (Yugoslav News), Sept. 22, and Oct. 6, 1951; also, *International Financial News Survey,* IV, 19 (Nov. 9, 1951), p. 152.

108 The turnover tax is applied to the sales of private individuals, cooperatives, and certain state enterprises. It consists of highly diversified rates according to the products considered, and is in principle levied only at *one stage* of the production and distribution of a commodity. Established in 1930 and modified in 1931 and 1949, the turnover tax is the mainstay of the Soviet budget. (Cf. Prof. K. Larionov, T. Golovanov, P. Tsyganov, *Dokhody Gosudarstvennogo Biudzheta ot Sotsialisticheskogo Khoziaistva (Revenues of the State Budget from the Socialist Economy*), Gosfinizdat, Moscow, 1954, pp. 35 ff.

109 The basic prices established for the producing enterprises are *planned production prices* which include planned production costs plus a planned profit markup. The prices at which enterprises normally sell to selling organizations are the planned production prices. However, if in any branch of industry planned production prices in some enterprises are above, and in other enterprises below, the selling price set for that branch, their prices may be equalized. If this results in a net deficit for the industry (i.e., when average planned production prices are above the selling price) the deficit is to be covered from the state budget. Retail prices are arrived at by adding to the selling price of goods at the factory administratively fixed, distributing and marketing costs. The planned profitability of various branches of production is regulated through the turnover tax. Cf., for instance, "The Polish Price System," in *Monitor Polski* (Official Gazette), May 17, 1950, as mentioned in *International Financial News Survey,* II, 49 (June 23, 1950), p. 392.

110 In order to spur lagging production, Yugoslavia abandoned the previous system of taxation and declared herself ready to replace it with a system of progressive taxation of profits. Under the previous system the federal budget was the collection center for taxes (mainly *turnover tax*), profits of enterprises, revenue of insurance, and loans subscribed by the population. The federal budget, in its turn, financed the investment program and covered the losses of state enterprises. Under the new system the scope of the federal budget is reduced; the collection of investment funds

A complementary measure in each country, aiming at checking the imbalances in demand and supply, is the utilization of rationing and of a dual price system. A common device is establishment of one price for a rationed portion of the supply of a type of goods, and sale of the remaining supply at a much higher price in a free market. Obviously, as each country of the area constitutes an autonomous economic unit, given goods are rationed in one East European country but not in the next; a double price system will be in effect at a given time in one or a certain number of East European countries but not in all of them. Thus in 1949 Poland and Hungary abolished their rationing system, whereas rationing remained in force in all the other East European countries. Later Poland had to revert to rationing and to a dual price system, the price of the rationed goods being placed at a level as high as the one previously established by the free market. The "free" prices increased further. Finally, as supply improved, Poland abolished its rationing system at the beginning of 1953. After a black market had developed in 1950, Hungary inaugurated a legal free market with prices 2 to 5 times as great as the prices established for rationed goods. At the end of 1951 there were established single prices which were higher than those for rationed goods but lower than those of the black market.

Schematically, the usual cycle runs as follows. Let us take as a starting point a situation in which consumers' goods are sold freely at the established prices. If, after a while, demand increases (or supply decreases), various quantities of goods will be withdrawn from the

has been withdrawn from it, and its scope for investment financing curtailed. The investments will have to be financed essentially by enterprises and by banks, the federal budget retaining the financing of purely defense investments. In order to assure the desired size of investment, the government may regulate the minimum obligatory investment funds in enterprises, increase income taxes, and limit earnings of the population by means of sales taxes. (Cf. J. V. Mladek, E. Sturc, and M. R. Wyczalkowski, *The Yugoslav Experiment in Decentralization*, International Monetary Fund, Staff Papers II, reprinted in *Readings on Contemporary Eastern Europe*, C. E. Black, editor, Mid-European Studies Center, New York, 1953, pp. 228 ff.) It is interesting to note that early in 1948 the Yugoslav Communist Central Committee was, among other things, accusing one of its former members, Žujovic (expelled then as "pro-Cominform"), of having "offered fierce resistance to the introduction of the turnover tax as a typically socialist form of socialist monetary accumulation, [given] preference to the capitalist form of profit in state economic enterprises, and the subjection of such profit to income-tax assessment, over the turnover tax on goods." Cf. B. Kidrič, *op. cit.*, p. 49. The Yugoslav experience is thus quite rich in reversals in this field.

TABLE 35. STRUCTURE OF BUDGETARY REVENUES, 1947 AND 1953

(percentages)

	Czechoslovakia		Poland		Yugoslavia		Hungary		Romania		Bulgaria	
Revenue	1947	1953	1947	1953	1947	1951	1947–48	1953	1946–47	1953	1946	1953
Turnover tax	32	51	39	76	44	76 (turnover tax and profits)	61	56	40	40	35	47
Profits	13	16	17	10	10		1	10	22	18	18	16
Direct taxes	20	8	25	10	21	9	28	6	9	7	25	7
Borrowing	[a]	[b]	[a]	1	25 (borrowing and other)	[c]	[c]	2	17 [d]	[b]	1 [d]	2
Other	35	25	19	3		15	10	26	12	35	21	28

[a] Deficit financed by Central Bank loan.
[b] Not available.
[c] Nil.
[d] Does not comprise all government borrowing.

Sources: For all countries except Yugoslavia: *ESE since the War*, op. cit., p. 28, and *Economic Bulletin for Europe*, Vol. 7, No. 2, (Aug. 1955), pp. 19 and 47. For Yugoslavia, 1947: Obren Blagojević, *op. cit.*, p. 80, and 1951: G. J. Conrad, *op. cit.*, p. 19.

market, hoarding will develop and, along with it, a black market. In order to "liquidate the speculators," absorb the surplus purchasing power, and also determine that at least a part of the supply available will be distributed as it considers fit, the government can place consumers' goods under rationing. This was done at times with both manufactured and agricultural goods, at other times with one or the other, and sometimes with some goods of each type. As the supply-demand imbalance becomes worse, a part of the available quantity of a given item may be rationed, the balance being sold freely at higher prices.

If a certain amount of a consumers' item is distributed under ration and the balance of the available quantity is sold at higher "free" prices through the state's special retailing outlets, the government will absorb the surplus purchasing power; if the amount available over the rationed quantity is sold by the peasantry at free prices, part of the surplus purchasing power will evidently flow to the countryside. (This will usually be permitted when there is a drop in the supply of agricultural goods owing to natural conditions and when it appears necessary to encourage the peasantry to bring the excess of their produce to the market.) Finally, as supply improves, or as the entire rationing system collapses because of the fact that the goods to be supplied at the (low) rationed prices are not forthcoming in the required quantities, rationing is dismantled, new single prices above the previously rationed prices (but equal to or below the "free" prices) are established, and wages and salaries are readjusted to the new price structure. Then, if a new discrepancy arises between the newly established single prices and the ones that will balance supply and demand, the cycle will start all over again.

As there is in each of these economies both a "suppressed" tendency toward inflation (because of the pressure of increases in employment and output in heavy industry) and a tendency toward underfulfillment of the plans for consumers' goods, the recurrent appearance of a black market and recurrent imposition of rationing are to be expected for a long period in the area as a whole.

As a last resort, when either the direct control or all the price manipulations described above fail to prevent the accumulation of cash in the countryside, a drastic monetary reform exchanging new money for old can immediately mop up the surplus. Such monetary reforms occurred in Poland in 1950, in Bulgaria and Romania in 1952, and in Czechoslovakia in 1953. They were patterned on the Soviet monetary refundings of December 1947 and February 1950.[111] These reforms established different conversion rates for various classes of holdings and reduced drastically various classes of cash holdings, mainly those of peasants, artisans, and small shopkeepers (see Table 36).

TABLE 36. THE SECOND WAVE OF MONETARY REFUNDINGS

Categories	Number of Units of New Currency Exchanged for 100 Units of Old Currency			
	Czechoslovakia	Poland	Romania	Bulgaria
Prices, wages, and state funds	20	3	5	4
Cash balances				
Lower portion	20	1	1	1
Upper portion	2	1	¼	1
Savings deposits				
Lower portion	20	3	2	3
Upper portion	3–10	3	½	1

Sources:
C: Monetary Reform Act of May 30, 1953.
P: Law of October 28, 1950.
R: Law of January 27, 1952.
B: Decree of May 10, 1952.

Generally, the reforms were followed by measures of derationing, especially of foodstuffs, by wage and salary adjustments mostly in favor of the lower brackets, and by the establishment for consumers' goods of single prices high above the previous ration prices. Thus the urban workers were also affected, up to a certain point, by the shifts in prices after the reform.

As already stated, the monetary reforms appear only as a last resort against dangerous inflationary pressures and for the realization of a large capital levy on certain social strata.[112] However, even this type

[111] For summaries on the monetary reforms, see *International Financial News Survey*, Vol. II, p. 261 (Soviet Reform); III, p. 142 (Polish Reform); IV, p. 238 (Romanian Reform); and IV, p. 368 (Bulgarian Reform).

For a detailed and competent study, especially of the Polish monetary reform, see Henri Wronski, *Le Rôle économique et social de la monnaie dans les democraties populaires, la réforme monnetaire polonaise 1950–1953* (The Economic and Social Role of Money in the People's Democracies, the Polish Monetary Reform, 1950–1953), Rivière et cie., Paris, 1954.

[112] Cf. Tsonu Tsontchev, Governor of the National Bank of Bulgaria, "Campaniata v Polza na Capitalizievaneto na Bankovite Depoziti" (The Campaign in Favor of Capitalizing on Bank Deposits). *PK*, No. 3, 1948, p. 11.

"Funds which are indispensable for building our country can be obtained in different ways: by an interior loan, by a monetary reform, or by a voluntary increase

of extremely drastic operation can produce results of only a very transient character. For instance, after the 1952 reform in Romania the peasants again succeeded in amassing substantial cash balances through the sale of consumers' goods on the free market, and the economic body became rapidly "swollen" again with cash concentrated in private hands.[113]

It is interesting to note that all the decrees on the above reforms pegged the new currencies to the ruble, which is usually referred to in the Soviet orbit as "the world's most stable currency." [114] Actually, the exchange rates in the orbit have no *direct* significance for foreign trade. Prices in foreign trade are negotiated, and, as a rule, correspond more to world market prices than to any relation between the prices in the various countries of the Soviet orbit. The rates are relevant only for foreign missions and for remittances.[115]

In summary, up to the end of 1948 financial policy was concentrated more and more on increasing the rate of investment in the public sector and "dislodging" the capitalist elements of the economy. The techniques used were mainly extending funds freely to public enterprises through bank credits or through the budget and limiting them for private enterprises; the utilization of discriminatory interest rates; and the resort to heavy levies on private capital either through taxation or through exchange of new currency for old, accompanied by the blocking of accounts above a given low ceiling.

After 1948, when large-scale liquidations of the non-agricultural private enterprises had been completed, the channeling of bank credits

of savings deposits. It is undeniable that it is more advantageous for the depositor that these funds be obtained by means of capitalizing on free deposits, for when he places, of his own free will, his excess means in credit establishments, he can draw them out, either in part or in whole."

[113] This situation caused the Central Committee of the Romanian Workers Party to state that the monetary reform had been "sabotaged" by the Ministry of Finance which: (1) during the preparation of the reform continued to press for the payments of taxes and debts to the state "thus ultimately inflicting substantial losses on the State"; (2) limited state spending on the eve of the reform instead of increasing it; and (3) did not limit the "abnormal" rise in savings deposits (which were later exchanged at a favorable rate). Cf. "Letter of the Central Committee of the Romanian Workers Party to All Party Organizations and All Party Members, concerning the Results of the Currency Reform and the Tasks of the Party, March 15, 1952," in *Documents Concerning Right Deviation in the Romanian Workers Party,* Romanian Workers Party Publishing House, Bucharest, 1952, pp. 12 ff.

[114] The expression was coined by the Soviet government on the occasion of the transfer of the ruble to the gold standard in February 1950.

[115] See below, Chapters 8 and 10.

as such lost its role as an "anti-capitalist weapon." Increasing the funds available to state enterprises for investment has been accomplished by (1) establishment of a new price structure (hence the increasing role of the turnover tax); (2) acceleration of the rate of increase in productivity as compared to the rate of increase in wages (hence the practice of norm revisions); (3) recurrent monetary levies on the remaining private enterprises, especially in agriculture, capable of recreating huge cash reserves (and hence the new type of monetary reforms).

The modest extension of credit to artisans, small traders, small and medium peasants (for private housing) after the 1953 crisis in the consumers' goods lines neither interferes with this basic mechanism nor prevents future monetary refundings against too heavy inflationary pressures.

CHAPTER

5

PROCESS OF NATIONALIZATION AND REORGANIZATION IN THE WHOLESALE, RETAIL, AND FOREIGN TRADE SYSTEMS

Definition of the Problem

As the multiple link between agricultural and industrial producers and consumers, the network of wholesale trade, jobbers, and retail trade was bound to feel strongly the impact of the nationalization process, especially as it affected industry and banking. The nationalization of certain channels of wholesale trade and jobbing was a "derivative" process. By its very complexity, the distribution system posed specific problems at each of its levels, both in the period of mixed economy with substantial private sectors and after the private sectors had been eliminated.

Up to 1948–49 the trade flows in each East European economy could be presented schematically as consisting of two primary and two secondary flows. The two primary flows of goods were one originating in the state and private industrial sector and flowing essentially through the commercial wholesale (and jobber) network, and one originating in the sphere of small-scale production, i.e., small industry, agriculture, and handicraft, both trickling through certain wholesale and jobber channels and coursing directly toward the consumer. The two secondary flows of goods were the transaction and movement of goods among commercial firms of all types and the flow of goods from the commercial firms to the final buyer.

Obviously, the first and part of the second primary flow and the first secondary flow together formed the *wholesale* trade; the second secondary flow and part of the second primary flow formed the *retail* trade. The main characteristics for the period that should be noted at this point were: (*a*) that capital goods (i.e., producers' goods in the broadest sense of the term) circulated in the primary as well as in the secondary flows; [1] (*b*) that the state sector could at the time either freely use traditional wholesale outlets or build alongside them its own distribution channels, the avowed aim of the period being not the liquidation of private trade but its *restriction;* (*c*) that organized retail trade, private, cooperative, or state-controlled, could have as suppliers either state or private (medium or small-scale) industry.

With the process of nationalization of the private industrial sector and the launching of the over-all plans, the problem of the allocation of goods was treated by the East European regimes, as in the Soviet Union, in two distinct categories: one relating to producers' goods, the other to consumers' goods. Allocation of the former became part of the system of organization of the so-called "material-technical supply" based on the scale of preference set by the planners, and *ad hoc* channels for their distribution began to be established. The allocation of consumers' goods (*a*) to industry for their further processing and (*b*) to the state and the cooperatives for further distribution to the population, and to institutions in the non-productive sphere (e.g., hospitals), became henceforth the newly limited domain of *domestic trade.*[2] *Pari passu,* with the centralization of agricultural produce through obligatory deliveries, payment in kind for the work of the state-owned agricultural machines and tractor stations, state agricultural contracting,[3] etc., it became impossible for the private wholesaler in agricultural and livestock produce to operate. Finally, the four trade flows assumed essentially the following aspects:

	Sellers		Buyers
1.	State producers (and collecting organizations)	→	State commercial organizations
2.	Private (part of handicraft and peasant) producers	→	Consumers
3.	State commercial organizations	→	State commercial organizations
4.	(State) commercial organizations	→	Consumers

[1] Primary goods produced in the state and private industrial sectors flowing through the commercial firms either toward the state and private industrial sectors or toward certain sectors of small-scale production.

[2] The former (*a*) represents in planning the so-called *extra-market* fund; the latter (*b*) the *market* fund.

[3] In the system of contracting, the state supplies the seeds, machinery, etc., whereas the contractor, be it a kolkhoz or a peasant, engages in a given production, generally

Wholesale trade, carried through the system of distribution both of certain industries and of the trade organizations, now became exclusively trade in consumers' goods; retail trade came to consist of the free or "unorganized" market plus the state-directed trade in state-produced commodity goods sold at fixed prices.[4] Thus not only the *type* of trade flows but also both the *scope* and the *commodity* structure of domestic trade underwent profound changes during the period under review.

We propose now to follow concretely the shifts in these flows, first, in the former Allied countries, where large-scale nationalization of industries was effected immediately after the war, and, second, in the former ex-enemy countries, where nationalization on a large scale was initiated at a later date. For a clear distinction between the organizations of domestic and foreign trade we propose to treat successively (1) wholesale and retail trade, and (2) the nationalization and organization of foreign trade.

Nationalization of Wholesale and Retail Trade in the Former Allied Group—Czechoslovakia

As stated in the chapter on industry (Chapter 3) after the 1945 nationalization of this sector in Czechoslovakia each nationalized enterprise was treated as an autonomous unit and managed accordingly. Up to the beginning of 1948 the nationalized undertakings continued to distribute their products through the available private wholesale and semiwholesale channels. Although as early as 1946 the Communist leaders had strongly attacked the system of private distribution of goods,[5] and some encroachments in that sphere had been envisaged at the time, the battle against the then-existing distributing system did not reach a climax until the end of 1947.

In the face of the scarcity of textile goods and a budding black market in textiles, the newly appointed Communist Minister of Do-

of industrial plants (e.g., flax, hemp, cotton, sugar-beet, etc.) which is afterwards delivered to the state. Incentives for contracting are the delivery of certain manufactured goods to the contractor, etc.

[4] See N. N. Riauzov and N. P. Titel'baum, *Statistika Sovetskoi Torgovli* (Statistics of Soviet Trade), Gostorgizdat, Moscow, 1951, pp. 16 ff.

In contrast to *domestic trade* which concerns only consumers' goods, *foreign trade* embraces both *consumers'* and *producers' goods.*

[5] Communist Premier Gottwald called the distribution system a "trade jungle." Cf. Jaromír Dolanský, *op. cit.,* p. 30.

mestic Trade, Alexej Čepicka,[6] proposed in December 1947 the immediate elimination of all textile wholesalers and the concentration of textile distribution in the hands of the state. The so-called "Čepicka Project" opened the battle in the wholesale field on a well-chosen strategic issue, for a large part of the textile industry (some 40 per cent of the weaving mills, finishing works, and dye works) was still operated by private enterprise, and the textile wholesale business had developed excessively during the war years to the point where the number of dealers in this branch alone had increased from the prewar 500–600 to 1,100–1,200 in 1946.[7]

The "Čepicka Project" was set in motion not by a vote of Parliament as the law required but by a simple Cabinet decree.[8] In January 1948, following the path taken by textiles, the important nationalized collieries repudiated their contracts with the private wholesale coal distributors, thus delivering a terrific blow to the private wholesale system just before the February Communist coup d'état. After the February coup the Communists nationalized the wholesale trade *en bloc* without any opposition. A simple decree promulgated April 18, 1948, took into the state sector the wholesale business [9] and the large department stores. A thorough reorganization was immediately undertaken, and by 1949 approximately 10,000 private wholesale firms with 54,000 employees were replaced by some 30 newly formed national trade monopolies with 22,000 gainfully employed.[10] The state completely reorganized the wholesale channels coming from and going to the villages. Early in December 1948 a newly organized Central Cooperative for Agricultural Products absorbed all the centers of the warehouse cooperatives, all

[6] It is interesting to note that Čepicka was subsequently made a general of the Army and put at the head of the Ministry of Defense. He was purged during the campaign against the so-called "personality cult," in 1956.

[7] Data given by Antonín Zmrhal, *Československý Vnitřní Obchod* (Czechoslovak Domestic Trade), USO, Prague, 1947, p. 39.

[8] For the political background to the "textile affair," see H. Ripka, *Czechoslovakia Enslaved: The Story of the Communist Coup d'État,* Victor Gollancz, London, 1950, pp. 143–144.

[9] Some of the nationalized property in both the industrial and the distributing spheres was American-owned. The largest in the distributing field was the property of Socony Oil, which had conducted an important distribution business in Czechoslovakia before the war amounting to several million dollars. Cf. Dana Adams Schmidt, *Anatomy of a Satellite,* Little, Brown & Co., Boston, 1952, p. 354.

[10] It should be noted that at the time these monopolies concerned both consumers' goods and machinery and accessories for handicraft, laboratory ware, and even products of the metallurgical sector. Cf. "The Companies for the Inner Trade," in *Adresář Československého Průmyslu 1949, op. cit.,* p. 14.

the dairy and distillery cooperatives, organizations for the sale of livestock, and so on. The new Central was given exclusive rights to the purchase of farm products, their distribution in the market, and the business of supplying implements and equipment to agriculture.[11] As the agricultural sector as a whole started to undergo profound changes, this system of distribution was modified. The above-mentioned Central was dissolved in November 1951, and its functions were transferred to a Central Purchasing Administration. Finally, in 1953, the collection and purchase of agricultural products became patterned on the Soviet model [12] centralized supply of agricultural products (viz., output of state farms, payment in kind to the state-owned Machine and Tractor Stations, obligatory deliveries and contracting),[13] and "decentralized" state purchase through the agricultural cooperative shops.

Nationalization, after the February coup, of the department and chain stores, some of which had been previously confiscated by the state, resulted in rapidly increasing competition for the smaller retail trader and craftsman, which, in conjunction with the administrative elimination of the medium retail trader, soon brought the larger part of the retail trade into the hands of the state. In 1948 state retail trade accounted for 12 per cent of sales and the cooperatives for some 15 per cent; by 1949 the former represented 36 per cent and the latter over 17 per cent.[14]

The "offensive" in the jobbing and retail fields was conducted simultaneously with respect to the direction of the flow of commodities (now controlled both at the level of production and at the level of wholesale), and the *form* and *size* of the retail outlets. Official policy from the outset encouraged the development of state department stores in the big towns [15] and reliance on consumers' and trade cooperatives

[11] Ladislav Feierabend, *Agricultural Cooperatives in Czechoslovakia*, Mid-European Studies Center, New York, 1952, p. 75.

[12] Václav Kopecký, Member of the Presidium, Central Committee of the Communist Party, notes:

> In order to ensure the new method of supply we have, in addition to other measures, introduced a new system of agricultural purchasing similar to that operating in the Soviet Union. [Cf. "Fifth Anniversary of February Victory of Working People of Czechoslovakia," in *FLP*, Feb. 20, 1953.]

[13] In exchange for technical crops, sugar-beets, chicory, flax, oil-bearing crops, and wool, the peasants were to be supplied with sugar, textiles, and building materials. Cf. Viliam Široký, "Currency Reform and Abolition of Rationing in Czechoslovakia," in *FLP*, June 5, 1953.

[14] *RP*, Aug. 2, 1952.

[15] From 1949 on the state-organized department store grew both in numbers and in volume of turnover. The new "giant" department store Obchodní Domy had

for the distribution of consumers' goods in the small towns and villages. By the end of 1948 only a few private trade establishments with more than 5 persons employed were still in operation. During 1949 the former Central Association of Czechoslovak Trade was absorbed into the Association of Czechoslovak Crafts, and the medium and some small trading establishments were transferred to the state sector. This process of liquidation of retail trade was carried out somewhat chaotically in a period of reorganization of the economy as a whole.[16] By 1951 the state enterprises conducted 65.5 per cent of the total retail trade and consumers' cooperatives 28 per cent. These two accounted for virtually all organized retail trade in 1952.[17]

The policy of extending the department stores into the smaller towns and increasingly limiting the cooperative activities to the villages was systematically implemented. From 1952 on, the consumers' cooperatives were primarily dealing in the villages with the object "of extending the trade between town and country, and extending the contracting for and the purchase of agricultural products." [18]

The liquidation of commercial retail trade had thus been essentially effected in 1949–50. According to the figures available for 1947, the operation involved a total of some 120,000 establishments, a number substantially below the prewar level.[19] In the sphere of consumer and trade cooperatives it affected 1,170 and 1,158 cooperatives, respectively.[20]

from the outset 65 establishments, 4,000 employees, and an annual turnover of around 3.5 billion Kčs, contrasted to the biggest prewar chain store Aso with 13 establishments, 1,000 workers, and a turnover of 200 million Kčs. Cf. Dolanský, *op. cit.*, pp. 30–31.

16 A Czech statistician notes that at the time the statistical office could not keep pace with the rhythm and forms of socialization: the work was hampered by delays in the reporting of changes in status of the trade establishment and by the profound administrative changes (creation of new provinces and new administrative districts) requiring a new regrouping of the data [cf. Dr. V. Trnka, "Representativní Šetření v Maloobchodě" (A Sampling Inquiry into Retail Trade), in *SZ*, X, 1949].

17 "Consumers' Cooperatives Active in Countryside," in *Prague News Letter*, IX, No. 14, July 4, 1953.

18 Jaromír Dolanský, "Towards Further Rise in Well-Being of Working People of Czechoslovakia," in *FLP*, July 3, 1953.

19 There were 10,500 wholesale, 82,000 retail establishments, and 23,000 commercial agencies in the Czech territories, and 35,000 commercial firms of all types in Slovakia in 1947 (*Statistical Digest of the Czechoslovak Republic, op. cit.*, p. 65). During prewar times there were 210,000 commercial firms in the Czech territories, and 35,000 in Slovakia (*Annuaire statistique . . . 1934, op. cit.*, p. 70).

20 These cooperatives played a quite significant role in the total retail trade of the country in 1947. Cf. Šimáček, *Czechoslovak Economy in a Nutshell, op. cit.*, p. 49.

POLAND

In contrast to Czechoslovakia, where the "equalizing factions in the national front" maintained up to the beginning of 1948 a fragile line between nationalized production and non-nationalized distribution, in Poland large-scale nationalization of industry and disorganization of the private sector brought about an early and growing intervention of the state in the wholesale channels. As early as 1945–46,

> . . . parallel to the formation of each link of the state industrial organization, commercial units were also created, which were intended on the one hand to supply the manufacturing establishments with new and auxiliary materials, and on the other hand to take over the production for distribution among consumers.[21]

The formation of *central trading offices* of the main state industries was intended both to expand the state network throughout the country, and to limit to the state sphere the sale of the products of state factories. In 1947 the central trading offices still depended heavily on private wholesale channels. At that time, out of a total of 5,879 wholesale establishments, 1,082 were managed by the cooperatives and 3,307 were run by private capital, which commanded 56 per cent of the total gainfully employed in wholesale trade.[22]

In order to eliminate the private sector, an all-out "battle for trade" was launched in 1947. The state wholesale and jobber outlets were multiplied, the "autonomy" of the cooperative movement was virtually liquidated, and a rigorous "administrative and social control" was established over private trade. The central trading boards of the individual industries, which "hitherto had recourse to cooperative and private wholesalers," were increasingly served by their own distributing system through a steadily growing territorial network.[23] At the end of 1948 total employment in the wholesale field had contracted from 90,000 to 78,000, and 58.3 per cent were now in the state sector, 28.4 per cent in the cooperatives, 13.3 per cent in the private sector.[24] In fact, the private wholesale trader was eliminated from trading in state-produced goods, keeping positions of importance only in supplying the towns with grains and meat. The structural modification of the cooperative movement, i.e., the replacement of its leadership, the amal-

[21] *Quarterly Review of the Bank Gospodarstwa Krajowego, op. cit.*, XV, 5, December 1946, p. 6.

[22] *Statistical Yearbook of Poland 1948, op. cit.*, p. 85.

[23] *Quarterly Review of the Bank Gospodarstwa Krajowego, op. cit.*, XVII, 3, September 1948, p. 17.

[24] *Rocznik Statystyczny 1949, op. cit.*, p. 91.

gamation of certain cooperative societies, and the rigorous delimitation of their respective spheres of operation, made them totally flexible instruments in the hands of the state, both as distributors and as purchasers of agricultural produce. The process of reorganization took place in the middle of 1948. A chief cooperative institution, the Central Cooperative Union, was created, and central boards were established for the agricultural cooperatives (Peasant Self-Aid), the consumers' cooperatives (Społem), and the dairy product cooperative societies.[25] The purchasing activities of the cooperatives of agricultural products were combined with the state apparatus of warehouses and storage into one organization,[26] which rapidly restricted the field of the private wholesale trader in supplying grain and meat. By mid-1950 all the wholesale trade was concentrated in the hands of the socialized sector.[27]

By early 1946 the state distributing system had organized only a few of its own retail stores for consumers. It was stressed at the time that:

> The latter [stores] have been created but for intervention purposes, and are in no way connected with any desire to promote direct retail trade through the State system. They may serve, however, as a comparing and controlling factor for private retail merchants in the matter of fixing a proper margin of profit connected with their sales.[28]

The 5,861 trading cooperatives played a limited role in trade. After the middle of 1947 this situation changed abruptly when, in the framework of the "battle for trade," the state organized a Central Board of

[25] On the reorganization of cooperatives see the *Quarterly Review . . . , op. cit.,* XVII, No. 2, June 1948, p. 19, and *ibid.,* No. 3, September 1948, p. 17.

[26] Thus for instance for grain and flour, the Polish Grain Establishments, and so on. Cf. Hilary Minc, *Poland's Economy Present and Future,* Documents and Reports on Poland, No. 5, Polish Research and Information Service, New York, 1949, p. 12.

[27] The combined state and cooperative wholesale trade in January 1949 accounted for 85 per cent of the total wholesale trade. [Cf. *Le Développement économique de la Pologne en 1948* (Economic Development of Poland in 1948), *Bulletin du Bureau d'informations polonaises* (Bulletin of the Bureau of Polish Information), Jan. 25, 1949.] This combined share equaled 98 per cent by the end of 1949. The distribution of both industrial and agricultural produce was concentrated for the towns in the hands of the State Central Trading Office, which had increased its wholesale branch stores and agencies from 109 and 121, respectively, in 1946 to 142 and 148 in 1950. For the villages, the wholesale trade in consumer goods was now handled exclusively by the Central of Agricultural Cooperatives (Peasant Self-Aid). (Cf. *Quarterly Review . . . , op. cit.,* XVI, No. 1, March 1947, p. 19; also Władysław Kowałczyk, "Handel Państwowy" (State Trade), in *Kultura,* Numer Krajowy, Vol. II, Paris, 1952, p. 204.)

[28] *Quarterly Review . . . , op. cit.,* XV, No. 4, September 1946, p. 4.

Retail Trade and a network of state department stores. By mid-1948 the department stores numbered 67, of which 30 were in the western territories, and a provision was made for the rapid extension of this network to all the towns of more than 10,000 inhabitants.[29] At the beginning of 1949 the state and the reorganized cooperatives, controlling respectively some 80 department stores and around 44,000 retail outlets, accounted for 35 per cent of the total sales in retail trade.[30] By the end of that year the percentage had increased to 56 per cent.[31] By 1950 it had risen to some 83,[32] in 1951 to around 90, in 1952 to 93, in 1953 to 96.[33] Nearly the totality of the organized retail trade, over 97 per cent of sales and over 118,000 retail outlets, was finally concentrated in the hands of the "socialist sector" by 1955.[34]

It can be seen that the elimination of the private trader from the various state channels followed this time pattern: elimination from (1) wholesale and state-produced goods, 1948; (2) wholesale and agricultural goods, 1949–50; (3) bulk of retail trade, 1951–52. Although there were 460,000 trade enterprises in 1938, only 101,000 had redeemed their trading licenses in 1946. The nationalization process, therefore, affected an already badly shrunken private distribution system. The idea of the administrative suppression of the private trader had been decisively rejected in 1948. Hilary Minc, notably, had insisted that the aim of the state was not "simply to suppress the private trading establishments and thus create a trying vacuum for the consumer." [35] However, in mid-1950 the same Hilary Minc, Poland's chief planner, suggested that the regime become interested, during the six-year plan, in even the minor trades undertakings such as kiosks, watch and optical stores, and even shoe-repairing.[36] In other words, no trad-

[29] *Ibid.*, XVII, No. 3, September 1948, p. 17. There were in Poland 135 cities and towns with more than 10,000 inhabitants in 1947. (Cf. *Statistical Yearbook of Poland 1948, op. cit.*, pp. 22–24.)

[30] *Le Développement économique de la Pologne en 1948, op. cit.*

[31] *Rocznik Statystyczny 1955, op. cit.*, p. 4.

[32] See: *A Survey of Poland*, Supplement to *The Statist, op. cit.*, p. 32. For policies concerning the period see: Janusz Litwin, *ABC Planu Szescioletniego* (The ABC of the Six-Year Plan), Warsaw, 1949; and Hilary Minc, *Ządania Gospodarcze na 1951 Rok* (Economic Tasks for 1951), Ksązka i Wiedza (Book and Science), Warsaw, 1951, p. 74.

[33] Cf., Boleslaw Bierut, "Report of the Central Committee to the Second Congress of the Polish United Workers' Party," in *FLP*, March 19, 1954.

[34] *A Survey of Poland*, Supplement to *The Statist, op. cit.*, p. 32.

[35] *Rzeczpospolita* (The Republic), Dec. 20, 1948.

[36] H. Minc, "Sześcioletni plan rozwoju gospodarczego i budowy podstaw socjalizmu w Polsce," *op. cit.*

ing line whatsoever was excluded from the nationalization of retail trade as it gained momentum in 1950 and 1951.

YUGOSLAVIA

Yugoslavia was the first country in the region to nationalize wholesale trade. Officially, the Yugoslav nationalization decree was enacted in December 1946; [37] in fact, private initiative has been excluded from wholesale trade since the liberation.

In nationalizing retail trade Yugoslavia also preceded the other East European countries. In 1945, 3 per cent of retail trade was handled by the state shops, 12 per cent by the cooperatives, and 85 per cent by the private shops.[38] In 1946 the state shops (viz. "people's stores," Narodni Magazin or NAMA) already accounted for 19 per cent of retail sales, the cooperatives 32 per cent, and the private sector 48 per cent. In 1947 the state share increased to 37 per cent and that of the cooperatives to 50 per cent. At that time the private trading sector

> . . . entered into the phase of liquidation. No nationalization law of retail trade was enacted; the final liquidation of the private trade was carried out on the basis of the special law on Private Trade, *through refusal of registrations and of giving out trading licenses to the speculators.*[39]

By the spring of 1948 the state share of retail sales reached almost 40 per cent, that of the cooperatives over 58 per cent. Thus in four years the share of the private sector had been reduced from 85 per cent to 1.7 per cent of total sales. In 1949 that share was limited further to less than 1.5 per cent, and the process of elimination of the private retailer rapidly approached its completion.

The comparison between the number of shops in the various sectors and the percentage distribution of sales reveals even more strikingly than do the figures for the countries analyzed above that the rapidly progressive Yugoslav nationalization contracted an already shrunken distribution apparatus. In 1938 there were in Yugoslavia some 89,000 retail shops.[40] At the end of the war their total number had fallen

[37] Nationalization Law of Dec. 5, 1946, *Službeni List* (Official Gazette), No. 98, 1946.

[38] Data on the distribution among the sectors of the trade for the years 1945–49 inclusive are from Peškovič and Čečez, *op. cit.*, pp. 73 ff., supplemented by *Statistički Godišnjak FNRJ 1954, op. cit.*, p. 235.

[39] *Ibid.* (Italics supplied.)

[40] This figure is given by the *Statistički Godišnjak FNRJ 1954, op. cit.*, p. 235, and concerns specifically the shops dealing in groceries and other retail trade. If we

to less than 41,000. After a temporary increase in 1946 to 53,000, the number decreased rapidly, reaching in 1948 a total of only 36,500. The trend toward "concentration," owing to the closing down of a number of shops apparently with little concern for their respective locations or the consumers' sources of supply, continued to 1951, when the total number of shops fell to 30,500. By 1953 the number had increased to 36,600, of which some 20,800 state shops carried 70 per cent of sales, the 15,000 cooperative and association shops a little less than 24 per cent, and some 800 private shops less than 0.1 per cent.[41]

Thus three-fourths of the retail trade of Yugoslavia is carried on by a network of less than 21,000 shops. Since in 1938 some 50,000 shops (grocery and other retail shops) were clustered around five centers (Belgrade, Zagreb, Novi Sad, Sarajevo, and Skoplje), and some 39,000 serviced the rest of the country, a very uneven distribution existed between these centers and the rest of the country, and a reduction of the *total* network of shops to 36,600 (a little over one-third of the prewar network) must have affected not only the centers but the country at large. Although the process has probably led to simplification and the reduction of overhead in the centers, it has evidently created country-wide shortages for the consumer.

Nationalization of Wholesale and Retail Trade in the Ex-Enemy Group—Hungary

As has been pointed out in the preceding chapters, the over-all nationalization of industry and banks (the basic objective of a Communist program of nationalization of an economy) was carried out in the ex-enemy countries either by stages or by all-embracing measures at the beginning of 1948. Given the logical sequence in the nationalization schedules, e.g., nationalization of production preceding nationalization of distribution, the latter was affected not only by the extent but also by the time period of the changes in production as a whole.

In Hungary, up to the middle of 1948, the state played only a minor role in wholesale trade. After the extension of the state sector in manufacturing in the spring of that year the planners turned their full attention to wholesale trade. The distribution agencies of the nationalized enterprises were reorganized, the area of activity of cooperatives

included all types of commercial establishments (such as hotels, taxi companies and other transport, commercial agencies, and offices), the total would be over 100,000. Cf. *Statistički Godišnjak 1938–1939, op. cit.*, pp. 290–291.

[41] *Statistički Godišnjak 1954, op. cit.*, p. 235, and 1956, *op. cit.*, p. 217.

was more clearly determined, and the private wholesalers were eliminated from the marketing of state-produced goods. As a consequence, the state share of wholesale sales increased in 1948 from 16 per cent in July to some 75 per cent in December.[42]

The systematic and overt elimination of the private wholesale trader from the channels of agricultural supply [43] led to the concentration in the hands of the state of almost the entire wholesale trade (93 per cent) by the middle of 1949,[44] even before legal dispositions specified that the state establishments should "conduct the large commerce and orient the entire commercial circuit."

State penetration into the jobbing and retail fields started with the organization in 1948 of such corporations as the National Department Stores, the People's Storehouse, the Municipal Food Store Company, and the National Hire-Purchase Office (for installment buying). However, the state share of total retail sales remained in 1948 only 20 per cent,[45] rising at the beginning of 1949, together with the cooperative share, to a combined total of 30 per cent. At the end of 1949 the extension of nationalization to industrial establishments with over 10 workers and the systematic reorientation of goods toward the state sector placed the remaining private trade sector in a very difficult position. Though it was specified at the launching of the 1949 nationalization wave that the measure ". . . does not concern crafts and retail trade and the government does not intend to nationalize the shops of craftsmen and retail trade in the future either, because they fill an important economic role . . ." [46] state control over supply and the competition of state shops confined the craftsman more and more to repair work and forced the closing of shop after shop. The control of supply and its distribution between state and private sectors were watched by

[42] "The more thorough application of planned economy to the distribution system resulted in the increase of nationalized commerce. The marketing agencies of nationalized industrial corporations, private firms and co-operatives were rearranged into a great number of national enterprises which are now conducting approximately three-quarters of wholesale trade." "Report of the Board of Directors of the National Bank of Hungary on the Business Year 1948," *op. cit.*, p. xviii; see also Kemény, *op. cit.*, p. 60, and *Today and Yesterday,* publ. by *HB,* 1949, p. 17.

[43] Taken over increasingly by the National Concerns (NC): Milk Industrial NC, Pig and Lard NC, Cattle Trading NC, Poultry Trading NC, etc. For the early data on trade, cf. *GT*, III, 2, February 1949.

[44] Data given by Mátyás Rákosi, August 17, 1949. Cf. *Bulletin économique,* Bureau hongrois de presse et documentation, *op. cit.*, Dec. 10, 1949.

[45] Kemény, *loc. cit.*

[46] Ernő Gerő, *HB,* 67, Jan. 15, 1950, p. 4.

the state as a gage of the relationship between those two sectors. In the last quarter of 1949 the share of the state sector in the supplies handled by the national wholesale business increased from 73 to 77 per cent, whereas the share of the private sector dropped from 26 to 23 per cent.[47] The data on wholesale transactions and on the relative position of various items in sales served as indicators to guide the offensive of the state against the private positions:

> Each large state commercial organization set up to supply a district was able to prepare the data on a nation-wide basis by districts and trade, necessary for the circulation and control of the majority of the centrally allocated basic goods through state, cooperative and small commercial stores. In this manner we were able to limit successfully the private sector *by branches and articles in the turnover,* according to the directives of our Party.[48]

By the end of 1950 the social share of total retail sales reached some 60 per cent, and by the end of 1951, 82 per cent.[49] The streamlining of the cooperatives and their transformation on the pattern already familiar in selling and purchasing organizations in the villages brought the socialized share of retail sales to some 90 per cent in 1952, the remainder representing less and less trade in state-produced goods and more and more small-scale artisan production and foodstuffs.

The limited output of consumers' goods and the closing down of private shops created in Hungary as elsewhere shortages for the consumer. In mid-1953, in the declaration inaugurating the reversal in economic policy, the new premier, Imre Nagy, stated that the over-extension of the state sector in retail trade and in handicrafts had disrupted the trading system of the country:

> In recent years the state extended its economic activity also to spheres where private initiative and private enterprise *can still play*

[47] "Fontosabb Mutatók a kereskedelmi statisztikában" (Some Important Indicators in Commercial Statistics), *SS,* 3rd year, No. 2, February 1951.

[48] Dr. József Selényi, "A belkereskedelmi statisztika időszerű kérdései" (Timely Problems of Domestic Commercial Statistics), *SS,* XXXI, 5, May 1953, p. 375.

[49] The figure for 1950 is from *Magyar Statisztikai Zsebkönyv 1956, op. cit.,* p. 141. The figure for 1951 is from *HB* 111, Feb. 1, 1952. It seems, however, that in practice no accurate evaluation of the capacity of small trade has been made. Thus a statistician notes:

> The lack of an accurate survey caused trouble in some sectors with planning of material allocations. The file cards established by the municipal, city and county councils do not give a sufficient basis for the determination of the status of small trade units and small private commerce. [Cf. Márton Major, "A kisipari és kereskedelmi adatfelvétel szervezési tapasztalatai" (Organizational Experiences in Collecting Data on Small Trade and Commerce), *SS,* III, 3, March 1951.]

a big role, and contribute to better satisfaction of the requirements of the population. This includes retail trade and handicraft industry. . . . Therefore, we shall provide a place for private businessmen; give those who are entitled to it the right to get permits and also ensure the necessary conditions and provide them with necessary goods, with credits, etc.[50]

Thus the "planned drive" which reached its climax in Hungary at the end of 1951 broke down an already narrow and imperfect distribution system (consisting of some 70,000 shops in the middle of 1948), the reconstruction of which, sought since 1953,[51] is a slow process, encountering enormous difficulties.[52]

Romania

In Romania the direct penetration of the state into both the wholesale and the retail fields dates from the closing days of 1947. The first state trading companies concerned themselves with the centralization and distribution of agricultural produce, in contrast to the pattern in the countries analyzed thus far, where wholesale and industrial channels were nationalized first. To the state trading companies for the collection and distribution of grain, pulse, oleaginous products, milk and dairy products, cattle, etc.,[53] there were added, after the nationalization of industry (undertaken from the middle of 1948 on), *centrals for distribution* of industrial products of various branches of state-owned industry.[54] By the end of 1949 virtually the entire wholesale business had passed into the hands of the state.

In Romania, the centrals for distribution of both industrial and agricultural produce typically engaged from the outset in jobbing and retailing in both the towns and the villages through the organization of three types of chain store, specializing in: (1) textiles and clothing,

50 Imre Nagy, "On Measures of Hungarian Working People's Party and Government Aimed at Raising the Standard of Living," in *FLP,* July 17, 1953. (Italics supplied.)

51 E.g., decrees enjoining the return to retail trade of store premises used for other purposes. Cf. *Magyar Közlony* (Official Journal), Dec. 29, 1954.

52 The total retail network, which had fallen to 54,000 shops in 1950, shrunk further to 24,000 shops in 1952. After the 1953–54 measures, the total of shops increased by 1955 to some 33,000 units (of which some 9,000 are privately owned). This still represents less than half the total of 1948. See: *Magyar Statisztikai Zsebkőnyv, 1956, op. cit.,* p. 146.

53 E.g., Romcereal (grain), Romlacta (milk and dairy products), Rompescăria (fish and fish products), etc. Cf. "State-Owned Trade," in *RR,* No. 12, October 1948, p. 34.

54 "Centrocoms" (commercial centrals): Centrocoms Textile, Metal, etc., *ibid.*

(2) agricultural implements and household hardware, (3) foodstuffs.[55] In principle, intervention in the retail field was to be limited. As stated by Gh. Gheorghiu-Dej early in 1949:

> We consider that in retail commerce, State and private commerce can and must act together, as a result of a normal goods circulation. The small merchant who is honest to the State and to his clients has to play an important part in the circulation of goods and will meet full cooperation on the part of the democratic regime.[56]

Actually, the small private retail trader, deprived both of commodities and of working capital (which had been previously confiscated through monetary manipulations), could not compete with the state stores and was rapidly driven out of business.[57] While in 1948 the "socialist sector" accounted for 25 per cent of the retail sales, by the end of 1949 its share was already 50 per cent. The cooperatives were invited to increase their role, but their development was inadequate; their share of total retail sales continued to be rather limited, amounting to less than one-third that of the state-owned shops.[58] The economic and administrative harassment of the small trader, his elimination from normal trade, the weakness of the cooperative apparatus, and the still insufficient spread of the state trade network brought about serious disturbances in the allocation and distribution of goods. Referring to the situation existing in mid-1950, the then Minister of Finance Vasile Luca harshly criticized the state centralized organizations dealing in both wholesale and retail agricultural produce:

> These too centralized and bureaucratic organizations have endeavored by administrative measures to abolish private trading by blocking the outflow of merchandise to the cities, removing village consumer cooperatives and organizing a sort of state ambulant trading.
>
> Undoubtedly the working peasant did not receive even those industrial products of which there was no shortage such as kerosene, matches, tobacco and salt.[59]

[55] "State Commerce in People's Republic of Rumania," in *RN,* May 22, 1949.

[56] Gheorghiu-Dej, "Report to the First Congress of the Romanian Workers' Party," in *RN,* May 22, 1949.

[57] Thus an official organ was writing at the close of 1949:

> Now several State stores have been opened in all districts and they are filled with all sorts of food articles. The citizens keep away from the old unsanitary stores in which the food is lying under the counter and is sold at exorbitant prices; they prefer to shop in the new State stores. [Cf. "State Companies Bring Down Food Prices . . . , *RN,* Oct. 23, 1949.]

[58] *La Roumanie Nouvelle* (New Romania), January 20, 1949, January 1, 16, and April 1951. *RN,* Jan. 1, 1950.

[59] *New York Times,* Aug. 20, 1950.

Nevertheless the "administrative" process of reorganization of trade continued on the same lines, and Luca was removed from power as a "right deviationist." By 1950, the socialist share in the organized retail trade increased to 60 per cent, and by 1951 to 76 per cent.[60] According to an official document of the Central Committee of the Romanian Workers' Party published subsequently, "even too many industrial goods" had gone to the villages against "too small" a volume of agricultural produce forthcoming from that sector.[61] In mid-1950 the co-operatives were purged and reorganized, and some of their town units were transferred to the state.[62] The cooperatives started to exercise their activity essentially in villages.[63] In fact, the regime seemed to be dissatisfied with the "slow progress" in the fight against the private sectors, the still "flourishing" private trade, and the lack of development of the cooperatives. Numerous decisions of the Council of Ministers and the Central Committee of the Party, taken even as late as 1953, concerned themselves with the "amelioration" of the work of the co-operatives and the development of exchanges between town and village.[64] Finally, at the launching of the "new course," in mid-1953, the Premier, Gh. Gheorghiu-Dej, proposed a comeback for the private trader at least in the sphere where the state had clearly failed:

[60] *Viaţa Sindicală* (Trade Union Life), Feb. 1, 1951, and March 28, 1952.

[61] V. Luca's price policy was subsequently branded as responsible for having caused, of all things, a

> . . . disproportion between the *large* volume of industrial goods distributed through village co-operatives and the *much smaller* volume of agricultural-foodstuff products purchased by cooperatives and State organs. [Cf. "Letter of the Central Committee of the Romanian Workers' Party, March 19, 1952," in *Documents Concerning Right Deviation in Romanian Workers' Party, op. cit.*, p. 10. Italics supplied.]

[62] During the purge of the "right deviationists" it was asserted that:

> As regards socialist State trade, the enemies of the people sought to disorganise and liquidate it, transferring certain units into the patrimony of co-operatives which in many places had become a shelter for exploiting and profiteering elements of town and countryside.

(Cf. "For Constantly Strengthening the Party," leading article published in *Scânteia,* June 3, 1952, reprinted in *Documents Concerning Right Deviation . . . , op. cit.,* p. 39.) This was given as a pretext in order to justify the transferring to the state of certain cooperative units.

[63] The "Central Union of the cooperatives of supply and distribution carries its activity through a large network of cooperatives especially in the countryside." Cf. Al. Sobaru, "Despre Metodologia Planificării Circulaţiei Mărfurilor cu Amănuntul" (On the Methodology of Planning the Circulation of Retail Trade), in *PE,* No. 5–6, June 1953, p. 163.

[64] Al. Sobaru, *loc. cit.*

It is necessary, simultaneously with strengthening state and cooperative trade, also to bring private trade into such spheres as sale of vegetables, fruit, dairy produce, eggs, poultry, fats, confectionery, the public feeding network, and sale of cottage-industry goods.[65]

Thus in Romania also the administrative elimination of the private trader evidently created shortages for the consumer as it did elsewhere in the area.

It can be estimated that in 1950–51, at the peak of the drive against the small private retailer, 40,000 "distributing units" at the most were in operation (of which 25,000 constituted the state sector).[66] This is one-third the prewar total.[67] Although the concentration process undoubtedly brought about the appearance in the main centers of large units with perhaps a lower overhead and operational cost than previously, it also resulted in a need to rely more heavily in these centers on the traditional peasant free-market supply (". . . . such spheres as sale of vegetables, fruit, dairy produce, eggs, poultry . . ."). It created obvious shortages for the consumer in the peripheral zones and especially in the villages. The press registered continuous protests about shortages in the villages, complaining that the cooperatives were failing to provide the villages not only with such goods as textiles, cement, nails, etc., but also with such basic products as salt, kerosene, and matches.[68]

BULGARIA

The process of nationalization of the Bulgarian wholesale channels started immediately after the Communist-led coup d'état of September 9, 1944. The channels affected were those for the marketing of agricultural products. Even before the war an autonomous government institution (Hranoiznos) was active in both purchase and sale of agricultural products. After the war only the state institution was author-

[65] Gh. Gheorghiu-Dej, "Towards Further Development of National Economy, Towards Further Rise in Well-Being of People!" in *FLP,* Aug. 28, 1953.

[66] Cf. Miron Constantinescu, Exposé sur le Plan Quinquennal à la seance du 14 Decembre 1950 de la Grande Assemblée Nationale (Speech on the Five Year Plan at the December 14, 1950, meeting of the Great National Assembly) in: *Le Plan Quinquennal Roumain* (The Romanian Five Year Plan), Notes et études documentaires (Notes and Documentary Studies), No. 1534, La Documentation Française (French Documentation), Paris, Sept. 28, 1951.

[67] The prewar number of commercial establishments was in the neighborhood of 130,000. *Anuarul Statistic al Romåniei 1939 şi 1940, op. cit.,* p. 360.

[68] See *Cronica Romånească* (Report on Romania), Anul V, March–April 1955, No. 3–4.

ized to buy and sell agricultural produce. It did so in accordance with the instructions of the General Commissariat of Distribution.[69] At the end of 1947 (after the nationalization of wholesale trade in tobacco, alcohol,[70] clothing and shoes, grocery articles, construction materials, metal and metal products, and petroleum products) an article in the nationalization law proclaimed the nationalization of the total wholesale system. The cooperatives alone or together with the state, and at times the state, the cooperatives, and private capital together, reorganized certain supply channels such as those for fruit and vegetables, eggs, etc., under the direction of the state.[71] Nationalization of the wholesale trade can be considered as essentially completed in the spring of 1948, when the participation of the state and cooperative sector reached, respectively, 64 and 36 per cent of total wholesale sales.[72] By 1953 the planned percentages for wholesale trade were to shift in favor of the state to 70 per cent, against 30 per cent for the cooperatives.[73]

A concerted attack against private retail trade was led by the state, the local authorities, and the cooperatives from 1947 on. The state-organized companies penetrated both the wholesale and the retail fields (viz., organization of "People's Stores," Naroden Magasin, "Narmags"); the local authorities took over the hotels and the restaurants (Horemags); the cooperatives turned their attention chiefly, though not exclusively, to the villages. In 1948 retail sales were divided as follows: 67.8 per cent by the socialized sector, 32.3 per cent by the private sector. By 1950 the share of the socialized sector rose to 85 per cent,[74] and by 1951 it reached 94 or 98 per cent.[75] In 1952 a decree of the Presidium of the National Assembly sharply increased the pressure on small traders and practically barred private initiative in this field. By the end of 1952 state and cooperative trade accounted for 99.3 per

[69] Professor Dinko Toshev, "Supply and Distribution," in *Free Bulgaria,* II, 7, April 1, 1947, p. 101.

[70] The monopoly of retail sale of tobacco, alcohol, etc., had existed before; what was now added was the monopoly of their production and wholesale distribution.

[71] The amalgamation of municipal cooperative and private initiative for the establishment of Plod-Zelenchuk (Fruits-Vegetables), Eggs Central, etc. Cf. "Economic Survey of 1947," in *Free Bulgaria,* III, 2, Jan. 15, 1948, p. 20.

[72] "Vătreshen Pregled, Bălgarskoto Stopanstvo" (Domestic Outlook of the Bulgarian Economy), *PK,* No. 2, 1948, pp. 68 ff.; also: *Les Nationalisations en Europe orientale, op. cit.,* p. 7.

[73] *Les Nationalisations en Europe orientale, loc. cit.*

[74] "Without Capitalists Trade Is Thriving," in *Free Bulgaria,* VI, 24, Dec. 15, 1951.

[75] The source quoted above gives 93.9 per cent; another source gives 98 per cent. Cf. *RD,* May 29, 1952.

cent[76] of retail sales, surpassing the planned percentage set for the end of 1953 of 95 per cent.

It is interesting to note that in the process of the socialization of retail trade the cooperatives in Bulgaria continued to play a role in distribution both in the towns and in the villages. The village consumer cooperatives (Selco-op) remained the basic channel of the trade in the villages; cooperative stores (Narco-op) continued to subsist in the towns, along with the state and city shops.[77] In the process of nationalization the state sector increased much more rapidly than the cooperatives, whose share of total sales remained almost stationary from 1948 until 1953: from 1948 to the beginning of 1952 the state share of total retail sales increased from 22.3 per cent to 51.3 per cent; the cooperative share increased in the same period from 45.5 per cent to 47.1 per cent.[78] The cooperatives maintained their share by substantially widening the sphere of their activity and by embracing both artisan production and some small-scale production (especially for formerly imported produce such as nylon goods, pistons and segments, emery powder, etc.).[79] Last, in Bulgaria also an increasing role in town trade is played by the free peasant market for such produce as vegetables, eggs, etc.

Summary on Area Trends

Nationalization of the wholesale channels in industry and agriculture followed differing time schedules in the various countries of the area. Nationalization of industrial wholesale channels was effected in Yugoslavia in 1945–46, in Bulgaria in 1947, in Poland and Czechoslovakia in 1948, in Hungary and Romania in 1949. Agricultural wholesale channels were completely nationalized in Yugoslavia and Bulgaria in 1945–46, in Czechoslovakia and Romania in 1948, in Hungary in 1949, and in Poland in 1950. The concentration of industry and the comprehensive nationalization measures that effected it facilitated the rapid nationalization of industrial distribution channels. The decentralized character of agricultural production and supply imposed both varying solutions in different channels and a more diversified approach in the reorganization of agricultural distribution.

[76] Vălko Chervenkov, "Along Trying Road of Building Socialism," in *FLP*, Sept. 11, 1953.

[77] For the respective fields of these shops see Svetoslaw Russev, "Home Trade," in *Free Bulgaria*, VI, No. 10, May 10, 1951, p. 154.

[78] *RD, loc. cit.*

[79] On craftsmen in Bulgaria, see *Bulgaria Today*, Vol. IV, No. 1, Jan. 1, 1955,

The general pace and the variation in the process of nationalization of retail trade from one country to another can be seen in Table 37.

TABLE 37. RELATIVE IMPORTANCE OF THE SOCIALIZED SECTOR IN "ORGANIZED" RETAIL SALES

(percentages)

Country	1948	1949	1950	1951	1952
Czechoslovakia	12	54	85 [a]	93	99
Poland	35	55	83	90	93
Yugoslavia	98	98	100	100	100
Hungary	20	30	60	82	91
Romania	25	50	60	76	80 [a]
Bulgaria	68	[b]	85	94	99

[a] Estimate.
[b] Not available.

Sources: See preceding text footnotes—for C: 14, 16, 17; for P: 31, 32, 33, 34; for Y: 38 and 41; for H: 48 and 49; for R: 58 and 60; for B: 74, 75, 76.

It should be noted that these statistics concern a very complex process, that the definitions of domestic trade sales have been shifted quite often, and, finally, that errors and discrepancies in various officially given percentages can easily be found. The data should be taken as indicating broadly that for Yugoslavia and Bulgaria, which entered first into the process of nationalization of retail trade, a large part of the private sector (in Yugoslavia nearly all) had been destroyed by 1948, and that in the other countries of the area this condition had been reached by the end of 1952.

What are the consequences of this process and the problems in this sphere facing these regimes?

So far as the organization of retail trade is concerned, two facts must be noted: (1) nationalization has mainly tended to utilize the existing (capitalist) department stores and large shops as its basic outlets; (2) it has tended to suppress many of the small private shops without having the means to create new ones. As a result of the utilization of the existing large stores the main stores are located in the town centers and peripheral areas are left without shops. Hence the following criticism:

> As a relic of the capitalistic commerce, the commercial trade is highly centralized. The stores which are very dense in the capital are all jammed together in the inner city, not considering the outer districts inhabited by workers or smaller rural centers available for the working peasantry. . . . It can, and it has been shown, that while in

some areas the number of people per store scarcely reaches 100–200, in other areas there are often several thousand people for one store.[80]

The elimination of the small private trader has resulted in an inaccessibility of retail outlets and the occasional utilization of former small (and often inefficient) shops by the state or by the cooperatives. In this connection Hilary Minc complained that the "tasks" of the cooperative trade "are not often well understood":

> The problem is not to replace small private shops, working with backward methods, by small state or cooperative shops, similar in all points to them. . . . The state and cooperative trade must be more efficient and dispose of more modern installations. Such a reorganization requires time and capital and can be accomplished only progressively.[81]

The nationalization of retail trade has thus left the state with a serious problem of shop location. The eventual solution of this problem, viz., the adaptation of the distribution system to the over-all shifts in the East European economies, would require substantial investments over a long period.

It would be erroneous to say that the liquidation of the private sector has "simplified" state problems of the *flow of goods*. During the period of rationing the state shops were in the favorable position of being able to distribute a given assortment of goods in a rigorously limited quantity at given prices. In the early period of these regimes the private and handicraft trades could supply but a small part of the market either at fixed or free-market prices. With the suppression of the private sectors and the end of rationing, the state distribution system has found itself faced with a host of problems. It is true that volume and nature of supply in the nationalized shops (now virtually the only existing ones) depend on a previously fixed rate of output of consumers' goods, and that, furthermore, both the assortment of goods and their prices are administratively established. However, even for the set output and without any private competition, account must be taken of the tastes and decisions of the consumers. Although the price mechanism does not adjust the composition of goods, the planners must remain keenly aware of the shifts in demand. As the chief of Soviet domestic trade notes, in almost lyrical terms:

> The planning of trade has its own specific features. It must take into account magnitudes that are subject to frequent fluctuation; it

80 "Fontosabb Mutatók a kereskedelmi statisztikában," *op. cit.*, p. 153.

81 *Poland's Economy Present and Future, op. cit.*, p. 20.

must take into account the relation between demand and supply, the tastes of the consumers, specific national and local features, and climatic conditions. More than all other kinds of planning, the planning of trade must be flexible, operative, and mobile. I would say that the man who plans trade must possess a vivid imagination, commercial intuition, to be able to take into account all these specific features.

Lenin said that not only the poet, but the mathematician too must have a vivid imagination. The good Soviet trade organizer must also possess it.[82]

The figures supplied by the East European statistical offices concern developments in the *registered* market in which the state, the cooperatives, and the reorganized handicrafts participate, with quantities determined by the plan. Outside this market part of the output of handicraft and peasant (individual or cooperative) enterprises passes through the so-called *unorganized* market where prices are established on the basis of supply and demand. No data have been published on the relative importance to the economies of the unorganized and organized markets. However, there is evidence that the unorganized market remains substantial[83] and that, in fact, the state encourages its development in certain lines of consumer supply (vegetables, fruit, eggs, butter, milk, etc.). Thus, if we consider the over-all balance sheet of nationalization in the retail sphere, it appears that the East European regimes tend to rely both on a newly "modernized" distribution system, which is limited and poorly located, and on an unorganized traditionally backward but pervasive system of peasant supply.

[82] A. I. Mikoyan, *The Camp of Socialism and the Camp of Capitalism.* Speech of March 10, 1950, Foreign Languages Publishing House, Moscow, 1952, p. 49.

[83] Thus, for instance, the Polish Institute of Agricultural Research gives the following indication of the structure of peasant income in Poland in 1951:

STRUCTURE OF PEASANT INCOME IN 1951

	Products, %		
	Vegetables	Animal	Total
Sold to state and cooperatives	41.2	28.4	33.4
Contracts	32.4	27.3	29.3
Free market	26.4	44.3	37.3
Total	100.0	100.0	100.0

Source: Wieś w Liczbach w Polsce Burżuazyjnoobszarniczej i w Polsce Ludowej (The Countryside in Figures in Bourgeois-Feudal Poland and in People's Poland), 1st ed., Książka i Wiedza (Book and Science), Warsaw, 1952, p. 66.

Content and Form of the Nationalization (Monopoly) of Foreign Trade

We turn now to the second subject of this chapter, the changes in the foreign trade system.

Foreign trade is concentrated in the hands of the state which has the exclusive rights of concluding foreign trade transactions and controls all imports and exports. The nationalization of foreign trade was effected for the first time in Soviet Russia immediately after the Communist Revolution,[84] its purpose being to assure the maximum possible protection for the Russian economy against any possible "capitalist economic intervention."[85] The monopoly as such has become a basic feature of the Soviet economic system, although both its role and its form have been continuously subject to change.

Absolute control over the movement of imports and exports, which is not necessarily tied to a specific over-all plan of interior development, can only have the object of protecting the economy against outright economic "intervention," but in over-all planning the monopoly becomes the direct instrument of such a plan. Hence, it serves to assure (in principle) that imports will consist solely of the commodities needed in relation to the plan and that exports will consist solely of such goods as are not stringently needed or are used as a means of payment for the required imports. In this sense, foreign trade serves to "convert" certain goods into others,[86] and therefore it can

[84] The basic decrees and laws concerning the establishment of the monopoly of foreign trade in Soviet Russia are:

1. Decree of Nov. 11, 1918 (Dec. 29, 1917, old style): "Decisions on the Import and Export of Goods."

2. Decree of April 22, 1918 (Apr. 9, 1918, old style). "Nationalization of Foreign Trade."

3. Decree of June 11, 1920: "Organization of Foreign Trade of RSFSR" (foundation of the Commissariat of Foreign Trade).

See G. P. Kaliuzhnaia, *Pravovye Formy Monopolii Vneshnei Torgovli SSSR v ikh istorickeskom Razvitii* (The Juridical Forms of the Monopoly of Foreign Trade in Their Historical Development), Izdatel'stvo Akademii Nauk SSSR (Publishing House of the Academy of Sciences of the USSR), Moscow, 1951, p. 28.

[85] Any form of protection other than the over-all nationalization of the foreign trade system was labeled by Lenin as "paper protectionism." *Ibid.*, p. 15.

[86] "Foreign trade proves itself necessary from the first division of the national income into funds of accumulation and into funds of consumption. The calculation of abstract values does not solve the problem of use values of the *material form* of the income which has to be distributed. . . . One cannot enlarge production with matches, leather, cereals. . . . The most determined will, will not succeed in trans-

be said that it is essentially the dynamics of the economic plan which determine the dynamics of imports, which, in their turn, condition the dynamics of exports.[87]

The rigorous control of the composition and *volume* of imports and exports will in part control the *direction* of foreign trade. However, not only economic but also political factors affect the direction of trade.[88]

Despite all attempts through control of foreign trade to "insulate" the national economy against fluctuations in the international ("capitalist") market, foreign trade cannot be conducted in a vacuum but remains subject to the fluctuations of supply and demand in the international market. Up to a point the planned economy can fight fluctuations in the foreign market by the establishment of long-term trade agreements, by credit manipulations, and so on, but the pressure of the foreign market will still cause displacements in the foreign trade plan (i.e., its non-realization in certain lines) and hence indirectly affect the basic economic plan.

As a function of both the changing objectives of the plan and a changing set of foreign relations the role of monopoly control of foreign trade can and does change. We shall examine the concrete

forming [these goods] into industrial equipment, into tractors and fertilizer. Foreign trade alone is able to operate this conversion. It is that [foreign trade] again which helps to solve the second problem, that of the division of the funds of accumulation among heavy industry, transformation industry and agriculture." [Lucien Laurat, *L'Économie soviétique—sa dynamique, son mécanisme* (Soviet Economy—Its Dynamics, Its Mechanism). Bibliothèque économique universelle (Universal Economic Library), No. V, Librairie Valois, Paris, 1931, p. 204.]

[87] D. D. Mishustin, *Vneshnaiaia Torgovlia SSSR* (The Foreign Trade of the USSR), Mezhdunarodnaia Kniga (International Book), Moscow, 1941, pp. 6–7. It should be noted that in this Soviet formulation it was foreign trade with the *capitalist* countries which was supposed to be adapted to a given structure of the domestic production of the Soviet planned economy.

On the question of trade with the socialist countries, it is argued now in Eastern Europe that the *production plan* itself should, to start with, take into account the possibilities of a "division of labor" existing among socialist states which in turn would somewhat modify the role of foreign trade. We shall turn to this problem in more detail in Chapters 8 and 9. Cf. Tibor Liska and Antal Máriás, "A gazdaságosság és a nemzetközi munkamegosztás" (Optimum Returns and International Division of Labor), *Közgazdasdgi Szemle* (Economic Review), No. 1, 1954, p. 81, as reprinted in *ESE* in 1954, pp. 131–135.

[88] "In our foreign trade, we must take into consideration what system of foreign trade exists in one country or another and what political relations exist between the USSR and this country, because commercial relations—their character and volume—are in direct connection with political relations." A. I. Mikoyan, "Speech to the Eighteenth Congress of the All-Union Communist Party," in D. D. Mishustin, *op. cit.*, p. 24.

impact of the changes subsequently, as functions of planning in Chapters 8 and 9, and as functions of specific foreign relations in Chapter 11. For the moment we propose to concentrate only on the *forms* of monopoly in foreign trade. They are undergoing changes basically related to: (*a*) the maintenance of the tie between distribution and production, and (*b*) the severance of this tie.

The Monopoly of Foreign Trade—Czechoslovakia

Before the second nationalization drive (i.e., before the February 1948 coup d'état) the private sector accounted for about two-thirds of the imports and from one-third to one-half the exports of Czechoslovakia. After the coup and the second nationalization drive the entire foreign trade of Czechoslovakia became a state monopoly. The control of imports, exports, of transit of goods of all kinds, and of international transport was placed under the direction of the Ministry of Foreign Trade and of such enterprises as it might establish by notification in the *Official Gazette*.[89] The state replaced the thousand private export and import firms that had previously participated in foreign trade with some twenty-three state monopoly joint-stock companies.

From the beginning the aim in Czechoslovakia was to separate distribution from production in both foreign and domestic trade. The guiding principle was the "restriction" of the industrial undertakings

> . . . to a purely manufacturing sphere, simplifying its organization, freeing it from the commercial risks and facilitating a better survey of the productivity and economy of the production especially by preventing the transfer of the productive losses to the distributive expenses and, inversely, the mingling of the productive and commercial results.[90]

The nuclei of the new companies were the export sections of the central managements of the nationalized industry. However, the financial and organizational sectors of foreign trade were not separated completely from those of production. As in the Soviet Union up to 1930, the various industrial centrals participated as stockholders in the formation of the foreign trade companies in order to maintain their "mutual cooperation and mutual supervision."

From 1948 to 1953 some of the original twenty-three companies were modified, with the aim of determining clearly their sphere of operations

[89] Law of April 28, 1948. Cf. *Bulletin of the National Bank of Czechoslovakia*, Annex to No. 2 (February 1949).

[90] "Companies for the Inner Trade," in *Adresář*, *op. cit.*, p. 13.

and avoiding overlapping activities. In 1953 the last tie between production and distribution was severed. The import-export joint-stock companies were converted, on the post-1930 Soviet pattern, into foreign trade corporations,[91] independent units operating in accord with the "khozraschët" system of accounting (i.e., with expenses to be covered from their own revenues after taxes). The companies now purchase the output planned for exports from the domestic wholesale organizations and aim at obtaining in the foreign market a given supply of foreign currency; the import agencies purchase on the foreign market and sell the goods obtained to the domestic purchasing organizations. For both types of operation the system of accounting seeks to establish the economic soundness of each foreign trade corporation.

POLAND

The Polish approach to the nationalization of foreign trade was in the beginning different from that of the Czechoslovak. At the outset of the postwar period the Polish government established practically a *de facto* monopoly of foreign trade. Although in the early period, notably up to the beginning of 1948, the cooperatives and the private sector also participated in foreign trade, they did so on the basis of licenses granted by the government and were under its absolute control. During that period the state enterprises engaged in foreign trade were (*a*) the Central Supply and Sales Offices of the nationalized enterprises, (*b*) a small number of limited liability companies, (*c*) one stock company.[92] In 1947–48 foreign trade was thoroughly reorganized with the aims of avoiding overlapping (hence the introduction of a uniform organizational type) and achieving the separation of production and distribution (hence the splitting up of the Ministry of Industry and Trade). The complete elimination of the private sector from production automatically precluded its participation in foreign trade. As for the cooperatives, their (controlled) participation was limited to exporting foodstuffs, cooperatively produced furniture, textiles, and handicrafts; on the import side, the central cooperative Społem (Together) was charged with meeting the requirements in foreign goods of the whole cooperative movement.

[91] The reform was carried out under orders 295 and 310 issued by the Ministry of Foreign Trade in November 1953. Cf. *CEB*, No. 278, November 1953, pp. 6, 17.

[92] See "Organization of Industry in Poland," *Quarterly Review of the Bank Gospodarstwa Krajowego*, XV, No. 5, December 1946, pp. 1 ff.; also, *Yearbook of the Foreign Trade of Poland*, Warsaw, 1948, quoted by Margaret Dewar in *Soviet Trade with Eastern Europe 1945–1949, op. cit.*, p. 37.

By the beginning of 1952 the foreign trade organizations were overhauled. Virtually all the former *central organizations for foreign trade* (both central bureaus for imports and exports and supply centers for given industries) were transformed into *national enterprises* with limited liability, and their field was further delineated in both the export and the import lines.[93] Thus the separation of production and of distribution was completed also in Poland, the organizations for foreign trade having been turned into independent units operating on the basis of the "khozraschët" system.

YUGOSLAVIA

The evolution of the Yugoslav organization of foreign trade has been directly inverse to that in the Soviet Union and in Czechoslovakia and Poland. Foreign trade was nationalized in Yugoslavia earlier than in the other countries, being conducted from the beginning of 1946 exclusively by (a) certain sales departments of the industrial directorates (e.g., mining), (b) newly setup trading companies, (c) the traditional state monopolies (e.g., tobacco, matches). Foreign trade policy was shaped by the Ministries of Industry and Foreign Trade, but the latter was responsible for the accomplishment of the plan and executed it through its export-import companies. Hence, according to later Yugoslav statements, serious conflicts arose between the foreign trade organs and industry over securing the goods needed for the foreign trade plan.[94]

[93] Compare lists of Polish central organizations for foreign trade in *Polish Foreign Trade*, No. 7, September–October 1951, pp. 64–65, with *ibid.*, No. 10, March–April 1952, pp. 82–83, and with *ibid.*, No. 15 (1), 1953, pp. 58–59. In the first source there are 30 Polish foreign trade organizations, namely: 21 *trading offices*, of which 19 are central bureaus of imports and exports and 2 supply centers (i.e., import bureaus for the iron and steel industry and for the Polish coal mines), 7 *foreign trade companies*, 1 *agency* (for chemicals and laboratory equipment), and 1 unclassified type of organization, namely, the Polish grain establishments. In the second source the total number of organizations engaged in foreign trade is 29, of which 28 are now *national enterprises with limited liability* (trading companies) and 1 *agency* (the same as previously). In 1953 the number of Polish central organizations for foreign trade was further reduced to 27, of which 24 are *national enterprises or companies with limited responsibility*, 1 *agency*, 1 *trading office* (for periodicals and books), and 1, the key company, Weglokoks, for coal exports, called both a national enterprise and a foreign trade office.

[94] Cf. Bernard Menashe, "O novom sistemu poslovanja u spoljnoj trgovini" (On the New System of Management in Foreign Trade), *Ekonomist*, No. 3–4, 1951, pp. 74–80.

As we have already noted, after the 1948 break with the Soviet orbit Yugoslavia engaged in the so-called "decentralized administrative planning system." By 1950 the foreign trade system had undergone a thorough reorganization. The previous state foreign trade monopolies were "turned over to the producers," i.e., were transformed into joint-stock companies the stock in which was owned by the various production directorates; [95] some state companies were abolished, part of their duties being transferred to the federal republics or to special directorates.[96] From then on, the producers (viz., the industrial and commercial directorates and the federated republics in given cases) were given planned objectives for the accomplishment of the centrally determined export and import plans. The objectives were determined in a detailed way for imports and exports of certain key items, and in a general way for secondary items. Thus a certain latitude of movement was allowed the producers as a special incentive for their participation in foreign trade: viz., the larger the amount of exports (i.e., overfulfillment of the export plan), the larger the share of foreign currency at the disposal of the producers.[97]

However, strong brakes were put on the actions of the producers through the system of appropriation and distribution of the funds earned in foreign trade. A large percentage of these funds, varying from 50 to 99.5 per cent, had to be turned over to the Central (Federal) Fund, and a varying percentage had to be turned over to the people's republic fund in the area in which the producer was located. These

[95] E.g., Agroprodukt (agricultural produce), Jugodrvo (wood), Jugolek (oily and pharmaceutical products), Jugometal (metal), Jugoelektro (electrical apparatus), Rudarsko Nabavno Preduzeće (mining), Technopromet (machinery), Hempro (chemicals), Centroprom (various manufactures), Centrotekstil (textile), and Investimport became joint-stock companies instead of state monopolies, the stock being held by the respective producing state central directorates (*ibid.*). Thus for instance the main stockholders of Jugodrvo apparently became Exportdrvo (Zagreb), Slovenijales (Ljubljana), Sipad (Sarajevo), Rudnik (Belgrade), Spoljopred (Hercegovina), and Vardar (Skoplje).

[96] Thus the transport monopoly *Transjug* was abolished, and its duties were transferred in the harbors to the Directory of Public Warehouses, in other fields to the transportation enterprises in the federal republic. Cf. Marko Perović, "Osnovni principi reorganizacije spoljne trgovine FNRJ" (The Basic Principles in the Reorganization of the Foreign Trade of FPRY), *Ekonomist,* No. 5–6, 1950, pp. 44–54.

[97] A certain relaxation of controls took place in mid-1952. License requirements for practically all exports and most imports were abolished, the exporters were given the right to use part of their export proceeds for their imports and were permitted to sell their "retained" exchange to other importers on the "free" foreign exchange market.

funds financed both the imports needed for national defense and other types of imports. Their varying percentage served as a deterrent against the export of given articles.

Thus, on the organizational plane, Yugoslavia has rather turned back to the pre-1930 Soviet system of foreign trade with certain modifications tending both to stimulate and to control the activity of the industries engaged in foreign trade. By the end of 1954, some 500 "economic organizations" were inscribed in the foreign trade register and were engaging in foreign trade.[98] By and large, the whole organizational system of foreign trade can, however, be considered as being still in a state of flux.

Hungary

Up to the end of 1947, 60 per cent of the total of Hungarian foreign trade was in the hands of the private sector.[99] However, both the import of certain merchandise (e.g., processed wood, charcoal, seed) and the export of certain others (e.g., spirits, wine and fruit distillates, oil-seed, pulses, seeds) were monopolized either by certain professional trading associations (Hungarian Wine Export Cooperative Society, Hungarian General Wood Import Cooperative Society) or by state concerns (Hungarian Foreign Trade Company, Ltd.). The creation of import and export monopolies was generally based on internal measures of the various departments and aimed at the establishment of foreign trade enterprises under state management. At times monopolistic restrictions were applied to certain commodities and certain countries.[100]

After the nationalization of the banks in November 1947, and of enterprises with more than 100 employees, March 1948, the state sector in foreign trade was consolidated: Its share was more than 70 per cent. In the autumn of 1948, in order to strengthen further state control of foreign trade, the government organized seven Hungarian export-import companies which took over virtually all the foreign trade of

[98] Cf. "Nekotorye Pravovye Voprosy Organizatsii Vneshnei Torgovli Iugoslavii" (Some Legal Questions Concerning the Organization of the Foreign Trade of Yugoslavia), *VT*, XXV, No. 1, January 1955, pp. 27–29.

[99] Iu Vanagas, "Reorganizatsia Vneshnei Torgovli Vengrii" (Reorganization of the Foreign Trade of Hungary), in *VT*, No. 1, 1949, pp. 31–32.

[100] For a study of the foreign trade system before its nationalization, see "Foreign Trade of Hungary since the Introduction of the Florin Currency," in *Monthly Bulletin of the National Bank of Hungary*, new series, III, 3–4 (March–April 1947), pp. 47–48.

the country.[101] Each of these companies had, to start with, an extensive area of operation.[102] Subsequently the original seven companies were split into various new foreign trade concerns, reaching by 1953 a total of some twenty-four companies, each specializing, as in the other East European countries, in a limited number of products: e.g., Agrimpex for grain, and Terimpex for animal products—a breakdown of the former Agricultural Export and Import Company; Chemolimpex for chemicals; Ligrimpex for wood; Metimpex for pharmaceuticals; Metalimpex for metals.

The new nationalization undertaken at the end of 1949, affecting not only all the foreign concerns except those belonging to the Soviet Union but also enterprises with over 10 workers, eliminated any possible participation in foreign trade other than that of the state, of the Soviet companies in Hungary, and of the joint Soviet companies formed with the Hungarian government. The agreements for the formation of these companies[103] placed them in a unique position vis-à-vis the monopolistic organization of foreign trade both in matters of trade and in utilization of the foreign currencies earned. Thus the Soviet companies (as well as the Soviet shares in the joint corporations with the Hungarian state) enjoyed, up to their liquidation in the autumn of 1954, a *de facto* extra-territorial status unaffected by whatever modifications occurred either in the specialization of the Hungarian companies for foreign trade or in their transformation from joint-stock companies into state units operating on the basis of the "khozraschët" system.

101 B. S. Vaganov: *Voprosy Organizatsii Vneshnei Torgovli Stran Narodnoi Democratsii* (Problems of the Organization of Foreign Trade of the Countries of People's Democracy), Vneshtorgizdat, Moscow, 1954, p. 17 ff.

102 Thus the Hungarian Foreign Trade Company, Ltd., had in its sphere not only the imports and exports of textiles, supply of the Hungarian leather industry with all types of materials, and the export of furs and leather, but also the import of colonial goods and the export-import trade with West Germany. The Agricultural Export-Import Co. (Agrimpex) had in its sphere both import and export of all types of agricultural products, processed or unprocessed. The East European Commerce, Ltd., concentrated in its hands the export and import of timber, chemicals, rubber, mineral oil, etc. Cf. "Planned Economy in Foreign Trade," *HB*, No. 39, Oct. 2, 1948, pp. 5–7.

103 The Soviet-owned corporations represented the consolidation of various former German companies inherited by the Soviet Union. For a description of the German heritage passed to the Soviet Union and of the joint companies, see below, Chapter 6, pp. 185–189.

ROMANIA

In Romania the penetration of the state into exporting and importing on a large scale dates from the closing months of 1947, when various juridical measures were taken such as authorization for the Ministry of Foreign Trade to establish joint-stock companies for imports and exports of any given commodity or group of commodities.[104] In the first half of 1948 several state companies were set up which continued to carry on foreign trade side by side with private capital.[105] By April 1948 a new constitution was adopted placing all foreign trade, whether conducted by state, cooperative, or private corporations, under complete state control. The subsequent nationalization of industry and all important commercial enterprises (June 1948) virtually liquidated the private sector and any possibility of participation in foreign trade by concerns other than the state companies, the state-controlled cooperatives, and the Soviet-Romanian joint-stock companies.[106]

The total trade of the country is now carried by some 15 state companies and managed by appointees of the Ministry of Foreign Trade; the shares of the companies are at the disposal of the Ministry of Trade; they do not pay dividends nor transfer their profits to the Ministry of Finance.[106] The Ministry of Foreign Trade was set up in Romania in October 1948.

The companies are far from being specialized in single products; their fields are in some instances extensive and overlapping. Such companies are Agroexport for grain, tobacco, fodder, etc.; Prodexport for horticultural products, cattle products, processed foods, etc.; Technoimport for the import and export of agricultural machinery and electrical appliances; Metallimport for the export of ores and the import of pig iron and ferroalloys; Maşinimport for the import and export of all types of machinery; Industrialimport for the import and export mostly of drilling equipment, etc.

The extensive holdings of the Soviet Union in Romania up to the autumn of 1954 (in the Soviet-Romanian companies dominating such fields as metal, oil, wood, chemicals, industrial machinery and equip-

[104] A. Lebedev, "Zakony Reguliruiushchie Vneshnuiu Torgovliu v Rumynii" (Laws Regulating Foreign Trade in Romania), *VT*, No. 11, 1948, p. 24.

[105] A. Lebedev, *ibid.*

[106] B. S. Vaganov, *op. cit.*, p. 20–21, and M. F. Kovrizhnykh, et al., editors, *Vneshniaia Torgovlia Stran Narodnoi Demokratsii* (Foreign Trade of the Countries of People's Democracy), Vneshtorgizdat, Moscow, 1955, p. 243 ff.

ment[107]) made fictitious the Romanian economic control of these Soviet-directed monopolies. These companies until their liquidation enjoyed *de facto* extra-territoriality and could dispose of their foreign currency holdings at their own discretion.[108]

BULGARIA

Since the end of the war the Bulgarian government has moved steadily toward the monopolization of foreign trade, taking under its direct management and control the key products entering into it. A monopoly for the import and export of grains and dried vegetables existed before the war; a state monopoly for the decisive export item *attar of roses* was established by decree in May 1945; the tobacco monopoly was established in April 1947. In the course of nationalization at the end of 1947 imports and exports passed from the hands of semistate or cooperative and private organizations exclusively into the hands of the state monopolistic centrals for imports and exports and of the central of cooperatives, both of which were placed under complete state direction.[109] Some 20 export-import companies, including the state monopolies participating in domestic and foreign trade, were formed in Bulgaria; as in the countries mentioned above, a separate Ministry for Foreign Trade was then created with the task of directing and controlling the country's foreign trade. The participation of the cooperatives remained limited to the export of cattle and sheep (undertaken by Tsentralen Cooperativen Săiuz, Central Cooperative Union) and certain items such as craftsworks products, the production of which is insured both by the state and the cooperative sectors.[110] Though limited in number, the Bulgarian import and export companies are quite specialized since exports and, to a certain extent, imports are limited to certain key products. In exports we find especially fruit, vegetables, poultry, eggs, and seeds,[111] each one

107 See below, Chapter 6, pp. 190–193.

108 See below, Appendix 2 to Chapter 6, documents on the formation of joint companies, especially Document 4, Convention for the Creation of the Soviet-Romanian Oil Company, Articles VI, VII, and VIII, pp. 219–220.

109 See "Vătreshen Pregled, Bălgarskoto Stopanstvo ot Sept. 1947 do Sept. 1948," *op. cit.*

110 For the specific fields of these companies, see "The New Foreign Trade Ministry," in *Free Bulgaria,* IV, 1 (Jan. 1, 1949), p. 13.

111 Thus at the International Economic Conference in Moscow, April 8–12, 1952, the Bulgarian delegate Prof. T. Vladigherov underlined the fact that the range of

with a specific company, whereas in all the other East European countries these exports are handled together by one company which monopolizes agricultural products. On the import side only a limited number of companies deal with commodities such as machinery, electrical appliances, and miscellaneous products.[112]

Summary on Area Trends

Thus nationalization of the foreign trade of the area as a whole had been effected by 1948. The first countries to nationalize foreign trade completely were Yugoslavia, as early as 1946, and Poland, which had a *de facto* monopoly from that period on but did not completely eliminate the private sector from foreign trade until later. Bulgaria, Hungary, and Romania formed monopolies of foreign trade by specific types of goods. The first to form them was Bulgaria, which engaged in the process as soon as the war ended. Czechoslovakia was the only country which nationalized its foreign trade in a single stroke—after the February coup d'état.

In contradistinction to the process of nationalizing domestic trade, in countries where multiple and far-reaching state controls and regimentations of foreign trade had always existed, the nationalization of foreign trade was effected without being directly and immediately correlated with the nationalization of production. Sometimes the nationalization of certain branches of foreign trade has effectively *preceded* the nationalization of the production sector supplying them.

The organization of the monopolies of foreign trade generally followed an evolution similar to that which had occurred in the Soviet Union. By and large, from 1948, when the monopolization of foreign trade was completed in the area, to 1953 the monopolistic state corporations remained tied to production, as was true in the Soviet Union up to 1930. With the development of planned economy in all directions, the monopolies tended to be patterned on the late Soviet models, that is, they became organizations under the control of the

Bulgarian export commodities has "grown wider." However, the concrete proposition for trade concerned only "grain, fodder, tobacco, fresh fruit, vegetables, and eggs." Another Bulgarian delegate, D. V. Dimitrov, Director of the state import company Himimport, indicated: "We can export wheat, corn, fodder, oil-seeds, fruit, vegetables, wine, poultry and eggs. . . ." Cf. *International Economic Conference in Moscow*, publ. by Commission for the Promotion of International Trade, Moscow, 1952, pp. 143, 190.

112 See below, the diversification of the Bulgarian companies as opposed to Czechoslovak and Polish diversification.

TABLE 38. CZECHOSLOVAKIA, POLAND, BULGARIA: FOREIGN TRADE COMPANIES

Items	Czechoslovakia	Poland	Bulgaria
Food Supplies and Agricultural Products			
All foodstuffs	Centrokomisie	Dalspo	Export-Import (E)
Wine, alcohol			Dărzhaven Spirten (E)
Agricultural products	Koospol [a]	Rolimpex	
Fruits, vegetables			Bulgarplodexport (E)
Tobacco			Dărzhaven Tiutiunev Monopol (E)
Seeds			Zemsnab (I)
Animal products		Animex	Tsentralen Cooperativen Săiuz (E)
Meat			Mesotsentrala (E)
Eggs, poultry			Iaitsetsentral (E)
Raw Materials and Semimanufactured Goods			
Ores and metals	Metalimex	Minex [a] Impexmetal	Bălgarrudaexport (E)
Coal		Centrala Zbytu Wegla (E)	
Oil		Cent. Produkt. Naftowych	
Timber	Ligna	Paged	
Chemical raw materials	Chemapol [a]		
Oily products			Bălgarska Rosa (E)
Medicinal herbs			Dărzhavno Sanitarno Aptechno [a] (E)
Fibers	Centrotex [a] (I)	Textilimport (I)	Industrialimport (I)
Hides, leather, furs	Exico	Skorimpex [a]	Kozhetsentral (E)
Manufactured Goods			
Metallurgical products	Ferromet	Impexmetal	
Plant assemblies	Technoexport (E)		
Heavy engine products	Strojexport (E) Strojimport (I)	Centrozap (I) Metalexport (E)	Metalimport (I)
All machines		Polimex (I)	
Ball bearings		Cebiloz	
Vehicles	Motokov	Motoimport (I)	
Agricultural implements	Koospol [a]		
Precision engines	Kovo		
Electrical equipment		Elektrim	Elprom
Ships' equipment		Centrala Morska	
Chemicals	Chemapol [a]	Ciech	Himimport (I) Dărzhavno Sanitarno Aptechno [a] (I)
Textile	Centrotex [a] (I)	Cetebe	
Leather goods		Skorimpex [a]	
Paper	Papco	Papexport	
Glass and ceramics	Glassexport (E) Czechoslovak Ceramics	Minex [a]	
Smallware	Pragoexport Jablonex		Bălgarindustrialexport (E)
Services and Other			
Shipping	Cechofract	Polcargo Baltona	
Forwarding	Metrans	Hartwig	
Trading	Darex	Dal	
Patents and technical advice	Technospol		
Books	Orbis	Prasa i Kziaska	
Films	Czechoslovak State Film	Film Polski[c]	
Miscellaneous	Artia	Varimex (E)	

(E) = export company, (I) = import company; all companies not followed by (E) or (I) are both export and import.

[a] Listed under two headings.

Sources:

C: *CEB*, No. 260, Dec. 1, 1952, and No. 278, November 1953.
P: *Polish Foreign Trade*, No. 15 (I), 1953.
B: *Free Bulgaria*, IV, 1, Jan. 1, 1949.

Ministry of Foreign Trade but operated separately as units of the "khozraschët" system. The only different evolution was that in Yugoslavia. After being the first to organize centrally controlled monopolistic companies, the country has now given the foreign trade companies a pre-1930 Soviet-type status, linked them again to the state-producing centrals and to the federated republics, and tried to develop new stimuli for the producers in the export field by rewarding, up to a point, their efforts to "over-fulfill" the plan of foreign trade.

Although the monopolies are patterned on the Soviet organizational scheme, it should be noted that they tend to fit given economies with varying characteristics. Consequently, the companies and monopolies operating in foreign trade in one country are not the same as those operating in another, as can be seen from Table 38, which compares the foreign trade companies in operation in Czechoslovakia, Poland, and Bulgaria. As contrasted to the first two countries, the Bulgarian companies are diversified in the agricultural-raw materials fields whereas the other countries are diversified in the manufactured goods groups. A comparison between Czechoslovakia and Poland reveals notable differences between those two countries both in the raw materials and in the manufactured goods group (see Table 38).

With the completion of the study of nationalization in the wholesale, retail, and foreign trade systems, we have completed the study of the nationalization of all the non-agricultural sectors except the special sphere formed by the Soviet enterprises and Soviet joint companies, to which we turn in the following chapter.

CHAPTER

6

THE SPECIAL CASE OF SOVIET RUSSIA'S ASSETS, COMPANIES, AND SHARE IN "JOINT PARTNERSHIPS"

AUTONOMY AND INTEGRATION

We now turn to the set of problems that concerns the functioning and growth of the only non-agricultural sector not engulfed in the nationalization process as it developed in the area up to 1954, namely, the Soviet companies in Eastern Europe and the so-called Soviet-East European "joint partnerships." The dismantling of *most* of these companies occurred in the autumn of 1954. The few remaining companies were liquidated in 1955 or 1956.

The study of the development and liquidation of these companies is in turn related to the question of the reparations paid to the Soviet Union. We have already indicated the legal foundation on which the obligations rest (cf. Chapter 2, pp. 34–35). Now we turn to the question of the fulfillment of these obligations and to the impact on the economies of the respective countries.

Both the study of reparations and the examination of the process of formation and growth of the Soviet-managed and -operated companies in some of these economies form indispensable parts of the general discussion of the reshaping of these economies and illuminate the interplay of tendencies of *autonomy* and *integration* at work in the Soviet bloc. In this context we mean by autonomy the autonomous development of each of these countries, by integration the direct or indirect coordination between their plans of development and the Soviet needs and plans. The framework in which these tendencies combine appears to be a continuously changing one. The object of the following analysis is to show precisely *how* these tendencies combine in *various degrees* at given time periods. A full view of the complex and conflicting tendencies at work in the region is possible only after examination of the problems connected with planning and trade, to which we shall turn in Section III.

Structure of Reparations Deliveries: Hungarian Metallurgical Products

As already noted,[1] Hungary and Romania were obligated to deliver to the Soviet Union from their current production over a period of six years, later extended to eight years, commodities valued up to 200 and 300 million 1938-dollars, respectively. These totals were reduced subsequently to 134.3 million and 226.5 million 1938-dollars, respectively. The main reparations requirements of the Soviet Union from Hungary were metallurgical products, from Romania petroleum and its derivatives. Furthermore, on the basis of a special convention concerning a part of the reparations deliveries from Germany to the Soviet Union, the latter also managed to obtain deliveries of Polish coal at a special price. In the analysis of the structures and impact of reparations we shall consider in turn these three groups of deliveries.

Hungarian reparations deliveries started in 1945 and were declared completed in January 1953. According to the official data, up to July 1948 the Hungarian reparations payments to the Soviet Union amounted to 68.6 million 1938-dollars (so-called gold dollars), of which 56.6 million dollars' worth of goods were from current production (see Table 39) and 12.0 million represented the value of certain shares of Romanian coal mines (Petroşani) in Hungarian possession which were transferred to the Soviet Union in the reparations account.

Useful indications of the composition of deliveries to the Soviet Union can be obtained from the official breakdown of the shipments from 1945 to 1947, inclusive. The sample is significant since it covers a total of 42.9 million gold dollars' worth of goods, i.e., over one-third of the total delivered.[2] The main commodities in the list are grouped in Table 40, from which it appears that agricultural products represented 15.5 per cent of the value of the goods delivered and consisted mainly of some 100,000 head of cattle and 120,000 tons of grain. The

[1] Cf. Chapter 2, pp. 39–40.

[2] The total bill was reduced, as stated, to 134.3 million gold dollars. If we deduct 12 million for the sale of shares, the goods delivered totaled 122.3 million, of which 42.9 million represents more than one-third.

TABLE 39. HUNGARY: REPARATIONS DELIVERIES JULY 1945–JULY 1948

(in millions of 1938-dollars)

Recipient Countries	1945 VII–XII	1946	1947	1948 I–VII	Total per Country
Soviet Union	4,909	19,878	18,175	13,638 [a]	56,600
Yugoslavia	401	3,042	10,163	[b, c]	13,606
Czechoslovakia	221	1,020	2,075	[c]	3,316
Total (per year or fraction of year)	5,531	23,940	30,413	13,638	73,522

[a] Obtained as a residual from total announced in July 1948.

[b] The deliveries to Yugoslavia ceased in 1948. Taking into account the eventual deliveries to Czechoslovakia, the total at the date considered (July 1948) amounted at the most to some 75 million 1938-dollars.

[c] Not available.

Source: *GT*, II, February 2, 1948, pp. 129–132.

raw and semimanufactured goods accounted for 36.9 per cent of the value of the deliveries and consisted of some 200,000 tons of bauxite, 170,000 tons of oil, 80,000 tons of iron and steel bars, and 26,000 tons of iron and steel plate. Manufactured goods, with emphasis on iron goods, machinery, and transport equipment, represented a total of 20.4 million gold dollars or 47.6 per cent of the value of deliveries. Including all the products of the metallurgical industry, they would account for over 65 per cent.

Reparations to the Soviet Union obviously had priority over reparations to Yugoslavia and Czechoslovakia. In August 1946 an agreement on reparations was signed by Hungary and Yugoslavia, and deliveries were increased in 1947, but in 1948 all deliveries were stopped following the political rift between the Cominform and Yugoslavia.[3] Hungary also reached an agreement with Czechoslovakia in 1946 extending the period of delivery to 1952.[4] The first agreement for deliveries to the Soviet Union, also in August 1946, extended the period of deliveries from six to eight years; a second agreement, signed in January

[3] An agreement regulating unsettled financial and economic questions between Yugoslavia and Hungary was signed at Belgrade on May 29, 1956. By the agreement Hungary assumed the responsibility to deliver to Yugoslavia, "as a balance of mutual claims and obligations" goods valued at 85 million dollars in equal installments over five years. (*Borba,* May 30, 1956.)

[4] Cf. *Monthly Bulletin of the National Bank of Hungary,* new series, III, 7–8 (July–August 1947), Budapest, p. 186.

TABLE 40. HUNGARY: STRUCTURE OF REPARATIONS DELIVERIES TO THE SOVIET UNION

(July 1945 to December 31, 1947)

Description of Goods	Unit[a]	Quantity	Quantity Total	Value $[b] 1,000 gold		%
Agricultural Produce	H		99,149		6,627	15.5
	Q		1,205,606			
Cattle	H	18,509		728		
Pigs	H	78,305		1,414		
Slaughtered pigs	Q	24,611		356		
Wheat	Q	562,111		1,470		
Rye	Q	475,531		1,104		
Raw and Semimanufactured Goods	Q		5,350,910		15,869	36.9
Bauxite	Q	1,980,615		1,227		
Oil	Q	1,723,841		1,839		
Iron and steel bars	Q	793,241		3,778		
Iron and steel plate	Q	263,516		1,396		
Raw metals	Q	30,562		1,025		
Manufactured Goods	P		14,770		20,466	47.6
	Q		698,376			
Iron goods	Q	427,116		5,222		
Steam boilers	Q	47,826		882		
Engines with pistons	Q	42,147		2,084		
Steam turbines	Q	21,592		925		
Machines for metal-processing	Q	46,382		1,587		
Other machines	Q	11,994		417		
Railway locomotives	Q	99,452		3,698		
Freight cars	Q	214,894		2,410		
Passenger cars	Q	14,454		837		
Tugboats	Q	30,314		1,005		
Total	H		99,149		42,962	100.0
	P		14,770			
	Q		7,368,811			

[a] Units: H = heads; Q = quintals (100 kg.); P = pairs of shoes.
[b] 1938 dollars.
Source: *GT*, II. 2, February 1948, pp. 129–130.

1948, reduced the reparations outstanding on July 1, 1948, a reduction chiefly in the delivery of agricultural products.[5] There was also a reduction in rolled-steel products, but all deliveries of industrial goods were to be metallurgical products.[6]

In order to gage the importance of these deliveries for the economy as a whole it must be noted that the reparations, including the shipments to Yugoslavia and Czechoslovakia (see Table 39), represented up to 71 per cent of the total exports of Hungary in 1946, 59 per cent of her exports during 1946–47 (July to July, i.e., the first "stabilization year" after the monetary reform), and 43 per cent of her total exports for the first three quarters of 1948 (see Table 41).

The total reparations bill increased in absolute terms from year to year (Table 41), but its relative share in total exports decreased owing to a steady increase in exports. In 1946–47 reparations deliveries exacted from Hungary by the Soviet Union, Yugoslavia, and Czechoslovakia were over 4 times as large as commercial exports to these countries (see Table 42).

On the basis of these tables the average Hungarian "reparations dollar" appears to have been equal in 1946 to about 43 forints or nearly 4 current dollars.[7] That is, to obtain credit for 1 dollar of reparations Hungary had to deliver goods worth almost 4 dollars at the current exchange rate. From 1948 on, because of the increase in prices at which reparations goods were valued after the beginning of that year, the value of the average reparations dollar decreased with respect to 1946.

The reduction of reparations granted in July 1948, i.e., the halving of the balance of 131.4 million, made the reparations due the Soviet Union from 1949 through 1952 a total of 65.7 million gold dollars or an average of 16.4 million gold dollars' worth of goods per year. However, the Soviet Union requested additional goods in payment of the

[5] Owing to the bad harvest, the agricultural surpluses of the country were very small, but the raising of industrial production "required a more voluminous import of raw materials and products, which had to be paid for mainly by the export of industrial goods, at a time when the bulk of the production of the heavy industry was claimed by reparations." "Report of the Board of Directors on the Course of Business in 1947," in *Reports to the 22nd Annual Meeting . . .*, National Bank of Hungary, *op. cit.*, p. xiv. Thus the change in the structure of the reparations due to the Soviet Union only shifted the burden, without alleviating it too much.

[6] *Monthly Bulletin of the National Bank of Hungary*, new series, IV, 5–6 (May–June 1948), pp. 127–128.

[7] The ratio is based on the 1946 figures in dollars and forints. Cf. Tables 39 and 41: 1,032 ÷ 23.9 = 43.17 forints per 1 "reparations dollar."

TABLE 41. HUNGARY: COMPREHENSIVE BALANCE OF FOREIGN TRADE

(in million forints)

	Exports			Imports		
	1946	1946–47[a]	1948 I–IX	1946	1946–47	1948 I–IX
Trade proper	420.5	836.4	1122.6	370.6	944.0	1473.6
Relief				232.5	254.2	122.3
Reparations	1032.0	1223.2	854.1			
Total deliveries	1452.5	2059.6	1976.7	603.1	1198.2	1595.9
		Percentages				
Trade proper	29.0	40.6	56.8	61.4	78.8	92.3
Relief				38.6	21.2	7.7
Reparations	71.0	59.4	43.2			
Total deliveries	100.0	100.0	100.0	100.0	100.0	100.0

[a] July 31, 1946, to July 31, 1947, first "stabilization year."

Source: Monthly Bulletin of the National Bank of Hungary, new series, III, 7–8 (July–August 1947), p. 186; and IV, 9 (September 1948), p. 212.

TABLE 42. HUNGARY: REPARATIONS AND COMMERCIAL EXPORTS, 1946–47

(in million forints)

Deliveries to	Commercial Exports	Reparations	Reparations, % to each country	2 ÷ 1·100
	1	2	3	4
Soviet Union	176.2	782.7	64	444
Yugoslavia	34.0	354.7	29	1,040
Czechoslovakia	88.8	85.6	7	96
Total	299.0	1,223.0	100	409

Source: GT, II, 2, February 1948, pp. 129–132.

so-called Hungarian debts to Germany. Following an agreement signed on December 9, 1947, the Soviet government reduced its claims for these debts from $200 million to $45 million,[8] of which $15 million were to be delivered in kind from 1949 through 1952 and $30 million were to be reinvested by the Soviet Union over a period of three years in the joint Soviet-Hungarian companies. Thus the reparations deliveries were to be maintained at about the level of some 19 to 20 million gold dollars per year until 1953, the same level as before the July 1948 reduction. These deliveries were in addition to Hungary's obligation to supply provisions for the Soviet occupation troops, especially up to 1947.

Romanian Oil and "Restitutions"

According to the Armistice Convention, one half of the Romanian reparations deliveries to the Soviet Union was to be petroleum and petroleum products, and the other half machinery, ships, timber, and grains.

The Armistice Convention foresaw the delivery of a total of 10 million tons of petroleum and its derivatives, valued at $150 million 1938-dollars or $15 per ton, to be transferred from September 1944 to September 1950 at the rate of 1.7 million tons per year. In July 1948 the Soviet Union stated that Romania had delivered in the reparations account goods in kind valued at a total of $153 million gold dollars but gave no breakdown of the commodities delivered.

In gaging the amount of petroleum shipments certain data appear significant. In spite of strenuous efforts to increase production, the Romanian petroleum output from 1945 through 1948 amounted to only some 17 million tons, out of which 10.6 million tons should have been available for export (see Table 43). As the Romanian export of petroleum to countries other than the Soviet Union during the same period did not amount to a total of more than 200,000 tons, at least 10.4 million tons must have been made available to the Soviet Union.

[8] Margaret Dewar indicates that the origin of this claim was the following: Germany had an adverse trade balance with Hungary [which towards the end of the war amounted to RM. 750 million] and was granted a credit through the Hungarian National Bank. The German Government in turn [through the Bank der Deutschen Luftwaffe] extended a credit of RM. 600 million to several Hungarian companies for the expansion of their war production [chiefly Messerschmitts] in a safe area, and for the purchase of machinery in Germany. Article 30, paragraph 4, of the Peace Treaty stipulated that Hungary waive all claims against Germany outstanding on May 8, 1945. The USSR, on the other hand, did demand payment of Hungary's debt to Germany and claimed $200 million. [Margaret Dewar, *Soviet Trade with Eastern Europe, 1945–1949, op. cit.*, pp. 67–68.]

Out of this total, hardly 1 to 1.5 million tons were considered as commercial exports.

It is possible to infer, then, that between 1944 and 1948 the Soviet Union received in the reparations account and as provision for its occupation forces some 9 million tons, i.e., as much as nine-tenths of the oil and oil products actually requested by the Armistice Convention. This inference is strongly substantiated by the detailed data which can be gathered for 1945 and 1946. As can be seen from Table 44, out of a total of 3.17 million tons exported in 1945, 3.14 million, or 99.03 per cent, went to the Soviet Union. In 1946, out of a total of 2.3 million tons counted as exports, 2.2 million tons, or 95.54 per cent, went to the Soviet Union. As appears from Table 45, which presents the detailed account of the reparations deliveries from September 1944 to September 1946, in both years deliveries *exceeded* the obligatory annual quota of 1.7 million tons. In 1945 they exceeded the quota by 47 per cent, with the emphasis placed on highly refined products such as gasoline, fuel oil, and paraffin. In 1946 the quota was exceeded by 6 per cent, with deliveries exclusively of refined products. At this rate it can be assumed that the full quota of oil deliveries was met by 1949 or early 1950.[9] However, no mention is to be found, around that period or later, of the completion of the Romanian reparations deliveries of oil. Apparently, since no larger oil amounts appear in the Romanian commercial agreements, they continued after that date at the same rate. It is possible to assume that a substantial amount of these deliveries was made in the account of the so-called "debts" to Germany.[10] Thus the most valuable item of Romanian exports, accounting in prewar times for 45 per cent of the country's total exports, remained mortgaged to the Soviet Union under one pretext or another for a long and still undetermined period.

The spot prices paid by the Romanian government for the purchase of oil earmarked for reparations were below the 1938 average in 1945 and in 1946 equal to it, i.e., $15 per ton.[11] These prices did not cover cost and taxes, a condition under which only the newly formed tax-exempt Soviet-Romanian Oil Company (Sovrompetrol) could thrive.

[9] In 1949 and in 1950 the total Romanian oil output reached 4.7 and 5.3 million tons, respectively. This left, consequently, over 2½ million tons per year for export.

[10] See above, Chapter 2.

[11] M. Pizanty, "Les Pétroles roumains," *op. cit.*, p. 66. On the basis of these prices the reparations oil deliveries amounted in 1945 to 28.9 million dollars and in 1946 to 27.7 million dollars, i.e., 56.6 million dollars in two years for oil products alone.

TABLE 43. ROMANIA: PETROLEUM OUTPUT AND EXPORT RESOURCES 1945–48

(in thousand metric tons)

Year	Output	Quantum 1938 = 100	Exports
1938	6,610	100	4,495
1945	4,680	72	3,172
1946	4,193	64	2,346
1947	3,810	58	2,476 [a]
1948	4,300	65	2,654 [a]
1945–48	16,983		10,648

[a] Estimates based on the average Romanian ratio of exports to output.

Sources:

Output, 1945–1948: UNSY 1955, New York, 1956, p. 144.

Exports, 1945: "Les petroles roumains" (Romanian Petroleum) in *EC*, II, 12 (May 1947), p. 65, based on data previously published by Mihail Pizanty in the *Monitorul Petrolului Românesc* (The Monitor of the Romanian Petroleum).

1946: E. A. Bell, "Romania to Revise Exports," in *World Petroleum*, New York, Nov. 4, 1947, p. 90. Also I. Schönfeld, "Problema Petrolului Românesc" (The Problem of Romanian Petroleum), *PE*, No. 1, February 1948.

TABLE 44. ROMANIA: EXPORTS OF PETROLEUM IN 1945 AND 1946

	1945		1946	
Destination	Tons	%	Tons	%
Soviet Union				
Art. X, Armistice Convention [a]	418,254	13.18	[b]	
Art. XI, Armistice Convention [c]	2,541,592	80.12	1,833,025	78.10
Commercial agreements	181,948	5.73	409,310	17.44
East European countries	8,893	0.27	76,030	3.24
Other	293		120	
Export as ship's fuel	21,020	0.66	28,300	1.20
Total	3,172,000	99.96	2,346,785	99.98

[a] Provisions for the Soviet occupation forces.

[b] Not available.

[c] Deliveries in the reparations account.

Sources:

"Les Pétroles roumains," *op. cit.*, p. 65, and E. A. Bell, "Romania to Revise Exports," *op. cit.*, p. 90.

TABLE 45. ROMANIA: DELIVERIES OF PETROLEUM PRODUCTS (ON THE BASIS OF THE ARMISTICE CONVENTION), SEPTEMBER 1944 TO SEPTEMBER 1946

(in tons)

	Sept. 12, 1944–Sept. 11, 1945			Sept. 12, 1945–Sept. 11, 1946		
Products	Quantity to be delivered	Actually delivered	Difference, %	Quantity to be delivered	Actually delivered	Difference, %
Gasoline	432,000	791,893	+83	870,000	890,750	+2
Kerosene	210,000	311,662	+48	270,000	301,768	+12
Fuel oil [a]	518,800	1,257,358	+142	180,000	207,656	+15
Paraffin	2,000	135,580	+6,679	400,000	430,540	+8
Other derivative products [b]	3,000	177	−94	2,000	2,311	+16
Petroleum crude	550,000	27,700	−95	[c]	[c]	
Total	1,715,800	2,524,370	+47	1,722,000	1,833,025	+6

[a] Including gas oil in 1944–45.
[b] Including residual oil in 1945–46.
[c] Nil.

Source: Unified table based on *Monitorul Petrolului Romănesc, op. cit.*; data communicated by M. Pizanty. Cf. "Les Pétroles roumains," *op. cit.*, p. 66.

At that time, as shown by the trend in the United States, the world market prices of refined products, gasoline, kerosene, and fuel oil, had increased substantially. The index of average United States prices for gasoline at refineries, on a basis of 1938 = 100, had risen to 112 in 1945, 128 in 1946, and 170 in 1947; for kerosene and fuel oil, on the same basis, to 104 in 1945, 121 in 1946, and 169 in 1947.[12] Yet the Soviet Union was receiving Romanian reparations deliveries of highly refined oil products at an increase of only 10 per cent over the average 1938 prices.

Article XII of the Soviet-Romanian Armistice Convention of September 1944 foresaw the "restitution, in good shape, to the Soviet Union, of all the goods and materials taken by Romanian troops from the territory of the Soviet Union." The value of the goods "evacuated or taken away from the Ukraine, Bessarabia, and Bukovina" (the last two had been Romanian provinces up to 1940) was established at 950 billion lei ($508.5 million at the 1945 rate of 1,868 lei per United States dollar). The deliveries were to consist mainly of 1 million tons of grain, over 300,000 head of livestock, 60,000 tons of various processed foods, and rolling stock. By the end of September 1945 roughly one-third of this total had been delivered, mainly 474,000 tons of grain

[12] Cf. *The Petroleum Data Book,* H. J. Struth, editor, Petroleum Engineer Publishing Co., Dallas, 1948, p. F, 44.

and 100,000 head of animals valued at 350 billion lei.[13] The balance of 600 billion lei due at that time was halved by the Soviet Union and the term of delivery extended for three years. These heavy levies, the requisitions made by the Soviet troops stationed in Romania, and a severe drought combined to overtax the resources of the country to such an extent that as early as 1945 the Soviet Union not only had to cancel some Romanian deliveries of cereals but also, apparently, to "credit" Romania with grain. In September of that year the Russians lent 300,000 tons of grain to the Romanians, and in April 1946 some additional hundred thousand tons "until the new crop" should be ready.[14]

Polish Coal

Although Poland was an ally during the war and therefore enjoyed a postwar status different from that of Hungary and Romania, a special convention enabled the Soviet Union to receive Polish coal at an admittedly low price. This convention, signed in Moscow August 16, 1945, exactly two weeks after the Potsdam agreement, provided that Poland would receive from the Soviet Union (1) 15 per cent of the material requisitioned by the latter in the Soviet zone of occupation in Germany during the period after the Potsdam conference; (2) 15 per cent of the industrial equipment that the Soviet Union was entitled to receive as reparations from the Western zones of Germany. The Soviet Union renounced all claims to German property located in Poland (including the part of Germany passed to Poland). In return, Poland agreed to send to the Soviet Union from 1946 on and during the occupation of Germany, *at a special price,* the following quantities of coal: 8 million tons during the first year, 13 million tons during the four subsequent years (1947–50), and 12 million tons each succeeding year of occupation.[15]

[13] The figures on the structure of these deliveries can be found in the London *Economist* of October 20, 1945. They are substantiated by the fact that the Soviet Union acknowledged the receipt of 350 billion lei' worth of goods.

[14] Listing these short-term credits of grain, but forgetting the previous heavy Romanian deliveries, the official *Romanian News* wrote in 1949:

> The fear of starvation has been eliminated [in 1945] thanks to the same true friend, the Soviet Union. [The working people] know that thanks to this brotherly help, welfare was able to start in the country. [Cf. "Romania's Economy Boosted by Soviet Help," *RN,* August 21, 1949.]

[15] Cf. Agreement between the Government of the USSR and the Provisional Government of National Unity of the Polish Republic for Damages Caused by German Occupation; Bulletin of US Department of State, *Polish-Soviet Treaties on the*

Commenting on this agreement early in 1946, the chief Polish economic planner, Hilary Minc, supported it in the following terms:

> The delivery of this coal (at a special reduced price) is tied to the delivery by the USSR of merchandise out of the German reparations, machines, motors, industrial installations, commercial ships, etc. These deliveries have been conceived in such a way that the losses incurred from the export of "reparations coal" at a reduced price should be entirely compensated, and even with a surplus, by the import of "reparations commodities," that is, without any detriment to our economic equilibrium.[16]

The large quotas foreseen in 1945 were modified in March 1947, and the Polish exports of "reparations coal" to the Soviet Union were cut from 13 million tons to 6.5 per annum. The Soviet deliveries stopped in 1948. In mid-1953, on the basis of a Soviet-East German agreement, both the Soviet Union and Poland renounced "all German reparations deliveries in any form as of January 1, 1954," [17] thus implicitly ending also the Polish obligation of counterpayment to Russia for reparations. However, the Polish coal deliveries at a low price apparently continued even afterwards. Thus, it seems that despite the early inclination of the Soviet leaders to place within legalistic frameworks their economic relations with the East European countries, in the long run, in such serious matters as Polish coal or Romanian oil, they simply ignored the question of whether or not those frameworks were still valid.

After the upheavals in the autumn of 1956 in Poland and Hungary, and the accession to power of Wladyslav Gomulka, the Soviet government was finally forced to liquidate the "past relations of inequality among socialist states" and reimburse Poland for the losses incurred because of the coal agreement. Consequently, as a compensation, the Soviet government cancelled the outstanding Polish

Frontier and Reparations, August 16, 1945, Vol. XIV, No. 348, March 3, 1946, p. 343. According to the Potsdam agreement the Soviet Union was to obtain 30 per cent of the reparations taken in the Western zones of Germany but had to furnish in turn Soviet merchandise as counterpayment for 15 of this 30 per cent. Poland thus undertook to rèimburse the Soviet Union for part of the German reparations, for which the Soviet Union itself was supposed to reimburse the Western powers.

[16] Speech at the Congress of the Soviet-Polish Friendship Association, June 2, 1946, *Rzeczspospolita,* June 4, 1946.

[17] A. Konoplev, "O znachenii ekonomicheskoi chasti Sovetsko-Germanskogo Soglasheniia" (On the Significance of the Economic Part of the Soviet-German Agreement), in *Novoe Vremia* (New Times), No. 36, Sept. 2, 1953, p. 10.

debts to Russia by half a billion dollars.[18] Thus, it took no less than the bloody upheavals of 1956 [19] which deeply shook the Communist regimes in the area, to force the Russians to bring to an end the low-paid Polish coal deliveries.

Impact of Reparations and Summary

The reparations deliveries just discussed began at a time when the East European countries had to cope with the grave problems of rehabilitation after the war, among them the reconstruction of the export and consumers' goods industries supplying the home market. After 1947–48 reparations continued until 1953 generally in what had become fully employed economies. Their effects were therefore different in the two periods.

In the past Hungary and Romania had relied on export surpluses (i.e., active commercial balances) in order to make financial and administrative payments. In the conditions of the early postwar period, when these economies were greatly disorganized, the necessity of achieving export surpluses for reparations deliveries led to the systematic depression of the level of imports. In Hungary, for instance, exports amounted to about a third of the prewar level (of this third 60 to 70 per cent were reparations), which meant that this country was deprived of foreign exchange with which to finance her imports. Depressed imports, restricted investment possibilities, and the necessity of meeting the fixed reparations obligations led to the selling of shares to the Soviet Union, as with the Petroşani mines. After 1947–48, as both national income and exports increased, the burden of reparations eased, notwithstanding the fact that the total of the goods delivered remained substantial. Thus, according to the estimates of the Three-Year Plan, reparations were to absorb some 10 per cent of the net material product (national income in the Marxian sense, i.e., excluding services) in 1946–47, and some 7 per cent during each of the Plan years, that is, 1947–48, 1948–49, and 1949–50.

If we try to illustrate the impact of reparations by the budget expenditures, some objections must be met. It is contended that the reparations "by no means represent[ed] an unmitigated burden,"—at least up to 1948. "Without this activity [created by the reparations

[18] See: *Discours de W. Gomulka du 29 Novembre 1956* (Speech of W. Gomulka of Nov. 29, 1956), publ. by *Bulletin* (Bureau of Polish Information), Paris, December 1956, p. 6 ff.

[19] See the Introduction.

obligations], unemployment would [have been] considerably higher than it is now," noted V. M. Dean.[20] The Russians asserted that the reparations deliveries "do not prejudice the fulfillment of the economic plans of these countries, but, on the contrary, help to raise their industrial production."[21]

These opinions seem to us hardly acceptable. There was an outlet for Polish coal and Romanian oil in the West as well as in the East. Furthermore, new imports of both raw materials and machinery could have been obtained in return without reducing domestic employment. The arguments about "unemployment" as the only alternative to reparations deliveries are not convincing.

As already stated, the goods to be delivered had to be purchased by the respective governments on the domestic market from the newly set up joint companies, and the value of the goods was a large budget item. Some indications of the magnitude can be obtained from the proposed budgets of Hungary and Romania for 1946–47 and 1947–48. It appears from the Hungarian figures (see Table 46) that reparations were to be 26.4 per cent of total expenditures in 1946–47 and 17.8 per cent in 1947–48. The reduction of reparations deliveries could have been accompanied by a rather substantial increase in the share of investments. If a reduction in reparations had been accompanied by an equal increase in investment, investment would have amounted to 10.6 per cent of expenditures in 1947–48 compared with 5.7 per cent in 1946–47.[22]

This impact of reparations on the level of investments can also be traced through the Romanian official figures (see Table 47). In Romania the reparations were scheduled to absorb from the total expenditures no less than 37.5 per cent in 1946–47 and to increase to 46.6 per cent in 1947–48! Similarly, the relative share of the invest-

20 Vera Micheles Dean, "Economic Trends in Eastern Europe, I, II," *Foreign Policy Reports,* April 1 and 15, 1948, p. 36.

21 D. Petrovski, "Economic Development in the Countries of People's Democracy," *New Times,* No. 8, 1949, pp. 6–10.

22 It is interesting to note that Kemény, in his valuable study already quoted, remarks in relation to this problem:

> The reduction of reparation [of July 1948] was calculated to save budget expenditure exceeding 600 million forint a year; it was assumed that this amount could be diverted to investment. Though later on these hopes turned out to be unfounded, the prospect of saving on reparation account was used as an argument in favour of stepping up the capital programme. In fact more than the amount of the reduction was required for the increase in defense expenditure, for the Plan, after its successful start, was more closely linked with military preparedness. [George Kemény, *op. cit.*, p. 61.]

TABLE 46. HUNGARY: BUDGETS (EXPENDITURE), 1946–47, 1947–48. PROVISIONAL ESTIMATES

(in million forints)

	1946–47			1947–48		
	Absolute figures		Percentages	Absolute figures		Percentages
	Detail	Main headings	% of total expenditure	Detail	Main headings	% of total expenditure
I						
Credits, general						
State administration		3,253.2	73.6		6,212.5	82.2
Transitory expenditure	1,699.9		38.5	3,015.8		39.9
Wages and pensions	1,170.0		26.5	2,097.2		27.7
Investments	253.7		5.7	800.0		10.6
Subsidy, public debt	129.6		2.9	299.5		3.3
II						
International obligations		1,167.5	26.4		1,341.1	17.8
Total expenditure		4,420.7	100.0		7,553.6	100.0

Source: *GT*, II, 3, March 1948, p. 177.

ments was to decrease from 5.4 per cent in 1946–47 to 3.1 per cent in the following year.

In fact, in both countries the forecasts of reparations costs turned out to be less than the actual charges. According to official Hungarian figures available for 1946–47, the actual results were as follows: total expenditure, 3,701.9 million forints; reparations, 1,436.1 million, or 38.8 per cent.[23] In Romania run-away inflation, still in full swing at the time, pushed the actual expenditures for the 1946–47 fiscal year from the 5.07 billion estimated to 11.35 billion lei.[24]

As could have been expected for small and underdeveloped countries, the burden of reparations taken from current output depressed the level of capital formation, absorbed a large part of their savings, and shook their financial structures to the very foundations.

Precisely because of these depressing effects the Russians constantly adjusted their reparations requirements, taking into consideration both

[23] *Monthly Bulletin of the National Bank of Hungary*, No. 7–8 (July–August 1947), p. 182, and No. 9 (September 1948), p. 213 (which also furnishes "actual results" for certain months of 1948).

[24] Same source as for Table 47.

TABLE 47. ROMANIA: BUDGETS (EXPENDITURE), 1946–47, 1947–48. PROVISIONAL ESTIMATES

(in million lei)

	1946–47			1947–48		
	Absolute figures		Percentages	Absolute figures		Percentages
	Detail	Main headings	% of total expenditure	Detail	Main headings	% of total expenditure
I						
Credits, general						
State administration		2,470.8	48.7		50,900.0	49.5
Interior	593.7		11.7	18,137.0		17.7
Military expenditure	434.5		8.6	5,714.3		5.5
National economy	218.4		4.3	6,507.3		6.3
Investments	274.8		5.4	3,164.6		3.1
Education, social security, and public debt	889.9		17.6	16,628.4		16.1
Debts, past accounts	59.5		1.1	748.4		0.7
II						
Special credits		700.0	13.8		4,000.0	3.9
III						
International obligations		1,900.0	37.5		48,000.0	46.6
Total expenditures		5,070.8	100.0		102,900.0	100.0

Source: "Le Budget général de l'état" (The General State Budget), *Bulletin d'information et de documentation*, National Bank of Romania, XIX, June 1947, pp. 57–60.

political and economic factors. Having imposed drastic conditions at the beginning, the Russians could continuously play the role of "lenient friend" by reducing the bill at the most critical moments.[25]

[25] Neither the Russians nor the Hungarian or Romanian Communists lost an occasion to praise these concessions skyhigh. Referring to the completion of the reparations, the Hungarian official Communist daily newspaper *Szabad Nép* (Free People) wrote on January 24, 1953:

> When the Soviet Union realized that the people of Hungary were making such a sincere effort to achieve economic stability and to strengthen democracy, she made increasingly great concessions. These concessions constituted a tremendous aid, assisting the country in recovery from the ravages of war, overcoming the damages of inflation and starting the country on the road of Socialist construction. . . . How infinitely stupid and inefficient is the slandering campaign of English-American reactionary imperialism which for eight years has been parroting that Hungary's economy will not survive the reparations.

According to this kind of logic the reparations to the Soviet Union are not a burden, but the Soviet concessions, i.e., the reduction of the reparations, are "a tremendous aid, assisting the country in recovery from the ravages of war . . ." (!)

To summarize:

Reparations and payment of the so-called "debts" to Germany decreased capital formation in reparations-paying countries, especially during the reconstruction period (1945–48). The burden was lessened in the second period (after 1948) not so much by the reduction of the reparations bills as such, since much of this reduction was offset by the obligation of now paying the German debts, but by the over-all increase in output and trade achieved after a very strenuous reconstruction period in which consumption had been reduced to a minimum.

The over-all contribution to the Soviet Union of reparations, restitutions, etc., was much more substantial than the value totals would suggest. For the period up to the reduction in July 1948 the per annum deliveries of Hungary and Romania amounted, respectively, to 18–19 million, and 40.8 million 1938-dollars and consisted not only of the key products already mentioned but also such goods as grain and cattle in a period marked by drought and scarcity. After the 1948 reductions the scheduled deliveries in the reparations account proper (not including the German "debt") were to amount per year, as already stated, for Hungary and Romania to 16.4 and 18.3 million 1938-dollars' worth of goods, respectively.

The reparations have been a clear expression of the fact that, from the economic point of view, the Soviet Union was considering the East European countries as *autonomous* units having their own problems of investment, balance of payments, and so on. Drastic requirements by the victor of the vanquished, low prices, and pressing demands for advance deliveries [26] highlighted the conflicting interests between the Soviet Union and the countries absorbed into its orbit both during the reconstruction period and during the period of "consolidation" of the Communist regimes.

The reparations were but one facet of Soviet policy: a second, to which we turn now, is that of the joint companies with Soviet partnership.

Various Types of Joint Companies

Before determining the structure and extent of the Soviet companies in Eastern Europe as they developed during the period extending from the beginning of 1945 to mid-1954, we should make some preliminary

[26] Cf. for Hungary, "Report of the Board of Directors on the Course of Business in 1947," *op. cit.*, pp. xiv–xv (concerning notably the 1947 deliveries); for Romania, see the section dealing with petroleum deliveries, pp. 172 ff.

remarks on the concept of "mixed companies" as it crystallized from the experience of the Soviet Union itself.

Before World War II many "mixed companies," i.e., companies with Soviet and foreign capital, functioned in the Soviet Union. In a documented study of these companies S. K. Margold supplies the following definition:

> A mixed company is a partnership between the Soviet Union and a foreign firm or a foreign government in which the Soviet Union retains 50 per cent. In this partnership the Soviet Union is represented by one of the State-controlled economic or trading enterprises. The company may be organized as a limited dividend corporation, a stock company or a corporation. Whichever it is, it is required to prepare annual plans and maintain definite import and export quotas as provided in the contract.[27]

Three basic types of joint companies functioned in the Soviet Union or with Soviet capital, carrying out, respectively:

1. Operating concessions, for mining, agricultural exploitation, and transport in the Soviet Union.

2. Technical aid contracts, for the establishment and equipping of plants, patents, consultative services, etc., in the Soviet Union.

3. Agency agreements, for marketing Soviet merchandise abroad.

Eager to obtain the cooperation of foreign capital, to master new technical skills, and to break the economic isolation of the country, the Russians set liberal conditions for foreign firms, granting profits ranging from 10 to 20 per cent per year and guaranteeing the companies opportunity to buy enough of their own output to assure them a specified profit. Most of the companies with operating concessions and even more of those with technical aid contracts (for advice and assistance on a royalty basis) were liquidated or had their interests purchased *in toto* by the Soviet Union in the thirties; the remaining ones were limited in number and played a quite minor role in the Soviet economy. The most successful expansion was in the agency agreement companies for the marketing abroad of various Russian produce such as grain, eggs, etc.

This past experience of Soviet association with foreign firms, capital, and governments, and with integration of joint companies in the planned structure, was put to ample use by the Soviet Union in the period 1945–54 in the establishment of various partnerships with the

[27] Stela K. Margold, *Let's Do Business with Russia,* Harper & Bros., New York, 1948, pp. 71–72.

East European governments. Now the prewar situation appeared, so to speak, reversed, and it was the Soviet Union that assumed the role of exporter of capital, not because she was actually exporting any funds but because the heritage of German assets placed in her hands an already established network of all types of firms and companies. The East European countries appeared to play the former role of the Soviet Union, not because they were eager to obtain Soviet cooperation but because, with the extensive positions acquired by that country in their economies, they were forced to accept this "partnership."

In the closing days of the war the Soviet Union seemed to have little concern for the formation of interlocked companies in Eastern Europe. Uncertainty as to the postwar political status of the region and the pressing nature of Soviet needs at first encouraged a policy of wholesale dismantlement of the former German plants and the transportation to the Soviet Union of any movable "war booty." This policy was subsequently abandoned as the Russians realized that such transfers usually represented only the squandering of equipment;[28] even when equipment could be successfully transported to the Soviet Union, obviously it was still necessary to construct a plant, to draw on Soviet labor, and to exert a drain on local resources in order to put it to use. From this and other considerations of a political nature, there evolved rapidly the conception of utilizing most of the equipment on the spot. Once the decision to abandon the dismantling of equipment had been reached, the Russians had to determine: (*a*) which enterprises should be kept as pure Soviet undertakings in the East European countries; (*b*) which assets should be used as the Soviet contribution toward the formation of joint companies, i.e., of Soviet partnerships with the respective countries; (*c*) which plants, machinery, or movables, such as ships or rolling stock, should be sold back to the respective countries. The comprehensive character of German companies, which is illustrated

[28] After an inquiry in Hungary early in 1948, a French observer described this first well-known period which left a trail of rusting equipment from the heart of Europe to the border of the Soviet Union:

> The Hungarian entrepreneurs talk with reticence about the equipment and the stock of raw materials taken by the Russians at the time when Hungary was still a zone of war operations. They avoided making estimates. The total is perhaps of the order of $200 million which should be added to the $600–800 million worth of goods taken by the Germans. But, curiously enough, the machines taken by the Russians have only rarely reached the plants for which they were meant. Directed towards the East, the equipment has almost always been unloaded at various train stations every time that the Russian commandery needed a train. We have seen pictures taken near the Csop region, in the Subcarpathian Ukraine: as far as the eyes can see, dismantled machines rust on each side of the rails, lost for everybody. . . . [Cf. *Le Monde* (The World), Paris, February 9, 1948.]

in the case of Hungary by the data presented below, in Appendix 1 of this chapter, made this choice a difficult one. In fact, the choice usually was neither immediate nor definitive. After the establishment of an exhaustive inventory of the goods,and assets considered as having been owned by the Germans, the Russians continually revised the status of certain enterprises, keeping them for a while as Soviet undertakings, making them the Soviet contribution in a joint company, swapping them against some other assets, or simply selling them back to the local government.

Broadly speaking, the Russians retained as pure Soviet companies (i.e., those directly managed by Soviet corporations) financial and distribution organizations. They used their shares in mining and manufacture mostly as contributions toward the formation of joint companies, a solution which left to the local partner the problem of supplying raw materials and labor. The mechanism of transferring shares to the various Soviet corporations and the process of forming the joint companies on the basis of these shares are illustrated with a series of documents in Appendix 2 of this chapter.

We turn now to the study of the development of the joint companies and Soviet undertakings in Hungary, Romania, and Bulgaria during the decade extending from the end of 1944 to the end of 1954. Then, after a brief examination of the Yugoslav experience with the Soviet economic partnership, we shall try to point out the prospects after the purchase by these countries of most of the Soviet-owned shares.

The Joint Companies and the Soviet Undertakings: in Hungary

The varied character of the German industrial enterprises which became the property of the Soviet Union at the end of the war can be seen easily from Table 48, based on an official list published by the Hungarian government early in 1947 on the occasion of the recording of claims referring to German assets.[29] There were transferred *in toto* to Soviet ownership 17 financial institutions, 82 mining and manufacturing firms of all types, 2 electric power-generating and -distributing companies, 1 provincial railroad line, 2 shipping companies (operating lines), 31 commercial agencies and bureaus, and 63 miscellaneous businesses. Out of the total of 201 firms, 132 firms organized as stock com-

[29] The nominal classification of the companies concerned is to be found below, in Appendix 1 of this chapter.

Table 48. Hungary: German Assets Transferred to the Soviet Union [a]

(classification by type of business)

Financial institutions		Mining and manufacturing		Fuel and power		Transport		Trade and commerce		Miscellaneous		Total
Stock Companies (Groups I and II of the official list)												
Banks	2	Metals and metal products	14	Electric power	2	Railroad	1	Shipping and travel bureaus	5	Miscellaneous	10	
Insurance companies	11	Mining and mining works	4	Charcoal products	1	Shipping	2	Commercial agencies	17	Not classified	13	
		Textiles	14			Moving	2					
		Construction materials	4									
		Chemicals	7									
		Laboratory and medical supplies	6									
		Electrical appliances	5									
		Food-processing	3									
		Lumber	3									
		Paper and packaging	1									
		Glass-manufacturing	2									
		Shoe-manufacturing	2									
		Ship construction	1									
Total	13		66		3		5		22		23	132
Firms Belonging to Individuals, Cooperatives, and Societies with Limited Responsibility (Group III of the official list)												
Savings banks	4	Metals and metal works	6	[b]		[b]		Commercial agencies	9	Miscellaneous	10	
		Textiles	3							Not classified	30	
		Industrial supplies and appliances	4									
		Other manufacturers	3									
Total	4		16						9		40	69
Grand total	17		82		3		5		31		63	201

[a] Data from the official list of March 8, 1947. Cf. Annex to Decree #3080-1947, *Magyar Közlöny, Rendeletek Tára* (Official Journal of Hungary, Collection of Decrees), No. 56, March 8, 1947, pp. 561–565.

[b] Nil.

panies were important in insurance, metal-manufacturing, textiles, and trade and commerce. Several of them were markedly important: the First Danube Steamship Corporation, for instance, which had left the shipping business (this had passed into the hands of a purely Hungarian company before the war), remained significant in the coal-mining business because of its control of the coal mines in the county of Baranya; Felton and Guilleaume Company had practically a monopoly position in the fields of steel cables, electrical insulation, and similar products; Domestic Textile Weaving and Cloth Manufacturing Company constituted a considerable part of the wool industry of the country; Linen, Jute, and Textile Industry Corporation had an outstanding position in the jute business. Although individually only one of them was important, the textile companies together accounted for a considerable part of the textile industry. Companies in various other branches, though relatively not so important, conducted a notable portion of the business in their fields (e.g., Otis Elevator Company, European Freight and Luggage Company).[30]

The Russians also acquired various blocks of shares, such as the shares of the National Bank of Hungary mentioned earlier, a block of shares of the Hungarian General Credit Bank which had previously belonged to the Dresdner Bank, and some shares of such key companies as the big metallurgical complex Manfred Weiss at Csepel.

Although most of the companies on the above list were at first operated as Soviet undertakings, the Russians moved early in 1946 toward the formation of joint companies in the fields of transportation and mining, of which the principal ones were:

1. The Soviet-Hungarian company for navigation on the Danube: Meszhart.[31] The Soviet contributions were some German shares and former Hungarian vessels retaken from the Germans. Hungary placed at the disposition of the new company her port facilities and the warehouses and buildings pertaining thereto. At its formation, Meszhart possessed a total tonnage of 30,500 tons, one-fourth the prewar Hungarian Danubian flotilla, consisting of various types of vessels, tugboats, etc.

2. The Soviet-Hungarian company for civil aviation: Maszovlet.[32]

[30] The author acknowledges with thanks the valuable comments on the importance and activity of the Hungarian companies kindly supplied by Dr. Victor Bátor.

[31] Status fixed by Order in Council of Ministers #4730/ME, Budapest, May 4, 1946.

[32] Status: Order in Council #4740/ME, Budapest, May 4, 1946.

The Soviet contribution consisted mostly of aircraft; Hungary guaranteed the use of *all* her civil airports and hangars. The Soviet Union extended a similar guarantee but only on the route connecting Hungary to the Soviet Union.

3. The Soviet-Hungarian company for prospecting, production, drilling (on behalf of this or any other company), and marketing of oil: Maszovol.[33]

4. The Soviet-Hungarian company for the processing of crude oil for Maszovol and other companies and the marketing of oil products: Molaj.[34] The companies converted into Maszovol and Molaj, respectively, were the former Manat, Ltd., and Ornstein and Koppel, Ltd.[35] The Soviet contribution was the former German General Crude Oil Refining Company and the concessions obtained during the war in the county of Bekes by the German firm Wintershall A.G. Hungary agreed to place at the disposition of these companies the oil royalties received from the Lipse oil fields (fields not included in the agreement), which were estimated at some 15 per cent of the production of these fields.[36]

5. The Soviet-Hungarian company for mining, by lease or purchase, and production of all kinds of minerals, especially bauxite, and for the manufacture of alum earth, aluminum, and alloys: Magyar Bauxite Banya (Hungarian Bauxite Mine)–Soviet-Hungarian Bauxite Aluminum Co.

6. The Soviet-Hungarian company for the construction and assembly of plants for the bauxite industry: Danube Valley Alum Earth Co. The interesting feature of this company is that its shares were held one-third by the Soviet Union, one-third by the Hungarian Treasury, and one-third by the Magyar Bauxite Banya Joint Company.[37] The Soviet contribution to these companies consisted mainly of the assets of the Transdanubian Bauxite Corporation.

Once constituted, these companies played an important role only in civil aviation and bauxite mining (in the latter case the two companies just cited controlled 40 per cent of the output).[38] It was at first

[33] Articles of association of Maszovol: cf. Order in Council #8170/ME, Budapest, July 23, 1946.

[34] Cf. Order in Council #8801/ME, Budapest, July 25, 1946.

[35] *Monthly Bulletin of the National Bank of Hungary*, new series, No. 7–9, (July–September 1946).

[36] *Ibid.*

[37] Cf. *Monthly Bulletin of the National Bank of Hungary*, new series, No. 7–9, (July–September 1946).

[38] "L'Industrie hongroise depuis la fin de la guerre" (Hungarian Industry since the War), in *EC*, IV, 3 (May–June 1949), p. 35.

rather modest in navigation, and insignificant in oil exploitation (where the Hungarian-American company, Maort, dominated the principal oil fields of Transdanubia).

According to data released early in 1948, the Soviet undertakings and the Soviet-Hungarian joint companies, 40 Soviet-owned corporations and 8 joint companies with a total of 3,876 plants, employed 2.6 per cent and 1.1 per cent, respectively, of the total gainfully employed in the manufacturing industries. The combined Soviet shares of the joint companies and the Soviet undertakings employed 3.1 per cent of the gainfully employed in manufacture, 1.7 per cent of the total number of generators, and 2.6 per cent of the operating electromotors. The combined share of the Soviet undertaking and the joint companies in mining and blast furnaces was 12.3 per cent of the total employed in these fields.[39]

Nationalization and the seizure of all foreign concerns except the Russian ones, completed in 1949, increased the economic importance of the Russian concerns in various fields. The existing joint companies were consolidated, and their field of operation was extended. According to data released in 1954, there were then in operation: 1. Meszhart, whose importance in the Soviet navigation of the Danube will be discussed below; 2. Maszovlet (civil aviation); 3. Masolaj, i.e., the consolidated group, Maszoval-Molaj, still excluded from the Transdanubian fields but accepted for contracting work on behalf of the Hungarian government in that region; 4. Maszobal, a consolidated bauxite aluminum company; 5. Danube Valley Alum Earth Co.

The German spoils helped in financing and consolidating the more thriving Soviet undertakings in Hungary. The already mentioned agreement on German debts supplied a fund of 30 million dollars for the financing of the companies with Soviet partnership. Various agreements between 1952 and 1954 provided for the sale by the Soviet Union to the Hungarian government of the former German holdings located in Hungary which were thus turned into ready cash for new Soviet purchases. Thus, by means of payments to the Soviet Union of the so-called "debts" to Germany, proceeds from the sale of undertakings, and profits, the Soviet enterprises fed upon themselves in order to consolidate their position in the Hungarian economy.

[39] Cf. *Közgazdaság* (Public Economy), Budapest, April 8, 1948, quoted in "L'Industrie hongroise . . ." *op. cit.*, p. 36; also *HB*, No. 26, May 10, 1948. The latter gives employment in the Soviet-owned group as 3.6 per cent of the total man power (instead of 3.1 per cent).

Romania

The Soviet Union acquired even more extensive German assets in Romania than in Hungary. In Romania they included some 397 commercial and industrial enterprises, 33 oil and mining firms, and 97 banks and insurance corporations.[40] These assets assumed immediate importance. As can be seen from Table 49, which lists the 15 joint

Table 49. Romania: The Soviet-Romanian Companies in Activity up to 1954

No.	Companies	Date of Respective Soviet-Romanian Convention [a]	Field of Operation [b]
1	Sovrompetrol	July 17, 1945	Oil exploitation
2	Sovromtransport	July 19, 1945	Road, river, and maritime transport
3	Tars	Oct. 26, 1945	Air transport
4	Sovrombanc	Oct. 26, 1945	Banking
5	Sovromlemn	Mar. 20, 1946	Wood exploitation
6	Sovromchim	Nov. 1, 1948	Chemical production
7	Sovromtractor	Nov. 1, 1948	Tractor-manufacturing
8	Sovromgaz	Feb. 20, 1949	Natural gas exploitation
9	Sovromcărbune	July 4, 1949	Coal exploitation
10	Sovrommetal	July 4, 1949	Metallurgy
11	Sovromconstrucţii	July 4, 1949	Construction
12	Sovromasigurări	Aug. 14, 1949	Insurance
13	Sovromutilaj	Aug. 15, 1952	Oil equipment
14	Sovromnaval	Aug. 15, 1952	Ship-building
15	Sovromcvarţ	Aug. 15, 1952	Uranium-mining

[a] The date of signature of the convention precedes, sometimes by months, the date of establishment of the company and the beginning of its activity.

[b] A Soviet-Romanian company, Sovromfilm, for film making, formed in 1949, was dissolved on July 20, 1952.

companies in activity up to 1954 and their respective dates of formation, the network of Soviet-Romanian companies expanded, so to speak, by waves, the most important of which occurred in 1945 (at the end of the war) and in 1949 (on the eve of the first Romanian Five-Year Plan).

[40] *Observations Concernant le Projet de Traité de Paix avec la Roumanie* (Observations Concerning the Draft Peace Treaty with Rumania), Ministère des finances de Roumanie (Ministry of Finance of Romania), Paris, 1946, p. 24.

Among the most significant Soviet-Romanian joint companies of the operating-concession type [41] must be noted the following:

1. The Soviet-Romanian company "for the exploration, exploitation, refining, and marketing of crude oil and its products": Sovrompetrol.[42] The Soviet contribution was the German oil shares of Romanian companies transferred to Soviet ownership, representing in 1945 12.5 per cent of the total capital of the active oil companies in Romania.[43] At its formation this company apparently played a secondary role; the British and American companies and the Romanian companies not merged with Sovrompetrol (the four big companies Astra-Română, Româno-Americana, Steaua Română, and Unirea) were still producing 60 per cent of the total oil output.[44]

2. The Soviet-Romanian company for road, river, and maritime transportation: Sovromtransport. The Soviet contribution consisted, *inter alia,* of previously Romanian-owned boats seized as war booty from the Germans by the Soviet troops. As appears from Table 50,

TABLE 50. ROMANIA: SHIPS PUBLICLY AND PRIVATELY OWNED, 1939 AND 1946

	1939		1946	
Ships	Number	Capacity, meter tons	Number	Capacity, meter tons
Romanian vessels				
Seagoing	25	120,732	2	[a]
Danube [b]	725	538,964	642	238,005
Sovromtransport				
All types			186	118,694

[a] Not available.

[b] Passenger boats, tugboats, barges, motor tankers, oil tankers.

Sources: Anuarul Statistic al României 1939 şi 1940, op. cit.; *CS*, No. 13, June 15, 1946; also, I. Zeigher, "La Collaboration roumano-soviétique" (Romanian-Soviet Collaboration), in *PE*, No. 3, 1948.

Sovromtransport took over probably the largest of the former Romanian vessels. From an average of 743 metric tons per inland-waterway vessel in 1939, the Romanian-owned vessels had dropped in 1946

[41] By extension we have included in the operating concessions the financial joint companies functioning in the banking and insurance fields.

[42] See below, Appendix 2, Document 4, Convention for the Creation of Sovrompetrol; also Appendix 2, Annex 1 to Document 2, the oil shares transferred to the Soviet Union.

[43] Cf. I. Schönfeld, "Problema Petrolului Românesc," *op. cit.*

[44] *Ibid.*

to an average of 370 metric tons per unit. The Sovrom average in 1946 was 638 metric tons per unit. As the total number of inland-waterway vessels had been increased from 725 in 1939 to 828 units, it can be assumed that the vessels added must have been of very small tonnage.

3. The Soviet-Romanian joint company for civil aviation: Tars. The Soviet contribution was mainly aircraft. Romania placed at the disposition of the company all her airports, hangars, and similar installations and granted to the company the right of establishing air routes over all Romanian territory. The Soviet Union granted the company the right of establishing civil air routes over the Soviet area of the Black Sea "between the airports of Izmail, Odessa, Nikolaiev, Kherson, Yevpatoriia, Simferopol" [45] (i.e., over the southern part of the former Romanian province of Bessarabia and the shores of the Black Sea down to the Crimea).

4. The Soviet-Romanian joint banking company for financing Soviet undertakings and joint companies in Romania and commercial transactions between Romania and the Soviet Union: Sovrombanc. The capital for this company was subscribed in equal parts by Soviet and Romanian incorporators, the Soviet Union contributing the numerous banking shares acquired from the Germans.[46] From the beginning Sovrombanc controlled a very substantial part of Romanian finance and industry.[47]

5. The Soviet-Romanian joint company for the exploitation of coal: Sovromcărbune. This company, created in the summer of 1949, had a distinctive feature: the Soviet contribution consisted of the Petroşani coal mine shares obtained as reparations from Hungary in 1946 and 1947.[48]

6. The Soviet-Romanian joint company for metal and metal-working: Sovrommetal. This company grew out of the holdings of former German shares, companies, and agencies, i.e., shares of Reşiţa and of the metal-working factory Malaxa [49] and the important German iron and steel distributing agencies located in Bucharest.[50]

[45] *Bulletin d'information et de documentation,* National Bank of Romania, XVIII year, No. 10–12, October–December 1945, p. 23.

[46] See below, Appendix 2, Annex 2 to Document 2.

[47] See below, Appendix 2, Document 2.

[48] Cf. *supra,* p. 167.

[49] Cf. *supra,* Chapter 2, p. 38.

[50] Namely: 1. The steelworks Poldihütte (representing Poldihütte of Prague); 2. Oţelul Boehler, Inc.; 3. Trei Inele, Inc. (representing Usine Krupp); 4. Băncotescu şi Nicolau, Inc. (representing Alpine Gesellschaft); 5. Sarcomex, Inc. (representing Schoeller Bleckmann Stahlwerke of Vienna); 6. Roechling, Inc. (representing Roch-

7. The Soviet-Romanian joint company for insurance: Sovromasigurări. This company was constructed on a foundation of the very large former German interests. The Soviet Union acquired four former German companies in toto and important blocks of shares in others, a total of over 20 per cent of all the capital of the insurance companies operating in Romania in 1945.[51]

Among the companies formed on the basis of technical aid contracts must be counted mainly Sovromchim, Sovromtractor, Sovromutilaj, and Sovromnaval. Some German assets were used to form these also, but no data on the form or size of the Soviet investment were released.

The joint Soviet company system in Romania finally penetrated every essential economic activity. The German holdings served not only for the setting up of the system but also for the financing of it through a series of agreements concerning the former debts to Germany, the liquidation of certain war booty, and so on.[52] The total of these so-called debts, increased, as we have seen, by the obligation imposed on Romania to return the gold received from Germany in payment for the grain and oil removed by the latter from Romania,[53] has not been revealed.

Bulgaria

The Soviet Union entered into only a few "partnerships" in Bulgaria. Early in 1946 it formed the Soviet-Bulgarian Mining Company Gorubso; in 1949, the joint Soviet-Bulgarian civil aviation company

lengestahl G.m.b.H. Volklingen); 7. Rudolf Schmidt, Inc. Cf. Ministerial Decision #54305 of Sept. 26, 1944, concerning the freezing of hard metals, *Bulletin d'information et de documentation,* National Bank of Romania, XVII year, No. 5–6, May–June 1945, p. 205.

[51] Total Soviet holdings of German shares amounted to 101 million lei, as can be seen from the nominal Tables 1 and 2 given in the annex to Document 3 in Appendix 2 to this chapter. The total capital of the insurance companies functioning in Romania amounted to 499 million lei in 1943. Cf. V. Galatescu, "Les Sociétés privées d'assurances de Roumainie et la régie autonome des assurances d'état-R.A.A.S." (The Private Insurance Companies and the State Autonomous Insurance Administration in Romania), *Bulletin d'information et de documentation,* National Bank of Romania, XVII year, No. 7–9, July–September 1945, p. 6.

[52] Referring in 1949 to the aid extended by the Soviet Union from 1945 on, the official *Romanian News* listed (under the title "Romania's Economy Boosted by Soviet Help") the following items which involved dealings with war booty: "The restitution of the entire rolling stock used by the Soviet Army; the *renting* for two years of 6,398 German cars belonging to the Soviet Union; the restitution of 35 warships and of 26 commercial ships." Cf. *RN,* Aug. 21, 1949 (italics supplied).

[53] See Chapter 2, p. 39, note 22.

Tabso; and, early in 1950, the Korbso Company for shipbuilding and Sovbolstroi for both construction and building materials.[54]

In mining the Soviet Union stepped into the position first held by the French and later by the Germans. Tabso was the Bulgarian counterpart of similar companies established in Hungary and Romania insuring Soviet control over all the air routes and airports of those countries. Since the Bulgarian Danube flotilla has always been negligible,[55] the Soviet Union did not set up in Bulgaria a joint company for navigation. The last two companies were essentially vehicles for "technical aid contracts" based on Soviet equipment and consultative services.

All other financial claims of the Soviet Union against Bulgaria were settled by a protocol signed in January 1948. The amount due the Soviet Union for various German assets transferred to Soviet ownership was reduced from $9 million to $4.5 million. The Soviet Union waived claims of 2,970 million leva ($10.4 million) for damages caused to former German assets in Bulgaria during the period when they were under Bulgarian administration. Finally, as stated in the official communiqué, the Soviet Union agreed to transfer to Bulgaria the Soviet-owned commercial and transport enterprises in that country, including a credit institution, two small power stations, and various buildings and land, the total valued at 576 million leva ($2 million), for half that sum payable in Bulgarian leva at the disposition of the Soviet Union.[56]

Yugoslav Experiences of Economic Partnership with the Soviet Union

We have seen that the network of Soviet undertakings and joint companies described thus far was established on a foundation of German assets in the former "ex-enemy" countries. The Soviet Union established strategically important joint companies in Danube navi-

[54] Cf. law concerning establishment of Gorubso, in *Dărzhaven Vestnik* (Collection of Laws), No. 71, Sofia, March 23, 1946; registration edict of Tabso, *ibid.*, No. 120, May 28, 1949. The first mention of Soviet technical aid in ship-building dates from the spring of 1950, when it was stated that thanks to this help the commercial Bulgarian maritime vessel *B. Kasabov* was constructed in the port of Varna. Cf. E. Valev, *Narodnaia Respublika Bolgariia, op. cit.*, p. 116.

[55] Before the war its tonnage was less than 10,000 metric tons or one-tenth that of any other East European country. The present tonnage is of the same order.

[56] Cf. *Free Bulgaria,* August 1, 1948.

gation and civil aviation also in a former Allied country, Yugoslavia, without the benefit of German assets.

Two joint Yugoslav-Soviet companies, the Yugoslav-Soviet Danubian shipping company Juspad and the Yugoslav-Soviet civil air transport Justa, were founded early in 1947 and liquidated in the middle of 1949.[57] They shed light on the role of the Soviet Union in this type of company, for the Yugoslavs published various documents and stenographic reports, notably on the discussions exchanged with the Russians at the time of the liquidation of these companies.[58] The companies were organized on the already familiar pattern of stock companies, half the stock being bought by the Soviet Union and half by Yugoslavia. Most of this stock was to be acquired by each government through the investment of equipment, and the rest was to be paid for in money. At the time of the liquidation of Juspad the Soviet Union had not invested the nominal capital it was supposed to invest, but the Yugoslavs had contributed to the company's shipping pool 137 of the *best craft they had* (i.e., 14 tugboats, 103 barges, and 20 tankers), selected from the Yugoslav flotilla by Soviet experts. The rest of the Yugoslav vessels were left for the utilization of the Yugoslav State River Shipping Company.[59] By the end of 1948 "the Soviet partner [had] paid only 9.83 per cent of its share to Juspad, while the Yugoslav partner [had] paid . . . 76.25 per cent of its share." [60]

Shortly after the formation of this company, and contrary to Yugoslav wishes, Juspad entered into an agreement with other Soviet (joint) companies and ignored the Yugoslav State River Shipping Company interests. The companies which entered into this practical agreement were:

[57] The companies were formed under a convention concluded on Feb. 4, 1947, on the basis of the Agreement on Economic Cooperation between the Soviet Union and Yugoslavia of June 8, 1946. The proposal for liquidation of the companies was advanced by Yugoslavia in a note of March 16, 1949, accepted by the Soviet Union on March 25, 1949.

[58] Cf. "The Yugoslav-Soviet Juspad and Justa Companies as a Form of the Policy of Unequal Economic Relations," section of *White Book on Aggressive Activities by the Governments of the USSR, Poland, Czechoslovakia, Hungary, Rumania, Bulgaria and Albania towards Yugoslavia,* Ministry of Foreign Affairs of FPRY, Belgrade, 1951, pp. 321–332.

[59] During the liquidation negotiations, the Soviet delegate noted in his answer that even the best Yugoslav craft were actually "obsolete and needed much overhauling." The Yugoslav replied that that was true, but they were, however, their *best. Ibid.,* p. 327.

[60] Cf. Declaration of Dr. Joza Vilfan, Yugoslav delegate, Second Committee of the Fourth Session of the UN General Assembly, UN press release, Oct. 7, 1949.

1. The Soviet Danubian State Shipping Co.
2. Meszhart (Soviet-Hungarian Shipping Co.).
3. DDSG (former Austrian Shipping Co., passed under Soviet control).
4. Sovromtransport (Soviet-Romanian Shipping Co.).

The proposed draft of the agreement, though bilateral in form, meant in essence

> the establishment of a cartel of the foregoing shipping companies with very broad cooperation in every respect—tugboating, mutual assistance, port services, agency services, tariff consultations, etc.[61]

The Yugoslavs had proposed without success that the agreement should be signed jointly with each of the above-mentioned companies by Juspad and the Yugoslav State River Shipping Company, but the Soviet partner refused. The draft of the agreement was withdrawn, and Juspad entered into a tacit agreement with the above-mentioned companies. The effects of this *de facto* understanding on tugging and freight rates are clearly visible. Avoiding recourse to the Yugoslav shipping company for tugboat services, Juspad exchanged such services with the Soviet Danubian State Shipping Company, which was well entrenched in the Romanian and Hungarian Danube ports. Thus, during 1948, Juspad employed the Yugoslav State Company for services valued at 39,207 kilats, and the Soviet Danubian Shipping Company for services valued at 509,307 kilats. In return Juspad did a slightly larger amount of business for the latter company,[62] the profits accruing at both ends in Soviet hands. The Yugoslav barges had to make unloaded trips either going to or returning from certain assignments. As for freight rates, the Yugoslavs noted that the transport of one *net-ton kilometer* of Yugoslav cargo in 1948 cost 0.40 dinar whereas the transport of one net-ton kilometer of Soviet cargo cost only 0.19 dinar, and the freight of other East European countries only 0.28 dinar. The Soviet representative at the liquidation discussions observed that evidently "the greater the transport distance, the less the charges per ton-kilometer," to which the Yugoslavs replied that there was no "need or reason for a difference so big that transport of Soviet freight cost less than half of the rate charged for transport of Yugoslav freight." [63]

[61] *White Book . . . , op. cit.,* Document 195 of April 1, 1948, pp. 321 ff.

[62] The Soviet representative did not contest these facts; he underlined only that the tugging services of one company (Juspad) were "compensated" for by the tugging of the other companies (the Soviet Danubian Shipping Company). *Ibid.,* p. 329.

[63] *Ibid.,* p. 332.

Turning now to the operations of Justa,[64] it appears that this company also appropriated the most profitable lines inside the country, leaving the Yugoslav company in a subordinate position. Moreover, the Soviet director of Justa

> . . . interpreting the [foundation] agreement arbitrarily . . . understood that Justa had received the right not only of commercial utilization of airports in FPRY, but also exclusive control of the entire air transport and even of all means of communication and radio-navigation.[65]

Such are the highlights of the Yugoslav experience of partnership with the Soviet Union as they appear from Yugoslav sources.[66] Early in 1946 the Russians submitted draft conventions for a series of other joint companies in Yugoslavia, notably for oil, banking, etc., but the negotiations did not succeed because of the Yugoslav dislike for the conditions offered.[67]

[64] The share capital of Justa was fixed at 100 million dinars ($2 million) for each side. Yugoslavia invested the airports, the means of communication, and 5 million dinars ($100,000) in cash. The Soviet Union invested the aircraft and technical installations. The Yugoslavs contend that their assets were valued low (i.e., at 1938 prices when the dinar was stronger) and that, moreover, the Russians acknowledged only the value of ordinary land and not of landing strips (i.e., they did not acknowledge the labor invested in that land). The Russian share was allegedly estimated at the higher 1946–47 prices. Cf. Vladimir Dedijer, *Tito,* Simon & Schuster, New York, 1953, p. 283.

[65] *White Book . . . , op. cit.*, p. 323.

[66] It should, however, be noted that the Yugoslavs had proposed at the negotiations for the liquidation of Juspad and Justa that *joint official records* be kept of the negotiations. This proposal having been turned down, the only available documents are now the published statements or shorthand records of the Yugoslav delegation at these negotiations. *Ibid.*, p. 323.

[67] Concerning the negotiations for the proposed joint Soviet-Yugoslav oil company, Dedijer notes:

> According to Soviet plans, the value of the oil fields in Yugoslavia was not to be recognized as Yugoslavia's share in the undertaking; he [the Soviet delegate Yatrov] invoked Marx, saying they were natural wealth with no direct social value. Our negotiators produced copies of agreements between the Soviet Union on one side, and Hungary and Persia, respectively, on the other. According to these agreements the Soviet Union had recognized the value of oil fields as representing 50 per cent of Persia's nominal share capital in the joint-stock company, and, in the case of Hungary, as representing 15 per cent.
>
> Moreover, the Soviets demanded that any oil products exported by Yugoslavia should go to the Soviet Union in accordance with Soviet requirements, free of all fiscal burdens and export duties during the first five years. The five-year period expiring, the Yugoslav government was entitled only to income tax and to no other fiscal dues or to customs. Yugoslavia could use the remainder of production for herself. . . .
>
> On top of all this, the Soviet plan required that all oil distribution in Yugoslavia, hat is, the whole retail network for gasoline and other oil derivatives, would be ı the hands of this company. [Cf. Vladimir Dedijer, *op. cit.*, pp. 278–279.]

THE STATUS OF THE JOINT COMPANIES AND THE CONDITIONS OF THEIR DEVELOPMENT

After a summary of the conditions that facilitated the development of the joint companies up to the autumn of 1954, and the basic pattern of conflict between them and the respective economies within which they developed, we propose to assess the impact of their liquidation on Soviet relations with the orbit.

At the time of their formation certain joint Soviet companies appeared, as we have noted, to be of minor importance when compared with the established position of other local or foreign concerns. In practice this relationship changed rapidly because of the following provisions built into the very foundations of the joint companies:

(*a*) A standard clause in all the agreements giving these companies complete exemption from taxes.

Here is a typical string of exemptions extended from the day of its foundation and for fifteen years to the Hugarian-Soviet crude oil company Maszovol:

> Exemption from the fees on documents, conveyances, and legal charges in connection with the formation of the company.[68]
>
> Exemption from any customs or other charges collectible on the goods imported as the contribution of the Soviet partner.[69]
>
> Exemption from the company tax, the company assets tax, in respect of property for the purposes of the concern and the equipment, machinery, employees' dwellings and buildings for cultural and welfare purposes pertaining thereto, the fee on conveyance of immovable assets, the fee on contracts of leases, equivalent fees on workers' dwellings, all fees payable on increases of capital and the issue of new shares, the conveyance fee on property and appurtenances brought into the company as a contribution in kind, and the fee for entry in the land register on debentures and bonds issued for business purposes; if the taxation system should be changed in place of these taxes and fees, the above full exemption extends to such new or higher taxes and fees; if the exemption does not extend to the new taxes, the Minister for Industry will refund the new or higher taxes and fees thus payable to the company.[70]

[68] Order in Council #9470/ME of Aug. 3, 1946. Cf. *Monthly Bulletin of the National Bank of Hungary,* new series, III, 1–2 (January–February 1947), pp. 12–13.

[69] Order in Council #8710/ME of July 31, 1946, *loc. cit.*

[70] Order in Council #1200/ME of January 30, 1947, *op. cit.*

These exemptions amounted to a virtual subsidy by the local governments to each of these companies.

(*b*) Complete latitude for these companies in the utilization of their foreign exchange.

Here is a typical disposition taken from the agreement for the establishment of the Soviet-Romanian Civil Aviation Company (Tars):

> In order to make expenditures abroad relating to the operation of the corporation, the acquisition of aircraft, installations and materials, the corporation shall obtain, without restrictions, from Romanian authorities, foreign exchange out of the amounts realized by the corporation from its operations.[71]

Furthermore, whereas the lack of foreign exchange prevented other companies from restoring their depleted facilities, the companies with Soviet partnership could be put back into operation by the use of installations taken by the Soviet Union as war booty, or eventually by some other installations supplied by the Russians.[72]

(*c*) Profits guaranteed to the joint companies from the moment of foundation. High costs and high taxes restricted the activities of the other companies whereas the spot prices paid by the local governments for the purchase of the output of the joint companies usually exported as reparations yielded a profit to the tax-exempt joint companies with Soviet participation.

(*d*) The strengthening of the joint companies by grants of extraordinary facilities in their respective fields.

In a concise summary of the facilities placed at the disposition of the (Soviet) joint companies for Danube navigation the Chairman of

[71] Article XI. Cf., *Bulletin d'information et de documentation,* National Bank of Romania, op. cit., XVII, 10–12, October–December 1945, p. 23. See also Appendix 2 to this chapter, Document 4, article V, paragraph 8 (Sovrompetrol Convention).

[72] In a study entitled "Some Post-War Aspects of the Romanian Oil Industry," the Romanian oil specialist, Mihail Pizanty, wrote at the end of 1946:

> One of the factors preventing the realization of a large program of trial drillings is the more and more pronounced scarcity of material implements and installations. Those required for new works are not available in satisfactory quantities and qualities. After all, it is not surprising that an industry which has discontinued relations with its suppliers and manages to live on only by utilizing its last remainders of stock, and replacing the worn-out material, cannot obtain the output ensured by a new and solid material.
>
> The cooperation of the U.S.S.R. with the Romanian oil industry through the intermediary of the "Sovrompetrol" Co. . . . was translated into fact by the supply of certain quantities of drilling material and of an important stock of motor trucks. [Cf. *RR,* No. 7, November 1946, pp. 50–51.]

the United States Delegation at the 1948 Belgrade Danube Conference, Mr. Cavendish Cannon, noted:

> Embarkation stations, factories, houses, warehouses, grain elevators, railway and communication routes have been placed under the control of these companies. This type of control has nothing to do with navigation. It is clear that this true monopoly can be used in order to put or not put the essential installations in the great Danube ports at the disposition of the ships of other nations, including the riparian nations.[73]

Obviously, a virtual *subsidy* by the local governments in the form of complete and perpetual tax exemption, complete latitude in the utilization of their foreign exchange balances, a competitive advantage over other concerns, and extended facilities in their respective fields insured the automatic growth and prosperity of the companies with Soviet partnership and operated against the growth of independent local or foreign-owned corporations.

Answering the critics who expressed doubts about the "equalitarian" bases of the joint companies, the late Andrei Vishinsky, then Chairman of the Soviet Delegation at the above-mentioned Danube Conference, declared:

> Mr. Cannon has explained that he has seen the agreements concluded between the U.S.S.R., Romania, Hungary and Yugoslavia on the creation of the joint companies for navigation. But it is necessary to examine more closely these agreements in order to see that the declaration of the American delegate lacks any foundation. If the text of these agreements is examined, it must be kept in sight that these companies *are not private companies,* but state companies. On the other hand, they are created on an *equalitarian basis,* with equal participation of representation of either country in the administration of the company in question, and are obligatorily and respectively *presided* [*over*] *by the Hungarian, Romanian, Yugoslav, representatives and never by the representatives of the U.S.S.R.*[74]

It is quite true that the companies were presided over by their respective nationals, but the president was only a figurehead since the real power in all these companies was vested in the hands of a *general manager, always a Soviet citizen.*

[73] Intervention on Aug. 5, 1948, of Mr. Cavendish Cannon, Chairman, U.S. Delegation at the 1948 Belgrade Danube Conference. Cf. *Dunaiskaia Konferentsia—La Conférence danubienne* (The Danube Conference), Russian-French official texts, Belgrade, 1949, p. 145.

[74] Intervention of Aug. 6, 1948, of Mr. Andrei Vishinsky, Chairman of the Soviet Delegation at the 1948 Belgrade Danube Conference. *Ibid.*, p. 186 (italics supplied).

Here are, for instance, the typical dispositions of the Statutes of the Hungarian Soviet Shipping Company (Meszhart), as summarized in the bulletin of the National Bank of Hungary:

> There are an equal number of Hungarian and Soviet members on the Board of eight directors and the supervisory committee of four. The Chairman of the Board of Directors is chosen from its members on the proposal of the Hungarian shareholders and the deputy-chairman on the proposal of the Soviet shareholders. The general manager is appointed by the board on the proposal of its Soviet members and the deputy general manager on the proposal of the Hungarian members. The sphere of authority of the *general manager* includes the making of contracts, the issue of obligations, the acquisition of movable and immovable assets, sea-going and river craft and other means of transport, their leasing, encumbrance or disposal, the effectuation of all banking and credit operations, the issue of powers of attorney, the establishment of freight regulations, matters connected with personnel and in general disposal of matters not placed within the sphere of authority of the general meeting of the Board of Directors.[75]

Thus, for all practical purposes, the joint companies were entirely in the hands of the *Soviet managers.*

A simple understanding among Soviet managers of various companies either in one country or in various countries was sufficient to create a *cartelized group* able to isolate any local state-owned company, as we noted above in the case of the Yugoslav Shipping Company.

Enjoying complete *extra-territoriality,* they could cut across both the local frontiers and the local planning. Although in principle they were supposed to adjust themselves to the local economic plans, in practice the local economic planners had to adjust their plans to the objectives of the joint Soviet companies.

Moreover, Soviet objectives were attained not only *directly* but also *indirectly,* through influence exerted by Soviet joint companies on other companies. Thus the Soviet Union, which through Sovromgas controlled the Romanian gas fields, could encourage the development of a joint Romanian-Hungarian company using gas facilities. Such a joint company, called Romagchim, was constituted in 1952 by an agreement which called for the creation of new branches of the chemical industries in Romania and Hungary, the natural gas in Romania

[75] Order in Council #4730/ME of May 4, 1946: Concerning the Statutes of Meszhart. Cf. *Monthly Bulletin of the National Bank of Hungary,* II, 1–6, January–June 1946, p. 12. (Italics supplied.)

being utilized as supply for the new installations in Hungary.[76] Other inter-East European joint companies such as a Romanian-East German joint company for the development of the chemical industry in Romania, utilizing local Romanian raw materials (a field in which Sovromchim operated),[77] and a Czechoslovak-Hungarian bauxite agreement,[78] providing for the production of aluminum in Czechoslovakia from Hungarian bauxites, indirectly served Soviet economic interests in these fields.

The extraordinary powers vested in the hands of the Soviet managers, the possibility of cartelization through a simple understanding among the managers, the *de facto* extra-territoriality of these companies, and the possibility of directly or indirectly extending their control in any bilateral or regional agreements gave the "joint" companies with Soviet partnership such strategical importance in these economies that they could keep the local state-owned companies at a mere subsistence level economically or force them to merge with the ever growing "joint" companies.

Dismantlement of This Network and Concluding Remarks

In the autumn of 1954 a series of bilateral agreements between the Soviet Union and Romania, Bulgaria, and Hungary, respectively, dismantled almost the entire network of joint companies in Eastern Europe. The Soviet-Romanian agreement, announced on September 17, 1954, liquidated twelve joint companies (including the Sovrombanc), but it made no mention of Sovrompetrol (oil) and Sovromcvarţ

[76] The concrete plans for Romagchim were elaborated in 1953. A Hungarian source wrote in this connection:

> Those engaged in preparing the plans are helped in their work by the experiences of experts from the Soviet Union and the German Democratic Republic. . . . The preparatory work in the field is to start in 1954. [Cf. *HB*, No. 142, May 16, 1953; see also *AIB*, III, No. 25, June 28, 1952.]

[77] The agreement concerning this company was signed in Berlin on Sept. 12, 1952. Cf. *AIB*, III, 36, Sept. 30, 1952.

[78] Lazlo Gay, Hungarian Deputy Minister for Foreign Trade, defined as follows the main features of these agreements: (*a*) one country places part of its vital natural wealth at the disposal of the other country until this raw material is exhausted or its utilization becomes superfluous; (*b*) the two sides, by their common efforts, produce materials and industrial equipment necessary for the realization of the agreement, mutually help each other in planning and in placing their technical experience at each other's disposal; (*c*) one of the sides supplies industrial equipment on credit. "Consolidating Economic Co-operation Between Soviet Union and Countries of People's Democracy," in *FLP*, Nov. 14, 1952.

(uranium). Sovrompetrol was finally dissolved in December 1955; Sovromcvarț was liquidated in November 1956.[79] The Soviet-Bulgarian agreement, announced on October 9, 1954, liquidated all the companies except the Soviet-Bulgarian Mining Company.[80] Finally, the Soviet-Hungarian agreement, announced on November 6, 1954, liquidated all the joint companies, including the Soviet Commercial and Industrial Bank inherited by the Soviet Union in Hungary.[81]

All the agreements concluded in 1954 stated:

1. That during the functioning period of the joint companies both sides had made large capital investments and that

> The Soviet party contributed large consignments of up-to-date equipment and material to the companies and gave technical assistance to the enterprise operating under the companies through sending experts, handing over technical documentation, and through participation in the drawing up of the building and reconstruction plans of the enterprises and in the training of highly qualified cadres.[82]

2. That the companies were being dissolved and the Soviet Union was transferring its shares in these companies to the respective East European partner because these companies had "carried out the tasks which had been set before them." [83]

3. That the parties to which the Soviet shares were transferred "shall pay back the value of the shares under favorable terms in several yearly remittances." [84]

[79] The Soviet Union now has bilateral agreements with each of the East European countries, including the former Allied countries, concerning the exploitation and the utilization of their uranium resources. According to official indications, the Soviet Union bears the expense connected with prospecting for uranium ore deposits in each of these countries and ensures the delivery of the materials and special instruments needed. In turn, these countries export their ore to Russia under "mutually advantageous conditions." The most important uranium mines are in Czechoslovakia and Hungary.

[80] Cf. *Otechestven Front* (Fatherland Front), October 13, 1954, and "Fraternal Aid," in *Bulgaria Today,* III, 21, November 1, 1954.

[81] Cf. "Soviet Union Transfers Its Shares in Hungarian-Soviet Mixed Companies to the Hungarian People's Republic," in *New Hungary,* V, 1, January 1955.

[82] *Ibid.*

[83] It is worth while noting that at each anniversary of the formation of the joint companies it had been customary in the past to stress that they were "an outstandingly efficient form of cooperation of a new type, based on equality and mutual aid and a factor of utmost importance in building socialism" in the respective country ("Soviet-Romanian Companies 7 Years Old," in *RN,* Aug. 3, 1952). Almost overnight this "factor of utmost importance in building socialism" had carried out the "tasks" set before it.

[84] *New Hungary, loc. cit.*

There can be little doubt that the decision to liquidate the joint companies represents a departure by the Soviet Union from some of the main forms of its pre-1954 policy toward both the ex-enemy countries and all the other states of the "socialist bloc." [85] Obviously, none of these countries was in a position to request the liquidation of the joint-companies network. Moreover, given the very conditions that prevailed at their formation, some of these companies were extremely prosperous, were growing automatically as their own output was growing, and had become a source of exogenous accumulation for the Soviet Union without requiring any net export of funds on her part. Only a political decision, deliberately taken by the Russians, can explain the changes occurring in the post-Stalin era, both in the Kremlin itself and in the Soviet bloc. The Soviet leaders undoubtedly sensed the pent-up pressures accumulated in the Soviet bloc against the presence of Soviet troops, of Soviet economic, technical, and administrative experts, and of Soviet agents of all kinds.[86] The dismantling of the largest part of the joint companies' network took place after the upheavals which shook East Germany in 1953. The final liquidation of all the companies and of the obligations arising from their dismantling occurred after the turmoil in Poland and Hungary in the autumn of 1956.

From 1954 to 1956 the Russians intended to use the liquidation of the joint companies as an important financial resource in the area. Both the former German assets which were at the basis of the joint partnerships and the new contributions of Soviet Russia were to be purchased, for unspecified sums, by the former enemy countries, where these companies were located. According to very rough estimates the gross value of the original German assets transferred by Romania to the Soviet Union in 1944–45, and incorporated in the Sovroms, reached some 200 million dollars.[87] The value of the respective assets involved in Hungary was somewhat less but

[85] The same policy was followed in respect to East Germany and immediately afterwards in respect to China.

[86] In this context, it is interesting to recall the incessant opposition of the Yugoslavs to this type of company.

[87] This estimate is given in the *Observations Concernant le Traité de Paix . . . , op. cit.*, p. 24. It is corroborated up to a point by the data available for most of the agreements concerning the Sovroms, for instance. Thus the original share of Soviet Russia in Sovrombanc can be estimated at some 4 million 1938-dollars, the share in Tars at 6.3 million dollars, the share in Sovromcoal at 12 million dollars. (The share in Sovrompetrol alone could be estimated at 17.7 million dollars, but this company does not appear in the original list of the companies dissolved.)

probably not below 150 million dollars.[88] Since the specific obligations arising from the liquidation of these assets actually resulted from the war period, this obligation can be legitimately called a "second round of reparations" to be paid to Russia. The case of the new Soviet contributions to the joint companies, made throughout the postwar period, is clearly of a different nature. The purchase of these contributions by the ex-enemy countries can be considered as a normal commercial transaction. However, it is interesting to note that the importance of this contribution was even more heavily stressed by the buyer than by the seller. The East European press was kept extremely busy enhancing the value of the Soviet contributions, whether made under the form of transfers of equipment or of services.

After the Hungarian upheaval, the Russians canceled the debts of the ex-enemy countries arising from the liquidation of the joint companies. It was started then that the total of these debts for Romania alone amounted to over 700 million dollars.[89]

In conclusion, the special case of *the sources, development, and liquidation* of Soviet assets in Eastern Europe suggests the following remarks:

1. It might be said that, notwithstanding the substantial political changes in these countries since the armistice, the cost of the war participation of Hungary, Romania, and Bulgaria on the Nazi side has placed on them a burden of debt to Russia for a period of not less than 12 years (1944–45–1956). First in the form of reparations, second in the form of joint companies, which grew mostly out of the German assets, and third in the form of the sale and transfer of those assets back to these countries, the Soviet Union has pressed its claims almost inflexibly. It is against this background that we should judge what the Soviet Union claims to have "given" these countries.

2. It is difficult to establish a dependable estimate of the peak of the heaviest claims of the Soviet Union as related to the capacity of payment of these countries. Specifically, it is difficult to decide whether this peak was reached during the period of reconstruction, i.e., up to

[88] On the basis of the data released at the formation of the joint companies, it can be estimated that the Soviet share in Maszobal (bauxite), for instance, amounted to some 3.7 million prewar dollars; that in Danube Valley Alum Earth, some 8 million; that in Maszovol and Molaj, some 4.7 million dollars, etc. No estimate is available to the author concerning the gross value of assets.

[89] "Satellite Unrest Costly to Soviet," in N. Y. *Times*, Dec. 23, 1956.

1948–49, when national income grew slowly and the reparations were extremely heavy, or during the first development period, i.e., from 1948–49 to 1953, when the net material product started to grow rapidly and reparations decreased substantially, but a large part of this net material product accrued to the joint companies and was controlled completely by Soviet Russia.

3. The coordination ("integration") of the plans and production of these economies with the plans and output of Soviet Russia was only partly the responsibility of the joint companies, for the joint companies cut across the plans, for instance, of Hungary and Romania and represented up to a certain point a self-sustaining network developing more *against* than *together with* the economies in which they prospered. Hence their liquidation should facilitate the organization of all-round planning, especially in Hungary and Romania. The coordination of the economic plans and foreign trade of the countries considered with those of Soviet Russia can be accomplished by other and more appropriate means such as, for instance, the Council of Economic Mutual Assistance (CEMA).[90] The sale and transfer to these countries of the Soviet share of the joint companies is thus a sort of *special extension of the process of nationalization* to the last spheres outside agriculture, which up to 1954 had not been under the control of the respective states.

4. The liquidation of the Soviet joint companies does not mean that other joint ventures are not to be formed in the area. The tendency of each of these economies to engage in more complex techniques and to develop the whole gamut of engineering industries, and the isolation of these countries from the West encourage the setting up of partnerships between the countries of the area, e.g., Czechoslovak-Hungarian, Hungarian-Romanian companies, etc. However, the conditions of the formation of such companies are different from those which presided at the formation of the Soviet joint companies. They are based on deliveries of equipment and installations by the industrialized partner and delivery of part of the output thus obtained by the less developed country.[91]

[90] See Chapter 11.
[91] See Chapter 9.

APPENDIX 1

MULTIPLE CHARACTER OF THE GERMAN ASSETS PASSED INTO THE OWNERSHIP OF THE SOVIET UNION

(Documents of Hungarian source)

In connection with the recording of claims and indebtedness referring to the former German assets located in Hungary, the Hungarian Government published on Mar. 8, 1947, as an annex to Decree 3080—1947, a list of 201 former German companies transferred to Soviet ownership.[92] The list, which reveals clearly the multiple character of the assets turned over to the Soviet Union, is comprised of three groups: I. 95 stock companies; II. 37 companies with state participation; III. 69 firms belonging to individuals, cooperatives, and societies with limited responsibility.

Less than a year after the publication of that document, an order in the Council of Ministers *cancelled* all the claims arising against these companies before Jan. 20, 1945.[93]

In the tables that follow, we have classified the assets by *type of business:*

1. Table 51 encompasses the firms listed in the annex to the official decree in Group I and Group II, i.e., 132 firms.
2. Table 52 comprises the firms of Group III, i.e., the balance of 69 firms.

Examination of both tables reveals clearly the secondary importance of the last-mentioned group of firms.

[92] Decree 3080—1947, *Magyar Közlöny, op. cit.,* No. 56, Mar. 8, 1947, pp. 561–565.

[93] Order 15/720/Korm of Jan. 4, 1948. Cf. *Monthly Bulletin of the National Bank of Hungary,* new series, IV, 1–2 (January–February 1948), p. 22.

TABLE 51. HUNGARY: FORMER GERMAN ASSETS TRANSFERRED TO THE SOVIET UNION, GROUPS I AND II [a]

Banks (2)

(I) 18. Creditanstalt Bankverein
54. Mercur Bank Co.

Insurance Companies (11)

(I) 4. Alliance Viennese Ins. Co.
7. Anker Gen. Ins. Co.
11. Berlin Victoria Gen. Ins. Co.
23. Danube Concordia Gen. Ins. Co.
24. Elem Gen. Ins. Co.
27. European Freight and Luggage Ins. Co.
51. Manheim Ins. Co.
77. Sudeten-German Union Ins. Co.
83. Turul Hung. National Ins. Co.
92. Victoria Fire Ins. Co.
94. Württemberg and Baden United Ins. Co., Helnbron

Metals and Metal Products (14)

(I) 12. Berndorf Metal Products Co. (Krupp)
19. Deichsel A. Hung. Barbed Wire and Steel Coil Corp.
26. First Hung. Type-Setting Manuf. Co.
30. Felten and Guilleaume Co.
32. Antal Freisler Elevator and Machine Manuf. Co.
36. Hutter and Schrantz Co.
55. Mezei Mines Ind. Railroad and Gen. Machin. Corp.
68. Schmidt Bros. Printing Press Manuf. Co.
76. Pumping Machin. Manuf. Co.
88. Steel Manuf. Corp. at Sopron
89. Iron and Steel Co.
(II) 1. Steel Wire and Barbed Wire Distr. Co.
26. Otis Elevator Co.
30. Stankö Chain and Crane Co.

Mining and Mining Works (4)

(I) 25. First Danube Steamship Corp.
81. Transdanubian Bauxite Corp.
95. Béla Zichy Urkut Mining Works
(II) 2. General Crude-Oil Refining Corp.

Textiles (14)

(I) 3. Albana Textile and Weaving Co.
35. Domestic Textile Weaving and Cloth Manuf. Co.
38. Linen, Jute & Textile Ind. Corp.
40. Kispet Silk Weaving Fact., Schiel Bros. Corp.
44. Hung. Cloth & Lining Manuf. Co.
57. Wool-Thread Textile Works Corp.
64. Salzmann Hung. Textile Indus.
70. Sopron & Ujpest Cloth & Rug Manuf. Co.
80. Tolna Textile Works Co.
87. Uwag Hung. Textile Weav. at Pomáz
93. Wellner Alpaca Co.
(II) 3. William Benger Textile Manuf. Co.
28. Plush & Velvet Weav. Co., Holzermann Bros. Co.
33. Textile Chemical Ind. Co.

Construction Materials and Related Products (4) (I) 13. John Biehn Roofing Mater., Tar and Asphalt Corp. 14. Bitumen Road Building Corp. 60. N. Rella and Cousin Constr. Co. 86. Road Building & Asphalt Products Co.	Chemicals (7) (I) 10. Beirsdorf Chemical Co. 71. Soroksár Chemical Ind. Corp. 75. Székesfehérvár Ind. Oxygen and Chemical Manuf. Corp. (II) 6. Braunsanilin Co. 11. Ferrocyan Chemical & Metal Co. 15. Perfumes and Cosmetics Co. 27. Persil Co.	Laboratory and Medical Supplies (6) (I) 9. Behring Serum Lab. Co. 43. Lab. Supply and Serum Material Distr. Co. 45. Hung. Odol Products Corp. 46. Hung. Optical Products Corp. 47. Hung. Pharmacological and Medical Supplies Co. 66. Schering Pharmacological and Chemical Products Co.
Electrical Appliances (5) (I) 1. AEG Union-Electrical Co. 48. Hung. Siemens Elec. Works Corp. 82. Tudor Battery & Transformer Co. 91. Elec. Manuf. and Distr. Co. (II) 13. Hoppecke Transformer Products Co.	Food-Processing (3) (I) 52. Gyula Meinl Co. 73. Stolwerk Brothers Co. (II) 25. Dr. A. Oetker Cereals and Special Food Products Co.	Lumber (3) (II) 16. East Carpathian Lumber Ind. Co. 18. Foreign Exchange Products and Lumber Ind. Corp. 34. Uzsok and Borsa Lumber Prod. and Distr. Co.
Paper and Packaging (1) (I) 58. Paper and Packaging Materials Co.	Glass Manufacturing and Distributing (2) (I) 61. Rosenthal China and Glass Manuf. Co. 74. C. Stolzle Sons Glass Products Corp.	Shoe Manufacturing (2) (I) 20. Del-Ka Shoe Manuf. Co. 63. Salamander Shoe Co.
Fuel and Power (3) (I) 21. Southern Hungarian Electrical Current Products Corp. at Bácsalmás 22. The Dráva Valley Electrical Current Products Co. at Szigetvár 41. Korom Industry Corp.	Railroads (1) (I) 39. The Railroad Trans. Co., Province of Keszthely	Ship Construction (1) (II) 19. Construction Co., building specialized ships
Shipping Companies (operating lines) (2) (I) 8. The Bavarian Lloyd Shipping Co. (II) 24. Norddeutscher Lloyd Co.	Shipping and Travel Bureaus (5) (I) 34. Hamburg-American Line Shipping (II) 9. Deutsche-Amerika Line Co. 12. Hanzá Shipping Bureau 21. Central European Travel Bureau 22. German Shipping Bureau Co.	Moving and Transportation (2) (I) 65. A. Schenker and Assoc. Internat. Moving and Trans. Co. (II) 36. Winkler and Fischer Internat. Trans. and Freight Co.

TABLE 51. HUNGARY: FORMER GERMAN ASSETS TRANSFERRED TO THE SOVIET UNION, GROUPS I AND II [a] (*Continued*)

Books (1)

(II) 23. German Labor Front Publishing Co.

Commercial Agencies (17)

(I) 2. Agfa Photographic Articles Distr. Co.
15. Budanil Paint and Chemical Sales Corp.
42. Book Distribution Corp.
53. Mercedes Benz Automobile Corp.
69. Singer Sewing Machine Corp., Berlin Agency
72. Steyr, Austro, Daimler, Puch Works Hung. Commercial Co.
78. Terra Co. Commercial Agencies
90. Chemical Products and Paper Import Co.

(II) 4. Meat Import Corp.
8. Csurgó Milk Export Co. at Kaposvár
14. Importex Commercial Co. Rep.
17. Commercial Information Svces., previously branch of Simmelpfeng
29. Press Article Distributing, Newspaper and Magazine Sales
31. Stova Watch and Photog. Equip. Sales Corp.
32 Wholesale Fur Distr. Co.
35. Vox Ind. and Comm. Co.
37. Zeiler Import and Export Co.

Not Classified (13)

(I) 28. Fattinger and Co.
29. István Felmayer and Sons Co.
33. Fülöp Haas and Sons Co.
49. Hung. Siemens Reiniger Works
50. Hung. City and Village Develop. Co.
59. Posnánsky and Strelitz Co.
62. Rudolf Mosse Co.
67. Schimmel and Partner Co.
79. Thiergartner and Stöhr Co.

(II) 5. Robert Bosch Co.
7. Feodor Burgmann Co.
10. Etam Co.
20. M. Catgut Products Co.

Miscellaneous (9)

Rubber:	(I) 37. East European Rubber Committee Corp.
Jewelry-cutting:	56. Naxos Jewel Cutting (Refining) Co.
Motion picture prod.:	17. Corvin Moving Picture Co.
	85. Ufa Movie Ind. and Movie Distr. Co.
Warehouses:	16. Centrum Warehouse Corp.
Grocery:	31. 5–6 Ferenc József Sq. (Gresham) Coffee House
Restaurant:	5. Alpine Village Restaurant Co.
Theaters:	84. Uránia Hung. Scientific Theater Assoc. Co.
Amusement park:	6. English Park Co.

[a] Table classification is by type of business. Group I, stock companies; Group II, companies with state participation.
All the companies are located in Budapest, unless otherwise stated. The arabic number preceding the company name is the number under which the company is listed in the respective group in the annex to the official decree of March 8, 1947.

TABLE 52. HUNGARY: FORMER GERMAN ASSETS TRANSFERRED TO THE SOVIET UNION, GROUP III [a]

(Small) Savings Banks (4) 1. Albrecht Bavarian Royal Prince Savings Deposit Co. 31. Holzermann Bros. Savings Dep. Co. 36. Koch and Partner Savings Dep. Co. 37. Ernö Krause and Co. Savings Dep.	Metals and Metal Works (6) 3. Augsburg-Nürnberg Machine Co. 7. Otto Bauer Ship Repair Co. at Baja 17. "Elhoma" Machine Ind. (Jungk and Neihardt Hung. Branch) 20. Erwerth and Co. Textile Machinery Manuf. Co., iron works at Komárom 25. Walter Fries Flour Mill Equip. at Pestszenterzsébe [b] 60. Schuchardt and Schuttex Constr. Machinery Co.	Textiles (4) 25. Walter Fries Sieve and Cloth Manuf. Co. at Pestszenterzsébe [b] 47. Neumann and Zimmermann Cloth and Lining Manuf. Co. at Vác 52. Rella Textile and Woolen Manuf. Co. 56. Lipót Saul Mechanical Weaving at Ujpest
Industrial Supplies and Appliances (4) 59. Schmiedt Ind. Supplies Co. 63. V. Strelow Gas Measuring Appliances Manuf. Co. 64. Rezso Strube Ind. Supplies Co. 65. V.D.O. Tachometric Co. Printing Establishments (2) 21. Fáklya Printing Establishment 62. Mrs. Steinlein and Frank Graphic Art Products Co.	Other Manufacturers (3) Rubber factory: 11. Ernö Bottke, Rákospalota Watch company: 27. Károly Güttert Lumber: 8. Otto Bauer Saw Mill and Lumber Factory at Baja	Commercial Agencies (9) 4. Australian Lumber Import Co. (Mahl and Co. Branch) 12. Brunsviga Adding Machine Distr. Co. (Günther Gelphe Branch) 14. Deutsche Buchgemeinschaft 35. Gusztáv Knapp Book Store 42. Károly Kösl, Subsidiary to Automobile Distr. and Mechanical Co. 45. János Nagy Medicinal Herbs Sales Co. 48. Pálgyörgy Neumann Elec. Appliances and Office Equip. Distr. Agency 58. W. Schimmelpfeng Information Bureau 67. Sándor Wery Von Limont, Agricultural Products, Colonial Imp. and Distr. Co.

TABLE 52. HUNGARY: FORMER GERMAN ASSETS TRANSFERRED TO THE SOVIET UNION, GROUP III[a] (*Continued*)

Miscellaneous (8)		Firms Belonging to Individuals—Not Classified (30)	
Dairies:	22. Bavarian Dairies at Cenye and Ujmajor	2. Hermann Anspacher	38. Dániel Krausz
		5. Barasch Bros. Co.	39. Kratzkow and Eifert
Flour mill:	46. Károly Godelmann at Nagyharsány	9. Dr. Block and Partner	40. M. Lánger
		10. Frigyes Bokisch	41. Károly del Medico, Branch
Construction:	34. Henrik Kling at Rákospalota	13. Alajos Chatelet and Son Co.	43. Bruno Meisner
		15. Arthur Dittrich	44. Munka, Hermann Birgert Co.
Moving:	32. Frigyes Jansen Co.	16. John Ede Duwensee	49. Albert Neuburger
Sign manuf.:	24. Károly Friciker Co.	18. Sándor Elbl	51. Kurt Prövig
Photoprint:	50. József Piesenberger	19. Áron Elsnberg	53. Otto Rieber Co.
Gold exchange:	57. G. A. Scheid Co.	23. Richard Flóderer	54. Károly Rindermann
Amusements:	6. Railroad Amusement Co.	26. Graeb and Sons Co.	55. Rudolf et Co., at Zittau
		28. Vilmost Hieber	61. J. F. Schwarzlose and Sons
		29. Károly Hins, Budapest agency	66. C. A. and Paul Vorsterer
		30. Igler and Partners	68. Justus Karl Friedrich Westhoff
		33. Dr. Rolaf Jürgensen	69. Ernö Wolf

[a] Table classification is by type of business. Group III, firms belonging to individuals, cooperatives, and societies with limited responsibility. All the companies are located in Budapest, unless otherwise stated. The arabic number preceding the company name is the number under which the company is listed in Group III in the annex to the official decree of March 8, 1947.

[b] The company is listed twice, under Metals and Metal Works and under Textiles, as it has two types of factory.

APPENDIX 2

PROCESS OF TRANSFER OF GERMAN ASSETS TO THE SOVIET UNION AND FORMATION OF JOINT COMPANIES

(Documents of Romanian source)

The five documents listed below [94] present the mechanism of transfer of German assets to the Soviet Union and the formation of the "joint companies."

Document 1 shows *to which* specific Soviet organizations the shares, assets, etc., which became Soviet property, had to be turned over.

Documents 2, 3 indicate *how this transfer was effected* in three different cases (the oil companies, banks, and insurance companies).

Documents 4, 5 explain how the shares and assets thus obtained by the Soviet Union *were placed subsequently in the joint companies as the Soviet contribution of capital.* (The two conventions referring to Sovrompetrol and Sovrombank can be considered typical.)

Document 1. Journal of the Council of Ministers No. 388 of March 30, 1946, dealing with the *delivery of German assets transferred to the ownership of the U.S.S.R.* by virtue of decisions reached at the Potsdam Conference.

ARTICLE I: (*a*) The shares, assets of corporations, assets of industrial, commercial, and other enterprises, movable and immovable property, and all other assets as well as the rights and interests belonging to German juridical or physical persons transferred to the ownership of the U.S.S.R. which are registered with the Bureau for the Administration and Supervision of Enemy Property (CASBI) shall be turned over, in accordance with the provisions of the present journal, to the following institutions accredited by the U.S.S.R.:

1. Union Ucrneft. 2. Union Sovfraht. 3. General Direction of Civil Aeronautics Aeroflot. 4. Union Tuzhnestrans. 5. (Union) Soiuzintorgkino. 6.

[94] Sources: *Bulletin d'information et de documentation,* National Bank of Romania, Document 1: XVIII, 4–6 (April–June 1946), p. 67; Document 2: XVII, 7–9 (July–September 1945), p. 26; Document 3: XVIII, 1–3 (January–March 1946), p. 21; Documents 4–5: XVII, 10–12 (October–December 1945), p. 21. (The present translation is from the French.)

Union Raznoexport. 7. Union Technoexport. 8. Union Exportkhleb. 9. Union Exportles. 10. Union Mezhkniga. 11. (Union) Soiuzpushnina. 12. Union Technopromimport. 13. Union Raznoimport. 14. (Union) Soiuzpromexport. 15. Administration of Romanian enterprises and real estate, Soviet Consulate, Bucharest.

(*b*) Any remaining movable and immovable property, shares, bonds, securities, etc., which are identified, as well as those which are identified after the publication of the present journal and those which are not registered with the CASBI, shall be turned over to the respective Soviet institutions within sixty days from publication of the present journal.

ARTICLE II: The turning over of German assets and shares provided for by Article I shall be carried out by the Commissioner-General of the Government for liaison with the Allied Control Commission, who shall draw up official reports separately for each item turned over, these reports being signed by the agents of the CASBI and the general manager of the corporation or enterprise on the one side, and by the representative of the Soviet institution which receives this item on the other side.

At the time when the official reports are drawn up, the corporations shall effect the transfer of shares to the names of the respective Soviet institutions, and shall also deliver a certificate proving that the transfer of shares has been made. The official report mentioned above constitutes proof of the turning over and shall specify the item and its location.

Document 2. Decree Law No. 2224 of July 18, 1945, providing for the *transfer of shares* which have become the property of the Soviet Union (oil and banking companies).

ARTICLE I: The shares of the oil and banking companies listed in the annexed tables constituting an integral part of the present law which belonged to German juridical or physical persons, and which have become the property of the Union of Soviet Socialist Republics as reparation for the war damage caused by Germany, shall be transferred in the shareholders' books kept by the respective companies to the long-term loan bank for industry and electrification Prombank, U.S.S.R.

ARTICLE II: The Presidency of the Council of Ministers shall indicate to the respective companies the shares the transfer of which must be carried out according to the provisions of the preceding article.

ARTICLE III: Within fifteen days from the receipt of such indication the companies shall effect the transfer of the shares, and they shall, at the same time, issue temporary certificates showing that the transfer has taken place; these certificates shall be delivered to Union Ucrneft and to Prombank, U.S.S.R., through the Presidency of the Council of Ministers.

ARTICLE IV: The holders, by whatever right, of the shares which have become the property of the Union of Soviet Socialist Republics must deposit them at the Presidency of the Council of Ministers within fifteen days from the publication of the present law, failing which these shares shall be cancelled.

ARTICLE V: In order to supervise the carrying out of the provisions contained in Article III, an advisory commission is established within the Presidency of the Council of Ministers; the commission is composed of the Secretary-General to the Presidency of the Council of Ministers, who shall be its President and have attributions of a political nature; of a Judge of the Court of Appeals of Bucharest, and of a delegate of the Ministry of Mines and Oil, each having an alternate.

Its members shall be appointed by decision of the respective bodies.

The Commission shall also examine the petitions of the persons concerned and decide by a majority.

ARTICLE VI: The director-generals, or in their absence the directors, and the managers of the oil or banking corporations who do not effect the transfer of the shares or do not issue the temporary certificates according to the present law shall be punished by one to five years' imprisonment—and in no case shall there be leniency granted because of extenuating circumstances.

The holders of the shares of the oil and banking companies coming under the provisions of the present law who do not deposit them within the period provided under Article IV shall be punished in the same manner.

ANNEX I. SHARES OF THE ROMANIAN OIL COMPANIES WHICH BELONG TO THE UNION OF SOVIET SOCIALIST REPUBLICS

Name of the Company	Nominal Amount of Shares, millions of lei
Concordia	755.8
Colombia	325.0
Petrol-Bloc	285.5
I.R.D.P.	115.5
Buna Speranţă	15.0
Explora	59.0
Meotica	21.3
Sardep	43.3
Sarpetrol	34.9
Transpetrol	4.5
Continenta	100.0
Total	1,759.8

ANNEX II. SHARES OF THE ROMANIAN BANKS WHICH BELONGED TO THE GERMANS AND WHICH HAVE BECOME THE PROPERTY OF THE UNION OF SOVIET SOCIALIST REPUBLICS

Name of the Bank	Nominal Amount of Shares, thousand lei
Banca Comercială Română	277,218.0
Societatea Bancară Română	196,908.0
Banca Hrissoveloni	22,000.0
Bancile Bănăţene Unite (Timişoara)	18,968.0
Banca de Credit Român	17,665.5
Institutul de Credit Funciar (Sibiu)	5,137.9
Banca Românească	3,075.0
Banca Generală de Economii (Sibiu and Braşov)	2,220.6
Total	543,193.0

Document 3. Decree Law No. 539 of February 16, 1946, concerning the turning over to the General Administrative Body for State Insurance of the U.S.S.R. of *property and shares which belonged to German insurance corporations and companies.*

The present decree provides:

(*a*) for the turning over of property belonging to German insurance companies and their Romanian branches, indicated in Table 2 below;

(*b*) for the transfer of shares of Romanian insurance companies which belonged to German juridical or physical persons, indicated in Table 1 below;

(*c*) that the Romanian Liaison Commission to the Allied Control Commission shall see that the provisions of the present decree are carried out.

TABLE 1. INSURANCE COMPANIES WHICH MUST TRANSFER SHARES TO THE GENERAL ADMINISTRATIVE BODY FOR STATE INSURANCE OF THE U.S.S.R.

Name of the Insurance Company	Nominal Value of Shares, thousand lei
Vatra Dornei	622.0
Compania Europeană	5,709.5
Steaua României	5,757.5
Generala	1,025.0
Naţionala	10,014.0
Dacia-România	3,170.0
Asigurarea Românească	72.0
Agricola Foncieră	156.0
Britania	14,855.0
Transilvania	21,316.0
Jauch and Hubener	1,220.0
Total	63,917.0

TABLE 2. GERMAN INSURANCE COMPANIES AND THEIR ROMANIAN BRANCHES WHICH ARE TO BE TURNED OVER TO THE GENERAL ADMINISTRATIVE BODY FOR STATE INSURANCE OF THE U.S.S.R.

Name of Insurance Company or Branch	Capital, thousand lei
Victoria (life insurance)	10,000.0
Victoria (fire insurance)	4,000.0
Alianţa	12,000.0
Danubía	12,000.0
Total	38,000.0

Document 4. Convention for the creation of the *Soviet-Romanian Oil Co.*[95] entered into between the Government of the U.S.S.R. and the Government of the Romanian Kingdom.[96]

ARTICLE I: The Government of the U.S.S.R. and the Royal Romanian Government establish by the present convention the organizations, companies, and groups which will constitute the Soviet-Romanian company for the exploration, exploitation, refining, and marketing of crude oil and its products:

For the U.S.S.R., Union Ucrneft and (Union) Soiusneftexport.

For Romania, the Companies Creditul Minier, Redevenţa, and the other companies or groups possessing shares of Romanian companies. (See Annex I, Document 2.)

The above-mentioned organizations, companies, and groups shall be given the necessary rights by the respective Governments in accordance with previous agreements so that they may be able to conform in every respect with the conditions provided in the present convention.

Consequently, the two Governments mutually guarantee the carrying out by the above-mentioned organizations, companies, and groups of the conditions of the constitution and financing of the Soviet-Romanian company.

ARTICLE II: The Soviet-Romanian company for the exploration, exploitation, refining, and marketing of crude oil and its products shall have the status of a Romanian private juridical organ of the type of a limited company according to the Romanian laws.

In the course of its activity the Soviet-Romanian company shall have the same rights as any other company with Romanian capital.

The duration of the company is unlimited.

The main office of the company shall be in Bucharest.

ARTICLE III: The purpose of the company shall be to prospect, explore, exploit, refine, and market liquid oil on areas belonging to the Romanian state or on areas belonging to private persons, directly or together with other companies or persons, as well as to refine and market the products of liquid oil.

ARTICLE IV: The company shall have a social capital of five thousand million lei to be paid in equal parts by the two contracting parties, Soviet and Romanian, mentioned in Article I.

The contributions of the two parties shall be covered as shown below:

A. The contribution of the Soviet party:

1. Installations, casing, and materials necessary for the exploration and exploitation of oil up to the total value of 740 million lei, according to a list

[95] The company was established on Oct. 24, 1945, by virtue of an order of the Council of Ministers #1337, confirmed by the decree law #1237 of Mar. 30, 1946. Cf. *Bulletin d'information et de documentation,* National Bank of Romania, XVIII, No. 4–6 (April–June 1946), p. 67.

[96] The translation of this document (without the Annex) may be found in Mid-European Law Project, *Economic Treaties and Agreements of the Soviet Bloc in Eastern Europe, 1945–51,* Mid-European Study Center, New York, 1952, pp. 24–30.

decided upon by the contracting parties and approved by the two Governments.

The evaluation of installations, casing, and materials shall be made on the basis of average prices of the first half of 1939 in Romania.

2. The shares of the companies mentioned in Annex I having a par value of 1,760 million lei.[97]

B. The contribution of the Romanian party:

1. Shares or assets of Romanian companies, at their nominal value.[98]

2. Areas that become available to the Romanian state as a result of the extension of prospected areas in the proportion of 50 per cent, and areas which are ceded as of now, in accordance with Article 95 of the Oil Law, to the companies of the Romanian group of the Soviet-Romanian company.

The above-mentioned lands shall be brought as a contribution by the Romanian group to the Soviet-Romanian company on the basis of an agreement between this group and the Soviet group.

The evaluation of the lands brought by the Romanian group as its contribution shall be made on the basis of the Romanian prices of the first six months of 1939 by a commission of experts in which the members of the two groups shall be in equal number. In case of non-agreement the commission of experts shall submit the matter for arbitration to the Romanian Government, which shall make a decision in agreement with the Government of the U.S.S.R.

3. 50 per cent of the royalties due yearly to the Romanian state until such time as the contributions of the two contracting parties become equal.

The crude oil shall be evaluated at the average prices in Romania in the first six months of 1939.

The capital subscribed by the two founder members shall be completely paid within three years of the date of the constitution of the company.

Within two years of the expiration of the first term of three years granted for the total payment of the subscribed capital, the two founder members shall contribute the assets (installations, land, etc.) up to the amount established as their contribution.

The difference resulting between the evaluation of the contributions and their real value, namely:

(*a*) between the par value of shares and the value of investments which constitute the assets by which these shares will be replaced within the aforementioned term, and

(*b*) between the evaluation of investments (materials, royalties, lands) at the average prices of the first quarter of 1939 and their commercial value at the time of their transfer to the society,

shall constitute a reserve of the company which shall be taxed as capital, according to Romanian laws, and not as profit, in view of the fact that it cannot be considered or used as profit.

As regards the transformation of shares, it is pointed out that the assets corresponding to the shares contributed or which will be contributed in exchange

[97] This is exactly the total value of the Romanian shares transferred to Soviet ownership. See above, Annex I to Document 2, p. 215.

[98] See below, Annex I.

for the share (*b*) of the Romanian contribution shall be evaluated as contributions to the corresponding par value of the respective share.

The difference between their evaluation and the real value of the shares shall be estimated at the end of the five-year period mentioned in Article IV, points 2 and 3, and shall also be entered into the accounts as a reserve fund.

If, as a consequence of these operations, there is a difference in the total value of the assets paid in exchange for shares by one of the contracting parties and that paid by the other contracting party, the group whose asset is smaller shall either be free to contribute the difference in similar goods evaluated on the same basis or shall compel the other group to withdraw its surplus in order to equalize the contributions.

This equalization shall be made by means of preliminary agreements as the need arises between the Soviet and Romanian groups of the company.

ARTICLE V: 1. The Soviet-Romanian company may obtain from the Romanian state rights of prospecting, exploration, and concessions for the exploitation of liquid oil in accordance with the present laws.

2. In general, at auctions in which several offers on equal terms are made for the same rights, among which is an offer of the Soviet-Romanian company, the offer of this company shall be preferred.

3. Besides the mining rights of the state, the Soviet-Romanian company may benefit also from the rights of private owners in accordance with conventions which it may conclude with them in conformity with present laws.

4. The Soviet-Romanian company may build the necessary pipelines to carry crude oil within the oil field and to carry it from the oil fields to the refineries.

5. After the contribution of royalties for the completion of the capital is effected, the Soviet-Romanian company may purchase and refine the royalties which it owes to the state from the oil produced on the company's own lands, as well as on the lands of the companies whose shares or assets enter into the composition of the capital of the Soviet-Romanian company.

6. The company shall be given the most favorable terms granted to oil companies for buying and selling of foreign exchange at the National Bank of Romania.

7. The company shall also be given the most favorable terms as regards the premiums granted by the Romanian state on imports and exports to oil companies.

8. The Soviet-Romanian company shall be granted by the Romanian authorities, without any difficulty, the foreign currency it requires for purchasing from abroad the materials and equipment necessary for its operations from the foreign currency that results from the company's own exports payable in such currency.

ARTICLE VI: Each of the founder members shall receive an equal number of shares of the capital subscribed.

The shares of the company shall be of nominal value.

The shares of the Soviet or Romanian group may be transferred only with the authorization of the respective government.

ARTICLE VII: 1. The administration of the company shall be carried out in accordance with the Romanian commercial code and with present Romanian laws, with the clarification contained in the following paragraph:

Special mention is made that the Board of Directors shall be composed of an equal number of members representing the Soviet and Romanian groups. The Chairman of the Board of Directors shall be Romanian, the Vice-Chairman Russian, the General Manager Russian, and the Assistant General Manager Romanian.

2. The liquidation of the company may be effected only after a preliminary agreement between the two Governments.

In that event the liquidation shall be made according to the Romanian commercial code.

3. All provisions concerning the organization and the functioning of the company shall be mentioned in a charter drawn up on the above-mentioned principles; the charter shall have a legal status in accordance with the Romanian commercial code.

ARTICLE VIII: The present convention shall be effective as of the date of signature. It shall be ratified by the two Governments within thirty days of the date.[90]

Annex I

List of the Romanian Oil Companies

whose shares and assets represent the Romanian contribution to the Sovrompetrol Company: Creditul Minier; Redevența; Subsolul Românesc; Astramina, Geosina; Neopetrol; Petrolul; Auxiliara Mineră; Sarver; Montana; Satelit; Luceafărul; Corana Română; Consorțiul Petrolifer; Compania Română de Petrol; Doicești; Socop; Integrupul (Petrolul Românesc, Petrol Govora, Forajul and Int. Grigorescu); Soc. Generală de Mine și Petrol; Titan; Int. Fr. Ciufu; Noris; Rasnov; Revoil; Petrol Obor.

[90] On February 18, 1948, a protocol was signed in Moscow for the partial modification of the agreement of July 17, 1945, regarding the creation of Sovrompetrol. According to this protocol, a series of oil lands among those specified in the Sovrompetrol charter was excluded from the obligation of the Romanian group, and other lands located in the rich Prahova district were added. The Romanian state was to contribute additional shares with a nominal value of 140 million lei and additional crude oil from state royalties. The Soviet group diminished its contribution in oil-field supplies, making up the difference with various shares of Romanian oil companies in its possession. The final contribution of the two groups was as follows:

Soviet Group		Romanian Group	
Shares and assets	1,769,337,000 lei	Shares and assets	1,182,800,000 lei
Equipment and supplies	730,663,000	Oil lands and crude oil	1,317,200,000
Total	2,500,000,000 lei	Total	2,500,000,000 lei

Cf. Constantin N. Jordan, *The Romanian Oil Industry*, Mid-European Studies Center and New York University Press, New York, 1955, p. 41.

Document 5. Convention for the creation of the *Soviet-Romanian Bank*[100] passed between the Government of the U.S.S.R. and the Romanian Kingdom.

ARTICLE I: The Government of the U.S.S.R. and the Royal Romanian Government appoint as incorporators of the Soviet-Romanian Bank:

For the U.S.S.R., Vneshtorgbanc (Bank for Foreign Commerce) and Prombank (Bank for Industry).

For Romania, The House of Her Highness the Princess Elizabeth, N. Malaxa Co., Usine de Fer şi Domenii Reşiţa (Reşiţa Iron Works and Domains), Banca de Credit Român (Romanian Credit Bank), Banca Hrisolveloni, Banca de Scont, Inc. (Discount Bank), and Dacia România-Asigurări, Inc. (Dacia-Romania Insurance Co.).

ARTICLE II: The Soviet-Romanian Bank shall be established in the form of a corporation, in accordance with Romanian laws, and shall enjoy all rights recognized to juridical persons of private law.

The corporation is exempted, as to its formation and the filing and the issuance of shares, from all stamp taxes and filing fees, and from all other fees due either to the state or to the Registry of Commerce and other public authorities.

In the performance of its functions the Soviet-Romanian Bank shall enjoy the same rights as banks whose capital is entirely Romanian.

ARTICLE III: The main activity of the Soviet-Romanian Bank shall be particularly directed toward the financing of commercial transactions between the U.S.S.R. and Romania and transactions which are carried on by companies established in Romania for the purpose of carrying out the Convention for Economic Collaboration between the U.S.S.R. and the Kingdom of Romania, signed at Moscow, May 8, 1945.

The Soviet-Romanian Bank shall perform all current banking operations.

ARTICLE IV: The Soviet-Romanian Bank shall have the right to acquire and to hold shares in Romanian corporations within the limits of its capital and its reserves.

ARTICLE V: 1. The authorized capital of the Soviet-Romanian Bank is 1,200,000,000 Romanian lei and is subscribed to in equal parts by the groups of Soviet and Romanian incorporators named in Article I.

2. The group of Soviet incorporators covers its subscription of 600,000,000 lei and receives in return 6,000 shares of the Soviet-Romanian Bank, in the following manner:

(*a*) For 456,700,000 lei subscribed, Prombank (Bank for Industry) contributes 533,426 shares of the Banca Comerciala Română (Romanian Commercial Bank) having a nominal value of 266,713,000 Romanian lei; 189,943 shares in the Societatea Bancară Română (Romanian Bank Corporation) hav-

[100] This convention was concluded on Oct. 26, 1945. The Bank was deemed to have come into existence as of Dec. 7, 1945. Cf. Decree Law #714 of Mar. 5, 1946. *Bulletin d'information et de documentation*, National Bank of Romania, XVIII, 1-3 (January-March 1946), p. 24.

ing a nominal value of 189,943,000 Romanian lei; and 264,000 current Romanian lei in cash, in return for 4,567 shares in the Soviet-Romanian Bank.

(*b*) For 143,500,000 lei subscribed, Vneshtorgbanc (Bank for Foreign Commerce) of the U.S.S.R. deposits 859,800,000 current lei in cash in return for 1,433 shares in the Soviet-Romanian Bank.

3. The group of Romanian incorporators covers its subscription of 600,000,000 lei, and receives in return 6,000 shares of the Soviet-Romanian Bank, in the following manner:

(*a*) The House of Her Highness Princess Elizabeth contributes 30 per cent of the total of shares issued by the Banca de Credit Român: out of a total issue of 2,400,000 shares it contributes 720,000 shares, receiving in exchange 2,057 shares in the Soviet-Romanian Bank having a nominal value of 205,700,000 lei.

(*b*) N. Malaxa Co. contributes 140,000 shares of the Banca Agricolă (Agricultural Bank) and 285,000,000 Romanian lei in cash, receiving in exchange 1,415 shares in the Soviet-Romanian Bank having a nominal value of 141,500,000 lei.

(*c*) The Usine de Fer şi Domenii Reşiţa contributes 102,000,000 Romanian lei in cash, receiving in exchange 292 shares in the Soviet-Romanian Bank having a nominal value of 29,200,000 lei.

(*d*) The Banca de Credit Român, Inc., contributes 285,000,000 Romanian lei in cash, receiving in exchange 815 shares in the Soviet-Romanian Bank having a nominal value of 81,500,000 lei.

(*e*) The Banca de Credit Român, Inc., acting in behalf of a group of clients, contributes 348,000,000 Romanian lei in cash, receiving in exchange 993 shares in the Soviet-Romanian Bank having a nominal value of 99,300,000 lei, which shares it is authorized to transfer to its clients.

(*f*) The Banca Hrisoveloni, Inc., contributes 54,000,000 Romanian lei in cash, receiving in exchange 154 shares in the Soviet-Romanian Bank having a nominal value of 15,400,000 lei.

(*g*) The Banca de Scont, Inc., contributes 54,000,000 Romanian lei in cash, receiving in exchange 154 shares in the Soviet-Romanian Bank having a nominal value of 15,400,000 lei.

(*h*) Dacia România Asigurări, Inc., contributes 42,000,000 Romanian lei in cash, receiving in return 120 shares in the Soviet-Romanian Bank having a nominal value of 12,000,000 lei.

4. The sum resulting from the difference between the amounts contributed by the two groups of incorporators in Romanian lei in cash to pay up shares of the newly created bank and the nominal value of the shares they have received in exchange shall be credited to the reserve account of the Bank.

The above-mentioned difference, and that which exists between the nominal value and the real value of shares contributed according to paragraphs 2 and 3 of the present article, shall not be considered, according to Romanian laws, as a gain to the Bank and shall not be subjected to taxes.

ARTICLE VI: Each group of incorporators, hereafter shareholders, shall be represented by an equal number of shares in the capital of the Soviet-Romanian Bank.

The shares of the bank shall be registered.

The shares of each group (Soviet and Romanian) may be transferred only with the authorization of the Board of Directors of the Bank.

ARTICLE VII: The management of the Bank shall be organized according to the commercial and banking laws of Romania, subject to the following exceptions:

The Board of Directors of the Bank shall be composed of an equal number of members representing the Soviet and Romanian groups, the Chairman of the Board of Directors being elected from the representatives of the Romanian group and the Vice-Chairman of the Board being elected from the representatives of the Soviet group.

The executive functions shall be entrusted to a general manager designated by the Soviet group and an assistant general manager designated by the Romanian group.

The articles of the bylaws of the Bank shall be drawn up in accordance with the principles laid down in the present convention and shall be approved by special Act, within seven days from the signing of the present Convention.

ARTICLE VIII: The Romanian Government shall lend all assistance to the Soviet-Romanian Bank in the conduct of its operations and, in particular, in the securing of the credit necessary to meet its needs with the National Bank of Romania or with other financial organizations of the Romanian Government.

ARTICLE IX: In the event of disagreement in general meeting of the shareholders relating to the operations of the Soviet-Romanian Bank, final decision concerning the disagreement shall rest with the Governments which have concluded this Convention.

The Governments party to this Convention can take the necessary steps to put an end to the disagreement.

ARTICLE X: The present Convention shall enter into force from the day of its signing and shall be operative until the termination of the activities of the Soviet-Romanian Bank.

It shall be ratified by each of the two states signatory within thirty days of its signing.

Liquidation may be effected only after an agreement between the Governments signatory to the Convention.

CHAPTER

7

THE TWO CYCLES OF CHANGES IN AGRICULTURE: LAND REFORMS AND COLLECTIVIZATION

Two Reorganizations of the Countryside

Immediately after the end of Nazi control of the area, the structure of private ownership in agriculture in Eastern Europe started to undergo rapid, and in some instances profound, changes. Mass colonization of the areas previously inhabited by Germans, such as the newly acquired Polish territories, the Sudetenland, and other historical German minority zones of the region, and most of the "parceling out" of the great domains were carried out from the last months of 1944 until 1946. Later measures of parceling out certain domains, for instance, of the church (in Poland) and the royal family (in Romania), put the seal on a process already basically completed.

Yet no sooner had the new socioeconomic relations been established in the rural sector than new and powerful forces started to challenge them. In effect, from 1949 on, stringent requirements of stepped-up industrialization and urbanization began to draw the rural areas into a new cycle of transformation. Various peasant strata were systematically set up one against the other; the state employed all the economic weapons at its command (taxation, obligatory deliveries of grain, credits, disposition of agricultural machinery, rental of state-owned lands, etc.) to "dislodge the capitalist element from the village," to bring the medium and poor peasants into agricultural collectives, and to increase both the crops and the marketable share of grains.

The first phase of this second cycle can be considered as completed in Yugoslavia in 1952. It ended for the area as a whole by the beginning of 1954.

The present chapter considers both the first cycle of transformation in the villages and the first phases of the second cycle. For the period extending from 1944 to 1949 a detailed account of the displacements in rural ownership is presented, with over-all tables on its structure as it emerged after the completion of colonization and land reforms. For the second period data are presented on the form, extent, and pace of collectivization drives. The disadvantageous results of forced collectivization are shown, followed by an outline of the subsequent shifts of policy in the rural area.

Remnants of Feudalism in Eastern Europe

One of the still widespread and generally accepted assertions about Eastern Europe after World War II is that a feudalistic system of agricultural land ownership had prevailed in this region as a whole until 1944, and that the new land reforms were aimed at destroying that system. The truth is that the structure of land tenure and ownership did not have any single characteristic for the area as a whole but rather a wide diversity from one country, and in many respects from one region, to the next. Moreover, the land reforms in the area had quite different aims and impacts in different countries.

If we look back to the prewar data (presented in Chapter 1, Tables 8 and 9) we recall that in three countries, Czechoslovakia, Poland, and Hungary, the domains over 100 hectares, which were only 0.5 to 0.6 per cent of the total number of agricultural holdings, covered 41 to 45 per cent of the farm land acreage. This structure of property, as well as other historical and national factors, served as the basis for the maintenance of precapitalist socioeconomic relations at least in some regions of the above-mentioned countries. The territorial changes at the end of the war partly changed this structure only in Poland, which lost to the Soviet Union the regions with predominant latifundia and forests but also acquired former German regions where the large estates of over 100 hectares covered 33 per cent of the farm land area.

In sharp contrast to these three countries, in Bulgaria and Yugoslavia the holdings of over 50 hectares, i.e., 0.1 per cent of the total number of holdings in Bulgaria and 0.5 per cent in Yugoslavia, covered only 1.6 per cent of the total Bulgarian farm land and 9.7 per cent of the Yugoslav. In both countries the process of so-called *territorialization* of the peasant was virtually completed. This process, consisting of the liquidation of large estates and feudal land tenure and the distribution of land to the peasants, had been under way in certain regions for more than a century and had entered its last phases before the end of the pre-World War II period.

Romania held a somewhat intermediate position. In the prewar period properties of over 100 hectares included 27.7 per cent of the Romanian farm land acreage; in the postwar years they covered some 21.6 per cent. However, successive land reforms had dissolved in Romania too most of the precapitalist socioeconomic relations in the countryside.

Thus, although it is legitimate to point to feudalistic remnants in the prewar structure of land ownership in Czechoslovakia, Poland, and Hungary, especially in the latter two countries, it is inaccurate to speak of the much divided farm lands of Yugoslavia and Bulgaria in the same terms.

Furthermore, at the beginning of the post-World War II period, the basic aim of the land reforms in Czechoslovakia and Poland was, as we shall presently see, not the pursuit of liquidation of "feudalistic remnants" but the mass *colonization* of previously German-held territories. Only in Hungary, representing the exception and not the rule for the region as a whole, did the extensive postwar land reform represent the first and last acts in the destruction of latifundia, or large landed estates.

Consequently we propose to study in turn: Czechoslovakia and Poland, i.e., *the process of colonization;* Hungary, i.e., the *process of destruction of latifundia;* Romania, Yugoslavia, and Bulgaria, i.e., the *process of recurrent land reforms* and continuous splitting up of land ownership.

"National Purges" of Land Ownership in Czechoslovakia and Poland

Before the complete liberation of Czechoslovakia from the Nazis the idea of a "radical solution" of the German and Hungarian minority problems in the border regions was embodied in the "Košice Program" in the form of a decision to confiscate *all the land* belonging to these minority groups. With liberation, this decision was translated into law. All the agricultural property belonging to German and Hungarian nationals and to traitors and enemies of the Republic was confiscated and, except for the forests which were taken over by the state, the land thus acquired was allotted to "persons of Slav nationality." [1]

According to the official data, these dispositions affected a total of nearly 3.1 million hectares, of which 2.5 million were in Czech lands and 550,000 in Slovakia. German agricultural ownership of Czech lands comprised 1.5 million hectares of agricultural land (i.e., arable land, pastures, and meadows) and 1 million hectares of forest and woodland. Of these, 100,000 hectares of agricultural land and 300,000 hectares of forests were situated in the interior, the rest in the border districts. The German land owners and agriculturists, big and small, were expelled together with the entire Sudeten population. The land affected was 36.5 per cent of the total agricultural and woodland area of the Czech provinces. Considering only the border zones as they were defined in 1936, i.e., the regions extending over 24,600 square kilometers in Bohemia and 12,400 in Moravia and Silesia [2] where most of the German settlers were, the percentage of land affected by the reform would rise to 70 per cent of the total available agricultural and woodland area. In Slovakia, where German and Hungarian land ownership was more limited, the reform affected only 11.4 per cent of the total agricultural and woodland areas of the province. Of the 550,000 hectares of land involved, of which about half was agricultural and half forest land, some 473,000 hectares belonged to German nationals, the rest to Hungarians and collaborationists.[3]

The total confiscated thus comprised 1.8 million hectares of agricultural land and 1.3 million hectares of forests. Out of the 1.4 million agricultural hectares in the border regions, 1.04 million hectares were handed over to 122,000 families of Slav settlers, of which over 100,000 families were from the agricultural regions in the interior of Bohemia, some 8,000 were Czech repatriates from neighboring countries (mostly Poland), and the rest were those of soldiers either in service or demo-

[1] Decrees No. 12 of June 21, 1945, on the confiscation of land; No. 28 of July 12, 1945, on the settlement of Slav farmers; No. 63 of Sept. 3, 1945, on the institution of the National Land Fund. See Dr. Valer Fabry, *Agricultural Laws of the Czechoslovak Republic, May 1945–March 1949*, Ministry of Agriculture, Library of the Czechoslovak Institute for International Collaboration in Agriculture and Forestry, Vol. 17, Brazda, Prague, 1949.

[2] The total surface area of the Czechoslovak provinces include: Bohemia—52,000 sq. km.; Moravia—22,300; Silesia—4,400; Slovakia—48,900. The total of the surface of the country, including Transcarpathian Ukraine (12,600 sq. km.) amounted to 140,400 sq. km. in 1937; after the postwar concession of the latter province to the Soviet Union it amounted to 127,800 sq. km. (See above, Chapter 1, Table 1, p. 3, and Chapter 2, Table 17, p. 32.

[3] Dr. J. Kořátko, *Land Reform in Czechoslovakia*, Orbis, Prague, 1948, *passim.*

bilized.[4] As for the forests, of 700,000 hectares which had formed part of large German estates and 300,000 hectares which had been in the hands of German farmers, 840,000 hectares were taken over by the state and 160,000 hectares were distributed to the villages. Individuals obtained allocation of forest land only in a few exceptional cases.

Thus after liberation the land reform consisted essentially of a "national purge of the Czech lands" which left "on the one hand, large-scale ownership of land by Czech and Slovak nationals untouched . . . and on the other hand completely [liquidated] not only German-owned big estates, but also the medium and small peasant holdings owned by Germans." [5]

The question of Slav-owned large estates was attacked only later through two basic legislative measures: revision of the first Land Reform Act (i.e., revision of the reform of post-World War I), and a New Land Reform Act. The first of these bills, adopted in 1947,[6] extended the principle of revision to landed property of over 150 hectares of agricultural land or over 250 hectares of land of any type which either had been exempt from sequestration during the prewar land reforms or had come, by concentration of land, to exceed the above-mentioned limits. In exceptional cases of urgent local need the estates in excess of 50 hectares could also be taken over by the state. According to Kořátko, the Czech and Slovak land-owner holdings thus affected, consisting mostly of residuary estates, could be estimated at some 700–800 thousand hectares,[7] an area equal to one-fourth that obtained at the liberation through the colonization of German-owned land. The second bill, the New Land Reform Act for "permanent regulation of ownership of agricultural and forestry land" of 1948,[8] fixed the limit of "the largest amount of land that may be owned by a working farmer and members of his family if they have their permanent domicile and a common household with the owner at 50 hectares," [9] the rest to be *purchased* by the state. The land expropriated through the New Land Reform Act can be estimated to have totaled some 700,000 hectares.

The total land expropriated attained finally 4.5 million hectares, of which 1.7 million were distributed to 350,000 small, medium, and landless peasants and 50,000 to workers and employees. The state retained

[4] *Ibid.*, pp. 23–24.

[5] *Ibid.*, p. 13.

[6] Bill of July 1947, No. 142 B.O.L. Cf. Fabry, *op. cit.*, pp. 13–14.

[7] Kořátko, *op. cit.*, p. 34.

[8] March 21, 1948. Cf. Fabry, *op. cit.*, pp. 13 ff.

[9] *Ibid.*

500,000 hectares of arable land and 2 million hectares of forests; 250,000 additional hectares were allotted to public institutions.[10] The changes in land ownership as they appeared in 1949 are compared to the prewar situation in Table 53. The total number of holdings and private acreage up to 50 hectares in the Czech lands had diminished approxi-

TABLE 53. CZECHOSLOVAKIA: CHANGES IN THE STRUCTURE OF LAND OWNERSHIP IN THE CZECH LANDS AND IN SLOVAKIA, 1949, COMPARED TO PREWAR

Size-Groups of Holdings by Total Acreage, ha.	1930		1949		Difference in 1949	
	Number of agricultural holdings 1	Total acreage, ha. 2	Number of agricultural holdings 3	Total acreage, ha. 4	Number of agricultural holdings, %, ± 5	Total acreage, %, ± 6
Czech Lands						
0–0.5	209,357	54,112	222,222	60,706	+6.1	+12.2
0.5–1	134,868	100,931	130,383	96,004	−3.3	−4.9
1–2	163,997	244,304	111,641	163,988	−31.9	−32.9
2–5	278,236	931,036	194,831	659,270	−30.0	−29.2
5–10	144,713	1,021,495	149,023	1,069,233	+3.0	+4.7
10–20	95,459	1,355,445	118,818	1,656,996	+24.5	+22.2
20–50	45,921	1,284,149	27,653	792,961	−39.8	−38.3
Total (under 50)	1,072,551	4,991,472	954,571	4,499,158	−11.0	−9.9
50 plus	8,138	2,547,497	7,045	2,606,678	−13.4	+2.3
Slovakia						
0–0.5	51,766	15,551	74,824	23,748	+44.5	+52.7
0.5–1	43,412	32,582	61,313	51,034	+41.2	+56.6
1–2	76,103	114,438	94,995	153,403	+24.8	+34.0
2–5	125,647	426,251	156,073	580,345	+24.2	+36.2
5–10	94,877	675,866	106,270	811,623	+12.0	+20.1
10–20	45,068	607,253	40,056	557,835	−11.1	−8.1
20–50	11,139	319,342	7,506	240,031	−32.6	−24.8
Total (under 50)	448,012	2,191,283	541,037	2,418,019	+20.8	+10.3
50 plus	6,943	2,496,343	4,444	2,203,586	−36.0	−11.7

Source: Dr. L. Stejskal, "Program Sčítání Zemědělských v. r. 1950" (Program of the Census of Agricultural Holdings in 1950), *SZ*, XIII, 2 (February 1950), p. 46.

[10] U.N. Department of Economic Affairs, *Progress in Land Reform: Analysis of Replies by Governments to a United Nations Questionnaire,* New York, 1954, p. 68.

mately 10 per cent. The extent of the colonization process is apparent not only in the very substantial decreases in the number of holdings and in acreage in the bracket from 20 to 50 hectares (a fall of almost 40 per cent) but also in the decreases in the low brackets of 1–2 and 2–5 hectares, where they are, significantly, about 30 per cent. Also, substantial increases are to be noted in the brackets 5–10 and 10–20 hectares, the usual size of new settlers' holdings.

In Slovakia, where the agricultural acreage available for distribution was more limited, a contrasting development can be noted. The number of holdings and the private acreage increased by 20 and 10 per cent, respectively, compared to prewar, with increases in all the brackets up to 10 hectares and a very substantial increase in holdings of 1 hectare or less, whereas the decreases are essentially in the brackets over 50 hectares. Thus, whereas in the Czech lands the expulsion of Germans permitted a relative consolidation of medium-sized peasant farms, in Slovakia the result of the displacements of ownership was further division of the land into dwarf and small holdings.

For the country as a whole, notwithstanding those changes in ownership up to 50 hectares, the total of the holdings over 50 hectares, now largely taken over by the state, had not diminished as compared to prewar. Before the war the acreage in holdings up to 50 hectares was 7.1 million hectares, or 58.7 per cent of the total of agricultural and woodland areas. After the postwar reforms this percentage remained approximately the same, 58.9 per cent. In other words, the state ultimately appropriated for itself the relative shares previously held by large estates and public ownerships combined, and it did *not increase at all* the total relative share of the private farmers (hence, the Slav settlers in general simply took the place of the small and medium German settlers).

In Poland land reform consisted of both mass colonization of newly acquired territories and of certain readjustments in the former territories.

The provisions of the reform were embodied in a decree which the Polish Committee for National Liberation (the so-called Lublin Committee) promulgated in the fall of 1944.[11] This decree provided for the confiscation of land owned (*a*) by citizens of the Reich not of Polish nationality by origin and by Polish citizens claiming German nation-

[11] Decree of Sept. 6, 1944, implemented by Executive Order of the Ministry of Agriculture and Land Reform on Mar. 1, 1945. See Stanisław Gryziewicz, "Rolnictwo" (Agriculture), in *Kultura,* Numer Krajowy, Vol. I, 1952, pp. 306–307.

ality; (*b*) by traitors; (*c*) by physical or corporate entities whose holdings exceeded 100 hectares. The properties of the Church were excluded from the decree up to the spring of 1950. Moreover, a special decree provided for the confiscation of forests and woodlands with an area of over 25 hectares and all real estate and movables utilized for the conduct of forest husbandry.[12]

According to official data, the total acreage affected by the reform was 13.8 million hectares of all types of land, of which 9.4 million were in the newly acquired territories and 4.4 million (of which one-fourth was German land) in the former Polish territories (see Table 54).[13] In

TABLE 54. POLAND: LAND REFORM AND RESETTLEMENT, SEPT. 6, 1944–JAN. 1, 1949

(in thousands of hectares)

Territories	Total Acreage Affected by the Reform and Resettlement	Distribution: Allotted to farmers (land reform proper)	Distribution: Left to local population	Distribution: Passed into public property: Taken over by various state and public administrations [a]	Distribution: Passed into public property: Forests, waterways, and roads (not for distribution)
Total	13,846.6	5,944.8		3,800.8	3,592.0
Newly acquired territories	9,437.6	4,004.9	459.0	2,702.1	2,271.6
Old territories	4,409.0	1,989.9		1,098.7	1,320.4
(of which former German lands)	(923.4)	(779.0)		(130.3)	(14.1)

[a] Administration of state farms, of state forests, for agricultural cooperatives, for schools, etc.

Source: Rocznik Statystyczny 1949, op. cit., Table 3*A*, p. 54, and Table 5, p. 58.

the West the acreage affected, 6.2 million hectares of arable land, 2.2 of forest, 1.0 of barren land, was virtually all the land available. Of this total, 459,000 hectares were left to the local (Polish) population and 4.0 million hectares were distributed to new settlers. In the pre-

[12] Decree of Dec. 12, 1944, implemented by Executive Order of Jan. 20, 1945.

[13] The data referring to the Polish land reform is based on the comprehensive coverage presented by *Rocznik Statystyczny 1949,* op. cit. Subsequently the Polish Institute for Agricultural Economics published a summary tabulation of the land distributed, which is at variance with the *Rocznik*. Thus, according to the second source, *Wieś w Liczbach,* op. cit., 3rd ed. (Warsaw, 1954), the total distributed to the peasants in the newly acquired territories attained actually only 3.685 million ha. (against 4.004 million indicated in 1950), and the land distributed in the old territories attained 2.384 million ha. (instead of 1.098 million). Throughout this section we shall, however, rely on the *Rocznik,* as the *Wieś w Liczbach* does not present the underlying data for its revised estimates.

war period some 1.1 million German estates under 100 hectares covered 6.2 million hectares; about 9 million estates over 100 hectares covered 3.2 million hectares. After the expulsion of the Germans there were established in the new territories a total of 483,000 agricultural holdings covering 4.0 million hectares of land, i.e., with an average of 8.3 hectares per newly created holding. The upper limit per holding was subsequently fixed at 15 hectares for land utilized in agriculture and 20 hectares for land used for livestock.[14] According to the figures released officially, most of the new settlers were repatriates from the East and landless peasants from the overpopulated former Polish territories, and families of demobilized soldiers and farm hands.[15]

In the former Polish territories, the land affected by the reform amounted to 21 per cent of the agricultural and woodland areas, distributed among 498,000 holdings. As can be seen from Table 55,

TABLE 55. POLAND: LAND REDISTRIBUTION IN THE NEWLY ACQUIRED TERRITORIES AND IN THE FORMER POLISH LANDS

Acreage and Holdings	Total: Newly acquired territories 1	Total: German lands in former territory 2	Total: Former lands (excluding German lands) 3	Detail in Former Polish Territory (excluding German-owned lands): New farms [a] 4	Expanded farms of owners of holdings: Under 2 ha. 5	Expanded farms of owners of holdings: 2–5 ha. 6	Expanded farms of owners of holdings: 5–10 ha. 7	Other 8
Acreage redistributed (thousands of ha.)	4,004.9	779.0	1,210.9	788.7	131.2	237.6	43.7	9.7
No. of holdings (thousands)	483.0	90.5	407.5	162.6	86.0	124.3	23.6	11.0
Average ha. per holding	8.3	8.6	3.0	4.9	1.5	1.9	1.9	0.9

[a] For farm hands and landless peasants.

Source: Rocznik Statystyczny 1949, op. cit. For col. 1, Table 3*B*, p. 54; for col. 2, Table 4*E*, p. 56; for col. 3, Table 5*C*, p. 59; for cols. 4–8, Tables 4*B* and 4*C*, p. 55.

90,500 holdings were redistributed from the previously German-owned land (column 2) with an average of 8.6 hectares per newly created

[14] The peasant holdings created under the resettlement scheme: ". . . remained for a long time indeterminate as far as boundaries and recorded titles of ownership were concerned. From the legal point of view the situation of these holdings was rather undefined and fluid. Three hundred thirty-eight thousand holdings of this kind [with an area of 2.9 million ha.] were affected in this way up to September 6, 1951, when a decree finally normalized their status." [S. Gryziewicz, *op. cit.*, p. 315.]

[15] *Życie Warszawy* on Sept. 6, 1949, gave the following figures· 200,000 families of repatriates; 40,000 families of former soldiers; 5,000 farm hands.

holding. On the Polish lands proper 162,600 new farms were created, with an average of 4.9 hectares per holding (column 4). Some 230,000 dwarf, small, and medium farms were expanded by an average of 1.5 to 1.9 hectares per holding (columns 5–7). According to the official data, a total of 788,000 new farms were created in the country as a whole and distributed to 572,000 families of farm hands and 216,000 families of landless peasants. Notwithstanding the large area available in the West and the comfortable size of the holdings allotted there to new settlers, many of the dwarf peasants, attached to their traditional locations in the former Polish provinces, apparently shunned transfer to the West.

The breakdown of the number of agricultural holdings in the newly acquired territories and former Polish lands reveals trends similar to those observed in Czechoslovakia (see Table 56). For the newly colo-

TABLE 56. POLAND: NUMBER OF AGRICULTURAL HOLDINGS IN THE NEWLY ACQUIRED TERRITORIES AND IN THE FORMER POLISH LANDS, 1947 COMPARED TO 1931

Size-Groups of Holdings by Total Acreage, ha.		Number of Agricultural Holdings within Present Boundaries, in thousands		
		1931	1947	Difference in 1949
Newly acquired territories	0–2	766.3	71.8	−163.1
	2–5	89.1	82.3	−7.7
	5–10	104.7	135.5	+29.5
	10–20	101.7	142.3	+39.9
	20–50	56.2	17.5	−68:9
Total	(0–50)	1,118.0	449.4	−59.8
	50 plus	19.8	7.1	−64.2
Former territories	0–2	377.8	759.2	+101.0
	2–5	638.5	910.1	+42.5
	5–10	440.7	701.1	+59.1
	10–20 [a]	124.7	253.1	+103.0
	20–50	77.9	51.1	−34.4
Total	(0–50)	1,659.6 [b]	2,674.6	+61.2
	50 plus	10.9	11.9	+9.2

[a] The divisions for 1931 are 10–15, 15–50.

[b] There were 113,500 holdings not accounted for specifically and labeled "unknown."

Sources:

1931: *Statistical Yearbook of Poland 1947, op. cit.*, pp. 38–39.

1947: *Statistical Yearbook of Poland 1948, op. cit.*, p. 38.

nized region, just as in the Czech lands, we note a sharp decrease in the total number of holdings and in the holdings on the fringes, i.e., in the dwarf holdings and in the holdings over 20 and 50 hectares. In contrast, in the former Polish territories, just as in Slovakia, the total number of holdings increased substantially (by 61 per cent over prewar), and there was a large increase in the number of dwarf holdings. The apparently unexpected increase in the holdings of 10–15 hectares can, at least in part, be imputed to some newly created farms on the German-owned lands in the former Polish territories.[16]

Thus the expulsion of the German population made possible the creation of an important stratum of medium-sized peasant holdings in the West without relieving *in toto* the pressure of rural overpopulation in the former Polish provinces.[17]

The Liquidation of Latifundia in Hungary

Turning to Hungary, let us note from the outset that of all the East European countries only Hungary had not witnessed any truly significant changes in its land-ownership structure in more than a century. In fact, for several reasons (socioeconomic importance of the large land holders, total failure of the 1919 revolutionary upheavals, etc.) the relative share of the large estates in the total farm land had continued to show a systematic increase. In pre-World War I Hungary estates of over 100 hectares covered 30.6 per cent of the farm land; in 1921 they covered 41.1 per cent; and in 1935, 43.1 per cent. Also in 1935, the privately owned estates of over 500 hectares represented 17.1 per cent, and those of over 1,700 hectares 11.5 per cent of the total farm land acreage. Hungarian post-World War I land reform was the least important in the region, affecting only some 600,000 hectares, of which 240,000 hectares went to the state in payment of land taxes, some 100,000 hectares were purchased by the state, and 250,000 hectares were

[16] Polish statistics supply data on farm land acreage distribution per groups of holdings for the country as a whole, but not by regions. Only a sample of this distribution is made available for the new territories, but the groups of holdings are differently tabulated (e.g., under 7 ha., 7–9 ha., 9–12 ha., 12–15 ha., over 15 ha.).

[17] In a rather roundabout way, Minc states that this overpopulation has only been *reduced,* thanks to the transfers to the West:

> The Recovered Territories are now inhabited by about six million Poles of whom five million are new settlers. The ethnical character of these lands has been changed completely and the agricultural overpopulation in Central Poland *materially reduced.* [Cf. *Poland's Economy Present and Future, op. cit.,* p. 21.]

willingly sold by the owners. Of this total less than 400,000 hectares were actually parceled out. There was no expropriation of land in Hungary until the post-World War II reform.

Introduced in the spring of 1945 by a decree of the provisional government,[18] the new land reform provided for confiscation and transfer into a state land fund of the estates of traitors and collaborationists and all large estates of over 1,000 cadastral acres (575 hectares).[19] The landed properties of the Church were included in the last category but with the specification that the Church could retain up to 100 cadastral acres (57.5 hectares) even when the original estate comprised more than 1,000 acres. The maximum for a private farm holding was established at 200 cadastral acres (115 hectares). This limit was raised to 300 cadastral acres only for a few anti-fascist agriculturists.

According to official data, the new land reform affected a total of 3.2 million hectares of agricultural and woodland area, or 38.8 per cent of the land available, of which some 1.9 million were rapidly redistributed to 642,000 claimants. The latifundia were thus annihilated. By 1947 there were only 21 *private* properties of the maximum size of 300 cadastral acres. The large estates of the Church, which before the war had extended over more than 1 million cadastral acres, were reduced to less than one-fifth that amount.[20] A representative sample of the distribution of land to 511,000 claimants (out of the total of 642,000) reveals that the new farms created by the reform averaged 3 hectares per holding, and that the dwarf and small holdings acquiring new land were expanded on the average by some 1.9 to 2.3 hectares per holding (see Table 57).

According to official data, the new land reform effected several changes in the structure of land ownership (see Table 58). There were very large increases in the acreage allotted to the low bracket of dwarf holdings (the "subsistence units" producing little, if at all, for the

18 Decree of March 17, 1945.

19 One cadastral acre = 0.575 hectare.

20 Out of a total of 1,006,311 cadastral acres belonging to churches of all denominations, 862,704 belonged to the Roman Catholic Church. Some were very large estates—like the Hungarian Catholic Religious Foundation which covered 122,000 acres; the Principal Chapter of Eger, 94,000 acres; the Holy Benedictine Order of Pannonhalma, 84,000 acres; the Archbishopric of Kalocza, 82,500 acres, etc. The total left to all religious denominations after the reforms amounted to 181,064 cadastral acres (about 104,000 ha.) of which about one-half were left to the Catholic Church. See *GT*, II, 9 (July 1948), p. 547; also Ilona Polányi, "The Issues in Hungary," in *World Affairs*, 2-3, 1948-49, pp. 138-139.

TABLE 57. HUNGARY: SAMPLE OF LAND DISTRIBUTION, NEW AND EXPANDED FARMS

Acreage and Holdings	Total	New Farms [a]	Expanded Farms of Owners of Holdings: Under 2.8 ha.	Expanded Farms of Owners of Holdings: 2.8–5.7 ha.
Acreage redistributed (thousands of ha.)	1,358.0	971.0	323.6	63.4
Number of holdings (thousands)	511.2	320.0	163.7	27.5
Average ha. per holding		3.0	1.9	2.3

[a] Farm hands, rural artisans, agriculturists.

Source: Information hongroise, Bureau hongrois de presse et de documentation (Hungarian Information, Hungarian Bureau of Press and Documentation), March 18, 1946.

TABLE 58. HUNGARY: CHANGES IN THE STRUCTURE OF LAND OWNERSHIP, 1947–48 COMPARED TO 1934–35

Size-Groups of holdings by total acreage, ha.	1934–35: Number of agricultural holdings [a]	1934–35: Total acreage, ha.[a]	1947–48: Number of agricultural holdings [a]	1947–48: Total acreage, ha.[a]	Difference in 1947–48: Number of agricultural holdings, %	Difference in 1947–48: Total acreage, %
	1	2	3	4	5	6
0– 2.8	1,358.0	1,030.2	1,229.8	2,081.8	−9.5	+102.0
2.8–11.4	362.4	2,106.3	631.0	3,930.3	+74.1	+86.5
11.4–28.0	81.8	1,383.1	56.4	959.1	−31.1	−30.7
28.0–57.5	15.7	613.9	9.1	371.2	−42.1	−39.6
Total	1,817.9	5,133.5	1,926.3	7,342.4	+5.9	+43.0
57.5 plus	14.1	4,092.8	6.6	1,862.3	−53.2	−54.5

[a] In thousands.

Source: GT, III, 4–5 (April–May 1949), pp. 227–228.

market).[21] Sharp decreases in the number of holdings of over 11.4 hectares reduced further the already relatively small number of medium

[21] The decrease in the number of holdings in the group up to 2.8 hectares and the total net increase of only 140,400 holdings for the combined groups from 0 to 11.4 hectares would suggest that here, too, an appreciable number of small holdings simply changed hands from their previous small owners (Germans or collaborationists) to new small owners.

and large peasant holdings. Finally, the decrease in the number of holdings of over 57.5 hectares (2.2 million hectares) clearly indicated the destruction of the private large estates. The combined share of the collective bodies and the state, some 19.7 per cent of the total land, or 1.8 million hectares before the reform, declined only slightly since most of this land was taken over by the state. Most of the forest areas, for instance, passed to either ownership or management by the State Forest Administration (Mallerd).[22]

It should be noted that the significant changes in the structure of land ownership effected by the reform neither provided land for all the landless peasantry nor solved the problem of overpopulation in the countryside. As against the 642,000 claimants who received small allocations of land, prewar data show that 779,000 poor peasants had neither land nor cottages of their own, and that there were some 3 million poverty-stricken peasants and their families in the villages.[23] Moreover, the former large estates employed more wage labor than did the new very small peasant households created through the reform.

The Land Reforms in Romania, Yugoslavia, and Bulgaria

In Romania, Yugoslavia, and Bulgaria, where only a small amount of acreage was available for colonization and where important land reforms had been carried out previously, the postwar reforms had a comparatively limited scope, affecting only 2 per cent of the total agricultural and forest area in Bulgaria and around 7 per cent in Romania and Yugoslavia.

The reform introduced in Romania in the spring of 1945 [24] provided for the expropriation of the lands of German nationals, traitors, and absentee land owners; properties of over 50 hectares "which have not been cultivated during the last seven years by their owners themselves"; and all private holdings in excess of 50 hectares.[25] The estates

[22] Cf. *GT,* III, 4–5 (April–May 1949), pp. 227–228.

[23] See *Today and Yesterday, op. cit.,* p. 27.

[24] March 22, 1945. Cf. *La Réforme agraire en Roumanie* (The Land Reform in Romania), Ministry of Information, Office of Foreign Cultural Relations, Bucharest, 1946, pp. 35 ff. Actually before the accession to power of the Groza government (March 6, 1945), the Communists encouraged the peasants to start dividing the large estates, thus placing the cabinet of General Radescu "in a very unstable position." Cf. *Le Puissant Mouvement populaire pour le renversement du gouvernement Radescu* (The Powerful Popular Movement for the Overthrow of the Radescu Government), Ministry of Foreign Affairs of the Romanian People's Republic, Bucharest, 1952, p. 29.

[25] *La Reforme agraire . . . , op. cit.,* p. 31.

of the King and of the royal family were excepted from the 1945 reform; at the end of 1947 they were transferred to the state after the abdication of the King and the proclamation of the Republic. Some so-called "model farms" or "agricultural centers," each extending up to 150 hectares, were left to private owners for the production of selected seeds, breeding of thoroughbred animals, etc. These farms, including all the holdings of 50 hectares, were subsequently labeled "feudal sabotage nests" and were expropriated with their inventories in the spring of 1949.[26]

The 1945 reform affected 143,000 estates and involved a total of 1.4 million hectares, of which 1.05 million were redistributed to 860,000 claimants, an average of 1.2 hectares per claimant.[27] The published provisional results of the agricultural census of 1948 supply the figures for the number of holdings and private land owners by groups of holdings but do not give data on their respective share in farm land acreage. They clearly suggest a further substantial increase in the total number (and probably acreage) of the subsistence units and dwarf and small estates. Some 50 per cent of the total of 5.5 million agricultural land owners were now owners of 0.5–1 hectare and 1–2 hectare estates. Over 78 per cent owned 0–3 hectares. From the point of view of agricultural *holdings* (which usually employ the acreage of two owners) at the end of the reform, holdings up to 3 hectares represented 1.6 million out of a total of 3.0 million, or over one-half. As the Romanian authors of the study on the 1948 census note:

> If 3 hectares represent generally the *minimum* land estate necessary for the maintenance in agriculture of an exploitation comprised of four persons, then more than one-half of the agricultural exploitations of Romania do not reach this level and are compelled to resort to some side-line income or to reduce their needs.[28]

The recurrent Romanian land reforms, trying, as it were, to catch up with progressive overpopulation in agriculture, thus admittedly brought about only limited and temporary relief to the situation in the villages. The laws of land expropriation became more and more severe, but their impact became progressively less extensive.

In Yugoslavia the land reform law was enacted in the summer of 1945.[29] The new Constitution of the Republic set a limit of 25 to 35

[26] *SC*, March 3, 1949.

[27] *CS*, No. 17 (1947), Tables 6 and 9.

[28] Golopenția and Onică, *Recensământul Agricol . . .* (Agricultural Census), *op. cit.*, p. 18.

[29] August 29, 1945.

hectares of arable land per holding, according to the region, and the total land per holding at 45 hectares. Areas exceeding 3 hectares were taken away from those who did not cultivate the land themselves. The reforms liquidated without compensation the large estates of private land owners, land corporations, and banks. The churches and monasteries were left 10–30 hectares of arable land and up to 30 hectares of forest area. Finally, here too all the German settlers were expelled. Notwithstanding these drastic measures, the total land expropriated amounted to only 1.566 million hectares (far less than after the first World War) of which 637,000 hectares were former German-owned land. Out of the total, 797,000 hectares were distributed among 316,000 families, of which 180,000 were families of poor peasants, 71,000 were families of landless peasants, and 65,000 were new settlers from other areas,[30] the distribution averaging 2.5 hectares per family. Furthermore, the government canceled all peasant debts.

The bulk of the land made available to new settlers was located in Vojvodina and Slavonia, where peasants from the grain-deficiency areas replaced the former German holders.[31] The state ultimately took 49 per cent of the total expropriated land (18.3 per cent for state farms, 4.3 per cent to the state forest fund, etc.).

The changes in private ownership are summarized in Table 59. The comparison between 1931 and 1950 reveals that the increase in acreage for owners of less than 10 hectares was approximately 600,000 hectares. (Obviously most of the beneficiaries of the reform were in this category). The shifts within this category increased the number of holdings of 2–5 and 5–10 hectares and reduced the *number* of dwarf holdings, while increasing their total *acreage*. There was a decrease in the total acreage of holdings of over 10 hectares from nearly 4.8 million hectares to 3.1 million. (The decrease represents most of the land expropriated.) The total number of holdings has decreased by some 42,000 units, and the average per holding for the group as a whole has decreased from over 20 to around 16 hectares, but the exact shifts between the two levels considered are blurred since the number of holdings accounted for in 1950 was not the same as in 1931.

Of all the East European countries Bulgaria least needed land reform of the type described above. In fact, the aim of land reform in Bulgaria was stated as being the liquidation of the "big *capitalist* landed

[30] *Statistički Godišnjak FNRJ 1954*, Belgrade, 1954, p. 115.

[31] Dr. Anton Melik, *Jugoslavija* (Yugoslavia), Državna Založba Slovenije (State Publishing House of Slovenia), Ljubljana, 1952, pp. 453 ff.

TABLE 59. YUGOSLAVIA: CHANGES IN THE STRUCTURE OF LAND OWNERSHIP, 1950 COMPARED TO 1931

Size-Groups of holdings by total acreage, ha.	1931		1950		Difference in 1950	
	Number of agricultural holdings [a]	Total acreage, ha.[a]	Number of agricultural holdings [a]	Total acreage, ha.[a]	Number of agricultural holdings, %, ±	Total acreage, %, ±
	1	2	3	4	5	6
0–2	671.8	693.5	598.8	719.0	−10.9	+3.6
2–5	676.3	2,287.6	790.3	2,690.7	+16.8	+17.6
5–10	407.2	2,873.1	433.4	2,994.2	+6.4	+4.2
10–20 [a]	174.0	2,380.8	110.6	1,343.4	−18.6	−35.1
20 plus [a]	56.3	2,410.9	76.9	1,769.3		
Total	1,985.6	10,645.9	2,010.0	9,516.6	+1.2	−10.7

[a] In thousands.
[b] In 1950, groups are 10–15 ha. and 15 plus.
Sources:
1931: *Statistički Godišnjak 1936, op. cit.*, pp. 88–89; also Melik, *op. cit.*, p. 453.
1950: *Socialistička Polioprivreda* (Socialist Agriculture), January 1952, as quoted by *Progress in Land Reform, op. cit.*, p. 16.

property."[82] A total of 45,000 hectares was taken from 2,450 "large owners," or 18.5 hectares per "large owner," and 120,000 hectares from the landed properties of the Church and monasteries, i.e., 165,000 hectares, of which 120,000 hectares were redistributed.[83] The end results, as they appear from Table 60, were a further increase of about 30 per cent in the dwarf and small holdings, a further reduction in the number and total acreage of holdings over 10 hectares, and a probable increase in the state-managed land not exceeding, however, a total of 200,000 hectares (see Table 60, rows 20–50 ha., 50 plus ha., and column 4).

As Chernokólev himself noted in 1948,

> The land reform has only a limited importance. It could not liquidate the scarcity of land or the excess of agricultural population. This problem remains to be solved by the intensive development of industry capable of absorbing the overpopulation from the countryside.[84]

[82] T. Chernokólev, "The Agrarian Policy of the Bulgarian Workers Party," in *FLP*, July 15, 1948.
[83] *Ibid.*
[84] *Ibid.*

TABLE 60. BULGARIA: CHANGES IN THE STRUCTURE OF LAND OWNERSHIP, 1946 COMPARED TO 1934 [a]

Size-Groups of holdings by total acreage, ha.	1934		1946		Difference in 1946	
	Number of agricultural holdings	Total acreage, ha.	Number of agricultural holdings	Total acreage, ha.	Number of agricultural holdings, %	Total acreage, %
	1	2	3	4	5	6
0– 2.0	239,417	233,147	309,291	304,487	+29.2	+30.6
2.0– 5.0	319,688	1,079,698	403,129	1,364,236	+26.1	+26.4
5.0–10.0	231,881	1,607,173	254,860	1,739,307	+9.9	+8.2
10.0–20.0	81,233	1,064,490	64,554	826,048	−20.5	−22.4
Total	872,219	3,984,508	1,031,834	4,234,078	+11.8	+10.6
20.0–50.0	12,089	314,786	6,968	172,381	−42.4	−45.2
50.0 plus	561	69,136	270	29,968	−51.9	−56.7

[a] Old Bulgaria, not including South Dobrudgea.

Source: MI, July 1947, p. 25.

SUMMARY ON AREA TRENDS

In the region as a whole land reform affected a total of close to 25 million hectares or one-quarter of the total agricultural and woodland areas. Over 56 per cent of that total was in Poland and consisted of former German lands. Furthermore, Czechoslovakia, Poland, and Hungary together account for close to 90 per cent of the total, only a little over 10 per cent being found in the other three countries (see Table 61).

As can be seen from Chart 8 on the comparative land reforms in Poland and Hungary, because of the extensive colonization process and the destruction of latifundia, the reform involved a far larger amount of land after World War II than after World War I. In Romania, Yugoslavia, and Bulgaria the amount of land expropriated and distributed was smaller after World War II than after World War I. In Czechoslovakia the changes closely parallel those which followed there after World War I.

On the basis of the official data available for the end of the land reform process (around 1949) a country-by-country comparison of the effects on the structure of ownership reveals the following trends:

TABLE 61. RATIOS OF LAND EXPROPRIATED AND DISTRIBUTED TO TOTAL AGRICULTURAL AND FOREST AREA UP TO 1948

Country	Total Agricultural and Forest Area	Total Expropriated	Total Distributed	Ratios		
				2 ÷ 1	3 ÷ 1	3 ÷ 2
	1	2	3	4	5	6
Czechoslovakia	11,729	4,500	1,700	38.4	14.5	37.8
Poland	27,773	13,868	5,995	49.9	21.6	43.2
Hungary	8,300	3,222	1,874	38.8	22.5	58.2
Romania	19,300	1,443	1,057	7.5	5.5	73.3
Bulgaria	8,000	165	120	2.1	1.5	72.2
Yugoslavia	22,300	1,566	797	7.0	3.6	50.9
Total	97,402	24,764	11,543	25.4	11.8	46.6

Sources:

C: Kořátko, *op. cit., passim;* also *Progress in Land Reforms, op. cit.*, p. 67–68.
P: *Statistical Yearbook 1948, op. cit.*, p. 44.
H: *GT*, I, 12 (November 1947), p. 632; also *Today and Yesterday, op. cit.*, p. 27.
R: Golopenţia and Onică, *op. cit.*
B: Chernokólev, article cited.
Y: *Statistički Godišnjak FNRJ 1954, op. cit*, p. 115.

1. The number of dwarf holdings ranged from some 30 per cent of the total number of holdings in Poland and Bulgaria to over 50 per cent in Romania and nearly 70 per cent in Hungary. The relative economic importance of the subsistence farms, however, increased in Poland and Bulgaria because of the importance of the small holdings from 2 to 5 hectares, representing in Poland over 30 per cent and in Bulgaria nearly 40 per cent of the total number of holdings (whereas in the other countries they were approximately 20 per cent).

2. The medium-sized holdings remained of some significance only in Poland and in Bulgaria; they played a decreasing role in Romania, Czechoslovakia, and Hungary.

3. The medium-large and large holdings together amounted to over 10 per cent of the total number of holdings only in Czechoslovakia and Poland and were roughly one-half that in the other three countries.

As to the acreage distribution of farm land, the official data further reveal that:

1. The subsistence units absorbed roughly one-fourth of the farm land in Czechoslovakia and Poland, nearly 40 per cent in Bulgaria, and over 50 per cent in Hungary.

2. The medium-sized holdings included up to 40 per cent of the farm land in Bulgaria and Poland and from about 20 to nearly 30 per cent in Czechoslovakia and Hungary.

3. The medium-large and large holdings together amounted to approximately one-fourth the land in Bulgaria and Hungary, over 30 per cent in Poland, and 47 per cent in Czechoslovakia.

Plotting along the horizontal axis of a graph the cumulative percentage of the number of holdings by size, and along the vertical axis

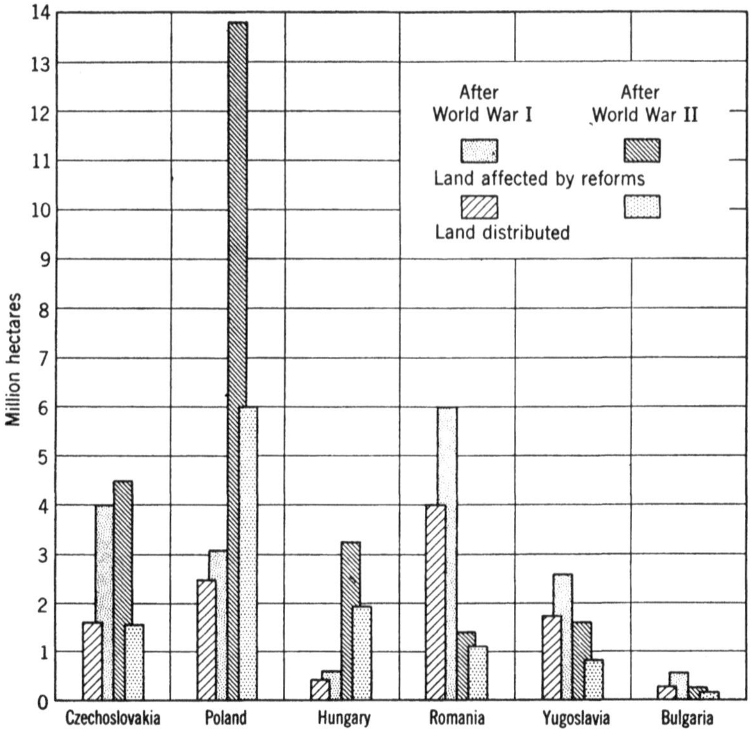

Chart 8. Land Reforms after World Wars I and II

the cumulative percentage of the private farm land acreage included in these holdings, we get a group of "Lorenz curves" which can be usefully compared with similar curves of the prewar distribution (cf. Chart 1, p. 16). Again all the curves diverge from the theoretical "line of equality," but they have now been brought quite close to the Bulgarian curve. Before the war, the degree of inequality in the distribution of private land varied considerably among the various countries of the area. These differences have now been substantially reduced. (See Chart 9.)

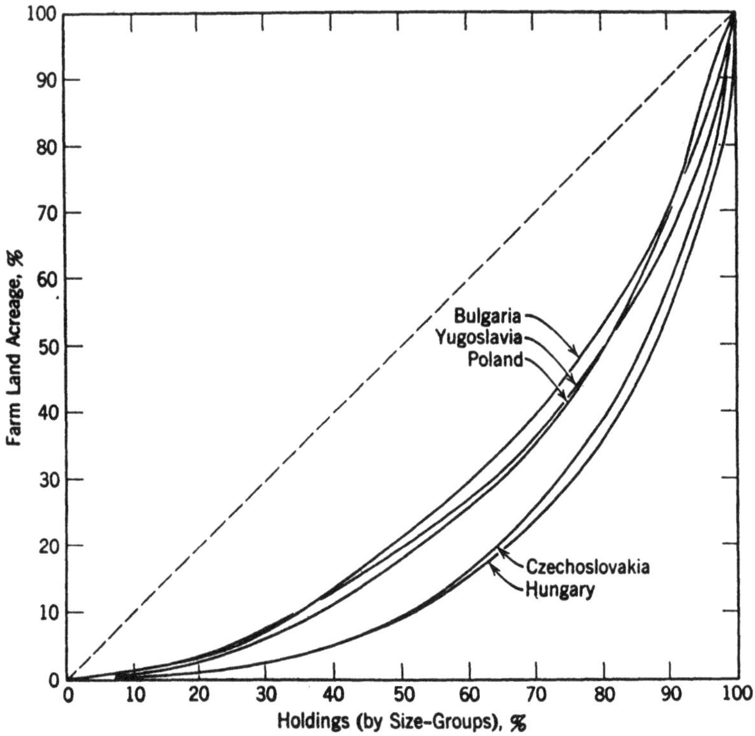

CHART 9. SIZE-GROUPS OF HOLDINGS AND SHARE IN FARM LAND ACREAGE ABOUT 1949

CHANGING THE PEASANT FROM AN OWNER INTO A LABORER

If H is an agricultural holding and F an agricultural family, the structure of agricultural land ownership in each of these countries could be broadly described as having three levels represented thus: [35] (1) the output of the holding does not cover the subsistence needs of the owner's family ($H < F$); (2) the holding covers exactly the needs of the family ($H = F$); (3) the output of the holding is larger than the needs of the family ($H > F$). Before the war the basic socioeconomic agricultural problem was to strike some "healthy balance" among the three. In Romania, Yugoslavia, and Bulgaria the pres-

[35] Prof. E. Cornăţeanu, "Cercetări asupra Rentabilităţii Agriculturei Rómâneşti" (Researches on the Profitability of Romanián Agriculture in *Economia Română* (Romanian Economy), XXVII (December 1945), Ministry of Commerce and Industry, Bucharest, 1946, p. 104.

TABLE 62. PRIVATE AGRICULTURAL HOLDINGS AND ACREAGE AROUND 1949, PERCENTAGE DISTRIBUTION [a]

Private Agricultural Holdings According to Size of Property [b]

Holdings, ha.		Czechoslovakia	Poland	Hungary [c]	Romania [d]	Bulgaria	Yugoslavia [e]
Small	0–2	46.5	28.8	68.6	53.1	29.2	29.8
	2–5	23.5	32.5	18.9	22.9	38.6	39.3
Medium	5–10	17.1	27.1	8.5	17.9	25.4	21.6
"Large"	10–20	10.6	10.4	3.4	5.0	6.8	5.5
	20–50	2.3	1.2	0.6	1.1		3.8
Total		100.0	100.0	100.0	100.0	100.0	100.0

Respective Share in Total *Private* Farm Land Acreage [b]

Holdings, ha.		Czechoslovakia	Poland	Hungary [c]	Romania [d]	Bulgaria	Yugoslavia [e]
Small	0–2	7.9	6.0	23.1	[f]	6.7	7.6
	2–5	17.9	21.5	27.3	[f]	30.9	28.3
Medium	5–10	27.2	38.8	22.4	[f]	41.5	31.4
"Large"	10–20	32.1	27.3	18.3	[f]	20.9	14.1
	20–50	14.9	6.4	8.9	[f]		18.6
Total		100.0	100.0	100.0	[f]	100.0	100.0

[a] The underlying data for Poland, taken from *Rocznik Statystyczny 1949*, are at variance with the data given in Table 56. The *Rocznik* covers a larger number of holdings and gives their corresponding share of farm land acreage, but does not supply the regional breakdown. The underlying data for Hungary are based on the 1947 computations and estimates of D. L. Tekal, settlement chief inspector, and are slightly at variance with the data given in Table 58. We had to resort here to Tekal's data, as the size-groups were more convenient.

[b] The raw data available referred to holdings: for Yugoslavia in 1950; for Czechoslovakia and Poland in 1949; for Romania in 1948; for Hungary in 1947; and for Bulgaria in 1946. All the data referred to *private* holdings and farm land except for Czechoslovakia. Our percentage distribution is computed by assuming that the holdings over 50 ha. (and in Bulgaria over 20 ha.) were taken over by the state in or around 1949.

[c] Divisions are: 0–2.8; 2.8–5.7; 5.7–11.4; 11.4–28.7; and 28.7–57.5.

[d] Divisions are: 1–3 and 3–5 in the Small group.

[e] Divisions are: 0–2; 2–5; 5–10; 10–15; and over 15.

[f] Not available.

Sources: (Computed from)

C: Stejskal, *op. cit.*, p. 46.
P: *Rocznik Statystyczny 1949*, *op. cit.*, p. 54.
H: *GT*, I, 13 (December 1947), p. 696.
R: Golopenţia and Onică, *op. cit.*, p. 7
B: *MI*, July 1947, p. 27.
Y: *Socialistička Poljoprivreda*, *op. cit.*

sure of overpopulation and the lack of surplus of any town outlets for farm labor for the labor available in the countryside encouraged the continuous splitting-up of the holdings in the group $H = F$. In spite of all the prohibitive provisions of the reform laws, further splitting-up occurred continuously even in the $H < F$ situation, thus inflating the unsound basis on which ownership and production in the countryside rested. The problem remained as stringent when the Communist parties started to press vigorously for power. However, they attacked the problem in a roundabout way. First they advocated immediately splitting up most of the holdings of the $H > F$ level and parceling them out into small lots (of about 1.2 hectares per claimant in Romania, 2.5 per claimant in Yugoslavia, and 3 per claimant in Hungary, etc.). It was obvious that these procedures increased the number of subsistence units in agriculture (and hence would further reduce the *marketable* share of grains) without solving in any way the serious problem of overpopulation in the countryside. But these measures were viewed by their authors only as an unavoidable political expedient to be employed before setting in motion new and far more complex readjustments in the villages.

The time for the more "complex readjustments," which were being prepared from the middle of 1948 on, arrived at the beginning of 1949. Having now been firmly installed in power, having virtually concluded the process of nationalization in the towns, and having drawn new and ambitious plans of development, the Communist regimes of Eastern Europe could turn their full attention toward the villages and start methodically to undo both the excessive subdivision of land and the increase in peasant ownership, which had occurred during the "first cycle of reorganization" of the rural areas.

The total liquidation of private property in agriculture, that is, in the largest sector of these economies, implies the ultimate transformation of the peasantry as a whole from *owners* into laborers on state-owned land. It should be recalled that in Soviet Russia nationalization and redistribution of land were jointly enacted by the revolution.[36] In Eastern Europe decades of land reforms had "territorialized" the peasantry, i.e., had transformed most of the peasants into owners of land. It was obvious that the peasants, with strong feelings about ownership, would view any attempt at outright land nationalization as a measure of personal expropriation and not as an act directed against

[36] The Russian fundamental land law of Feb. 19, 1918, "abolished forever *private ownership of land,* mineral resources, waterways, forests," etc.

the "big estates." [37] Therefore the expropriation of the peasants and their transformation in to "usufructuaries" in Eastern Europe had to be attempted in a succession of moves.[38]

Such moves as the successive isolation and destruction of the upper layers of the peasantry, the systematic expansion of state-owned and state-managed agricultural undertakings, and the formation of peasant collective undertakings (i.e., the combined measures that characterize the "second" cycle of reorganization of the countryside) can and do have other objectives and results than merely the nationalization of land. They aim at creating conditions of large-scale exploitation of the land, at liquidating backward methods of cultivation, at employment of mechanization, and so on. They aim also at bringing as completely as possible into the sphere of planning the largest private sector outside of total state control. Thus the cycle would not be considered complete until both the reduction of the peasantry as a whole into a mass of agricultural workers and the possibility of combining agricultural land and undertakings at the will of the planners were achieved.

[37] In 1948, at the outbreak of their rift with the Russians, the Yugoslavs stressed with much ado the idea that the Balkan peasant was not a land tenant whom the nationalization of land could have allowed to "gain land," but a small owner to whom this measure would have meant loss of ownership. Actually, stern regulations on land buying and selling and wide expropriation rights conferred upon the state had limited substantially this ownership. (Cf. Kidrič, op. cit., pp. 18 ff.) It is interesting to note that the Yugoslavs, who had stressed this idea, were to be the first in the region to enact wide measures of land nationalization, as we shall see immediately.

[38] "The nationalization of land signifies that its sole owner is the State. . . . Thus, while with us in Russia the building of Socialism was effected from the very beginning under the conditions of the nationalization of all kinds of land, in the People's Democracy countries, the nationalization of land will be accomplished as an outcome of *a number of moves* undertaken during the process of constructing Socialism." Cf. N. D. Kazantsev, "Zemelnye Reformy i Puti Preobrazovaniia Selskovo Khoziaistvo v Stranakh Narodnoi Demokratsii Tsentralnoi i Iugovostochnoi Evropy" (The Land Reforms and the Road toward the Reorganization of Agriculture in the Countries of People's Democracy of Central and South-East Europe), *Izvestiia Akademii Nauk SSSR, Otdelenie Ekonomiki i Prava* (News of the Academy of Science of the USSR, Section on Economy and Law), No. 4, Moscow-Leningrad, July–August 1950, pp. 257 and 285, as quoted by Gryziewicz, *op. cit.*, p. 316. (Italics supplied.)

Restricting, "Dislodging," and Restricting Again the Kulak

Even before 1949 a series of measures—progressive land tax, increased obligatory deliveries according to the size of the holding, orientation of credits, state distribution of seeds, concentration of agricultural machinery in the hands of the state, etc.—had been limiting the income and freedom of action of the upper strata of the peasantry. By and large, each country had perfected the method that it considered most appropriate to its agricultural structure; only later did a more unified course take shape in the area as a whole.

In Czechoslovakia before 1948 the proprietors holding up to 20 hectares could sell their produce to the state at the highest price, those holding from 20 to 50 at a lower price, and those holding over 50 hectares at the lowest price.[39] After 1948 the land tax, which was collected in kind, assessed according to the acreage of the holding and the quality of arable land, and exacted at the beginning of the crop threshing and surrendered along with the quota of obligatory deliveries, was progressively increased for holdings of over 10 hectares.

In Poland in 1951 the land tax was about 3.5 per cent of the poor peasants' cash income "while 378,000 kulaks and the most wealthy middle peasant households paid taxes amounting to 27.6 per cent of their cash income." [40]

In Hungary from the summer of 1949 holdings with more than 40 cadastral acres (over 23 hectares) were compelled to surrender to the state 3.5 times more grain per acre than the small holdings of 5 acres (2.8 hectares); moreover, all the farmers with over 10 acres (5.7 hectares) were required to contribute extra grain to a "special fund for the development of agriculture." [41]

In Romania a highly discriminatory system of grain collection was established at the end of 1948. The peasant holdings up to 1 or 3 hectares of poor land were exempt from the grain quota. The holdings of 50 hectares and over were taxed at quota deliveries 4 to 5 times larger than those required of the middle peasants.[42] The system proved

[39] Cf. N. Kazantsev, *op. cit.*

[40] R. Zambrowski, "Development of Agriculture in Poland," in *FLP*, Sept. 14, 1951. The figure given by this source covers almost entirely the groups of holdings over and above 10 ha. (See below, Table 63.)

[41] Ernő Gerő, "The Policy of Hungarian Workers' Party in Countryside," in *FLP*, Dec. 1, 1948.

[42] Ion Berceanu, "New Regime of Grain Collection in Romania," in *RR*, III, 11 (September 1948).

unworkable, and in March 1949 these farms (of 50 hectares and over) were expropriated.[43]

In Yugoslavia compulsory purchase of agricultural produce at low, controlled prices ranged from 50 to 90 per cent of the "surplus" of peasant produce and increased progressively, as did the income tax. This system, established from the early period of the Communist regime, was discarded in the summer of 1951.[44]

A major additional instrument in the policy of "restricting rural capitalism" was the familiar combination of credit orientation and discriminatory interest rates.[45]

Finally, private agricultural machines and implements were taken over by ad hoc Machine-Tractor Stations, and the sale of machinery to private persons was prohibited.

At the opening of the second cycle of reorganization of the villages, i.e., at the beginning of 1949 (except for Yugoslavia, which engaged earlier in this process), the policy of "restricting the kulak" [46] was replaced by the policy of "dislodging" him from the economy.

According to the data available for 1949, there were then in the area some 1.1 million private holdings of over 10 hectares, that is, some 8.5 per cent out of a total of 13 million holdings (see Table 63).[47] Of those of over 10 hectares some 300,000 holdings may have

[43] See above, p. 238.

[44] The list of farm products subject to compulsory deliveries was then greatly reduced. Compulsory deliveries of grains (wheat, rye, corn, oats, and barley) were abolished as of June 30, 1951. Agricultural producers could dispose of all grains and other farm products, except wool, *at current free market prices.* Cf. *Les Nouvelles yougoslaves,* June 21, 1952, and *Neue Züricher Zeitung,* July 2, 1952, as quoted in the *Economic Digest,* V, 10 (October 1952), pp. 446–447.

[45] The turn toward the familiar pattern already noted in the non-agricultural sectors is clearly detailed here for Poland:

> The problem of credits is an important problem in the economic policy in the countryside. In it are already appearing the basic lines of the class fight in the villages. This year [1948] all the private peasant holdings have obtained more than 13 billion zlotys of credit which were destined for the medium and poor peasants. In practice, the major part of this credit went to the rich instead of going to the poor. This is due to the fact that our banking apparatus does not yet function in the spirit of the government and does not apply in the matter of allocation of agricultural credits any differentiation, treating, on the contrary, the rich as the most solvent customer. The party has the task of watching to see that the current of credits goes in the direction of the intentions of the government and supplies the poor and medium peasants. [*Glos Ludu* (Voice of the People), September 8, 1948.]

[46] As already stated (cf. Note 4, Ch. I) Kulak designates the peasant who resorts to hired help (that of the poor and landless peasant) and who is in the position of renting to other peasants his implements, draft animals, grains, or money for profit.

[47] Compare to prewar Table 8, Chapter 1, p. 14.

TABLE 63. STRUCTURE OF FARM LAND OWNERSHIP, AROUND 1949 [a]

Holdings, ha.		Czecho-slovakia	Po-land	Hun-gary [b]	Ro-mania [c]	Bul-garia	Yugo-slavia [d]	Total	%
Small	0–2	696	962	1,404	1,636	316	599	5,613	43.0
	2–5	351	1,084	387	707	418	790	3,737	28.6
Medium	5–10	255	906	174	551	276	433	2,595	19.9
"Large"	10–20	159	347	55 [e]	154	74	111	900	6.9
	20–50	35	39	27 [e]	34	[f]	77	212	1.6
Total		1,496	3,338	2,047	3,082	1,084	2,010	13,057	100.0

[a] Number of private farms in *thousands*, and *percentage distribution* according to the size of holdings (in hectares).

[b] Divisions are: 0–2.8; 2.8–5.7; 5.7–11.4; 11.4–28.7; 28.7–57.5.

[c] Divisions are: 1–3 and 3–5 in the Small group.

[d] Divisions are: 0–2; 2–5; 5–10; 10–15; over 15.

[e] Estimate.

[f] Nil.

Sources: Same as in Table 62.

had more than 15 hectares and only 210,000 more than 20 hectares.[48]

The attack against the kulaks during the period extending from 1949 until the middle of 1953 was aimed at different types of peasants in the various countries and did not have uniform results in the area as a whole. The policy of "dislodgment" generally consisted of very steep taxation of the holdings to be "liquidated," prevention of the peasants involved from joining the agricultural cooperatives organized by the other peasants, and direct pressure in order to force them off the land. The kulak designation was applied, according to the intensity of the drive, to a range of holdings. Thus in Romania in 1949 there were officially designated as kulak farms a total of between 50,000 and 60,000 holdings, by and large, those of 20 hectares and over. Subsequently the Central Committee of the Romanian Workers' (Communist) Party redefined the term and indicated that it had "intended" from 1949 on to consider as kulak holdings some 150,000 peasant farms, or generally those of over 15 hectares.[49] In Hungary in 1949 there were officially designated as kulak holdings the farms of over 15 hectares; however, the implementation of this policy in the villages led

[48] It is important to note that the number of peasant owners is usually *larger* than that of the number of holdings *in the lower brackets*, as the latter often belong to two small owners (husband and wife, father and son, etc.). In the upper brackets the reverse holds true: the number of holdings is larger than the number of owners. Cf. Golopenţia and Onică, *op. cit.*

[49] This "upward adjustment" of the number of kulaks was made in the spring of 1952 during the fight against the former Minister of Finance, Vasile Luca, purged at the time as a "right deviationist." Cf. "Letter of the Central Committee of the Romanian Workers' Party, March 15, 1952," *op. cit.*, pp. 8–9.

to such extensive "dislodgment" of peasants with even less than 10 hectares that official warnings had to be given against too zealous application of the law.[50]

In some countries, especially Hungary, these policies drove so many kulaks off the land that enormous tracts were left fallow. By 1953 the new Hungarian premier, Imre Nagy, defined the situation in the following terms:

> The measures taken against the *kulaks,* which assumed a nationwide character and went beyond the policy of restricting the *kulaks,* meant, in addition, that the government, year after year, *had to worry more and more what to do with the so-called reserve land,* abandoned or handed over to the state, and which remained uncultivated because of the uncertainty in agriculture and because of the difficult conditions for cultivating the land.[51]

In Czechoslovakia and Yugoslavia the agricultural cooperatives were left open to all the peasants, including the kulaks. The heavy taxation on the private medium-large and "large" holdings even drove some of their owners into cooperatives, whereas the medium peasant (generally with 8 to 10 hectares), who was not so heavily taxed, usually remained outside. The social composition of cooperatives reflected the effects of this system of incentives. Thus in 1950 in the Czechoslovakian villages where cooperatives had been established, only 38 per cent of the peasants owning less than 2 hectares of land joined, 40 per cent of the peasants with 2–5 hectares, and 48 per cent of those with 5–10. The percentage was 62 per cent for those of 10–15, 53 per cent for those of 15–20, and 45 per cent for those of over 20 hectares (usually the so-called "model farms").[52] In order to prevent the rich peasant from retaining, up to a point, either his land or his livestock by joining a cooperative of the so-called "lower type," and in order to avoid his exercising a leadership role in the cooperatives, a whole series of measures was put into operation. The peasant owners of a given size of holding were either barred from leadership posts or simply forbidden to join cooperatives; they were expelled from those to which they

[50] In an admonition reminiscent of a famous Stalin "tactical retreat" of the early thirties, Rákosi declared in 1949:

> Another serious deficiency has been the fact that our organizations do not discriminate between middle peasants and *kulaks* in most places. We consider in general those to be *kulaks* who own more than 25 cadastral acres [15.7 ha.] of land, but our comrades in the villages have considered farmers owning more than 15 cadastral acres [i.e., 8.6 ha.] as *kulaks.* [Cf. *SN,* March 24, 1949.]

[51] Imre Nagy, "On Measures . . . ," *loc. cit.*

[52] Cf. *RP,* Feb. 25, 1951.

had been previously admitted.[53] Part of their land was taken by the state through new land laws. This method was applied in Yugoslavia, and deserves particular attention.

After having preceded, up to 1949, all the other East European countries in the drive for collectivizing agriculture, Yugoslavia slackened the pace of that drive in 1951 in connection with the structural changes undergone by the economy in all the other spheres. In 1951–52, after the change in the system of taxation and agricultural deliveries, the Yugoslavs were faced by massive flights from the cooperatives. The movement became so extensive that it had finally to be authorized officially. As the flight of the richer and medium peasant from the collectives reduced their land, the Yugoslavs devised a new and far-reaching countermove. On May 22, 1953, a new federal law (the "General People's Land Pool and the Allocation of Land to Agricultural Organizations") *nationalized all cultivable land exceeding a maximum of 10 hectares* and proclaimed it "common social property." Holdings exceeding 10 hectares of cultivable land were *expropriated* (with a nominal indemnity payable over 20 years) and taken over for cultivation by the state or by the cooperatives. If the state or the cooperatives could not take over the land, it was left for cultivation to the previous owner and his family. By this move the Yugoslavs achieved one of the main goals of Communist policy in the second cycle of reorganization of agriculture: they restricted further the sphere of private ownership (up to 10 hectares) and at the same time transformed all the peasants working on any plot of land exceeding 10 hectares into workers on state land. By June 1954 the expropriation had involved 268,954 hectares of land taken from 66,248 households (or an average of 3.3 hectares per household except in Vojvodina, where this average was 5 hectares). About one-third of this land was taken over by the state farms and one-third by the peasant working cooperatives; the rest was still to be allocated.[54]

[53] In Hungary the kulaks were first prevented from "managing" the cooperatives, later simply from joining them. The ban against the kulak joining cooperatives was enforced from the outset in Poland and in Romania. See Kazantsev, "*Zemelnye Reformy* . . . ," op. cit., and Gerő, *op. cit.*

[54] Jovan Djordjević, "Two Federal Laws and Their Significance," in *Review of International Affairs,* IV, 11 (June 1, 1953).

The data on the land expropriations and distributions is from *Ekonomska politika,* November 18, 1954, p. 925, as quoted by Prof. Jozo Tomasevich: "Collectivization of Agriculture in Yugoslavia" (mimeo.), April 1955 (presented at a Seminar on Collectivization of Agriculture, at the University of Kentucky). Prof. Tomasevich seems to imply that the reform had been completed by June 1954. Actually, as indicated

After the end of the first phase of the reorganization of agriculture (the middle of 1953) there was a tendency, in the area, to abandon the policy of "dislodging" the kulak and to return to the policy of "restricting" him in various ways, e.g., by expropriation (but of only part of his land), by lowering his taxes to a level which would enable him to continue the cultivation of his land, by removal of other vigorous restrictions which had previously driven him away from the village, and so on. This milder course was tied closely to a series of other measures which we shall discuss below, after a survey of the development of the state and cooperative agricultural sectors.

Expansion of the State Sector

Postwar reforms and the expulsion of the Germans added tremendously to the area of state lands. As a rule, all forests were declared state property and managed under boards set up *ad hoc*. The state agricultural land (arable land plus pastures and meadows) was considerably augmented, in some of these countries amounting to 2 million or more hectares of first-class land. The state share of the combined agricultural and woodland areas ranged from 17 per cent in Yugoslavia to as much as 36 per cent in Poland and 41 per cent in Czechoslovakia. However, immediately after the war and up to 1949, in farming and agricultural exploitation state initiative remained centered on the prewar state-owned and operated farms. The rest of the new state land was generally leased to landless or poor peasants. In contrast to Poland where the state farms expanded greatly after the war, the state-managed farms in other East European countries played a rather limited role up to the beginning of 1949. As can be seen from Table 64, they encompassed fewer than 30,000 hectares in Hungary and Bulgaria, fewer than 70,000 hectares in Czechoslovakia, and some 150,000 hectares in Romania (most of which represented the newly confiscated royal farms).

After the beginning of the second phase of reorganization of the villages in 1949, the state farms expanded rapidly either by simple extension of state cultivation on state lands formerly leased to peasants, by outright expropriation of privately owned "model farms" or "kulak farms." By 1950 the state farms had increased the land under their cultivation more than threefold in Bulgaria, more than six-fold in Czechoslovakia and Romania, and over 26 times in Hungary. In

previously in Table 59, a far larger amount of hectares is to be found in the private holdings exceeding 10 hectares.

TABLE 64. DEVELOPMENT OF STATE FARMS, 1948, 1950, 1953, 1955

Country	Arable Land in State Farms, thousands of hectares				Per Cent of Arable Land in State Farms		
	1948	1950	1953	1955	1950	1953	1955
Czechoslovakia	67	466	482	490 [a]	9.8	10.0	10.0 [a]
Poland [b]	1,506	2,200	2,489	2,580	11.0	12.0	13.0
Hungary	28	793	793	1,401	13.5	13.5	24.3
Romania	153	953	1,329	1,329	9.3	14.4	13.7
Bulgaria [d]	27	85 [e]	170	200 [a]	1.9 [e]	2.5	3.5
Yugoslavia [b]	[c]	323 [e]	469 [f]	680	2.3 [e]	3.3 [f]	5.6

[a] Estimate.
[b] Agricultural land for all years.
[c] Not available.
[d] Cultivated land for all years.
[e] 1949.
[f] 1952.

Sources:

C: Dolansky, *Three Years of Planning . . . , op. cit.*; B. Kiesewetter, *Statistiken zur Wirtschaft Ost- und Südosteuropas* (Economic Statistics of East and South-East Europe), Deutsches Institut für Wirtschaftsforschung (German Institute for Economic Research), Special Series No. 33, Vol. II, Duncker & Humblot, Berlin, 1955, p. 16; *ESE in 1955*, UN, ECE, Geneva, 1956, p. 196.

P: *Rocznik Statystyczny 1949, op. cit.*, p. 100; *FLP*, Jan. 30, 1953; *ESE in 1955, op. cit.*, p. 196.

H: *GT*, II, 13 (November 1948); Vas, *A hároméves terv befejezése . . . , op. cit.*; Rákosi in *SN*, Dec. 16, 1952; Kiesewetter, *Statistiken . . . , op. cit.*, p. 18; also *Magyar Statisztikai Zsebkönyv 1956, op. cit.*, p. 92.

R: Gheorghiu-Dej: *Raportul de Activitate . . . Congresul al II-lea, op. cit.*, p. 94; *ESE in 1955, op. cit.*, p. 196.

B: Kiesewetter, *Statistiken . . . ; op. cit.*, p. 17; *P.K.*, No. 2, 1948, p. 80; Chervenkov in *FLP*, September 11, 1953; *ESE in 1955, op. cit.*, p. 196.

Y: Ivanović in *Review of International Affairs*, Vol. V, No. 16, April 1954; *Statistički Godišnjak FNRJ 1954, op. cit.*, p. 118; *Statistički Bilten* (Statistical Bulletin), No. 11, July 1952, p. 62; and *Zadružni Vjesnik* (The Cooperative Messenger), June 14, 1956.

Yugoslavia, also, there was a progressive expansion of state farm land accompanied by substantial increases of the state-owned acreage.[55] By 1953 the state farms had under cultivation around 3 per cent of the agricultural or arable land in Yugoslavia and Bulgaria, and from 10–13 per cent in the other countries of the area. The land under

[55] According to data for January 1953, the Yugoslav *state-farmed land* comprised 220 state farms covering a total agricultural area of 373,000 hectares (an average of close to 1,600 ha. per farm), and 446 local agricultural farms covering a total of 59,000 hectares (or an average of 130 ha. per farm). Including also some small state farms and the farms belonging to institutions, the land utilized by the state amounted to a total of 732,000 hectares, compared to 75,000 hectares before the war. The 732,000

cultivation in the state farms has thus increased from around 2 million hectares in 1948 to 5 million hectares in 1953.

Various Types of Agricultural Producers' Cooperatives

Pari passu with the policy of restricting the kulak and expanding the state-owned acreage, a whole series of measures was adopted in 1949 to induce the peasantry to form joint agricultural undertakings, officially designated as *agricultural producers' cooperatives.* To draw the peasants more easily into the collectivization process, various "organizational forms" were devised, taking into consideration the attachment of the peasant to his plot of land, his cattle, and draft animals. Basically, however, these forms centered generally on two main models: (1) a model considered "inferior," which recognized in some way the principle of private-land ownership of the cooperator; (2) a model called a "superior" type of cooperative, closely patterned on the Soviet kolkhoz, which was based on the absorption of the land of the cooperator into the common property of the undertaking. In the second type the individual ownership was limited, henceforth, to a small housing-gardening plot only and a specified number of (small) livestock.

Here are the varying characteristics of the organizational forms employed from 1949 on in the area as a whole after the liquidation of the previously existing peasant cooperatives or their arbitrary fusion into so-called "unified producers' cooperatives."

In Czechoslovakia four types of producers' cooperatives were created:

Type I: Joint tillage of land; private ownership of land, draft animals, implements, and the respective crop.

Type II: Joint cultivation of plots with boundaries to be plowed over after being grouped in "land-compounds";[56] land ownership still recognized, the peasant receiving land rent; draft animals and implements remain private property and can be lent for money to the cooperatives.

Type III: Crop and animal production cared for collectively, the basic means of production being *purchased* by the cooperative; rent still recognized, but limited to 10–20 per cent of the cooperatives' income, the rest being distributed according to the work done.

hectares represented a little over one-third of the total *state agricultural acreage.* The latter amounted for its part to 2.54 million ha., of which 2.07 million were pastures. Most of this land was leased to the cooperatives and individual peasants. Cf. *Statistički Godišnjak FNRJ 1954, op. cit.,* pp. 116, 118.

[56] In this type and in the following types of cooperatives the owners' small gardening plots are excepted from joint cultivation.

Type IV: Both land and means of production common property; land rent abolished as "unearned income," and each member paid according to work units (the kolkhoz type).

Poland also devised four types of producers' cooperatives (the second one created in 1951):

Type I: Joint tillage, similar to Type I of the Czech cooperatives.
Type II: Joint tillage, private ownership of draft animals which are lent to the cooperatives, payment of rent to the peasant, who is recognized as owner of his land.
Type III: Crop and animal production carried out collectively; division of net income up to 30 or 40 per cent in proportion to land, livestock, and equipment contributed by each cooperator; division of the rest of 60 or 70 per cent according to each one's labor outlay.
Type IV: The kolkhoz type.[57]

In Hungary three types of producers' cooperatives were established:

Type I: Collective plowing and sowing of plots grouped in land compounds; individual reaping. Cost of plowing and sowing burdens each member according to the land contributed; the crop belongs to him after cost deduction.
Type II: Collective plowing, sowing, harvesting, and threshing. Proportionate distribution of profits and expenses according to the land and draft animals contributed.
Type III: The kolkhoz type.

In Romania two types were established:

Type I: Simple "tillage association" in which the peasants joined their lands in compounds, either *partly* or *entirely*, for a *season* or *permanently*, and remained the owners of the land cultivated within the association, of the agricultural implements, and of the crops obtained.[58]
Type II: The kolkhoz type.

In Bulgaria a single type of producers' cooperative was established with distinctive features:

[57] Considerable confusion has developed concerning the Polish cooperatives. This is due to the fact that the second type of cooperative, introduced in 1951, is usually described as the "fourth type" of cooperative (cf. Gryziewicz, *op. cit.*, pp. 318 ff.). The categories here are based on the official Polish system of classification: I. Land Cultivation Association (ZUZ); II. Agricultural Cooperative Association (RZS, Type I); III. Agricultural Cooperative Societies (RSW, Type II); IV. Agricultural Cooperative Groups (RZS, Type III). Cf. *Wieś w Liczbach*, 1st ed., Warsaw, 1952, p. 131.

[58] From 1951 on the official statistics record only the *permanent* tillage associations.

> The cooperators brought all their land, implements, and cattle to the cooperative. Crop and animal production were tended collectively, the income being distributed on the basis of (1) labor outlay, (2) surface and quality of the land brought to the cooperative, (3) importance of the equipment furnished to the collective.

Thus in Bulgaria the principle of land ownership was still recognized although the plot borders were plowed over and private ownership lost its distinctiveness.

In Yugoslavia four types of producers' cooperatives were put into operation:

Type I: Joint tillage, somewhat similar to the respective type established in the other countries; land *rent* paid according to the *income* of the joint undertaking.

Type II: Crop and animal production tended collectively; land *rent* paid according to the *value* of the land contributed to the cooperative by each member, plus payment by work units.

Type III: Recognition of the cooperative member's land ownership for three years and of his right to leave the cooperative after this period; private ownership temporarily recognized, but the peasant renounced his right to receive rent, and after the three years the land became collective property; payment by work units.

Type IV: The kolkhoz type.

All the "intermediate" types between the simple joint land tillage and the kolkhozy were considered *transitional forms,* meant to facilitate the passage of the peasantry from an "inferior" type of cooperation to the "superior" type, i.e., the collective ownerships.

During the first phase of the collectivization drive, and more specifically in the first years, many poor and landless peasants flocked to the "superior" type of cooperative (kolkhozy). As aid in the formation of these they were given state land and other state endowments. The medium-large and especially the medium peasant either joined the "inferior" type of cooperative or continued to tend his own land. The result of the process was that the intermediate forms of cooperatives did not play the role for which they were intended, since from the outset the kolkhozy tended to be a concentration of landless peasants, and the medium peasantry, which was supposed to be drawn into the cooperatives, tried desperately to remain outside.

The impatience of the state with this situation and the changing moods of the policy makers in the area can be easily observed if we survey closely the process of growth and development of the cooperatives over the period considered.

TABLE 65. PRODUCERS' COOPERATIVES: ABSOLUTE FIGURES 1949–55, AND YEARLY INCREASES AND DECREASES, 1949–53

Country	Total Producers' Coopera-tives, 1949	Yearly Increases or Decreases					Total Producers' Cooperatives	
		1949	1950	1951	1952	1953	1953	1955
Czechoslovakia	1,911	1,911	3,204	1,135	532	568	7,350 [a]	7,016 [a]
Poland	243	190	1,956	857	1,422	3,294	7,772	9,963
Hungary	1,520	1,140	1,100	2,032	663	−638	4,677	4,817
Romania	56	56	971	956	1,647	400	4,030 [b]	6,325 [b]
Bulgaria	1,608	508	979	152	8	[c]	2,747	2,747
Yugoslavia	6,625	5,307	343	−171	−2,572	−2,967	1,258	[d]

[a] Excluding simplest type of cooperative.
[b] Including joint tillage associations.
[c] Nil.
[d] Not available.

Sources:

C: *CEB*, Feb. 1, 1953, p. 264; *RP*, Dec. 17, 1952; *ESE in 1955*, p. 196.

P: *Rocznik Statystyczny 1955*, *op. cit.* p. 107; and *ESE*, *ibid.*

H: *Le Problème agraire dans les democraties populaires* (The Agrarian Problem in the Popular Democracies), II, Notes et études documentaires, No. 1799 (September 1953); *SN*, Dec. 30, 1953, *ESE*, *ibid.*

R: *PE*, No. 5–6 (June 1953); Gheorghiu-Dej, in *FLP*, May 29, 1953; *La Roumainie nouvelle*, VI, 109 (March 15, 1953). "Plan Fulfillment Report for 1953," in *FLP*, Feb. 12, 1954, April 15, 1955; *ESE*, *ibid.*

B: *Zemedelsko Zname* (Peasant's Banner), Sept. 28, 1951, Sept. 2, 1953; *FLP*, Sept. 11, 1953; and *ESE*, *ibid.*

Y: Conrad, *op. cit.*: Pavao Rastovčan, *Pravo zemljoradničkih zadruga* (Law on Agricultural Producers' Cooperatives), Zagreb, 1950; *Statistički Godišnjak FNRJ 1954*, *op. cit.*, p. 141; *Borba*, March 23, 1954.

Pace of Development of the Producers' Cooperatives

Although the existence of various types of cooperatives would suggest a certain official concern with the free will of the peasant, since various choices were offered to him, an inspection of the figures referring to the yearly formation of cooperatives in the period under survey reveals an opposite official attitude. As can be seen from Table 65, certain years reveal a brusque official tendency to force *the supposed free will of the peasant.* In Czechoslovakia the drive gained momentum in 1950 and again in 1951, as compared to the pace in 1949, 1952, and 1953. In Poland the faster pace occurred between 1952 and the first half of 1953, after which, the number of cooperatives being almost 8,000, no new cooperatives were formed for a while. An obvious acceleration occurred in Hungary in 1951, in Bulgaria in 1950, and in Yugoslavia in 1949, followed by a series of crises. A decline finally set in, resulting in 1953 in the dissolution of numerous cooperatives, notably in Yugoslavia and in Hungary.

We shall discuss below the various reasons for this decline. Let us note for the moment that in 1953 the producers' cooperatives held the following share of the total arable land: nearly 7 per cent in Poland; 11 per cent in Romania; 26 per cent in Hungary; 33 per cent in Czechoslovakia; over 60 per cent in Bulgaria. The total arable land held by the cooperatives rose in these five countries, between 1950 and 1953, from 3.8 million to 7.5 million hectares (see Table 66).

Table 66. Development of Cooperatives: Arable Land, 1950, 1953, 1955

	Arable Land in Cooperatives (Million Hectares) at end of			Per Cent of Arable Land in Cooperatives at end of		
Country	1950	1953	1955	1950	1953	1955
Czechoslovakia	0.81	1.61	1.60	14.8	33.0	33.0
Poland	0.20	1.06	1.80	1.2	6.7	11.4
Hungary	0.39	1.38	1.28	6.0	26.0	22.2
Romania	0.27	0.97	1.20	2.7	10.6	12.8
Bulgaria [a]	2.19	2.51	2.53	43.6	60.5	60.5
Yugoslavia	2.20 [b]	2.50 [bc]	0.43	18.0 [b]	21.0 [bd]	3.6

[a] Cultivated land for all years. [c] 1952.

[b] Agricultural land.

Sources: Economic Bulletin for Europe, Vol. 7, No. 3 (Nov. 1955), p. 25; *ESE in 1955*, p. 196; Kiesewetter, *Statistiken . . ., op. cit.*, pp. 16–19; for Y: *Statistički Godišnjak FNRJ 1956, op. cit.*, p. 99.

There were also some interesting differences in the percentages of peasant farms drawn into the cooperatives. In Poland, some 2 per cent of the peasant farms were incorporated in 1950, as against 48 per cent in Bulgaria. In 1953 the percentage had risen to 5.8 per cent in Poland as against 53 per cent in Bulgaria. The low percentages in Poland, Romania, and Hungary reveal the strong reluctance of the peasants to be drawn into cooperatives. It should be noted that the relative share of cooperating households tended to be smaller than the share held by the cooperatives in arable land, a fact which underlines the policy of endowment of cooperatives with land from the state-owned acreage. The cooperative farms of the area, excluding Yugoslavia, totaled at the end of the first phase of the collectivization process, in 1953, over 1.6 million or roughly 15 per cent of the peasant homesteads (see Table 67).

TABLE 67. DEVELOPMENT OF COOPERATIVES: INCORPORATED FARMS, 1950, 1953, 1955

	Incorporated Farms in Thousands at end of			Percentages of Total Farms at end of		
Country	1950	1953	1955	1950	1953	1955
Czechoslovakia	[a]	344	335	[a]	23.0	22.3
Poland	66	192	200	2.2	5.8	6.0
Hungary	89	263	228	4.3	12.8	11.1
Romania	[a]	300	382	[a]	8.8	11.3
Bulgaria	537	569	600	48.0	53.0	60.0
Yugoslavia	418	420 [b]	[a]	25.0	25.0	[a]

[a] Not available. [b] 1952.

Sources: As in Table 66. For some percentages, data based on Table 62; for R: Gheorghiu-Dej, *Raportul de Activitate, . . . Congresul al II-lea, op. cit.*, p. 105.

The total land under cultivation in the socialist sectors in the area, excluding Yugoslavia, amounted in 1950 to some 8.2 million hectares. By 1953 the total rose to 12.7 million hectares. In Poland and Romania the share of the socialist sector was around or below 25 per cent, in Hungary and Czechoslovakia about 40 per cent, and in Bulgaria over 63 per cent (see Table 68).

That the formation and operation of many of the cooperatives were made possible essentially by extending all kinds of state facilities proved to be a liability rather than an asset for the socialized sector and ultimately played a decisive role both in the 1953 agricultural crisis and in the subsequent changes in official attitude toward the rural areas.

TABLE 68. THE "SOCIALIST SECTOR" IN AGRICULTURE, 1950, 1953, 1955

Country	Arable Land (Thousand Hectares) 1950	1953	1955	Per Cent of Arable Land 1950	1953	1955
Czechoslovakia	1,276	2,092	2,090	24.6	43.0	43.0
Poland [a]	2,400	3,549	4,380	12.2	18.7	24.4
Hungary	1,183	2,173	2,681	19.5	39.5	46.5
Romania	1,223	2,299	2,529	12.0	25.0	26.1
Bulgaria	2,275	2,680	2,730	43.6	63.0	64.0
Yugoslavia [a]	2,523	2,969 [b]	1,117	18.0	24.0 [b]	9.2

[a] Agricultural land for all years.
[b] 1952.
Sources: Totals from Tables 64 and 66.

THE SOCIALIST SECTOR: MEANS AND ACHIEVEMENTS

As we have seen, both the state farms and the agricultural producers' cooperatives expanded enormously from 1949 to 1953. This expansion was accompanied by the concentration of a large part of the farm machinery and tractors on the state farms and in the creation of *ad hoc* Machine and Tractor Stations (MTS) primarily to service the cooperatives and also, if possible, to service the private sector. The MTS received as stock not newly produced machines and tractors but agricultural machinery purchased or confiscated by the state from the private sector, with these results: (*a*) the MTS started to operate with a stock of largely worn-out machines and tractors; [59] (*b*) the private sector was compelled to work under even more backward conditions than previously.

Soon this stock was renewed and expanded. As can be seen from Table 69, significant increases were achieved in 1953 as compared to 1950. However, the rapid collectivization drive increased in 1953

[59] Let us recall that in Romania, for instance, an inventory of the available tractor stock taken in 1946 indicated that that country possessed 9,286 tractors, of which 6,618 were in working condition, 2,239 were in need of repair, and 429 were considered unusable. Of this total the state held at the time 3,621 tractors, of which 3,129 had been obtained through expropriation. Of this group 1,627 were in working condition, 1,220 were considered in need of repair, 282 were considered unusable. Cf. *La Réforme agraire en Roumanie, op. cit.,* p. 27. In 1948, on the eve of the collectivization drive, the available tractor stock was still around 9,000, of which 3,500 were in the hands of the state. Cf. *PE,* No. 1, 1948, pp. 9–12. It should be noted that the years 1946 and 1947, drought years, were not favorable for the renewal and improvement of the existing tractor park.

the ratio of hectares per tractor and hence lowered the degree of mechanization in that year, as compared to 1950. The ratio remained stabilized afterwards at the 1953 level, except in Hungary and Bulgaria. In these two countries the ratio declined, due to the decrease in the number of cooperatives in Hungary and to the stabilization of cooperatives at the 1953 level in Bulgaria (see Table 69).

TABLE 69. MECHANIZATION OF AGRICULTURE IN 1950, 1953, 1955

	Number of Tractors in the MTS (Thousand 15 hp Units)			Arable Land in Cooperatives per Tractor Unit (Ha/Tractor)		
Country	End 1950	End 1953	Mid-1955	End 1950	End 1953	Mid-1955
Czechoslovakia	15.80	19.02	17.00	51	68 [a]	93
Poland	5.00	16.40	20.00	40	91	90
Hungary	6.53	8.67	11.00	60	160	91
Romania	6.10	12.50	16.00	44	78	81
Bulgaria	10.87	13.47	17.20 [b]	201	186	147
Whole area	44.30	70.06	81.20	125	113	103

[a] This calculation takes into account the tractors owned by cooperatives as well as those on MTS.

[b] Estimate.

Source: Economic Bulletin for Europe, Vol. 7, No. 3 (Nov. 1955), Table 14 and Table 66.

Even though the producers' cooperatives had concentrated their efforts on grain production and had actually become grain-producing enterprises, at the peak of the first phase of the new reorganization the private sector in all countries except Bulgaria continued to supply around three-fourths of the marketed grain. In Czechoslovakia, Hungary, and Romania the share of the socialist sector was considerably larger in arable land than in marketed grain, a fact which suggests that this sector lagged in output, since the share of output marketed tends to be larger in the socialist than in the private sector. In contrast to these three countries, the share of the socialist sector in Poland was larger in marketed grain than in arable land. However, data on output indicate that even in Poland the socialist sector accounted for a far smaller part in production than suggested by its respective share in arable land.[60] Only in Bulgaria did the relative share in marketed

[60] According to *Wieś w Liczbach*, 3rd ed., *op. cit.*, p. 29, the share of the socialist

grain significantly exceed the share of the socialist sector in cultivable land. Except in that country, the bulk of the marketed grain was furnished by the poor and middle peasants, as Table 70 indicates.

TABLE 70. PERCENTAGE SHARES IN MARKETED GRAIN IN OR AROUND 1952

	Czecho-slovakia	Po-land	Hun-gary	Ro-mania	Bul-garia	Yugo-slavia
Socialist Sector	30.0	23.4	31.4	15.0	75.0	24.2
State	[a]	16.9	[a]	9.8	[a]	5.0
Cooperatives	[a]	6.5	[a]	5.2	[a]	19.2
Private Sector	70.0	75.6	68.6	85.0	25.0	75.8
Kulaks	[a]	19.0	7.2	12.3	[a]	[a]
Other peasants	[a]	57.6	61.4	72.7	[a]	[a].
Total	100.0	100.0	100.0	100.0	100.0	100.0

[a] Not available.

Sources:

C: Plan fulfilment report for 1953, *FLP*, Feb. 5, 1954.

P: *TL*, Dec. 31, 1953.

H: *Tarsadalmi Szemle* (Social Review), April–May 1953.

R: *Dokumentacioni Bilten* (Bulletin of Documentation), No. 8–9, 1954, p. 149.

B: Kostiukhin in *VT*, XXII, 7 (July 1952), p. 6; also, *Bulgaria Today*, II, 23–24 (December 1953), p. 7.

Y: Ivanović in *Review of International Affairs*, Vol. IV, No. 13 (July 1953, p. 17).

Data on livestock output also suggest a poor performance by the collectivized sector. By 1952, the share of this sector in the total number of cattle, pigs, and sheep, ranged from 33 to 38 per cent in Czechoslovakia, from 9 to 14 per cent in Poland, and from 17 to 25 per cent (cattle) in Bulgaria, far out of proportion to the respective shares of land.[61] The poor performance of the socialist sector *in relation to the means at its disposal* finally brought about a serious examination of the role and efficiency of some of the agricultural producers' cooperatives. It appeared at the end of 1952 that many of them were nonviable units which often did not even produce enough to cover the cost of labor. This situation was brought into the open first in

sector in total grain production was, in 1952, 13.5 per cent. Its share in arable land was 16.5 per cent.

[61] Cf. *RP*, February 1953, *Wieś w Liczbach*, 3rd ed., *op. cit.*, p. 26, and *FLP*, Sept. 11, 1953. For a detailed account of the respective importance of the production of crops and livestock in the collectives of Czechoslovakia and Poland, see Ernest Koenig, U.S. Dept. of Agriculture, "Collectivization in Czechoslovakia and Poland" (mimeo.), April 1955 (presented at a Seminar on Collectivization of Agriculture at the University of Kentucky, April 1955).

Yugoslavia, and subsequently, from the middle of 1953 on, in the rest of the area.

In a declaration about the state of the Czechoslovak cooperatives, Nepomutcky, then Minister of Agriculture, noted that in 1952 only 14.1 per cent of the producers' cooperatives had fulfilled or overfulfilled the 1952 plan; 41.7 per cent had distributed profit over and above the current wages although they had not fulfilled the plan; and 44.2 per cent had not even produced enough to cover the cost of the work of their members.[62] This poor balance sheet was also stressed by the new Premier Široký:

> Together with the leading cooperatives which are managing their economy successfully and which have had obvious economic and financial success, there are cooperatives which, because of failure to utilise advanced agrotechnical and zootechnical methods and owing to the low level of the organisational work and bad labour discipline, have poor economic and financial results.[63]

In Poland, after the intensified pace of the collectivization drive during the first half of 1953, the following declaration was made by the Secretary of the Polish Communist Central Committee, E. Pszczolkowski:

> The formation of new producers' cooperatives must not lead to the weakening of those already functioning. The principle "not a single bad cooperative" is being taken up more and more by the Party organizations and people's councils.[64]

In Hungary the then newly named Premier Nagy remarked similarly:

> The too rapid numerical development of the cooperatives and violation of the voluntary principle contributed undoubtedly to the unfavorable development of agriculture as a whole. . . . Some of the cooperatives, owing to the absence of the necessary conditions, could not become consolidated economically and organizationally. On the other hand, this hindered normal work and led to a decline in the investments necessary for developing agriculture.[65]

In Romania, Gheorghe Gheorghiu-Dej noted in the same vein that compulsion in the creation of cooperatives, mismanagement, lack

[62] *Le Problème agraire dans les democraties populaires, II, op. cit.*, pp. 11–12.
[63] "Currency Reform . . . ," *op. cit.*
[64] *FLP,* June 12, 1953.
[65] Nagy, "On Measures . . . ," *op. cit.*

of inner democracy, and lack of work discipline had all but "discredited" the "idea of Socialist transformation of agriculture."[66]

Thus in the region as a whole, including Yugoslavia, all the official declarations and articles pointed toward the necessity of applying to agriculture the criterion of *productivity* for determining which cooperatives should survive and which should be discarded.

THE "NEW COURSE" AND ITS IMPACT

The main negative elements of the balance sheet of five years of the second cycle of reorganization of the rural areas (1949–53), which finally compelled a thorough reappraisal of the previous agricultural policies, can be summarized as follows:

1. Waste of part of the available land by leaving it fallow after forcing the kulaks and the peasants with medium-large farms off their land.
2. Reluctance, if not refusal, of the medium peasantry to join cooperatives.
3. Multiplication of the nonviable, economically unsound producers' cooperatives.
4. Low output both inside and outside the socialist sector[67] due to: (*a*) overcentralized, bureaucratic planning, (*b*) lack of proper incentive, (*c*) worn-out equipment and low level of investment in agriculture as a whole, and (*d*) lack of technicians and managers in the cooperatives already set up and in the MTS.

Reappraisal of the agricultural policies was undertaken consecutively by all the countries in the area. As always, this important political reversal, called the "new course," coincided with a series of significant events, such as the death of Stalin, the outburst of street revolts in East Germany, and, above all, the open avowal that the agrarian policy of the Soviet Union itself had led during the last twenty-five years to a catastrophic drop in both agricultural output and livestock breeding.[68] Although it is certain that the Communist world, because of ideological affinity and ingrained discipline, tends to follow

[66] In *FLP*, May 29, 1953, Dej notes with some ingenuousness:

What kind of collective is it that is made up of people brought together by chance, people who lack conviction of the superiority of the collective farms and who *all the time are looking backward at their tiny plot of land?*

[67] The figures on the total output will be presented in Chapter 9.

[68] It would hardly be possible to determine even the approximate share of each of the various events in this reappraisal.

the Russian lead in the establishment of its policy line, it should be noted that (*a*) this reversal was preceded by the Yugoslav crisis, which indicates that the problem was already there and did not need to be "induced" by outside influence; (*b*) the reappraisal took a different form in such countries as, say, Hungary and Poland; and (*c*) although the reversal took place in the Soviet orbit as a whole in the last part of 1953, a substantial difference *in time* exists between the Soviet reappraisal and the reappraisal in Eastern Europe. In the Soviet Union it was possible to conceal a critical situation for twenty-five years, but in Eastern Europe it was next to impossible to sustain even the scheduled development in industry with a declining agricultural output and a smoldering crisis in the rural areas. This political and economic reappraisal affected, as we shall see below,[69] all the economic sectors of these countries.

The following agricultural measures were intended to correct the errors of the first phase of collectivization:

1. Utilization of all land available, and hence: (*a*) stopping the expulsion of the medium and large peasants from the land; (*b*) a more "liberal" attitude toward the peasants ready to rent state-owned land; (*c*) release of *peasant-workers* working part-time in industry and part-time on the farm from their contracts or other obligations to given plants or factories.

2. More leeway in the formation of cooperatives and more liberty for the peasants to join or quit. Although, except for Yugoslavia, no country of the area repudiated the fixed types of cooperatives, all acquiesced in the formation of "hybrid" cooperatives which adapted the characteristics of one of the officially established types to the interests and needs of a given group of peasant cooperators. As a liberalizing measure, Hungary legalized a simple type of cooperative similar to the Romanian seasonal or permanent joint-tillage association.

As indicated above, only Yugoslavia discarded more or less completely the previously established rigid types of agricultural producers' cooperatives. A decree, the "Property Relations and Reorganization of the Peasant Working Cooperatives," of March 28, 1953, legalized the withdrawal of peasants, singly or in groups, from the cooperatives. The result was the virtual collapse of the previously existing system, and the Yugoslav regime attempted to merge the agricultural working cooperatives with the general type of cooperative existing in the vil-

[69] See Chapter 9, pp. 354 ff.

lages (e.g., consumer cooperative). The principle of flexibility in the form of cooperative was implemented by "pulling down the Chinese wall which has existed between the so-called general type agricultural cooperative and the peasant working cooperative," that is, by merging the various forms "one into another." [70]

3. Stopping the "administrative" pressures for collectivization and liquidation of some of the nonviable cooperatives. The principle of *productivity* was stressed as a decisive factor but not used as a final criterion for selecting and maintaining the existing cooperatives. As a result, only in Hungary and Yugoslavia was there liquidation of an appreciable number of cooperatives. In the other countries of the area the process was merely temporarily stopped at the point reached by the middle or the end of 1953.

4. Decentralization in planning and state collection, and stronger incentives for the producers. Hence: (*a*) increased prices, lowering the quota of obligatory deliveries, and less rigidity in the taxation system; (*b*) increased investment in agriculture and the eventual supply of *credits, technical aid,* and *seeds* to the individual peasant; (*c*) increased goods made available to farmers, e.g., building materials, and consumer goods; (*d*) reorganization of the management of the already established cooperatives and MTS.[71]

Long-Term Policies in Agriculture

The principles and methods summarized above were officially labeled as a "new course" in agriculture. They were supposed to guide the over-all planning not only from the middle of 1953 to 1955 but also for the period of the second quinquennium starting in most of these countries in 1956. However, less than two years after its launching some of these postulates were discarded as "right-wing deviations." Thus again it became questionable whether the peasant would flock freely to cooperatives without at least some mild "administrative" pressure, whether planned industrial economy could coexist for "a long period" with a privately owned small-scale producing agriculture, whether enough means were available for increasing the share of investments in both agriculture and the light industries.

[70] Cf. Moma Marković, President of the Main Cooperative Federation of the FPRY, at the fourth annual assembly of that body, in *Borba,* Apr. 6, 1954; also *Borba,* Mar. 29, 1953.

[71] Subsequently some countries, *e.g.,* Poland, envisaged the possibility of dissolving the MTS and selling the agricultural machinery to the cooperatives.

Except in Yugoslavia, "marking time" in the producers' cooperative movement was ended, and in Poland and Romania the number of cooperatives again started to climb (see Tables 65 and 66). By mid-1955 most of the losses in collectivized land incurred from 1953 on had been made up in the whole area, excluding Yugoslavia (see Table 68). Having again inaugurated a vigorous policy in the countryside,[72] the East European leaders started to fix tentative dates for the completion of the process of collectivization.

The Bulgarian regime has set for itself the task of completing the collectivization of agriculture by 1960. The Polish, Hungarian, and Romanian regimes have affirmed their desire to render collectivization during the second long-term plan the *predominant* form in agriculture. Thus liquidation of private property in agriculture was to be carried out in the area, excluding Yugoslavia, throughout the second and eventually part of a third planned quinquennium. In Yugoslavia, where the organization of agriculture has its distinctive features—such as nationalizing land holdings above 10 hectares and merging cooperatives into general-type cooperatives (consumer, sales cooperatives, etc.)—the development of the multi-purpose agricultural cooperatives was to be further encouraged.

The problem of the scale of investment priorities during the period up to 1960 is discussed in Chapter 9. Let us note here that the idea of a higher priority for investments in agriculture, advanced during the new-course period, was scheduled to influence the allocation of resources during the second quinquennium. However, the increases in agricultural investment were to be extremely modest. On the other hand, parsimonious investments were envisaged in the light industries. The flow of "productive means," such as cement and building materials and the flow of consumer goods toward the villages, was to continue to remain extremely limited.

All these plans have been thrown out of balance by the June 1956 Poznań riots and the Hungarian uprising of October–November 1956. Under these pressures numerous agricultural cooperatives have collapsed in both Poland and Hungary. At least these countries must

[72] Thus Rákosi stated in the spring of 1955:

Alongside the steadily rising level of production in the existing cooperatives, we must see to it, primarily by explanatory work, that this year *there is an end to simply marking time in the producer cooperative movement,* that the peasants begin to join cooperatives and that new cooperatives are set up side by side with the old ones. ["On the Political Situation and Tasks of the Party-Resolution of the Central Committee of the Hungarian Working People's Party" (March 2–4, 1955, *FLP,* March 11, 1955.]

operate under an "emergency program" for a few years, and the target of all-out collectivization must clearly be pushed further into the future. However, this is only a transitional phase.

In evaluating the long-range prospects of the reorganization of agriculture, two groups of factors need to be considered. On the one hand, the inner convulsions of the Soviet Union during the period of its mass collectivization, the difficulties encountered by each East European country during the first quinquennium, and the danger of open uprisings, are constant warnings against a relentless speed-up in agriculture and in the other spheres.[73] On the other hand, in the long run these regimes cannot and will not accept the coexistence of a nationalized economy outside agriculture, and a privately conducted agriculture. These two groups of factors might again set the stage for spasmodic increases in the collectivization of agriculture. Combined with such spasmodic increases it can be expected, as in Yugoslavia, that there will be measures for a progressive nationalization of land starting from a limit of, say, 8 or 10 hectares, and for a further extension of the state farms. In the last analysis, the solution chosen in East Europe seems to be the approach by *stages* toward the basic Communist aim, which remains, in agriculture as in the other spheres, the elimination of private property, whatever the consequence might be in respect to output.[74]

[73] In contrast to the pace of collectivization in East Europe, let us recall that the "first phase of the second cycle" in the reorganization of the rural areas extended in the Soviet Union from 1929 to 1933. In this short span of time there were forced into the collectivized sector 14 million peasants, 65.6 per cent of the peasant households, and 83 per cent of the total sown area. On the eve of the collectivization drive there were, as of 1929, only 1 million peasants in the collectives, 3.9 per cent of the peasant households, and 4.9 per cent of the total sown area. Cf. L. M. Zaltsman et al., *Organizatsiia Sotsialisticheskih Selsko-Khoziaistvennykh Predpriiatii* (The Organization of the Socialist Agricultural Undertakings), Ogiz-Soc'Khogiz, Moscow, 1947, p. 29.

[74] As stated by Gheorghiu-Dej: "Socialist construction cannot rest for any great length of time upon two different bases—upon socialist industry and small-scale farming." (See "Carrying Out the Great Leninist Teaching on the Alliance between the Working Class and the Peasantry," in *FLP*, April 15, 1955.)

SECTION III

PLANNING AND DEVELOPMENT

INTRODUCTORY NOTE TO SECTION III

The section just concluded has traced the process of *structural* changes both in the perspective of planning and during the carrying out of the plans. The present section focuses on *planning itself* as it evolved in a continuously changing setup, and discusses two closely interrelated sets of problems: the first concerning economic growth and the relevance of the Soviet planning model to the six East European economies with their specific budget of resources; the second relating to economic autonomy vs. integration in the Soviet orbit as a whole.

In the context of development problems this section briefly reviews previous debates on the industrialization of the area centered on the problems of surplus population and terms of trade. It analyzes the first economic plans and traces their relationship to the parallel lines of development. It examines in detail the performance of each of the economies in the key sectors during the first planned quinquennium and appraises the relevance of the Soviet planning model (sharply differentiated sectoral rates of growth) to the set of countries under survey. After analyzing the "new course" and its significance as far as resource allocation, rates of growth, and division of labor in the orbit are concerned, it concludes with the analysis and appraisal of the prospects for the *second* planned quinquennium, 1956–60.

Some data relevant to the problems of autonomy vs. integration have already been presented in Chapter 6, in the discussion of the problems of reparations and joint companies. In the present section are knit together: (*a*) the impacts of planning and industrialization on the foreign trade of each of these countries during the first planned quinquennium, with the assumption of a lack of detailed coordination at the level of output; (*b*) the character of the attempts at *coordination* of foreign trade; (*c*) the relation of Soviet Russia's positions in some of these economies to the pattern of trade and trade settlements in the area.

Thus this section discusses the mechanism of planning (Chapter 8), the sectoral performance and prospects (Chapter 9), the specific problems of man power and management (Chapter 10), and, last, the problem of trade and trade relations among these countries (Chapter 11). A series of graphs and a statistical appendix to Chapter 9 present data for all the basic products for all the countries considered up to 1955.

In examining the data concerning the indices of production given in the plans (Chapter 8) and the results of the plans (Chapter 9), it should be taken into consideration that in Eastern Europe, as in the Soviet Union, the index numbers of industrial production are based on production data including duplications. The data for each period are the sum of the value of output of all industrial enterprises; goods produced by one enterprise that are sold to another and used by it in production are thus included more than once. In technical terms, these indices are based on the *sum of the total value of output* of each enterprise and not on *value added* (i.e., excluding duplications). If the degree of double counting remains constant from one year to the next, the indices will not be distorted, but if the double counting increases, as happens in a period of industrialization, the indices will tend to overstate any increase in output.[1] The Soviet indices tend to be biased upward not only for this reason but for other reasons as well: the computation of the value of outputs in 1926–27 rubles, a year in which the prices of industrial products were abnormally high relative to other prices, so that increase in industrial output increases the value of total output by an abnormally high percentage; the pricing of new products, not at their prices when they are produced in volume, but at the high prices of their first year of production; the absorption of small-scale industrial enterprises into the statistics for large-scale industry, whose increase in output is thus exaggerated; and other factors.[2]

Some of those factors have also played a role in the East European type of indices in degrees varying among the different countries. The distorting factor of the pricing of new products has played a substantial role in the East European countries, probably more so in Romania or Bulgaria, which were beginning industrialization, than in Czechoslovakia, which was already industrialized. The base year for those countries, however, has been either 1937 or 1939, which for some of them was a normal year and provided a more appropriate weighting system than the 1926–27 prices for the Soviet Union. It would not be safe, however, to state that the degree of exaggeration of the annual rate of increase in output indicated by the data cited below either is or is not less than that in the Soviet Union. We do not have sufficient data to be sure. Because the indices present valuable information even in their uncorrected form, they are presented here without any attempt at recomputation. They must be used with caution, with consideration for their built-in

[1] In an explanatory note concerning the East European type of indices, the United Nations' *ESE Since the War,* UN, ECE, Geneva, 1954, stresses also the following problems:

> If there is a switch from butter-making on farms to factory production of butter, the gross output of industry is increased by the full value of the butter made, whereas the gross output of agriculture is reduced only by the difference between the value of the butter and that of the milk from which it is made. (It is this type of change which is mainly responsible for the huge increases in the output of the food-processing industries of the East European countries.) If, as has been the case, animal husbandry increases in importance at the expense of production of crops for human consumption, the gross output of agriculture increases because the crops fed to animals are counted twice. If, for purposes of administrative control, the output of an integrated plant is recorded at several stages, the gross output of the plant becomes a function of the number of administrative units into which the plant is split. [Cf. p. 25.]

[2] For a summary of these defects and an explanation of the need to recompute the Soviet indices, see Professor Donald R. Hodgman's paper "Industrial Production in Soviet Economic Growth," in A. Bergson, editor: *Soviet Economic Growth,* Row, Peterson & Co., Evanston, Ill., 1953, pp. 225 ff.

upward bias and their more and more limited value as the span of time increases and the errors in them are compounded.

The concept of national income presently used in East European and Soviet statistics is "net material product." It excludes services except for those connected with production and transport of goods. Notwithstanding numerous deficiencies, to be discussed in Chapter 12, let us note for the moment that income data for two basic reasons give a more accurate impression of the overall changes in the economy than the indices of gross value of output. First, they exclude duplication. Second, a shift of output from small-scale industry and crafts will cause the increase of industrial output to overstate the increase in the output of goods, whereas national income data will record the value of total output of goods without this error. The utility of the indices of gross value of output is mainly to gage the degree to which desired changes have been attained, i.e., in what measure the plan fulfillment figures expressed by those indices correspond to the goal set, computed by the same procedure.

CHAPTER

8

THE PLANS: MODEL, SCOPE, AND RELATIONS IMPLIED

Industrialization in Eastern Europe

The problem of industrialization of Eastern Europe is not a new one. The area is densely populated, and a high percentage of its population is engaged in agriculture. The low per capita output of the peasantry relative to per capita output in industry has long since raised two sets of problems in every country in the area, the first concerning surplus population in agriculture, and the second, the terms of trade and what goods should be produced for export and what goods imported rather than produced at home.

The existence of a surplus population in agriculture implies the presence of agricultural workers whose productivity is zero on the land, and whose removal from the land hence would not cause a fall in agricultural output. Although the phenomenon has been evidenced many times by inquiries on the spot, and there has developed among economists a broad consensus on the existence of this "disguised unemployment" in agriculture in the so-called underdeveloped countries, no generally accepted measurement of this surplus has been devised, and the differences in the various estimates made are often substantial. The determination of the excess is ascertainable with a set of assumptions in relation, for instance, to an optimum population density and conditions of production on the land. According to the estimates of a study group directed by Dr. P. N. Rosenstein-Rodan, and combining social methods for estimating the *actual* agricultural surplus population (as contrasted to the *theoretical* surplus), this surplus for the six countries was in 1937 approximately 15 million out of an agricultural population of 61 million, a "disguised unemployment" of almost 25 per cent. The largest surpluses were in Bulgaria and Yugoslavia, 28 and 35 per cent of the respective agricultural populations, the lowest in Czechoslovakia, 13 per cent. Hungary is said to have had a surplus of about 18 per cent, Romania about 20 per cent, and Poland (in its prewar territory) 24 per cent.[1] The existence of a surplus and growing agricultural population coupled with the inability of industry to absorb even the annual increase in the labor force was a distressing problem in this region long before World War II.[2]

The crises of the 1930's, when the purchasing power of agricultural produce fell sharply in relation to that of industry, coupled with the belief that the secular trend in their purchasing power was down-

[1] The study group conducted by Dr. Rosenstein-Rodan indicated that four methods were available for estimating the actual surplus agricultural population: (1) *empirical inquiry* (by means of questionnaires addressed to owners, and inquiring about the number of surplus people on each holding); (2) computation on the basis of the census of the *average number of man-hours' work* by the active agricultural population, and then estimation of the number of man-hours required to achieve the same amount of output, the difference—converted into persons—representing the surplus; (3) calculation of the *existing density* of agricultural population, as compared to a *"reasonable" density* on the assumption of "reasonable" methods of production; (4) calculation of the number of persons who could be supported on the land, assuming the existing conditions of production, at *a given minimum standard of living that is "reasonable."* It is on the basis of all these methods that the group estimated the *actual* surplus indicated above. Cf. "Agricultural Surplus Population in Eastern and South Eastern Europe," compiled by Dr. P. N. Rosenstein-Rodan as part of the materials for a study of *Economic Development of Eastern and South Eastern Europe,* undertaken for the Royal Institute of International Affairs, Chatham House, 10 St. James's Square, London, S. W. 1, during the years 1943–45.

What could be called the "theoretical surplus" has been calculated for the area by W. E. Moore on the basis of a completely different set of estimates. Moore related agricultural population to total arable land, computed in terms of *arable equivalent for all types of land,* and assumed the Western (French) yield per hectare of arable land. His computations show surpluses of as much as 40 to 80 per cent of the agricultural population existing on the land. (Cf. Moore, *Economic Demography of Eastern and Southeastern Europe,* a League of Nations study published by Princeton University Press, Princeton, N. J., 1945.) Moore's *method of converting the existing land into arable equivalents* and the utilization of the Western yield set rather arbitrary limits, in contrast to the concrete approach referring to the surplus in the framework of the existing conditions on the land.

[2] See, for instance, an interesting paper by O. Franges, "L'Industrialization des pays agricoles du Sud-Est de l'Europe" (The Industrialization of the Agricultural Countries of South-East Europe), in *Revue économique internationale* (International Economic Review), XXX, 2 (July 1938), pp. 27 ff., which summarizes the state of the problem on the eve of the Second World War.

ward, led the countries of Eastern Europe to foster industrial production at home by extremist protectionist policies. In a much discussed theory at the time, a Romanian economist suggested in the late 1920's that choice by the agricultural countries in the production of commodities should be determined, not by *how much a given commodity costs on the international market compared to how much it would cost to produce it at home,* but by the *productivity attainable per man in the production of these goods.* As the attainable value of the output per man engaged in agriculture is smaller than the output per man in industry, agriculture was described as presenting "an intrinsic inferiority" as compared to industry, and the trade of agricultural goods, as against industrial, was characterized as "implicitly unequal." [3] The famous Swedish economist, Bertil Ohlin, naturally pointed out that, pushed to its logical conclusion, this theory would make absurd the continuation of agricultural output even in a well-endowed agricultural country like Romania.[4] However, it is not necessary to push the argument to either extreme, stressing exclusively either the problem of productivity or the static aspects of "factor endowment." The crux of the matter is that, where there is surplus agricultural population, moving part of it into industry tends to increase both output per man in agriculture and the total national product.

However, unless the government takes active and skillful steps, surplus agricultural labor may not move into non-agricultural employment, for any or all of several reasons:

(1) Because of family structure, the nature of village life, or other social influences it may be difficult to induce the surplus labor to leave the agricultural villages.

(2) The effective demand for non-agricultural products may not be great enough to induce the development of new or enlarged non-agricultural industries. Aggregate demand may be too low.

[3] M. Manoilescu, *Théorie du protectionnisme et de l'échange international* (Theory of Protectionism and of International Trade), Bibliothèque internationale d'économie politique (International Library of Political Economy), Girard, Paris, 1929; also *A New Conception of Industrial Protectionism* (English text), Regia Monitorului Official Imprimeria Naţională (The Official Gazette, National Printing House), Bucharest,1931; also "Arbeitsproduktivität und Aussenhandel" (Labor Productivity and Foreign Trade), in *Weltwirstschaftliches Archiv* (Archives of World Economy), XLII, 1, 1935, pp. 13–43.

[4] B. Ohlin, "Protection and Non-Competing Groups" (English text), in *Weltwirtschaftliches Archiv,* XXXIII, 1, 1931, pp. 30–45.

(3) Entrepreneurial talent or technical knowledge necessary for the development of new enterprises may be lacking.

(4) Even though there are idle workers and other idle resources, the financial machinery necessary for the financing of new enterprises may be lacking.

(5) Capital formation in new industries may require the importation of capital equipment, and the foreign exchange necessary to purchase it may not be available.

Even before World War II the passive attitude of the governments of the East European countries toward these problems had given place to government financing of private investment or to direct investment by government.[5] However, government action remained haphazard and was unable to effect sufficient increased employment even to keep abreast of the increase in the labor force.

In addition to the problem of stimulating adequate demand and an adequate level of capital formation there is the problem of selecting the most advantageous projects for investment. Any one entrepreneur may assume that the economy as a whole remains as it is or develops only gradually. If, however, the government or private investors as a group take actions which will change materially the size and nature of the economic system as a whole, the individual decisions may be in error, or, specifically, may be too timid and not the most advantageous ones. East European governments have tended increasingly to judge the desirability of investment on the basis of a future situation conditioned by an intervening period of economic growth and development, an attitude having little in common with the protectionist theories of the 1920's, which advocated developing domestic industries without regard to the cost of production of the products.

As is indicated below, analysis on the basis of anticipated future changes in the general structure of the economy establishes quite clear-cut boundaries to growth and development, just as conventional planning by a single entrepreneur on the basis of the existing situation does, although in the first circumstance the boundaries are more distant than those determined by analysis based on present costs, present yields, and the present international division of labor.

The above should not be taken to imply that the planning of the East European governments was far-sighted and correct. Their plans were also based on Marxist ideas of the basic desirability (virtually

[5] For a discussion of these problems, see the extensive and valuable comment of K. Mandelbaum, *The Industrialization of Backward Areas,* Institute of Statistics, Monograph 2, Basil Blackwell, Oxford, 1947, Part A.

without analysis of cost or yield) of the development of industry and especially of "heavy" industry, steel, machinery, etc.

Erecting the Planning Framework

After a first phase of "stock-taking" extending up to the end of 1946 the period of planning opened in 1947 with the launching of the so-called "reconstruction plans." As can be seen from Table 71, Czechoslovakia and Bulgaria each established a two-year plan, Poland and Hungary, a three-year plan. Romania alone started its reconstruction plans at the end of 1948 and had two one-year plans up to the end of 1950. Yugoslavia put into execution at the beginning a plan for both reconstruction and development which was to last from 1947 to 1951, inclusive, and which was subsequently extended for one year (to 1952). Reconstruction plans were concluded in 1948 in Czechoslovakia and Bulgaria and in 1949 in Poland and Hungary. Romania concluded its reconstruction period at the end of 1950, when the whole region was engaged in the first national plans of development. The first long-term plans of development were scheduled to be completed either in 1953 (Czechoslovakia and Bulgaria), 1954 (Hungary), or in 1955 (Poland and Romania). Actually, toward the end of 1953 a "new course" was inaugurated in the area, implying substantial reorientations of the plans and important shifts in the allocation of available resources. Finally by the turn of 1956 Czechoslovakia, Poland, Hungary, and Romania launched simultaneously with Soviet Russia a new long-term plan. Bulgaria, having proclaimed completion of its first five-year plan in four years, that is in 1952, launched its second five-year plan in 1953 for the period 1953–57, and decided to launch a three-year plan between 1958 and the end of 1960, and thus fall in step with the other countries.

Let us now consider closely the problems these countries faced in the erection of their planning framework. Except in Czechoslovakia and Bulgaria, which had suffered less during the war than the other countries of the area, and which had consequently set as an objective a two-year period of reconstruction, the plans envisaged a longer period and were set in the framework of badly shattered, war-damaged economies, some of which were facing complicated problems of territorial integration (Poland) or heavy and multiple international obligations (Hungary and Romania). The plans had to take into account the interweaving in the economy of *six* types of ownership: nationalized enterprises, joint state-private enterprises, joint state-Soviet com-

TABLE 71. PLANS OF RECONSTRUCTION AND DEVELOPMENT, 1947–60

Country	(*R*) Plans of Reconstruction [a]						(*D*) First Plans of Development [a]			Second Plans of Development	
	Period				Officially completed end of	Number of years	Period Jan. 1–Dec. 31	Officially completed end of	Number of years	Period Jan. 1–Dec. 31	Number of years
	Year	First of	Year	End of							
Czechoslovakia	1947	Jan.	1948	Dec.	1948	2	1949–1953	1953	5	1955–1960	5
Poland	1947	Jan.	1949	Dec.	1949	3	1950–1955	1955	5	1955–1960	5
Hungary	1947	Aug.	1950	July	1949	2¼	1950–1954	1954	5	1955–1960	5
Romania	1949	Jan.	1950	Dec.	1950	2	1951–1955	1955	5	1955–1960	5
Bulgaria	1947	Apr.	1949	Mar.	1948	1¾	1949–1953	1952	4	1952–1957 [b]	5
Yugoslavia	1947	Jan. ————					→ 1951	1952	6	yearly plans	1

[a] Throughout this chapter, in the tables, *R* refers to plans of reconstruction and *D* to the first plans of development.
[b] A three-year plan, 1958–60, is to follow the Second Five-Year Plan.

panies, Soviet and other foreign companies, private capitalist companies, and private small-scale ownership predominant in agriculture. Moreover, the planners were confronted by three types of organization of production: state ("socialist"), private (capitalist), and very small-scale production (in craft trades, cottage industry, and agriculture).

The technical conditions of the elaboration of the reconstruction plans were extremely precarious. At the time there existed no reliable data or even good estimates concerning many aspects of the economy, for example, the crafts, the sown areas, and the livestock population. Most of the plans used as a point of reference the 1938–39 data because no reliable measurement was available for either 1945 or 1946. The determination of the capacity of production in certain industries or the degree of its utilization, or the level of the national income and its sources, had to be based, in many countries, on extrapolations and expert opinions rather than on solid data.[6] To start with, in most of these countries planning consisted of organizing a given output in the nationalized enterprises and establishing a system of constantly expanding controls in the other spheres.[7] During the first year the planned sector faced enormous difficulties in its relations with the private sector, which except in Yugoslavia was then profiting by the scarcity of consumers' goods, together with increased incomes created by increased expenditures by the nationalized sector. As we have already noted, these difficulties were overcome, not by the establishment of some *modus vivendi* with the private sector or even with small producers, but by extensive nationalizations and by increased nationalization as an operating policy throughout the economic body.

[6] See for instance, for Hungary, the very interesting article of Dr. Béla Gorácz, "A Magyar Hároméves Terv Statisztikai Felépítése" (The Statistical Construction of the Hungarian Three-Year Plan), in *Magyar Statisztikai Szemle* (Hungarian Economic Review), XXVI, 16 (January–June 1948), pp. 3–7.

[7] Thus, for instance, the Czechoslovak government memorandum on the Five-Year Plan reads:

> The Two-Year Plan was . . . fragmentary in character and its scope was confined to a number of sectional aspects of the Czechoslovak economy, chief among which was production. Fundamentally, the Two-Year Plan was a production programme for the key sectors of the economy, supplemented by the most important balance sheets of raw materials, investment, man power, and foreign trade, which were to ensure the harmonious and complementary development of the various sectors. The production plans setting out target volumes of output in individual sectors were supplemented in the second year of the two-year period by certain qualitative indicators, providing directives for the planning of the quality of certain key products and of production economy, i.e., in particular the productivity of labour, as well as consumption of raw materials, fuel, auxiliary materials, power, etc. [The Czechoslovak Economic Five-Year Plan . . . p. 202.]

The *first development plans* were launched under completely new objective and technical conditions. Nationalization had reduced both the forms of ownership and the methods of production in the economy. In the former Allied countries the enormously expanded socialized ownership now faced both a sharply reduced capitalist ownership and an important aggregate of small private ownership in agriculture. In the ex-enemy countries these three *types of ownership* coexisted with two other important forms: the Soviet companies and the joint companies with Soviet participation. The whole economy was now reorganized along two basic lines of *methods of production:* state-socialist and private, very small-scale producers. Capitalist production (in this context, private property with hired labor) survived only to a limited extent in crafts, trade, and agriculture. Planning under such conditions approached more and more the post-1928 planning in Soviet Russia. It became progressively less flexible than in the reconstruction period, and it embraced more and more of the economy.

Finally, the *second long-term plans* of development were launched under conditions basically similar to those existing at the moment of the launching of the first development plans, the only difference being that in the meantime the state had increased substantially its sphere of ownership and direct control in agriculture, the last sector of private small-scale production.

Schematic Outline of a Plan

What, in essence, is a plan? How is it constructed? How is it implemented?

A plan represents a comprehensive set of accounts linking a series of output, investment, and consumption targets with the projected factor commodity and money flows required to assure their attainment. Contrary to Western practice, in the Soviet Union and Eastern Europe these accounts, called *balanced estimates,* do not constitute just a series of forecasts or provisional models based on varying hypotheses and assumptions, but a definite set of tasks which must be accomplished and which are binding as a law for society as a whole.

The accounts are balance sheets, with one side of the account showing resources and the other side their distribution. One set of balance sheets is expressed in physical units, as balances between supply and distribution of productive resources or inputs: man power, productive capacity (machines), and raw materials. Another set, in value terms, deals with output and its use, or with productive capacity and its allocation among alternative types of output. These accounts trace product, income, and expenditure flows.[8]

The point of departure in Soviet-type planning is the definition of objectives by the top political authority. This authority takes upon itself the formulation of targets for: (*a*) the allocation of national product among investment, government consumption, and personal consumption, and (*b*) the production of a series of key final and intermediate products. Broadly speaking, these various targets and the order of priority accorded to their fulfillment or overfulfillment reflect primarily the planners' scale of preferences, with consumers accorded a largely advisory role, within the constraints imposed by physical and human resource limitations. Planning directives are formulated on the basis of detailed accounts for the preplan period prepared by the National Planning Board (NPB). This Board has to translate the general directives into specific and closely coordinated plans for use of inputs and interindustry relationships. In constructing these prospective balances the NPB works with technical coefficients (combinations of present and future estimated inputs needed to produce given outputs).[9]

In general terms, the process of plan formulation is based on a system of successive approximations rather than on a simultaneous adjustment of all variables in the system. Concretely, this means that an imbalance between targets on the one hand and resource and capacity limitations on the other hand is resolved according to a definite order of priorities, with plan fulfillment in low-priority areas

[8] For a detailed discussion of these concepts, see Prof. J. Marczewski, "Le Rôle des comptes nationaux dans les économies planifiées du type sovietique" (The Role of National Accounts in Planned Economies of the Soviet Type), in *Income and Wealth*, Series IV, International Association for Research in Income and Wealth, London, 1955.

[9] Here is, for instance, an example of the character of the technical productive coefficients and their utilization during the Second Soviet Five-Year Plan. In order to determine the output of sugar-beets needed for a given index of sugar production, the Planning Board devised coefficients for the utilization of labor, fuel, etc., consolidated in the following table:

	1932	1937
Extraction of sugar per 100 kilos of sugar-beets	13.10	14.00
Losses of sugar during manufacture, percentage	2.87	2.40
Expenditure of labor force in man-hours, per sugar quintal	5.60	3.00
Expenditure of fuel, per 100 sugar quintals, in tons	7.90	6.45

Cf. Bettelheim, *La Planification soviétique, op. cit.*, p. 108.

being sacrificed if necessary in order to fulfill or overfulfill targets in high-priority areas, or "leading branches," of the economy.[10]

Once the general objectives and key targets have been defined by the political authority, the full and detailed elaboration of the plan by the NPB involves a two-way process of communication and adjustment. Thus the NPB distributes the tasks among the various technical ministries, which in turn allot projects to their subordinate national corporations and branches, which finally allocate tasks among individual plants. At this point the process of elaboration starts in the opposite direction. The plant faced with specific goals elaborates these into concrete operational plans that involve planning of production, investment, and basic repair and requirements of labor, fuel, and materials. Actually, given the production targets, cost and financial plans are formulated on the basis of so-called technical-economic coefficients or *norms,* which in effect provide one of the strategic links between the enterprise and the national plan. These enterprise plans are consolidated at each level, and finally at the national level by the NPB. Once this consolidation is effected, the plan is submitted for approval by the government. Within the framework of this more or less general and long-range plan, detailed annual plans are promulgated by government decree.

Paralleling this process of detailed plan elaboration, the planning authorities formulate aggregate national product, income, and expenditure accounts. In a sense, Soviet planning proceeds first from a definition of objectives in aggregate terms to plan elaboration involving a great deal of disaggregation. Then this process is reversed with the consolidation of specific detailed accounts into a new set of national accounts. In the course of this operation, attention is paid to the "household account," i.e., consumer income and expenditures, in order to make sure that the various financial, fiscal, and production plans will be such as to maintain an equilibrium between the flow of

[10] As Marczewski notes, the plan *in toto*

is not a simple technical operation, consisting in the solving of a system of *n* equations with *n* unknowns. This would be the case, only if there were neither political objectives to be achieved nor political variables and if the system would serve only to extrapolate trends observed statistically, which would be conceivable only in a completely liberal regime of pure competition. [Cf. "Le Rôle des comptes nationaux . . . ,"] *op. cit.*, p. 7.

For each specific product the margin of error can, however, be determined mathematically as any error is conditioned by three factors: the margin of error of the basic statistical data, the error connected with the prediction of future economic trends, and the deviation allowed from the trends contemplated in the future. Cf. Dr. Béla Gorácz, *op. cit.*, p. 5.

disposable income and the flow of consumers' goods and services. However, disequilibrium in this sphere need not lead to a revision of production targets, since the government is in a position to re-establish an equilibrium through resort to various fiscal devices and other means at its disposal.[11] On the basis of past experience a major revision in the production and investment plan is likely to be contemplated on this account only if the scarcity of consumers' goods threatens to undermine political stability.

The plans discussed in this section are the long-range economic plans. These do not contain detailed plans for each year of the plan period. They state the scheduled increases in specified products (in physical terms), the planned increases in output of various branches of production (in value of gross output only), and the expected national income. As the value of output by branches is not given in terms of net output, it is difficult to analyze the planned contribution of each sector to the increase in national income. Various methodological differences sometimes render an over-all tabulation extremely difficult (e.g., certain countries give the gross value of engineering, whereas others give the gross value of output of machine tools only, etc.). No detailed and systematic information is given on foreign trade; the plans for this sector were presented in greater detail only in the reconstruction plans. As a rule, the long-range plans constitute only the *framework* within which adaptations and revisions are unavoidable during the plan period.[12] However, sometimes these revisions are not published or are released only in a very summary fashion which of course greatly complicates the task of the analyst.

Having thus briefly sketched the planning framework in the area, let us turn now to the planning model and to the scheduled changes in the economy.

Basic Characteristics of the Model

In an article on the problems of industrializing Eastern and Southeastern Europe written during World War II, Dr. P. N. Rosenstein-

[11] See above, Chapter 4.

[12] The forecasts are valid not only so far as the described structure and the predicted estimates correspond to the real structure and to the deliberate choices made, but also so far as the hypotheses concerning the *unpredictable variables* (climatic condition, foreign trade policies, etc.) are verified. Cf. Marczewski, "Le Rôle des comptes nationaux . . . ," *op. cit.*

Rodan noted that there were two fundamentally different ways of industrializing open to the area:

> (i) That Eastern and South-Eastern Europe should industrialise on its own, on the "Russian model" (by which we do *not* mean communism), aiming at self-sufficiency, without international investment. That would imply the construction of all stages of industry, heavy industry, machine industry, as well as light industry, with the final result of a national economy built like a vertical industrial concern. This way presents several grave disadvantages. . . . It can only proceed slowly, because capital must be supplied internally at the expense of a standard of life and consumption which are already at a very low level. It implies, therefore, a heavy and, in our opinion, unnecessary sacrifice. . . . It will lead finally, since there are appropriate natural resources in the area, to an independent unit in the world economy implying a reduction in the international division of labour; i.e., the output of the world as a whole would be less than it might be, the world would be poorer in material goods. . . .
>
> (ii) The alternative way of industrialisation would fit Eastern and South-Eastern Europe into the world economy, which would preserve the advantages of an international division of labour, and would therefore in the end produce more wealth for everybody. It would be based on substantial international investment or capital lending.[13]

As we shall see presently, industrialization was attempted along the lines of the "Russian model": "the construction of all stages of industry" with emphasis on "heavy industry," i.e., on one type of producers' goods only rather than on other producers' goods or on consumers' goods, and that emphasis applied not by the area as a whole but by each nation.

Let us now follow concretely the global outputs planned by each of these countries in industry and agriculture, in the basic sectors of industry (heavy and light), and in their main branches. As already stated in the Introduction, we propose to examine jointly the reconstruction and the first development plans in order to compare their targets to the results achieved first up to 1953, then up to the end of 1955. Only afterwards will we turn to the new goals of the second long-term plans.

As can be seen from Table 72, the reconstruction plans set the prewar level as a general objective in agriculture (except in Poland, whose population was appreciably reduced and whose goal was substantially below the prewar level, and in Bulgaria, which suffered less from the war and set a higher goal). During the reconstruction period

[13] "Problems of Industrialisation of Eastern and South-Eastern Europe," in *The Economic Journal*, LIII, 1943, p. 203.

Table 72. Planned Outputs in Industry and Agriculture during the Reconstruction and First Long-Term Plans [a]

	R		*D*	
Country	Indus.	Agric.	Indus.	Agric.
Czechoslovakia	110	100	213	138 [b]
Poland	148	76	417	115
Hungary	127	90	434	140 [b]
Romania	117	100	306	160
Bulgaria	167	134	403	135
Yugoslavia			494	151

[a] Prewar = 100. Gross value of output.
[b] Revised Plan.

Sources:

Plans of Reconstruction:

C: *First Czechoslovak Economic Plan: Act and Memorandum*, 2nd ed., Orbis, Prague, 1948.

P: *Polish National Economic Plan of Economic Reconstruction for the Period of January 1, 1946–December 31, 1949*, Warsaw, 1946.

H: *Hungarian Three-Year Plan*, publ. by *HB*, Budapest, 1947.

R: 1949: "Romania's Economic One-Year Plan," in *RN*, Washington, Jan. 16, 1949; 1950: Bill on the State Plan of the RPR, in *Planned Development of the RPR*, Bucharest, 1950.

B: *Law on the Two-Year Economic Plan, 1947–1948*, Ministry of Information and Arts, Sofia, 1947, with an Introductory Report by Dobri Terpeshev.

First Plans of Development:

C: *Czechoslovak Economic Five-Year Plan; Act and Government Memorandum, op. cit.*: Revised Plan in *RP*, Feb. 25, 1951; also *ESE in 1951, op. cit.*, p. 62.

P: *The Six-Year Plan of Building the Foundations of Socialism, 1950–1955*, Pol-Gos, Warsaw, 1951.

H: *Le Plan quinquennal de la RPH* (The Five-Year Plan of the PRH), publ. by *HB*, Budapest, 1950; also *Planirovanie Narodnogo Khoziaistva Vengrii, Sbornik Materialov* (Planning the People's Economy of Hungary, Collection of Materials), Izdatel'stvo Inostrannoi Literatury, (Publishing House of Foreign Literature), Moscow, 1950. Revised Plan in *SN*, May 16, 1951; also *ESE in 1951*, UN, ECE, Geneva, 1952, p. 62.

R: *Le Plan quinquennal roumain* (The Romanian Five-Year Plan), Notes et études documentaires (Notes and Documentary Studies), No. 1534, La Documentation Française (French Documentation), Paris, 1951.

B: Dobri Terpeshev, *Doklad o Piatiletnem Plane, Piatyi S'ezd B.K.P.* (Report on the Five-Year Plan at the Fifth Congress of the BWP), Izdatel'stvo Direktsii Pechati (Published by the Department of Printing), Sofia, 1947.

Y: *Law on the Five-Year Plan of the FPRY, op. cit.*

the goals scheduled in industry called for increases over the prewar levels ranging from 10 to almost 70 per cent.

The tendency to accelerate rapidly the process of industrialization is clearly illustrated by the goals set for the first development programs. Agricultural production was scheduled to reach one and one-third or one and one-half times the prewar volume simultaneously with a growth of industry to more than double the prewar level in Czechoslovakia, more than triple in Romania, and more than quadruple in Poland, Hungary, Bulgaria, and Yugoslavia.

In every country the emphasis in industry was placed squarely on the producers' goods industries, and in this group on certain of its key branches (see Table 73).

TABLE 73. PLANNED INCREASES IN GROSS VALUE OF OUTPUT OF KEY INDUSTRIAL BRANCHES DURING FIRST PLANS OF DEVELOPMENT [a]

Country	Total Industry 1	Producers' Goods Industries 2	Metal-working Industry 3	Machine-building Industry 4	Consumers' Goods Industry 5
Czechoslovakia	198	233	231	352	173
Poland	258	254	300	360	211
Hungary	310	380	490	[b]	245
Romania	244	[b]	220	216	[b]
Bulgaria	219	320	266	680	175

[a] Preplan year = 100.
[b] Not available.
Sources: As in Table 72.

The first development plans set as a goal for the value of gross output of the producers' goods industries a total from 2 to nearly 4 times the preplan total. Furthermore, the center of *each plan* was established in the metal-working industry; in this branch everything was focused on the construction of machinery.

In the words of the Czechoslovak Government Memorandum on the (first) Five-Year Plan:

> The centre of the whole plan is the *metal-working industry* . . . and again the entire plan is focused on the *heavy engineering sector* [14] within the metal-working industry. . . . Stalin's reference to the "chief link" of the economic plan applies in this context: *"In order to carry out such a plan it is necessary first of all to find its main link;*

[14] The term "engineering" sector as used here for Eastern Europe is comparable to the American term "heavy machine industries."

for only after this main link has been found and grasped can all the other links in the plan be pulled up." [15]

Each country built its plan around this "center." The Czechoslovak development plan scheduled increases in the metal-working industries and in the heavy engineering branch of 93 and 138 per cent, respectively. The goals were raised during the middle of 1951 to 131 and 252 per cent, respectively. (The Revised Plan also raised the target for equipment of mining, steel, and building industries, and for rolling stock and lowered the targets for agricultural machinery and tractors.) In Poland the metal industry was scheduled to reach a level 3 times higher than previously and to extend considerably its assortment of products. In Hungary the initial plan set a target for increase in the engineering branches of 125 per cent, which was subsequently increased to 390 per cent, and for the machine-building industry scheduled the manufacture of a whole range of heavy machinery not produced before in that country. In Romania the accent was placed on production of drilling equipment, machine tools, heavy electrical equipment, compressors, and tractors. Substantial increases and equally ambitious plans were scheduled even by the smallest country of the area, Bulgaria, which planned to develop especially building machinery, cement mixers, compressors, etc.

Compared to the centralization in the metal-working industries, the planned increases in the consumers' goods industries appear moderate in each nation and in the region as a whole.

Thus all these countries patterned their plans on the "Russian model," focusing on expansion of the heavy goods industries, and concentrating their efforts on "broadening" their respective "bases of industrialization" in order to achieve that end.

Broadening the "Industrial Base" in Each Unit

This decision resulted in: (*a*) the planning of substantial increases in the outputs of the key products, coal, iron and steel, electric power, and cement; (*b*) the planning of expanded geological research and prospecting, and large utilization of whatever limited national sources of raw materials were available; (*c*) a newly established pattern of industrial location.

As far as the key products were concerned, the reconstruction plan set a goal of 133 million tons for coal in the region as a whole, a total

[15] Cf. *The Czechoslovak Economic Five-Year Plan, op. cit.*, p. 53.

slightly above the prewar output of the area (see Table 74). The development plans then set a target of 202 million tons, about 157 per cent of the output of the area in the prewar period. In view of the nature of the deposits available, the main increases in all these countries, except Czechoslovakia and Poland, were scheduled for lignite, a fact implying dependence on imports for most of the hard coal and coke needed. The expected increases in the Czechoslovak output of hard coal, lignite, and coke were planned by that country so as to insure relative coverage of domestic needs for hard coal (usually dependent up to a point on imports) and to leave margins for exports for the other products. The Polish planned output of 100 million tons, leaving very substantial surpluses for export, represented an increase of 30 per cent compared to the prewar output in the present territory, a rather impressive target if we consider the fact that many mines and their equipment were destroyed at the end of the war.

TABLE 74. PLANNED OUTPUTS OF COAL, STEEL, AND ELECTRICITY

	Hard Coal and Lignite, millions of tons			Steel, millions of tons			Electricity, billions of kwhr.		
Country	1938	*R*	*D*	1938	*R*	*D*	1938	*R*	*D*
Czechoslovakia	31.8	41.6	52.0	1.87	2.40	4.30 [a]	4.1	7.4	12.3
Poland	77.0	77.8	100.0	1.89	2.00	4.60	7.0	8.0	19.3
Hungary	9.3	9.3	18.5	0.64	0.80	2.20 [a]	1.1	2.0	6.0
Romania	2.4	2.9	8.5	0.27	0.35 [b]	1.25	1.1	2.6	4.7
Bulgaria	2.1	2.0	6.5	[c]	[c]	0.01	0.2	0.9	1.8
Yugoslavia	5.8	[c]	16.5	0.23	[c]	0.76	1.1	[c]	4.4
Total	128.4	133.6	202.0	4.90	5.55	13.12	14.6	20.9	48.5

[a] Revisions of 1951.
[b] Estimate.
[c] Nil.
Sources: As in Table 72.

In the steel industry in all the countries (excluding Yugoslavia) the scheduled output by the end of the reconstruction period was to be 5.5 million tons, or 118 per cent of prewar output. By the end of the development plans it was scheduled to reach 12.3 million tons, or 261 per cent of prewar, and, including Yugoslavia, 13.1 million tons, or 267 per cent of prewar. It is interesting to note that such an output from the beginning implied planned dependence of the region on imports of iron ore. Before the war the domestic iron ore output of Czechoslovakia, Poland (present territory), Hungary, and Romania in terms of iron content had amounted to some 1.1 million tons, as related to an output of 5.1 million tons of steel. The scheduled output for the end of the first development plans was to reach about 2.4 million tons in iron content, as related to an output of 12.3 million tons of steel. The problem of fulfilling the plans became acute after the Yugoslav break with the Soviet orbit and the region's loss of significant supplies of iron ore from Yugoslavia, but achievement of many of the forecast outputs was from the outset conditioned on overcoming enormous difficulties, given the state of depletion of certain mines and the kind of equipment available.

In all the plans the greatest efforts were centered on electric output. The reconstruction plans set a goal of 20.9 billion kilowatt-hours, as compared to 13.5 billion in the prewar period (excluding Yugoslavia), an increase of 55 per cent for the region as a whole. By the end of the first development plan the total output was to increase to 48.5 billion, as compared to 14.6 billion in prewar times, i.e., more than 3 times the prewar production. The increases were to be obtained by fuller utilization of existing capacity and new construction, and were to serve as the basis for new power-consuming industries. Planned *increases* ranged from 175 per cent for Czechoslovakia and Poland to 280–320 per cent in Hungary, Yugoslavia, and Romania, and to 800 per cent in Bulgaria.

With the stress on new constructions, plans included extensive developments for construction materials and a complete reorganization of the building industry as such. The goals in cement outputs are characteristic of the magnitude of the changes envisaged. The production of cement was to rise from a prewar output of 5.9 million tons to 14.2 million by the end of the first development plans, a net increase of 140 per cent.

The planned expansion of prospecting and utilization of all types of national raw materials can be gaged by the development scheduled by each country for the output of non-ferrous metals and for the development of "local" resources. Each country listed increased outputs of zinc, copper, lead, as well as oil and natural gas, even when their past resources were known to be extremely small and their exploitation cost prohibitive. Except for Yugoslavia with its large resources of non-ferrous metals and Poland with its zinc, the region was known to be poor in these resources, and many of the mines slated for reopening had been abandoned for many years. Furthermore, the plans stressed "local" resources, both for construction and for local manufacture, in order to broaden the pool of total available resources and to relieve the pressure of local demand on the centrally allocated materials.

The plans to enlarge the industrial base and to change the preplan pattern of location of both individual plants and industrial concentrations resulted in the preparation of detailed schemes of development for various backward regions and the decision to construct there a substantial number of the large new projects.[16] A systematic effort to this end was envisaged in the Czechoslovak plan for Slovakia, in Poland for localities "outside the highly industrialized areas of Upper and Lower Silesia, and of Łódź," and, in the Yugoslav plan, for certain of its most backward federated republics. The importance of the Czechoslovak effort can be measured by the fact that about 30 per cent of the total planned investment was earmarked for Slovakia. The Polish plan called for the development of industrial centers at Krakow, Częstochowa, and Warsaw, and indicated that "80 per cent of the new plants would be built outside the existing industrialized areas."[17] The other countries also stressed the development of certain specific regions or towns non-industrialized until then. In Hungary particular emphasis was placed on backward agricultural regions like the right bank of the Tisza and the Transdanubian region. In Romania a major construction project, the Danube-Black Sea Canal, and several plants were scheduled to be developed in Dobrogea and other backward areas.

Thus the plans aimed at simultaneously changing the *importance, structure,* and *location* of the industrial sectors. The first development plans took into account the fact that, in order to achieve these changes, there would have to be substantial increases in the number of workers in manufacture proper, the gainfully employed in industry in the broadest sense of the term (including building, transport, and industry of local interest), and the total labor force employed in the socialized sector. As can be seen from Table 75, the scheduled increases in industry proper involved a total that can be estimated at around 1.5 million; the total of gainfully employed in manufacture can be estimated at an additional 1.5 million. Finally, the total to be

[16] Evidently the new locational pattern of industry not only met the economical objective of exploiting locally thus far unused resources; it also served certain political and social objectives, whose significance and implications are actually outside the scope of this study.

[17] Only Krakow and Częstochowa can be considered as *new* locations for industry; they were to receive the new steel industries, which accounts for the large percentage of new plants to be built outside the "existing industrialized areas."

absorbed in the socialized economy (i.e., all the state sectors including civil service) might be estimated at about 5 million persons, less than 6 per cent of the total population, which in turn was expected to rise by some 6.2 per cent during the same period. Thus the first development plans did not contemplate solution of the problem of surplus agricultural population for the region as a whole. However, the impact on this surplus population was to vary greatly from one country to the next.

TABLE 75. SCHEDULED INCREASES IN THE LABOR FORCE DURING THE FIRST DEVELOPMENT PLANS

Country	Increase of Workers in Manufacture Proper	Increase of Gainfully Employed in Industry (including other than manufacture proper) [a]	Total Increase of Gainfully Employed in the Socialized Economy
Czechoslovakia	239,000	359,000	482,000 [b]
Poland	300,000	1,000,000	2,100,000
Hungary	340,000	480,000	[c]
Romania	[c]	570,000	825,000
Bulgaria	90,000	138,000	[c]
Yugoslavia	175,000	[c]	[c]

[a] Including building, transport, handicrafts, and industry of local interest.
[b] The revised 1951 figure increased the total to 780,000.
[c] Not available.

SCHEDULED DEVELOPMENTS IN AGRICULTURE

As we have already noted above, the planned increases in total agricultural output appear quite modest when compared to the proposed accelerated growth of industry. However, two factors have to be taken into consideration in gaging the scheduled developments in agriculture: the point of departure and the envisaged changes in the nature of the output.

The point of departure in agriculture was extremely low, and one of the basic factors preventing the restoration of output was the losses incurred in all types of livestock in all the countries except Czechoslovakia and Bulgaria. The plans listed growth of production simultaneously in three directions which competed in various ways among themselves: grain, industrial crops, and livestock. In Czechoslovakia and Hungary the emphasis was on the output of livestock; in Bulgaria and Yugoslavia it was on crops. The planned increases in grains indicate that the region as a whole was to reach only the prewar level during the development plans (see Table 76). The return to the prewar level and the later surpassing of it were to be done by reducing the area sown and appreciably *increasing* the yields by mechanization and extensive use of fertilizers. The mechanization of agriculture was to absorb up to one-half the total investment earmarked for agriculture.

TABLE 76. PLANNED PRODUCTION OF GRAINS [a]

	Czechoslovakia	Poland	Hungary	Romania	Bulgaria	Yugoslavia	Total
Prewar [b]	5.5	13.3	6.1	8.0	3.5	8.2	44.6
R	5.0	11.5	5.6	[c]	3.3	[d]	[c]
As % of prewar	91	86	84	[c]	94	[d]	[c]
D	5.5	14.5	6.6	8.9	4.5	9.4	49.4
As % of prewar	100	109	108	111	129	115	110

[a] Quantities are in millions of tons.
[b] Prewar data refer to present territory.
[c] Not available.
[d] Nil.

Substantial reclamation projects and the land released from grain production were to make possible a tremendous expansion of industrial crops. Before the war such crops had been intended for the foreign market (poppies in Yugoslavia, roses in Bulgaria, soybeans in Romania, much of the tobacco crop in all the countries). In addition to the continuation and expansion of these traditional crops, the plans prescribed the growth and rapid increase in the crops of textile fibers. For flax and hemp the Hungarian plan slated an increase of output of 30 to 40 per cent over 1949, the Romanian plan an increase by 1955 to 3 times the prewar output of flax and 10 times that of hemp, and the Yugoslav plan to 5 and 10 times prewar, respectively. All these countries projected considerable expansion in cotton acreage and output. The Romanian plan proposed an increase of cotton acreage from 3,000 hectares before the war to 300,000 hectares in 1955, with the output in that year to reach 700 per cent over that of 1950. The Bulgarian output was to increase to 25,000 tons of cotton, against 7,000 in the prewar period. In Yugoslavia an increase in cotton acreage of over 400 per cent was to be accompanied by an increase in output of 1,000 per cent above that of prewar. Substantial increases were also planned for oleaginous plants such as sunflowers and soybeans.

As already mentioned, plans called for a substantial recovery in livestock and an expansion of the "fodder base." Czechoslovakia planned an increase in the fodder crops area of some 200,000 hectares, 6 per cent over the fodder area of 1948, together with a decrease of some 3 per cent in the area under bread-grains. In Hungary the fodder area was to be extended by approximately 100,000 hectares, and the area under wheat and rye was to be reduced. In Romania the increase in the fodder base was to be 380,000 hectares, a 44 per cent increase over 1950, and a reduction was scheduled in the acreage for corn. In Bulgaria some 55,000 hectares of wheat and corn land were to be taken for green fodder crops. In Yugoslavia and Poland increases were scheduled in both wheat and fodder acreage, to be effected in Yugoslavia by extension of the total arable area and in Poland by cultivation of fallow land. As far as livestock is concerned, Czechoslovakia and Bulgaria, which had less severe losses than the other countries, planned to attain their prewar level during the reconstruction period. Bulgaria even foresaw substantial increases over prewar levels. The other countries planned to reach the prewar level and to surpass it eventually during the reconstruction period in somewhat the following order: Romania, Hungary, Poland, Czechoslovakia (see Table 77).

TABLE 77. PLANNED LIVESTOCK DEVELOPMENT

(1938 = 100)

	R				*D*			
Country	Cattle	Horses	Pigs	Sheep	Cattle	Horses	Pigs	Sheep
Czechoslovakia	95	[a]	100	[a]	88	[a]	105	256
Poland	49	63	119	32	77	77	146	126
Hungary	76	67	152	54	104	80	175	88
Romania [b]	97	50	81	85	138	58	195	128
Bulgaria	144	[a]	273	107	133	102	319	101
Yugoslavia					100	100	100	100

[a] Not available.
[b] Plan of reconstruction refers to the 1949 plan.

Comparison of the absolute figures for livestock population to be attained by the end of the development plans with prewar figures reveals an emphasis on increasing the number of pigs and sheep. The planned increase in cattle was limited by the fact that a large number would be beef cattle, whose feed requirements affect both grasses and concentrates. The very heavy losses of horses incurred during the war in the whole region, especially in Poland and in Yugoslavia, were to be *only partially replaced* since the intended mechanization would lessen the need for draft animals (see Table 78).

TABLE 78. PLANNED LIVESTOCK POPULATION AT END OF FIRST DEVELOPMENT PLANS [a]

Livestock	Prewar	*D*	% of Prewar
Horses	9.4	7.4	71 [b]
Cattle	26.5	26.4	99
Pigs	21.5	33.4	155
Sheep	35.6	40.4	113

[a] In millions of head.
[b] Estimate.

It should be noted that the rates of recovery proposed in all the countries were higher than the rates of recovery after World War I. After World War I "it took grain production in these countries seven years to recover, while livestock did not recover until 1928, and in some countries not until 1936." [18] Thus, though the planned output in agriculture was moderate as compared to the growth envisioned in industry, greater problems were created in agriculture by the task of *changing* substantially the *structure of output* in this vast sector of the economy, dominated by a vast number of small owners utilizing a large part of the land for crops for their own subsistence.

SOURCES OF FINANCING AND STRUCTURE OF INVESTMENT

The development of an economy depends, among other things, on the rate and character of investments; these in turn depend on the rate and character of development of the economy.

To sustain the growth proposed by these plans, each country relied essentially on its own capital. The former Allied countries benefited during the reconstruction period from substantial UNRRA grants; the former enemy countries had to deliver reparations, which substantially reduced their capital.[19] Except in Poland and Hungary,

[18] Cf. *Agricultural Recovery in Continental Europe during the 1914–1918 War and the Reconstruction Period,* League of Nations, Economic and Financial Series, 11/A/7, Geneva, 1943.

[19] According to the Hungarian Three-Year Plan, during the reconstruction period, the Hungarian national income was to be burdened with reparations to the amount of 6.6 to 6.8 per cent from 1947–48 to 1949–50, as compared to 10 per cent

which in the reconstruction plans foresaw "eventual foreign investment" in their countries,[20] the plans indicated that the growth process was to be financed exclusively from national resources. The ratio of gross investment to anticipated national income during the reconstruction era was scheduled at about 9 to 10 per cent in Bulgaria and Hungary and 20 to 21 per cent in Czechoslovakia and Poland. In all the countries, during the first development plans, the share of investment in the anticipated national income was planned to amount to between 20 and 27 per cent. These rates compare to an average rate of investment of 4 to 6 per cent of the national income in the prewar period.[21]

The basic sources of funds envisioned for these planned investments were: (1) the state budget–revenues from the turnover tax and the profits from state undertakings (including the National Bank and the Investment Bank); [22] (2) sinking funds (used specifically as coverage for renewals and capital reparations); [23] (3) creation of credit through increases in bank deposits, (4) loans from the public, and (5) funds of the various undertakings themselves (obtained by liquidation of inventories, sale of rejects, etc.).[24]

in 1946–47. No comparable data are available for Romania; however, it can be estimated that the rate was as high as or higher than 10 per cent. In relation to the budgets, see above, Chapter 6, pp. 179–181 ff.

20 The Polish investment policy during the reconstruction period was established by assuming that foreign capital would cover between 15 and 20 per cent of the total value of the foreseen investment. Cf. *Polish National Economic Plan . . . , op. cit.* The Hungarian reconstruction plan indicated:

> The investments provided for in the Three-Year Plan were decided upon the assumption that the economic, social, and cultural rehabilitation of the country will have to be ensured even if we are left to our own resources alone. Nevertheless, there are also supplementary plans ready for the event of foreign loans, on non-political terms being forthcoming which—no doubt—would speed up the process of recovery. [See the *Hungarian Three-Year Plan, op. cit.*, p. 50.]

21 The figures of the reconstruction plans relate gross investment to national income as computed by the "Western methods" (i.e., including all goods and services produced). The development plans relate gross investment to national income in the Marxian sense (i.e., limited to material goods and productive services only). In both cases, the percentages are somewhat inflated since they relate gross to net. The prewar ratios, on the other hand, relate net investment to net income.

22 For the changed role of the budget in the new decentralized Yugoslav system, see above, Chapter 4, pp. 124–125, note 110.

23 Cf. *The Czechoslovak Economic Five-Year Plan, op. cit.*, p. 179.

24 The planners can establish the turnover tax and the profit markup so that, if the market is cleared at the set prices, the government receives in return as budget receipts its outlay on investment, defense, and services.

Some of the plans stressed that a large part of investment was to be forthcoming

In order to sustain the sector growth scheduled by the plans, both the reconstruction and the development plans concentrated from 40 to 50 per cent of total investment in industry (mining, manufacturing, and building) (see Table 79). For all the countries the relative

TABLE 79. SECTOR INVESTMENT IN THE PLANS, 1947–55

(percentages)

Country	Plans	Industry and Building	Transport and Communications	Agriculture	Housing	Public Services	Other
Czechoslovakia	*R*	38.4	20.7	7.2	20.5	13.2	[a]
	D	40.6	15.7 [b]	8.0	11.7	24.0	[a]
	r [c]	40.6	15.7 [b]	8.0	11.7	24.0	[a]
Poland	*R*	39.0	24.0	13.0	9.0	11.0	4.0
	D	42.9	14.9	11.9	8.3	21.4	0.6
Hungary	*R*	32.0	27.0	9.0	12.0	20.0	[a]
	D	41.8	14.8	15.7	10.0	12.9	5.0
	r [c]	51.7	11.8	12.9	7.6	10.1	5.9
Romania	*R*	47.0	21.0	9.0	5.0 [d]	16.0	2.0
	D	53.4	16.2	10.0	3.2 [d]	14.4	2.8
Bulgaria	*R*	45.0	15.0	6.0	11.0	17.0	6.0
	D	43.1	18.8 [b]	13.0	4.5	19.5	2.6
Yugoslavia	*R* and *D*	43.0	26.0	8.0		23	

[a] Nil.
[b] Roads, bridges, and other public works included in public services.
[c] Revised plans in 1950.
[d] Only investment in workers' housing, other housing, and public services.

share of industry increased from the reconstruction to the first development plans, markedly so for Czechoslovakia and Hungary in the revised plans. In the total allocated to industry, the relative share of heavy industry (producers' goods industries) represented from 80 to 90 per cent of the total, compared to 10–20 per cent for the light industries (consumers' goods industries).

from "cost reduction due to increases in productivity." See: Poland's *Six-Year Plan . . . , op. cit.,* and Christo Popov, "Natsionalniiat Dokhod i Kapitalovlozheniia" (National Income and Investment), in *PK,* No. 4, 1949, p. 65. This seems to imply that the planners were expecting cost to fall more than the selling price and thus increase the volume of profits.

The second item of importance in total investment was transportation and communication (i.e., rail, road, water, and air transports, and post, telegraph, and telephone). Their relative share of some 15 to 25 per cent of the total investment tended to decrease in the first development period, generally to below 15 per cent.

Agriculture (specifically, state and collective farms and land reclamation projects) was to receive only a very small share of investment, generally around 8 to 12 per cent of the total.

Three investment items, housing, public services, and "other," need some qualification. The share of housing was actually to be greater than it appears in the table, since some investments of this type were also included in the public services. The public services included social and cultural investments, other state administration, and trade (the latter absorbing up to 2 per cent of the total investment).

Thus, on the one hand, the plan prescribed the utilization of a heavy share of the national income for "accumulation," i.e., for investment. On the other hand, the model of the plan required a heavy concentration of investment in the *main links* of the plans, i.e., in the *metal-working industries* and in *heavy industries in general.*

"Strategic" Ratios Underlying the Plans

In summary, the average scheduled yearly rates of increase of the gross value of industrial output during the first development plans were set at 14 to 17 per cent in all the countries except Hungary, where the revised rate was raised to over 25 per cent (see Table 80). These rates may be compared with the average claimed increase of the gross industrial output of Soviet Russia, during its first two five-year plans, of over 20 per cent per year (computed in 1926–27 rubles). The average rates of increase for producers' goods industries were to be slightly higher but to remain in the neighborhood of the rates of increase of industry as a whole, except for Bulgaria. The average rates of increase of the quantities of basic materials produced, more significant than the indices of gross output, vary widely from country to country and from product to product. As can be expected, the increases in the gross output were somewhat but not much greater than those in the output of materials.[25]

[25] As Professor A. Gerschenkron remarks in connection with data concerning Soviet Russia, the rates of growth of the *value* of industrial output tend to exceed that of quantities of basic industrial materials because of *the increase of*

TABLE 80. SCHEDULED YEARLY RATES OF INCREASE OF INDUSTRIAL OUTPUT AND OF BASIC INDUSTRIAL MATERIALS DURING THE FIRST DEVELOPMENT PLANS

	Average Yearly Rates of Increase Compounded Annually						
	Industrial Output			Basic Industrial Materials			
Country	All Industry	Producers' Goods Industry	Consumers' Goods Industry	Coal	Pig Iron	Steel	Electricity
Czechoslovakia	14.6	18.1	11.2	5.2	13.4	10.5	7.7
Poland	14.6	16.8	13.3	3.8	17.9	12.6	15.4
Hungary	25.4	30.5	19.6	8.8	24.5	20.9	13.8
Romania	17.5	[a]	[a]	21.5	19.0	17.5	17.4
Bulgaria	17.0	26.6	22.2	11.3	[b]	[b]	29.2

[a] Not available.
[b] Nil.

The strategic figures that knit together all the data in the plans and that express the global targets of the economy were: (*a*) the projected increases in the national income [26] during the planned period, (*b*) the capital-output ratios (i.e., the increment in capital required to bring about the given increase of the national income), (*c*) the division of the manufacturing output between producers' and consumers' goods output, (*d*) the division of total output between industrial and agricultural output, and the changes in the structure of agricultural output itself.

As can be seen from Table 81, both the reconstruction and the first development plans projected very high average yearly rates of increase in the national income. The plans of reconstruction obviously relied on a rapid recovery from the very low levels of 1946 and on the full utilization of the capacity of plant and machinery available. The rates of increase in the national income set for the first period of development, while smaller than the ones set for the reconstruction years, were still highly optimistic as to the possibilities of expansion of the economy.

value added per unit of basic materials employed. Thus the closeness of the rates of increase of, say, steel to the higher rates of increase in the value of the industry as a whole appears quite normal. For a discussion of this point in connection with the rates of increase for Soviet Russia, see Norman M. Kaplan, "Capital Formation and Allocation," in A. Bergson, edit., *Soviet Economic Growth, op. cit.*, pp. 72 ff.

[26] Throughout this discussion national income is taken in the restrictive Marxian sense used in East Europe (i.e., limited to material goods).

If we relate the total investment during the plan period to the increase to be brought about in the national income in the last year of the plan, we get a table closely related to Table 81. Table 82 clearly

TABLE 81. PLANNED AVERAGE YEARLY RATES OF INCREASE IN NATIONAL INCOME [a]

Country	*R*	*D*	*Dr.*[b]
Czechoslovakia	23.9	8.2	13.0
Poland	32.9	13.4	
Hungary	20.1	10.3	18.0
Romania	25.0 [c]	19.2 [d]	
Bulgaria	[e]	13.0	
Yugoslavia	[f]	14.1	

[a] Net material product, excluding "nonproductive" services.
[b] Revised plans. [c] Plan for 1950. [d] Estimated. [e] Not available. [f] Nil.

shows that overoptimistic assumptions prevailed as far as the capital-output ratios were concerned. The reconstruction plans implied very low ratios, expecting the unusual result that a given amount of investment would bring about equal or larger increases in the national income. During the first development plans the capital-output ratios were expected to continue very low for Bulgaria and Poland, though higher than in the previous period. Finally, they were expected to be far higher for Czechoslovakia and Hungary, where a given increment in the national income was considered to require 3 times as large an investment.

The ratios suggest that expectations during the first plans of development were that the return on capital invested would, on the average, be *higher in the less industrialized countries of the region* (and with a lower per capita income) than in the others.[27]

[27] The capital-output ratios are given here as an indication of the *expectations of the respective governments as implied by the plans,* rather than as a particularly significant economic measurement. It is very risky to make generalizations on the basis of this type of series. (The underlying assumption seems to be that the ratio of added capital to added production would be the same in all countries with a given level of income, an assumption which is rather arbitrary, since it implies that differences in national resources per capita do not cause significant differences in the capital per worker needed to yield a given increment of output.) Moreover, in the short run, any variation in aggregate income owing, for example, to the changes in the contribution of agriculture would be liable to cause sharp variations in the capital-output ratio and thus affect very much comparisons of it from one year to the next or from one country to the next.

With these qualifications it is interesting to note that, according to the planned ratios (i.e., Table 82), a curve relating capital on the vertical axis to income per

TABLE 82. PLANNED CAPITAL-OUTPUT RATIOS

(billions of national currencies [a])

	Czechoslovakia	Poland	Hungary	Romania	Bulgaria	Yugoslavia
			Reconstruction Plans			
Increase in Investment [b] (ΔC)	69.8	10.0	6.6	[c]	6.8	
Increase in Output [d] (ΔO)	44.5	11.5	11.0	[c]	27.8 [e]	
Ratios $\frac{\Delta C}{\Delta O}$	1.5	0.9	0.6	[c]	0.2 [e]	
			First Long-term Plans			
Increase in Investment [b] (ΔC)	336.2	44.1	50.9	1330.0	425.0	278.3
Increase in Output [d] (ΔO)	110.0	21.3	15.6	595.0	278.7	122.0
Ratios $\frac{\Delta C}{\Delta O}$	3.3	2.0	3.2	2.2	1.5	2.2

[a] C: Pre-1953 Korunas, 1946 and 1948 prices; P: prewar zlotys, 1937 prices; H: 1947 forints at plan prices; R: 1950 prices; B: prewar leva for reconstruction plan, 1948 leva for long-term plan; Y: 1947 dinars.

[b] Total investment during the plan period.

[c] Not available.

[d] Increase in last plan year over last preplan, of the net material product excluding "nonproductive" services.

[e] Estimate.

All the plans forecast a substantial change in the ratio of producers' goods to consumers' goods within the *total gross value of manufacturing* output. Thus Czechoslovakia foresaw that by the end of the

capita on the horizontal axis would tend to have a positive slope and be concave upward. The increment of capital needed for a given increment in productive capacity *would be lowest in the countries with the lowest per capita output (or income) and would increase up to a point as the level of per capita income rises.* From these relations it might be assumed that the marginal productivity of capital would be higher in the less developed countries of the area. This relation is the opposite of the one indicated by Colin Clark, according to whom the increment of capital needed for a given increment in productive capacity is higher, the lower a country's per capita income. (Cf. *Conditions of Economic Progress,* Macmillan & Co., London, 1951.) Any attempts at generalization can thus lead to entirely conflicting results. It should be noted that in Eastern Europe each of the countries had the same general pattern of investment, e.g., each allocated the same relative share for transportation, etc.

development plans this ratio would be 62:38 (as compared to 44:56 before the war); Poland, 63.5:36.5 (as compared to 47:53 in the prewar territory); Yugoslavia, 57:43 (as compared to the reverse ratio, 43:57); Bulgaria, 45:55 (as compared to 24:76).

Some of the plans allow the computation of scheduled changes in the ratio of industrial output to agricultural output. Thus Czechoslovakia planned that by the end of the development plan this ratio would be 80.8:19.2 (as compared to 72.4:27.6 before the war); Poland, 75.5:24.5 (as compared to 52:48 before the war in the prewar territory); Yugoslavia, 64:36 (as compared to 45:55); and Bulgaria, 47:53 (as compared to 27:73). These changes were to be accompanied by substantial shifts in the share of livestock relative to grain in the total value of agricultural output.

These ratios are "controlling" aggregate figures indicating how all the scheduled sector developments should translate themselves in the structural changes of the gross national product. They will be used subsequently as points of reference in the discussion of the actual performance achieved. Let us note here that thus, from the outset, the sector targets and the combined, structural results are uniquely related; the one could not be altered without altering the other.[28]

The Soviet Model and the Relationship It Conditions

The plans aimed at the industrialization of each economy, except, of course, for Czechoslovakia, where industrialization had already been attained, and where the object of the plan was to change sharply its industrial structure by shifting the emphasis from light to heavy industries. As we have seen, all the plans followed the same model. All placed the emphasis on the metal-working industries, then on the broad group of heavy industries, then on industry as a whole as compared to agriculture. All aimed at increasing the output of electricity, coal, iron, and steel rapidly. All reveal, by their emphasis on engineering industries and output of construction materials, a systematic policy of increasing capital formation and enlarging productive capacity. Since each of these countries aimed at "all-round" development, each stressed the necessity of producing within the economy every type of goods, even those whose cost had previously appeared prohibitive. All followed the same pattern of distribution of investment. Centered on each na-

[28] Compare this statement to the Introduction and to the contention that two bookkeeping accounts might exist in these economies.

tional unit, each plan clearly was drawn up independently and, in this specific phase of development, implied only marginal, if any, coordination with the others. There were only two officially stated examples of collaboration between two pairs of countries. One concerned Czechoslovakia and Poland, the other Yugoslavia and Bulgaria. Both were drawn up in 1947 and had only limited implementation. The more detailed of the two, the Czechoslovak-Polish agreement of July 4, 1947, was to operate in four fields: (1) trade, (2) transportation, (3) collaboration among various economic sectors, and (4) planning. Concerning points 3 and 4, which interest us at present, it was agreed that certain industries of the two countries would envisage the coordination "little by little [of] their programs of production in order to apportion the fabrication of determined products." [29] The long-term objectives, extending over various plan periods, were to be achieved within the framework of the plans by agreements secured "step by step" when required. Thus no close coordination of output, which would affect the pattern of sector growth in each economy, was envisaged.

The plans proposed all-round developments for each economy, whatever its past evolution and its resources might be. The tendency to follow closely the Soviet model cannot be considered simple mimicry. With the exception of Czechoslovakia, all the countries were underdeveloped, and the Russian model may well have appeared to them as being the *only* way of fostering development. On the other hand, the attempt to solve all the problems of industrialization in each nation separately, whatever its resources, fostering autarkic tendencies in every nation, developing even the most uneconomical type of national resource [30] involved abandoning international specialization *and lowering the efficiency of investment.* Actually, the countries completely lacking basic resources on which to erect the industrial structure [31] placed themselves in an extremely precarious position from the outset, since their planned development

[29] It is interesting to note that this collaboration was envisaged "in order to facilitate the industrial progress of both sides and *avoid unnecessary investments.*" [Cf. *Sprawy Międzynarodowe* (International Affairs), I, 1 (October–December 1948).] This same objective could have been set with no less reason for the region as a whole.

[30] This involves not only the exploitation of previously cost-prohibitive natural resources but also the utilization of low-grade products, and substitutes (e.g., charcoal instead of imported coke for the production of steel, etc.).

[31] See below, Chapter 9.

would lessen their ability to export and hence to make good their deficiencies through imports.

As related to this scheme of development, Soviet Russia's position was shaped by its status as receiver of reparations from some of these countries and also by its large foreign trade possibilities, as supplier of raw materials and as potential importer of certain semifinished and manufactured goods. The plans did not assume any "Soviet aid" other than the eventual import from Russia of given raw materials (e.g., iron ore, cotton, etc.), eventual credits of grains, and technical aid (rather than a direct supply of equipment), coupled with possibilities of "large" exports to the Russian market.

As for the limitations and possibilities of each of these countries, an example seems appropriate. Taking the per capita steel consumption as an indicator of the "level of industrialization" of a country, United Nations statisticians suggested that an annual consumption of 200 kilograms of steel per capita would correspond to a "level of industrialization" approximately comparable to that of France in 1950; of 300 kilograms, to a level comparable to that of Sweden and the United Kingdom; of 545 kilograms per capita to the level of the United States, and so on, in the year considered.[32]

On the assumption that the plans would be carried out and that the domestic steel consumption would be equal to the expected output except for exports of steel from Poland, we could say that, at the end of the first development period, Romania was scheduled to reach a "level of industrialization" comparable to that of prewar Hungary; the latter a level comparable to that of prewar Czechoslovakia; and Czechoslovakia a level close to that of prewar Sweden. Thus the industrialization scheme, as conceived in the first plans of development, was evidently not intended to result in a leveling-off of the *inequalities existing in the area:* it was only to shift the region as a whole to a higher level of industrialization, *keeping the countries basically in their relative positions in respect to each other.*

[32] *World Iron Ore Resources and Their Utilization,* UN, Dept. of Economic Affairs, New York, 1950, p. 43.

CHAPTER

9

SECTOR GROWTH, PACE OF INDUSTRIALIZATION, AND PROSPECTIVE DEVELOPMENT

Note and Qualification

As indicated in the Introduction to Section III, this chapter will focus on performance as compared to planning, and will attempt an appraisal of the second development plans which are to extend up to 1960.

In establishing the balance sheet of the first phase of development, both before 1953 and during the "new course" up to 1955, we do not propose to examine every branch of industry or agriculture. We intend to concentrate on some key branches which appear to us as indicative of both the present strength and the future possibilities of those countries, e.g., fuel and power, iron and steel, chemicals, and construction, and shall dwell only briefly on the question of the light industries. We consider again in detail the developments in agriculture which are determinant factors in industrialization and urbanization. This choice is perforce imperfect and open to criticism since it neglects such decisive aspects as transportation. However, no claim is made that this examination is exhaustive. Not only might other aspects be examined, but further detailed work can and should be done even under the headings chosen. Our main object is to present an integrated, even if simplified, scheme, upon which it should be possible to construct some meaningful appraisal of future possibilities.

To facilitate a comparison of today's trends, we present a series of graphs (Charts 11–15) on basic outputs from 1913 (or from 1920) to

1955.[1] For the purpose of comparison among countries, each graph presents on the left the main producer or producers and on the right all the others.

In contrasting Yugoslav achievements with the goals set it must be kept in mind that the break with the East substantially modified the course of the Yugoslav plan and required major readjustments from 1948–49 on. There is, therefore, a wide discrepancy between Yugoslav goals and achievements.

ENERGY SOURCES

The autarkic industrialization of a country is dependent on its energy resources, its supply of iron and steel, and the potential plant capacity available for their production.

Energy sources may be classed as *primary* (coal, oil, natural gas, and hydroelectricity, and, to an important extent, fuel wood) and *secondary* (coke, synthetic fuels, thermoelectricity). Let us consider first the primary sources.

The countries of the region are very unequally endowed with coal, most of the coal fields being concentrated in Poland and Czechoslovakia. The hard coal of the region is in Polish Upper Silesia and the nearby Szechoslovak Ostrava-Karvinná deposit, which together comprise the Silesia-Ostrava Basin, one of the four major hard coal deposits of Europe. Less important coal fields are in Polish Lower Silesia, Bohemia, Hungary, Romania, and Yugoslavia. Poland and Czechoslovakia again are the two most important countries for brown coal and lignite, but important reserves are also to be found in Yugoslavia, Romania, Hungary, and Bulgaria.[2] (See Chart 10, p. 308.)

The development of the output of hard coal and lignite for the region as a whole from 1913 to 1955 can be observed in Chart 11. An

[1] The underlying data for the charts has been gathered from the statistical yearbooks of the League of Nations, for the interwar period, and from the Yearbooks of the United Nations, for the postwar years, complemented by the statistical yearbooks of the countries considered whenever necessary. For the data in physical terms for the key years 1938, 1948, 1953, 1955, see the Appendix to this chapter, pp. 366–380.

[2] The best brown coal of the region, i.e., the highest in caloric value, is that of Czechoslovakia and Hungary; for these countries 1.6 tons of brown coal is considered equivalent to 1 ton of hard coal, whereas for the other countries of the area this ratio is usually given as 3 to 1.

For a detailed discussion of the mineral resources of the area see: Victor H. Winston, "Mineral Resources," in *Resources and Planning in Eastern Europe,* N. Pounds and N. Spulber, eds., Slavic and East European Series, Vol. 4, Bloomington, Indiana University Publications, 1957, pp. 36–86.

enormous effort to increase production from the low of 1944–45 was made in every country of the area. However, in considering the past

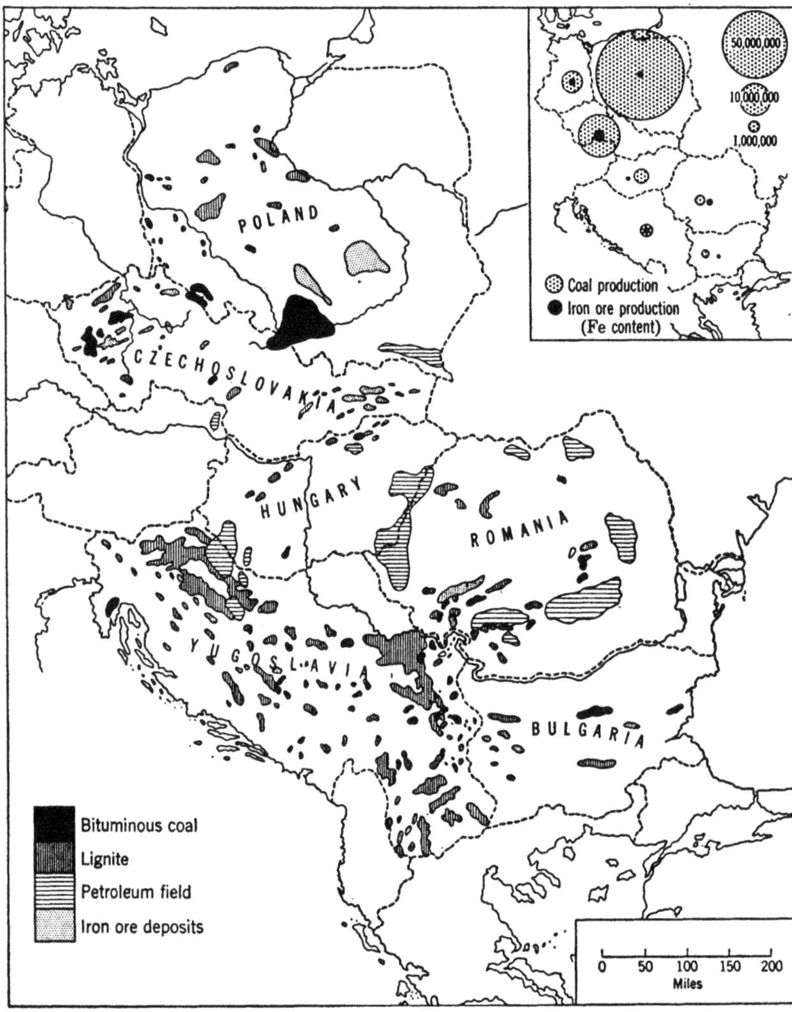

CHART 10. COAL, IRON, AND OIL RESOURCES OF EASTERN EUROPE

trends, it can be seen that the highest levels of output up to 1950 were attained in the peak years 1913 and 1943. It is only in the second part of the first plan of development that most of the small producers substantially raised those levels. Table 83 shows that it

TABLE 83. SECULAR TRENDS IN THE OUTPUT OF HARD COAL AND LIGNITE, 1913, 1943, 1953

Country	1913, in thousands of tons	1943, in thousands of tons	1953, in thousands of tons	1943 as % of 1913	1953 as % of 1943
Hard Coal					
Czechoslovakia	14,271	24,617	20,300	172.5	82.5
Poland	58,000	92,000	88,725	158.6	96.3
Hungary	850	1,260	1,993	148.2	158.2
Romania	453	306	400	67.5	130.7
Bulgaria	11	204	575	1,854.5	281.9
Yugoslavia	26	420 [a]	925	1,615.4	220.2
Lignite					
Czechoslovakia	23,137	27,583	32,763	119.2	118.7
Poland	[b]	7,611 [c]	5,900	[b]	77.5
Hungary	5,514	10,789	19,016	195.7	176.3
Romania	2,566	2,604	4,100	101.5	157.5
Bulgaria	342	3,811	8,400	1,114.3	220.4
Yugoslavia	2,825	6,916 [a]	10,321	244.8	149.2

[a] 1940.
[b] Not available.
[c] 1937.

Sources: 1913, 1943, 1953: For all countries excluding Poland and Yugoslavia: *Annuaire Statistique International* (International Statistical Yearbook), 1927, League of Nations, Geneva, 1927, p. 94; *UNSY, 1953*, UN, New York, 1954, pp. 105, 108; *ESE in 1955, op. cit.*, pp. B37–B41.

P: *The European Coal Problem*, UN, New York, 1952, p. 10, and *Monthly Bulletin of Statistics*, UN, New York, May 1956, p. XIV.

Y: *Annuaire Statistique International, ibid.*, and *Statistički Godišnjak FNRJ 1954, op. cit.*, p. 156.

is precisely the key producers of hard coal of the region that had not reached the 1943 peak level by the end of 1953. For hard coal, the Czechoslovak output in 1953 represented only 82 per cent of the 1943 output, the Polish output 96 per cent. For lignite, Czechoslovakia, like all the lesser producers of the region, surpassed the previous peak, but Poland was producing only 77 per cent of the estimated 1943 level. For both lignite and coal the Czechoslovak output fell substantially below the goal set after the 1951 plan revisions: thus the combined output of the two types of coal in 1953 reached 53.0 as against 63.6 million tons projected in 1951. Achieving these results required severe straining of both human beings and equipment. Even by 1955, the combined coal output had reached just 62 million tons, that is 1.6 million tons short of the goal scheduled for 1953.[3] In view of the terrific strain on labor and machines, it is open to question whether Poland, which reached 100.5 million tons in 1955 and is the

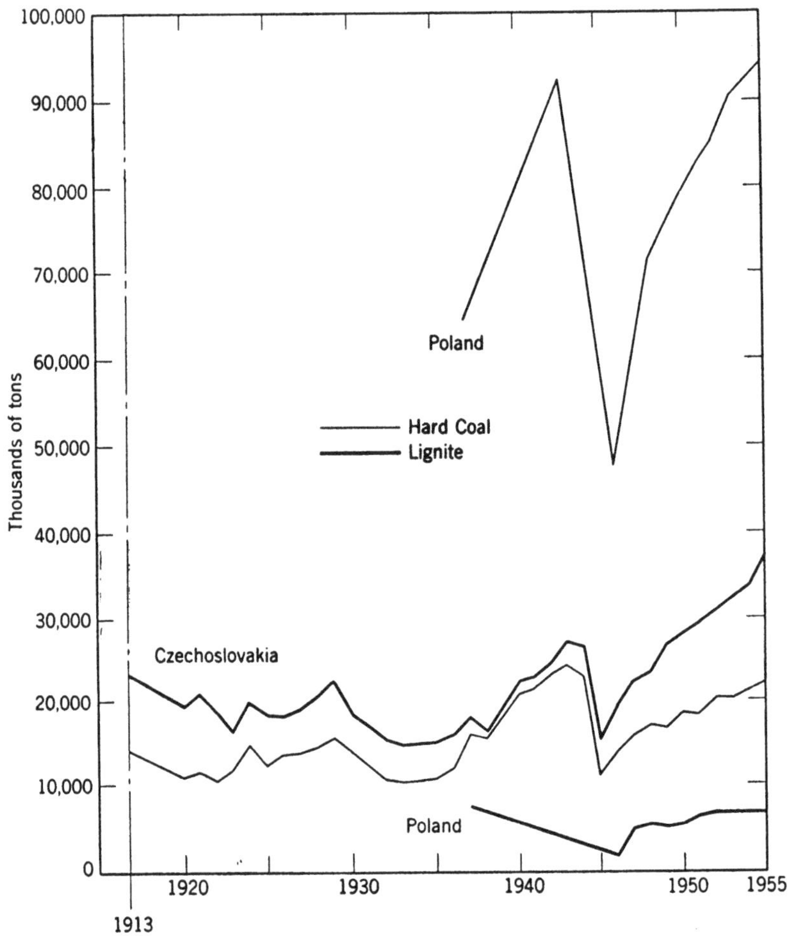

CHART 11. COAL PRODUCTION, 1913–55

main producer and exporter of coal of the area, will be able to reach by 1960 the goal of 110 million tons of coal it set for itself.

The increases achieved by the smaller countries of the area are of very modest scale, especially in hard coal, when compared both to

[3] See Table 96, Appendix to this chapter, pp. 367–68.

their needs and to the output in the highest producing countries, Czechoslovakia and Poland. Also, especially in lignite production,

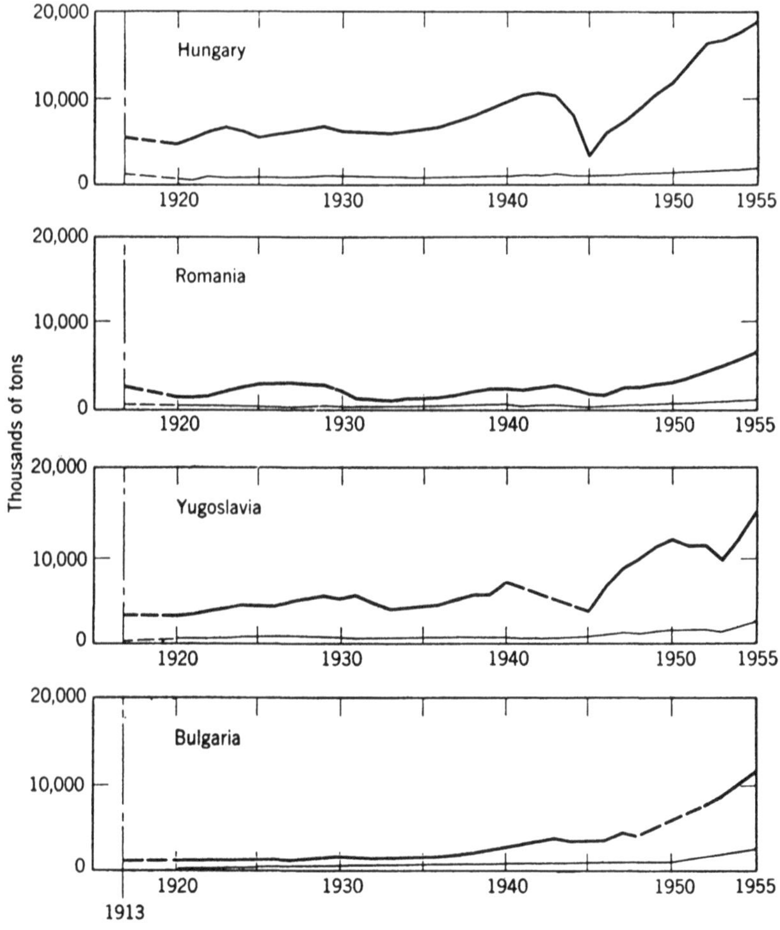

CHART 11 (*Continued*).

the increases have fallen short of the goal and the quality of the fuel has deteriorated, despite the disregard for cost and effort.

The area has far fewer oil and natural gas than coal resources. The main producer is Romania, whose oil output increased steadily during the interwar period up to 1936, when it began to decline. By 1947 production had fallen to 3.8 million tons, a level comparable to that

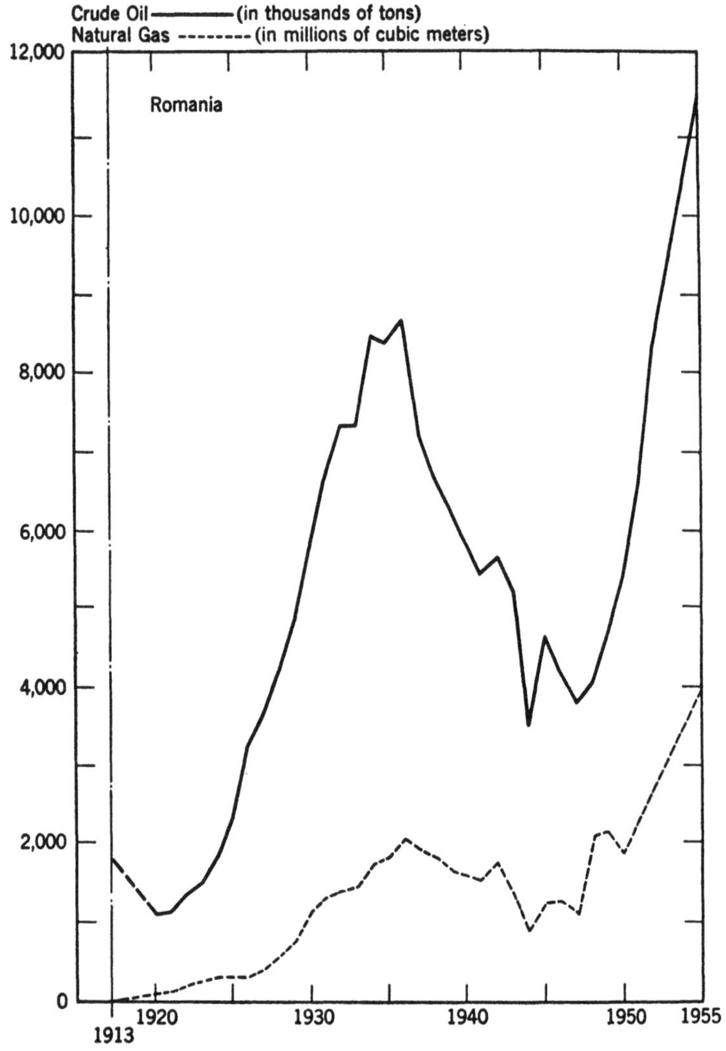

CHART 12. CRUDE OIL PRODUCTION, 1913–55

of 1927 (see Chart 12). Since 1947, according to the official data, output has increased continuously until it finally surpassed the 1936 high mark in 1953 (8.7 million and 9.3 million, respectively). Production has increased further, according to the official data, to more than 10.5 million tons in 1955. The target for 1960 is 13.5 million.[4]

[4] See Table 96, Appendix to this chapter, pp. 367–68.

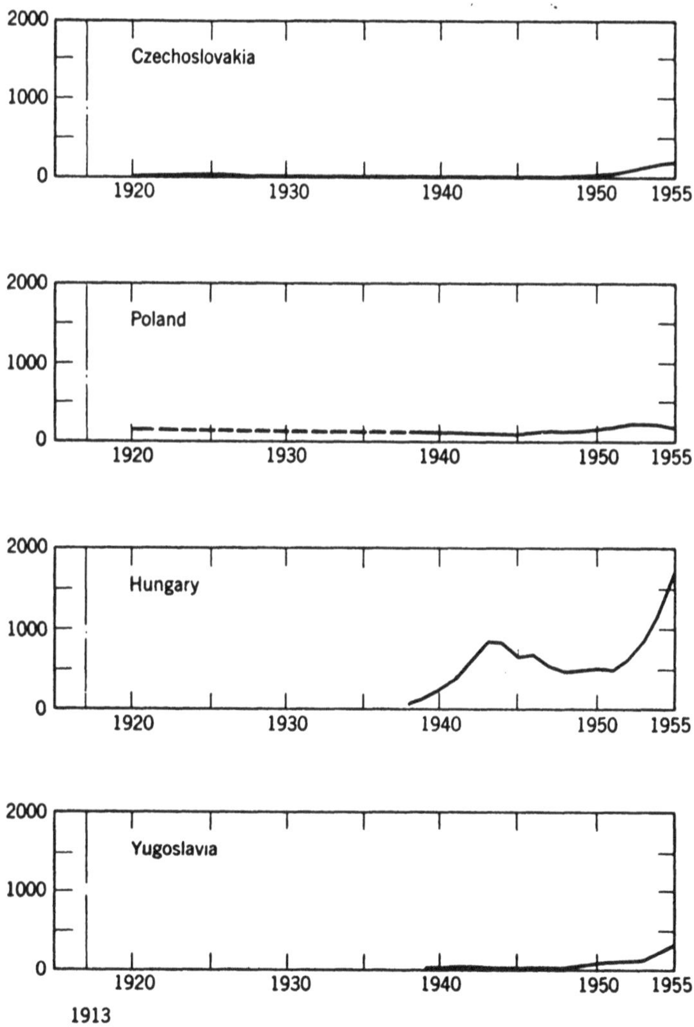

CHART 12 (*Continued*).

The impressive performance claimed since 1950 may be due not only to discovery of new oil structures and ruthless exploitation of previously known fields, including those considered "a reserve for the future" (e.g., the oil pools of Moldavia),[5] but also to substantial tech-

[5] In spite of the ruthless exploitation of all known reserves, refugee specialists are skeptical of the official claim and believe these data are somewhat inflated. Cf. Constantin Jordan, *The Romanian Oil Industry, op. cit.*, p. 218 ff.

nical changes. This would parallel the big upsurge in the Soviet oil output in the 1930's.[6]

Except for Hungary, efforts to increase oil output in other countries have not been rewarding; the necessary deposits have not been found. Hungary, which produced over 1.6 million tons in 1955, is scheduled to produce 2 million tons in 1960.[7]

Romania, the foremost producer of natural gas, is stated officially to have produced some 2.0 billion cubic meters in 1950 as compared to 2.1 billion in 1936, and in 1955 almost double that level, 3.9 billion cubic meters. Compared to Romania, output elsewhere is very limited, the other important producers being Poland (some 200 million cubic meters in 1952) and Hungary (the last data available was 175 million cubic meters planned for 1950). The output of Yugoslavia is 14 million cubic meters, and that of Czechoslovakia only 2 million.

Potentially the hydroelectric resources of the region are very substantial, but development is still limited. Hydroelectric power generated in 1950 may be estimated at but 1 per cent of what is possible in Romania, 2 per cent in Yugoslavia, 4 per cent in Hungary, 6 per cent in Bulgaria, 9 per cent in Poland, and 16 per cent in Czechoslovakia. Considerable expansion has been envisaged both during the first development plans and, in a broader perspective, up to 1965. The development of hydroelectricity is generally slow and requires large investment and utilization of materials, so that it may be assumed that substantial increases in hydro-generating capacity will not be achieved until the last part of the second quinquennium of development. Detailed plans for Romania project for 1960 a hydro-generating capacity equal to the 1950 total of Romania and Yugoslavia combined. Both countries could play a very significant role as exporters of hydro-produced current. An old project, abandoned after the

[6] As has already been noted (note 72, p. 199), the Romanian oil equipment was in a very poor state in 1946. The scarcity of implements and installations prevented large-scale trial drillings. It was firmly believed then that recovery of the old working capacity and the start of "vigorous activity of drilling and refining" were dependent on resuming trade relations with the old Western sources of supply. (Cf. Mihail Pizanty, "Prewar Aspects of the Romanian Oil Industry," *op. cit.*) The high increases in output, especially since 1950, coincide not only with large imports of Soviet drilling equipment, but with the development of a new Romanian industry of manufacture of drilling material.

[7] For data on the Hungarian industry, see: *The Hungarian Oil Industry*, Mid-European Studies Center, New York, 1954.

break with Yugoslavia but revived since 1956, is a large-scale plan for the development of Danube power resources in the area of the Iron Gates.[8] There are various projects for developing other Yugoslav hydro resources by importing equipment for the plants from Austria and Italy in exchange for the newly produced current.[9]

The over-all structure of *commercial* sources of energy in 1950 (all primary sources, excluding fuel wood) reveals only minor changes from prewar conditions (see Table 84). These consist of increases in the relative shares of solid fuels in the total supply of Romania and Bulgaria and of liquid fuels in Hungary, and slight increases in the share of hydroelectricity in Czechoslovakia, Poland, Hungary, and Romania. With the exception of Romania, the chief energy source remains the solid fuels, which comprise from 85 to 99 per cent of the total. The first development plan has not brought about any decisive changes. Only large-scale development of hydroelectricity could substantially alter this pattern, and such development, as already indicated, is perforce slow.

Fuel wood is a significant source of energy in the region, especially in the less developed countries. The share of fuel wood in the total sources of commercial and non-commercial energy, computed in coal equivalent, is estimated for 1949 as 1.7 per cent in Poland, 4.5 per cent in Czechoslovakia, 14.7 per cent in Hungary, 23.0 per cent in

[8] For the original Romanian plan of electrification see: "Electrification Plan of the Romanian People's Republic 1951–1960," Report of Gh. Dej, October 14, 1950, *RN*, October 31, 1950.

The question of the construction of Yugoslav-Romanian hydro installations in the zone of the Iron Gates is apparently considered as a project of interest for the area as a whole. The eventual output of hydro power at the completion of this project would be 9 to 12 billion kilowatthours and the cost, at 1956 prices, about one billion dollars. See: *The New York Times*, July 29, 1956.

[9] See: *Prospects of Exporting Electric Power from Yugoslavia*, UN, ECE, Geneva, January 1955. The study examines four key hydro projects to be developed eventually in Yugoslavia, up to 1965–66. The projects would represent a total installed capacity of over 1,700 mv. with a total yearly output of 5.8 billion kwhr., that is, an output of hydro origin destined for export larger than the total Yugoslav electrical output of 1955.

Concerning both the transport of electricity between countries and the organization of a transportation grid in each of the countries of the area, see *Quelques aspects techniques du transport de l'énergie électrique* (Some Technical Aspects of the Transport of Electric Power), UN, ECE, Geneva, August 1952, pp. 72 ff. See also *Transfer of Electric Power across European Frontiers*, Study by the Electric Power Section, UN, ECE, Geneva, August 1952 (mimeo.), pp. 197–199.

TABLE 84. COMMERCIAL SOURCES OF ENERGY, 1937 AND 1950[a]

	1937				1950			
Country	Solid fuel	Liquid fuel	Natural gas	Hydroelectricity	Solid fuel	Liquid fuel	Natural gas	Hydroelectricity
Czechoslovakia	98.5	0.1	[b]	1.4	98.0	0.2	[c]	1.8
Poland	96.1	1.9	1.9	0.1	99.0	0.3	0.3	0.4
Hungary	99.5	0.2	0.1	0.2	88.5	8.6	2.4	0.5
Romania	6.6	70.3	22.7	0.4	12.0	63.6	23.3	1.1
Bulgaria	88.2	[d]	[d]	11.8	91.0	[d]	[d]	9.0
Yugoslavia	86.0	0.1	0.1	13.8	85.2	2.5	0.3	12.0

[a] Percentages of total computed in coal equivalent.
[b] Negligible.
[c] Not available.
[d] Nil.

Source: Computed from *World Energy Supplies in Selected Years, 1929–1950,* UN Statistical Papers, Series J, No. 1, New York, 1951, pp. 50–51.

Romania, 38.3 per cent in Yugoslavia, and 43.5 per cent in Bulgaria.[10] Its importance in the total supply of energy is due not only to a low level of industrialization but also to rather limited supplies from other sources and difficulties in their use. It can hardly be expected that this share will decline substantially during the next few years in Romania, Yugoslavia, and Bulgaria. It might even increase because of a greater demand for energy, the limited possibilities of adding to the coal output, and the likelihood of more exports of current, once the new hydroelectric facilities are in operation.

Concluding the discussion of energy we turn directly to thermoelectricity and to total electricity output, leaving the output and de-

[10] Cf. *World Energy Supplies . . . , op. cit.* According to estimates of a German source, the relative share of fuel wood in the output of energy in Romania represented only 17 per cent in 1950 (given the increase in oil output) as compared to 20 per cent in the 1930's and 33 per cent in 1913. In Yugoslavia this source estimates that fuel wood accounted for 37 per cent of the total in 1950 and 1951, as compared to as much as 60 per cent in 1937. Cf. Deutsches Institut für Wirtschaftsforschung (Abt. Bergbau und Energiewirtschaft), DIW, *Mitteilungen* (Nos. 3 and 4) *über die Industrie und Energiewirtschaft der Sowjetischen Besatzungszone Deutschlands* (SBZ) *und der osteuropäischen Länder* [German Institute for Economic Research, Section of Mines and Energy, Information (Nos. 3 and 4) on Industry and Energy of the Soviet-Occupied Zone (in Germany) and the East European Countries], Berlin, 1953, pp. 16–17.

velopment of metallurgical coke for discussion in relation to the supply of iron and steel.

The rapid and systematic increase in electric power generating capacity and production is considered the cornerstone of the industrialization and "socialist transformation" of the area, just as it has been and is still considered in Soviet Russia. The data available on the electric generating capacity in 1952 indicate substantial increases over prewar capacity. As can be seen from Table 85, by

TABLE 85. ELECTRIC GENERATING CAPACITY (MV)

Country	1938 1	1948 2	1952 3	% Increase, 3 ÷ 1 4
Czechoslovakia	1,850	2,740	3,100	67
Poland	[a]	2,460	3,830	[a]
Hungary	690	823	1,310	89
Romania	510	600	710	39
Bulgaria	120	170	430 [b]	258
Yugoslavia	505	673	750 [b]	48

[a] Not available.
[b] 1951.
Sources:
Col. 1: C, P, H, R, B: *Statistical Yearbook of the World Power Conference*, No. 4, 1948, publ. by the Central Office WPC, London, 1949, Tables 19A and 20. Y: *Indeks*, II, 10 (October 1953), p. 10.
Cols. 2, 3: *op. cit.;* UNSY, 1955, pp. 279–280.

1952 the increases over prewar output were generally from 40 to nearly 90 per cent; in Bulgaria the increase was 258 per cent. By 1955 the region had probably already doubled its prewar generating capacity. The results of the several national efforts are strikingly apparent in Chart 13. Although all the countries of the area materially increased their production, Poland and Czechoslovakia each produced nearly as much as, or more than, the other four countries combined.[11]

In considering the sources of electric production at the key turning points of 1929, 1937, and 1950, it appears that the coal-producing countries have developed their hydro resources, whereas in the countries endowed with high hydro potentials the share of hydroelectricity

[11] For underlying data, see Appendix to this chapter, p. 367.

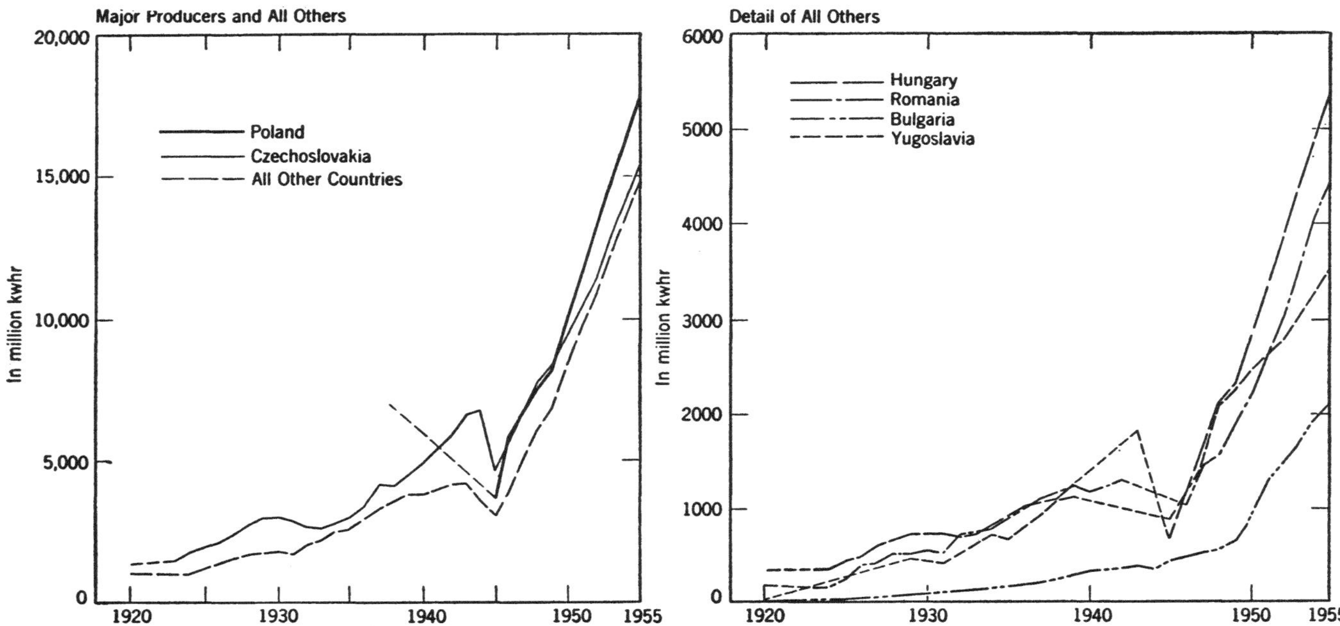

CHART 13. ELECTRIC POWER OUTPUT, 1920–55

TABLE 86. SOURCES OF ELECTRICITY PRODUCTION, 1929, 1937, 1950

(percentages)

	1929		1937		1950	
Country	Hydro	Thermal	Hydro	Thermal	Hydro	Thermal
Czechoslovakia	7.3	92.7	13.5	86.5	12.1	89.9
Poland	1.6	98.4	1.4	98.6	5.3	94.7
Hungary	0.8	99.2	1.2	98.8	2.5	97.5
Romania	10.5	89.5	8.3	91.7	9.5	90.5
Bulgaria	57.0	43.0	66.3	33.7	38.4	61.6
Yugoslavia	36.7	63.3	49.3	50.7	48.9	51.1

Source: World Energy Supplies . . ., op. cit., p. 87.

has decreased in 1950 as compared both to 1929 and 1937, with a very slight exception for Romania (see Table 86).

To summarize, the goals set after the revision of 1951, for the output of coal, oil, electricity, and other energy sources combined were not always achieved; the average (compound) rates of growth for coal output for the period considered fell short of those set by the plans (notably in Hungary). In all the countries the increases in coal output were accompanied by a marked deterioration in quality, and there appear to be marked difficulties in the way of a further systematic increase during the second planned quinquennium. So far as oil is concerned, prospective developments are limited. The results obtained in the key producing country, Romania, are rather difficult to appraise, in view of the scanty data available and the great decline in output since the end of the war. The efforts to develop electricity, both hydro and thermal, resulted in an average rate of growth generally above that projected. The outlook for a systematic increase in the production of electricity, both by water power and by steam power utilizing low-grade coals, is good. In 1955 the per capita output of electricity increased to close to 1,200 kilowatthours in Czechoslovakia, 550 to 650 in Hungary and Poland, 200 to 275 in the other three countries. By 1960 the per capita outputs are scheduled to reach over 1,850 kilowatthours in Czechoslovakia, some 800 in Poland and Hungary, and around 350–400 in the other countries.[12] These outputs could sustain a further increase in industrialization.

[12] See Table 102 in the Appendix to this chapter, p. 374.

Supply and Potentialities of Iron and Steel

For the region as a whole the iron and steel industry depends by and large on local resources of metallurgical coke and on some imports (from the Donbas) as well as on large imports of iron ore (from Krivoi Rog). The main deposits of coking coal are concentrated in the western part of the Silesia-Ostrava Basin.[13] Hence the Czechoslovak present and potential outputs are high as related to estimated reserves.[14] Before the war German and Czechoslovak Silesian coal could produce more coke than Poland could produce in the eastern part of the Basin. However, since the war Poland's position has improved by the addition to Upper Silesia of the high-grade coking coal of Lower Silesia.[15] In addition to these main sources, there are secondary fields in Hungary, Romania, and Yugoslavia.

The peak of Czechoslovak output of metallurgical coke, reached in 1944, was 5 million tons. The output of the prewar eastern territory of Germany taken over by Poland, estimated at 3.0 million tons, plus the 2.0 million of old Poland makes a total of 5.0 million tons for the prewar Polish output in the postwar territories. In 1948 the Czechoslovak output was 4.6 million tons and the Polish output 5.2 million. In 1953, their output increased to 5.9 and 7.9 million, and in 1955 to 7.0 and 10.0 million, respectively. Strenuous efforts have been made by all the other countries to increase their production of coke, but,

[13] See Jan H. Wszelaki, *Fuel and Power in Captive Middle Europe*, Mid-European Studies Center, National Committee for a Free Europe, New York, 1952, p. 22.

[14] The estimates of the reserves of coal and those of coking coal vary substantially. Two United Nations publications, *World Iron Ore Resources and Their Utilization*, *op. cit.*, pp. 66–67, and *Transfers of Electric Power across European Frontiers*, *op. cit.*, pp. 177–178, give, respectively, 6.4 and 6.0 billion metric tons of hard coal as probable reserves of hard coal for Czechoslovakia, and 60 and 193 billion, respectively, for Poland. Another study, *European Steel Trends in the Setting of the World Market*, UN, ECE, Geneva, 1949, p. 116, gives 30.1 billion metric tons probable hard coal reserves for Czechoslovakia and again 193 billion for Poland. However, all the sources note the well-known fact that the Czechoslovakian coking coal is of high grade, whereas it is considered of only moderate grade for Poland. The discrepancies between these sources concerning the reserves of the other countries of the area which have small deposits are not very wide.

[15] Cf. Wszelaki, *op. cit.*, p. 22. According to *European Steel Trends . . . , op. cit.*, p. 116, the proportion of coking coal to the estimated hard coal reserves of Lower Silesia would be over 50 per cent, whereas they are less than 10 per cent as compared to the reserves of Upper Silesia. However, it must not be overlooked that the total reserves of the latter are far larger than those of the former.

the results have been rather modest.[16] Yugoslavia produced 731 thousand tons of coke in 1955. Romania planned an output of 700 thousand tons for the end of 1955, eight times its 1938 production, but produced only 300 thousand tons, an amount far below needs. The Hungarian output remains very limited; the Bulgarian output is negligible (22,000 tons). In view of their projected continued increase in steel production, the last four countries will continue to depend heavily on imports. On the other hand, Czechoslovakia and Poland will continue to be substantial coke exporters.[17]

All the countries have iron-ore deposits. In Czechoslovakia they are found at Nučice-Zdice (west of Prague) and Košice (in Slovakia); in Poland at Kielče-Radom (in the southeast part of the country) and Częstochowa (to the north of the Upper Silesian complex); in Hungary at Rudabanya (in the north, close to the Ózd-Diosgyör area); in Romania in Banat at Resiţa and in the Ghelar region (western part of the country); in Bulgaria at Kremikovtsy (close to Sofia), at Haskovo (in the south) and around Burgas; in Yugoslavia in Bosnia (at Liubija in the northwest part of the country), and at Vareš (north of Sarajevo). Except in Bulgaria and in Yugoslavia, which have richer ore, all the ore resources of the area are of low grade, with only 35 to 40 per cent iron content. Traditionally, the local output has been complemented by large imports of iron ore from Sweden and, since the Second World War, the Soviet Union (Krivoi Rog). The strenuous effort to develop local iron-ore resources has not eliminated the need for large imports of both iron and scrap, a need which, in view of projected increasingly higher targets for steel, will be multiplied.

The main iron and steel centers in Czechoslovakia are at Trineč (Morávska-Ostrava complex), Kladno (north of Prague), Plzeň, and in Slovakia; in Poland, in the Ostrowiecz area and in the Upper Sile-

[16] Efforts have been made by Hungary, Romania, and Yugoslavia to produce coke from low-grade coal. In Hungary: the coal from the main basin of Pećs is improper for coking purposes and attempts have been made to utilize the nearby Komlo coal output for coking. In Romania: a concentration plant was under construction in Hunedoara to produce coke from the low-grade coal of the Jiu Valley. In Yugoslavia: attempts have been made to use for coking local coal combined with foreign coke. See "L'Industrie hongroise depuis la fin de la guerre," *op. cit.*, p. 50; *FLP,* May 30, 1952; Werner Markert, editor, *Jugoslawien. Osteuropa Handbuch* (Yugoslavia. East Europe Handbook), Böhlau Verlag, Köln-Graz, 1954, p. 259.

[17] It takes somewhat over one ton of coke to make one ton of steel. In 1955 the combined Czechoslovak and Polish steel outputs reached 8.9 tons as compared to a combined coke output of 17.0 million tons.

sian complex; in Hungary, at Ózd-Diosgyör and at Csepel Island (Budapest); in Romania, in Banat (Reşiţa) and Transylvania (Hunedoara-Calan area); in Yugoslavia, at Jesenice, Sisak, and Vareš-Zenica.

Almost all these countries have made determined efforts during the first long-term plans for the development of new iron and steel works. However, many of the key planned projects were abandoned. Czechoslovakia built the new Gottwald steel mills, with a capacity of 1 million tons, at Kunčice, in the Morávska-Ostrawa complex, but discontinued the construction of a much-publicized project near Košice (Slovakia), the Huko complex, which was also to possess a capacity of 1 million tons. The directives for the second quinquennium foresee construction of two new giant furnaces at the Gottwald steel mills. Poland completed the first stage of the construction of the Lenin Steel Works in Nowa Huta (New Foundry) near Krakow, the biggest industrial investment of the six-year plan. She also expanded tremendously the former Rakow Foundry, now Bierut Foundry, near Częstochowa, and erected a special foundry near Warsaw. The present capacity of the Lenin and Bierut works is, respectively, 1.5 and 1.1 million tons of steel per year, and this capacity will be considerably increased after the completion of the second stage of construction during the second long-term plan. Hungary finished, after many delays, only one-half of the planned expansions in her metallurgical capacity. She constructed one blast furnace of the Lenin Steel Works and two open hearth furnaces of the Stalin Iron Works at Sztalinváros (Dunapentele). One-half of the original project, a second giant blast furnace scheduled to be completed before 1954, is now included in the second long-term plan. The Romanian Hunedoara works have been enlarged and modernized. Yugoslavia failed to carry out plans for erecting large iron works at Skoplje. Finally, Bulgaria's first steel mill, the Lenin Steel Mill, started its production in 1953 with an "experimental" output of 50,000 tons a year.

All these developments have not basically changed the location pattern of iron and steel works, and no radical changes in that pattern appear to be envisaged.

Chart 14 depicts the over-all increase up to 1955 in total iron-ore production (Fe content), pig iron, and crude steel since 1938 for Poland and since 1913 for the other countries of the region. Production of pig iron and steel, like that of coal, generally remained stable up to 1940. In Czechoslovakia sharp changes in the world market caused wide fluctuations. Since 1948 all the countries of the region have surpassed former peaks in the output of both pig iron and steel and have continued systematically to increase production. In the region as a whole the output of pig iron increased from 3.2 million tons in 1938 to 3.6 million in 1948, 6.6 million in 1953, and 8.0 million in 1955. The largest increases were achieved by Poland and Czechoslovakia; Hungary encountered major difficulties in raising her output to the planned level.[18] Steel production in the entire area increased from 5 million tons before the Second World War to 6 million in 1948, nearly 11 million in 1953, and over 12 million in 1955. The goals of the new quinquennium are a total output for the area of roughly 18 million tons in 1960.

Analysis of the *rates* of growth up to 1955 and comparison of these rates with those set by the plans reveal a conspicuous failure in the area so far as pig iron is concerned. The rates of growth of pig-iron output have been below those projected. The rates of growth for steel have been approximately equal to those projected in the plans for Czechoslovakia and Poland only, an achievement made possible by increased utilization of scrap.[19] All the other countries failed to meet the requirements. Hungary and Romania fell far below their goals. As a result, the total steel output of the area dropped below the levels scheduled for the end of the first development plans.[20]

As compared to the peak prewar year 1929, the per capita steel consumption increased in 1953 from 110 to 174 per cent in Yugoslavia, Bulgaria, and Czechoslovakia, 256 per cent in Hungary, and over 400 per cent in Romania.[21] The per capita outputs reached in 1955 some 350 kgs. in Czechoslovakia, about 160 kgs. in Poland and Hun-

[18] Thus Imre Nagy, then Hungarian Premier, stated in 1954:

> Of special significance are the extraordinary tasks which we must solve in the mining, iron and steel, and power industries. Development of these decisive branches has not kept pace with the general rate of our industrialization, and their technical re-equipment lags despite the increased demands made on them. [Cf. "For Steady Rise in Standard of Living of Hungarian People," in *FLP,* Feb. 5, 1954.]

[19] The shift of the ratio of scrap to pig iron for the output of steel has represented an advantage from various points of view. Notably, it has allowed a higher blast-furnace output and has diminished the coke consumption. Moreover, it has conditioned a better steel quality, assuming that the pig iron now produced is of lower quality, as it is produced with coke with a high sulfur content. The known lack of scrap in the area makes it impossible to keep the ratio attained during the first development plans. Concerning the lack of scrap, see *The European Steel Market in 1954,* UN, ECE, Geneva, June 1955, pp. 30–31.

[20] Compare Table 74, p. 290, to Table 98, p. 370, in the Appendix to this chapter.

[21] *The European Steel Market in 1953,* UN, ECE, Geneva, January 1954, p. 43.

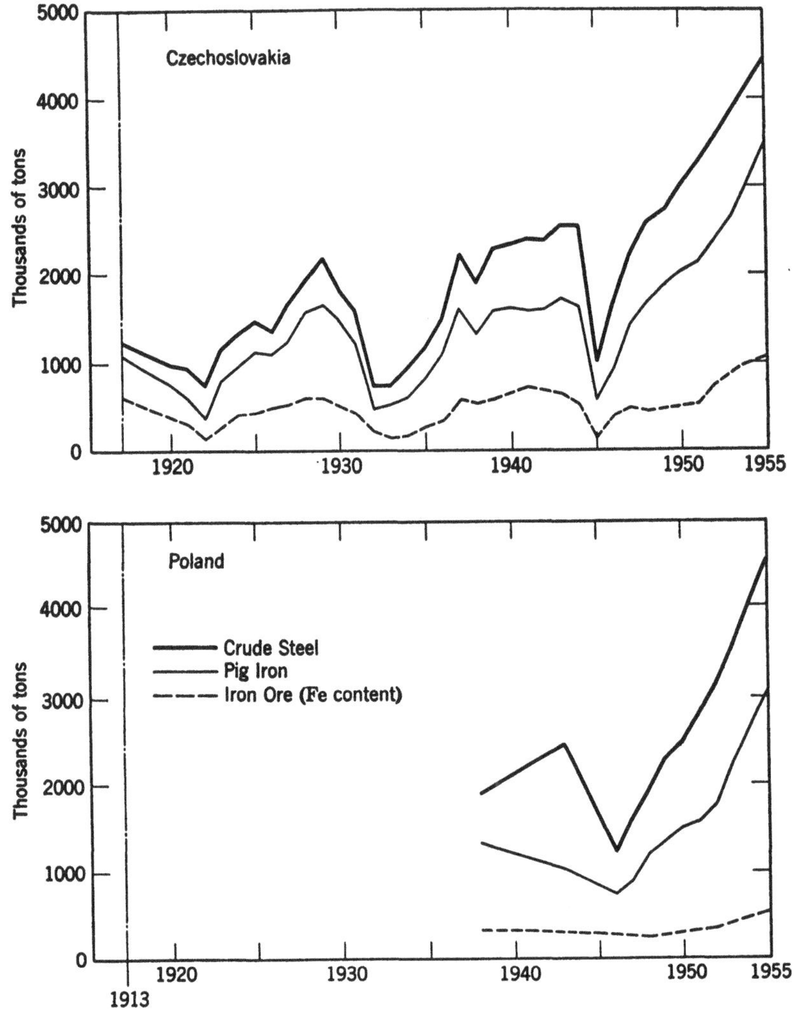

CHART 14. IRON AND STEEL PRODUCTION, 1913–55

gary, and from 35–45 kgs. in Yugoslavia and Romania. By 1960 the per capita outputs are scheduled to reach 480 kgs. in Czechoslovakia, between 220 and 240 kgs. in Poland and Hungary, and from 40–90 kgs. in the other three countries.[22]

The growth of the iron and steel industry continues to be hampered by the lack of sufficient iron-ore resources and, in some of the coun-

[22] See Table 102, p. 374, in the Appendix to this chapter.

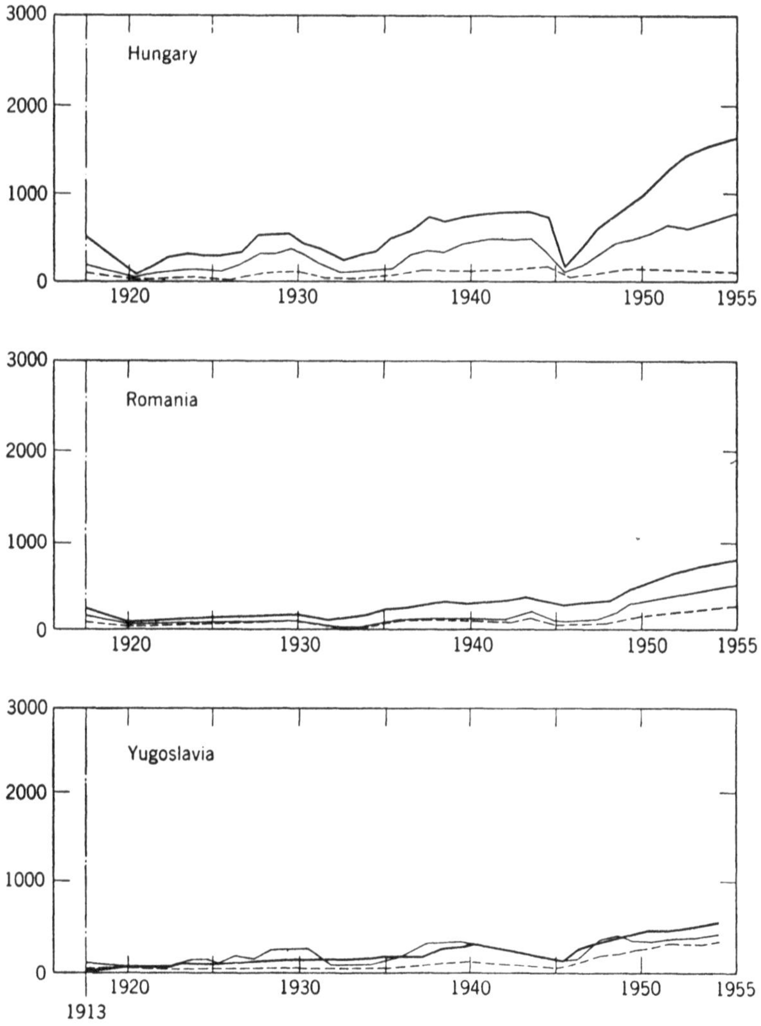

CHART 14 (*Continued*).

tries, lack of coking coal. Although the iron and steel industries can develop on the basis of substantial imports of iron ore from outside the area and trade in coke within the area, the difficulties encountered in increasing the production of coal, coke, and pig iron during the first plans of development portend even more formidable obstacles during the second quinquennium.

Engineering

The engineering industry[23] of the area is concentrated mainly in Czechoslovakia, Poland, and Hungary. In each of these countries the industry has markedly different national characteristics.[24]

Before the war Czechoslovakia had a well-established engineering industry composed of *all the principal sectors:* all types of transport equipment, machine tools, electrical equipment, agricultural machinery, and a large world-wide exporting armament industry (the famous Škoda works). It grew steadily both during the war and in the period of reconstruction and development. As can be seen from Table 87,

Table 87. Czechoslovakia, Poland, Hungary: Engineering Industry 1938, 1948, and in or about 1953 (estimated)

(in million US dollars)

	Czechoslovakia			Poland			Hungary		
Sectors	1938	1948	1952	1938	1948	1953	1938	1948	1954
Road transport	27.8	48.1	96.0	0.2	27.0	50.0	7.8	2.4	39.3
Rail transport	12.9	88.0	108.0	5.5	130.0	173.8	11.8	37.1	89.0
Water transport	[a]	[a]	[a]	[a]	8.5	[a]	3.0	5.2	[a]
Power	12.7	19.5	18.0	1.2	[a]	[a]	[a]	[a]	[a]
Electrical material	9.5	17.2	14.7	8.9	146.3 [b]	246.0	32.0	47.4	117.9
Electronics and signalling	9.8	19.8	25.3	10.6		109.0	[a]	[a]	[a]
Machine tools	25.0 [b]	39.6 [b]	50.0	2.3	20.0	51.4	0.4	5.9	51.6
Agricultural machinery	20.1	33.4	74.0	8.0 [b]	25.0	50.0	4.3	12.5	11.1
Various	15.0	20.5	25.0	198.3 [c]	53.2	122.0 [c]	91.1 [c]	85.0 [c]	324.4 [c]
Engineering stores	239.3 [c]	262.9 [c]	645.4 [c]				[a]	[a]	49.6
Total	372.1	549.0 [b]	1,056.4 [b]	235.0	410.0	802.2	150.4	195.5	977.3 [d]

[a] Not available.
[b] Estimate.
[c] Includes all sectors for which details are not available.
[d] Equals: heavy machine industry, $653.1 million; hardware industries, high power electric industry, and telecommunications industry, $324.2 million.

Source: Étude générale des industries mécaniques en Europe, op. cit., pp. 162, 167, 172 (Appendix).

substantial increases were achieved by 1948 in all branches of the engineering industry, and further significant increases were expected during the first development plan in such branches as transport (23 per cent increase in volume for rail transport and 100 per cent for

23 See above, Chapter 8, note 14, p. 288.

24 Some of the data concerning these three countries are based on *Étude générale des industries mécaniques en Europe* (Survey of European Engineering Industries), UN, ECE, Geneva, 1951, pp. 103–106.

road transport), electronics (28 per cent), machine tools (39 per cent), agricultural equipment (121 per cent). The projected total output of the engineering industry, which may include part of the armament output,[25] was to attain in 1953 more than three times the prewar output. Notwithstanding a systematic effort, the level reached in 1953 was 224 per cent of 1937.[26] Data for 1955 indicate that the Czechoslovak output of machine tools reached some 15,700 units, as compared to 5,500 in 1937 and 11,800 in 1948. In the branch of agricultural machinery, the output of tractors in 1955 reached 12,300 units as compared to 200 before the war and 9,100 units in 1948.[27]

In contrast to Czechoslovakia, Poland has concentrated mostly on light engineering, with the chief emphasis on rail transport, electrical high-power machinery, agricultural machinery, mining machinery, and metal-working machinery. Although since the war relentless efforts have been made for "all-round development of engineering," even in 1953 Polish heavy engineering was still considered to be underdeveloped. However, the acquisition of a key German plant in Wrocław (Breslau) contributed to the postwar development of the rolling-stock industry, which is now important in the export of railway coaches and heavy and light locomotives. Moreover, the key sector of machine tools increased its output remarkably, from a total of 5,600 units (6,800 tons) in 1948 to a total of 13,900 units (27,800 tons) in 1955. Among the productions of the engineering industry which have been scheduled for larger development are output of cars, trucks, and tractors. By the end of 1955 7,900 tractors were manufactured, as compared to 6,900 in 1953 and 2,500 in 1949.[28] However, production remained below the plan targets. Poland is still dependent on imports for generators, machinery for rolling mills, various

[25] In a study on the Soviet iron and steel industry, Professor M. G. Clark has suggested that all munitions production was concealed in the Soviet statistics under the title "Miscellaneous Machine Building." On the basis of various computations, Prof. Clark indicated that from 1932 until 1938 the munitions could have increased from 17.1 per cent to 30.6 per cent of all Soviet machine construction. (Quoted by Harry Schwartz, *Russia's Soviet Economy,* Prentice-Hall, New York, 1951, p. 248.)

[26] CEB No. 306, March 1956, p. 2.

[27] The interest attached to these industries does not concern agriculture alone. As is known, these types of plants are among the most easily transformed for the production of tanks and war material.

[28] For a concise account of the Polish machine-building industry and of its chief establishments see: *A Survey of Poland,* Supplement to *The Statist, op. cit.,* pp. 21–22.

types of machine tools, and equipment for the production of industrial chemicals.

Hungary's long-established machine industry produces electrical equipment, rail transport, agricultural machinery, and certain types of machines. Hungary is also a significant producer and exporter of light electrical products, railway engines, and tools. The plan placed a special emphasis on machine tools, and by 1953 the machine-tool output increased sharply while that of tractors was cut below the 1948 level. In 1954 the output of tractors was stepped up and in 1955 Hungary produced 5,750 tractors, compared to 1,190 units in 1948 and 800 units in 1953. During the first five-year plan, a whole series of new types of machines was devéloped, such as street cars, harvesters and combines, construction and road-building machinery, machinery for the chemical industry, automatic looms for the textile industry, trucks,[29] etc. It is claimed officially that the gross value of engineering during the first five-year plan increased up to 267 per cent over the pre-plan year 1949.[30]

The engineering industry has been small in Romania and Yugoslavia and nonexistent in Bulgaria.

Romania engaged after 1949–50 in the development of an all-round engineering industry. The official announcements claim the beginning of production of domestic machinery, especially for the oil industry (oil drilling motors, oil derricks), and locomotives and various types of machinery for electrical engineering, such as ball bearings.[31] Moreover, Romania produces tractors—some 5,000 units in 1955—combine harvesters, and other kinds of equipment. According to the same sources, Romania imports most of the required heavy machine tools, either from the Soviet Union or from Czechoslovakia, East Germany, and Hungary, whence come also heavy electrical equipment and heavy road and building construction machinery (excavators, compressors, dragline excavators, etc.).

[29] The production of the first ten Csepel trucks (6.5 tons each), mass-produced, was announced in 1950. Cf. *Revue commerciale hongroise* (Hungarian Business Review), No. 1, 1950, p. 7.

[30] Report of the Central Bureau of Statistics on Economic Progress and the Trends of Material and Cultural Standards of the Population During the First Five Year Plan 1950–1954, *Hungarian Review*, No. 6, June 1955, p. 9.

[31] A portrayal of the achievement of the Romanian machine industry organized in the form of an exhibit, "The Planned Economy of the RPR in Full Progress," opened in Bucharest at the beginning of 1953. The various machines on view were reproduced in *RN*, Jan. 28, 1953, and Feb. 4, 1953.

By Western standards Bulgaria did not have what might be called even one engineering *plant;* nevertheless, like all the other countries, she engaged in the production of machine tools, metal-working machines, and related machinery. Although the announced increases as compared to prewar figures are meaningless (it is claimed that the output of machine tools in 1952 was 120 times the 1939 production [32]) it is certain that engineering has started to develop. Its main achievements are the production of machinery of all types (800 types, but not mass-produced), transport equipment (more assembly work than actual output), electrical material, and some construction machinery. Agricultural machinery accounts for one-third of the engineering output, but Bulgaria does not yet produce tractors or combines. She imports all kinds of machinery from the other countries of the area: heavy electrical equipment mostly from Czechoslovakia, rolling stock from Poland, electrical material and electronics equipment from Hungary, and agricultural machinery from the Soviet Union.[33]

Yugoslavia has also made serious efforts to attain an all-round development of heavy and light engineering. Outstanding among the machinery plants are the new Železnik and Litostroj constructions. The Yugoslav output of machine tools increased between 1948 and 1953 from some 637 tons to over 2,300 tons, that of "other machine and industrial equipment" from 9,500 tons to over 24,000 tons.[34] Production of tractors, nonexistent in 1948, accounted for some 1,100 units in 1955. Engineering, as all the other industrial branches, has recovered after experiencing a marked decline in 1952–53.

It may thus be seen that the first development period was characterized by a significant increase of engineering output in the area as a whole, diversification of production in each country, and encouragement of certain new industries in some of these countries (such as production of heavy machine tools in Poland, or equipment for the oil industry in Romania). Each country set itself the task of developing a complete engineering industry, almost regardless of cost and the duplication of efforts entailed. As George Kemény remarked:

[32] F. T. Konstantinov, *Bolgariia na puti k Sotsialismu* (Bulgaria on the Road to Socialism), Gosudarstvennoe Izdatel'stvo Politicheskoi Literatury (State Publishing House of Political Literature), 2nd ed., Moscow, 1953, p. 142.

[33] E. Valev, *Narodnaia Respublica Bolgariia, op. cit.*, p. 83; also, D. Kostiukhin, "Pod'em Narodnogo Khoziaistvo Bolgarii," (The Advance of the National Economy of Bulgaria), in *VT*, No. 7 (June 1952), pp. 6 ff.

[34] Cf. *Statistički Godišnjak FNRJ 1956, op. cit.*, p. 145, and also Table 99, p. 371, in the Appendix to this chapter.

. . . No policy aiming at a division of labor on a broader regional scale has been pursued. For the rest, each of the satellite governments is intent on building industry along the line of self-sufficiency. . . . Production programs in each of the small or medium-sized economies are unduly varied, with a view to providing the market with a wide range of home-made products. In this concept, considerations of the advantages of large-scale production are discarded. Government spokesmen boast of the achievements that would be regarded as misconceptions if measured by standards of up-to-date industrial development.[35]

However, to a certain degree circumstances have dictated a sort of division of labor in the area. Czechoslovakia has continued to supply most of the heavy equipment, Poland the rolling stock, Hungary the electrotechnical supplies. The problem of the division of labor has presented itself to systematic consideration of planners during the "new course" and since then has remained a key problem.

Chemicals

The increased output of coal, oil, iron, and steel has markedly enlarged the raw-material base of the chemical industry,[36] which has undoubtedly made appreciable strides in the area.

Before the war the chemical industry of Czechoslovakia played a decisive role in East Europe, and the largest Czechoslovak chemical combine, Aussiger Verein, had important domestic and foreign holdings.[37] During the war the Germans began the largest and potentially the most important single enterprise in this industry, the synthetic gasoline works at Most. This plant has remained intact, and its projected output in 1953 was 525,000 tons of synthetic oil.[38] The plan

35 "East European Developments in Social Economic Structure," in *World Politics,* VI, 1 (October 1953), pp. 78–83.

36 For main chemicals, see Table 100, p. 372, in the Appendix to this chapter.

37 The Aussiger Verein fuer Chemische und Metallurgische Produktion accounted directly or through its patron bank the Živnostenská for more than 60 per cent of the country's total chemical production and had important holdings in Zorka (First Yugoslav Chemical Industry Co., Subotica) and Mărăşeşti (Romanian Chemical Works, Ltd., Bucharest). In combination with the Solvay Co., Brussels, it had a share in the Solvay companies in Romania and Yugoslavia. Cf., US Dept. of Commerce, Bureau of Foreign and Domestic Commerce, *World Chemical Developments in 1937,* Trade Promotion Series No. 177, US Govt. Printing Office, Washington, 1938, pp. 30–35.

38 Jan H. Wszelaki contends that this plant, declared a war trophy in 1945 and taken over by the Russians, was subsequently returned by them to the Czechoslovakian government, *in exchange for the Jachymov uranium mines.* (Wszelaki quotes

called for the production of nitric acid, nitrogenous acid, ammonia, potash, soda, artificial fertilizers, and synthetic fabrics, and envisaged extending the range of the industry to effect "reduced dependence of the country on foreign products." [39]

The continued activity in the steel industry and the increased production of coke have provided, and will continue to do so, a large output of crude tar and of coal-tar byproducts. Also by 1955, there were substantial increases in the production of sulfuric acid, which more than doubled as compared to prewar output, and fertilizers, which nearly quadrupled. The targets for 1960 for these items are very high.

Prewar Poland had some one thousand chemical plants, the most important being the government-owned United Explosive and Nitrogen, Ltd., Warsaw. Over a hundred gas plants and nine coke plants constituted the nucleus of the prewar coal-tar industry. The chemical industry, which suffered less destruction than was at first assumed, recovered rapidly, and the ample supply of local raw materials, including hard coal and brown coal, rock salt, anhydrite, gypsum, and various minerals and ores, furnishes it with a solid base.

In 1947–48, after attaining and surpassing the prewar output for most of the key products, the main efforts have been directed toward the increased production of sulfuric acid, artificial fertilizers, and sodium products, as well as the development of synthetic fuels.[40] By 1955 Poland was the leading producer of chemicals in the area and was playing an increasing role in the exports of organic and inorganic chemicals, carbon derivatives, and paints.[41] Prospects for further expansion are good.

Hungary had nearly 300 chemical plants, but war damage was considerable, particularly to factories producing industrial chemicals.[42]

an unpublished study on the Czechoslovakian industry by Dr. V. Paulat of New York.) Cf. *Fuel and Power . . . , op. cit.*, p. 34. The actual output of the plant is not indicated by the Czechoslovak sources.

[39] Cf. *Czechoslovak Economic Five-Year Plan, op. cit.*, p. 82.

[40] Two plants, the Wiżow Works, based on anhydrite, and the Busko Works, based on gypsum, are to produce a quantity of sulfuric acid equal to the combined production of all the works previously in operation. For fuels, the main new constructions are near Óswieçim. Other combines are at Gorzow. Cf. "New Chemical Works in Poland," *Polish Foreign Trade,* No. 14 (November–December 1952), pp. 19 ff.; see also Jozef Wasowicz, *Outline of Economic Geography,* Polonia, Warsaw, 1955, p. 39.

[41] "Poland's Coal Mining and Chemical Industries," in *Polish Foreign Trade,* No. 28–29 (3–4), 1955.

[42] US Dept. of Commerce, Bureau of Foreign and Domestic Commerce, *World*

Not having sufficient raw materials for this industry, Hungary must import them. Thus, for instance, in 1947–48 most of the caustic soda needed for the treatment of bauxite had to be imported, despite Hungary's having increased her output of caustic soda above the prewar level; this specific situation was improved by 1955. However, since the chemical industry in Hungary is heavily dependent on imports, particular attention has been paid to this problem. A joint company has been formed with Romania for the importation of Romanian natural gas.[43] The second five-year plan strongly emphasizes manufacturing organic chemicals from this raw material; the Tiszavidek chemical combination is already scheduled to be the "greatest achievement" of the second five-year plan, making possible the mass production of synthetics. Hungary has, moreover, continued to produce, from both local and imported raw materials, appreciable amounts of superphosphates and pharmaceuticals and will continue to play an important role in drug production.[44]

Romania before the war had 230 plants making industrial chemicals, explosives, fertilizer, dyes, soap, and miscellaneous products. The chemical industry there has been closely associated with the petroleum industry, and before the war official statistics grouped them together. Although Romania possesses important raw materials (wood, coal, oil, salt, and natural gas) she was before the war an importer of such chemicals as coal-tar dyes, pharmaceuticals and medicinals, pigments, and paints. During the war German investments facilitated significant progress in some of these fields. After the war, by an intense effort, the damaged oil refineries were restored so that by 1946 they could process the limited crude-oil production; however, this operation could be characterized only as "patchwork." During the first planned quinquennium the cracking capacity was apparently increased,[45] and it is claimed that the total production of 1955, 10.5

Chemical Developments 1940–46, Industrial Series No. 75, US Govt. Printing Office, Washington, 1947, pp. 33–34.

43 Cf. Romagchim, Chapter 6, p. 202, particularly, note 76.

44 The largest chemical plant of the first five-year plan, the Nitrogen Fertilizer Works of the Borsod Chemical Combine at Kazincbarcika in Northern Hungary, was opened in 1955. Production in the pharmaceutical industry was, in 1955, ten times that of the peak period during the war. See: Árpád Kiss, Minister of Chemical Industries and Power Supply, "Ten Years' Progress of Hungary's Chemical Industry," *Hungarian Review,* No. 5, May 1955, p. 13.

45 C. N. Jordan doubts that the provision of the first five-year plan concerning the increase in cracking capacity was fulfilled. Cf. *The Romanian Oil Industry, op. cit.,* p. 255.

million tons of oil, was refined domestically. Among the other achievements claimed during that period are the opening of a large chemical plant utilizing natural gas, of a plant for the production of electrodes and abrasives, and of other factories.[46] Development of petrochemicals is potentially great, and the second plan gives particular attention to this possibility.

Before the war the Bulgarian chemical industry consisted of about 80 plants, mostly small, for manufacturing soap, perfumery, toilet preparations, explosives, varnishes, ink, insecticides, industrial gas, and limited quantities of fertilizer and plastics. Only soap and toilet preparations, alcohol, matches, and rose oil were manufactured in sufficient quantities to satisfy domestic needs, and there were exportable surpluses of such specialties as mint oil. Imports included chemicals for raw materials, large supplies of copper sulfate for crops, and all types of finished products.[47] By 1948 the available plants were concentrated in fewer than 50 enterprises. The plans stressed the necessity for developing new and modern units to utilize domestic raw materials such as coal, pyrites, salt, and wood. The largest constructions during the first development plan were a fertilizer plant and some caustic soda plants.[48] The second quinquennial development foresees progress along the same lines.

Before the war Yugoslavia had a significant chemical industry, in which industrial chemicals predominated. Besides such basic products as sulfuric acid, calcium carbide, caustic soda, copper sulfate, aluminum salts, and fertilizers, she also produced considerable amounts of matches, cellulose, acetic acid, acetone, methanol, sodium acetate, calcium acetate, and formaldehyde.[49] Before the war Yugo-

[46] The new Berea plant at Braşov (Oraşul Stalin), using natural gas, is described in Romanian sources as "one of the lagrest plants in Southeast Europe." For abrasives the new plant is Carbochim at Cluj. See: *RN*, April 1, 1953 and December 2, 1953.

[47] US Dept. of Commerce, Bureau of Foreign and Domestic Commerce, *Chemical Developments Abroad, 1939: Effect of Munitions and Preparedness upon Chemical Production, Consumption and Foreign Trade,* Trade Promotion Series, No. 211, US Govt. Printing Office, Washington, 1940, p. 14; also *World Chemical Developments 1940–46, op. cit.*, pp. 16–18.

[48] The largest Bulgarian fertilizer plant is the Stalin plant at Pernik (Dimitrovgrad). The caustic soda plants are at Provadia. See: Valev, *Bolgariia . . . , op. cit.*, pp. 202–203, and *Narodnaia Respublica Bolgariia, op. cit.*, p. 85.

[49] US Dept. of Commerce, Bureau of Foreign and Domestic Commerce, *World Chemical Developments 1938,* US Govt. Printing Office, Washington, 1939, p. 92.

slavia's main chemical exports were pyrites, sodium carbonate, caustic soda, and calcium carbide.[50]

The chemical industry made notable progress in certain fields, as illustrated both by new constructions and by the increased output of such products as sulfuric acid, chloric acid, and caustic soda. The Yugoslav regime has turned now its attention to fertilizers, which up to 1955 have sorely lagged behind. A nitrogenous fertilizer plant, and a superphosphate and sulfuric acid factory are to be built with Soviet credits and equipment.[51]

To summarize, the principal features of the postwar growth of the chemical industry in the area were the upsurge of the Polish chemical industry and the substantial diversification of products in every country. Polish strides can be gaged by the production of sulfuric acid. By 1948 it was slightly larger than the Czechoslovak output, though still below prewar level; by 1955 it was 167 per cent of prewar and double the 1948 production. The available data also indicate large increases in the production of caustic soda and fertilizers.

In the area as a whole there are good prospects for further expansion of such key products as sulfuric acid and fertilizers, and for development of new and more advanced branches, such as organic chemicals in Hungary and petrochemicals in Romania.

The diversification of chemical output has demonstrated, as in all the other industries, an effort by each country to provide homemade products and become "independent" of imports. Only subsequently were there specific attempts at cooperation between countries based on imports of equipment in exchange for chemical raw material (for example, the Romanian-Hungarian cooperation in Romagchim).

Building

There have been two simultaneous efforts in the building industry in the area as a whole: one to transform the building trades into an integrated industry with modern construction equipment, and one to expand the output of building materials. The first has been sustained largely by using the heavy building machinery manufactured by

[50] *Chemical Developments Abroad 1939, op. cit.,* p. 70.

[51] The yearly output capacities of the promised nitrogenous fertilizer plant and the superphosphate factory are to be 220,000 and 250,000 tons, respectively. *Borba,* Sept. 3, 1955. It is, however, uncertain whether the Russians will actually deliver these goods.

Czechoslovakia and East Germany, the second by increasing the cement output and exploiting to the utmost the local materials.

As seen from Chart 15,[52] the leading producer of the area in total cement output is now Poland, whose production reached 3.8 million tons in 1955. For the area as a whole, the total output in 1955 was double that of 1938, increasing from 6.0 to 12.2 million tons. However, even this was below the goals set by the plans.

Among the most important new factories in the field during the first long-term plan were those in Poland, where there are local supplies of raw materials of all types, including inferior grades of coal and granulated slag,[53] and those in Hungary[54] and Romania.[55] On a per capita basis the output of cement in 1955 was 224 kgs. in Czechoslovakia, 115 to 140 kgs. in Poland, Hungary, and Romania, and 84 to 87 kgs. in Yugoslavia and Bulgaria. The outputs scheduled for 1960 are: 330 kgs. in Czechoslovakia, 180 to 190 kgs. in Hungary and Romania, and about 160 kgs. in Bulgaria. These represent roughly a fourfold increase over prewar figures.[56]

Equally important has been production of bricks and window glass. In 1955 the output of bricks was 7.8 million units as compared to 5.4 million before the war. During the first long-term plan a substantial share of these outputs has served for plant and other state constructions, with extremely modest provision for private housing, especially in Poland, Romania, and Bulgaria. Apparently Poland met the modest targets she set for herself, while Hungary, with higher targets, failed to reach them. Bulgaria overfulfilled her plan. In Czechoslovakia, Poland, and Hungary the annual average rate of dwelling

[52] See also Table 101, p. 373, in the Appendix to this chapter.

[53] The most important Polish cement factories are situated in Silesia and in the Malopolska Uplan. Among the newly built plants are Wierzbica in the Kielce region and Rejowiec II in the province of Lublin. The Wierzbica apparently has been built with Soviet equipment. See "Expansion of Poland's Cement Industry," in *Polish Foreign Trade,* No. 15 (1953), pp. 5–6; "The Quality of Polish Cement Improves from Year to Year," *ibid.*, No. 10 (March–April 1952), p. 50; and J. Wasowicz, *Outline of Economic Geography, op. cit.*, pp. 39–40.

[54] The largest cement works constructed are those of Hejőcsaba, near Miskolc. The most important cement factory of the country in construction during the first quinquennium is located at Vác at the northern end of the Danube River. No indications are given for the origins of machinery. Cf. "The Hungarian Building Materials Industry," *HB,* No. 143 (June 1, 1953), p. 16.

[55] The new plants are located at Medgidia, on the site of the abandoned Danube-Black Sea Canal project, and at Bicaz. The automatic cement factory at Medgidia is of Soviet make. AIB, III, 34 (September 13, 1952).

[56] See Table 102, p. 374, in the Appendix to this chapter.

space built, related to total population, during the first long-term plans, varied between 80 and 110 square meters (or the equivalent of about 2–3 dwellings) per 1,000 inhabitants. In Yugoslavia, the rate of private building was probably similar; in Romania it was smaller, less than 1 dwelling per 1,000 inhabitants, and in Bulgaria somewhat larger, over 4 dwellings per 1,000. Most of the new dwellings, built

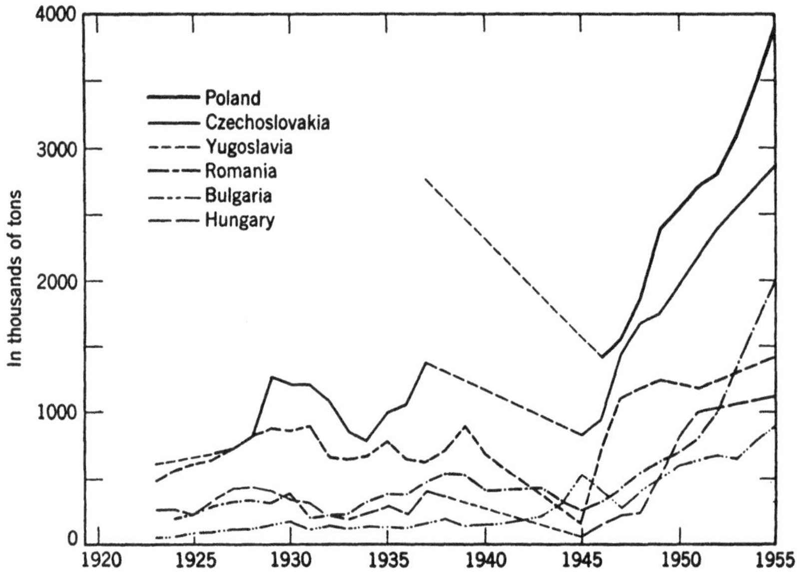

CHART 15. CEMENT PRODUCTION, 1920–55

in towns related to key projects, were allocated to industrial workers, with constructions in the capital cities comparatively limited. Even so, in certain countries the overcrowding was more serious in the new centers than in the already heavily congested capitals. In the countryside, private construction by peasants, using essentially local raw materials, did not ordinarily need official allocations of building materials.[57]

SOME CONSUMERS' GOODS

No other information on the area is so difficult to analyze as that pertaining to the production of consumers' goods and their availability in the home market. First, the data on the changes in produc-

[57] See *ESE in 1954, op. cit.*, pp. 53–54.

TABLE 88. YEARLY RATES OF HOUSING CONSTRUCTION DURING THE FIRST LONG-TERM PLANS

Yearly average	Unit	Czechoslovakia, 1949–53	Poland, 1950–55	Hungary, 1950–54	Romania, 1950–55	Bulgaria, 1949–53	Yugoslavia, 1953
Plan	Thous. in.[2]	1,940	2,008	1,760	560	260	[c]
Actual		1,416	2,088 [a]	880	353 [a]	1,373 [b]	1,640
Plan	Sq. meters per 1,000 inhabitants	152	75	183	33	35	[c]
Actual		111	82	92	20	180	96

[a] 1950–54.
[b] 1949–52.
[c] Not available.

Sources: ESE in 1954, op. cit., p. 53 and *Quarterly Bulletin of Housing and Building Statistics for Europe*, Vol. III, No. 2, UN, ECE, Geneva, October 1955, pp. 104–106. For Bulgaria: also, *Bulgaria Today*, Vol. V, No. 18, September 1955, p. 4.

tive capacity are scant. Second, the changes in output of such basic products as cotton fabrics are not indicative of the state of supply in the domestic market, since some of these industries are traditionally exporting industries; and, moreover, industries which previously produced for the home market have had to export in order to pay for some of the cotton imported. Third, since a substantial proportion of the consumers' goods available in the domestic market is manufactured from local materials, no complete tabulation on this type of output is furnished.

Before the war the important centers of Czechoslovakia (especially northern Bohemia and Brno in Moravia), Poland (Łódź—cotton; Bielsko—wool; Żyrardów—linen), and Hungary (Budapest, Győr, Miskolc) not only supplied domestic needs but also played an important role as exporters. Hungary was, however, very dependent on imports of raw materials. The industries of Romania (mainly Buhuşi, Braşov, and Bucharest) and Yugoslavia (centers of Serbia and Croatia) supplied most of the needs of the domestic market, the demand of higher quality textile goods being met by imports. The Bulgarian textile centers (Gabrovo and Sofia) supplied part of the local needs but never succeeded in meeting foreign competition.

The extensive war damage, especially to the Polish textile industry, was repaired by 1948–49. Poland was able to re-enter foreign markets.[58] In the area as a whole the additions to plant capacities seem to have

[58] See, for instance, *Polish Foreign Trade*, September–October 1952, p. 49, and March–April 1952, p. 43; also B. Puczyński: *Geografia Gospodarcza Polski* (Economic Geography of Poland), Nakładem Państwowego Wydawnictwa Naukowego (State Scientific Publishing House), Warsaw, 1953, p. 135.

been modest for the period considered. The data available, for instance, for cotton spindles in 1951, as compared to 1938, point toward a decrease in the capacity available in Czechoslovakia and Poland; data for 1952 indicate increases in Romania, Hungary, Bulgaria, and Yugoslavia.[59] The most significant changes in the location of industry are those which occurred in Czechoslovakia, the new funds invested in textiles being earmarked for Slovakia, where some new plants have been constructed,[60] while various old plants were closed in the Czech lands and the equipment available was concentrated in fewer plants.[61]

The data available on the output of cotton goods, woolen fabrics, and leather footwear have been assembled in the Appendix (see Table 103, p. 375). The changes in output are summarized in Table 89. In 1948 the output of cotton goods was substantially below prewar levels in Romania; it had not changed in Hungary; it had increased in the other countries. However, a comparison of the data available for fabrics in meters and in tons reveals that in Poland and in Romania, for instance, the increases in output measured in meters were accompanied by a decrease in the weight of the fabrics. By 1953 the prewar level had been surpassed in the region as a whole. The largest increase, registered in Bulgaria, was due not only to the increases in capacity indicated above but also to the full utilization of the capacity available, much of which had been idle in the base year. The woolen fabric output presents basically the same trends, but with some variations. In 1948, excepting Ro-

[59] Cf. the data presented in *ESE Since the War, op. cit.*, Table 25, "World Capacity for Cotton Textile Production," p. 270, and *Processes and Problems of Industrialization in Under-Developed Countries*, UN, Dept. of Economic and Social Affairs, New York, 1955, p. 145.

[60] See, for instance, Dorothy W. Douglas, *Transitional Economic Systems: the Polish-Czech Example*, Routledge and Kegan Paul, London, 1953, p. 99.

[61] The first Czechoslovak plan was built on the premise that a great opportunity was opening for the products of heavy industry and that there was no reason whatsoever to keep the consumers' goods industries in their previously held foremost position. The textile industry was to lose its prewar position since, as Gottwald stated,

> That place corresponded more to the needs of the Austro-Hungarian monarchy, where our textile industry had a large stable market, than to the needs of to-day. It is known that already before the Second World War we had to face some difficulties when our textile industry, which had originally been built up as an industry producing principally for the home market, was to become our main export industry. [See *Long-Term Planning in Czechoslovakia*, a speech by Prime Minister Gottwald at the Extraordinary Meeting of the Central Planning Commission on Oct. 10, 1947, Czechoslovak Ministry of Information, Prague, October 1947, pp. 7–8, quoted by D. W. Douglas, *ibid.*, p. 107.]

TABLE 89. INCREASES AND DECREASES IN CONSUMERS' GOODS OUTPUT, 1948 TO 1955 [a]

(1938 = 100)

Country	Cotton [b]			Wool [b]			Footwear		
	1948	1953	1955	1948	1953	1955	1948	1953	1955
Czechoslovakia	7	28	[c]	38	66	[c]	17	31	14
Poland	19	73	96	11	73	100	[c]	[c]	[c]
Hungary	[d]	49	66	−28	−18 [e]	18	5	140	297
Romania	−33	89	135	−8	135	152	[c]	[c]	[c]
Bulgaria	76	250	308	7	76	[c]	[c]	[c]	[c]
Yugoslavia	45	16	57	131	39	108	96	−4	58

[a] Cotton goods, woolen fabrics, leather footwear.
[b] Underlying data for Czechoslovakia in tons; for all the others, in meters. Cf. Appendix, Table 103, p. 375.
[c] Not available.
[d] Nil.
[e] 1952.

mania and Hungary, all the countries of the area were producing more than before the war. By 1953, all except Hungary surpassed their prewar output. In 1955 Hungary, in her turn, surpassed that level; the increases in the area ranged from 30 to 150 per cent over prewar output.

By and large, the outputs of both cotton and woolen goods range substantially below those of the key industries, in line with the low priority assigned to the light industries during the first development plans.

The data available indicate a significant increase in the production of leather footwear since the war in all the countries except Czechoslovakia and Yugoslavia. The explanation for this increase may lie in the reorganization of the dispersed craftsmen's shops and the introduction of more advanced methods, although, as already noted in another context, the mere pooling of craftsmen's shops does not create a modern industry. It is interesting to note that Czechoslovakia, who had long had a highly developed shoe industry, hardly increased her output in 1955 and has relatively modest targets for 1960.[62]

The stress on consumers' goods both in the Soviet Union and in the area as a whole at the close of 1953 opened new prospects for the consumers' goods industries, especially textiles, of the exporting coun-

[62] See Table 103, p. 375, in Appendix to this chapter.

tries. However, the conversion of these economies from heavy to light industries proved to be costly and difficult. The new policy defined at the start of 1955 restored high priority to heavy industry and closed the promising prospects opened earlier for the modernization and substantial increase of the light industries of the area.

Industrial Growth and Shifts in Basic Ratios

Over-all industrial output expanded sharply during the period considered, as can clearly be inferred from the preceding data concerning key industrial outputs. However, the measurement of the *over-all* performance of industry remains extremely uncertain. As already stated, the official index numbers of industrial production are indices of the *gross* value of output and are subject to serious methodological deficiencies.[63] Even these indices are often revised and are not quite consistent from period to period. For a time it seemed to be common practice to release optimistic index numbers at the completion of each phase of a plan and to subsequently revise these same indices downwards so that the new performance appeared enhanced. Sometimes the reverse has happened, and indices released at an earlier date have been revised upwards. As a result the high yearly rates of growth at the beginning of the plan have been lowered and brought in line with the smaller rates at the end of the plan. Whatever the reason for these revisions, poor methodology and dubious statistical practices have conspired to make it hazardous to manipulate these indices.[64] They can be considered only as *broadly indicative* of the general trends in output. According to these indices, by 1955, Yugoslavia, Czechoslovakia, and Romania increased their industrial output by 2 to 3 times the prewar level, Hungary, Poland, and Bulgaria by over 3, 4, and 5 times, respectively. The exceptionally high Bulgarian and Polish index numbers are undoubtedly attributable to substantial changes in the structure of output and to high "priced-in" products as the plan unfolded.

[63] See introductory note to Section III, pp. 272–274.

[64] Here are some examples illustrating these points. For the base year preceding the first long-term plans (1948 for Czechoslovakia and Bulgaria, 1949 for the others) the following indices of gross industrial output have been made available: C: 107 and 111; P: 157, 167, or 177; H: 139 and 153, R: 97 and 117; B: 170 and 184. The same holds true for the indices of gross agricultural output (e.g., for Bulgaria the indices 98.3 and 115 for 1948, etc.). In order to make the indices as consistent as possible we have tried to derive the indices for the earlier years from the data released in 1953–55. See Appendix, Table 104, p. 376.

The actual rate of growth in the gross value of industrial output tended to decline yearly during the first long-term plans and fell, on the average, below the targets set. This trend is discernible for both producers' and consumers' goods.[65] The high rates of 1949–50 were due in part to employment of idle resources, human and material, as well as to a reallocation of the resources already in use (as from one type of capital formation to another).[66] Both processes can be considered as having reached their limits by 1950. After this date it became more and more difficult to expand output at the same rates[67] even though there was considerable new capital construction, as the stepped-up production of steel machinery and the intense activity in the building industry clearly indicate.

Yugoslavia deserves some specific comments. The Yugoslav indices (which, it should be noted, expressly exclude the armament industry) are indicative both of the loss in impetus after 1949–50 and of the recovery in 1953 and after.

Up to 1948–49 Yugoslavia, who first benefited from particularly favorable conditions such as UNRRA aid and reparations, was in a position rapidly to increase her gross industrial output. Subsequently, having lost her import sources of coal and coke, pig iron and steel, oil, and certain machinery, and being compelled to make radical changes in plans and investments, Yugoslavia suffered a period of imbalance in the economy as a whole, and her gross industrial output not only ceased to advance but declined in certain years. The Yugoslavs started to "underutilize" the industrial capacity available while continuing to import machinery to complete various constructions.[68]

[65] Cf. Tables 104 and 105, pp. 376 and 377, in the Appendix to this chapter.

[66] Although any utilization of previously unused resources can bring about an increase in the total output (since the productivity of these resources was previously zero), there is a limit to the increase which can be brought about by reallocation of resources already in use. It is evident that shifts from one sector to another and a reallocation of resources might at a certain point not only not bring about any increases but even cause a decrease in total output if the marginal efficiency of the resources shifted was higher in their previous utilization.

[67] It should be noted that the official yearly increase of the gross value of Soviet industrial output, whose upward bias is well known, has been indicated as being, from 1928 to 1932, of the order of 22 per cent, 1933–37 of 17.1 per cent, 1938–40 of 13 per cent, and, only after readjustments and reconstruction after the war, again around 20 per cent for the period 1946–50. Cf. B. Puczyński, *Geografia Gospodarcza Polski, op. cit.*, p. 79.

[68] Yugoslavia had to curtail the imports of certain raw materials while continuing the import of machinery. The result was a "planned underutilization" of the

It is an open question whether this situation was brought about by circumstances or simply by poor planning.[69]

For the area as a whole, given the nature of the data available, the best measurement of the fixed investment can be obtained from the relation of gross investment (including expenditure on replacements but not on repairs) to the national income as defined in Eastern Europe and Russia, that is, as net material product.[70] According to the official data the average rates of growth of national income fell, for all the countries except Czechoslovakia and Bulgaria, below the plans, while the average rate of growth of the gross fixed investment was above that set by the plans. Gross fixed investment oscillated around 25 per cent of national income, four to five times higher than during the prewar period. The high level of investment was accompanied by an equally high allocation of resources for defense purposes. The two combined led to a very sharp curtailment of consumption. The government share not otherwise accounted for represented in 1952–53 from 14 to 18 per cent of the national income in Czechoslovakia, 17

industrial capacity available:

. . . According to the provisions of the social-economic plan for 1953, the capacities of industry and mining will be utilized by almost 70%. The limits of capacity utilization are established by the amount of raw materials industry can be supplied with from domestic and foreign sources. Utilization of capacity in the processing industries is on the average below 60% and for some plants even falls to 40%. About 90% of the capacities of the basic industries will be utilized; with mining at 100% and those basic industries depending on raw materials, especially imported ones, at 90%. . . . The underutilization of capacities resulting from the unfavourable relationship between the basic and the processing industries, and the deficit in the balance of payments can, as the plan provides, be solved in several years. The economic plan for 1953 has made this its aim by putting the emphasis on completion of the key basic capital construction that has begun. This will also augment the utilization of industrial capacities in 1953. . . . [Cf. "1953 Economic Prospects," in *Review of International Affairs,* IV, 3 (Feb. 1, 1953), p. 19.]

69 *ESE in 1953,* UN, ECE, Geneva, 1954, notes that according to official statements sufficient capacity has been built by Yugoslavia in 1952 to produce the target outputs set for the end of 1951. However, the *Survey* notes that this does not prove that the plan to start with was realistic, since "there is no way of knowing whether, if things had been different, sufficient material would have been available for the balance of demands such as to utilize this capacity." This leads the *Survey* to conclude that those who attributed at the time the greater part of Yugoslavia's difficulties to the change in the political climate and those who insisted on the Yugoslavs' own failures in planning were thus both right. *Ibid.,* p. 113.

70 The data on the planned average yearly rates of increase in the national income are given above, in Chapter 8, Table 81, p. 301. A short discussion of the conceptual problems involved in the *net material product* (national income) in Eastern Europe, the actual figures on income, and its structure are to be found below, in Chapter 12, pp. 469–471 and 477–479.

per cent in Hungary, and as much as 20 to 24 per cent in Yugoslavia; but in Yugoslavia from 4 to 5 per cent was covered from other than domestic sources. Roughly, the share of consumption has thus represented some 60 per cent or less of the net physical product over the period considered. In the reparations-paying countries the delivery of reparations implied a reduction in either investment or consumption.

Given the pattern of investment, the ratio between producers' goods and consumers' goods in the gross value of industrial output shifted constantly in favor of the first, as Table 90 indicates. In or around

TABLE 90. RATIOS OF PRODUCERS' GOODS TO CONSUMERS' GOODS IN GROSS VALUE OF INDUSTRIAL OUTPUT

	1937–39	1948	1953
Czechoslovakia	44	56	62
Poland	47	54	62
Hungary	39	48	58
Bulgaria	23	34	39
Yugoslavia	43	[a]	[a]

[a] Not available.

Sources:

C: 1938: A. Kuibyshev, in *VT*, No. 3, 1952, p. 62; 1948 and 1953: V. Široký, in *FLP*, Sept. 18, 1953.

P: 1937 and 1948: *L'Économie polonaise au seuil de plan de six ans* (Polish Economy on the Threshold of the Six-Year Plan), Notes et études documentaires (Notes and Documentary Studies), No. 1070, Documentation Française (French Documentation), Paris 1949, p. 3; 1953: computed from B. Bierut in *FLP*, Mar. 19, 1954.

H: 1938 and 1949: *Today and Yesterday*, *op. cit.*, p. 9; 1952: *ESE in 1953*, *op. cit.*, p. 61; for 1953, on the basis of the first half-year, this percentage is estimated at 65.

B: All years: V. Chervenkov, in *FLP*, Mar. 5, 1954. The percentage included timber industries and fishing. Excluding these, the percentage would rise in 1952 to 44.

Y: *Law on the Five Year Plan*, *op. cit.*, which gives the 1939 figure; an increase scheduled in producers' goods to 57 in 1951.

1953 the relative share of the producers' goods industry increased as follows: up to 40 per cent of the gross value of industrial output in Bulgaria (compared to 23 per cent prewar and 34 per cent in 1948); up to 58 per cent in Hungary (from a level of 40 per cent prewar and 48 per cent in 1948); up to 62 per cent in Czechoslovakia and Poland (compared to 44–47 per cent prewar and 54–56 per cent in 1948). It should be noted that in Soviet Russia the relative share of producers' goods industries was said to represent 73 per cent in 1952–53 (as against 61 per cent in 1940, 58 per cent in 1937, and 34 per cent in 1924–25).

Compared to the planned capital-output ratios for the period considered, those actually achieved appear to have been on the average somewhat lower for Czechoslovakia and Romania but higher for all the others (compare Table 82, p. 302, to Table 91). In other words, investments were larger than planned and/or income increases were smaller than forecast. However, as already noted, the analysis of these ratios is subject to numerous qualifications.[71]

TABLE 91. ACTUAL CAPITAL-OUTPUT RATIOS DURING THE FIRST LONG-TERM PLANS

(billions of national currencies) [a]

	Czechoslovakia	Poland	Hungary	Romania	Bulgaria
Increase in Investment [b] (ΔC)	338.0	170.8	67.4	1,260.0	400.0
Increase in Output [c] (ΔO)	125.0	62.0	19.5	640.0 [d]	160.0
Ratios $\frac{\Delta C}{\Delta O}$	2.6	2.7	3.4	1.9 [d]	2.5

[a] C: Pre-1953 Kčs, 1948 prices; P: 1950 prices; H: 1949 prices; R: pre-1952 lei, 1950 prices; B: pre-1952 leva, 1948 prices.

[b] Total investment during the plan period.

[c] Increase in last plan year over preplan of the net material product excluding "non-productive" services.

[d] Estimated.

Source: ESE in 1955, op. cit., pp. 236, 239, 241, 243 and 245.

Detailed examination of the balance sheet of the reconstruction and the first development plans demonstrates that: (*a*) the targets set for the key industrial products, such as iron, steel, and electricity, have not always been met, notwithstanding the increasing amount of resources allocated to these purposes; (*b*) the outputs obtained have not corresponded to the outputs scheduled, in many fields. The claims of fulfillment and "overfulfillment" of the plans in terms of gross value of outputs thus mask the fact that the economy does not reach the specific targets set by the planners and that *the product mix obtained at the end of any plan period does not bear a close resemblance to the product mix scheduled.* Notwithstanding wide controls, large

[71] See above, Chapter 8, note 27, pp. 301–302.

enforcement powers concentrated in the state, and complete centralization of investment means, targets and results diverge substantially. While we cannot discard the impact of such factors as poor planning or the influence of various "circumstantial" factors (such as the ones which we will discuss immediately in relation to the new course), the experience of these six countries shows that centralized planning with all its controls cannot actually "push" the economy on the exact positions scheduled, even when the results are officially proclaimed as "overfulfilled."

Let us add also that an inseparable part of the picture of the expanding industrial output in Eastern Europe was the deterioration of quality brought about by the human reaction to the ruthless pressures of the system. There have been complaints in all the countries about the poor quality of the basic materials (such as coal mined and pig iron and steel produced) and constant recrimination against increased waste of social property,[72] widespread theft, and depletion of resources.[73] Innumerable decrees have imposed severe sentences[74] for such "offenses," but they have continued to grow and multiply.

[72] Apparently, this occurs from top to bottom of the social pyramid. Thus, Ernő Gerő writes concerning Hungary:

> We have to take stern action against those who put their hands into the pocket of the state as if it were their own. It was found, for instance, that the so-called "miscellaneous expenses" of the enterprises considerably increased in comparison with the previous year. . . . This can be explained by the fact that they concealed under "miscellaneous expenses," which are less controlled, other superfluous, exaggerated, unnecessary and unauthorized expenses. All this, however, shows only a minor part of that waste and squandering of State funds, of irresponsible management which still can be found to a fairly broad extent in our country. [Ernő Gerő, "The Position of the Hungarian National Economy in 1952 and the Tasks in Its Development," publ. by *HB*, Budapest, 1952, pp. 30–31.]

[73] The Yugoslavs have constantly pointed out these deteriorations and depletions in the other East European countries, which they attributed to the fact that "the workers do not regard as their own the social property but as the wealth appropriated by a caste of rulers for their own preservation." (Cf. "Four New Decrees in Poland," *Review of International Affairs*, IV, 11 (June 1, 1953). However, one of the most striking pictures of waste and squandering "with careless and often ruthless attitudes toward social property" is given by Tito himself about Yugoslavia. Thus, he says,

> One can often see various industrial and agricultural machinery and tools lying in the rain and snow, exposed to rust and decay, while we are short of them and are making great efforts to obtain foreign currency in order to import them or manufacture them ourselves. Furthermore, transport facilities, lorries and passenger cars, and fuel are used to a large extent without need every day. We can see empty lorries and passenger cars rushing to and fro. I am convinced that often they do so without any need. . . . [See Marshal Tito, *For Independence and Equality*, Jugoslovenska Knjiga (Yugoslav Book), Belgrade, 1950, pp. 58–59.]

[74] Poland has introduced the innovation of punishing producers of poor-quality

The Lag in Agriculture: Grains, Livestock

During the first long-term plan, agriculture developed, as already noted, under the following conditions: state discrimination in favor of the socialist sector, heavy taxation on the upper layers of private holdings, compulsory collectivization, and, generally, low priority in investment as compared to all the other sectors of the economy.

According to the plans of reconstruction and development, the areas sown in grain were to be reduced progressively, this reduction to be compensated for by larger yields obtained by increased use of fertilizer and mechanization. The land removed from grain cultivation was to provide an increase of land for industrial crops and to enlarge the "fodder" base in order to sustain an increased livestock population. On almost all counts, and in every country, the results have been very different from those expected, with the exception, perhaps, of the reduction in the area sown. The "unknown variable," the weather, dealt heavy blows to output in certain years (mainly 1947, 1950, and 1952).

Up to 1948 the problem of reducing the fallow land was closely related to the general readjustments of the postwar period.[75] After 1949 the land left fallow became a political problem directly related to the policy of restricting and dislodging the richer strata of the peasantry.[76] It affected more and more adversely the objectives set by the plan. Furthermore, the reduction of the sown area was not compensated for by increases in yields, which for the period from 1948 to

goods for home consumption by prison terms up to five years, and producers of poor-quality goods earmarked for export by terms up to ten years. The Yugoslav publication quoted in note 73 notes that "there is no known instance in the legislation of a sovereign country providing for two measures and two different sentences for one offense." The *Review of International Affairs* adds that the explanation of this fact is that most of Poland's exports are sent to the Soviet Union.

[75] In a country like Poland, where the problems of the expulsion of the Germans and the colonization of the western regions were of great magnitude, the surface left fallow in 1946 was around 6 million hectares. This surface was reduced to 2.5 million hectares in 1947 and 1.5 million in 1948, i.e., at that later date, 9 per cent of the total surface of arable land. Cf. "L'Économie polonaise au seuil du plan de six ans," *op. cit.*, p. 4. In the other countries the question of fallow land was also very significant; thus for instance in Romania in 1947, fallow land represented 564,000 hectares or close to 6 per cent of the arable land of the country. (Cf. *CS*, No. 19, p. 24.)

[76] See above, Chapter 7, p. 251, the typical statement of the then Hungarian Premier, Imre Nagy.

1952 were, by and large, *below* the prewar averages for all types of grains and far from the targets set for 1953–55 (see Table 92).

The poor crops of wheat and corn (the latter a staple food in most of the Balkan villages) made it next to impossible to sustain the planned level of supplies in either the towns or the villages; the better results achieved in potato crops did little to relieve a critical situation. The output of bread-grains in 1951–52 was some 80 to 90 per cent of the prewar output, and the output of coarse grain a little higher. In 1955 the agricultural outlook had not changed substantially. Czechoslovakia and Hungary increased their coarse-grain output by 12 to 15 per cent, but produced only 80 to 90 per cent of their prewar bread-grain output. Poland increased her bread-grain but failed to increase her coarse-grain production. Romania claimed a sudden high increase in her total grain output of more than 51 per cent over prewar, but it is rather difficult to account for this increase given the very low levels up to 1955. Bulgaria increased both her bread-grain and her coarse-grain by 12 and 52 per cent, respectively. No significant changes were reported for Yugoslavia. Thus, by and large, the area as a whole produced an amount of grain roughly equal to that of prewar times (see Table 93).

A computation of the per capita output of bread-grain, coarse-grain, and potatoes for 1948 and 1953 [77] reveals that the per capita supply was generally lower than before the war in all the countries, except for Poland, where it was slightly higher. Some increases over prewar outputs can also be noted for the other countries but only for some outputs (e.g., bread-grain for Bulgaria, coarse grain for Czechoslovakia, potatoes for Romania). While the comparison with the 1934–38 period in terms of output gives little indication of the problem of domestic supply, since much of the grain available was exported before the war, it should be noted that the postwar period created new needs through the agrarian reform and increasing urbanization, and that these needs developed coincidentally with the falling off of the per capita output.

The problem of increasing output by applying "modern techniques" was aggravated by lack of investment, the very poor state of the equipment available, and the reluctance of the peasants to join the cooperatives, even when the latter were endowed with state-owned land. (This explains why in every country the state had at its disposal large tracts of land often left fallow.) In Czechoslovakia, the most advanced

[77] See Table 107, p. 379, in the Appendix to this chapter.

TABLE 92. AVERAGE YIELDS, SELECTED PERIODS

(quintals per hectare)

	Wheat				Corn			
Country	1934–38	1948	1948–52	1953–55	1934–38	1948	1948–52	1953–55
Czechoslovakia	17.2	16.1	18.6	19.6	21.1	20.9	21.4	24.0
Poland	14.6	11.7	12.2	17.0	14.3	[a]	[a]	[a]
Hungary	13.7	11.6	13.1	16.0	19.9	21.5	19.3	23.0
Romania	10.3	7.8 [d]	[a]	12.5	10.4	12.3 [d]	[a]	14.0
Bulgaria	12.5	7.2 [d]	[a]	15.0	11.3	10.3 [d]	[a]	[a]
Yugoslavia	11.4	14.1 [b]	12.0	[a]	17.6	16.1 [b]	13.3	[a]

	Potatoes				Sugar-Beets			
	1934–38	1948	1948–52	1953–55	1934–38	1948	1948–52	1953–55
Czechoslovakia	135	119	127	152	286	230 [b]	246	235
Poland	138	108	124	150	265	189	188	240
Hungary	73	66 [b]	64	87	204	[a]	204 [c]	209
Romania	89	[a]	[a]	[a]	153 [e]	[a]	[a]	177
Bulgaria	61	[a]	[a]	[a]	164	117 [be]	[a]	[a]
Yugoslavia	57	88 [b]	73	[a]	188	122 [b]	140	[a]

[a] Not available. [b] 1949. [c] 1948–53. [d] 1947. [e] Estimate.

Sources: 1934–38, 1948–52: *ESE Since the War*, *op. cit.*, p. 272 (also for P, *Wieś w Liczbach*, 3rd ed., *op. cit.*, p. 166), and "Podaci o poslератnom privrednom razvitku SSSR i zemalja Istočne Evrope" (Data on the Postwar Economic Development of the USSR and of the East European Countries), *Dokumentacioni Bilten*, Institut za Medunarodnu Politiku i Privredu (Bulletin of Documentation, Institute for International Politics and Economics), No. 8–9, 1954, *passim*; 1947–48: *Rocznik Statystyczny 1949*, *op. cit.*, and *FAOY*, *1949*, *I. Production*, *op. cit.*. 1953–55: Plans.

TABLE 93. INDICES OF PRODUCTION OF MAJOR CROPS, SELECTED YEARS

(1934–38 = 100)

	Bread-Grain			Coarse Grain			Potatoes			Sugar-Beets		
	1948	1953	1955	1948	1953	1955	1948	1953	1955	1948	1953	1955
Czechoslovakia	81.8	83.0	81.1	97.8	107.9	112.0	55.2	71.7	[a]	74.5	94.7	[a]
Poland	89.8	76.0	108.8	75.3	79.0	82.9	70.3	114.5	98.6	70.8	162.8	172.0
Hungary	80.8	94.1	92.4	97.1	105.3	115.9	103.2	93.8	98.6	123.0	265.0	220.0
Romania	90.4	75.7 [b]	151.4 [b]	104.3	[b]	[b]	87.8	185.3	[a]	203.5	326.6	502.5
Bulgaria	99.0	132.3	112.0	81.5	105.9	151.9	89.2	[a]	[a]	178.1	344.1	349.3
Yugoslavia	104.2	105.6	101.1	87.7	85.4	84.1	100.0	140.9	153.9	294.8	298.0	271.7

[a] Not available.

[b] All grain included under bread-grain.

Sources: For underlying data, see Table 106, p. 378, in Appendix to this chapter.

country of the region, agriculture was only 26 per cent mechanized in 1951 and 30 per cent in 1952. More specifically, plowing had been mechanized up to 20 per cent, sowing 30 per cent, and the tending of crops as little as 0.08 per cent. The Czechoslovak Premier, Široký, stated:

> Especially here in Czechoslovakia we had all the prerequisites for ensuring that socialist industry would effectively contribute to the development of agricultural production both in the state farms and in the co-operatives and in the private sector. However, the aid on the part of the state and socialist industry was and remains inadequate.[78]

Judging by the performance of the most advanced country of the region, certain claims of rapid mechanization of other East European countries have to be taken with much skepticism. Thus, for instance, the Bulgarians claim "over-all mechanization" in agriculture in 1952 of 34.7 per cent.[79] Actually, the available figures on the surface plowed with tractors from 1947 to 1949 reveal that the surface so plowed was about 5.1 per cent (1947), 6.4 per cent (1948), and 8.3 per cent (1949) of the arable area of the country. The claimed rapid increase from that level to 1955 seems rather difficult to account for.[80] As already stated, although these changes are by no means negligible,[81] it has long been pointed out that, even if the initially scheduled transfers of tractors to agriculture were realized at the foreseen pace, "this . . . will still leave agricultural mechanization in Eastern Europe far behind Western standards." [82]

The switching from food and feed crops to industrial crops has come up against the atomized character of private property in the countryside and the necessity for the peasantry to stick to consumers' crops for its own subsistence. By 1953–54, the bureaucratic extension of industrial crops to regions unsuitable for their cultivation has brought about situations in which the planned sown acreage has been realized but the expected crop has not been obtained. However, by

[78] Viliam Široký, "For Steady Advance of National Economy, for Raising Well-Being of the People of Czechoslovakia," in *FLP*, Sept. 18, 1953.

[79] V. Chervenkov, in *FLP*, Sept. 11, 1953.

[80] See Chapter 7, p. 262.

[81] *Ibid.*, Table 69, p. 262.

[82] *European Tractor Industry in the Setting of the World Market*, UN, ECE, Geneva, 1952, p. 112.

and large, in all the area some successes have been achieved in this respect.

Livestock totals per thousand inhabitants remained, up to 1953, generally below prewar levels except for pigs and sheep. The head of *cattle* per thousand inhabitants remained at the prewar level in Poland, Hungary, and Bulgaria, and surpassed that level in Czechoslovakia, Romania, and Yugoslavia. However, the increases were obtained at the cost of decreases in quality and productivity. As the Czechoslovak Premier, Široký, noted:

> In the sphere of animal husbandry we must proceed from the fact that of late the head of cattle has increased without a corresponding extension of the fodder base. Consequently, the head of cattle has grown to the detriment of the quality of the stock and its productivity. Without a serious extension of the fodder base it will be impossible to ensure improvement in the productivity of the stock which, from the point of view of supplying the working people with high-grade meat and other high-grade products of animal husbandry, is a most urgent matter.[83]

In fact, a complexity of causes, such as inadequate methods of livestock husbandry, fodder shortages, failure to cultivate sown grass on a large scale, low grass output per hectare and retarded hay harvesting, causing substantial losses in forage and diminution of its nutritive value, sharply diminished both the quality and the output of livestock.[84]

The inadequate methods of livestock husbandry are to be attributed generally to the low priority of investment in agriculture, and in particular to the fact that the small peasant homesteads were compelled to manage their livestock and cultivate land under the most primitive conditions.[85] The low priority of investment resulted in lagging construction of shelters for animals and lack of training and employment of an adequate number of agricultural specialists and

[83] V. Široký, article cited in note 78.

[84] *SC*, Jan. 5, 1954.

[85] Although much reliance was placed on the peasant and on his primitive methods of livestock breeding as a primary source of meat, milk, wool, etc., supplies, officially much was attributed to "new Soviet zootechnical methods." Thus, for instance, an *Agerpress* article on the improvement of livestock claimed the following achievements:

> By the Soviet Ivanov method of sheep crossing, a new variety was obtained much more productive of wool and meat. . . . As a result of adopted Soviet methods, fecundity of sheep was raised from 93 to 97 . . . the birthrate of foals was raised from 68 to 77.4 per hundred mares . . . etc. [*AIB*, III, 35, Sept. 20, 1952.]

cadres in the "socialist sectors." The lack of credits for the peasant and the fact that he retained only the residual share of his output left after the state levies combined to make it impossible for him to insure "unbroken fodder supplies" for livestock breeding. Without such supplies the state of livestock deteriorates and its productivity is imperiled in the years of poor weather,[86] for, when the peasantry lives on the margin of subsistence and has no possibility of falling back on reserves or on loans, each variation in crops which brings about a fall in the production of concentrates, especially corn, automatically causes a decline in the quantity of meat and lard and imperils the supply of the towns. Lack of incentive for private livestock breeding for the market, upon which we have previously dwelt,[87] also contributed to lowering production.

In the early postwar period and up to 1948 certain countries (Poland, for instance), where the number of horses had fallen to half the prewar total (cf. Table 108 in the Appendix), imported horses as draft animals. During the development period mechanization was supposed to compensate for a slow rate in the increases in draft animals, but the scattered evidence available indicates that the lack of horses in the private sector and the lack of machinery and the prohibitive cost of utilization of the machinery of the Machine and Tractor Stations compelled the poor peasants to resort to their cattle as draft animals, with a resultant further reduction of the output of milk and high-grade meat. The following Bulgarian statement on this aspect of the situation, referring to cooperatives which, as is known, have a privileged position as compared to the private homesteads and have access to the machinery of MTS, is illuminating:

> In 1952, the average productivity of a TKZS (agricultural producers' cooperative) milk cow was 583 liters of milk, while up to October 1953 the average was only 555 liters. The low livestock productivity

[86] "The principal cause of the low yields in livestock breeding lies in the failure to ensure unbroken fodder supplies. In years of unfavorable weather the state of livestock deteriorates and its productivity declines." *SN*, Dec. 24, 1953.

[87] Before the 1953 revisions it was customary to recognize the role of the drought in the reduction of meat supplies to the towns; however, it was denied that lack of incentive also played an important role in this sense and any fall in supply was usually attributed to "the activities of the class enemies." Thus, for instance, the Polish *Trybuna Ludu* wrote on Feb. 16, 1952:

> A certain slow-up in raising of domestic animals took place in 1951, and the number of pigs even decreased slightly. The reason for this was to be found not only in the insufficient reserves of fodder, aggravated by the drought of 1951, but also in the weakening of the interest of peasants in raising domestic animals, which was caused, among other things, by the activities of the class enemy.

is due to faulty and inadequate feeding, and to the general lack of care given animals. *The low milk productivity in TKZS is due to the fact that 45 per cent of the animals are still used for work.*[88]

After the 1953 crisis and the launching of an "all-out effort for increase of the agricultural output" there was no further pretense either that mechanization had already replaced draft animals or that it would eventually replace them. It was claimed instead that *both* mechanization and an increase in horse breeding were the latest signs of progress. Thus the Hungarian Minister of Agriculture and member of the Hungarian Political Bureau of the Communist Party, Andras Hegedűs, wrote:

> With a view to developing horse breeding it is necessary first of all to do away with the incorrect conception that mechanised agriculture lessens the significance of horse breeding and will result in a big reduction in the number of horses.
>
> Experience shows that more intensive agriculture, even given large-scale mechanisation, not only does not lessen the significance of horse breeding, but even makes for a definite increase in the number of horses.[89]

As can be seen from Table 108 in the Appendix, the actual number of horses was, in 1955, far below the prewar levels.

To summarize, there were certainly substantial changes in the composition of agricultural output during the reconstruction period and during the first long-term plans as compared to prewar. Grain acreage and output generally declined, whereas those of industrial crops rose as a result of the efforts to solve the problem of the domestic supply of fibers, oil, and sugar. The share of livestock in the total volume of agricultural output increased. However, livestock remained below the needs of the towns, and its quality, as noted, sharply deteriorated.

Many of the changes did not correspond to those planned. The decrease in grain acreage was not accompanied by remarkable increases in yields except in *certain* state or cooperative undertakings;[90]

[88] *Zemedelsko Zname*, Dec. 2, 1953. (Italics supplied.)

[89] Cf. "Tasks of Raising Agricultural Production in Hungary," in *FLP*, Jan. 8, 1954.

[90] According to Andras Hegedűs, average crop yields in quintals (100 kg.) were 17.3 and 16.1 quintals in 1953 in the state and cooperative farms, respectively, for ordinary sowing of winter wheat, as compared to an average of 13.1 for the country at large. However, as Hegedűs himself notes, in order to solve the Hungarian grain problem, it would be necessary to increase yields per hectare *in the country at large*

on the average, the yields fluctuated from year to year, and for certain crops (e.g., corn) systematically fell below the prewar level.

The increase in industrial crops was due not to appreciable increases in yields but to the expansion of acreage (which at times reached a point where it was detrimental to grain and fodder crops).

Mechanization lagged to the point where the role of draft animals had to be officially emphasized.

Finally, so far as the gross value of output is concerned, although the figures released are contradictory, it appears that by the end of the reconstruction plan, the volume of production oscillated between 77 and 98 per cent of prewar volume and by the end of the first long-term plans, between 90 to 130 per cent. The extent of the failure in agriculture can be judged by the fact that the actual outputs at the end of the first long-term plans for all countries except Romania were *below the ones scheduled initially for 1948–49* at the end of the reconstruction period.[91] (Compare Table 94 with Table 72, p. 287.)

THE "NEW COURSE" PREFACE TO THE SECOND PLANS

By mid-1953 sharp imbalances had appeared in all these economies. In the producers' goods industries themselves the relentless pressure for the "fulfillment" and "overfulfillment" of the plan brought about a marked wearing down of both man power and machines as well as a continuous deterioration in the quality of output and an alarming

by some 250 kilograms per hectare (i.e., from 100 to 150 kilograms per "hold"), a goal which is still far off (*ibid.*).

According to Yugoslav figures, the yields per hectare in quintals for wheat were in that country in 1951: 16.3, 13.5, and 12.6 for the state, cooperative, and private sectors, respectively. As the Yugoslavs themselves note, all these results should be appraised in the light of the fact that the *average* yield of wheat is 22.6 quintals in Germany, in Belgium 24.6, and in Denmark 28.5 per hectare. Cf. Milan Ivanović, "The Development of Yugoslav Agriculture," *op. cit.*

It should be recalled here that the cost of production per unit of output is far higher in the state farms than in any other type of farms. Cf. Andras Hegedűs, "The Hungarian State on the Road to Socialism," in *FLP*, June 17, 1955.

[91] It must be noted that in the case of Romania the figures released for 1955 are not consistent with those released for previous years. For Bulgaria the indices of agricultural output were higher in 1951 than in 1952 when the plan was proclaimed completed. The volume of Bulgarian agricultural production moved as follows from 1948 to 1952: on the basis of 1939 = 100, the volume was 98.3 in 1948, 87.1 in 1949, 91.3 in 1950, 129.8 in 1951, and 108.1 in 1952. Cf. Zoltan Kenessey, "A Mezőgazdaság Fejlődése Bulgáriában" (Development of Agriculture in Bulgaria), *Statiztikai Tajekoztato*, No. 4, 1953.

TABLE 94. ACTUAL GROSS VALUE OF AGRICULTURAL OUTPUT AT THE END OF THE FIRST LONG-TERM PLANS

	Czecho-slovakia	Po-land[a]	Hun-gary	Ro-mania	Bul-garia	Yugo-slavia
End of Reconstruction Plan	90	77	91	86	98	[b]
End of First Long-Term Plan	103	92	102	129	109	109

[a] Gross output in the postwar area as percentage of gross output in the prewar area.

[b] Nil.

Source: Derived from *ESE Since the War, op. cit.*, p. 24, and *ESE in 1955, op. cit.*, p. 191.

increase in the share of rejects. The lack of all sorts of manufacturing goods for broad consumption, the poor quality and high prices of the consumer goods made available to the domestic markets, imperiled for their part the normal flow of trade between town and countryside. As already indicated in Chapter 7, the policy of low prices for agricultural produce, and high prices for manufactured goods, discouraged the expansion in agricultural output and trade, and jeopardized the towns' supply of foodstuffs and raw materials.

The stresses and strains of these imbalances in the economy of the East European countries were brought into the open in the middle of 1953. Regardless of what special circumstances prompted the frank revelation of them in the different countries, at that time all the countries sharply revised their general plans and, up to a point, the pattern of their investment. Whereas in 1952 in every country there were many announcements that the plans would be fulfilled in *four years instead of five,* and Bulgaria proclaimed that she had finished her first development plan in four years, in mid-1953 such declarations ceased, and official spokesmen started to stress the fact that for the balance of the year and for 1954 and 1955 the plans would be short-term with the object of changing the situation in agriculture and improving in general the situation of the consumer. The slogan of 1952, "acceleration of the pace of industrial development," was replaced by "consolidation of the results achieved," the slowing down of the development of industry, as the slogan of 1953–54. The reasons for the retreat were briefly summarized thus by the premier of Czechoslovakia:

> . . . The serious lag in agriculture leads to violation of the proportionate development of the national economy of our Republic, gives

> rise to constant difficulties in supplying the working people with food and the light and food industries with raw materials and acts as a serious brake holding up a still more rapid rise in the standard of living of the working population. While industrial production in 1953 compared with 1948 will increase twofold, agricultural production during the same period will increase only one-third, and will still be below the prewar level. Clearly such a state of affairs cannot satisfy the growing demands of society.[92]

The nature of the retreat was summarized in the following way by Rákosi:

> The main question of our entire further development, the next decisive link which we must tackle with vigor, is development of agriculture. It is the focal task of the day *and for the next two or three years.* A slow-down in development of heavy industry, consolidation of the results achieved and, at the same time, rapid and extensive development of agriculture constitute in their entirety one of the important features of the *new stage* which we began to work on after the adoption of the decisions by the Central Committee and Government.[93]

After these decisions, the volume of investment was reduced, as were the scheduled rates of development for industrial production in general and for capital goods in particular, and increases in both investment and output in light industry and agriculture were projected. The reduction in the rate of investments in Czechoslovakia, according to official statements, was 16.1 per cent. The other countries of the area slowed down or abandoned some of their "big projects" (the expansion of the Sztalinvaros mills in Hungary, the Danube-Black Sea Canal in Romania, etc.). The rates of development for industrial production and for the producers' goods industries were substantially lowered. In Czechoslovakia the rates for pig iron and steel were set, respectively, at 8.3 per cent and 4.5 per cent in 1954, as against a planned rate of 13.4 and 10.5 per cent,[94] respectively, during the first development plans.

On the other hand, the shares of light industries and agriculture in total investment were increased, the first on the average by 3–5 per cent of the total investment, the latter by 5–7 per cent. Thus the investment plans for 1954–55 allocated roughly some 10–15 per cent

[92] Široký, article quoted in note 78 above.

[93] Report at the Central Committee of the Hungarian Working People's Party, Plenum of Oct. 31, 1953, in *FLP,* Nov. 20, 1953. (Italics supplied.) The "decisions" refer to those of June 28, 1953.

[94] *CEB,* No. 282, Mar. 1, 1954, pp. 4 ff. Compare to Table 80, p. 300.

of the total investment to light industries, contrasted to 7–11 per cent during the 1948–53 period.[95] The new (yearly) plans also allocated 13–20 per cent for agriculture as against 8–13 per cent previously. Taking the investment share earmarked for the light industries and for agriculture during the first period as 100, the *increases* envisaged were 35–45 per cent for the light industries and 60 per cent or more for agriculture.

The division of output between capital formation, plus government use not otherwise accounted for, and consumption was altered in favor of consumption to a total of between 5 and 10 per cent and perhaps as high as 12 per cent. In Czechoslovakia the share of capital formation was lowered from 25 per cent of the national income in 1953 to 22 per cent in 1954, and that of government use not otherwise accounted for from 18 to 14 per cent, thus increasing the share of personal consumption from 57 per cent of national income to the higher but still very low level of 62 per cent.[96] In Hungary the share of consumption increased from a low of 58 per cent in 1953 to 70 per cent in 1954.[97]

The "new course" as defined at the end of 1953, higher priorities for light industries, and specifically food-processing industries, and for agriculture, increase in the output and import of consumers' goods, shift in output in favor of consumers' goods, was substantially modified less than a year later, and many of its formulations and objectives were discarded as "right-wing deviations." Thus both the shift in emphasis toward the *light industries* and any substantial shift in output in favor of *consumption* were discarded. The all-out effort of "increasing and strengthening heavy industry," the "basis of socialist construction," was reaffirmed in the area as a whole. Even in 1954 the shift in favor of light industry in some countries (e.g., Poland) was limited since any radical shift would have entailed loss of many previous investments. By the end of 1954 the undisputed priority of heavy industry with emphasis on the producers' goods sector, had been reaffirmed in every country in the area,[98] with great stress placed on the necessity of increasing production and reducing consumption. In

[95] In the 1948–53 period only the Hungarian investment percentage allocated to the light industries was lower, namely, 6 per cent during the initial plan, and 5 per cent after the 1951 revisions.

[96] *CEB,* No. 282, Mar. 1, 1954, pp. 4 ff.

[97] Both Rákosi (*FLP,* Nov. 20, 1953) and Nagy (*ibid.,* Feb. 5, 1954) give the same figures.

[98] Cf. *Pravda,* February 18, 1955.

Hungary, where the 1953 shift had been given the most publicity, it was stated now:

> Inasmuch as our country's economic forces have not developed satisfactorily in the recent period the higher living standards of the working people do not rest on a firm, solid foundation.[99]

The East European regimes did not revert simply to the pre-1953 agricultural policy. A slightly higher share of total investment was allocated to agriculture, and substantial changes were made in crop selection and production plans. The new emphasis was now on corn instead of industrial crops, in order to improve the livestock situation, on extension of the area cultivated, on increase of qualified manpower in agriculture, and on a better balance between the advance of industry and the growth of agriculture.

The Soviet Model and the New Plans

The second long-term plans of Czechoslovakia, Poland, Hungary, and Romania were started at the same time as the sixth Five-Year Plan of the Soviet Union, on January 1, 1956. Whereas the first long-term plans were established at various times in the different countries, all the second long-term plans except for that of Bulgaria were framed and launched *simultaneously*. It was stated during the new course that only simultaneity in the preparation and completion of the plans could insure an effective coordination of the output and trade plans by taking into consideration from the outset the conditions of demand and supply in the "intraplanned market." [100]

Numerous statements indicating rejection of some of the most outrageously autarkic features of the first long-term plan were released from then on, by all the countries of the bloc. All stressed the fact that the "division of labor on an international scale," actually limited to the intraplanned market, implied that the energies of each country should be concentrated on those branches which have "a sound domestic basis of raw materials." However, stressing these principles,

[99] Resolution of the CC of the Hungarian Working People's Party, "On the Political Situation and Tasks of the Party," *FLP*, March 11, 1955.

[100] Thus a Czechoslovak source stated in 1954:

> The actual future plan will be compiled for the year 1955 and for the years 1956 to 1960 in order to make it possible to avail better of the mutual economic cooperation of the People's Democracies and of the Soviet Union where in 1956 further long-term plans commence, and for the period of 1956 to 1960, further mutual long-term agreements will be concluded between Czechoslovakia and those states. [*CEB*, No. 282, March 1, 1954, p. 4.]

the chief planners indicated, would not imply abandonment of the cardinal theory of the undisputed priority of heavy industry in each and every country. Thus Miron Constantinescu, the chief Romanian planner, stated:

> Each country gives special, and in future will undoubtedly continue to give even more, attention to those particular branches of heavy industry that it is most capable of developing (coal and some branches of the chemical industry in Poland, heavy machine building in Czechoslovakia, the aluminum industry and machine-tool building in Hungary, and so forth). Special consideration must be given to the economic expediency (the profitability) of producing certain goods in this or that country, to the specialization and cooperation of production, to the elimination of harmful parallelism and the introduction of line production. . . . Nevertheless, the all-round development of the machine building industry is a major necessity for all the countries. . . . [Lenin] developed the Marxist tenet that accumulation in department I [production of the means of production] is a factor making for the proportional development of these two departments [I and II—producers' and consumers' goods] and consequently that department I must play the leading role in extended reproduction. . . . From this springs the need for accelerated rates of development of heavy industry, a need that is common to all countries building socialism.[101]

Simultaneity in launching the plans, consideration at the planning stage of the other countries' availabilities and structure of investment and output, limitation of certain autarkic tendencies and coordination of some of the key tasks but also reaffirmation of the "undisputed priority" of heavy industry as the basis of "socialist construction" in each unit, allocation of a slightly higher share of investment to agriculture than during the first plans of development—these were the main principles stressed during the preparation of the new plans.

The draft directives of the second five-year plans, most of which were published only in mid-1956, impress, however, by the striking similarity of their basic design. All the plans again scheduled the highest increases in producers' goods industries as well as in industry as a whole as compared to agriculture. In contrast to the drafts of the first five-year plans or to the revised drafts of these plans, the new draft directives foresaw a far *slower rate of growth* during the second period of development. Thus in the producers' goods industries the increases over the quinquennium were to range from 57 to 78 per cent as

[101] Miron Constantinescu, "On the Road of Building Socialism, Some Problems of Economic Development in Rumania in the Light of the Economic Tasks of the People's Democracies," in *FLP,* Sept. 9, 1955.

compared to 130 to 280 per cent scheduled for the first quinquennium in their revised versions. In industry as a whole the increases were to range from 50 to 75 as contrasted to 98 to 210 per cent during the preceding period. In the consumers' goods industries the increases were to be from 40 to 55 as compared to 73 to 145 per cent. Finally, in agriculture the increases were to range from 30 to 66 as compared to 37 to 88 per cent (see Table 95). Thus, so far as industry is concerned, as higher and higher plateaus of output are reached, it evidently becomes increasingly difficult to expand production at continuously higher or even constant rates. Planning cannot accomplish what it is often alleged to accomplish, namely, sustained growth at *expanding* rates.

In the draft directives the emphasis was not on new spectacular projects, but on the completion of *unfinished* tasks of the preceding plans, such as the construction of two blast furnaces at the Gottwald mills in Czechoslovakia, of one giant blast furnace at Sztalinvaros in Hungary, etc. The directives were essentially concerned with completion of the projects deemed indispensable to the further progress of these economies and not with the revival of the "white elephants" of the first plans, such as the Huko Combinat, which was to be constructed in Slovakia, and the Romanian "Danube-Black Sea" canal. Better utilization of the plant and machinery available, completion of previous projects (namely, in the steel industries), new constructions in more carefully selected fields (such as power including atomic-power plants, chemicals, and others), and introduction of labor-saving devices, instead of haphazard constructions of labor-intensive projects, increase in productivity [102]—these were in brief the basic directives of the new plans. It should be noted that the emphasis on a lower absorption rate of new workers into industry would tend to increase the pressure of overpopulation in agriculture and would eventually lower the per capita output in this sector.

The directives set competing tasks for agriculture, by requiring simultaneous increases in grain, industrial plants, and fodder output.[103] They stressed for this purpose eventual progress in mechanization, in fertilizer utilization, and so on. The collectivization of agriculture was to be completed in Bulgaria by 1959–60 and was to become the predominant form of organization in the other countries by 1960. Thus complete elimination of private small-scale property was set to be ac-

[102] This question is discussed in Chapter 10.
[103] Compare to the first quinquennia, Chapter 8.

TABLE 95. PLANNED AND ACTUAL INCREASES IN GROSS OUTPUT DURING THE LONG-TERM PLANS, 1949–60

		First Long-Term Plans [a]			Second Long-Term Plans [b]
		Targets			
		Original plan	Revised plan	Actual	Targets
		1	2	3	4
Czecho-slovakia	Producers' goods	66	133	119	57
	Consumers' goods	50	73	80	40
	All industry	57	98	100	50
	Agriculture	37	53	14	30
Poland	Producers' goods	154		180	57
	Consumers' goods	111		134	49
	All industry	158		166	53
	Agriculture	50		19	25
Hungary	Producers' goods	104	280	188	60
	Consumers' goods	73	145	127	40
	All industry	86	210	113	50–52
	Agriculture	42	54	12	27
Romania	Producers' goods	[c]		131	70–75
	Consumers' goods	[c]		97	50–55
	All industry	144		110	60–75
	Agriculture	88		50	[c]
Bulgaria	Producers' goods	220		150	78
	Consumers' goods	75		100	48
	All industry	119		119	60
	Agriculture	59		11	66

[a] Base year is year preceding the plan. C and B, 1948; P and H, 1949; R, 1950.
[b] For all, excluding Bulgaria, base year 1955; B, 1952.
[c] Not available.

Sources: Cols. 1–3: Table 73, in Chapter 8 and Table 103 in Appendix to this chapter. Producers' and consumers' goods actual results: *ESE in 1955, op. cit.*, pp. 191 and 237.

Col. 4: C—Návrh Směrnic Ústředního výboru KSČ pro sestavení druhého pětiletého plánu rozvoje národního hospodářství ČSR na léta 1956–1960 (Draft directives of the CC of the Czechoslovak Communist Party for the second Five-Year Plan of development of the economy of Czechoslovakia). Supplement to *RP*, May 4, 1956.

P—J. Cyrankiewicz: "O założeniach planu 5-letniego na lata 1956–1960" (On the Premises of the 5-Year Plan for 1956–1960), *TL*, July 26, 1956, and "O Rozwoju Rolnictwa v latach 1956–1960 i Zadaniach Partii na Wsi, Uchwała V. Plenum Komitetu Centralnego PZPR" (On the Development of Agriculture during the years 1956–1960 and the tasks of the Party in the Countryside. Resolution of the Vth Plenum of the CC of the Polish Workers' Party), *TL*, Feb. 11, 1956.

H—"Irányelvek a magyar népgazdaság fejlesztésének masodik ötéves tervéhez" (Directives on the Development of the Second Five Year Plan of Hungary), *SN*, April 27, 1956.

R—Gh. Gheorghiu-Dej: *Raportul de activitate al Comitetului Central al Partidului Muncitoresc Romîn la Congresul al II-lea Al Partidului, op. cit.*

B—F. T. Konstantinov, edit.: *Vtoroi Piatiletnii Plan Razvitiia Narodnoi Respubliki Bolgarii, op. cit.*

complished during the second, and part of an eventual third, planned quinquennium. Finally, some minor "decentralization" measures were stressed by certain plans in respect to collection of obligatory deliveries by local authorities, but there were no significant changes concerning planning of output.

The scheduled average yearly rate of increase in national income was set at 8–10 per cent in all countries except Bulgaria. The scheduled rates were to be, of course, lower than during the first long-term plan. Investment was, however, to be increased appreciably, by 60–75 per cent, as compared to the preceding quinquennia, again around 25 per cent of the national income.

The data available on the investment pattern indicate that the relative share of industry was to oscillate between 40 and 50 per cent of the total, and the share of agriculture around 15 per cent. The light industries were to continue with a very low priority, notwithstanding the past experience that the peasant has no incentive to sell over and above compulsory deliveries, if there are few consumer goods to buy.

The June 1956 uprising in Poznań and the nationwide Hungarian revolt shook the entire Soviet bloc, imperiled the validity of the draft directives for the second quinquennium, and prompted, moreover, the serious questioning of the underlying assumptions of Communist planning itself. The Hungarian revolt had already revealed that the Soviet planning model was breaking down in the area and that industrialization *à la russe* could not be carried out "administratively" by each and every country, whatever its endowment of resources or its political traditions might be. The Russians themselves had to recognize publicly the limitations of the Soviet "model" and to accept the unpleasant task of exposing the absurdity of its mechanical transplantation to all the countries. Thus, *Pravda* appraised as follows the "errors" which led to the Hungarian revolt:

> In the economic field serious miscalculations were made:
>
> A considerable part of the means was earmarked for the building of new large enterprises that were beyond the powers of a small country like Hungary.
>
> A fast rate of industrialization which is correct under conditions in the Soviet Union was mechanically adopted in Hungary. Large enterprises were built without provision being made for raw materials.
>
> The former party and state leadership of Hungary mechanically copied the experience of the Soviet Union in the field of industriali-

zation despite the fact that the leaders of the Hungarian Workers party were repeatedly given comradely advice not to do this.

The planning of economic development should have proceeded from the concrete conditions of Hungary and account should have been taken of the fact that it is not up to every country to create all branches of industry as it has the possibility of relying on all the Socialist countries.

More means should have been expended on the development of agriculture and on increasing the production of consumer goods, which would have made it possible steadily to improve the living standards of the population.

The road taken by the Soviet Union's creating its own powerful industry within a short space of time was conditioned by the Soviet Union then being the only country of socialism in a capitalist encirclement.[104]

The breaking down of the Soviet model in Hungary and its partial breakdown in Poland,[105] the necessity of operation for at least one or two years on the basis of hastily improvised emergency programs, the disruptions provoked in the intraplanned market by the shifts in output and planning, have seriously jeopardized the realization of some of the main 1960 targets. Czechoslovakia and East Germany, for instance, are forced to scale down some of their output targets in view of the scheduled fall in Polish supplies of coal and steel, and this in turn affects the Soviet imports of machinery and manufactured goods.[106]

[104] See *Pravda,* Nov. 23, 1956, as translated in the N. Y. *Times,* Nov. 24, 1956.

[105] The Polish economists suggest that the Polish planning "model" should differ from both the Soviet and the Yugoslav models. This model should preserve the principle of central planning notably in respect to the basic outputs of the key industries, the basic raw materials supplies, the distribution of funds for main capital investments, and the prices of articles produced by key industries. The central plan should not deal, on the other hand, with "the detailed range of production, which should be defined by the factory in consultation with the purchasers, the plan concerning employment and average wages, the system of wages and money grants, the plans for minor investments, and the distribution of the works fund." (See for instance: "New Economic Model" in *Polish Facts and Figures,* No. 534 of Dec. 8, 1956, reprint of an article by M. Lesz originally published in *Życie Warszawy* of Nov. 27, 1956.) Most of the Polish articles on the subject emphasize the necessity of a "departure from the bureaucratic methods of economic planning and budgeting."

[106] It should be noted that increased interdependence in planning even at the level of output (as well as at the level of trade) did in no way imply abandonment of the principle of autonomous allocation in each unit and did not aim to reduce each plan to part of an integral "master plan." Long before the launching of the second quinquennium some students of East Europe were already speaking of the

Whatever the immediate impact of the upheavals on the pattern of investment in this or that country, on the degree of the new decentralization tendencies in industry and on the economy as a whole, on the limited liberty granted to the small craftsman and agricultural producer, or on the temporary slowing down of the collectivization drive, one fact is certain: the Soviet dogma of industrialization, with its stress on building a "heavy industrial base" in each national unit, its skewed pattern of investment, its highly centralized character, its complete disregard of the consumer, and its patent failures, is now being seriously challenged, for the first time since 1928; and it will, in all likelihood, be challenged more and more in the years to come in the entire Soviet orbit.

At the border of the Soviet bloc, Yugoslavia affirms now that she has already built her *heavy industrial base* and is turning more and more resolutely toward a policy similar to that of the "new course." In the plan for 1953 the question of a gradual change in the "basic proportions in investments" was already being considered; the idea gained momentum throughout 1954 and 1955. Even though some key projects of the first development plan were delayed by one, two, or three years, and some were for all practical purposes abandoned, Yugoslavia continued generally, up to 1953–54, to complete many industrial enterprises depending essentially on imported raw materials. As the country found it difficult to pay for some of these imports she had to leave unused much of the newly built plant capacity.[107] When the relations with the Soviet bloc were "normalized," in 1955, the Yugoslavs envisaged concurrently a decrease in certain imports from the West, an increase in certain exports, notably to the Soviet bloc, and a relocation of the resources on hand. The period opened in 1956 was characterized by a decrease in the share of investment in national income and by a new pattern of investment allocation. The guiding principle for investment in what is called by Belgrade the "new phase" is "to achieve the quickest economic result for the smallest expendi-

existence of a Soviet "master plan" of which the East European plans were but a component part. Actually an integrated plan for an area would propose not only simultaneity, coordination in drawing of the plans, and limitation of autarkic tendencies (especially in the weakest links of the area), but also extensive division of labor and perhaps a *central decision concerning the allocation of resources in the entire area.* Before as well as after the current changes, the plans rest on decentralized autonomous decisions on investment by each nation.

[107] Cf. above, note 68, pp. 340–341.

ture of funds." This means concretely the following measures: (*a*) continuing investment in electric power, oil, and coal, not only because certain projects are in advanced stages but more so because they depend on or supply local raw materials; (*b*) sharp curtailment of investment in the metal-working industries, review of the work in process, and abandonment of the completion of certain steel works or plants for nonferrous metals and certain projects related to machinery manufacture, etc.; [108] (*c*) emphasis on modernization, on consumers' goods production, and on agriculture.

The new orientation is valid for the few years coinciding broadly with the second planned quinquennium. Thus, the divergence between the planned development of Yugoslavia and that of the other East European countries may be less accented in certain respects throughout this period. It is difficult to determine whether the departures of Yugoslavia from her first planning model (and hence from the underlying assumption that sustained growth is inseparable from continuous enlargement of the means of production) were due more to the hard realities of a small country which has experienced a period of isolation, or to the political intelligence of its leadership.

[108] For a detailed outline of these policies, see particularly S. Vukmanovič-Tempo, "Principi društvenog plana za iduću godinu" (Principles of the Social Plan for the Next Year), *Borba,* Oct. 18, 1955; and also, Vukmanovič-Tempo, "Uskladjivanje privrednog razvitka i podizanje životnog standarda" (The Coordination of Economic Development and Raising of the Living Standard), *Borba,* Oct. 11, 1955.

APPENDIX

TRENDS IN BASIC EAST EUROPEAN INDUSTRIAL AND AGRICULTURAL OUTPUT

This statistical appendix presents data in physical terms for the main constituents of industrial and agricultural production in the key years 1938, 1948, 1953, 1955, 1960. The 1938 data for Poland refer only to the present territory. The figures for 1960 are the targets of the second five-year plan. For Bulgaria, instead of 1960, the data refer to 1957, the end of the Bulgarian second five-year plan.

The statistics for 1938 and 1948 are generally based on the statistical yearbooks of the League of Nations and of the United Nations, respectively, complemented by the statistical yearbooks of the countries considered, whenever necessary. The data for 1953 and some of the data for 1955 come from the Economic Surveys of Europe of the United Nations, completed and checked against the data released by the countries discussed in various other sources. The data for 1955 and the targets for 1960 come from the official directives of the second five-year plans.

TABLE 96. FUEL AND POWER [a]

	1938	1948	1953	1955	1960 Goal
		Hard Coal			
Czechoslovakia	15,836	17,746	20,300	23,250	29,300
Poland	69,400	70,262	88,725	94,500	98,300
Hungary	1,042	1,238	1,993	2,692	[b]
Romania	299	200	400	400	[c]
Bulgaria	146	327	575	[b]	[b]
Yugoslavia	450	952	925	1,133	[b]
		Lignite			
Czechoslovakia	16,027	23,591	32,763	38,790	57,790
Poland	7,611 [d]	5,040	5,900	6,000	11,700
Hungary	8,306	9,377	19,016	19,624	[b]
Romania	2,097	2,461	4,100	5,800	[c]
Bulgaria	1,942	3,544	8,400	10,300	14,000 [e]
Yugoslavia [f]	5,287	9,692	10,321	14,074	[b]
		Oil			
Czechoslovakia	19	49	196	202	[b]
Poland	141	139	189	180	[b]
Hungary	43	485	846	1,600	2,000
Romania	6,610	4,300	9,500	10,575	13,536
Yugoslavia	1	36	172	257	[b]
		Electric Power			
Czechoslovakia	4,052	7,715	12,400	15,080	25,340
Poland	7,000	7,514	13,600	17,740	29,803
Hungary	1,109	2,000	4,580	5,400	8,350
Romania	1,135	1,511	3,400	4,300	7,740
Bulgaria	236	560	1,620	2,100	2,800 [e]
Yugoslavia	1,090	2,061	2,982	4,340	[b]

[a] Coal and oil in thousand metric tons, electricity in million kwhr.
[b] Not available.
[c] Total coal output scheduled to increase to 11.1 million tons.
[d] 1937.
[e] 1957 plan.
[f] All subbituminous coal.

(*Sources for this table are on page 368.*)

Sources:

Hard Coal and Lignite:

1938–53: *UNSY 1955, op. cit.*, pp. 139–142, completed for:
P: *The European Coal Problem, op. cit.*
B: *FLP*, February 5, 1954.
Y: *Statistički Godišjnak 1954, op. cit.*, p. 156.

1955–60: C: Návrh Směrnik . . ., *op. cit.*
P: *Monthly Bulletin of Statistics*, May 1956, *op. cit.*, p. XIV; Cyrankiewicz: O założeniach . . ., *op. cit.*; and "O wynikach wykonania Planu Sześcioletniego i Podstowowych Założeniach Planu Pieciołetniego v latach 1956–60. Uchwała VII Plenum Komitetu Centralnego Pzpr" (On the Results on the Fulfillment of the Six Year Plan and on the Basic Premises of the Five Year Plan 1956–60. Resolution of the VII Plenum of the Central Committee of the Polish United Workers' Party), *TL*, August 3, 1956, and *Survey of Poland*, Supplement to *The Statist, op. cit.*
H: *UNSY, ibid.*, and *Magyar Statisztikai Zsebkőnyv, 1956, op. cit.*
R: *Economic Bulletin for Europe*, Vol. 7, No. 1 (May 1955). Gheorghiu-Dej: *Raportul . . ., op. cit.*, p. 40.
B: *ESE in 1955, op. cit.*, p. B36.
Y: *Statistički Godišnjak 1956, op. cit.*, pp. 140 ff.

Oil:

1938–53: *UNSY 1955, op. cit.*, p. 144, completed for:
P: *Petroleum Industry Record 1918–1948*, Oil Industry Information Committee, New York, 1949, Table 15b; *Monthly Bulletin of Statistics, ibid.*

1955–60: C: Návrh Směrnik, *op. cit.*
P: *Monthly Bulletin of Statistics, ibid.*
H: Irányelvek . . ., *op. cit.*
R: Gheorghiu-Dej: *Raportul . . ., op. cit.*, p. 40.

Electric power:

1938–53: *UNSY 1953, op. cit.*, pp. 260–261; *UNSY 1955, op. cit.*, pp. 286–287.

1955–60: *ESE in 1955, op. cit.*, pp. B36–B41, completed for: C, H, R with same sources as given for coal and oil above.

TABLE 97. METALS [a]

	1938	1948	1953	1955
	Iron Ore (Fe content)			
Czechoslovakia	525	430	690	747
Poland	322	224	392	556
Hungary	74	80	102	100
Romania	68	94	310	200
Yugoslavia	279	377	382	500
	Lead Ore (Pb content)			
Czechoslovakia	4 [b]	[c]	[c]	[c]
Poland	[c]	17	[c]	[c]
Romania	6	4 [d]	[c]	[c]
Yugoslavia	85	63	85	90 [e]
	Zinc Ore (Zn content)			
Yugoslavia	45	37	60	70 [e]
	Pyrites (S content)			
Czechoslovakia	8	[c]	[c]	[c]
Poland	[c]	25	[c]	[c]
Romania	5	[c]	[c]	[c]
Yugoslavia	63	38	3	1
	Bauxite			
Hungary	540	400	1,394	1,241
Yugoslavia	405	144	478	791
	Manganese (Mn content)			
Hungary	9	[c]	[c]	[c]
Romania	22	16	60	90
Yugoslavia	1	4	3	3

[a] Mining of main metal ores, in thousand metric tons.
[b] 1937.
[c] Not available.
[d] 1947.
[e] Estimate.

Sources:

1938–53: For all, *UNSY 1955*, pp. 149, 152, 155, 157, 175. Completed for P with: *Quarterly Bulletin of Steel Statistics*, Vol. V, No. 4, UN, New York, 1954, p. 52.

1955: Same sources as for coal and oil, same years, Table 96.

TABLE 98. METAL-MAKING

(in thousand metric tons)

	1938	1948	1953	1955	1960
		Ferrous Metallurgy			
		Pig Iron			
Czechoslovakia	1,323	1,660	2,800	2,990	4,780
Poland	1,294	1,208	2,360	3,112	5,200
Hungary	335	403	720	855	1,410
Romania	133	191	456	575	1,150
Yugoslavia	108	172	270	514	[a]
		Crude Steel			
Czechoslovakia	1,873	2,650	4,400	4,480	6,540
Poland	1,897	1,955	3,604	4,426	7,200
Hungary	648	762	1,540	1,620	2,240
Romania	277	340	716	765	1,600
Yugoslavia	230	368	515	806	[a]
		Nonferrous Metallurgy			
		Copper			
Yugoslavia	42	37	31	28	
		Lead			
Czechoslovakia	5	8	[a]	[a]	
Poland	[a]	17	[a]	[a]	
Romania	6	3 [b]	[a]	11	
Yugoslavia	9	49	71	71 [c]	
		Zinc			
Czechoslovakia	9	2 [b]	[a]	[a]	
Poland	[a]	108 [c]	138	156	
Yugoslavia	5	7	15	15 [c]	
		Aluminum			
Czechoslovakia	[a]	[a]	3	25	
Hungary	1	9	28	37	
Yugoslavia	1	2	3	11	

[a] Not available.
[b] 1947.
[c] 1949.

Sources:

Ferrous metallurgy:

1948–55: For all, excluding P: *UNSY 1955*, *op. cit.*, pp. 255–257; completed with *ESE in 1955*, *op. cit.*, p. B36–B41.

1948–55: P: *Quarterly Bulletin of Steel Statistics*, Vol. V, No. 4, *op. cit.*, p. 12; *Monthly Bulletin of Statistics*, May 1956, *op. cit.*, p. xv; and *Survey of Poland*, Supplement to *The Statist*, *op. cit.*, p. 18.

1955–60: For all, same sources as for coal and oil, same years, Table 96.

Nonferrous metallurgy:

1948–53: *UNSY 1955*, *op. cit.*, pp. 260, 261, 263, 265. Completed for:
C: *CEB*, No. 315, Dec. 1956, pp. 12.
P: *Monthly Bulletin of Statistics*, May 1956, *op. cit.*, p. xv.
H: Irányelvek . . ., *op. cit.*, and *Magyar Statisztikai Zsebkönyv, 1956*, *op. cit.*, p. 60.

TABLE 99. ENGINEERING: MACHINE TOOLS AND TRACTORS

		1938 [a]	1948	1953	1955
		Machine Tools			
Czechoslovakia	Pieces	5,500	11,810	[b]	15,690
Poland	Pieces	[b]	5,643 [c]	11,275	13,900
Hungary	Pieces	120	1,880	6,115	5,121
Poland	Tons	3,060	6,800	21,300	27,800
Yugoslavia	Tons	84	1,105	2,395	3,120
		Tractors			
Czechoslovakia	Units	200	9,100	8,100	12,300
Poland	Units	[b]	2,510 [c]	6,900	7,900
Hungary	Units	550	1,190	800	5,750
Romania	Units	[d]	800	5,100	5,000
Yugoslavia	Units	[d]	3 [c]	1,360	1,100

[a] Czechoslovakia, 1937.
[b] Not available.
[c] 1949.
[d] Nil.

Sources:

1938–53: For all excluding Yugoslavia: *ESE in 1953*, *op. cit.*, pp. 272–276 and *ESE in 1955*, *op. cit.*, pp. B36–B41.
Y: *Statistički Godišnjak 1956*, *op. cit.*, p. 145.

1955: *ESE in 1955*, *op. cit.*, completed for:
P: *Survey of Poland*, Supplement to *The Statist*, *op. cit.*, p. 31.
H: *Magyar Statisztikai Zsebkőnyv, 1956*, *op. cit.*, p. 61.
Y: *Statistički Godišnjak*, *loc. cit.*

TABLE 100. MAIN CHEMICALS

(in thousand metric tons)

	1938	1948	1953	1955	1960
		Sulfuric Acid			
Czechoslovakia	165.6 [a]	215.0	312.0	375.1	560.0
Poland	267.0	222.0	370.3	448.5	768.0
Hungary	45.0	18.2 [c]	[b]	124.2	200.0
Romania	45.2	26.3	73.6	92.0	211.6
Bulgaria	6.9	11.6	25.5	32.4	39.9 [d]
Yugoslavia	23.0	43.6	40.2	73.0 [e]	[b]
		Caustic Soda			
Czechoslovakia	[b]	101.9	61.0	60.5	141.0
Poland	23.0 [a]	47.7	82.0	101.0	[b]
Hungary	2.7	4.2	[b]	11.7	40.5
Romania	13.8	12.5	23.8	52.0	[b]
Yugoslavia	13.6	18.5	22.5	30.6	[b]
		Nitrogenous Fertilizer (N content)			
Czechoslovakia	24.5	29.0	38.0	98.4	156.5
Poland	[b]	55.1	83.9	154.4	352.0
Hungary	5.5	10.8 [f]	12.1	12.7	[b]
Yugoslavia	8.2	1.9	6.7	6.7	[b]
		Phosphorous Fertilizer (P_2O_5 content)			
Czechoslovakia	22.4	35.0	74.0	90.0 [e]	[b]
Poland	[b]	73.6 [f]	103.8	130.3	252.0
Hungary	9.5	15.4 [f]	30.8	28.5	[b]
Yugoslavia	4.4	8.4	6.9	[b]	[b]

[a] 1937.
[b] Not available.
[c] 1947.
[d] 1957.
[e] 1954.
[f] 1949.

Sources:

1948–53: *UNSY 1955, op. cit.*, pp. 233, 235, 238; *ESE in 1953, op. cit.*, pp. 271–276, and *ESE in 1955*, pp. B36–B41. Completed for:
H: *Magyar Statisztikai Zsebkönyv, 1956, op. cit.*, p. 68.
Y: *Statistički Godišnjak 1954, op. cit.*, p. 159.

1955–60: *ESE in 1955, ibid.*, and same sources as for coal and oil, same years, Table 96.

Table 101. Building Materials [a]

	1938	1948	1953	1955	1960
		Cement			
Czechoslovakia	1,350 [b]	1,652	2,300	2,900	4,520
Poland	2,770	1,800	3,294	3,812	6,785
Hungary	343	320	1,060	1,200	1,860
Romania	532	650	1,900	2,000	3,600
Bulgaria	194	380	714	825	1,210 [d]
Yugoslavia	878	1,169	1,241	1,533	[c]
		Bricks			
Czechoslovakia	1,128 [b]	924	1,300	1,600 [e]	[c]
Poland	3,210	975	2,206	2,590	3,990
Hungary	548	700 [f]	1,140	1,250	1,950
Romania	121	43 [g]	[b]	1,122 [e]	[c]
Bulgaria	50	130	567	655	[c]
Yugoslavia	380	722	664	799	[c]
		Window Glass			
Czechoslovakia	[c]	131	147	[b]	[c]
Poland	[c]	76	113	114 [f]	[c]
Hungary	12	26 [g]	[b]	[b]	[c]
Romania	13	23	33	39 [f]	[c]
Bulgaria	7	8 [g]	[b]	[b]	[c]
Yugoslavia	12	18	24	36	[c]

[a] Cement and window glass in 1,000 metric tons. Bricks in million units.
[b] 1937.
[c] Not available.
[d] 1957 plan.
[e] Yearly plan.
[f] 1949.
[g] 1947.

Note: The raw data for window glass were given in metric tons for Czechoslovakia, and Romania; in m^2 for Hungary, Bulgaria, and Yugoslavia; sometimes in tons, sometimes in m^2, for Poland. In order to obtain a uniform tabulation we converted the square meters into tons by using as conversion factor: 1 sq. ft. = 24 oz. of flat glass. This figure was chosen as an intermediate between the so-called "single-strength" glass (18 oz. per sq. ft.) and the "double-strength" (26 oz. per sq. ft.).

Sources:

Cement:

1938: All except Poland: *Annuaire Statistique International* (International Statistical Yearbook), League of Nations 1938–39, Geneva, 1939, pp. 131, 144.
P: *ESE in 1953*, p. 275.

1948–53: C, R, Y: *UNSY 1955, op. cit.*, p. 250 and *ESE in 1955, op. cit.*, p. B37–B41.
P: as for 1938; *Monthly Bulletin of Statistics*, May 1956, *op. cit.*, p. xv.
H, B: *ESE in 1953, op. cit.*, p. 271; *ESE in 1955, op. cit.*, B37.

1955–60: Same as for coal and oil, same years, Table 96.

Bricks and Window Glass:

For all: *ESE in 1953, op. cit.*, pp. 271–276 and *ESE in 1955, op. cit.*, pp. B36–B41.
Completed for: H: Irányelek . . ., *op. cit.*
B: *ESE in 1952*, UN, ECE, Geneva, 1953, p. 276.
Y: *Statistički Godišnjak, 1956, op. cit.*, p. 144.

TABLE 102. PER CAPITA OUTPUTS OF ELECTRIC POWER, STEEL AND CEMENT [a]

	1938 [b]	1948	1953	1955	1960 [b]
		Electric Power			
Czechoslovakia	266	625	975	1,162	1,859
Poland	199	313	512	648	1,011
Hungary	123	217	475	547	810
Romania	57	95	198	247	416
Bulgaria	37	78	217	275	360
Yugoslavia	69	130	176	247	[c]
		Steel			
Czechoslovakia	123	215	346	345	480
Poland	54	81	136	162	244
Hungary	72	83	160	164	217
Romania	14	21	42	44	86
Bulgaria			[c]	[c]	32
Yugoslavia	15	23	30	45	[c]
		Cement			
Czechoslovakia	89	134	181	224	332
Poland	79	76	124	139	230
Hungary	38	16	110	121	180
Romania	27	28	110	114	193
Bulgaria	31	54	96	84	156
Yugoslavia	56	72	73	87	[c]

[a] Electric power in kwhr; steel and cement in kgs.
[b] Czechoslovakia, 1937. Bulgaria and Yugoslavia, 1939.
[c] Not available.

Sources: As in Tables 96, 98, and 101.

TABLE 103. LIGHT INDUSTRIAL PRODUCTS [a]

		1938	1948	1953	1955	1960
		Cotton Fabrics [b]				
Czechoslovakia	Million meters	[c]	280	347	340	439
Poland	Million meters	288	344	501	565	681
Bulgaria	Million meters	34	60	119	139	147 [d]
Hungary	Million meters²	140	140	209	233	247
Romania	Million meters²	104	79	197	245	300
Yugoslavia	Million meters²	111	161	129	174	[c]
Czechoslovakia	Thousand tons	55.7	59.6	71.5	[c]	[c]
Poland	Thousand tons	68.6	58.9	[c]	[c]	[c]
Romania	Thousand tons	21.1	9.3	30.8	[c]	[c]
		Woolen Fabrics [b]				
Czechoslovakia	Million meters	[c]	34.0	48.0	39.3	47.0
Poland	Million meters	37.7	41.9	70.5	75.7	86.8
Bulgaria	Million meters	5.2	5.1	9.8	[c]	13.0 [d]
Hungary	Million meters²	20.0	14.4	16.1	25.7	34.7
Romania	Million meters²	12.3	11.4	28.9	31.0	[c]
Yugoslavia	Million meters²	12.4	28.7	17.2	25.8	[c]
Czechoslovakia	Thousand tons	17.2	23.8	28.6	[c]	[c]
Poland	Thousand tons	27.6	23.4	[c]	[c]	[c]
Romania	Thousand tons	5.5	3.4	[c]	[c]	[c]
		Leather Footwear [b]				
Czechoslovakia	Million pairs	55.0	64.4	72.5	62.8	76.1
Poland	Million pairs	[c]	4.9	20.8	24.1	[c]
Hungary	Million pairs	3.5	3.7	8.4	13.9	16.2
Romania	Million pairs	[c]	2.6	9.0	17.7	25.7
Bulgaria	Million pairs	[c]	0.5	1.3	2.0 [e]	4.8 [d]
Yugoslavia	Million pairs	2.4	4.7	2.3	3.8	[c]

[a] Cotton and woolen fabrics, and footwear.
[b] Czechoslovakia, 1937; Yugoslavia and Bulgaria, 1939.
[c] Not available.
[d] 1957.
[e] 1954.

Sources:

ESE in 1953, *op. cit.*, pp. 271–276. *ESE in 1955*, *op. cit.*, pp. B36–B41. Completed for:

Y: *Statistički Godišnjak, 1956*, *op. cit.*, p. 147.

TABLE 104. YEARLY RATE OF GROWTH OF GROSS INDUSTRIAL OUTPUT

(percentages)

	Gross Output [a] in 1948	Yearly Rate of Growth (previous year = 100) 1949	1950	1951	1952	1953	1954	1955	Gross Output [a] in 1955
Czecho-slovakia	108	17	16	15	17	11	4	11	251
Poland	140	16	31	24	20	18	11	11	443
Hungary	107	30	38	24	24	11	3	8	322
Romania	85	15	40	29	23	14	7	11	290
Bulgaria	184	28	23	19	17	9	9	10	528
Yugoslavia	150	11	3	−3	−1	11	13	12	234

[a] Base year: C: 1937; P, H, R: 1938; B and Y: 1939.

Sources:

C: 1948: *Statistical Bulletin of Czechoslovakia*, VIII, 7, and Dolanský, *Three Years of Planning . . ., op. cit.*, p. 14; 1949–52: Dolanský in *FLP*, July 3, 1953: 1953–55: *ESE in 1955, op. cit.*, p. 171.

P: 1948 derived from Minc, *Poland's Economy Present and Future, op. cit.*, p. 3, and *Wieś w Lizbach*, 3rd ed., *op. cit.*, p. 103; 1949–53: Yearly indices in Bierut, *FLP*, March 1954; also, *Poland of Today, op. cit.*, p. 60; 1954–55: *ESE, ibid.*

H: 1948: *Bulletin Economique pour l'Europe*, IV, 2 (August 1952), p. 64; 1949: *Le Plan quinquennal, op. cit.*, p. 3; 1950–53: based on Rákosi, in *FLP*, May 28, 1954, and May 25, 1954. 1954–55, *ESE, ibid.*

R: 1948 and 1955: Gheorghiu-Dej, *Raportul de Activitate, op. cit.*, p. 39, and in *FLP*, Aug. 28, 1953, Aug. 27, 1954, also *RN* No. 252, Sept. 16, 1953.

B: 1948, 1952–53: Chervenkov, in *FLP*, March 5, 1954, and Konstantinov, edit., *Vtoroi Piatiletnii . . ., op. cit.*, p. 5. For other years, *ESE in 1955, op. cit.*

Y: 1948–53: *Statistički Godišnjak FNRJ 1954, op. cit.*, p. 162. 1954–55: Vukmanović-Tempo in *Borba* Nov. 29, 1955.

TABLE 105. ACTUAL AND PLANNED YEARLY RATES OF GROWTH OF GROSS INDUSTRIAL OUTPUT OF PRODUCERS' AND CONSUMERS' GOODS

(percentages)

		1st Long-Term Plans, Yearly Average	Actual Rates of Growth (previous year = 100)						2nd Long-Term Plans, Yearly Average, 1956–60 [b]
			1950	1951	1952	1953	1954	1955 [a]	
		1	2	3	4	5	6	7	8
Czecho-slovakia	Prod.	19	16	23	27	5	4	8	10
	Cons.	14	15	9	10	19	5	13	11
Poland	Prod.	30	27	25	22	17	11	6	[b]
	Cons.	22	25	18	12	19	11	11	[b]
Hungary	Prod.	56	38	41	33	18	−6	7	12
	Cons.	29	39	25	16	4	9	9	8
Romania	Prod.	[b]	43	30	27	17	4	16	14
	Cons.	[b]	32	28	18	11	11	10	10
Bulgaria	Prod.	24	18	17	14	18	17	[c]	15
	Cons.	35	20	21	9	10	3	6	10

[a] Provisional.
[b] Bulgaria 1953–57.
[c] Not available.

Sources:

Col. 1: as in Table 73.

Cos. 2–7: *ESE in 1955, op. cit.*, p. 228 and *Economic Bulletin for Europe*, Vol. 8, No. 1 (May 1956) pp. 56 and 58.

Col. 8: same as in Table 96.

TABLE 106. PRODUCTION OF MAIN CROPS

(in thousand metric tons)

	Czechoslovakia				Poland				Hungary			
	1934–38	1948	1953	1955	1934–38	1948	1953	1955	1934–38	1948	1953	1955
Bread-grain	3,081	2,520	2,558 [a]	2,500	8,819	7,924	6,709	9,600	2,920	2,360	2,750	2,700
Of which wheat	1,510	1,398	1,558 [a]	1,500	1,900	1,620	1,854	2,120	2,220	1,580	[b]	[b]
Coarse grain	2,504	2,450	2,703 [a]	2,800	4,462	3,360	3,528 [c]	3,700	3,190	3,100	3,360	3,700
Of which corn	173	252	300 [a]	400	[b]	[b]	[b]	[b]	2,306	2,862	2,600	[b]
Potatoes	11,914	6,578	8,551	[b]	38,014	26,760	31,800	26,400	2,130	2,200	2,000	2,100
Sugar-beet	5,986	4,463	5,668	[b]	5,962	4,226	6,880	7,272	1,000	1,230 [d]	2,650	2,200

	Romania				Bulgaria				Yugoslavia			
	1934–38	1948	1953	1955	1934–38	1948	1953	1955	1934–38 [e]	1948	1953	1955
Bread-grain	2,765	2,500 [f]			2,052	2,033	2,715	2,300	2,663	2,775	2,814	2,692
Of which wheat	2,600	2,360			1,057	[b]	2,465	[b]	2,429	2,524	2,506	2,430
			6,000	12,000 [g]								
Coarse grain	5,156	5,380 [h]			1,510	1,231	1,600	2,300	5,432	4,768	4,640	4,568
Of which corn	4,032	5,279 [h]			913	890	897	[b]	4,690	4,071	3,831	3,900
Potatoes	1,241	1,090 [d]	2,300 [i]	[b]	112	100	[b]	[b]	1,468	1,468	2,069	2,260
Sugar-beet	398	810	1,300	2,000	229	408	788	800	508	1,498	1,514	1,380

[a] Plan (for 1953). [b] Not available. [c] 1951–52. [d] 1949. [e] Prewar area. [f] Estimate.
[g] The figures are apparently not consistent with those released for previous years.
[h] 1947. [i] 1952.

Sources:

1934–38: For all excluding Yugoslavia (FAO computations), *ESE Since the War*, *op. cit.*, pp. 274–275, and *FAOY 1952*, UN, FAO, Rome, 1953, pp. 45 and 49.
Y: *Statistički Godišnjak 1954*, *op. cit.*, pp. 121–122 and *ibid.*, *1956*, pp. 101–106.

1948–49: *Rocznik Statystyczny 1949*, *op. cit.*, International Section, pp. 273–275.
Y: *Ibid.*

1953–55: For all, excluding Poland and Yugoslavia, "Podaci o posleratnom Privrednom Razvitku SSSR i Zemalja Istočne Evrope," *op. cit.*, *passim*; *ESE in 1954*, *op. cit.*, p. 41; *ESE in 1955*, *op. cit.*, p. 174; and *Economic Bulletin for Europe*, Vol. 8, No. 1, (May 1956), p. 56.
P: *Monthly Bulletin of Statistics*, May 1956, *op. cit.*, p. XIV.
Y: *Statistički Godišnjak*, *1956*, *op. cit.*

TABLE 107. PRODUCTION PER CAPITA OF MAIN CROPS

	Czechoslovakia			Poland		
	1934–38	1948	1953	1934–38	1948	1953
Bread-grain	210	204	201	251	330	253
Coarse grain	171	198	212	127	140	133
Potatoes	815	533	672	1,083	1,116	1,198

	Hungary			Romania		
	1934–38	1948	1953	1934–38	1948	1953 (bread-grain and coarse grain combined)
Bread-grain	318	256	285	176	157	309
Coarse grain	349	336	349	329	339	
Potatoes	232	293	207	78	69	134

	Bulgaria			Yugoslavia		
	1934–38	1948	1953	1934–38	1948	1953
Bread-grain	313	286	364	191	175	165
Coarse grain	240	173	214	389	301	273
Potatoes	18	14	[a]	105	93	121

[a] Not available.

Sources: As in Table 106.

TABLE 108. LIVESTOCK BREEDING

(in thousands)

	Czechoslovakia				Poland			
	1938	1948	1953	1955	1938	1948	1953	1955
Horses	662	629	[b]	700 [c]	3,916	2,307	2,720	3,000
Cattle	4,376	3,461	3,842	3,890	10,554	6,390	7,400	8,100
Pigs	3,538	2,566	3,456	4,770	7,525	6,630	9,700	11,000
Sheep	519	387	1,106	1,327	3,411	1,410	3,300	4,300
	Hungary				Romania			
	1938	1948 [a]	1953	1955	1938	1948	1953	1955
Horses	939	569	681	729	2,042	939	1,073	1,200
Cattle	2,372	2,070	2,200	2,128	3,494	4,277	4,581	4,800
Pigs	3,886	5,200	4,500	5,818	2,296	1,823	3,634	5,600
Sheep	1,868	591	1,637	1,857	9,767	10,900	[b]	12,500
	Bulgaria				Yugoslavia			
	1938	1948	1953	1955	1938	1948	1953	1955
Horses	584	550	460	470	1,273	973	1,127	1,250
Cattle	1,512	1,910	1,700	1,900 [c]	4,225	5,260	4,995	5,300
Pigs	752	1,080	2,070	2,400	3,504	3,439	4,520	4,780 [c]
Sheep	9,935	9,000 [d]	7,872 [d]	8,500 [c]	10,153	9,970	11,400	12,000 [c]

[a] 1948–49.
[b] Not available.
[c] Projection.
[d] Estimate.

Sources:

1938: For all: *Rocznik Statystyczny 1949, op. cit.*, International Section, p. 275.

1948: *ESE Since the War, op. cit.*, p. 273, completed for:
C: *Statistical Digest of the Czechoslovak Republic 1948, op. cit.*, p. 69.
P: *Wieś w Liczbach, op. cit.* (1st ed.), p. 96.
H, Y: *FAOY 1948*, UN, FAO, Rome, 1949, pp. 110, 111, 118, 122, 126.
B: *ESE in 1954*, p,. 271.

1953: For all, excluding Poland: *ESE in 1954, op. cit.*, p. 271.
P: *Monthly Bulletin of Statistics*, May 1956, *op. cit.*, p. XIV.

1955: For all excluding Hungary and Yugoslavia: *ESE in 1955, op. cit.*, p. 175 and projections.
H: *Magyar Statisztikai Zsebkőnyv, 1956, op. cit.*, pp. 118–120.
Y: *Statistički Godišnjak 1956, op. cit.*, pp. 113–114.

CHAPTER 10

MANPOWER AND MANAGEMENT

Changes in the Manpower Base: Population 1930–60

We have concerned ourselves up to now with the material aspects of the implementation of the plans. We now turn to the human aspects, i.e., to manpower and management. The manpower base of a country is determined by its population—its size, its age-group structure, its potential expansion, and its skills. The development of managerial groups is dependent on the general level of technology and scientific activity of the country and on the training facilities in plants and enterprise and in schools of all types.

The total population in the *present* territories of Eastern Europe [1] can be estimated at some 87 million in 1930 and some 97 million in 1938. At the end of the war, as a result of war casualties and population displacements, the total population in the present territories amounted to around 84 million. By 1953 it had increased to over 90 million. Assuming these trends have continued, the total population must have been almost 93 million in 1955 and will be over 99 million (2.5 million over the 1938 level) in 1960. Thus, the war losses and displacements will have been made up in some fifteen years (see Table 109).[2]

[1] It should be noted that these figures are different from those presented in Chapter 1, Table 1, p. 4, since the latter refer to prewar territories.

[2] The projections, based on the period 1948–53, or 1953–55, have been obtained by means of the formula $P_1 = P_0(1r)^t$, where P_0 is the population at the beginning of the period, P_1 is the population at the end of the period, t is the number of years

TABLE 109. CHANGES IN TOTAL POPULATION IN PRESENT TERRITORIES, AND PROJECTIONS

(Selected years, 1930–60. In thousands.)

	1930	1938	1948	1953	1955	1960
Czechoslovakia	13,998	14,603	12,339	12,712	12,967	13,625
Poland	30,000	35,090	23,970	26,511	27,341	29,450
Hungary	8,688	9,159	9,205	9,632	9,865	10,305
Romania	14,282 [a]	15,682	15,873	17,150	17,400	18,600
Bulgaria	6,110	6,737	7,090	7,460	7,609	7,995
Yugoslavia	13,780	15,384	15,817	16,927	17,557	19,118
Total	86,858	96,655	84,294	90,392	92,739	99,093

[a] 1932.

Sources:

1930: C: *Statistical Bulletin of Czechoslovakia*, II, 8 (October 1948).
P: *Statistical Yearbook of Poland, 1947, op. cit.*, p. 12.
H: *Annuaire statistique hongrois, 1937, op. cit.*, p. 13.
R: *UNDY 1948*, UN, New York, 1949, p. 104.
B: *Statisticheski Godishnik' . . . 1938, op. cit.*, p. 15.
Y: *Statistički Godišnjak . . . 1938–1939, op. cit.*, p. 111.

1938: *UNDY 1948, op. cit.*, pp. 102–104, 147 (Poland). Both 1930 and 1938 for Bulgaria corrected by adding population of southern Dobrogea.

1948: *UNDY 1952*, UN, New York, 1953, pp. 97–98, 126–129.
Y: *Statistički Godišnjak FNRJ 1954, op. cit.*, p. 54.

1953: P: *Rocznik Statystyczny 1955, op. cit.*, p. 1.
H: *New Hungary, op. cit.*, Vol. V, No. 5 (July–August 1955), p. 4.
Y: Same as for 1948.
C, R, B: Estimated.

1955, 1960: (except Yugoslavia) author's projections.
Y: Same as for 1948.

The two world wars and the post-World War II displacements significantly affected the age structure of the population. As can be seen from Table 110 a notable ageing of the population as a whole is registered in the region. Thus by 1948–49 in Czechoslovakia 21.7 per cent of the population was over 50 years old as against 19.8 per cent before the war; in Poland 16.3 per cent as against 15 per cent; in Hungary 23.2 per cent as against 20.3 per cent; in Bulgaria 17.1 per cent as against 15.3 per cent; and in Yugoslavia 16.7 per cent as against

intervening, and r is the annual rate of change. Given the character of the data on population by ages, no use could be made of mortality tables, and we had to resort for projections to the general formula. The annual rate (per cent) has been computed as being around 1.0 for Czechoslovakia, Hungary, Romania, and Bulgaria, around 1.5 for Poland, and 1.6 for Yugoslavia.

15.5 per cent. The same trend is apparent in Romania.[3] Of those over 50 years old the number over 65 has substantially increased in Czechoslovakia, where it represented 7.6 per cent as against 6.7 per cent before the war, Hungary, 8.0 per cent as against 7.0 per cent, Yugoslavia, 5.7 per cent as against 5.4 per cent; probably the same is true in the other countries.

TABLE 110. PERCENTAGE DISTRIBUTION OF POPULATION BY AGES, PREWAR AND POSTWAR

	Prewar					Postwar (1948–49) [a]				
Country	−14	15–49	50–64	65+	Un-known	−14	15–49	50–64	65+	Un-known
Czechoslovakia	25.7	54.5	13.1	6.7	[b]	24.3	53.9	14.1	7.6	0.1
Poland	32.5	52.5	7.3	7.7	[b]	28.4	55.3	11.3	5.0	[b]
Hungary	26.0	53.7	13.3	7.0	[c]	24.5	52.3	15.2	8.0	
Romania [d]	33.5	52.5	9.0	4.5	0.5	28.9	(47.0)	(15.9)	(8.2)	[b]
Bulgaria	35.5	49.2		15.3		27.7	55.2		17.1	
Yugoslavia	34.6	49.9	10.1	5.4	[c]	32.1	51.2	11.0	5.7	[c]

[a] Czechoslovakia, 1947; Bulgaria, 1945.
[b] Included in the 65+ age group.
[c] Negligible.
[d] The Romanian figures for the postwar period comprise the following age groups: −14; 15–44; 45–59; 60+.

Sources:
C: *CEB*, III, 5 (May 1948), pp. 79–80.
P: *Kultura*, Numer Krajowy, IV, *op. cit.*
H: *Trends in Economic Growth. A Comparison of the Western Powers and the Soviet Bloc*, prepared for the Joint Committee on the Economic Report (83d Congress), Legislative Reference Service of the Library of Congress, Washington, 1955.
All others: *UNDY 1948* and *1952*, *op. cit.*

In proportion to total population the productive age groups in 1948–49 were as large as and sometimes even slightly larger than before the war except in Czechoslovakia. The group from 15 to 49 in Poland was 55.3 per cent of the total population as compared to 52.5 per cent before the war; in Bulgaria, 55.2 as against 49.2; and in Yugoslavia, 51.2 as against 49.9. However, in the examination of these figures two facts should be taken into consideration: first, the decline of almost 50 per cent in the birth rate in the period from 1915 to 1918; second, that the slight increases in the relative share of the 15–49 group are due to the very significant decrease in the age group through

[3] Dr. A. Golopenţia and Dr. D. C. Georgescu, *Populaţia Republicii Populare Române la 25 Januarie 1948, Rezultatele Provizorii ale Recensământului* (The Population of the People's Republic of Romania on January 25, 1948. The Provisional Results of the Census), Institutul Central de Statistică (Central Statistical Office), Bucharest, 1948, *passim*.

14 years of age. Before the two world wars the age pyramid rested on a large youth base. In 1948–49 the youth base was much smaller, the proportion of population in the 0–14 age group having decreased in Czechoslovakia from 25.7 per cent in the 1930's to 24.3 per cent; in Poland from 32.5 to 28.4, in Hungary from 26.0 to 24.5, in Romania from 33.5 to 28.9, in Bulgaria from 35.5 to 27.7, and in Yugoslavia from 34.6 to 32.1.

During the second, and possibly third, planned quinquennium the impact of the Second World War will be strongly felt. Relatively fewer persons than normally were born between 1940 and 1945 and this fact is reflected in deficits at ages 1 to 5 in 1945, 11 to 15 in 1956, and 21 to 35 in 1966. Only during the latter part of the third quinquennium will this trend be overcome.

Expansion of the Population Outside Agriculture

War losses, postwar displacements, and nationalization sharply changed both the number and structure of the total non-agricultural population. As can be seen from Table 111, in 1948 in most of the countries of the area this total had fallen below the levels reached in the thirties, both absolutely and proportionately to the total population. After 1948 and through the first period of development up to 1953 a powerful expansion appears to have taken place, resulting in increases in both the total and the ratio of active to total population. Between 1948 and 1953 there was a net increase of the non-agricultural labor force of about 400,000 in Bulgaria, 465,000 in Yugoslavia, close to 600,000 in Czechoslovakia, 750,000 in Hungary, 825,000 in Romania, and over 1.9 million in Poland. It is interesting to note that these great changes did not affect the three-part pattern of development already observable before the war.[4] Czechoslovakia is the only country in which the ratio of active population is over 32 per cent; in Poland and Hungary it is 23–27, and in the others it is 15–16.

At the core of the expansion of the total, active non-agricultural population lies the expansion of the labor force in mining and manufacture. Other important increases took place in building, transportation, and the state bureaucracies.

The increases in mining and manufacture during the period considered ranged from over 100,000 in Bulgaria and Yugoslavia to 270,000

[4] See Chapter 1, Concluding Remarks.

TABLE 111. TOTAL LABOR FORCE OUTSIDE AGRICULTURE

Country	Prewar		1948		1953	
	Absolute (in thousands)	% of total population	Absolute (in thousands)	% of total population	Absolute (in thousands)	% of total population
	1	2	3	4	5	6
Czechoslovakia	4,864	34.8	3,541	28.7	4,125	32.4
Poland	5,253	17.5	4,500	18.7	6,443	24.3
Hungary	1,967	22.6	1,800	19.5	2,550	25.4
Romania	2,095	14.7	1,875	11.8	2,700	15.7
Bulgaria	688	11.5	809	11.4	1,192	16.0
Yugoslavia	1,583	11.5	2,046	12.9	2,511	14.9

Sources:

Col. 1: Same as for Table 2 (prewar frontiers), Chapter 1, p. 5

Col. 2: C: *Zprávy Státního Úřadu Statistického*, Series D-F-G, Vol. XXX (1949), No. 1–3.

P: Minc, in *FLP*, Jan. 15, 1949, and *ESE in 1954*, *op. cit.*, p. 38.

H: *HB*, March 11, 1950, and *ESE in 1954*, *op. cit.*, p. 38.

R: Dr. A. Golopenţia and Dr. D. C. Georgescu, *op. cit.*, p. 11.

B: D. Terpeshev, *op. cit.*,

Y: U. S. Dept. of Commerce, Bureau of the Census: *The Population of Yugoslavia*, by Paul F. Myers and Arthur A. Campbell, International Population Statistics Reports, Series P-90, No. 5, U.S. Govt. Printing Office, Washington, 1954, p. 73.

Col. 5: For some countries the data refer to the "socialist economy" and hence include technicians and other personnel of MTS and state farms.

C, H, R: *ESE in 1954*, *op. cit.*, p. 38.

P: *Rocznik Statystyczny 1955*, *op. cit.*, p. 199.

B: For 1948–52 inclusive, *Bulgaria Today*, III, 1 (January 1954), 1953, *FLP*, Feb. 5, 1954.

Y: *Statistički Godišnjak FNRJ 1954*, *op. cit.*, p. 94.

Cols. 2, 4, 6: Computed; data on population from Table 109.

in Czechoslovakia, over 300,000 in Romania, and 460,000 in Hungary,[5] increases by and large more substantial than those projected in the plans for a five-year period (see Tables 112 and 75). The increase in Poland was probably around 650,000, appreciably more than forecast. Although in absolute figures employment in mining and manufacture in Poland became larger than in any other country of the area (close to one-third the total of over 6.4 million in the area as a whole) it should be noted that in the ratio of employment in mining and manu-

[5] The increases in "new" workers were actually smaller, as these figures include some of the handicraft absorbed in the nationalized sector.

TABLE 112. EMPLOYMENT IN MINING AND MANUFACTURE, 1948 AND 1953

	1948		1953	
	Absolute (in thousands)	% of total population	Absolute (in thousands)	% of total population
Czechoslovakia	1,362	11.0	1,630	12.9
Poland	1,494	6.2	2,472	9.2
Hungary	440	4.7	900	9.3
Romania	400 [a]	2.5	716	4.0
Bulgaria	165	2.3	247	3.3
Yugoslavia	452	2.8	594	3.5

[a] Estimate.

Sources:

1948: C: *L'Evolution economique de la Tchecoslovaquie*, *op. cit.*, p. 39.
P: See Chapter 3, Table 28, p. 63.
H: *ESE in 1954*, *op. cit.*, p. 38.
R: M. Biji, "Intreprinderile Industriale Particulare . . .," *op. cit.*,
B: F. T. Konstantinov, edit.: *Vtoroi Piatiletnii Plan . . .*, *op. cit.*, p. 47.
Y: *Privreda FNRJ U 1952 Godini, S Osvrtom na Posleratni Razvoj* (The Economy of FPRY in 1952 with reference to its postwar development), Ekonomski Institut FNRJ (Economic Institute of the FPRY), Belgrade, 1953, p. 113.

1953: C: *CEB*, No. 282, Mar. 1, 1954.
P: *Rocznik Statystyczny 1955*, *op. cit.*, pp. 2, 83.
H: *ESE in 1954*, *op. cit.*, p. 38, and *Economic Bulletin for Europe*, Vol. 7, No. 2 (Aug. 1955), p. 90.
R: Index from the *Economic Bulletin for Europe*, Vol. 2, No. 1 (July 1950), p. 95 (applied to the 1948 figures).
B: As above for 1948.
Y: *Statistički Godišnjak FNRJ 1954*, *op. cit.*, p. 96.

facture to *total* population the three levels of development already familiar to us are still noticeable. In Czechoslovakia this ratio was close to 13 per cent; in Hungary and Poland it varied around 9 per cent, and in the other three countries of the area, around 3–4 per cent.

As might be expected, the major part of the expansion in industry was in engineering. Total employment in engineering in the three most developed countries increased between 1948 and 1953: in Czechoslovakia from some 400,000 to nearly 500,000; in Poland from 280,000 to nearly 500,000; and in Hungary from 84,000 to 135,000. In the same period employment in the textile industry decreased in Czechoslovakia from 270,000 to 220,000, remained stationary in Poland at around 330,000, and increased in the other countries, but far less than in engineering, for instance, from 70,000 to 90,000 in Hungary.

The increases in total industrial employment over and above the targets set by the plan reveal both the drive for the fulfillment of production goals and the failure to achieve planned gains in productivity. In order to achieve production goals, many plants had resorted to hiring additional unregistered labor, and others had created manpower reserves as a hedge against turnover, absenteeism, cases of sickness, etc. In an over-all analysis of the development of output during the period 1948–53 in the entire area Stefan Jędrychowski, a member of the Central Committee of the Polish United Workers' Party, remarks:

> The growth of industrial output in recent years has been determined only partially by increased labour productivity. *It was mainly due to the significant growth in the numbers* employed in industry.[6]

If we apply the index numbers of *gross output* of industry, we note certain changes in the level of output per man. As may be seen from Table 113, by 1948 this level appears to have fallen below prewar in

TABLE 113. LEVEL OF OUTPUT PER MAN IN INDUSTRY, 1948 AND 1953

(prewar = 100)

	1948			1953		
Country	Index of output 1	Index of employment 2	1 ÷ 2 3	Index of output 4	Index of employment 5	4 ÷ 5 6
Czechoslovakia	108	111	97	218	134	147
Poland	140	180	77	360	299	120
Hungary	107	110	97	290	225	128
Romania	85	107	79	250	191	130
Bulgaria	184	160	115	441	240	183
Yugoslavia	150	147	102	183	187	97

Sources: Output indices, cf. Table 104, p. 376. For 1938 employment, cf. Chapter 1, Table 5, p. 10 (for Hungary, 400,000, instead of 469,000, employment capacity). For 1948, 1953, see above, Table 112, p. 386.

all the countries except Bulgaria and Yugoslavia. After 1948 and up to 1953 the prewar level seems to have been reached and surpassed in the area as a whole, except for Yugoslavia. Leaving out Bulgaria, the most substantial increase in productivity was in Czechoslovakia, an increase of 47 per cent over prewar. In the other countries of the

[6] Stefan Jędrychowski, "Concern for Well-Being of Working People in People's Democracies," *FLP,* Jan. 29, 1954. Italics supplied.

area, excluding Yugoslavia, the increases ranged from 20 to 30 per cent over prewar. However, it should be noted that *the upward bias of the index numbers of output also distorts the figure on the level of output per man.* For Bulgaria, this is quite obvious, and the figure should be discarded as highly inflated.

The high increases in the labor force over and above the plan targets definitely reduced the validity of the forecasts about the "wage fund" and the possibility of obtaining investment funds from increases in productivity.

Concurrent with the influx of labor in mining and manufacture, notable increases were achieved, as already noted, in building. In Czechoslovakia the total number gainfully employed in construction between 1949 and 1953 rose from 270,000 to 420,000, in Poland from 340,000 to 740,000, and in Hungary from 100,000 to 270,000.

Last, there were large additions to the state bureaucracies. We can distinguish in turn: (1) the central government, excluding the Ministries of Interior and War, (2) the Ministries of Interior and War, (3) teachers, (4) state monopolies and enterprises, and (5) local governments.

1. The central government, excluding Interior and War Ministries, included before the war some 60–80,000 persons in Hungary and Czechoslovakia, approximately 100,000 in Romania and Yugoslavia, and about 110,000 in Poland.[7] There were various changes in these administrations, *but their total numbers apparently did not change drastically.*[8]

2. There are many indications of large expansions of the Ministries of Interior and of War; however, no over-all completely reliable tabulation can be secured.[9]

[7] See above, Chapter 1, Table 11, p. 21.

[8] Thus, for instance, the central government proper, excluding 2, 3, and 4, as above, was around 60,000 in Hungary in 1946–47. Cf. *GT*, I, 2 (1947), p. 78. For Poland, cf. data from 1946 through 1949 in *Rocznik Statystyczny 1949, op. cit.*, p. 142.

[9] According to a series of articles by Casimir Smogorzewski, a Polish writer now a member of the editorial staff of the *Encyclopedia Britannica,* the interior and armed forces of these countries (excluding Yugoslavia) were as follows in 1952:

	Interior Forces	Armed Forces
Poland	100,000	450,000
Romania	70,000	255,000
Czechoslovakia	60,000	190,000
Hungary	50,000	135,000
Bulgaria	40,000	170,000
Total	320,000	1,200,000

(Footnote continued on p. 389.)

3. There was certainly an increase in the number of teachers, in some countries as many as to double the total in the prewar period.

4. There was a substantial reorganization in the state monopolies and enterprises. Most of the former state monopolies became autonomous units like the nationalized enterprises. Only the public services, administration of forests, and such were grouped under the budgetary heading of state undertakings, and their personnel treated as state employees. There are numerous indications of substantial increases in this category of personnel. In transportation (state railways) in the area as a whole, for instance, there were large increases during the reconstruction period, at a time when railway traffic had not even recovered its prewar level.

5. Large increases occurred also in the *local governments* whose sphere of operation had been extended so that it embraced the "industries of local interest." [10]

Town Labor Reserves and Women's Labor

The large expansion in the non-agricultural population during the first plan of development drew first on the *town labor reserves* of the young, the unemployed, the displaced, those engaged in less essential

(Footnote continued from p. 388.)
(Cf. "Au Service de Staline" [In the Service of Stalin], in *Le Monde,* May 13, 1952.) Scattered data seem to substantiate at least the order of magnitude represented by these figures. Thus, for instance, the Hungarian state police force and other security forces were officially given as about 36,500 in 1946–47, as well as in 1949. (Cf. *GT,* as in note 8 above, and *Társadalmi Szemle* [Social Review], Budapest, March–April 1949.) This would compare to some 20,000 before the war (cf. above, Chapter 1, p. 22). The Yugoslavs claim that their police force decreased from 41,200 in 1950 to 28,000 in 1953 (cf. *Yugoslav Review,* III, 1–2 [January–February 1954], p. 12).

For the armed forces, various estimates given in the Western press set the armies of the five countries mentioned at around 1 million (cf., for instance, *New York Times,* Aug. 22, 1950). The Yugoslav army is said to be of the order of 500,000. A study of the armed forces of these countries written by a Yugoslav officer gives for each the number of divisions and their types, on the basis of which an estimate could be made of the total forces involved. (Cf. Colonel Ivan [pseud.], a series of articles, "On the Development of the Armed Forces of Cominform Countries," in *Review of International Affairs,* IV, 2, 4, 5, and 6 [January to March 1953].)

It should be noted that the armed forces as such are not usually counted in the labor force but represent a separate category. Their importance is relevant here in relation to the "weight" of the War Ministry.

[10] Thus, for instance, in Poland, the staff of the local authorities amounted in 1948 to 192,524 people, of whom 100,348 were in the local administration proper and 92,176 in the administration of financial enterprises and plants. Cf. *Statistical Year book of Poland 1948, op. cit.,* p. 227.

occupations, and, more than ever before, on the female labor pool, and second on the man power available from the *countryside*. Labor available in towns was more easily trained for semiskilled and skilled jobs, and was already on the spot; it was more difficult to sustain a flow from agriculture. Land reforms had anchored some small peasants, landless peasants, and farm hands to their new land, and the attractions of the towns were offset by the bad housing situation and rationed distribution of food there.

There was a strong appeal to the young in the fact that many of them were entrusted with high positions in management. The re-entrance into the labor force of various people previously employed in less essential occupations is indicated by the decrease in workers in handicrafts, domestic servants, etc.[11]

The increase in the female labor force, perhaps the most significant of the increases mentioned, deserves some elaboration. According to the official data, in 1953–55 the female labor force in the three most developed countries of the area, Czechoslovakia, Poland, and Hungary, oscillated between 31 and 35 per cent of the total labor force in mining and manufacture as compared to some 25 per cent before the war. In the smaller countries of the area, where the demand for labor was not so great, the proportion of women was smaller. In Romania, for instance, it was 24 per cent of "the total number of wage-earners in all the spheres of activity." [12]

The large increase in the total female labor force (e.g., one-half the net increase in industrial employment in Czechoslovakia from 1950 to 1952) was accompanied by wide diversification in the jobs

[11] Paragraph 9 of the Act instituting the two-year plan in Czechoslovakia indicated clearly the sources from which additional labor should be recruited and how labor should be channeled:

(*a*) persons who can be dispensed with in their present work will change over to branches where they are urgently required; (*b*) skilled workers will gradually return to their original trade; (*c*) the recruitment of juvenile workers will be planned; (*d*) persons who are capable of work but have not yet taken up any employment will be recruited for productive work; (*e*) the number of gainfully employed women will be increased; (*f*) persons of impaired working capacity will be recruited; (*g*) re-immigration of Czechs living abroad will be encouraged; (*h*) work-competitions will be organised, in order to raise the efficiency of all workers. [In summary:] (1) re-deployment of labour from over-staffed occupations into industry, agriculture and the building trade; (2) recruitment of new workers; (3) raising of efficiency. [Cf. Dr. B. Glos, *The Mobilisation of Labour in Czechoslovakia,* Orbis, Prague, 1948, pp. 29–30.]

[12] Cf., for Czechoslovakia, *ESE in 1953, op. cit.*, p. 73; for Poland, *Rocznik Statystyczny 1955, op. cit.*, p. 84; for Hungary, *SN*, May 21, 1952; for Romania, *RN*, Nov. 25, 1953. Also, *Economic Bulletin for Europe*, Vol. 8, No. 3 (November 1956), p. 39.

open to women. Because of war losses, shifts in the age groups, maintenance of armed forces, and the over-all new employment pattern, women in industrial employment were working not only in textiles, clothing, glass and ceramics, and food-processing industries (that is, in their traditional labor roles), but also in mining, iron and steel works, and building. Furthermore, significant numbers of women replaced male workers in post offices, the civil services in general, transportation, trade, and banking.

Official literature reveals the employment of women at blast furnaces, in shipyards, and as bricklayers, tractor drivers, deep-sea fishermen, lumberjacks, firemen, and so on. Detailed data released by Poland for 1954 indicate that female labor represented in that year 11.0 per cent of the labor force in the fuel industry, 18.2 per cent in ferrous mining and metallurgy, 23.1 per cent in nonferrous mining and metallurgy, 20.8 per cent in power plants, 23.1 per cent in the lumber and wood-working industry. In Hungary in 1952 the relative share of female labor was 4 times as large as before the war in the iron and metal industries and 13 times as large in building; moreover, 42.5 per cent of the railroad and streetcar conductors and 62 per cent of the post-office employees were women. In all these countries women figure prominently among the "stakhanovites," in the "shock brigades," and in the higher technical posts including engineers and certain executive jobs.[13]

The increase in the supply of female labor was undoubtedly due to such factors as the desire for higher pay (in reward for both very heavy work and higher skills), better social care for their children (nurseries

[13] In a rather lyrical mood *Szabad Nép* wrote:

> Women are now operating lathes, huge cranes, conduct streetcars, direct street traffic. . . . Our hearts are filled with proud joy when we see them in military and police uniforms, when we hear their reports as heads of producers' cooperatives, leaders of brigades . . . 100 factory managers, 658 foremen, 696 crane operators, roughly 4,000 streetcar conductors, over 700 automobile drivers, over 600 tractor drivers, 111 heads of producers' cooperatives, 305 council chairmen—these figures are a vivid proof of the equality between men and women. [April 1, 1952.]

And the Romanians added:

> In the past, the working women of Romania were deprived of the most elementary right, subjected to ruthless exploitation and kept in a state of inferiority to men. . . . Compared with 1948, in 1951 the number of women employed in industry was 200 per cent greater; it increased 157.1 per cent in trade, transport and banks, and by 191.3 per cent in the civil service. An ever increasing number of women from the ranks of the people are being entrusted with responsible jobs which they carry on successfully. . . . There are 1,650 women stakhanovites and 18,000 leaders in production; 17 women are chairmen of collective farms, and in 1951, 1,105 women were on the managing boards of collective farms. [Cf. *RN*, Nov. 25, 1953.]

for children of factory workers),[14] and the fact that the income of one wage earner is often insufficient to support a family.

Agricultural Labor Force

Since there was a high demand for labor and insufficient surplus labor from the countryside, labor shortages appeared once the reserves of the town were absorbed. The industrialization process attracted youth, i.e., the natural increase, but not the non-productive surplus agricultural population.

The scanty data available on rural population, population in agriculture, and agricultural labor force, are grouped in Table 114. The figures concern two postwar periods: 1946–49 and 1953–56. As appears from column 1, the rural population represented in the first period some 51 per cent of the total population of Czechoslovakia, from 65 to 68 per cent in Poland and Hungary, and from 75 to 84 per cent in the other three countries. The data for the second period, though incomplete, point clearly toward a marked drop in these percentages, in the area as a whole during the first long-term plan. Actually it should be noted that this sharp drop in percentages was often due not to an absolute reduction in the rural population, but to increases in total population. Thus in the case of Poland, the rural population numbered 16.1 million persons in 1946, 15.6 million in 1949 after the expulsion of the Germans, 15.6 million in 1953 and again 15.6 million in 1954.[15] The rural population of Hungary was estimated at 6.0 million in 1949 and 5.6 million in 1953.[16] The rural population of Romania, according to the census data, reached 12.1 million at the beginning of 1948 and 12.0 million in early 1956.[17] The only exception to this trend is in Yugoslavia, where the rural population decreased between 1948 and 1953 from 13.2 million to 12.1 million.[18] Actually the Yugoslav statistical definitions of rural

[14] Although usually extended social protection is stressed for women in general and mothers in particular, there are also cases in which the new "equality between men and women is pushed to the point where expectant mothers are kept on night shifts, standing by the blast furnaces." Cf. *Życie Gospodarcze,* Sept. 19, 1952, *TL,* Aug. 25, 1953, as quoted by Z. Jordan, "Structure of Population," in *Polish Affairs,* II, 7–9 (September 1953).

[15] *Rocznik Statystyczny 1955, op. cit.,* p. 1.

[16] Data derived from *SS,* 3rd Year, No. 6, June 1951, p. 529, and *SN,* May 25, 1954.

[17] *SC,* May 6, 1956.

[18] Myers and Campbell: *The Population of Yugoslavia, op. cit.,* p. 31.

and urban population have been changed essentially between the two censuses and hence these data are difficult to evaluate. Judging by the Polish, the Hungarian, and the Romanian data, it appears that, at least in certain countries, the increases in urban population have been roughly equal to the increases in total population, while the rural population has remained stationary.

TABLE 114. POPULATION IN AGRICULTURE

	Rural population, as per cent of total population		Population in agriculture, as per cent of total population		Labor force in agriculture, as per cent of total labor force	
	1 1st Period [a]	2 2nd Period [b]	3 1st Period	4 2nd Period	5 1st Period	6 2nd Period
Czechoslovakia	51.2	[c]	28.0	24.0 [d]	37.8	30.2
Poland	68.6	58.1	51.6	48.7 [e]	30.1	[c]
Hungary	65.5	58.8	48.9	45.0	[c]	[c]
Romania	76.6	68.7	[c]	[c]	[c]	[c]
Bulgaria	75.4	[c]	[c]	[c]	[c]	[c]
Yugoslavia	83.8	71.5	71.7	61.7	75.0	61.4

[a] First period 1946–49 (C: 1947; P: 1948; B: 1946; H: 1949; R and Y: 1948).
[b] Second period 1953–56 (C, P, H: 1953; R: 1956).
[c] Not available.
[d] Estimate.
[e] 1951.

Sources:

Col. 1, excluding R: *UNDY 1955*, UN, New York, 1956, pp. 185, 472 ff.; R: *SC*, May 6, 1956.

Other cols.: C: *FAOY*, I, 1952, *op. cit.*, pp. 16, 18; *RP*, June 12, 1954.
P: *TL*, Dec. 28, 1949, *Wieś w Liczbach*, *op. cit.*, p. 15, *Rocznik Statystyczny 1955*, *op. cit.*, p. 1.
H: *SS*, 3rd year, No. 6, June 1951, p. 529; and *SN*, May 25, 1954.
Y: Derived from *Statistički Godišnjak 1954*, *op. cit.*, p. 56; and Myers and Campbell: *The Population of Yugoslavia*, *op. cit.*, p. 31.

The ratios of total population in agriculture (labor force and dependents) to total population have also fallen in the two periods considered as compared to prewar. In Czechoslovakia the ratios fell from 33:100 before the war to 28:100 and then 24:100 in the postwar periods; in Poland, from 60:100 to 51.6:100 and then to 48.7:100; in Yugoslavia from 76:100 to 71.7:100 and finally to 61.7:100. These falls, considered as characteristic for the process of industrialization, require, however, some qualifications. In certain countries, such as Czechoslovakia and Poland, the ratios have shifted in the first period considered, mostly because of the changes in frontiers and total population. In the second period, they have changed partially because of the increase in total population, while the agricultural population has tended to decrease only slightly. Thus the agricultural population of Poland numbered 12.6 million in 1949 and 12.4 million in 1951, the year for which the official ratio is furnished. In Yugoslavia the shifts in ratios are clearly indicative of a significant fall in agricultural populations. Thus, according to the 1948 and 1953 censuses the agricultural population has fallen from 11.1 million to 10.1 million. The data supplied by the censuses on the labor force indicate, however, on the other hand, that this fall was due not to the absorption of agricultural labor into industry, but to widespread unemployment. According to the official data, the total labor force fell in Yugoslavia from 9.4 to 7.4 million in the years considered, while the agricultural labor force for its part fell from 7.4 to 5.2 million.

By and large it appears, thus, that during the first phase of development the total population of the villages has tended to remain stationary while the agricultural population has, for its part, decreased slightly. By attracting essentially the *youth*, the *skilled workers*, and the *craftsmen* into the towns, the process of industrialization, not powerful enough to bring about marked decreases in total agricultural population, has, however, conditioned substantial changes in the age structure and composition of the villages. The systematic drawing of the youth into the towns has left many villages with no future generations to cultivate the soil. This factor, plus the low level of investment in agriculture, has imperiled output. Because of ". . . the desire to prevent a further deterioration in the age structure of the agricultural labor force and to maintain it at its present strength until more capital has been put into agriculture . . ." [19] certain countries envisaged the slowing down of industrial recruitment during the new course and again for the second quinquennium.

Drawing the craftsmen and skilled workers from the villages left the countryside without even rudimentary facilities.[20] Furthermore, it deprived the "socialist sector" itself of the cadres needed to man its

[19] *RP,* Apr. 27, 1954, as quoted in *Economic Bulletin for Europe,* Vol. 6, No. 1 (May 1954), p. 17.

[20] See above, Chapter 3, p. 75, note 45.

Machine and Tractor Stations, its agricultural cooperatives, etc.,[21] a development that necessarily aggravated the crisis in agriculture. Hence, new campaigns have been launched in all these countries for the return to the villages of the partially employed, while the emphasis of the new plans has been shifted from labor intensive to labor-saving investments.

THE ACCELERATED PROCESS OF CREATION OF TECHNICAL CADRES

How to accelerate the process of creating technical cadres, i.e., "production leaders," from the skilled worker to the foreman, technician, engineer, manager, and executive; how to produce an increasing number of cadres and allocate them first to meet the needs of both industry and agriculture and second to meet the various needs within industry; where to get those production leaders and how many were needed in the economy—these were the problems confronted during the period of reconstruction up to 1948–49 and the first period of development, and they still confront the area at the present. The attempted solutions to these problems have changed substantially since the first period.

At the end of the war the former Allied countries had suffered wholesale liquidation of their native leaders during the German occupation and faced a dearth of specialists caused both by the closing down of schools during the occupation and the flight or expulsion of foreign specialists of all types. In the first days of the liberation the transition from the occupation to the new regime was assured by the appearance of so-called "works councils" which assumed control of industry, but the power of these councils was short-lived. Young and inexperienced administrators were given responsibility by the various parties, especially the Communist Party. Top management of the nationalized enterprises was exercised by a council of delegates from various parties, as in Czechoslovakia, or by one centrally designated manager who shared direction with the head of the Communist Party section and the head of the trade union.

In the ex-enemy countries liberation had less drastic effects. Until the beginning of extensive nationalization in 1948 there was less pres-

[21] Thus in his report at the Central Committee Plenum of the Hungarian Workers' Party, on Oct. 31, 1953, Rákosi said:

> We must bear in mind that in recent years industry has so sapped agriculture of labor that producers' cooperatives, state farms and machine and tractor depots are experiencing a serious shortage of labour. Hence we must spare no effort to facilitate the return of industrial workers, who had recently quitted agriculture, to the countryside. [Cf. *FLP,* Nov. 20, 1953.]

sure to push the young and inexperienced into responsible jobs. After nationalization there developed the same general pattern of management as in the other countries.

The period of improvisation was followed by an all-out effort in technical training both for youth and for adults already placed, even at the highest posts of responsibility. The chief Polish planner, Hilary Minc, said:

> We cannot limit ourselves to the training of youth in order to form a new popular elite. This would oblige us to wait too long, and time is pressing. The Six-Year Plan, with the tasks it implies, will not wait. Fortunately, we dispose among the popular strata of elements susceptible of furnishing these cadres. During the last four years, there developed in the midst of the working class a category of people fulfilling the conditions necessary to form an elite. These are the workers who are now directors, assistant directors, foremen—i.e., specialized workers of a high value. These people have practical knowledge of industrial matters; many of them have administrative and organizational notions, and many of them have a high social consciousness. The only thing they lack is a general cultural training and a scientific education a little more developed. This training must be conveyed to them by directing them toward adequate schools and replacing them with other people. Only in this way can be realized an accelerated formation of cadres coming from the people.[22]

Let us examine the measures for adult training and those for youth. The formation of a "technically trained popular elite" was undertaken through (*a*) the training of skilled workers on the job, (*b*) special technical adult preparatory schools (for foremen and technicians), (*c*) the establishment of special university sections for the rapid training of the worker technicians as engineers, and (*d*) the training of all types of "higher cadres" in the Soviet Union.

It is difficult to disentangle information concerning this type of training from the data concerning the regular schooling system, but some idea of the magnitude of the effort can be gathered from the following comment on Romania:

> The rapid training of tens of thousands of skilled workers is accomplished not only by training new personnel, but also by retraining older workers. . . .
>
> The practice of training workers—young and old—at their places of work became more and more widespread. Thus, in 1951, 27,000

[22] Cf. *Rzeczpospolita,* Dec. 20, 1948, as quoted by *L'Économie polonaise au seuil du plan de six ans, op. cit.,* p. 20.

> workers took training courses or courses for training foremen in the enterprises of the Ministry of Metallurgy and the Chemical Industry, and over 71,000 employees of enterprises of the Coal and Oil Ministry took courses to improve their technical qualifications. . . .
>
> The Workers' Faculties, too, play an important part in the training of new personnel. There are 17 workers' university courses in various parts of the country, in which workers are trained to be engineers. In 1950–1951, there were 2,516 students enrolled in these courses.[23]

The number of cadres sent to the Soviet Union for training steadily increased after 1948–49. The cost of their Soviet training and the payment of Soviet specialists "on loan" often reached significant figures in the balance of payments of Eastern Europe, as we shall see subsequently.[24]

Parallel to the more specialized training of the best adult cadres was the concentration on the development of larger and larger strata of "stakhanovites," i.e., leaders in increasing productivity, rationalizers, and innovators with a purpose of training the working mass as a whole. Workers were encouraged to compete in attempts to increase output and improve quality by campaigns for the "improvement in utilization of materials and of machinery," for "helping those who are behind," for "a rhythmic increase," i.e., cessation of irregular output and rush work at the end of the month in order to reach the targets, for "improving the quality of the work," "to reduce waste," and so on.[25]

In addition to this training of the working force as a whole, an integrated system copied from Soviet Russia, a systematic expansion of the technical training of the youth outside the factories was organized through the development of *apprenticeship centers, tekhnikums* (specialized technical schools for the training of youth between 14 and 18), and *engineering schools,* the so-called "organiza-

[23] "Creative Initiative of Working People Develops under People's Democracy," *RN*, June 3, 1953.

[24] See below, Chapter 11.

[25] "How Socialist Competition Works" is briefly explained in an article by the same title in the *Prague News Letter,* IX, 14 (July 4, 1953):

> Socialist competition finds its expression in pledges of individual workers, of work teams, of factory shops or whole factories for plan fulfillment and over-fulfillment, savings, improved quality of products and all the other above-mentioned features. It also takes the form of challenges between workers and factories in other people's democracies and in the Soviet Union. The same applies to farmers, agricultural cooperatives and State Farms.

tional foundations" of the labor reserve system, aimed at replenishing and increasing the technical strata. Both the tekhnikums and the higher engineering schools developed at a swift pace: in 1953–54, Poland had an enrollment of 120,000 in these schools, Hungary an enrollment of 62,000, Romania, 50,000.[26] The tekhnikums, with a very wide variety of specializations,[27] graduated in Poland some 60,-000 in one year.[28] From the higher engineering schools the number of yearly graduates had increased in Czechoslovakia by 1946–47 to over 8,300 as compared to 2,200 in 1937.[29] In Poland it had reached 4,000 per year, in Hungary, 1,800 as against 150 before the war, and in Romania over 1,000 as compared to 200 before the war.[30]

As the economies expanded, many former technical specialists who had been discarded during nationalization were brought back into service. Gheorghiu-Dej, for instance, remarked:

> We must be guided by Stalin's direction: "It would be stupid and unwise to regard practically every expert and engineer of the old school as an undetected criminal and wrecker. We have always regarded and still regard 'expert-baiting' as a harmful and disgraceful phenomenon." Every old specialist determined honestly to serve the interests of our homeland, the interests of the socialist construction, will find support and sympathy in the Party and the Government. For such specialists, conditions suitable to their activity must be created, as well as the prestige and authority necessary to their activity.[31]

To cope with shortages of both skilled and unskilled workers, a more and more complex system of compulsory labor was devised, and reliance on "administrative measures" became the tacit rule. There can be little doubt that the system of *forced labor* developed apace with the increased needs imposed by over-all centralized plan-

[26] For Poland, *FLP,* May 24, 1953; for Hungary, *Magyar Statisztikai Zsebkőnyv, 1956, op. cit.,* p. 184; for Romania, *RN,* No. 243, July 15, 1953.

[27] For the mining industry, for example, the following tekhnikums were available in Hungary: deep drilling, mine surveying, mining art, mining machines, mineral-oil mining, geology. Cf. "Technical Schools—New Type Secondary Schools in Hungary," *HB,* No. 141, May 1, 1953.

[28] Brian Simon, *Education in the New Poland,* Lawrence & Wishart, London, 1955, pp. 27–28.

[29] Cf. Dr. B. Glos, *The Mobilization of Labor in Czechoslovakia, The Problem of Manpower,* Orbis, Prague, 1948, p. 138.

[30] For sources, see note 26 above.

[31] Gh. Gheorghiu-Dej, *Speech to the National Conference of Miners,* State Publishing House, Bucharest, 1952, p. 53.

ning and had become one of its most significant features.[32] Together with the development of an "administratively managed labor pool," complex state controls were devised for the channeling of the youth trained in the vocational schools or in paramilitary formations. Typical in this sense is a Polish law concerning the distribution within the economy of the graduates of tekhnikums and higher institutions. The introduction to the law reads thus:

> The growing needs of the socialist economy demand that a planned policy should be conducted in the sphere of employment of newly trained cadres, and above all of technicians. The People's State, which is spending enormous sums for the education of youth in vocation and other higher schools, should direct in a planned fashion the inflow of graduates of these schools into the socialized establishments of work and ensure the youth of the possibility of immediately participating in the socialist construction.[33]

On the other hand, wage differentials were created in order to promote stakhanovite movements to increase production and "break" the norms, to encourage technical training at all levels, and to assure up to a point the distribution of labor according to the needs and targets of the plans. Up to 1949 wages were paid partly in cash and partly in produce in kind, which varied according to occupation and rank. With the launching of the development plans, wages were paid only in cash, all wages being based on a common minimum, a spread according to the type of work, and individual productivity. Generally, the average wage in the highest-paid categories of industrial workers has been up to 2.3 times that in the lowest-paid, and within each category wages have varied according to the respective skill of the worker, the highest wages in the category being 8 or 10 times the lowest. The highest wages for clerical, technical, and executive personnel have been 5 or 6 times the lowest. Since 1949, and more so from 1953 on, continuous efforts have been made in order to increase the sphere of the piecework system as compared to the wage system by time unit (hour, day, week). Piecework is based on given norms: wages are computed by multiplying the number of

[32] The most complete assemblage of official documents and allegations concerning forced labor in the East European countries is to be found in the UN, International Labour's Office: *Report of the Ad Hoc Committee on Forced Labor, Supplement No. 13,* in the Official Records of the Sixteenth Session of the Economic and Social Council, and No. 36 in the Studies and Reports (new series) of the International Labour Office, Geneva, 1953.

[33] *Dziennik Ustaw* (Journal of Laws), No. 10, 1950, p. 106.

units produced by the appropriate rate, plus bonuses over the established norm in the given industry. Other types of piecework are the so-called pure piecework, in which the number of units produced is multiplied by a given rate per unit, progressive piecework where higher rates are applied after a given output, etc. Pay by time, now called in Eastern Europe "the lowest type of payment," varied according to the category (i.e., the range 1–2.3) and also the type of work (e.g., higher in mining as compared to textiles).[34]

New large strata of "production leaders" or "engineering-technical cadres" are developing. They include (1) recently trained technicians or engineers arising from the top layers of the working classes (usually party members), (2) new young technicians from the technical schools and higher management schools who have been selected not only for their capabilities but also because of their social origin (children of workers, peasants, or state employees), and (3) some of the old technical specialists re-integrated in the new economic setup. In the words of an official publication:

> The new intelligentsia in the countries of the people's democracy is being formed . . . from the ranks of the leading workers, from the new section of the working class which, jointly with graduates from the higher educational establishments, constitutes the core of the working-class intelligentsia, the core of the leading staff of the new intelligentsia. . . .
>
> The best part of the old intelligentsia in the people's democratic countries is also taking an active part in socialist construction.[35]

The strenuous pace of development, the necessity of drawing from given social strata, and the traditional backwardness of most of the economies create a situation which is still marked by the following officially recognized shortcomings: a definitely "reduced technical level of the cadres"; [36] a continuous process of discarding managers after

[34] For the relations between wages in general, productivity, and total money supply, see above, Chapter 4.

[35] "Powerful Upsurge of Culture in Countries of People's Democracy," *FLP,* Feb. 12, 1954.

[36] Thus Gh. Gheorghiu-Dej remarks,

> Another shortcoming is the fact that many of the cadres finishing various qualifying schools possess a reduced technical-vocational level owing both to an unsatisfactory selection of students and to the unsatisfactory level of teaching in these schools. [*Speech to the National Conference of Railwaymen,* Publishing House of the Romanian Institute for Cultural Relations with Foreign Countries, Bucharest, 1953, p. 24.]

a short period of trial and failure at their new assignments; [37] an avowed irrationality in the numbers of persons assigned to different functions (overconcentrations, especially in the administrative machinery, and dearth of specialists at the level of the plant); [38] mass fluctuation of the cadres available owing to the necessity of sending them from one place to another wherever the need appears more pressing.

"One-Man Management" and the New Role of the Party and the Trade Unions

From 1948 on it appeared, as in Russia in the 1930's, that it was necessary to strengthen the hand of the manager in order to obtain the increases required by the plans and assure "labor discipline" all along the production line. With the over-all reorganization of industry,[39] the principle of responsibility for one administrator at each level was emphasized. Simultaneously the role of the secretary of the Party in the enterprise was redefined and that of the trade union oriented in a new direction. The principle of "one-man management" may be summarized as follows:

> Each unit of production is led by a chief who assumes the entire responsibility for his sector, who enjoys unlimited powers, and who is subordinated directly to the chief of the next echelon.[40]
>
> The minister is responsible for the entire work of his ministry. And in exactly the same way the team-leader is responsible for the

[37] Some of the reasons are given in the speech referred to in note 36, above:

> The schooling plans elaborated without taking into account the requirements of the concrete situation on the spot . . . ; the bureaucratic and indifferent attitude toward the constant raising of cadres and towards their living and working conditions; the posting and promoting of cadres without knowing them, by way of administrative decisions taken from the office chair, etc. [*Ibid.*, p. 26.]

Also, for instance, a Bulgarian source indicates that often the cadres are selected either solely for political or for professional merits, and adds ". . . such a one-sided approach leads to mistakes in the matter of promoting cadres and is one of the main reasons for the great fluctuation in personnel." *RD,* as quoted by *FLP,* Oct. 9, 1953.

[38] Thus, for instance, *SN,* of Dec. 13, 1953, writes: "Skilled and well-educated agricultural experts work in agriculture only in small numbers; the greater part is engaged in administrative work." On the other hand, a Polish source indicates that, out of a total of 6,000 engineers in the Ministry of Machines Industry, only 72 were working in factories for agricultural machinery, notwithstanding the launching of the "new course."

[39] See above, Chapter 3, pp. 57 ff.

[40] Cf. J. Dolanský, in *RP,* Sept. 9, 1951.

> work of his team, for its labor discipline, for quantity and the quality of work. It follows that leadership and responsibility are very closely linked, that they organically supplement each other. The higher the post of the leader, the greater his responsibility.[41]

Starting from the top of the pyramid, the leading organs were not to interfere in all the affairs of a plant or enterprise but to limit themselves to approving plans, helping in their execution, nominating the direction cadres, and establishing in principle the indices for the utilization of capacity, consumption of raw materials and energy, and so on.

The role of the party cadres in factories and undertakings was defined as follows:

> The Party organizations must from time to time hear reports from leaders on their work; they must develop on a wider scale criticism and self-criticism, helping thereby to eliminate shortcomings and mistakes quickly. However, the Party organizations must not—on the pretext of effecting control or on any other pretext—violate the principle of one-man management; must not substitute manager, engineer, head of department or foreman. The Party organization in the factory cannot give operative instructions to a production leader; it cannot cancel or change instructions to a production leader; it cannot cancel or change instructions issued by leaders of enterprises.[42]

The activity of the trade unions, which, up to 1948, during the period of "mixed economy" with large private sectors, had spearheaded the attack against the latter and exercised control over management at every level, was oriented in a completely different direction. Their essential aims now were to "help to make the most of the working day,"[43] organize competition and emulation, abolish absenteeism and fluctuation, and be, in fact, the watchdog to see that the plan was fulfilled and overfulfilled. The trade union leaders were supposed to "cooperate" with management and at the same time express the "workers' interest" by helping to frame the collective agreements between management and workers in such a way that "on the one side the state plan should be fulfilled and exceeded and on the other hand the living conditions and the status of the work-

41 Cf. "For Strengthening One-Man Management in Industry in Hungary," *FLP*, Nov. 16, 1951.

42 *Ibid.*

43 Raiko Damianov, "Bulgarian Trade Unions Fight to Carry Out Five-Year Plan," *FLP*, Mar. 1, 1949.

ers should be improved."[44] The official press frequently complained that the trade unions tried to "organize" emulation by issuing decrees, and "proclaimed" in the name of the workers, but without their participation, "pledges" to fulfill and overfulfill the plans.[45] Notwithstanding the fact that the trade union had nothing to do with the "defense" of the workers' interests, they embraced almost all the wage and salary earners since membership was virtually compulsory.[46]

The basic purpose of the establishment of the system of "one-man management" was, and still is, to make "the chain of relations, Ministry–to Central Administrations–to single establishments, direct, so that plan fulfillment could be exactly located and insisted upon."[47] However, Party interference and control continue to operate haphazardly all along the line. The role of the Party sections, especially of the section to develop "criticism and self-criticism, helping thereby to eliminate shortcomings and mistakes quickly," is such that management is under their *de facto* tutelage. The following Bulgarian statement is typical.

> The Party Committee in the factory, helped by the city and district committees, analysed in detail the reasons for the lag and worked out concrete measures for better work by the enterprise. No. 2 shop

[44] "Labour Collective Agreements," in *AIB,* III, 35 (Sept. 20, 1952).

[45] Thus, for instance, István Kristóf, a member of the Politbureau of the Hungarian Workers' Party, writes:

> In some enterprises the development of emulation is hindered by bureaucratism. We still have among us economic, Party and trade union leaders who, without the participation of the working people "proclaim" the pledge of the enterprise, and, in doing so, distort the idea of emulation. They often try to "organise" emulation by issuing decrees, failing to understand that the initiative of the masses is the most essential element in emulation. [Cf. "Socialist Emulation in Hungarian People's Republic," *FLP,* April 3, 1953.]

This fact is repeated quite often in each of the other "people's democracies." See, for instance, Wiktor Klosiewicz, "New Attitude towards Labour in People's Poland," *FLP,* May 22, 1953.

[46] In 1948 in Czechoslovakia and Poland the trade unions embraced the majority of the labor force outside agriculture. After 1948, the trade unions increased extremely rapidly in the other countries also, reaching by 1953 as much as 75 to over 90 per cent of the total labor force: 1.77 million in Hungary, with a labor force of 2.41 million (cf. István Kristóf, "Report to the Eighteenth Trade Union Congress," *Népszava,* Feb. 28, and Mar. 3, 1953); 2.3 million in Romania with a labor force of 2.5 million (cf. "The Third Congress of Trade Unions of the RPR," in *AIB,* IV, 5 (Feb. 7, 1953).

[47] Dorothy W. Douglas, *Transitional Economic Systems: The Polish-Czech Example, op. cit.,* p. 172.

> was the "bottle-neck," being 50 per cent behind plan. The Party Committee took the shop under constant supervision. The leadership was strengthened on its initiative, greater mechanisation was introduced and other concrete and effective measures were taken. The carrying out of these measures yielded positive results: work in the shop considerably improved.[48]

Thus control and "supervision" and strengthening of "leadership" do not follow the establishment of the one-man management chain as they are supposed to do; this is true not only at the level of the plant but also at district, regional, and other levels. The press of all the countries is full of complaints about the "bureaucratic approach to the problem of management," "arbitrary interferences," and so on. The following illustrates an extreme case:

> A typical example of this departmental approach was the system of work practiced by the district committee in Kamienna-Gora (Wroclaw region). The economic department of this committee displayed no interest in the election of the Party bodies in the factory organisations with which it maintained close contact, assuming that it should occupy itself with economic problems and that the organising department should handle questions of the Party organisations. It is not surprising, therefore, that the instructors of the economic department appropriated the right of issuing orders to the managers and of exercising control over industrial enterprises, that they ignored the branch organisations and acted over their heads.[49]

The Yugoslav Type of "Decentralized Management"

Up to 1948–49 Yugoslavia was the most rapid and faithful follower of the latest Russian model of management. As early as 1946 Yugoslavia endorsed the system of one-man management, i.e., one-man direction and responsibility at each echelon, as the way to put an end to the waste in efficiency and the irresponsibility growing in the state economic sphere. Strongly worded speeches were made during the discussion of the 1946 budget. One of the top officials of the regime remarked:

> . . . Too many people seem to think that because the enterprises are state-owned, their managers can function without responsibility. They calmly budget for losses, and expect the state to compensate them for their inefficiency.[50]

[48] See "Party Control in Enterprise," by O. Khranova, Secretary, Party Organisation, September 9th Factory, in *FLP,* July 24, 1953.

[49] Antoni Alster, "Some Questions of Organising Work in the Polish United Workers' Party," *FLP,* Oct. 9, 1953.

[50] Žujović, as quoted in J. Morris, *Yugoslavia, op. cit.,* p. 87.

After the intervention of Edvard Kardelj, Deputy Prime Minister, who underlined that "the managers and organizers on the spot must have the greatest possible freedom of action, but they must also show the greatest initiative and responsibility," the debate was closed with the conclusion:

> Managements will be completely responsible for the conduct and profitability of their concerns, for the conditions of work and for relations between employees and managements. . . . They, and all our people must rely on themselves alone, try to increase the productivity of their work, and lower production costs.[51]

After the break with the Soviet bloc the Yugoslav leadership sounded a new note, stressing the necessity of "control from below and mass initiative" in the new theoretical framework, according to which "the operating functions should become more and more decentralized and transferred to the organs closest to the masses, while the function of planning accounting, control and organizational and political education should be centralized as the principal means of general management from the center." Kardelj remarked now:

> It is necessary to strengthen personal responsibility, but not in one direction only. The manager must be personally responsible for his work both to his superiors and to those in whose name he manages the enterprise, institution, etc. In this instance, also, the principle of individual responsibility is being bureaucratically vitiated in that an attempt is being made to destroy the control over the manager from below. If we adopted this road, we would strengthen bureaucracy and prevent a broad development of mass initiative. This would in effect, be a bureaucratic administrative method of management which would immediately slow down the progress of Socialist construction.[52]

In 1950, in the framework of the over-all reorganization of industry,[53] the federal parliament adopted a new "Basic Law concerning the Management of State Industrial Enterprises and Higher Industrial Associations by the Working Staffs." This Act laid down the principle and the method for the establishment of *elective workers' councils* and *management boards,* the latter to be elected by the former from their membership.

According to the law, the workers' council of an enterprise and the

[51] *Ibid.*, p. 88.

[52] *On People's Democracy in Yugoslavia,* Yugoslav Information Center, New York, 1949, p. 67.

[53] See above, Chapter 3, pp. 69–70.

workers' council of a higher industrial association were to be henceforth elected by the working staff of the enterprise or the association; in smaller enterprises the whole labor force was to constitute the workers' council. These councils were to take over the planning of work, bookkeeping and records, and all personnel matters. The management boards were to be elected for one year, and a new management board was not to include more than one-third of the members of the previous board. Such boards were to draw up proposals for basic plans, issue a monthly operation plan, take any measures necessary to increase production and meet the set production quotas. In order to insure both expert direction and government supervision of every enterprise and higher industrial association, the managers of enterprises were "to be appointed by the management board of a higher industrial association, or otherwise by a competent state organ (if the enterprise is not associated), while the manager of a high industrial association is to be appointed by the appropriate state organ." [54]

This reform is continuously stressed by the Yugoslav regime as one of its basic contributions to "socialist theory and practice." The alleged aim is to prevent the "bureaucratization" of the economic apparatus and assure an equilibrium between the workers and the central economic organs of the state. However, in any decisive case the central state organs decide the course to be followed.[55] Moreover, since the beginning of 1955 new modifications have been introduced in respect to both the standard of productivity in the enterprise and the role of the trade unions.

Up to 1950 the main role of the trade unions was, as in the other East European countries, to promote plan fulfillment pledges and whip up the "rationalizers," "innovators," and various campaigns.

[54] Cf. the Law concerning the Management of State . . . etc., of July 21, 1950, and comments by Dr. Borbe Miljević et al., *Razvoj privrednog sistema FNRJ* (Development of the Economic System of the FPRY), *Znanje,* Belgrade, 1954, pp 63–70.

[55] In an article on workers' self-management in Racovica, the largest tractor factory of Yugoslavia, counting a personnel of over 1,500, the following passage is illustrative of those relations:

> The interference of the State organs in the affairs of the factory is looked upon by the working collective with a great deal of indignation. Last December, the Economic Council suggested to the collective that it should change its Director, explaining this suggestion by the fact that their factory, in view of its importance, should be headed by an expert. But despite this plausible argument and the undeniable well meaning of the Economic Council, the Workers' Council rejected that suggestion at three successive meetings as being an interference from outside. But at its fourth session, the collective accepted it "with understanding but sorrow," and their old Director, a former locksmith, Nikola Polimas, was given a really warm sendoff. [Cf. N.O., "Workers' Self-Management in Rakovica," *Review of International Affairs,* IV, 11 (June 1, 1954.)]

From 1950 to the end of 1954 the trade unions, though embracing the majority of the active population outside agriculture (1,700,000 members), played only a secondary role and assumed essentially cultural, social, and insurance responsibilities rather than any task connected with production or work problems. Since 1955 they have had a more significant role. Their representatives, along with the representatives of the state and of management, form commissions having the final say in the establishment of *work norms.* These, abandoned in 1953 and replaced by the introduction of various incentives aiming to encourage factories and enterprises to operate independently, have been re-introduced in the economy as a whole.[56]

Since the 1956 Polish and Hungarian upheavals, the Yugoslav system of workers' councils is exercising a strong influence in the neighboring countries. It is, however, hard to determine how at least some of the elements of this system will be adopted by the other countries of the area.

Summary and Prospects

In summary, it may be noted that through the second quinquennium, i.e., up to 1960, the population of the area will reach over 99 million, a level higher than that of 1938. With the prospect of the slowing down of the rate of growth in industry, the necessity of increasing the agricultural output in the shortest span possible, little if any increase in the labor force outside agriculture will come from the villages. The prospect is, in fact, for an increase in the surplus (non-productive) agricultural population while the regimes continue to create gradually the conditions for a future substantial change in agriculture by means of increased mechanization and the formation of large farm units.

The expansion of the labor force outside agriculture above the prewar level occurred only in the last phase of the first development plan. The sources of this labor force have been a redeployment of the working force available, the drawing into industry of the young from towns and villages, and the entrance of women into non-agricultural production on a large scale and in a far wider range of jobs than previously. The increases have been due essentially to lagging production and the desire to reach the targets set. The shortages of labor that have developed have been due to the exhaustion of these

[56] For a clear and detailed outline of these changes, see the *New York Times* report of its Belgrade correspondent, March 18, 1955.

labor pools. With the new course and the directives established for 1956–60 and the relative easing of the demand for new labor, the shortage of labor should be less than that experienced during the first development plans, even though the replenishment of the labor force will be limited by a smaller addition of young people. Clearly, more decisive efforts will have to be made to increase the productivity per man in industry, i.e., just the opposite of what is planned in agriculture, where these regimes seem to settle on the idea that, during the next quinquennium, output per head in agriculture will in all likelihood remain low.

The effort to increase productivity per man in industry will continue to be accompanied by a further development of the technical cadres, i.e., skilled workers, foremen, technicians, engineers, "production leaders," employing the experience already gained in training at the level of the plant, the enlarged school facilities, and the larger numbers of technical cadres already engaged in production. Thus much of the improvisation and inefficiency that characterized the first development plans will probably be avoided, and a certain consolidation will take place all along the production line.

During the first development plans there was a constant tendency toward an increase of the white-collar and managerial groups as compared to the mass of industrial workers. The first group, which is accounted in Communist economic literature as overhead cost, increased in Czechoslovakia, for instance, from some 14 per cent of the total gainfully employed in industry in 1946 to close to 16 per cent in 1949. It can be expected that substantial efforts will be made to "stabilize" this ratio so as to avoid the proliferation, especially in industry, of "bureaucratism."

CHAPTER

11

THE PATTERN OF TRADE AND THE KEY POSITION OF SOVIET RUSSIA

A "Second World Market"

In his last work Stalin suggested that "the most important economic sequel of the Second World War and of its economic consequences" was "that the single all-embracing world market disintegrated, so that now we have two parallel world markets . . . confronting one another." [1] Stalin thus stressed the fact that the existence of several economies of the Soviet type created a specific trade bloc whose member economies deal only among themselves. Although it is true that a restricted market with specific features has been created in the East, it is not quite accurate to speak of it as a "world market" all by itself. First, this market has highly selective membership, participation in it being preconditioned by the modification of the political and economic structure of each country, a condition necessary but not sufficient (e.g., Yugoslavia); second, the participants in this market still continue to trade in the extra-orbit markets and contemplate enlarging their trade relations there; third, the relative importance of international trade within the restricted intra-planned economies

[1] J. Stalin, *Economic Problems of Socialism in the U.S.S.R.*, International Publishers, New York, 1952, p. 26. The subject has since been extensively elaborated by both Soviet and East European economists: Among the latter, notably by O. Lange, "Rozpad Jednolitego Rynku Światowego i Ukształtowanie się Dwóch Równoległych Rynków w Gospodarce Światowej" (Disintegration of the Single World Market and the Formation of Two Parallel Markets in the World Economy), *Ekonomista,* I (1953); among the former, notably by V. Alkhimov and I. Dudinskii, *Raspad Edinogo Mirovogo Rynka* (Disintegration of the Single World Market), Gospolitizdat, Moscow, 1953. These and numerous interpretative studies are largely repetitious.

market is extremely limited compared to that in the extra-orbit markets. In any event, a regional or other type of grouping, whatever its particular features, remains in fact but *a part* of the world market. Let us turn now to more specific features of this restricted market.

The principal directions of the flow of international trade of the East European countries in 1937, 1948, and 1952 are presented in Table 115. As can be seen from columns 8 and 11, in 1948 from 66

TABLE 115. SHARES OF MAIN AREAS IN TOTAL TRADE OF EACH EAST EUROPEAN COUNTRY, 1937, 1948, 1952

(percentages)

	Soviet Union			People's Democracies			Combined Share			Rest of World		
Country	1937	1948	1952	1937	1948	1952	1937	1948	1952	1937	1948	1952
	1	2	3	4	5	6	7	8	9	10	11	12
Czechoslovakia	1	16	35	10	14	36	11	30	71	89	70	29
Poland	1	22	32	6	12	35	7	34	67	93	66	33
Hungary	[a]	11	29	13	23	42	13	34	71	87	66	29
Romania	1	25	58	17	46	27	18	71	85	82	29	15
Bulgaria	[a]	54	57	12	20	32	12	74	89	88	26	11

[a] Nil.

Sources:

1947: *PE*, No. 5–6 (May–June 1952), p. 66, corrected on basis of *The Network of World Trade*, League of Nations, Geneva, 1942.

1948, 1952: *Ibid.*; *VT*, XXII, 10 (October 1952), and XXIII, 11 (November 1953).

to 70 per cent of the trade of Czechoslovakia, Poland, and Hungary and 30 per cent of the trade of Romania and Bulgaria were transacted in the extra-orbit market. By 1952 that proportion had fallen in the first three countries to between 29 and 33 per cent and in the last two to between 11 and 15 per cent. Thus by 1952 from 67 to 89 per cent of the total international trade of all the countries was in the intra-planned economies market, consisting of the Soviet Union and the so-called "people's democracies" (the East European countries), and China.[2] The expansion of the intra-bloc trade was due to an increase both of the trade with the Soviet Union and of the trade between the people's democracies. However, the table (especially columns 3 and 6) clearly indicates that the share of the Soviet Union alone is nearly as big for Poland and Hungary as, and far larger for

[2] Other countries included in this market, but of secondary importance, are Albania, the Mongolian People's Republic, North Korea, and North Vietnam.

all the others than, the share of all the people's democracies. Thus the development of the intra-planned economies market has been characterized by the enormous expansion of the trade with the Soviet Union, which is the decisive buyer and seller in this market. Since the Soviet Union's share in the trade of the area in 1937 was negligible, its rise is striking.

There are available no absolute data for either the total trade of the countries or the total bloc trade. On the very imperfect basis of data derived from export and import statistics of countries outside the bloc some idea of the magnitude of the total trade, as well as of the bloc trade, can be obtained from the official percentages. As appears from Table 116, the *total* international trade [3] of the Soviet bloc countries was 5.2 billion dollars in 1948. This total had increased by 1952 to over 9 billion dollars, and together with East Germany and China to close to 12.5 billion dollars. Out of these totals the intra-bloc trade can be estimated to have represented, respectively, 2.3 billion and 9.4 billion.[4] The bloc trade of Soviet Russia increased during this period from 1.1 billion dollars to close to 3.8 billion dollars.

Between 1948 and 1952 the largest increase in total trade has been secured by the Soviet Union. The largest increase in the "eastern world market" has been secured by Hungary, followed by the Soviet Union, Poland, and Czechoslovakia. The trade of the Soviet Union alone amounted to some 40 per cent of the total bloc trade. Let us survey now briefly the changes in the structure of this trade.

[3] This figure includes *outside exports toward the bloc* valued f.o.b., and *outside imports from the bloc* valued c.i.f. The normal data for the bloc would, of course, consist of a reverse set: own exports f.o.b. and own imports c.i.f.

[4] These estimates diverge from the figures presented by the *ESE in 1954, op. cit.*, p. 113, and *ESE in 1955, op. cit.*, p. 179. Whereas we build the total trade of each country on the basis of its known trade with the West and the utilization of the official over-all percentages of the distribution of trade, the United Nations statisticians derived their totals from the official trade statistics either for recent years, as in the case of the Soviet Union, or from 1947 and 1948 data carried forward by means of officially published indices of total trade. Both methods have serious drawbacks. They produce the same results for 1952, for Poland, Romania, and Bulgaria, but diverge for the other countries. According to the UN estimate, the total international trade of the Soviet Union and of the East European countries amounted in 1952 to 10.2 billion dollars, as against 9.1 estimated in our table.

TABLE 116. SOVIET BLOC: ESTIMATED TOTAL TRADE AND BLOC TRADE, 1948 AND 1952 [a]

Country	Total Trade 1948 1	Total Trade 1952 2	Total Bloc Trade 1948 3	Total Bloc Trade 1952 4	Percentage Increase 2 ÷ 1 5	Percentage Increase 4 ÷ 3 6
Czechoslovakia	1,216	1,406	365	998	15	173
Poland	1,053	1,589	358	1,065	51	197
Hungary	292	564	99	400	93	304
Romania	341	578	242	491	69	103
Bulgaria	163	302	121	269	85	122
Soviet Union	2,181	4,716	1,156	3,772	116	226
East Germany		1,018	[b]	804		
China		2,265	[b]	1,631		
Total	5,246	12,438	2,341	9,430	137	302

[a] Based on derivative data; millions of U.S. dollars in current prices.
[b] Countries not included at that time in that market.
Sources: Data based on U.S. Dept. of Commerce, International Economic Analysis Division, Bureau of Foreign Commerce, Value Series, combined with percentages from sources in Table 115.

DEVELOPMENT AND STRUCTURE OF SOVIET TRADE WITH THE AREA

As noted elsewhere,[5] the prewar trade of Soviet Russia with Eastern Europe was very limited. In the period extending from 1924–25 to 1938 the relative share of East Europe in the total of Soviet exports varied between 0.6 per cent (in 1925–26) and 2.8 per cent in 1926–27, and in the total of Soviet imports from 1.6 per cent in (1938) to 6.2 per cent (in 1930). In absolute values of trade with Eastern Europe, the prewar peak of Soviet exports was attained in 1926–27 and the peak of Soviet imports in 1931. During the ensuing prewar years exports declined more than 50 per cent, and imports steadily contracted until, in 1937–38, they were less than 10 per cent of 1931. In fact, the sharp downward trend of Soviet imports from East Europe followed, on a lower plane, the global downward trend of Soviet imports during the period considered.

By far the largest part of prewar Soviet trade with Eastern Europe was with Czechoslovakia and Poland, about 10 times as much as with Hungary, Romania, and Yugoslavia together. There was no prewar

[5] Cf. above, Chapter 1, pp. 5 and 9.

TABLE 117. USSR: SHARE OF THE MAIN COMMODITIES IN SOVIET TRADE WITH CZECHOSLOVAKIA AND POLAND, 1925 TO 1936

(value percentages)

	1925–26	1926–27	1927–28	1929	1930	1931	1932	1933	1934	1935	1936
Exports to Czechoslovakia											
Bladders, casing, sausage skins	6.1	7.7	11.9	10.1	[a]	[b]	[b]	[b]	[b]	[b]	[b]
Bristle	33.5	32.9	[b]	[b]	[b]	[b]	[b]	[b]	[b]	[b]	[b]
Iron ore	[b]	[b]	9.9	28.7	53.0	73.1	16.4	16.7	[b]	[b]	[b]
Manganese	[a]	[a]	[a]	[a]	[a]	12.6	[b]	[a]	[a]	11.7	9.7
Furs	[a]	[a]	[a]	[a]	[a]	[a]	[a]	6.5	11.7	12.4	6.1
Flax	[a]	[a]	[b]	[b]	[a]	[b]	[b]	[b]	[b]	13.7	37.4
Imports from Czechoslovakia											
Ferrous metals	[a]	20.2	30.0	38.0	54.9	54.3	[a]	29.5	40.4	27.8	18.7
Iron, steel manufacture	8.9	16.1	26.3	22.6	27.6	25.9	39.7	20.0	24.5	42.1	18.3
Machinery equipment and spare parts	[a]	7.7	9.3	16.8	7.5	8.2	42.3	29.9	10.8	10.4	30.9
Agricultural machinery	21.5	15.8	[a]	9.3	[b]	[b]	[b]	[b]	[b]	[b]	[b]
Electrical appliances and machinery	[a]	[a]	[a]	[a]	[a]	[a]	[a]	[a]	[a]	[a]	[a]
Exports to Poland											
Grains	[b]	58.7	[a]	[b]	[b]	[a]	[b]	[b]	[b]	[b]	[b]
Fish	36.5	6.2	8.7	[a]	8.1	16.5	5.4	6.6	[a]	[a]	[a]
Oil cakes	[a]	5.2	8.1	9.2	8.9	[a]	[a]	[a]	[a]	[b]	[b]
Timber	[a]	[a]	11.4	23.9	18.0	5.6	11.5	[a]	[a]	[a]	[b]
Iron ore	14.5	6.1	21.2	18.4	6.1	13.2	[a]	19.2	7.1	8.0	9.4
Manganese	21.4	[a]	[a]	[a]	[a]	5.9	[a]	8.2	[a]	[a]	17.0
Furs	[a]	[a]	[a]	[a]	[a]	15.3	25.0	17.6	24.4	18.7	40.8
Imports from Poland											
Ferrous metals	[a]	6.1	12.0	31.2	70.0	71.5	65.3	78.3	53.2	36.0	63.1
Non-ferrous metals	[a]	31.4	46.4	30.7	14.0	12.6	21.1	[a]	[a]	[a]	[a]
Iron, steel manufacture	8.9	[a]	[a]	[a]	[a]	8.5	[a]	[a]	32.4	6.0	[b]
Machinery equipment and spare parts	[a]	10.9	7.5	[a]	[a]	[a]	8.2	5.3	[a]	[a]	[a]

[a] Less than 5 per cent.
[b] Nil.

Source: S. N. Bakulin and D. D. Mishustin, *Vneshniaia Torgovlia SSSR za 20 let, 1918–1937* (Foreign Trade of the USSR for 20 Years, 1918–1937), Statisticheski spravochnik (Statistical Handbook), Moscow, 1939, pp. 31 ff.

Soviet trade with Bulgaria. The even trend of these levels over the entire prewar period suggests the careful planning of Soviet foreign trade.

Soviet trade with Czechoslovakia and Poland, which made up the bulk of Soviet trade with Eastern Europe, did not exhibit either a stable inner pattern or a great variety. As Table 117 shows, the emphasis shifted from year to year from certain main commodities to others. The principal Soviet exports to Czechoslovakia from 1925 to 1929 were sausage skins, bristle, and iron ore; from 1929 to 1933 iron ore was predominant, representing up to 73 per cent of the total; from 1934 on, the emphasis was on manganese, furs, and flax, the other items mentioned completely disappearing from this trade. In Soviet imports from Czechoslovakia the ferrous metals predominated in the early 1930's, when they accounted for 55 per cent (1930) of the value of these imports; their relative share, which remained important, fell off in 1936 to 18.7 per cent, the emphasis having shifted toward iron and steel products, machinery, and equipment.

The Soviet exports to Poland from 1925 to 1931, except for a large delivery of grain in 1926–27, were fish, oil cake, timber, and iron ore; from 1931 to 1936 the emphasis shifted to iron ore, manganese, and furs. The bulk of Soviet imports from Poland from 1929 on was ferrous metals; nonferrous metals played an important role from 1926 to 1931, when the emphasis shifted first to machinery and subsequently to iron and steel manufacture.

On the whole, Soviet exports to these countries consisted of iron ore, furs, and occasionally grains; Soviet imports were mainly metals, ironware, and machinery.

The largest expansion in Soviet trade with Eastern Europe in the prewar period (which ended for Russia in June 1941, with the German invasion) occurred in 1940 and the first half of 1941, i.e., at a time when Russia's trade relations outside the German bloc were hampered by the war.

The 1940–41 Soviet trade agreements with Hungary, Romania, Bulgaria, and Yugoslavia provided for Soviet exports of superphosphates, timber, and machine oil, mainly to Hungary and Romania, and cotton, iron, and flax, mainly to Bulgaria and Yugoslavia. In exchange, Hungary was to send to the Soviet Union railroad wagons, river ships, machinery, and spare parts; Romania, mainly petroleum and mineral oil; Bulgaria, processed cotton, tobacco, certain agricultural products, pork, and skins; Yugoslavia, processed cotton and metals.

The notable characteristics of these agreements were: (1) the small part played by agricultural produce (only Bulgaria was to send some), (2) the strong emphasis on finished industrial products, and (3) the import by these countries of Russian raw materials on a "contracting" basis for processing in the importing country and re-export to the Soviet Union.

Despite the limited importance of the prewar transactions between the Soviet Union and Eastern Europe (and hence the risks involved in generalizing on the basis of limited data) it can be asserted that on the whole, up to 1941, the Soviet Union seems to have viewed Eastern Europe as a limited "subsidiary" market mainly for the export of her industrial raw materials and the import of metals and manufactured goods—the last purchased in the ordinary way—or for the export of Russian raw materials to be processed and re-exported by the East European countries.

Turning now to the postwar period, it is essential to note that up to 1948 the increase in trade between the Soviet Union and the East European countries occurred under the conditions of (1) the increased commercial isolation of the Soviet Union and severance of commercial ties between certain East European countries and their former industrial suppliers; (2) a substantial decline in output and available resources in war-devastated countries, some of which also were burdened with reparations payments to the Soviet Union. In this general framework increased trade with the Soviet Union (and the multiplication of inter-East European transactions) resulted not so much from an attempt to adjust services as from a sustained effort to make up for lost sources of supply under the least propitious conditions.

Notwithstanding the difficulty of disentangling trade proper from non-commodity payments ("invisibles," such as the schooling of East European students in the Soviet Union), military agreements, liquidation of "enemy property," reparations deliveries, and so on, it can be asserted that the postwar pattern of trade between the Soviet Union and Eastern Europe up to 1948 did not deviate substantially from the prewar pattern. The Soviet Union exported as before, but now on a far larger scale, mainly iron ore, iron and steel, raw cotton, and grain. It imported mainly machinery, ironware, cotton fabrics, and, under special agreements, primary products such as coal, petroleum, and metals. Since a substantial part of the Soviet industrial raw materials sent to Eastern Europe during that period was processed and re-exported to Russia, the large Soviet exports of iron ore and cotton were balanced by large Soviet imports of ironware and cotton fabrics (see Table 118). Even in Romania, where the import of Soviet iron was

TABLE 118. COMMODITY STRUCTURE OF TRADE WITH THE SOVIET UNION IN 1947

(in thousand metric tons)

Commodities	Czechoslovakia	Poland	Hungary	Romania	Total
Imports from USSR					
Grains	76.6	310.4	[a]	[a]	387.0
Iron ore	513.2	256.3	80.7	95.0	945.2
Iron and steel	12.0	[b]	[b]	35.0	47.0
Coal and coke	[a]	[a]	90.0	115.9	205.9
Cotton, raw	5.6	38.3	10.0	17.0	70.9
Exports to USSR					
Petroleum	[a]	[a]	[a]	500.0	500.0
Coal and coke	[a]	8,196.6	[a]	[a]	8,196.6
Ironware	0.1	11.1	[b]	[a]	11.2
Cotton fabrics [c]	[a]	30.0	11.0	30.5	71.5
Machinery	6.6	3.5	[b]	[a]	10.1

[a] Nil.
[b] Not available.
[c] In million meters.

Sources:
C: *Zachranicni Obchod 1947* (Foreign Trade 1947), Vol. 179, Prague, 1948.
P: *Statistical Yearbook 1948, op. cit.*
H: *GT*, January 1949.
R: *RR*, No. 9, July 1948.

not "directly counterbalanced" by Romanian exports of ironware and the like, the Soviet raw material made possible the fulfillment of planned Romanian production in which the Soviet Union was highly interested. Thus, in the words of a Romanian Minister:

> Due to the massive imports of pig iron, cast iron and coke and minerals (from the Soviet Union), the Hunedoara, Reşiţa and Titan Nadrag Calan Works will manufacture the iron and steel required by the Malaxa works which in their turn will be able to manufacture the casing and pipe required by the petroleum industry. . . .[6]

As has already been emphasized, a large part of the petroleum production was earmarked for reparations payments to the Soviet Union, and only a small portion of it entered into Romanian trade proper.

[6] "The New Economic Romanian-Soviet Agreements," by Ştefan Voicu, then Minister of Industry, in *RR*, No. 11–12 (April 1947), p. 41.

The basic similarity of this pattern of trade with the prewar pattern is apparent in the relative importance, in value terms, of the finished goods, raw materials, and foodstuffs in the over-all structure of the Soviet-East European trade. As may be seen from Table 119, the relative share of the finished goods and the total value of the imports of these countries from the Soviet Union ranged from 1 to 4 per cent for the more developed countries of the region and from 15 to 24 per cent for the others. The bulk of the East European imports was raw materials and semifinished products, mostly raw cotton and iron ore, and, for Czechoslovakia and Poland, grain and livestock. The Soviet imports from all the countries except Bulgaria and Yugoslavia had a substantial content of industrial products ranging from 27 to close to 40 per cent of the imports from Poland, Hungary, and Romania, and amounting to over 90 per cent of the imports from Czechoslovakia. Soviet imports from Bulgaria were largely agricultural produce such as foodstuffs and tobacco, and from Yugoslavia mainly metals. As for the finished and semifinished products, it should be noted that the Soviet Union manifested a particular interest in consumers' goods (such as footwear and all types of textiles, mainly cotton fabrics) and building materials (such as cement and window glass), both of which figure in varying quantities in the Soviet imports from all the East European countries.

Trade relations between the Soviet Union and East Europe underwent significant changes during the period from the end of 1948 to the end of 1955. In addition to such factors as the industrialization of the area and the Western "strategic embargo," which we will discuss below, the lessening of the reparations burden for the ex-enemy countries (East Germany, Hungary, Romania, Bulgaria) played an important role. While remaining an essential supplier of raw materials, which continued to make up the bulk of the Soviet exports to these countries, the Soviet Union began to export fully equipped plants and heavy machinery under a series of so-called investment agreements. Investment goods, which up to 1948 represented an insignificant part of Soviet exports to the region, came to represent probably around 20 per cent of their yearly value. As we have already noted in Chapter 9, a variety of fully equipped plants were sent from, or scheduled to come from, the Soviet Union (e.g., the Polish steel mills of Nowa Huta, various cement factories, etc.).[7]

On the other hand, the launching of the various national develop-

[7] See also below, section on Soviet Aid, pp. 432–437.

TABLE 119. STRUCTURE OF TRADE WITH THE SOVIET UNION AROUND 1948 [a]

Type of Commodities	Czechoslovakia (1949 = 100)	Poland (1947 = 100)	Hungary [b] (1947 = 100)	Romania [b] (1945–48 = 100)	Bulgaria (1946 = 100)	Yugoslavia (1948 = 100)
Imports from the Soviet Union						
Finished products	3.6	3.7	1.0	23	24.2	15.7
Raw materials, semifinished products	40.3	50.3	97.6	77	55.2	84.3
Notably: Cotton, raw	11.8	35.4	44.7	24		
Iron ore	6.8	4.6	16.5			
Foodstuffs and animals	56.1	46.0	1.4		11.8	
Exports to the Soviet Union						
Finished products	90.6	27.5	38.4	32	2.0	1.8
Notably: Textiles	13.8	20.8	34.2	25		
Footwear	13.3					
Raw materials	1.8	52.5	46.8	68	77.9	88.5
Notably: Coal or oil		49.0	15.4	18		
Tobacco					70.0	
Foodstuffs and live animals	7.6	20.0	14.8		20.1	9.7

[a] Value percentages. For each country: Imports from the Soviet Union = 100; Exports to the Soviet Union = 100.
[b] For Hungary and Romania: commercial trade only (i.e., excluding reparations).

Sources:

C: *Zachranicni Obchod 1947, op. cit.*

P: Based on data of the Ministry of Commerce and Industry. Cf. E. Zaleski, *Les Courants commerciaux au cours de la première moitié du XX siècle* (Commercial Currents in Danubian Europe during the First Half of the 20th Century), Librairie Générale de Droit et Jurisprudence (General Library of Law and Jurisprudence), Paris, 1952, p. 367.

H: *GT*, Jan. 1949.

R: *La Roumanie nouvelle*, Nov. 15, 1948, and *RR*, No. 14 (April 1947), pp. 39–43.

B: *Statistikata Na Vănshnata Tărgoviia 1946* (Statistics of Foreign Trade 1946), Sofia, 1948.

Y: Milentije Popović, "O ekonomskim odnosima izmedju socijalističkih država" (On the Economic Relations among Socialist States), *Communist*, July 1949, pp. 98 ff.

ment plans and the reorientation and diversification of national outputs made possible a substantial increase and diversification in the exports of the region to the Soviet Union. These were increases in the variety of aggregates (fully equipped plants, particularly from Czechoslovakia), heavy machinery, locomotives, and transport equipment, and increases in the variety and relative importance of textiles, footwear, light metals industries products, appliances, foodstuffs, tobacco, mass consumers' goods, raw materials, and semifinished products.

According to Czechoslovak data, the imports of Czechoslovakia from the Soviet Union increased by 85 per cent between 1949 and 1954. During the same period the structure of imports shifted as follows, on the basis 1949 = 100: machinery and equipment reached the index 666, raw and other materials 164, foodstuffs 159, and consumers' goods 203. The structure of the Czechoslovak exports to the Soviet Union changed as follows, on the basis 1949 = 100: machinery and equipment 395, raw and other materials 75, foodstuffs 137, and consumers' goods 23. Notable among the Czechoslovak imports were mining, agricultural and construction machinery, iron ore, oil and oil products, and foodstuffs. Among the Czechoslovak exports were machines which Czechoslovakia formerly did not produce, for example, ships, mobile power plants, and special machine tools.[8]

According to Polish data, the imports from the Soviet Union in 1955 consisted of machinery and parts, representing up to 13 per cent of the total value of Polish imports, raw and other materials such as oil (480 thousand tons), iron ore (3 million tons), cotton (70 thousand tons), grain and foodstuffs (400 thousand tons of grain, etc.). The exports consisted of vessels, machinery and equipment accounting for some 10 per cent of the total Polish exports, raw and other materials, namely, coal (8.2 million tons), coke (434 thousand tons), cement (69 thousand tons), some foodstuffs and consumers' goods (such as 9 million meters of cotton and woolen fabrics).[9]

Basically, the structure of this trade in the period considered appeared as indicated in Table 120. The Soviet Union exported aggregates in order to increase outputs in which she had a long-range interest (steel, cement, and oil), and provided the region with the

[8] "The Balance Sheet of Czechoslovak-Soviet Trade Relations," *CEB*, No. 304, Jan. 1956, pp. 1–6.

[9] "La Structure du Commerce Exterieur Polonais" (The Structure of the Polish Foreign Trade) in *Bulletin, Bureau of Polish Information*, No. 365, May 7, 1956, pp. 4–7.

TABLE 120. STRUCTURE OF TRADE WITH THE SOVIET UNION, 1948–55

Soviet Exports						Soviet Imports					
Goods	C	P	H	R	B	Goods	C	P	H	R	B
Aggregates[a]		+	+	+	+	Aggregates[a]	+				
Heavy machinery	+	+	+	+	+	Heavy machinery	+	+	+		
Agricultural machinery	+	+	+	+	+	Ships	+	+	+		
						Locomotives	+	+	+		
						Transport equipment	+	+	+	+	
						Light metals industries		+	+		
						Chemicals		+	+	+	
						Textiles	+	+	+	+	+
						Footwear	+				
Oil and oil products	+	+			+	Oil and oil products			+	+	
Steel				+		Cement	+	+		+	+
Coke			+	+		Coal and coke		+			
Pig iron and cast iron			+	+		Metals		+			+
Iron ore	+	+	+	+		Ores	+		+		+
Other ores	+	+									
Nonferrous metals	+	+	+	+							
Cotton	+	+	+	+	+	Tobacco					+
Wool	+	+	+	+	+						
Rubber	+	+	+	+							
Timber	+		+			Timber				+	
Grain	+	+				Sugar	+	+			
Other foodstuffs	+					Other foodstuffs			+	+	+

[a] Fully equipped plants.

Sources: Trade agreements for the period 1948–55.

bulk of its raw materials, part of which returned to the Soviet Union as finished goods. Moreover, Soviet exports facilitated the industrialization process of the area, an industrialization carried out, as we have already noted, in the individual framework of each country striving for "all-round development" and therefore implying a substantial lowering of the efficiency of industrial investments in the entire area. With its exportable surplus of iron ore, oil, steel, coke, and grain as well as its machinery and equipment, the Soviet Union is evidently again holding the commanding positions in the supply of the countries of the area during the second long-term plans.

DEVELOPMENT AND STRUCTURE OF INTRA-EAST EUROPEAN TRADE

In the decade preceding the Second World War intra-East European trade fell sharply from the levels attained in 1929. Some of the countries were competing fiercely in the world market for some of their surpluses; [10] in the crisis years of the 1930's they were in the grip of autarkic tendencies; moreover, the entire region was dependent on given patterns of trade settlements in which the Central and West European countries played a decisive role. The vigorous German drive toward the East ultimately attached the agricultural countries of Eastern Europe directly to the expanding economy of the Reich and reduced substantially the intra-zone trade of Czechoslovakia, which had developed promising intra-zone trade relations in the late 1920's.

In 1928 the East European countries absorbed 20 per cent of the Czechoslovak exports and provided 17 per cent of her imports. In the following ten years this trade, instead of increasing, decreased. By 1938 they were absorbing 14 per cent of the Czechoslovak exports and providing 16 per cent of Czechoslovak imports.

After the war Czechoslovakia turned resolutely toward the East. Although also aiming at enlarging her global trade, Czechoslovakia systematically developed her expansion in this area mostly toward Poland and Yugoslavia since the other countries were burdened with reparations and could engage only in a limited way in trade proper. The success of the all-out effort of Czechoslovakia can be measured by the following indices: on the basis of 1937 = 100, in 1948 her export index for cars was 598, for railroad cars 1,665, for steam engines 2,258, and for consumers' goods in large demand in the East, such as bicycles and motorcycles, 6,672 and 53,010, respectively.[11] At that time Czechoslovakia exported ironware, agricultural machinery and equipment, and footwear and other consumers' goods to Poland; coke, textiles, and motorcycles to Hungary and Romania; power-driven machines and some machine tools mainly to Yugoslavia and in very limited amounts to Bulgaria. Czechoslovakia imported coke and steel from Poland; corn, seeds, and mineral oil from Hungary and Romania; ores and metals from Yugoslavia; and tobacco from Bulgaria.

After 1948, as Czechoslovakia geared her industrial production more and more toward heavy goods, her heavy industry exports to the area increased substantially. In the period from the end of 1948 to 1955, Czechoslovakia exported all types of aggregates, e.g., electric power stations (notably, the key Hungarian power station Inota), transformers, all types of heavy equipment, transport equipment, heavy construction materials, and limited amounts of coke and coal.

[10] See above, Chapter 1, pp. 6–7.

[11] *Czechoslovak Economic Bulletin,* Czech Embassy, Washington, I, 9 (October 1949).

In 1951, for instance, 75 per cent of the exported industrial products were sold to the Soviet Union and the people's democracies as compared to 55 per cent in 1949. Between 1948 and 1954 the export of complete industrial installations rose more than 14 times.[12] With the decline of trade with the West, Czechoslovakia entered into substantial trade in equipment, machinery, and fuel (coal and coke) with East Germany, from which she obtained chemical products, fertilizers, and some raw materials. She obtained coal, iron, and steel from Poland; oil from Romania; and nonferrous metals from Poland and Bulgaria. The demand for consumers' goods did not increase in the area as a whole, and they did not play an important part in the intra-orbit trade of the area until after 1953, when Czechoslovakia began to import cameras, photo equipment, and watches from East Germany and increased shipments of foodstuffs from the other countries of the area, while increasing her exports of motorcycles, bicycles, radio sets, sewing machines, furniture, and leather goods.[13] However, it is as supplier of heavy equipment that Czechoslovakia's role will continue to grow in the Soviet bloc.

Prewar Poland played a very limited role in East European trade. In 1920 the other countries of the area absorbed 10 per cent of her exports; in 1938 they absorbed 6.6 per cent. Over the same time span Poland's imports from the East European countries fell from 15.0 per cent to 6.5 per cent.

Immediately after the war Poland, with its new resources and increased industrial potential, began to have a very significant part in the area trade. The Soviet Union and Eastern Europe (including Yugoslavia) accounted for 36.7 per cent of Polish exports and 41.7 per cent of her imports in 1948. In that year Polish trade in Eastern Europe was turned mainly toward Czechoslovakia and Yugoslavia. Czechoslovakia supplied her with machinery and equipment, and Yugoslavia with a variety of metals; Poland supplied Czechoslovakia with raw materials, and Yugoslavia with raw materials and equipment. Polish trade with the reparations-paying countries, Hungary, Romania, and Bulgaria, remained at the low prewar levels.

After 1948–49 there was a substantial increase in Polish trade with East Germany and Czechoslovakia, her suppliers of heavy equipment,

[12] *Hospodář,* February 22, 1951; also, *CEB,* No. 304, January 1956, p. 14.

[13] See R. Dvořák, Czech Minister of Foreign Trade, "Economic Co-operation of Countries of Democratic Camp," *FLP,* Feb. 12, 1954. Also: "Some Data on Mutual Trade," in *CEB,* No. 307, April 1956, pp. 6–14.

machinery, and certain raw materials, and the buyers of coal, coke, steel (East Germany only), and all types of metals and foodstuffs. There was a lesser increase in trade with the other East European countries, to which Poland exported, in addition to coal and steel, railway rolling stock, chemicals, and various equipment in exchange for industrial raw materials and some finished goods, mainly from Hungary.

Polish trade with East Germany and Czechoslovakia has marked possibilities of development during the second quinquennium, since Poland can get from them both essential equipment and manufactured mass consumers' goods.

The other East European countries, Hungary, Romania, Bulgaria, and Yugoslavia, played a limited part in each other's trade during the prewar period. Two features of their trade relations were of some significance: the Hungarian-Yugoslav trade and the Bulgarian imports from Romania. In 1939 Hungary absorbed 5.2 per cent of the Yugoslav exports and provided 3.6 per cent of Yugoslav imports, levels which had remained about the same since 1929, Hungary obtaining from Yugoslavia mainly ores and metals and supplying Yugoslavia with manufactured goods. Romanian-Bulgarian trade had a significant role so far as Bulgarian imports were concerned, Romania providing as much as 4 per cent of Bulgarian imports (contrasted with over 7 per cent in 1929), mainly oil products. Other trade among the four countries varied from as little as 0.1 per cent to a little over 2 per cent.

After the war, outside the traditional Hungarian-Yugoslav and Romanian-Bulgarian trade relations, no significant developments occurred up to the end of 1948. An attempt at broad cooperation and interchanges was undertaken by Yugoslavia and Bulgaria but failed to materialize since Yugoslavia left the bloc in 1948.

With decreasing reparations burdens and the necessity for Hungary to compensate for her former Yugoslav partner, during the period 1948–55 the foundations were laid for a closer collaboration among the three small countries, Hungary, Romania, and Bulgaria. Prospects for the development of close trade relations among these countries are good, since Hungary can export industrial goods to the two other countries in exchange for Romanian oil, gas, salt, and metals or for Bulgarian metals and concentrates; and Romania can activate its trade with Bulgaria by supplying her with oil and oil products, electricity, and implements. However, Romanian imports from Bulgaria can hardly be increased to any significant amount.

During the 1948–54 period Yugoslavia turned completely toward the West for trade since, after its political break with the Cominform, the Soviet Union, followed by the other East European countries, cancelled all agreements with Belgrade.[14] Since 1955 new and significant trade relations have been established by the Soviet Union and the East European countries with Yugoslavia, and it seems possible that during the second long-term plan this trade will eventually expand. Yugoslavia could supply mainly metals and agricultural produce and import machinery and equipment, oil, coke, etc.[15]

Basically, three channels of intra-East European trade as it developed from 1948 to 1955, listed in decreasing order of importance, were: (*a*) trade among Czechoslovakia, East Germany, and Poland; (*b*) trade between these three countries and the other three countries of the area; (*c*) trade among the last three. In the first channel moved mostly machinery and manufactured goods, some raw materials, mostly ferrous and nonferrous metals, and coal. In the second channel moved machinery, such industrial raw materials as Czechoslovak and Polish coal and coke, Polish steel, etc., other industrial raw materials, and foodstuffs. In the last channel moved small electrical ware, transport equipment, other types of equipment, raw materials, metals, oil, etc.

Trade with the Asiatic people's democracies, mainly China, had varying importance for the different countries. In this trade East Germany exported machinery and vehicles, Czechoslovakia machine tools and equipment, Poland machinery and metals, Hungary equipment and raw materials, Romania oil-drilling equipment, and Bulgaria chemicals. In return China sent ores (wolfram, molybdenum, and even iron ore, tin, and cobalt), fibers (cotton), fats, and oil. Allowing for the difficulties of transport, the prospects are that this trade will be strongly increased during the current quinquennium.

[14] Thus for political reasons the Soviet Union established an embargo on the bloc's trade with Yugoslavia. It is worth noting that at the same time the Soviet writers were bitterly complaining about the "unjustified strategic embargo" to which the Soviet Union itself was subjected. The Yugoslav trade with the West represents a development distinct from that occurring in the bloc; its scope, development, and character fall outside the limits of this study.

[15] For a discussion of the Yugoslav trade relations with the bloc, see N. Spulber, "On Yugoslavia's Trade Relations with the Soviet Bloc," *Economia Internazionale* Vol. IX, No. 2, Genoa, May 1956.

Mechanism of Trade in the Orbit and Role of CEMA

In principle the planning and control of all foreign trade transactions of the Soviet Union and the East European countries are worked out through their respective Ministries of Foreign Trade, which unify the export and import plans of the various national export and import corporations, decide within the limits of the over-all economic plan the transactions to be carried out, and participate in the negotiation of commercial agreements between these corporations and the other states. Theoretically, the plans of these corporations are based on the "balances of production-consumption" drawn up by each control agency, establishing the production of a given commodity and checking the present and potential domestic production against present and future needs. Both import and export plans are components of the over-all plan of economic development and are drawn up with definite aims in view, aims which "are subject to change to suit the planned development of the country's economy in the current period; in their turn, the plans themselves are subject to the influences of development taking place in the national economy and in the world market." [16]

From 1945 to 1948 both trade proper (i.e., excluding reparations) between the Soviet Union and the East European countries and trade among the latter were conducted on the basis of bilateral agreements, usually of one year's duration, which rigorously fixed the methods of trade and payment. They specified that the quantities and kinds of goods to be exchanged were to be fixed in special protocols (quota lists); that the delivery of the commodities was to be effected on the basis of contracts between the respective Soviet and East European organs of foreign trade; [17] that the prices established in these contracts were to be "fixed in United States dollars on the basis of the world market prices prevailing on the date the contract is signed"; that the payment for this trade was to be made through the respective State Banks of the trading partners, which, for this purpose, "shall open for each other special non-interest-bearing accounts in United States

[16] See A. Baykov, *Soviet Foreign Trade*, Princeton University Press, Princeton, N. J., 1946, especially Chapter III, "The Organization of Soviet Foreign Trade on the Eve of the Second World War," pp. 23–141.

[17] At the time in many of the East European countries the respective "organs of foreign trade" referred simply to the Ministries of Foreign Trade as such. Only subsequently were foreign trade corporations organized as in the Soviet Union by branches or commodities. Cf. above, Chapter 5, pp. 163 ff.

dollars"; and that trade should balance over each 3 (or 6) months.[18]

Although prices, contracts, and accounts were to be established in "United States dollars," *no use of foreign exchange was actually required.* At the inception of the trade the State Bank of each contracting party opened a special non-interest-bearing account to the credit of the other country. All payments for goods to be delivered and for accruing charges were made by the respective banks in national currency and entered in the books in dollars when the goods crossed the national frontier. In other words, for any delivery the central bank of the exporting country debited the account of the country to which the goods were sent, and credited its own Ministry of Foreign Trade, and upon the receipt of imported goods it made opposing entries.

After 1948, in view of the dangers of economic isolation and schisms (as the Yugoslav one), the Soviet Union and the other Communist bloc countries adopted a series of measures such as the constitution of a "Council of Economic Mutual Assistance" (CEMA),[19] the ruble reform, and increasing interchanges in the bloc which paved the way for a closer integration of the bloc as a whole that would be substantially different from that existing up to 1948.

The CEMA was organized by the Soviet Union together with five East European countries (Czechoslovakia, Poland, Hungary, Romania, and Bulgaria) half a year after the break with Yugoslavia. The official communiqué, dated from Moscow, January 25, 1949, invited any country of Europe which shared the principles of "mutual assistance" and "wished to participate in broad economic cooperation with these countries" to join the Council, but the only country which hastened then to accept the invitation, Yugoslavia, was turned down. Ultimately the Council "accepted" Albania and East Germany.

How the Council was supposed to bring about the "mutual assistance" and "broad economic cooperation" among its members has not been clearly explained. Nevertheless, some valuable clues can be found in an analysis of a similar type of cooperation envisaged in the preceding period by certain East European countries and of certain acts which followed the creation of the Council.

We may take as an example of the preceding system of collaboration in Eastern Europe the Czechoslovak-Polish agreements concluded July 4, 1947, which were to operate in four economic fields: (1) trade

[18] See Appendix 1 to this chapter, pp. 455–457, for a "typical" Trade and Payments Agreement, also covering a credit agreement.

[19] The official Russian title of CEMA is "Sovet Ekonomicheskoi Vzaimopomoshchi."

between the two economies, (2) transportation problems, (3) permanent collaboration between the various sectors of the economies, and (4) collaboration in the field of planning.

Mutual trade was fixed by an agreement for five years at a total of 150 million dollars, or 30 million dollars per year. The commodity structure of this trade was determined provisionally, and a procedure for its modification was devised.

The agreement on transportation provided for access to each other's ports on the Oder (Poland) and on the Danube (Czechoslovakia), and provided for the construction over a period of eight years of a canal between the two rivers.

The industries of the two countries accepted "coordination little by little of their programs of production in order to apportion the fabrication of determined products." At the same time the two states decided to establish jointly certain industrial installations.

Trade and investment objectives were to be attained by the mutual submission of "provisional lists" of orders for a given planned period. Such a provisional list of orders for the period 1948–53 was, for example, submitted by Poland to Czechoslovakia in the spring of 1948.[20]

The long-term objectives extending over various planned periods (of five years or more) were to be achieved within the framework of "long-term projects" by agreements secured step by step when required. In fact, the long-term projects have remained limited so far, as compared to each country's over-all plan.

The administrative structure set up for carrying out these agreements was to consist of a "Council of Economic Cooperation" with a given number of joint committees, each for a specific field of collaboration.

As pointed out above, no similar data were released for CEMA. After its creation trade continued to flow in bilateral channels, national over-all long-term plans on parallel lines were established by each country, and the joint companies continued to expand on the already established lines of development. However, within these limits the role of the Council became more and more apparent.

During the period up to 1948 there was no coordination whatsoever of the aggregate magnitude of the foreign trade of the various countries. Any serious non-fulfillment of the planned foreign trade (reflecting both the lack of coordination among the intra-planned econo-

[20] *Sprawy Międzynarodowe*, I, 1 (October–December 1948), Polish Institute of International Affairs, Warsaw.

mies and the displacement brought about by the stronger bargaining power of some countries) was reflected in the production plans of the various countries.

In order to achieve some coordination at the level of trade among the various countries, two measures had to be taken: the establishment of provisional lists of the structure of trade of each country for a longer period, say, up to 1955, and the signing of long-term agreements between countries.

The establishment of provisional consolidated lists of future orders addressed to each country could be effected only by a central *ad hoc* organ such as CEMA. Up to a point this centralization placed the Council in the position of "allocating" the exportable surpluses and controlling the imports of each country. Moreover (and this time in contrast to the limited Czechoslovak-Polish agreement referred to above), such a consolidated list of the key products entering into the trade of the more isolated countries might have exerted very strong pressure on their plans despite the fact that such plans had been drawn separately with a view only to "domestic" requirements. However, the very absence of an integrated multilateral pattern of trade and trade settlements, and the continuance of a strictly bilateral system of trade agreements, indicates that the countries retained a very large measure of control over their foreign trade up to the end of the period under review.

In addition to the establishment of provisional consolidated *lists* by CEMA, from 1950 on there were established long-term *bilateral* agreements, usually of five years' duration, first between the Soviet Union—the central buyer and seller in the intra-planned economies market—and all the other East European countries,[21] and second between pairs of East European countries. Obviously, the centralized establishment of provisional consolidated lists for each country and the linking of trade partners through a network of bilateral agreements, which characterized the system of trade as it evolved between 1948 and 1955, were in conflict. One measure aimed at coordination and the other at keeping intact the bargaining power of the partners.[22]

[21] Such agreements have been signed by the Soviet Union with Czechoslovakia for the period 1951–55, with Poland for 1953–58, with Hungary for 1952–55, and with Romania for 1952–55. Cf. A. Korolenko, "Printsipi Ravenstva i Vzaimnoi Vygody v Torgovle SSSR s Evropeiskimi Stranami Narodnoi Demokratii" (Principles of Equality and Mutual Benefit in the Trade of the USSR with the European Countries of People's Democracy), in *Voprosy Ekonomiki,* March 3, 1952.

[22] "Of vital significance for the establishment of planned trade between the democratic countries are the long-term trade agreements concluded between them. At

The two measures can, however, coexist since provisional consolidated lists, as well as the long-term agreements themselves, are only *minimum* agreements. In this framework, the mutual deliveries of commodities are established on a *yearly* basis, i.e., by specifying the quantities and kinds of goods to be exchanged (quota lists), by signing contracts between the respective partners' organs of foreign trade, and so on, just as in the preceding period. The extent of the mutual exchanges is not limited by these agreements and annually surpasses their scope.[23]

After 1948–49, prices, contracts, and reciprocal accounts opened by the trading partners with their State Banks were increasingly in rubles instead of United States dollars as previously. In February 1950 the ruble was officially transferred to the gold standard, and the Soviet state bank established a new set of rates of exchange with the foreign currencies.[24] The decision was presented both as an outgrowth of the "strengthening of the ruble" as compared to the "depreciation of currencies in the Western countries," and as a measure destined to place the trade in the Soviet bloc on a "firm basis." From that date on, *all* prices, contracts, and reciprocal accounts in the bloc have been

first the situation was such that, while a country with a planned economy could calculate for years ahead its vital import requirements and its export possibilities, it could not be sure for years in advance that it would definitely get everything it needed from the other countries with planned economy, or that it would definitely supply them with certain goods. Today, however, the long-term trade agreements serve as a solid basis for planning foreign trade for years in advance and in this way create prerequisites which will enable the countries marching along the pathway to Socialism to *co-ordinate plans for production and capital investments in individual branches of the economy by means of international trade agreements,* i.e., by means of ensuring supplies of certain goods over a period of several years. The year 1952 is the first year when the bulk of the foreign trade between the Soviet Union and countries of people's democracy is being already conducted on the basis of long-term trade agreements." Cf. László Gay, *op. cit.*

23 "Czechoslovak Foreign Trade with the European People's Democracies." *CEB,* No. 305, Feb. 1956.

24 The Soviet state bank established its purchasing price for 1 gram of fine gold at 4.25 rubles, the rate of exchange passing from 5.30 to 4 rubles for 1 dollar, and from 14.84 to 11.29 for 1 pound sterling, etc. The rate of exchange of the foreign currencies was lowered by 25.66 per cent, which corresponds to a 34.55 per cent revaluation of the ruble. It has been constantly indicated in the West, since that reform, that the ruble is overvalued and that its real rate might be around 30 rubles to 1 dollar. It is interesting to note that, even after the transfer of the ruble to the gold standard, as the world price of gold is determined in the final analysis by the official. price fixed by the United States Treasury, the ruble is attached to a standard whose price depends on the United States.

expressed in rubles.[25] During the previous period the entering in these accounts of the goods delivered in dollars, or even in the currency of one of the trading partners, was a means of putting the respective transactions on a common basis. Any monetary unit would have served for accounting purposes for this type of trade if it had been defined in terms of gold or dollars so as to remain "stable" as a measure of the prices and transactions concerned.

The "new" ruble could certainly easily replace the "fictitious dollar" of the special accounts and become the new *"fictitious* bookkeeping unit" of the bloc, without need for any reform. In fact, any fictitiously defined ruble, at any rate of exchange, could have served the purpose without the spectacular decision of February 1950. However, establishing the ruble on a "firm basis" not only made it possible to carry on all future trade in the bloc on a uniform basis, with an over-all view of all the trade relations involved, *but also made the Soviet Union the final judge of the rates of exchange in the bloc as a whole.*[26] A byproduct of the revaluation undertaken in 1950 was its effect on the total value of "invisibles,"[27] the prices of which are

[25] Concerning the clearing system operated on the basis of the Soviet ruble (allegedly "the hardest and most stable currency in the world"), see A. F. Ramzaitsev, *Pravovye Voprosy Vneshnei Torgovli SSSR* (Legal Questions of the Foreign Trade of the USSR), Vneshtorgizdat, Moscow, 1954, pp. 61 ff., and V. V. Ikonnikov, editor, *Denezhnoe Obrashchenie i Kredit SSSR* (Money Circulation and Credit in the USSR), Gosfinizdat, Moscow, 1954, pp. 430 ff.

[26] It has been suggested that the East European countries themselves have an important interest in seeing that this rate is a meaningful one. The profit or loss of each Ministry of Foreign Trade depends on three factors independent of each other: (1) the domestic wholesale prices at which this Ministry carries its domestic transactions concerning its trade program; (2) the clearing ruble prices at which are carried the transactions with foreign countries; (3) the exchange rate at which "revenue or expenditure of the Ministry in clearing rubles are converted into domestic currencies." In these conditions, both the size of any imbalance in clearing rubles and the total money supply will be dependent upon the adopted exchange rate (since the rate will determine the amount of financing that the respective treasury has to undertake in order to cope with this trading imbalance). Thus "even though the exchange rate may not affect the trade program itself (as it would in a market economy) it can still play a definite role in determining the impact of the trade program upon the money supply and hence upon domestic monetary equilibrium." Cf. Edward Ames, "The Exchange Rate in Soviet Type Economies," *Review of Economics and Statistics,* XXV, 4 (November 1953), pp. 337–342. Actually, as the Soviet Union is directly interested in these rates, it is open to question whether *each* East European country can establish a "correct" rate so as to avoid undesirable domestic monetary consequences.

[27] Such items are: payments for training groups of students in the military and technical schools of the Soviet Union, transportation services by Soviet companies, wages of various Soviet technicians "lent" to the other countries.

fixed in rubles and which sometimes play a significant role in the balance of payments with the Soviet Union of the least developed of East European countries. However, the long-term objectives of the reform seem more important. It opened the way not only for the exchange of intra-bloc balances (expressed in clearing rubles) into gold or foreign currency balances held by countries with extra-bloc export surpluses, *but also at some later date for the exchange of ruble balances into Soviet goods within some established limits.* This possibility would require, however, that the intra-bloc trade *switch from the international price pattern to the Soviet price pattern,* and then each "interior" economic measure in the Soviet Union itself would have a direct repercussion in the network of all the intra-bloc transactions. These are, however, only *long-term prospects,* in relation to which the centralization of the trade lists operated by CEMA and the utilization of the new ruble as the standard of value in the intra-orbit transactions were only the preliminaries.

Other special agreements (such as investment agreements, coordination of certain planning aspects between two countries, and technical aid contracts) have also been "cleared" in some instances through CEMA.

Although the role of CEMA has been growing it has by no means supplanted negotiation and establishment of bilateral technical-aid contracts. Thus, it is thanks to agreements concluded *directly* between various countries (as between Czechoslovakia and Hungary and between Hungary and Poland for specialization in certain types of rolling-mill products) that there was some progress toward output coordination during the first long-term plans. As already stated,[28] during and after the new course, the necessity of a broad division of labor was emphasized. The current long-term plans take into consideration specific output and delivery plans of the other countries and recognize that certain countries are in a better position for producing certain types of goods.[29] But planning is still encompassed in the framework of each "sovereign" state and coordination is achieved only piecemeal through laborious negotiation both *in* and *outside* the CEMA. For the second quinquennium, if not also for a third, the piecemeal approach seems to have the better chance to prevail. Transportation is

[28] See above, Chapter 9, p. 358.

[29] See: "National Plans Coordinated" in *Prague News Letter,* Vol. 12, No. 10, May 12, 1956; V. Široký: "Ekonomicheskoe Sotrudnichestvo na uroven vozrosschikh zadach, Sotsialisticheskiĭ Gosudarstv" (Economic Cooperation on the Level of the Growing Tasks of the Socialist States), *Pravda,* April 6, 1956.

the sole field in which extensive cooperation has already developed, and led to establishment of a single tariff for freight and mutual utilization of railway rolling stock.[30]

Soviet Aid

East European political and economic literature places exaggerated emphasis on "Soviet aid." It consistently refers to Soviet exports to these countries as "aid" and magnifies their significance in every aspect of economic activity. It pictures the Soviet Union as generous creditor, investor, and industrializer of the area.[31]

It is true that the Soviet Union has supplied a substantial portion of East European needs. The Soviet Union is the source of 70 to 100 per cent of the iron-ore imports of the East European countries (70 per cent for Czechoslovakia, 68 for Poland, 100 for Hungary and Romania, in 1954 and 1955), all the manganese, large quantities of ferro-alloys, oil, 30–100 per cent of the cotton, and so on. The new steel industries of the area depend heavily on iron-ore imports from the Soviet Union. She, in turn, absorbs a large proportion of the exports of both raw materials and manufactured products of the East European countries: from 30 to 80 per cent of their steel products for export, from 30 to 100 per cent of their textile exports, around 30 per cent of the Polish coal, large quantities of Romanian oil, much of the Bulgarian tobacco. The share of East European domestic output exported to the Soviet Union appears very large: from 5 to 15 per cent of their steel products, from 5 to 30 per cent of their output of cotton fabrics, and 9 per cent of their coal output (Poland). These figures do not indicate the drain of such exports on East Europe: the

[30] V. Klochek and K. Viriasov, "Ekonomicheskoe Sotrudnichestvo Stran Lageria Sotsializma" (Economic Cooperation of Countries of the Socialist Camp), *VT*, XXII (February 1952), p. 8.

[31] A familiar technique of stressing Soviet aid through trade is to emphasize every link of the chain through which a given Soviet import goes, e.g., a reference to a Bucharest exhibition on Romanian-Soviet collaboration:

> From the numerous stands featuring the fruitful results of economic collaboration between Romania and the USSR, we shall mention only the important ones. In the field of textile industry alone this collaboration resulted in the import of 18,017 tons of cotton which secured work to: 23 spinning mills with 290,000 spindles, 390 weaving mills with 16,000 looms, 245 knitting and stocking mills, and 120 thread, lace, and ribbon factories. These enterprises are employing over 40,000 workers. [Vasile Luca, "New Orientations in Romanian Finances," *RR*, II, 5–6 (1948), p. 95.]

The entire story hinges on Romanian imports of 18,000 tons of cotton, of which a large part was ultimately exported to the Soviet Union as finished goods.

diversion for export of even a small part of the total output of one product might be a burden, whereas the diversion of a major part of the output of another product might be an advantage. They do indicate, however, not only the heavy dependence of these countries on the Soviet market but also the significant contribution of these countries to Soviet supply.

A second aspect of "Soviet aid" is the grants and credits given to the area. According to the data available, the Soviet Union played only a modest role as creditor up to the end of 1955, *except for armaments,* for which no data have been released.

The Soviet credits are of 3 main types: (1) credits in gold or foreign currency, (2) credits for the purchase of raw materials in the Soviet Union, and (3) investment credits. Through 1956 the credits extended to the area, excluding Yugoslavia, and specifically mentioned by either Soviet or East European sources, have represented a total of not more than 850 million dollars (see Table 121).

Before 1948–49 the Soviet Union had extended some 25 million dollars essentially for the purchase, from the Soviet Union, of grain and foodstuffs, had transferred some transport equipment (especially in the early postwar period and from her war booty) for a total which can be estimated at perhaps as much as 15 million dollars, and made two straight loans in foreign exchange to Czechoslovakia and Poland for the purchase of machines, equipment, and some foodstuffs from the West, totaling about 50 million dollars. Most of these credits were extended in a period when the East European economies were partly disorganized and when some of them were sending reparations to the Soviet Union at a rate of over 40–50 million gold dollars per year (over 20 million from Hungary and substantially more from Romania). Furthermore, up to a certain point, many of the so-called special commercial loans were offset by other types of short-term commercial credits, as we shall see immediately.

The most important credits to be extended by the Soviet Union were the "investment loans," which assumed real importance only from 1948 on. A credit of this type, of 135 million dollars for the purchase of equipment from the Soviet Union, was extended to Yugoslavia in 1947, but only 0.6 per cent of this credit took the form of actual deliveries to Yugoslavia before the 1948 break, when the rest of the credit was canceled. Small investment credits have been extended to Hungary, Romania, and Bulgaria. The most important credits of this type have been granted to Poland (and, outside the area, to

TABLE 121. USSR: CREDITS TO EASTERN EUROPE THROUGH 1956

	Type of Credit [a]	Dollars [b] (millions)	Total by Country
Czechoslovakia			
1948	1)	23	23
Poland			
1947	1)	28	
1948	3)	450	
1950	3)	100	
1956	2)	125	703
Hungary			
1948	3)	[c]	[c]
1956	2)	25	[c]
Romania			
1947	2)	10	
1956	2)	[c]	[c]
Bulgaria			
1948	2), 3) [d]	11	
1956	2)	17.5	
1956	3)	70	98.5
Yugoslavia			
1947	2), 3) [d]	19 [e]	
1947	3)	135 [e]	154
1955	1)	30	
1955	2)	54	
1955	3)	110	194

[a] 1) Credits in gold or foreign currency; 2) credits for the purchase of raw and other materials; 3) investment credits.

[b] After 1950 the credits have been labeled in rubles. They are here converted into dollars at the official rate of 4 rubles to 1 dollar.

[c] Unspecified amount.

[d] Including transfer of transport equipment from the Soviet war booty.

[e] Only part of the scheduled goods were actually delivered; the rest of the credits were canceled in 1949.

Sources: EE General: *Pravda*, July 2, 1950, *Planovoe Khoziaistvo* (Planned Economy), No. 3 (March–July 1952), pp. 65 ff., M. F. Kovrizhnykh et al., *Vneshniaia Torgovlia*, *op. cit.*, pp. 43–47; *Economic Bulletin for Europe*, Vol. 8, No. 3 (November 1956), p. 43.

Y: Tito, *For Independence and Equality*, *op. cit.*, pp. 72–77; *Borba*, January 15, 1956; *New York Times*, April 28, 1956.

China [32]). Poland obtained a first investment loan of 450 million dollars in 1948, anticipating the delivery of investment goods during

[32] China obtained from the Soviet Union an investment loan of 300 million dollars, at 1 per cent interest per year, in 1950, and a second investment loan in 1954, of 520 million rubles (130 million dollars). According to an agreement

the period from 1948 to the end of 1955. These deliveries were to consist of the Nowa Huta steel mills complex, electrical generating plants, cement plants, and various equipment, repayable in exports of steel, cement, etc., produced by these plants over a period of 10 years at a 3 per cent rate of interest. A similar loan of 100 million dollars for various investment goods for the period 1951–58 was extended by the Soviet Union to Poland in 1950. Deliveries under both loans were to be used for building 30 new industrial plants in Poland over the period 1948–58. After re-establishing her relations with Belgrade in 1955, Moscow extended 3 credits to Yugoslavia, of which the most important, the investment loan, concerned the purchase of fertilizer plants from the Soviet Union.

The Soviet Union is becoming more important as creditor [33] and as supplier of certain plants in whose output she is directly interested (such as steel plants for Poland). She is, furthermore, compelled for political reasons to shoulder at least part of the economic burden conditioned by the convulsions which occurred in 1956 in countries like Hungary and Poland.

It can be easily foreseen that the East European pressures for larger Soviet credits of grain and raw materials and for the cancellation of previous debts will probably increase as the difficulties of these countries deepen. Let us note finally that some of the East European countries are also supplying to the other countries of the area plants and equipment on credit in order to increase outputs in which they are directly interested (Czechoslovak plants for Hungarian bauxite, Hungarian plants for Romanian gas, etc.).

The last and one of the most heavily stressed aspects of Soviet aid is the "mutual exchange of scientific-technical aid." Such exchanges have occurred and continue to occur both between the Soviet Union and the people's democracies, and among the latter countries themselves.

signed in 1956, the USSR will "help China construct 55 new enterprises in addition to 156 plants the construction of which is provided for by the previous agreements" (*Pravda*, April 8, 1956). The exact total of the credits extended is not specified.

[33] According to a declaration of Nikita Khrushchev at the XXth Congress of the Communist Party of the USSR, the Soviet credits extended to the "people's democracies" amounted by mid-1956 to 21 billion rubles, or 5.240 billion dollars at the official rate of exchange. These figures diverge so substantially from the indications of the specific credits extended by the Soviet Union that it might be assumed they include military credits as well as some special arrangements like the one concerning purchase by Hungary and Romania of the Soviet share in the former joint companies.

In principle, the system of interchange of experience has been as follows up to the present. CEMA acted as the centralizer of requests, but the actual technical agreements were concluded on a *bilateral* basis. These agreements, usually of five years' duration, called for the formation of a joint commission of the two partners meeting twice a year and submitting *recommendations* to the respective governments. These joint commissions established the general plan of exchange, for instance, of licenses and patents.[34] Although Soviet literature and the literature of the other countries insist that these interchanges were gratuitous, such a characterization oversimplifies the situation. It must be noted from the outset that certain countries of the area, like Czechoslovakia, East Germany, and also in certain respects even Hungary, had, in some fields, far greater industrial experience and technical know-how than the Soviet Union, so that the "gratuitous interchange" might have been either more beneficial to the Soviet Union or equally beneficial for both partners. For the more backward countries such as Romania and Bulgaria, and also for certain branches of Hungarian and Polish industry, exchange would be more beneficial to the East European countries than to the Soviet Union.

During the first long-term plan there was rarely a simple transmission of licenses and patents from the Soviet Union to the other countries; usually the transfer either was made to the existing joint companies or was used for the setting up of new "joint" ventures. Currently, the exchange of "scientific-technical aid" plays a key role in the field of atomic energy. Evidently in the area the Soviet Union

[34] Thus, for instance, at the 1953 session of the Soviet-Polish Committee on Scientific and Technical Cooperation, the two countries signed a protocol according to which the Soviet Union agreed to furnish scientific and technical assistance to Poland by transferring to it the plans for a chemical factory, a building materials plant, blueprints of types of metallurgical and power-generating equipment, of machine tools, and technical data for the production of dyes, medicinals, etc.; moreover, the Soviet Union "at the request of the Polish side, will undertake to examine various projects drawn up by the Polish planning agencies"; finally, the Soviet Union undertook to play host to Polish specialists for practical training in factories, bureaus, research outfits, etc. In return, the Soviet Union obtained technical data for the production of various types of chemicals, glass, and other industrial products; furthermore, Poland "will make it possible for a group of Soviet specialists to familiarize themselves with the progress made in various branches of the national economy." (Cf. official communiqué in *Pravda,* Nov. 5, 1953.) It might appear from this communiqué that the technical cooperation aimed also at giving a very detailed view to the Soviet experts of the inner workings of each East European economy.

is the undisputed leader in this field. However, the transmission of "scientific aid" is dependent on the conclusion of bilateral contracts between each of these countries and the Soviet Union concerning the exploitation and the exports of uranium.[35]

Regarding "acceptance of engineers and workers for training in the Soviet Union," except for organized trips to the Soviet Union compensated for by trips of Soviet experts to the other countries, a normal arrangement in any group of countries having friendly relations, it must be noted that the Soviet Union derived substantial monetary benefit from the training of large groups of students from East Europe, as we shall see below.

Prices, Balances of Trade, and Balances of Payments

A question often raised in relation both to trade and to Soviet "aid" is that of the *specific* prices of the commodities involved in the exchanges between the Soviet Union and the East European countries, and among the latter countries.

After the break with the bloc, the Yugoslavs strongly attacked the principle of utilization of the *international price pattern* among "socialist countries" on the grounds that, following a Marxian postulate, such practices are by definition favorable to the industrialized countries, which derive an "automatic" advantage from trade (considered as interchange of "materialized labor") because of the higher productivity per man in precisely the branches of goods that form most of their exports.[36] Nevertheless, in pointing to the Hungarian prices of industrial goods and stressing that they were supposedly "very high in relation to the prices of Yugoslav raw materials which Hungary obtained as imports," the Yugoslavs failed to make a case against the Soviet Union, even though they purported to be doing so. The Russians also export mostly raw materials, and hence these price relations would work against them just as against the Yugoslavs.

It would appear that under certain conditions the Russians did benefit from their terms of trade with East Europe. A specific example is the Russian-Polish agreement on Polish coal. A more general case can be made from the terms of trade secured by Russia from

[35] See Chapter 6, note 79, p. 203.

[36] See, for instance, Vladislav Malenković, "O pitanju ekonomskih odnosa izmedju SSSR—ą i njemu potčinjenih zemalja" (On the Question of Economic Relations between the USSR and the Countries Subjected to Her), in *Ekonomist*, III, 3 (1950), pp. 39 ff.

certain East European countries, which were much more favorable than the terms of trade secured by the East European countries or by some Western countries, and from indirect evidence concerning the prices secured by Russia from resale in extra-bloc markets of produce obtained from her intra-bloc trade.

Since our data relating to these general cases are very incomplete, any relevant computation is perforce crude. However, a certain pattern is clearly apparent, and some interest attaches to such computations. The data available for 1948 for Czechoslovak exports will serve to illustrate the point. That year the Soviet bloc absorbed 50 per cent of the Czechoslovak exports of ironware and steel, 70 per cent of her exports of power-driven machines, 72 per cent of her exports of electrical machinery, and 80 per cent of her exports of footwear. The Soviet Union alone absorbed 45 per cent of the iron and steel, 57 per cent of power-driven machines, 53 per cent of the electrical machinery, and 39 per cent of the footwear.

A comparison of the unit value indices of (*a*) total exports, (*b*) exports to the Soviet Union, and (*c*) exports to East European countries (excluding the Soviet Union) reveals that, for the articles considered, the unit value indices of the exports to the Soviet Union were systematically *lower* than the average and those to the other East European countries frequently *higher* than average. Although no breakdown is available for each type of machinery, and there is no certainty that the structure of each subcategory would be exactly the same in the cases considered, the general comparison is quite clear. On the basis of 1937 = 100, the unit value indices of exports to the Soviet Union were: for footwear 605, whereas the average index for all footwear exports was 764; for cotton fabrics 316, average 433; for iron and steel wares 137, average 270; for electrical machinery 215, average 300; for other power machinery 264, average 372; for machine tools 388, average 430. Since the Soviet Union bought all these items in large quantities, these discrepancies cannot be merely statistical accidents due to derivation of an index from a small number of units.

The other East European countries paid usually more than average and always more than the Soviet Union. For cotton fabrics the unit value indices of exports to Eastern Europe were 569, average 433; for iron and steel wares 320, average 270; for agricultural machinery 327, average 278; for power machines 548, average 372; for machinery and spare parts 819, average 458. The inference is that the Soviet Union paid, at least to certain East European countries in the year considered, prices lower than the average received in their current trade. The higher prices charged the other "socialist" countries appear characteristic of a general tendency to inflate all the prices in the interchanges among the "socialist" economies at a time when there was a progressive decrease in supplies from the West; for each of the East European countries, and here we can include the Soviet Union, tried to benefit from its special bargaining position in the intra-bloc market.[37]

There is indirect evidence of possible Soviet profits from her trade with the East European countries, from Soviet attempts to undersell some East European producers in the extra-bloc markets. Thus Bulgaria is reported to have attempted to sell essence of roses in the United States in 1950 at 80 dollars for seven-eighths of an ounce, whereas the Russian Amtorg is reported to have offered this typical Bulgarian export product at a price of only 67 dollars for the same quantity. There have been numerous situations when the Soviet Union appeared to be underselling East European producers, but much of the supporting evidence comes from Yugoslav sources and is difficult to verify.[38]

From 1949–50 on, two basic principles were stressed in relation to prices in the intra-bloc trade: their *stability* over the period of long-term contracts, and their *uniformity* for all the transactions of a given country concerning a given product. With respect to the maintenance of the same prices over the period of a long-term contract, the ideas stressed were the independence of the bloc from the "chaotic fluctuation of prices in the world markets" and the possibility of long-term planning on a "firm basis." With respect to the *single prices* established in the bloc for any given product of a producer, the idea stressed was "justice" in trade, whatever the bargaining strength of a supplier in respect to her buyers.[39] As stated by a Romanian source:

> Prices are established for a one-year period, and in the large majority of cases remain constant for a period of years, over the duration of the agreement between the signing parties. . . . In contrast to the capitalist market, on the democratic market there are no multiple prices for one and the same commodity. For the same commodity, and for all the countries of this camp to which it is delivered, each

[37] Computations are based on *Měsíční Přehled Zahraničního Obchodu* (Monthly Reports on Foreign Trade), December 1948, and *SZ*, XII, 4, 1949.

[38] For an extensive presentation of these cases, see E. Zaleski, *op. cit.*, pp. 383–388.

[39] See, for instance, I. Dudinskii, "Ekonomicheskoe Sotrudnichestvo SSSR i Stran Narodnoi Demokratsii" (Economic Cooperation of the USSR and the Countries of People's Democracy), in *Bolshevik*, No. 6 (March 1950), pp. 9 ff.

country establishes a *single price,* with little differences only, in the *limit* of differences in the cost of transportation.[40]

The principle of a "single price" for any given commodity was adopted in order to avoid the very situation that had prevailed up to 1949–50, *multiplicity of prices and large variations in prices* according to the bargaining strength of the partners. Since 1949–50 a price concession to one trader partner has brought about price revisions for the same commodity when sold and even delivered to other partners in the bloc.[41] It should be noted, however, that this measure is by no means a protection against a powerful purchaser, since, in principle, this purchaser can lower the price whenever she signs her contract. Hence the only result is that weaker purchasers get the same advantage at the expense of the supplier. Outside of this change, no innovations have been introduced as far as prices are concerned.

None of the East European countries has published its balances of trade since 1949. The data available up to 1948 for Czechoslovakia, Hungary, Bulgaria, and Poland can be combined to get an over-all view of trade relations in the area. The data given by the first three countries were in their national currencies, with Poland's in dollars. All indicate the practice of liquidating imbalances over a short period, usually from one year to the next. On close examination, it is the group of smaller countries (Bulgaria, Romania, and Yugoslavia) which emerge as the *commercial creditors* of Czechoslovakia, Poland, and Hungary.[42]

[40] M. Horoviţ, "Despre Decontările Internaţionale şi Relaţiile de Credit dintre Ţările Lagărului Socialist" (On International Payments and the Credit Relations among the Countries of the Socialist Camp), *PE,* No. 7, July 1954, p. 107.

[41] In an article by Hsu Hsueh-han (Vice-Minister for Foreign Trade), "China's Trade with the European People's Democracies," we read, for instance:

Prices of goods which do not conform with the above principles and seem unreasonable are subject to voluntary readjustment by both sides. Even after an agreement has been signed or the goods have already been delivered, the price of a given article which is discovered to be against the policy will be adjusted. For instance, Hungary voluntarily lowered by 12 per cent the prices of her steel measuring tapes, locks and balls; Czechoslovakia brought down by 600,000 rubles the price of statistical machines for the railways when a recalculation was found to be necessary after the conclusion of the trade contracts. Democratic Germany cut the price of fluoroscopic screens by 36.69 per cent. All these reduced prices were made in an atmosphere of cordial friendship. When China fixed a lower price for cotton exported to Poland she immediately lowered correspondingly the price of cotton formerly fixed in trade agreements with Romania and other European People's Democracies. China also cut by 25 per cent the prices of animal casings sold to Hungary even after they had been shipped. [Cf. *People's China,* XVII, Peking, 1953, p. 13.]

[42] See below, Table 124, Appendix 2 to this chapter.

The unusual situation in which the smaller and less developed countries were creditor countries is a direct result of the relative bargaining strength they possessed *at the time* in the area. The smaller countries needed the processing facilities of Czechoslovakia, Poland, and Hungary and were in the least favorable condition. Although the agreements contained the provision that "the amount of payments effectuated by each contracting party in the special credit account must remain equal between themselves and this equality must be maintained in the course of each three months," the little countries could hardly stop deliveries to a stronger partner even when the value of their exports to such a country had exceeded that of their imports from it. Hence it was this group of smaller countries which usually carried the burden of commercial short-term credits free of interest. Only in special circumstances was the situation reversed, the Soviet Union assuming this position of short-term creditor.

The balance of payments between the Soviet Union and the East European countries is influenced by factors other than this commercial trade. The consolidated Soviet-Yugoslav balance of payments for 1945–49 which can be constructed from Yugoslav data[43] furnishes some helpful indications of the relations between the Soviet Union and the East European countries during the period. The balance of payments data indicate that the Soviet Union extended to Yugoslavia a credit of around 85.5 million dollars in the exchange of commodities. The Yugoslavs imported Soviet goods to the amount of 192.4 million dollars and exported goods worth 114.9 million dollars. In fact, the entries for merchandise show that the Yugoslav imports, both under ordinary and special trade agreements and under the investment loan, were actually slightly *smaller* than the Yugoslav exports (i.e., 114, 394,000 as against 114,804,000 dollars). The creditor position of the Soviet Union resulted at the time only from the Soviet sale of (surplus) military equipment and of transport equipment from war booty. Of the total 85,486,000 dollars of credit extended by the Soviet Union, the short-term credit outstanding in 1949 amounted to only 7.7 per cent of the total and the long-term credits to over 92 per cent. Of the latter, 85.2 per cent was from military loans, and 7.0 per cent from the transfer of transport equipment from war booty.

As already stated, since 1949 investment loans tended to rise substantially, especially for Poland. For the other countries, the balances of payment with the Soviet Union probably differed from that estab-

[43] See below, Tables 125–127, Appendix 2 to this chapter.

lished for Yugoslavia only in the following respects: (1) larger debit entries under *current transactions* for such items as foreign travel (specifically, training of technical and military cadres in the Soviet Union), transportation (e.g., on the Danube), and investment income (from the joint companies); and maintenance of the rule of tight balancing for merchandise transactions covered by ordinary trade agreements, usually over a six-month period; (2) substantial liabilities incurred by all East European countries for Soviet military equipment.

Pattern of Multilateral Trade and Settlements

Because of the economic structure of the region and the structure of its foreign trade, the following multilateral regional system of trade and trade settlements might emerge: (1) only a part of the Soviet claims against Hungary, Romania, and Bulgaria arising from any source, including certain indispensable Soviet exports to these countries, would be compensated for by exports from them to the Soviet Union; (2) the largest part of these claims would be met by exports from Hungary, Romania, and Bulgaria to Czechoslovakia, Poland, and East Germany, which in turn would export to the Soviet Union; (3) any eventual "non-compensable" surplus of exports or imports would be financed within given limits through credits extended by a centrally managed fund.

The system could then rest on two regional groups: one, composed of Hungary, Romania, and Bulgaria, would "industrialize" mainly on the basis of the Hungarian industrial complex; the second, composed of Poland, Czechoslovakia, and East Germany, would nourish and expand its present industrial structure on the Polish steel and coal base.

The first group could be brought to reduce its imports from the second, but at the same time this group could direct a large flow of exports varying from oil to foodstuffs toward the second group, enabling the latter to export finished goods to the Soviet Union (see Chart 16).

In order to keep the groups in balanced operation, Soviet exports of iron ore, metals, and cotton would have to continue, and in contrast to general practice in the preceding period, not all these exports would be processed for immediate re-export to the Soviet Union.

Such a pattern of integration could ultimately permit a quite rigid coordination of the future "trade orders" without necessarily hindering limited agreements for given planned production.

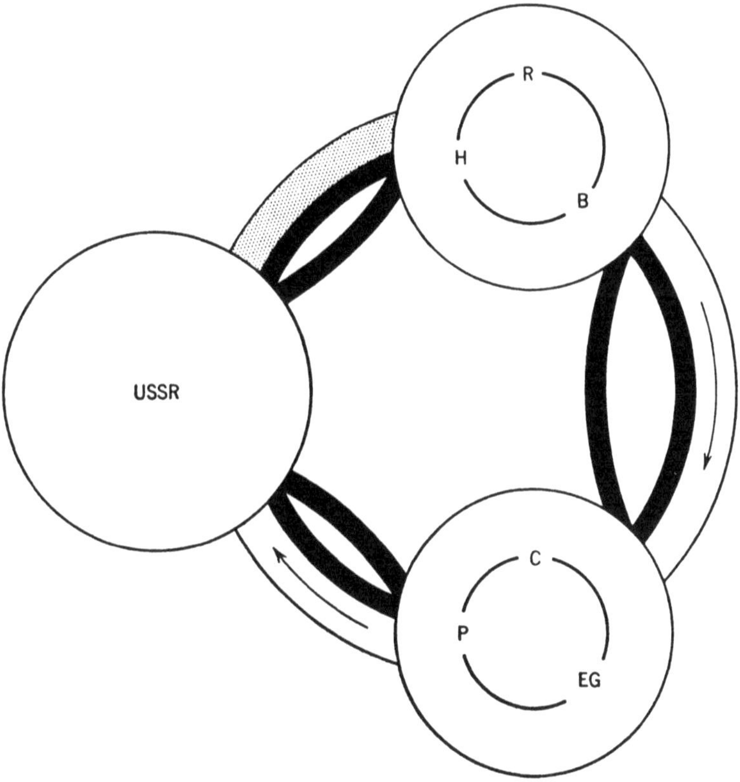

Trade bilaterally compensable

Soviet purchasing power from all sources

Trade multilaterally compensable within the system as a whole

H, R, B Hungary, Romania, Bulgaria

P, C, EG Poland, Czechoslovakia, East Germany

CHART 16. PATTERN OF MULTILATERAL TRADE AND SETTLEMENTS IN THE SOVIET BLOC IN EUROPE

Such multilateralization of trade and settlements inside the bloc would eventually affect the transactions of each unit with the countries outside the bloc, and could lead ultimately to a centralized management of bloc resources in foreign currency.

During the first development period, some East European economists expressed the idea that "the full socialist development of a world market" requires "evidently not only bilateral agreements but the coordination of trade and coordination of plans of production between all the countries of the socialist camp." [44] However, the concepts of a broad division of labor and of multilateralization of trade and trade settlements face two serious obstacles. As already stated, the Marxian concept of "enlarged reproduction" seems to be interpreted by East European countries of the Soviet bloc as implying the necessity of the creation, by each one, of a national heavy "industrial base." The multilateralization of trade still seems, on the other hand, to be considered unfavorably by the Soviet Union, who so far has systematically stressed the utility for "planning" purposes of strictly controlled bilateral trade flows.

Factors Affecting the Extra-bloc Trade

The foreign trade of the bloc exhibited two symmetrical characteristics in the period extending from 1948 to 1955: a methodical increase in intra-bloc trade, offset by a sharp decline in the extra-bloc trade. In nominal values, the latter trade fell continuously up to and including 1954, but increased in 1955 over the 1948 level.[45] In volume, the drop in this trade was striking when compared to prewar volume. The registered exports and imports of Western Europe to and from the bloc were in 1953 but 31 per cent and 22 per cent of their prewar volume.

Two basic factors have affected the trends in the extra-bloc trade, especially with Western Europe: the industrialization of the area and a policy of trade restrictions applied by the West, known as the "strategic embargo."

The process of industrialization has significantly changed the struc-

[44] O. Lange, "Rozpad Jednolitego Rynku Światowego i Ukształtowanie się Dwóch Równoległych Rynków w Gospodarce Światowej," *op. cit.* See also: N. Spulber, "Economic Thinking and its Application and Methodology in Eastern Europe outside of Soviet Russia," *The American Economic Review*, Vol. XLVI, No. 2 (May 1956), p. 379.

[45] See Table 127, Appendix 3.

ture of exports and the demand for imports of the countries of the area.

The share of manufactured goods in Czechoslovakian exports increased from around 72 per cent in 1937 to 82 per cent in 1948, and probably to more than 85 per cent in 1953.[46] Textiles and clothes accounted for 25 per cent of these totals in 1937, but 16 per cent in 1948, and only 7 per cent in 1953. The share of machinery and vehicles increased from 6.8 per cent in 1937 to 20 per cent in 1948 and 40 per cent in 1953. In Polish exports the share of transport equipment and machinery increased from 2.4 per cent of the total exports in 1949 to 12 per cent in 1953. Hungary had large increases in the export of machinery, transport equipment, and electrotechnical products. The share of manufactured goods in Romanian exports increased from less than 2 per cent in 1938 to nearly 18 per cent in 1953.

On the other hand, the striking changes undergone by the rural areas (land reforms and the collectivization drive) affected adversely both the amount and nature of the so-called "traditional" agricultural exports of some countries. In Hungary, for instance, the staple products of the larger estates fell off after the land reform and were replaced by products characteristic of small holdings: poultry, goose liver, eggs, feathers, seeds, vegetables, game and fish, bowels and bladders. The collectivization drive failed to reorganize the countryside rapidly and secure increased yields from reduced acreage. On the contrary collectivization and the domestic demand for industrial crops brought about a further reduction in the traditional agricultural outputs and, therefore, in the exportable margins.

Simultaneously, both industrialization and the structural modifications in agriculture conditioned substantial shifts in the nature and the volume of the demand for imports. There was an increased demand for industrial raw materials (coal, steel, ores, etc.), heavy and light machinery, transport equipment, and the like. The demand for consumers' goods, textiles, shoes, household goods, etc., fell off sharply. Because of the postwar disruptions, structural changes, and some severe drought years, the demand for foodstuffs increased rapidly up to 1948, but started to taper off toward the end of that period.

Only Poland, with her decisive exportable surpluses of coal, and

[46] For some underlying data, see mainly A. Chistiakov, "Razvitie Economicheskogo Sotrudnichestva Stran Sotsialisticheskogo Lageria" (Development of Economic Cooperation between the Countries of the Socialist Camp), in *Komunist,* Moscow, Vol. XXXI, No. 15, October 1954 and Kovrizhnykh, et al., Vneshniaia Torgovlia, *op. cit., passim.*

Soviet Russia, with the period of structural changes in agriculture already completed, could maintain a higher stability in the structure of their exports and, hence, in their extra-bloc trade. Romania might have been in a strong position, given her oil, had not a large part of it been mortgaged to Soviet Russia (following the reparations obligations and the formation of the joint Soviet-Romanian Oil Company).

The second basic factor affecting the trade relations of these countries has been a series of trade restrictions established by the West. The February 1948 Prague coup d'état marked dramatically the break of the Soviet area with the West. The United States and some of the Western powers immediately started to create a system of "security export control" for East-West trade flows. From the beginning this implied the application of *selective* controls with the stated aims of: (1) *denying* to the Soviet bloc goods which could imperil Western security (i.e., applying an "embargo" in respect to goods of primary strategic importance: not only arms but also specialized machinery for the production of armaments, machine tools, transport equipment, etc.); (2) *limiting* exports of goods which could be turned rapidly from civilian to military use (i.e., fixing "quantitative controls" in respect to a series of goods of secondary strategic importance: specialized machinery and the like); (3) *establishing* a *surveillance* list for certain key commodities such as rubber. Thus the emphasis was placed from the beginning on the *composition* and not on the *volume* of this trade.

The United States initiated its exports controls in March 1948. Other Western countries established controls over certain war materials. Through the Economic Cooperation Act of 1948 (cf. Section 117*d* as amended) Congress directed the ECA administrator to prevent the shipment to the Soviet bloc of ECA-financed products that were banned for export to the Soviet bloc by the United States itself. Early in 1950 the United States, Canada, and the West European powers, some of which had already instituted tighter security controls on their trade with the East, established an informal joint committee for determining the areas of controls and agreement, and for common action.[47] As stated in one of the official reports to Congress:

[47] The Consultative Group (CG) of the 15 Western powers concerned formed a working committee (COCOM), which never issues communiqués and the details of whose discussions are not revealed. Cf. the Revision of Strategic Trade Controls, Mutual Defense Assistance Control Act of 1951 (the Battle Act), Fifth Report to Congress, First Half of 1954, Washington, 1954, p. 16.

> . . . The setting up of controls acceptable to all allied nations has been a difficult process. Roughly, it has involved the specific definitions of commodities which they wished to embargo, which commodities shipments they wished to restrict in quantity, and which should be kept under surveillance. In addition, the experts have had to agree on effectiveness of enforcing these controls.[48]

The continuing discussions resulted in a steady expansion of the lists of commodities for control up to 1953. At the same time, Congress adopted the Battle Act, which provided for an embargo list of goods which the United States government "believes the free world should withhold from the Soviet bloc," and for the maintenance of some sort of controls (either quantitative controls or surveillance) concerning other goods.[49]

By the end of 1953, besides munition and atomic energy items, 260 items had been placed on the international embargo list; 90 items figured on the quantitative control list; 100 were placed on the surveillance list.[50]

Step by step, a vast network of export controls was thus established by the countries participating in the COCOM. However, though the aims were clearly defined, varying attitudes toward trade with the Soviet bloc were bound to manifest themselves in the West, arising from the immediate interests of the countries involved, changes in the international political situation, economic difficulties at home, and conditions prevailing in the world market.

[48] The lists established by the COCOM have to do only with exports to the European Soviet bloc, not to Communist China. The embargo applied against China is carried out under another control system, based on a United Nations resolution.

[49] If a country which is receiving military, economic, or financial aid from the United States *knowingly* permits an item on the Battle Act embargo list to be shipped to the Soviet bloc, the President must decide whether to cut off such aid or to order its continuance.

[50] The Battle Act embargo list included at the end of that period the combined lists of items accepted for embargo by the Consultative Group mentioned in note 9. As stated, this list concerns potential exports to the bloc from other countries than the United States. The United States' *own* export lists, unified in a "master export security list" comprise: the munitions list, compiled and administered by the Department of State; the atomic energy list, compiled and administered by the Atomic Energy Commission; and the export security list, compiled and administered by the Department of Commerce. See Hearing before the Subcommittee on Foreign Economic Policy of the Committee on Foreign Affairs of the House of Representatives, 83rd Congress, Second Session on *East-West Trade,* US Printing Office, Washington, February 16, 1954.

The Soviet bloc attempted to counter the embargo in various ways. It tried to deepen any "conflicts" among the Western powers, promoted "international trade conferences," participated lavishly in international trade fairs, and invited to Soviet Russia trade missions of "honest businessmen." It also resorted to systematic contraband on a large scale. These efforts to break the embargo often involved purchase by a neutral agent of certain goods with a false bill of lading, shipment of these goods to a free port, and then their transfer to a bloc destination. This kind of effort was, however, thwarted by a control system called "import certificate–delivery verification" (ICDV).[51] But contraband trade implies a continuous search for new methods. It is evident that numerous firms, especially in such border countries as West Germany, Austria, and Italy, have repeatedly cooperated in such deals.[52]

Whatever the real volume secured through contraband, one thing is certain: contraband is a very expensive item; in this situation, it might be added, the larger its scale the more expensive it is. Hence, decisive efforts were made by the Soviet Union in April 1952 to present, at an International Conference in Moscow of businessmen and economists from all over the world, vast prospects for the expansion of the East-West trade flows. At that conference the countries of the Eastern bloc indicated the possibility of their exporting yearly, over the period 1953–55, twice or three times as much as before (see Table 122). Actually, these exportable surpluses never materialized. East-West trade continued to flow, but very slowly, and trade with the United States stopped completely.[53]

[51] Under this system

"a government, before granting an export license, may require the exporting firm to present an import certificate executed by the importing firm and certified by *his* government. After the goods have been shipped, the exporting country may further require that the exporting firm produce a 'delivery verification' in which the importing country verifies that the goods were really delivered to the country for which they were originally licensed." [Cf. World-Wide Enforcement of Strategic Trade Controls, Mutual Defense Assistance Control Act of 1951 (the Battle Act), Third Report to Congress, First Half of 1953, Washington, 1953, p. 13.]

[52] See, for instance, a strongly dramatized but interesting report by David Douglas Duncan, "To Messrs. Dulles, Stassen, Conant: A Memo on Western Aid for Red Build Up," *Life,* Vol. 34, No. 4, January 26, 1953, pp. 23–33.

Actually, official reports to Congress also contain a series of examples of when the contraband did not succeed. (See, for instance, the Revision of Strategic Trade Controls, *op. cit.,* pp. 25 ff.) At one point, no fewer than 87 West German firms were blacklisted for "improper trade" with the orbit. (Cf. *New York Times* June 4, 1952.

[53] See Tables 128 and 129, Appendix 3 to this chapter.

TABLE 122. SOVIET BLOC IN EUROPE: EAST-WEST TRADE IN 1952, AND LEVEL PROPOSED FOR 1953–55 BY THE MOSCOW CONFERENCE

(in millions of dollars, and percentage increases)

Country	Estimated Trade, 1952	Eventual Yearly Trade, 1953–55 (Moscow Conference estimates)	Percentage Increase
Czechoslovakia	408	900–1,000	+120 or +145
Poland	524	700– 800	+ 34 or + 53
Hungary	164	300– 400	+ 83 or +144
Romania	87	200– 300	+130 or +245
Bulgaria	33	100	+203
Soviet Union	944	2,500–3,300	+165 or +249
Total	2,160	4,700–5,900	+118 or +173

Sources:

1952: See above, Table 116.

1953–55: Data grouped in *Economic Bulletin for Europe*, Vol. 4, No. 3 (November 1952), on the basis of the data released at the Moscow Conference of April 1952.

While the Soviet efforts were not successful in removing the main Western trade restrictions, the Western powers themselves had to continuously adjust their system of controls both in specific cases and in a more general framework. The Western nations "marched always together but not always in perfect step": [54] the necessity of adapting the controls to individual situations was expressed in the official United States acceptance of some limited exports of even primary *strategic goods* from certain countries receiving American aid. During 1952 and 1953, for instance, the first two years of the Battle Act, the total export of Battle Act *embargo* items knowingly permitted by countries receiving United States aid was in the neighborhood of $15 million, actually a small sum compared to the total exports to the bloc.[55] On the other hand, by 1954 a "streamlining" of the International control lists (deletion of some items, redefinition of others, etc.) reduced the embargo list to 170 items (instead of 260 in 1953), the quantitative control list to 20 (instead of 90), and the surveillance list

[54] Cf. the Revision of Strategic Trade Controls, Mutual Defense Assistance Control Act of 1951 (the Battle Act), Fifth Report to Congress, First Half of 1954, Washington, 1954, p. 1.

[55] East-West Trade Trends, Mutual Defense Assistance Control Act of 1951 (the Battle Act), Fourth Report to Congress, Second Half of 1953, Washington, 1954, p. 59.

to 60 items (instead of 100).[56] In 1956 the US Commerce Department canceled the previous requirements of export licenses for 700 items in 57 categories, mostly consumers' goods but including also such "embargo items" as machinery for construction, excavating, and mining.[57] Thus the system of controls is not and cannot be conceived as rigidly as some people probably thought it could in 1948 or in 1953. As it applies to a fluid situation, it must take into account changes occurring both in and outside the bloc.

Let us see now the combined results of all these factors on the extra-bloc trade during the period up to 1955 inclusive.

Structure and Pattern of Extra-bloc Trade

The commodities exported by the Soviet Union outside its orbit were principally grain, wood and timber, hides and skins, and nonferrous metals. The East European countries exported raw materials, agricultural products, timber, light manufactures, and other goods. Although some of the commodities exported were essential to the importing countries (Soviet grain for the United Kingdom),[58] the total value of this trade accounted for only a small percentage of the foreign trade of most of the importing countries.

In imports, the area made a decisive effort, up to 1953, to receive a relatively larger share of machinery and equipment than ever before, even if this equipment was of "secondary" strategic value. Thus, in 1938 the share of equipment and other producers' goods amounted to 53 per cent of the bloc imports from Western Europe; in 1948 it represented 57 per cent; in 1950, 65 per cent; in 1951, 61 per cent.[59]

In this connection, some interesting differences are apparent between the Soviet extra-bloc trade and the East European extra-bloc trade, with Great Britain, for instance. In the Soviet imports from the United Kingdom the *value* of such secondary strategic goods as

[56] The Revision of Strategic Trade Controls, Mutual Defense Assistance Control Act of 1951 (the Battle Act), Fifth Report to Congress, *op. cit.*, p. 2.

[57] See list in *New York Times,* April 27, 1956.

[58] The United Kingdom obtained from the Soviet Union in 1953, for instance, wood and timber (34 per cent of the Russian deliveries), nonferrous metals (24 per cent), hides and skins (16 per cent), grain (9 per cent), and other produce. The share of grain, very large in 1951 or 1952 (45–60 per cent of the deliveries), fell sharply in 1953. From the satellites, the United Kingdom obtained mainly meat (48 per cent of the deliveries), wood and timber (16 per cent), and grain (6 per cent).

[59] Computed from *Economic Bulletin for Europe,* Vol. 3, No. 2 (October 1951); underlying data in constant prices, exports of eleven Western countries, f.o.b.

nonferrous metals, machine tools, other machinery, and electrical generators fell in comparison to prewar, but in the structure of imports their relative share became much more substantial.[60] In 1951, out of the total imports from the United Kingdom (excluding re-exports), the relative share of electrical generators represented 21.6 per cent, that of machine tools 27.0 per cent, that of other machinery 21.6 per cent. In 1953 the largest relative share in the Soviet imports from the United Kingdom (excluding re-exports) was represented by electrical goods, 33.3 per cent (i.e., £1.1 million), and electrical generators, machine tools, and other machinery accounted for 18 per cent (£0.6 million). The East Europeans also obtained machinery of secondary strategic importance, some of which probably figured only on the quantitative control lists. The *relative* share of electrical apparatus, electrical machinery, other machinery, and vehicles, though increasing as compared to prewar, remained, however, for all these countries at a total not exceeding £4.5 million. All these sums were quite *small.* They do not indicate a major deal for the bloc. What they do suggest, however, if taken in conjunction with all the data concerning the extra-bloc trade of the area, is that the "quantitative restrictions" may have hit the East European countries harder than they did the Soviet Union. This distinction is meaningful so long as these countries remain economically "autonomous" units, i.e., so long as each is supporting its own burden of trade deficits, investment problems, and the like.

Since 1954–55, both the Soviet Union and the East European countries have made decisive efforts to expand their trade with the "underdeveloped areas": Far East, Middle East, Africa, and Latin America. Soviet and East European machinery and equipment on credit or on a barter basis have been sent in increasing amounts to various countries (such as India, Ceylon, Burma, Afghanistan, and Egypt). Soviet and East European technical assistance has been offered on a broad basis to some countries.[61] There is a growing interest in the whole area (including Yugoslavia) in these relations. The bloc's capacity for absorbing raw materials such as rubber, cotton, wool, and metals, is susceptible to growth; at the same time its capacity for de-

[60] Cf. *East-West Trade,* British Information Service, Reference Division, New York, August 1954.

[61] United States Congress, Subcommittee on Technical Assistance Programs, *Soviet Technical Assistance in Non-Communist Asia.* Printed for the Committee on Foreign Relations, 84th Congress, 1st Session, US Government Printing Office. Washington, 1955.

livering equipment as well as manufactured goods in demand in the underdeveloped areas is also growing.

The pattern of extra-bloc trade presents during the period under review some noteworthy characteristics. The common feature of both Soviet and East European extra-bloc trade is the increased share of Europe up to 1953, when this share represented over 80 per cent of the total, and the fall in this share after 1953. In 1955 this share represented 70 per cent of the total while the relative shares of the Far East, and especially of Latin America, gained ground lost previously, or took new positions.

The difference between the Soviet and the East European pattern of extra-orbit trade is "localized" in Europe. There, two customers, the United Kingdom and Finland, took in 1953 over 53 per cent of the total extra-bloc exports of the Soviet Union and provided a corresponding amount of her extra-bloc imports. The same countries absorbed a significant share of East Europe's exports, namely, 33 per cent, but provided only 10 per cent of her imports. As a rule the East European countries maintained a wider distribution than Soviet Russia over the main trading areas of the world.[62]

While the increases forecast by the Moscow 1952 Conference have failed to materialize, some gains have been registered both in the total extra-bloc trade and in the trade with Western Europe. Considering the case of each country separately these increases seem spasmodic, with noticeable fluctuations from year to year. There is no guarantee whatsoever that these flows will continue to grow. Given the framework in which this trade is bound to operate, determined as its structure is by both planned requirements and embargo limitations ("adjusted" to the degree of political tension at any given moment), the prospect seems to be for *spasmodic* increases and decreases in East-West trade rather than for a systematic development of these trade flows. In any event, in the context of the present intra-orbit relations and under conditions of the bloc's increasing capacity for expanding trade with underdeveloped areas, the East-West trade has lost and is losing a certain amount of its previous importance.

Role and Scope of the "Second World Market"

The prospects for a further development of the intra-bloc trade can be considered good. The Western trade controls have had considerable effect but, in the last analysis, this is more on the periphery

[62] See Tables 131 and 132 in Appendix 3 to this chapter, p. 406.

than on the center of power in the bloc.[63] The structure of Soviet exports has generally enabled Russia to fare better than most other countries of the bloc and to obtain from extra-bloc sources, even through normal trade, some limited amounts of strategic goods. In other words, the countries of the bloc, offering different types of commodities, some of which are in more pressing demand than others, have succeeded in varying degrees in cutting through the embargo lines. The embargo, with its emphasis on security and long-range perspectives, was and still is perhaps less responsible for the low levels of East-West trade than is the lack of given exportable surpluses in the bloc itself. What the embargo policy has actually prevented is the further development of the Soviet industrial machine *on the basis of Western deliveries of heavy equipment or vehicles on long-term credit.*

By its very scope and character the embargo has probably facilitated indirectly the strengthening of Russia's central position in regard to the East European countries, in view of their increased dependence on Soviet deliveries of industrial raw materials and capital equipment not obtainable from other sources.

An increase in certain key imports (machinery, other producers' goods, or raw materials) would ease the situation. This is especially true of some smaller countries of the Soviet bloc now at the mercy of stronger partners placed in a monopoly position by the embargo itself; but it is highly improbable that additional imports would essentially modify the pattern and the structure of trade that evolved in the area mostly during the period of the first development plan.

Even though it has grown up within the period considered, the "second world market" is far more limited than its geographical size would suggest. In 1948 the intra-bloc trade of the Soviet bloc amounted to some 2.3 billion dollars, and in 1953 to 12.9 billion.[64] In these years the total world trade, excluding that of the Soviet bloc countries, represented a total of 111.2 billion and 149.4 billion dollars.[65] In other words, the "second world market" represented but 2.0 per cent and 8.6 per cent, respectively, of the trade transactions outside that restricted market.

[63] See, N. Spulber, "Effects of the Embargo on Soviet Trade," *Harvard Business Review,* XXX, 6 (November–December 1952); and, "Problems of East-West Trade and Economic Trends in the European Satellites of Soviet Russia," *Economia Internazionale,* Vol. VIII, No. 3, August 1955.

[64] For 1948, see above, Table 116, p. 412. The 1953 estimates here are from: *ESE in 1954, op. cit.,* p. 113; and *ESE in 1955, op. cit.,* p. 179.

[65] Cf. *UNSY 1955, op. cit.,* pp. 386–387.

In principle, the increase in interchanges between the planned economies was supposed to be the way out of the "chaos of the world market" and the means of assuring *a stable base for each plan.* As we have already indicated, during the period ending with the break with Yugoslavia, the countries in a strong bargaining position in this region were able to throw out of gear the plans of the weaker countries. After 1949 only a degree of centralization of orders and a limited number of consolidated lists could be effected by CEMA since each of the national long-term plans had been drawn and put into execution without taking into consideration the development of the other countries. In an attempt to avoid such a situation in the period that opened in 1956, each national plan took all the others into consideration. Will doing so transform the market within the group into one which will offset for each economy fluctuations and deficiencies in its production? We have strong doubts that it will. Even with the attempt to adjust output to trade in this market during the second quinquennium, imbalances are bound to arise both in the output of each economy and in its trade. Only the countries with a stronger bargaining position will be able to correct these imbalances by forcing certain of their goods into the intra-bloc market and by obtaining needed goods from it. In this sense this market would play a *compensatory role* primarily for the central buyer and seller, i.e., the Soviet Union. In fact, the existence of such a market would certainly alleviate for the Soviet Union certain of the consequences of her economic isolation. With three markets and sources of supply open to her (the large Soviet market itself, a progressively integrated East European market, and certain Asiatic outlets, three markets which can function as a unit in meeting the requirements of the Soviet plan), the Soviet Union can effectively "gain independence of outside economic fluctuations and crises." This cannot hold true for each country in this vast complex. The plan of each small country may aim at modeling the future so as to attain its own over-all industrial development, but the concrete adjustments forced by Soviet needs will inevitably take precedence over these plans and determine, in the long run, the evolution of each national economy.

APPENDIX 1

A "TYPICAL" SOVIET-EAST EUROPEAN TRADE AND PAYMENTS AGREEMENT

(Soviet-Romanian Trade and Payments Agreement, February 20, 1947, Official Text [66])

In order to develop trade relations between the two countries, the Government of the U.S.S.R. and the Romanian Government are agreed upon the following:

ARTICLE 1. The Government of the U.S.S.R. shall assure the delivery to Romania, from the signing of the present Agreement until December 31, 1947, of goods provided for in list I, attached to the present Agreement.

The Romanian Government shall assure the delivery to the U.S.S.R., from the signing of the present Agreement until December 31, 1947, of the goods enumerated in list II, attached to the present Agreement.

Lists I and II may be modified and completed by common agreement of the two parties.

ARTICLE 2. The two Governments bind themselves to take all the measures necessary for the development of the exchange of commodities in accordance with the present Agreement.

Competent authorities of the two countries will deliver, in accordance with the laws in force, authorizations to import and export goods in accordance with the present agreement.

The Romanian Government will take all adequate measures required by the level of prices in Romania in order to ensure at the realization of the commercial transactions (in pursuance of the present agreement and in accordance with the prices provided for under Article 3 of the present Agreement) normal conditions for the exchange of commodities between the two countries.

ARTICLE 3. The deliveries of goods provided for under Article 1 of the present Agreement shall be carried out on the basis of contracts between the

[66] *Bulletin d'information et de documentation,* National Bank of Romania, XIX, 1–3 (January–March 1947), pp. 17–18.

respective Soviet organizations for foreign trade, on the one side, and Romanian physical and juridical persons, on the other side.

The prices of commodities shall be fixed in the contracts mentioned in United States dollars on the basis of current prices in the world markets.

ARTICLE 4. Contracts may be concluded between the Soviet organizations for foreign trade, on the one side, and Romanian physical and juridical persons, on the other, within the limits of the laws in force in the two countries concerning the imports and exports of commodities, also for the delivery of commodities not included in the lists indicated under Article 1, as, for example, compensation operations.

ARTICLE 5. Payments for the commodities which will be delivered in accordance with the agreements provided in Article 3 of the present Agreement, as well as payments for accruing charges concerning the exchange of commodities, shall be effected in the U.S.S.R. by the State Bank of the U.S.S.R. and in Romania by the National Bank of Romania.

To this purpose, the above-mentioned Banks shall reciprocally open special, non-interest-bearing accounts in United States dollars and shall immediately notify one another of all entries in these accounts.

Upon receiving such notice, the Bank concerned will effect the payment to the institution or persons concerned, on presentation of the corresponding documents, whether or not funds are available in the account.

ARTICLE 6. In accordance with the separate convention signed today relating to the granting by the Government of the U.S.S.R. to the Romanian Government of a loan in goods, the net balance at the end of each quarter in the accounts mentioned in Article 5 in favor of the State Bank of the U.S.S.R. shall be transferred to the special loan account provided for under Article 5 of the loan Agreement.

These transfers shall be effected each quarter to the extent of 40 per cent, at most, of the total amount of payments made by the Romanian party during the quarter for the Soviet goods delivered pursuant to the present Agreement and in the limits of the sum total of the credit of 10 million United States dollars.

ARTICLE 7. The amounts of all payments effected by each State, with the exception of the payments transferred in accordance with Article 6 of the present Agreement to the special loan account, must be equal and this equality must be maintained in the course of each quarter during the application of the present Agreement.

ARTICLE 8. The State Bank of the U.S.S.R. and the National Bank of Romania shall determine together the terms of discount between them in accordance with the present Agreement.

ARTICLE 9. The Government of the U.S.S.R. and the Romanian Government shall designate representatives who shall meet every three months alternately in Moscow and in Bucharest to examine the carrying out of the reciprocal delivery of commodities pursuant to the present Agreement, and the situation of payments, and to formulate, if necessary, needed recommendations.

When the equilibrium between payments is not maintained during any quarter of the period of application of the present Agreement, taking into consideration payments due for deliveries effected in accordance with lists I and II of the present Agreement, the Governments of the two countries will take measures to restore the equilibrium as quickly as possible.

ARTICLE 10. Apart from contracts provided for under Articles 3 and 4 of the present Agreement, the Soviet organizations of foreign trade and the Romanian physical and juridical persons, with the authorization in each case of authoritative organs of the two Governments, may conclude contracts for the delivery of goods not included in the lists indicated under Article 1, the payment for these goods being made in the currency established by the contracts.

In such cases payment shall be made in conformance to the conditions provided in such contracts, with the exception of the terms of discount established under Article 5 of the present Agreement.

ARTICLE 11. Upon the termination of the present Agreement, the State Bank of the U.S.S.R. and the National Bank of Romania shall continue to receive payments to the accounts indicated under Article 5 and to effect payments on these accounts in accordance with the provisions of the present Agreement for all contracts which will have been concluded within the period of application of the present Agreement.

If at the termination of the payments provided for under the present Agreement there appears in the accounts indicated under Article 5 a debit balance for one of the parties, this party is obliged to make it good after an agreement between the parties, either by deliveries of additional goods at prices in conformance with the provisions of Article 3 of the present Agreement and within a period of three months from the date when the present Agreement has ceased to be valid, or by the transfer of free currency, convertible at the Bank indicated by the creditor State, or in gold.

ARTICLE 12. The present Agreement shall enter into force on the day of its signing and shall be valid until December 31, 1947.

Drawn in Moscow on February 29, 1947, in two original copies, each in Russian and Romanian, both texts being authentic.

APPENDIX 2

BALANCES OF TRADE AND PAYMENTS

This appendix contains a series of figures on Balances of Trade of each East European country with the Soviet Union and the area, as well as some data on the Yugoslav Balance of Payments with the Soviet Union. The tables refer to the first postwar period 1945–48 or 1949, and are based on the national statistics of the countries considered.

TABLE 123. BALANCES OF TRADE WITH THE BLOC[a]: 1945–48

Czechoslovakia
(in million koruna)

Country	1945	1946	1947	1948	1945–48
Soviet Union	−186.4	+360.9	−331.7	+195.1	+37.9
Poland	+3.1	+113.6	−211.1	+618.9	+524.5
Hungary	−173.9	−206.4	+230.5	+74.3	−75.5
Romania	−6.4	−2.8	+148.1	−281.7	−142.8
Bulgaria	−5.7	−81.7	−260.5	+182.4	−165.5
Yugoslavia	−6.1	−282.2	+416.0	+214.9	+342.6
Total	−375.4	−98.6	−7.7	+1,003.9	+522.2

Poland
(in million dollars)

Country	1945	1946	1947	1948	1945–48
Soviet Union	+4.6	−42.6	−9.0	−7.2	−54.2
Czechoslovakia	[b]	+1.8	+8.6	−9.9	+0.5
Hungary	+0.2	+0.7	−0.2	+0.2	+0.9
Romania	[b]	+0.4	+0.3	−0.3	+0.4
Bulgaria	[b]	+0.4	−4.2	+1.3	−2.5
Yugoslavia	[b]	[b]	+2.2	−4.5	−2.3
Total	+4.8	−39.3	−2.3	−20.4	−57.2

Hungary
(in million forints)

Country	1946	1947	1948	1946–48
Soviet Union	+29.7	−9.1	+42.8	+63.4
Czechoslovakia	−21.8	−0.1	−5.5	−27.4
Poland	−9.8	−14.2	−8.7	−32.7
Romania	−19.7	−31.4	−23.0	−74.1
Bulgaria	+1.5	+0.6	−0.5	+1.6
Yugoslavia	−1.9	−49.3	−130.5	−181.7
Total	−22.0	−103.5	−125.4	−250.9

Bulgaria
(in million leva)

Country	1945	1946	1947	1948 (Jan.–May only)	1945–48 (1948, Jan.–May only)
Soviet Union	+7,158.9	−4,476.2	−250.0	−4,959.6	−2,526.9
Czechoslovakia	[b]	+512.2	+1,247.5	−769.5	+990.2
Poland	[b]	+184.0	+1,045.1	−254.9	+974.2
Hungary	−14.4	+14.0	−12.5	+29.6	+16.7
Romania	−105.8	+290.2	−169.0	−218.0	−202.6
Yugoslavia	−27.2	−1.7	+390.7	+910.1	+1,271.9
Total	+7,011.5	−3,477.5	+2,251.8	−5,262.3	+523.5

[a] Import surplus: −, Export surplus: +. Trade proper only.
[b] Nil.

Sources:
C: Zahraniční Obchod (Foreign Trade), Vol. 177 (1946), and 179 (1947); *Měsíční Přehled Zahraničního Obchodu* (Monthly Survey of Foreign Trade), December 1948; also *SZ*, XII, 4 (1949).
P: *Statistical Yearbook 1947* and *1948*; also "Les Relations extérieures de la Pologne" (Foreign Relations of Poland), *EC*, IV, 5.
H: *GT*, 1946 (June 1947); 1947–48 (January 1949).
B: *MI*, 1945–47 (XXXV, 1 [January 1948]); I–V, January–May, 1948 (XXXV, 6 [June 1948]).

TABLE 124. YUGOSLAVIA–USSR: CURRENT AND CAPITAL TRANSACTIONS, 1945–49

(in thousand dollars)

Current Transactions

	Credit	Debit	Net Credit
1. Merchandise	114,804	192,440	−77,636
2. Non-monetary gold movement	[a]	[a]	[a]
3. Foreign travel	[a]	7,500	−7,500
4. Transportation	[a]	[a]	[a]
5. Insurance	[a]	[a]	[a]
6. Investment income	[a]	600	−600
7. Government, not included elsewhere	[a]	[a]	[a]
8. Miscellaneous	2,150	1,900	250
9. Donations	[a]	[a]	[a]
10. Total current transactions	116,954	202,440	−85,486

Movement of Capital

	Assets	Liabilities	Net Assets
11. Official long-term capital	[a]	78,846	−78,846
Official loans	[a]	800	−800
Bank loans	[a]	[a]	[a]
Portfolio securities	[a]	[a]	[a]
Amortization	[a]	[a]	[a]
Other contractual repayment	[a]	6,046	−6,046
Other	[a]	72,000	−72,000
12. Short-term capital	116,954	123,594	−6,640
Payments and clearing agreements	114,804	105,426	9,378
Other liabilities	[a]	8,768	−8,768
Other	2,150	9,400	−7,250
13. Total movement of capital	116,954	202,440	−85,486

[a] Nil.

Source: Constructed from data in Tito, *For Independence and Equality*, *op. cit.*, pp. 73 ff.

TABLE 125. YUGOSLAVIA–USSR: MERCHANDISE TRANSACTIONS

(in thousand dollars, 1945–49)

	Credit	Debit
Ordinary trade agreement	114,804	105,426
Special trade agreement	[a]	8,168
Investment agreement	[a]	800
Transport equipment from (Soviet) war booty	[a]	6,046
Military equipment	[a]	72,000
Total	114,804	192,440

[a] Nil.

Source: Same as for Table 124.

Table 126. USSR: Structure of Soviet Credits to Yugoslavia, 1945–49

(in thousand dollars)

	Planned Credits	Actual Deliveries in Credits	Per Cent from Total Delivered
Short-Term Transactions			
Special commercial credit	9,000	8,168	45.0
Training of Yugoslav cadets in the Soviet Union	[a]	7,500	41.3
Liquidation of Soviet-Yugoslav joint companies	[a]	600	3.3
Other non-commercial payments	[a]	1,900	10.4
Total	9,000	18,168	100.0
Yugoslav repayments by current exports or other	[a]	11,528	100.0
Total Soviet short-term credits outstanding	[a]	6,640	7.7
Long-Term Transactions			
Transport equipment from war booty	10,000	6,046	7.0
Military loan	72,000	72,000	85.2
Investment loan	135,000	800	[b]
Total	217,000	78,846	92.2
Total Soviet credits outstanding		85,486	100.0

[a] Nil.

[b] Negligible.

Source: Same as for Table 124.

APPENDIX 3

EXTRA-BLOC TRADE OF EASTERN EUROPE AND OF THE SOVIET UNION

This appendix presents the data collected from the official trade statistics of the extra-bloc countries by the International Economic Analysis Division, Bureau of Foreign Commerce, US Dept. of Commerce. The data are tabulated in unclassified statistical tables entitled "Value Series: Free World Imports and Free World Exports," which are released irregularly. Tables 128–131 uniformly give data for the years 1948, 1950, 1953, and 1955.

TABLE 127. EXTRA-BLOC TRADE OF EASTERN EUROPE AND THE SOVIET UNION, 1947–55

(Unadjusted data. Millions of current US dollars)

	1947	1948	1949	1950	1951	1952	1953	1954	1955 [a]
Exports of:									
1. US	335.3	122.7	61.7	26.4	2.7	0.5	0.6	5.9	7.2
2. OEEC [b]	562.1	609.4	759.5	591.1	657.1	624.7	560.5	679.1	800.7
3. Total (1 + 2)	897.4	732.1	821.2	617.5	659.8	625.2	561.1	685.0	807.9
4. Total extra-bloc	1,235.7	1,271.1	1,305.5	966.2	1,137.6	1,038.5	934.7	1,212.7	1,426.5
Imports of:									
1. US	108.2	113.0	67.5	80.5	63.8	32.3	29.9	42.2	55.5
2. OEEC [b]	630.3	940.1	915.8	700.3	827.8	756.0	663.2	754.1	1,014.2
3. Total (1 + 2)	738.5	1,053.1	983.3	780.8	891.6	788.3	693.1	796.3	1,069.7
4. Total extra-bloc	908.1	1,347.6	1,281.8	1,039.3	1,243.1	1,120.2	1,005.2	1,183.7	1,571.2

[a] 1955 preliminary and incomplete.

[b] Austria, Belgium-Luxembourg, Denmark, France, West Germany, Greece, Iceland, Ireland, Italy, Netherlands, Norway, Portugal, Sweden, Switzerland, Trieste, Turkey, United Kingdom.

Sources: "Value Series: Free World Imports and Free World Exports," prepared by the International Economic Analysis Division, Bureau of Foreign Commerce, US Dept. of Commerce, Washington, D. C. For 1947–52, May 1953; for 1953, May 1954; for 1954, January 1955; for 1955, June 1956

TABLE 128. UNITED STATES AND OEEC [a] EXPORTS TO EASTERN EUROPE AND THE SOVIET UNION

	United States Exports				OEEC Exports			
Countries	1948	1950	1953	1955 [b]	1948	1950	1953	1955 [b]
Czecho-slovakia	21.6	10.5	[c]	2.1	235.9	176.4	79.0	123.9
Poland	55.5	8.9	0.6	3.3	172.4	163.2	142.9	183.7
Hungary	8.0	3.5	[b]	0.8	50.2	92.4	65.6	148.5
Romania	7.5	2.0	[b]	0.2	17.7	24.9	57.6	53.3
Bulgaria	2.1	0.8	[b]	0.1	11.7	13.9	24.6	21.5
Soviet Union	28.0	0.7	[b]	0.2	121.5	120.3	190.8	269.8
Total	122.7	26.4	0.6	6.7	609.4	591.1	560.5	800.7

[a] Austria, Belgium-Luxembourg, Denmark, France, West Germany, Greece, Iceland, Ireland, Italy, Netherlands, Norway, Portugal, Sweden, Switzerland, Trieste, Turkey, United Kingdom.

[b] Preliminary and incomplete.

[c] Negligible.

Source: As in Table 127.

TABLE 129. UNITED STATES AND OEEC [a] IMPORTS FROM EASTERN EUROPE AND THE SOVIET UNION

	United States Imports				OEEC Imports			
Countries	1948	1950	1953	1955 [b]	1948	1950	1953	1955 [b]
Czecho-slovakia	22.1	26.6	2.3	3.8	280.2	212.8	125.6	173.8
Poland	1.2	11.1	14.3	26.6	287.1	231.9	199.0	224.6
Hungary	1.6	1.9	1.7	2.0	74.1	81.4	41.9	94.7
Romania	0.5	0.3	0.4	0.3	31.6	11.4	28.5	66.1
Bulgaria	0.8	2.3	0.4	0.4	13.6	7.9	24.5	19.7
Soviet Union	86.8	38.3	10.8	16.9	253.5	154.9	243.7	435.3
Total	113.0	80.5	29.9	50.0	940.1	700.3	663.2	1,014.2

[a] Austria, Belgium-Luxembourg, Denmark, France, West Germany, Greece, Iceland, Ireland, Italy, Netherlands, Norway, Portugal, Sweden, Switzerland, Trieste, Turkey, United Kingdom.

[b] Preliminary and incomplete.

Source: As in Table 127.

TABLE 130. TOTAL EXTRA-BLOC TRADE OF EACH EAST EUROPEAN COUNTRY AND OF THE SOVIET UNION

(Unadjusted data. Millions of current U.S. dollars)

Country	1948	1950	1953	1955 [a]
1. Exports to extra-bloc unadjusted (Imports of extra-bloc) [b]				
Czechoslovakia	404.8	346.3	204.7	321.4
Poland	338.7	292.7	269.0	342.7
Hungary	84.9	103.1	60.7	140.8
Romania	42.6	32.3	63.4	117.9
Bulgaria	18.6	12.9	29.7	24.1
Soviet Union	458.0	252.0	377.7	624.3
Total	1,347.6	1,039.3	1,005.2	1,571.2
2. Imports unadjusted [b] (Extra-bloc exports to the bloc)				
Czechoslovakia	342.8	250.0	133.4	249.4
Poland	309.8	245.2	211.9	319.7
Hungary	67.1	117.5	82.0	187.3
Romania	47.8	44.2	63.0	77.6
Bulgaria	15.6	16.2	28.7	25.4
Soviet Union	488.0	293.1	415.7	567.1
Total	1,271.1	966.2	934.7	1,426.5
3. Total (1 + 2) [b]				
Czechoslovakia	747.7	596.4	338.1	570.8
Poland	648.6	537.9	480.9	662.4
Hungary	152.1	220.7	142.7	328.1
Romania	90.5	76.5	126.5	195.5
Bulgaria	34.3	29.2	57.4	49.5
Soviet Union	946.0	545.1	793.4	1,191.4
Total	2,619.2	2,005.8	1,939.0	2,997.7

[a] Preliminary and incomplete data.
[b] Extra-bloc includes Yugoslavia in all years except 1948.
Source: As in Table 127.

TABLE 131. PATTERN OF IMPORTS OF THE SOVIET BLOC IN EUROPE FROM EXTRA-BLOC AREAS [a]

	Soviet Union				Eastern Europe [b]			
	Per cent of total imports from extra-bloc				Per cent of total imports from extra-bloc			
	1948	1950	1953	1955	1948	1950	1953	1955
United States	5.3	0.3	c	c	10.6	3.3	0.2	0.8
Canada	c	c	c	0.5	2.1	0.5	0.1	0.6
Europe	58.8	63.1	80.9	74.8	68.4	76.2	80.3	67.7
Of which *United Kingdom*	*5.4*	*13.6*	*29.6*	*15.7*	*10.2*	*7.3*	*6.0*	*5.8*
Finland	*27.5*	*22.1*	*23.7*	*24.2*	*1.4*	*2.9*	*4.2*	*4.1*
Near East and Africa	12.0	11.4	9.1	12.1	4.1	3.8	5.8	9.5
Far East	15.1	15.9	2.0	1.7	3.9	3.0	4.5	6.8
Oceania	6.5	8.9	8.0	1.1	2.0	5.4	5.6	5.1
Latin America	2.3	0.4	c	9.8	8.9	7.8	3.5	9.5
Total	100.0	100.0	100.0	100.0	100.0	100.0	100.0	100.0

[a] Based on derivative data, i.e., extra-bloc exports to bloc f.o.b. Rounded percentages by main trading areas.

[b] Includes East Germany for 1950 and 1953. Data for 1955 preliminary and incomplete.

[c] Negligible.

Source: Data computed from sources in Table 127.

TABLE 132. PATTERN OF EXPORTS OF THE SOVIET BLOC IN EUROPE TO EXTRA-BLOC AREAS [a]

	Soviet Union				Eastern Europe [b]			
	Per cent of total exports to extra-bloc				Per cent of total exports to extra-bloc			
	1948	1950	1953	1955	1948	1950	1953	1955
United States	17.7	15.2	2.9	3.5	2.6	4.5	3.2	3.5
Canada	c	c	0.2	0.4	0.5	0.6	0.5	0.4
Europe	68.8	70.9	88.3	72.7	84.3	78.2	81.8	72.7
Of which *United Kingdom*	*22.2*	*38.0*	*29.6*	*28.2*	*9.8*	*8.6*	*12.0*	*11.8*
Finland	*10.4*	*9.4*	*23.7*	*13.9*	*4.0*	*4.9*	*11.5*	*9.9*
Near East and Africa	10.1	11.0	7.3	8.6	6.0	6.9	7.8	8.6
Far East	3.2	2.4	0.8	5.1	1.7	2.9	2.9	5.1
Oceania	c	0.5	0.5	0.8	1.4	1.7	0.8	0.8
Latin America	0.2	c	c	8.9	3.5	5.2	3.0	8.9
Total	100.0	100.0	100.0	100.0	100.0	100.0	100.0	100.0

[a] Based on derivative data, i.e., extra-bloc imports from the bloc, c.i.f. Rounded percentages, by main trading areas.

[b] Includes East Germany and Albania in 1950 and 1953. Data for 1955 preliminary and incomplete.

[c] Negligible.

Source: Data computed from sources in Table 127.

SECTION IV

CONCLUDING REMARKS

CHAPTER

12

INVESTMENT AND NATIONAL INCOME

Introductory Note

Throughout this study we have focused on three main questions: (1) the process of nationalization of the East European economies, (2) the establishment of centralized planning and the performance of these economies within that framework, and (3) the problem of *autonomous* development versus *integration,* the relations between these countries and the Soviet Union and their own interrelations. This chapter briefly re-examines these subjects in terms of their dynamic interconnection, the purpose here being not to review previous summaries but to recombine the basic elements in the book so as to gain an over-all view of the structural changes in the economy of Eastern Europe.

These dynamic interconnections are best understood if related to changes in the size and composition of the national income. The sequence, pace, and ultimate objectives of nationalization can be fully grasped only if related to national income. The processes of both planning and development are dependent on and conditioned by national income. The present and prospective relationships in the bloc are ultimately determined by differences in national income, hence, by differences in the capacities for saving and capital formation, and in long-run rates of growth.

Two types of official computations on national output are available for the East European countries, as has already been noted: those of "total gross product" and those of "net material product" in current or constant prices. Basically, Marxian methodology [1] postulates that national income includes only income created in production of material goods and of "productive services," valued at market prices, i.e., prices including the "turnover tax" which is essentially a sales tax. Material production has the following branches: agriculture; industry; construction; transport and communications; trade and catering; and miscellaneous.[2] Services not directly related to production and distribution (nearly all personal and government services) are not included in national income. National income is computed from the side of production. The gross yearly product is computed as the sum of the gross output (including duplications) in all the above-mentioned sectors of "material production." The total is readily obtained by multiplying quantities produced times market prices, for each enterprise and for each sector. This total, in turn, is broken down in (1) cost of production (c)—i.e., cost of materials and fuels as well as depreciation allowances; (2) wage bill and contributions to social security (v); and (3) "surplus value" (m) absorbed by the state in the form of the turnover tax and by the enterprises as "profit."

From the total $c + v + m$, net material product is obtained, in its turn, by the subtraction of c and, hence, by elimination of duplications, is given as equal to $v + m$.

National income is divided (distributed) into a consumption fund (C) and an accumulation fund (A). The first comprises the outlay on consumer goods and material services of the whole population (personal consumption) as well as the material consumption of institutions, e.g., hospitals, state administration, armed forces, etc. (social consumption). Evidently, C is larger than v since a new redistribution of means occurs in the broader framework determined both by all the transactions on goods and services and by the budget. Accumulation—which is correspondingly smaller than m—is equal to gross fixed investment (including changes in stocks of goods in progress and expenditure on capital replacements but not on repairs).

The data released are total figures, for certain years in current prices, for other years at constant, prewar, or postwar prices, various percent-

[1] For a detailed analysis in English of Soviet methodology (the "model" of the East European computations), see P. Studenski, "Methods of Estimating National Income in Soviet Russia," in *Studies in Income and Wealth,* Vol. 8, National Bureau of Economic Research, New York, 1946.

[2] There are slight variations from one country to the next in respect to these branches, e.g., some show handicraft production separately, others include it in industry, some do not account at all for banking services while others do, etc.

ages relating the share of accumulation in income, and a series of index numbers concerning income growth in certain years. A whole set of indispensable figures is not released: thus the nexus between current and constant prices is not given, so that the series cannot be connected, no data in any form are released on personal consumption, etc. Moreover, the information available is unclear as to what it covers and what is being compared from year to year.[3] Known deficiencies in collecting and processing the basic data, incorrect evaluation of new commodities entering into the stream of production, and other shortcomings typical of both Soviet [4] and East European present-day statistics, place extremely serious limitations on the data available. Against this background the following computations must and should be appraised. Undoubtedly, full exploration of all interrelationships developing in these economies would require recomputation of national income as the end product of a series of interrelated sector and global accounts of incomes; that is, an effort similar to the one attempted by Western economists for Soviet Russia's income.[5] However, as they stand, the data on net material product, though precluding comparison with Western national accounts and requiring very serious reservations, do allow comparisons *among the countries of the area.* They also underline the broad structural shifts in these economies and furnish some basis for checking other figures appearing in this book obtained from different sets of data.

Dynamics of Nationalization and National Income

The rationale of the nationalization processes so far as both sequence and ultimate objectives are concerned can be more readily grasped with the help of Chart 17. The magnitudes represented on the chart are roughly indicative of the "average" condition in the East European countries. Each rectangle on the chart (I, II, III, IV) represents the national income (as in East European computations, the

[3] A critical analysis of both the content and the general shortcomings of this method can be found in E. F. Jackson, *Social Accounting in Eastern Europe,* in Income and Wealth, Series IV, International Association for Research in Income and Wealth, London, 1955, pp. 242–259.

[4] See, for instance, A. Bergson, Introduction to *Soviet National Income and Product in 1937, op. cit.,* p. 5.

[5] Cf. A. Bergson, op. cit., and subsequent studies: Abram Bergson and Hans Heymann, Jr., *Soviet National Income and Product, 1940–1948,* and Oleg Hoeffding, *Soviet National Income and Product in 1928,* both published by Columbia University Press, New York, 1954.

net material product (*Y*)). A yearly rate of increase of 10 per cent of *Y* is assumed throughout the chart. Each rectangle is divided by vertical lines into segments; each represents the sector of the economy

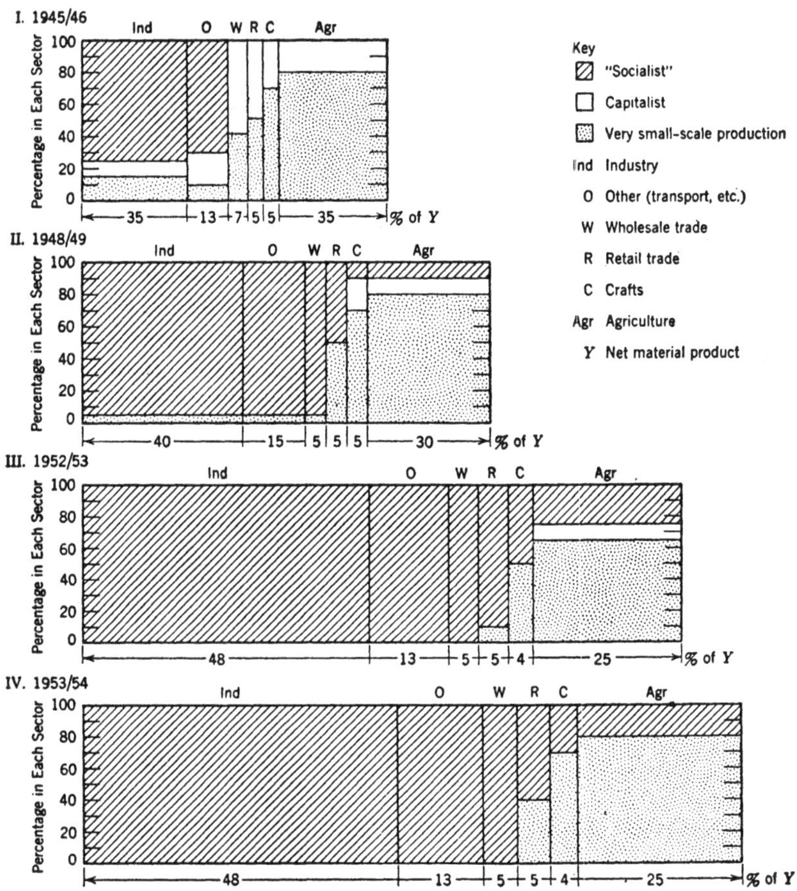

CHART 17. DYNAMICS OF NATIONALIZATION AND NATIONAL INCOME IN EASTERN EUROPE AND THE SYSTEMS OF PRODUCTION; SCHEMATIC DEVELOPMENT, 1945–54

indicated. The width of each of these segments indicates the magnitude of *Y* originating in the respective sector. Each segment in turn is divided into layers indicating the importance in the sector of nationalized and cooperative enterprises, together termed the "socialist sector," large-scale or "capitalist" private enterprises, and very small-scale enterprises, respectively. The very small-scale enterprises are those in which economic activity is centered around the owner and his family, and where hired labor is resorted to in a limited way, including "industries of local interest" (like tiny flour mills, carding workshops, plants to make vegetable oils, soap, shoe polish), handicraft production, small trade, and small and "medium" peasant farms (those up to 8 or 10 hectares in size). The sectors, from left to right, are arranged in the order of increasing importance of very small-scale production. The increase of net material product from one period to the next is indicated by an increase in the length of the rectangle. The area of a segment in any of the four rectangles is thus comparable with that in any other.

Let us now consider in turn rectangles I, II, and III, illustrating schematically the relations between the process of nationalization, the growth of net material product, and the system of production and ownership in a "typical" East European economy in the decisive years 1945–46, 1948–49, and 1952–53.

I. The first rectangle presents .economic relations after the first nationalization wave and the land reforms.

By sectors, 35 per cent of net material product originates in industry, 35 per cent in agriculture, and 30 per cent in all the other spheres of activity. By systems of production, a little over 35 per cent originates in state enterprises (75 per cent of industry and 70 per cent of "other" being nationalized); slightly more than 21 per cent originates in the "capitalist system," still present in every sector; and 43.5 per cent originates in very small-scale private enterprises, mostly in agriculture, where it is the dominant form. The major part of "capitalist" production had previously been in industry, in which it predominated, but by 1945–46 most "capitalist" industrial enterprises had been nationalized.

II. The second rectangle presents the situation in 1948–49. Both the relative importance of the three basic systems of production and ownership and the contribution of each sector to net material product have been drastically changed. As contrasted with 1945–46, the state and cooperative system, now together termed the "socialist sector," have absorbed not only enterprises that were previously "capitalist" but also some very small-scale enterprises. Many of these undertakings have been taken over by the local bodies of the state machine or by the newly organized cooperatives. The "capitalist system," i.e., "private enterprises resorting to hired labor," has been liquidated in all sectors but crafts and agriculture.[6] Finally, the private, very small-scale sectors, sharply reduced in various spheres of activity, remain predominant in agriculture and crafts, and of substantial importance in retail trade.

During the development of nationalization in the various sectors, substantial shifts have occurred in the share of income from net material product originating in these sectors. At the end of the reconstruction period the share originating in industry, into which substantial amounts of investment were channeled during that period, has increased to 40 per cent of the total and that of "other" to 15 per cent, whereas that of agriculture has fallen to 30 per cent. This decline is due both to the decrease in agricultural production and to the increase in net material product. The "socialist sector" now accounts for some 62 per cent of net material product, private, very small-scale production accounts for 33 per cent, and the share contributed by so-called "capitalist" ownership has been reduced to a bare 5 per cent.

III. The third rectangle presents schematically the situation in 1952–53, on the eve of the "new course." The relative importance of both the basic systems of production and the sectors have shifted further from the 1945–46 and 1948–49 relations. The "socialist sectors" have been extended to the whole sphere of industry, "other" activities, and wholesale trade; they have engulfed large segments of retail trade and crafts; and they have developed a foothold in agriculture. Very small-scale private enterprises are now limited to agriculture, crafts, and a very restricted position in retail trade. Finally, the "capitalist" system has been liquidated, though the word is still applied to the so-called "kulak strata," a loosely defined group of peasant owners of plots of land varying from 8 to 10 hectares up to 15 to 25 hectares.

Pari passu with the development of nationalization, new and marked shifts have occurred in the share of each sector in the net material product. Industry alone now accounts for close to 50 per cent of the net material product. The share of agriculture has fallen to 25 per cent; all the other activities together contribute around 25 per cent. As for systems of production, the "socialist sectors" now account

[6] Actually, it is rather ludicrous to speak of the subsistence of the "capitalist system," since the term now refers only to some large workshops and to farms up to and around 50 hectares; it has lost all relevance in the capitalist fields *par excellence,* manufacturing and banking. However, official terminology is being quoted here.

for close to 80 per cent, very small-scale private enterprises for 17.5 per cent, and the "capitalist" sector for 2.5 per cent.

Before commenting on the last rectangle of the chart, let us note some concrete differences, as well as similarities, between each of the economies and the one described as "typical" in our scheme.

In the former Allied countries (Czechoslovakia, Poland, and Yugoslavia) the first large wave of nationalization occurred in 1944–45, whereas in the ex-enemy countries (Hungary, Romania, and Bulgaria), as we have already noted, nationalization was effected between 1947 and 1949. Thus in fact the first and second graphs represent fairly well the situation in the former Allied countries whereas, so far as the ex-enemy countries are concerned,[7] the first and second graphs should be telescoped into one.

During the entire period there were substantial differences in the several countries in the shares of each sector in the formation of the national income, with Czechoslovakia at one extreme and Bulgaria at the other. The percentages in the first two graphs have been selected so as to approximate the situation in the middle group, namely, Poland and Hungary (the group of agricultural and raw-material-producing countries which, however, had substantial industrial facilities).

By 1948–49, the importance of nationalized and cooperative enterprises combined in the various countries had reached the proportions indicated in Table 133.

In industry, except in Romania, 92 per cent or more of the gross output then originated in the "socialist sector"; there was no private activity in the banking field; from 75 to 100 per cent of the wholesale trade was concentrated in the hands of the state. Although in each of these countries nationalization had engulfed all the other important service sectors (insurance, transportation, foreign trade), there were still wide differences in the secondary sectors such as retail trade. Finally, the process of "socialization" was just beginning in the key sector of the very small-scale production system, i.e., in agriculture. Except in Bulgaria, where the agricultural sector was very large, upwards of 60 per cent of the national income originated in the socialist sectors. Thus, by that time, each of these economies resembled our "typical" economy fairly closely, except for considerable variation in the percentage of agriculture that had been socialized.

[7] Also in this group the Soviet share in Soviet-owned companies and joint ventures could have been distinguished; we avoided it, however, for the purpose of simplification.

TABLE 133. SHARE OF THE SOCIALIST SECTOR IN VARIOUS ECONOMIC SECTORS AND IN THE NATIONAL INCOME, 1948–49

(percentages)

Country	Industry (gross output) 1	Banks (transactions) 2	Wholesale Trade (sales) 3	Retail Trade (sales) 4	Acreage (arable land) 5	Net Material Product 6
Czechoslovakia	94	100	100	54	9.2	61
Poland	96	100	87	55	7.1	64
Hungary	92	100	75	30	7.9	66
Romania	85	100	90 [a]	50	6.5	59
Bulgaria	93	100	100	68	12.2	45
Yugoslavia	100	100	100	98	28.6	70 [a]

[a] Estimate.

Sources:

Cols. 1–5: Chapters 3, 4, 6, and 7.

Col. 6: N. Spulber, "National Income and Product" of C, P, H, R, B, Y, published respectively in Mid-European Studies Center, *Handbooks of C., P., H., R., B., Y., under the Communists*, F. A. Praeger, Inc., New York, 1957.

From 1948–49 to 1952–53 the course of development of all the countries considered, including Yugoslavia, was, so far as the extension of the state sectors and their shares in investment are concerned, more consistent than ever before. By the end of that period, the contribution of the socialist sector toward the formation of the net material product had risen to 73–75 per cent in all the countries of the area except Czechoslovakia where it was higher. The share of very small-scale private production in the net national material product had thus been reduced to between 20 and 30 per cent, as depicted in our "model."

IV. Let us turn now to the fourth rectangle, illustrating schematically the shifts in the relations envisaged by the "new course." New outlets have been opened to very small-scale private production in crafts and in retail trade, and some cooperatives have been disbanded in agriculture, thus reducing the "socialist sector" in this sphere. On the other hand, the state has limited the size of farm available to *private ownership* to 10 or 15 hectares. Only two systems of ownership and production exist, and the share of one of the two, i.e., very small-scale private production, notwithstanding the concessions obtained in the secondary fields of crafts and retail trade, amounts to less than one quarter of the net national material product, an increase of some 5 per cent as compared to the combined share of capitalist and very small-scale private production in 1952–53.

These marginal concessions thus do not affect the basic positions attained in all the spheres of economic activity through the coupled processes of nationalization and planning. As appears from the dynamics of this whole development, its rationale is to reduce methodically and finally to *annihilate the possibility of productive investment* in the private sectors. That is why the process of nationalization does not stop in the various sectors of the economy at the limits of the very small-scale, private production system but attempts to take it over, control it, and reduce its importance, and is in constant conflict with it in every sphere of activity. That is also why, although capitalism in any Western sense of the word has disappeared from the economy, its specter continues to haunt the East European planners.

Structural Changes in National Income

The development of the national net material product during the whole period under survey is shown in Table 134. The compound yearly rate of increase for the period 1949 to 1953 has varied in the region from some 11 to approximately 16 per cent.

Table 134. Net Material Product, 1947–55 [a]

(in billions of national currencies in constant market prices) [b]

Country	1947	1948	1949	1950	1951	1952	1953	1954	1955
Czecho-slovakia	51.4	59.8	63.6	68.2	78.1	90.5	95.1	102.4	[c]
Poland	14.7	18.0	19.2	23.2	25.9	28.5	30.9	35.2	40.7
Hungary	19.8	27.0	38.0	44.0	52.0	54.0	58.0	57.5	[c]
Romania	[c]	498.0	564.0	605.0	815.0	939.0	1,021.0	1,058.0	1,245.0
Bulgaria	38.1	51.4	63.8	[c]	[c]	78.7	91.3	99.8	[c]
Yugoslavia	756.0	919.0	1,001.0	956.0	1,030.0	936.0	1,134.0	1,200.0	1,361.0

[a] For Yugoslavia, the figures include depreciation allowances.

[b] 1937 prices for Czechoslovakia and Poland; 1939 prices for Bulgaria; 1949 prices for Hungary; 1950 prices for Romania; 1953 prices for Yugoslavia.

[c] Not available.

Sources: Summary data from references listed in Table 133, Col. 6.

If we consider the sources of the net material product by sectors during three decisive periods, 1938, 1948, and 1953, we obtain the tabulations in Table 135.

In the prewar period, in Czechoslovakia some 53 per cent of the income from the net material product originated in industry. This percentage was 30 to 35 per cent in Poland and Hungary, and 24 to 28

Table 135. Net Material Product by Origin

(percentages)

Country	From Industry 1938	From Industry 1948	From Industry 1953	From Agriculture 1938	From Agriculture 1948	From Agriculture 1953	From Other 1938	From Other 1948	From Other 1953
Czechoslovakia [a]	53.2	61.9	70.0	23.2	17.6	13.0	23.6	20.5	17.0
Poland [bc]	30.1	42.4	52.7	44.7	29.9	28.0	25.2	27.7	19.3
Hungary [b]	35.5	47.1	56.6	34.5	26.7	15.0	31.0	26.2	28.4
Romania	28.4	40.2	53.6	53.2	46.0	31.4	18.4	13.8	15.0
Yugoslavia	24.6	36.4	42.1	50.3	38.1	30.3	25.1	26.5	27.6
Bulgaria [d]	24.3	31.9	47.2	56.9	52.2	34.3	19.8	15.9	18.5

[a] 1937 instead of 1938.
[b] 1949 instead of 1948.
[c] 1952 instead of 1953.
[d] 1939 instead of 1938.

Source: As in Table 133, Col. 6.

per cent in the other three countries. A three-way pattern is also clearly marked in agriculture. About 23 per cent of income originated in this sector in Czechoslovakia, less than half the share from industry alone. From 35 to 45 per cent came from agriculture in Hungary and Poland, a share equal to that of industry in Hungary, and higher by one third than that of industry in Poland. Finally, from 50 to 57 per cent of the income was from agriculture in the other three countries of the area, double the share from their industries. The three-way pattern is less apparent so far as the share of income from all other sources is concerned; these sectors vary greatly in volume in the different countries.

By 1948 notable changes appear in the origin of income from the net material product. According to official data, close to 62 per cent originated in industry in Czechoslovakia. In Poland and Hungary this percentage was respectively 42 and 47 per cent, the higher increase, in Poland, being due to the structural change in the country as a whole. Finally, from 32 to 40 per cent are the proportions given as originating in industry in the third group of countries. The share originating in agriculture is less than 18 per cent in Czechoslovakia, from 27 to 30 per cent in Poland and Hungary, and around 40 to 52 per cent in the last group.

The marked structural changes during the first development plan were reflected in a further shift in favor of industry. By 1953, income from the industrial sector rose in Czechoslovakia to 70 per cent of the total, while it varied from 42 to 57 per cent in the other countries. The share originating in agriculture continued to decline, falling to 13–15 per cent for Czechoslovakia and Hungary, 28 per cent for Poland, and to 30–34 per cent for the other three countries.

As illustrated in Chart 17, p. 472, along with this enhanced importance of industry and diminished importance of agriculture, new relationships have developed between the socialized sector and very small-scale private production with its low level of output.

Variations in Total and Per Capita Income

A comparison of index numbers of total national income and per capita income based on official data on net material product reveals some interesting variations in the region as a whole (see Table 136).

Table 136. Index Numbers of Total and Per Capita Net Material Product in Constant Prices:[a] 1947–55

(prewar = 100)[b]

	Czechoslovakia		Poland		Hungary		Romania		Yugoslavia		Bulgaria	
	Total	Per capita	Total	Per capita	Total	Per capita	Total	Per capita	Total	Per capita	Total	Per capita
1947	91	114	95	132	65[c]	64[c]	d	d	d	d	83	74
1948	106	130	117	161	88[e]	86[e]	79	98	d	d	111	99
1949	113	137	125	168	124	120	90	110	d	d	138	121
1950	121	149	151	198	144	138	96	117	d	d	d	d
1951	138	169	168	219	170	161	135	157	d	d	d	d
1952	160	195	185	236	176	166	150	178	d	d	170	145
1953	168	201	201	252	190	177	163	191	138	126	198	167
1954	181	213[f]	228	281	188	173	175	195	145	126	216	180
1955	d	d	264	319	d	d	199	226	d	d	d	d

[a] 1937 prices for Czechoslovakia and Poland; 1938 prices for Yugoslavia; 1939 prices for Bulgaria; 1949 plan prices for Hungary; 1950 prices for Romania.
[b] 1937 for Czechoslovakia; 1939 for Bulgaria; 1938 for all others. Index numbers are rounded.
[c] 1946–47.
[d] Not available.
[e] 1947–48.
[f] Derived from plan figures.
Source: As in Table 133, Col. 6.

So far as the total net material product is concerned, by 1948 only Czechoslovakia, Poland, and Bulgaria had reached or surpassed the prewar level. The countries mortgaged by heavy international obligations, Hungary and Romania, reached or surpassed the prewar level in 1949 or 1951. By 1953, the increases over the prewar level ranged from 60 to 100 per cent in the entire area, excluding Yugoslavia, where the increase was around 40 per cent.

Given the widespread population changes, the variations in per capita income were noticeable from one country to the next. The population changes over the period considered can be broadly summarized as follows: Czechoslovakia, Poland, and Romania (and, of course, mostly Poland) suffered great population losses due to the war, territorial displacements, and expulsions. Hungary approached its prewar population level, and Bulgaria registered increases through annexation. Hence, in Czechoslovakia, in Romania, and especially in Poland, per capita income has risen more rapidly than total income since the prewar period; in Hungary the per capita indices and the total indices moved along roughly parallel lines; and in Bulgaria the increase in per capita income was less than that in net material product. Thus, according to the official data, Czechoslovakia and Poland had reached and surpassed the prewar per capita product only in 1949, almost at the same time as Romania. In 1953 per capita income rose in Czechoslovakia, Poland, and Romania to double the prewar level (in Poland to two and one-half times prewar); while in Hungary and Bulgaria the level was between 167 and 177 per cent of prewar. Computed in current dollars the prewar and 1954 per capita incomes reached in Czechoslovakia are 244 and 519 dollars, respectively; in Poland 116 and 468 dollars; in Hungary 224 and 387 dollars; in Romania 139 and 314–329 dollars; in Yugoslavia 133 and 167 dollars; in Bulgaria 163 and 285 dollars.

The increases of per capita product do not indicate corresponding increases in "public welfare." Services not included in the net material product did not increase as did the net material product, so that the net material product probably increased more than national income as measured in Western countries. Further, as already stated, the shares of investment and of military expenditure were enormously increased as compared to prewar, and conversely the share of personal consumption was substantially depressed. Thus it was openly recognized in Poland after the June 1956 outbursts at Poznań that the average real wages have been lowered for many categories of workers during the first long-term plan. According to the then Premier E. Ochab, a commission of the Communist party officially established in 1956 that "a considerable number of working people did not improve their situation in comparison with 1949 and also that there are groups of working people whose situation somewhat worsened." [8]

[8] This statement reversed previous equally official claims of increases in real wages of 27.6 per cent during the first long-term plan. Ochab placed the blame for this situation on military expenditures:

The plans for the second quinquennium aim at a far lower average rate of growth of the net material product than did the first long-term plans: the planned rate of increase in net material product is 8 to 10 per cent (compared to 11 per cent and above during the first quinquennium). Only if the military expenditures are curtailed as scheduled, will it be possible to achieve under these conditions a slow increase in the workers' share of consumption, without a long-run sacrifice of investment outlays.

Rates of Growth and Some "Controlling Figures" in the Net National Product

A summary of the indicators of growth of the net material products at the end of the first long-term plans is shown in Table 137. As can be seen from the table, all the countries have failed to meet the targets set by their plans and in most cases there have been substantial discrepancies between targets and achievements.

The index of the net material product originating in industry nearly doubled in each country and increased more rapidly than the index of the net income. In all countries except Czechoslovakia, it also increased faster than the index of per capita income. In contrast to those originating in industry, only Poland, Hungary, and Romania indicate increases in the index of income originating in agriculture.

Comparisons of the index number of gross value of output and of net value underline the upward bias of the indices of gross value (see Table 138). The discrepancy becomes even greater if the two sets of indices are based on prewar prices. Thus, at 1938 prices the index of gross value of output rose in Poland at the end of the six-year plan to 443, while the derived index of net value reached only 349. In Bulgaria at 1939 prices the index of gross value rose to 403 at the end of the first long-term plan, while the derived index of net value reached only 332. Thus we can note again that the indices of gross value are

The defence industry absorbed cement, steel and non-ferrous metals of which we had very little; it absorbed, as we are saying in the resolution, the best workers and engineers; it absorbed raw materials in short supply and devoured tremendous sums in foreign currency for the import of installations. The value of the production of the defence industry represents many thousands of millions. But these thousands of millions should be multiplied several times if we want to arrive at the value of the goods which the same human cadres could have thrown on to the market, utilising the same raw materials and the equally expensive equipment for another and easier civilian production. [Statement by Edward Ochab, Seventh Plenum of the Central Committee of the P.U.W.P., *Polish Facts and Figures*, No. 515, July 28, 1956.]

TABLE 137. NET MATERIAL PRODUCT (Y): SUMMARY OF INDICATORS OF GROWTH DURING THE FIRST LONG-TERM PLANS

Indicators		Czechoslovakia 1948 = 100 1953	Poland 1949 = 100 1955	Hungary 1949 = 100 1954	Romania 1950 = 100 1955	Yugoslavia 1939 = 100 1951	Bulgaria 1948 = 100 1952
Total Y	Plan	148 [a] 170 [b]	212	163 [a] 230 [b]	260	193	185
	Actual	159	210	150	187	157 [c]	153
Per capita Y	Actual	154	190	144	175	146 [c]	146
Net Y originating in	Agric.	80	120	105	150	[d]	100
	Indus.	200	246	192	193	[d]	197
	Build.	270	289	206	[d]	[d]	[d]
	Other	107	167	111	266	[d]	215

[a] Original plan.
[b] Revised plan of 1951.
[c] Estimate.
[d] Not available.
Sources: Same as for Table 134, and *ESE in 1955*, Geneva, 1956, p. 237.

TABLE 138. INDEX NUMBERS:[a] GROSS VALUE OF OUTPUT AND CONTRIBUTION TO NET MATERIAL PRODUCT

Countries	Industry Gross	Industry Net	Agriculture Gross	Agriculture Net
Czechoslovakia (1953)	202	200	114	80
Poland (1955)	266	246	120	120
Hungary (1954)	213	192	112	105
Romania (1955)	210	193	150	150
Bulgaria (1952)	219	197	108	100

[a] Base year = Year preceding plan.
Sources: As in Tables 104 and 137.

only of limited importance, and that their manipulation must be done with circumspection.

AUTONOMY VS. INTEGRATION: CONFLICTING ELEMENTS IN THE SOVIET BLOC

The relationships in the bloc have substantially changed throughout the period 1944 to 1955. The antithesis: *development toward autarky* (of each economy) as against *integration* (into the Soviet economic sphere) is far less clear-cut than currently assumed. The frameworks both of autonomous development and of integration are extremely flexible, and they combine in varying degrees at various historical points. In 1944–45 the Soviet Union was occupying some of these countries and was exacting heavy reparations from them. Moreover, she was shipping home as so-called "restitution" or simply as war booty whatever movable assets she could lay her hands on. However, one might have quite clearly spoken of "autonomous development" of these occupied countries, since they were effectively supporting the occupation and restitutions burdens, and their own availabilities for investment and development were limited by those levies. After 1944–45 the Soviet Union renounced this early policy and started to build the network of joint companies in these countries. Economic integration at that time meant the systematic building of Soviet purchasing power in these countries and the continued shipment to the Soviet Union of large quantities of reparations. "Autonomous development" meant, among other things, the possibility for some of the countries of the area to trade extensively with the West, as was true, for instance, of Czechoslovakia and Poland. After 1948 and the break with Yugoslavia, the combination of autonomous and integrating factors changed further. Reparations were sharply reduced, and East Germany moved from an outright colony into a status comparable to that of the East European countries in 1945–46. Freed from a substantial part of the reparations burden, the commercial trade of the reparations-paying countries developed substantially. As difficulties arose in trade with the West, and as all the East European countries entered into the period of their first plans of industrialization, their trade with the Soviet Union developed very rapidly. During the first "planned quinquennium" and the "new course," integration implied the heavy dependence of these countries on Soviet imports and exports. An incipient structure of more clearly determined trade channels and a pattern of trade settlements began to develop on the basis of this increased trade and the key position of the Soviet Union as between the Soviet market itself, the East European market, and the Asiatic (Chinese) market.

On the basis of these past trends, one may venture the prognosis that, whatever the future adjustments between the conflicting purposes of autonomous development and integration, used here in the economic sense without precluding any "distorting" interventions of a political nature at any moment, they will be determined by the two factors that clearly dominated the entire period from the end of the war to the end of 1955, namely: (*a*) the stressed "preeminence" of the Soviet Union, and (*b*) the responsibility of each country for its own burden of investment and development. The stressing of the preeminence of the Soviet Union does not necessarily imply "voluntary" sacrifices in favor of the Soviet Union so far as, say, quantity, quality, and prices of goods are concerned; it is, nevertheless, a reminder of the fact that, by its sheer weight, that country is bound to dominate a small group of countries isolated at its boundaries, and that their destinies are largely in Soviet hands. The stressing of the *economic* autonomy and "national independence" of each country does not spring from any generous limitation of the Soviet power at its own borders but simply from the fact that such national development, in the framework of all-round planned economies with no private sectors and led by subservient Communist parties, best serves the long-range economic interests of the Soviet Union itself. Each East European country is increasingly compelled by the very isolation of the region to shape its economic plans primarily to serve Soviet, and only secondarily other East European, import needs and export availabilities. Conversely, the Soviet Union finds in these countries both a ready workshop for its raw materials without actual sacrifices in terms of the Soviet Union's own investment resources and a market serving as a perfect cushion for any imbalances of its own plan. From this point of view, the economic autonomy of each unit serves the interests of Soviet economic development infinitely more than the absorption of those countries into the Soviet Union would. Of course, frontiers can be moved backward and forward for strategic or other reasons. Economically, however, both from the point of view of Soviet investments and from the point of view of cushioning the imbalances of the Soviet plan, the *autonomy* of each unit appears to be much more useful. In any event, this autonomy does not and would not in any way prevent the mobilization of all the resources of the area in case of war.

The uneven development of the region, the very unequal capacity for investment of the countries of the area, their reliance on those capacities, and the planning of each country for all-round development even during the second planned quinquennium will tend to engender substantial conflicts between these countries and the Soviet Union and among themselves. Up to a point, it might be said that the 1948 Yugoslav crisis illustrated this fact since it brought to the fore, among other things, the conflict between an autonomous plan and the requirements of all the other countries of the area, above all the Soviet Union, so far as trade and investment are concerned.

There is no doubt that the concentration of ownership and the possibility of channeling all available savings places enormous resources in the hands of the state. So long as the system holds together, it is possible to increase capital formation over a given period and to achieve economic growth in certain sectors following the priorities set by the planners. But this is paid for by the sharply reduced share of private consumption in the net material product, a factor which creates enormous imbalances and pent-up pressures and generates deep processes of dislocation which can ultimately lead to the complete disintegration of the system itself. The deterioration of the standard of living, notwithstanding the growth achieved in total product, the development of an increasingly cumbersome and inflexible planning machinery, the breaking down of the system of incentives, and the corrosion of the will to work in wide strata of the society, have already created a series of decisive obstacles to further growth at the rates previously achieved. The reduction of the share of investment in total product, the shift in its pattern, the decentralization in respect to certain industrial outputs, the liberty of craftsmen, small tradesmen, and peasants to produce and trade, are now to be permitted in order to check these processes of dislocation. Thus, these regimes must return in a limited way to some of the pre-1948 orientations. It remains to be seen, however, what success can be secured by reinstating, up to a point, the "three-sector" economy—i.e., by the official reacceptance of limited growth of the private and cooperative sectors, and by such measures as decentralization. It is already apparent, however, that the economic growth of the area for the next five to ten years can be secured only at substantially lower rates than those claimed to have been achieved during the first planned quinquennium.

The convulsions in Poland and Hungary and the new disruptions engendered in the intraplanned market by the falling outputs of these two countries indicate that, instead of diminishing, the orbit conflicts are deepening and increasing in scope. The saddling of countries and peoples with a stifling bureaucratic regime, and the reluctance of Russia to concede even limited political freedom to her satellites, are bound to initiate new and even more powerful centrifugal tendencies in the Soviet bloc. Neither the passage of time nor the lessons of the past are likely to alleviate these basic conflicts.

PUBLICATIONS CITED

Periodicals Frequently Cited, in Abbreviated Form

AIB	*Agerpress Information Bulletin,* Bucharest.
CEB	*Czechoslovak Economic Bulletin,* Prague.
CS	*Comunicări Statistice (Statistical Information),* Bucharest.
EC	*Études et conjoncture, économie mondiale, Serie economique et financière* (Studies and Business Trends, World Economy, Economic and Financial Series), Paris.
FLP	*For a Lasting Peace, for a People's Democracy!,* Bucharest.
GP	*Gospodarka Planowa* (Planned Economy), Warsaw.
GT	*Gazdaságstatisztikai Tájékoztató* (Economic and Statistical Bulletin), Budapest.
HB	*Hungarian Bulletin,* Budapest.
IN	*Indeks* (Index), Belgrade.
MI	*Mesechni Izvestiia na Glavnata Direktsia na Statistikata* (Monthly Bulletin of the Central Office of Statistics), Sofia.
PE	*Probleme Economice* (Economic Problems), Bucharest.
PK	*Pari i Kredit* (Money and Credit), Sofia.
RD	*Rabotnichesko Delo* (Workers' Deed), Sofia.
RN	*Romanian News,* Romanian Embassy, Washington, D. C.
RP	*Rudé Právo* (Red Right), Prague.
RR	*Romanian Review,* Bucharest.
SC	*Scânteia* (continued after 1953 as Scînteia) (the Spark), Bucharest.
SN	*Szabad Nép* (Free People), Budapest.
SS	*Statisztikai Szemle* (Statistical Review), Budapest.
SZ	*Statistický Zpravodaj* (Statistical Information), Prague.
TL	*Trybuna Ludu* (People's Tribune), Warsaw.
VT	*Vneshniaia Torgovlia* (Foreign Trade), Moscow.
ESE [1]	*Economic Survey(s) of Europe,* Economic Commission for Europe, Department of Economic Affairs, United Nations, Geneva.
FAOY	*Yearbook of Food and Agricultural Statistics,* Food and Agricultural Organization of the United Nations, Rome.
UNDY	*Demographic Yearbook(s),* United Nations Department of Economic Affairs, New York.
UNSY	*Statistical Yearbook(s),* United Nations Department of Economic Affairs, New York.

[1] Since these United Nations publications are also very often referred to, we have included them with the periodicals.

Other Periodicals Used

American Economic Review, Evanston (Illinois).

Annals of the American Academy of Political and Social Science, Philadelphia.

The Banker, London.

Biuletyn, Polish Research and Information Service, New York.

Biuletyn Instytutu Gospodarstwa Narodowego (Bulletin of the Polish Institute of National Economy), Warsaw.

Bolshevik, Moscow.

Borba (Struggle), Belgrade.

Bulgaria Today, Sofia.

Bulletin d'information et de documentation (Bulletin of Information and Documentation), Banque Nationale de Roumanie, Service des Études Economiques (National Bank of Romania, Economic Studies Service), Bucharest.

Bulletin du Bureau d'Informations Polonaises (Bulletin of the Bureau of Polish Information), Paris.

Bulletin économique, Bureau hongrois de presse et de documentation (Economic Bulletin, Hungarian Bureau of Press and Documentation), Paris.

Bulletin of the National Bank of Czechoslovakia, Prague.

Cronica Românească (Report on Romania), New York.

Czechoslovak Economic Bulletin, Czechoslovak Embassy, Washington, D. C.

Dărzhaven Vestnik (Collection of Laws), Sofia.

Deutsches Institut für Wirtschaftsforschung, Abt. Bergbau und Energiewirtschaft, *Mitteilungen über die Industrie und Energiewirtschaft der Sowjetischen Besetzungszone Deutschlands und der osteuropäischen Länder* (German Institute for Economic Research, Section of Mines and Energy, Information on Industry and Energy of the Soviet-Occupied Zone in Germany and the East European Countries), Berlin.

Dokumentacioni Bilten (Bulletin of Documentation), Institut za Medjunarodnu Politiku i Privredu (Institute for International Politics and Economics), Belgrade.

Droit social (Social Right), Paris.

Dziennik Ustaw (Journal of Laws), Warsaw.

Economia Internazionale (International Economy), Genoa (Italy).

Economia Română (Romanian Economy), Bucharest.

Economic Digest, London.

The Economic Journal, London.

The Economist, London.

Ekonomist (Economist), Belgrade.

Ekonomista (Economist), Warsaw.

Ekonomska Politika (Political Economy), Belgrade.

Federal Reserve Bulletin, Washington, D. C.

Finansi i Kredit (Finance and Credit), Sofia.

Finansije (Finance), Belgrade.

Free Bulgaria, Sofia.

Głos Ludu (Voice of the People), Warsaw.

Harvard Business Review, Cambridge.

Hospodář (Economist), Prague.

Hungarian Review, Budapest.

Information hongroise, Bureau hongrois de presse et de documentation (Hungarian Information, Hungarian Bureau of Press and Documentation), Paris.

International Financial News Survey, Washington, D. C.

Izvestiia Akademii Nauk SSSR, Otedelenie Ekonomiki i Prava (News of the Academy of Science of the USSR, Section of Economy and Law), Moscow-Leningrad.

Journal de la Société hongroise de statistique (Journal of the Hungarian Statistical Society), Budapest.

Komunist, Belgrade.

Komunist, Moscow.

Közgazdaság (Public Economy), Budapest.

Közgazdasagi Szemle (Economic Review), Budapest.

Kultura (Culture), Paris.

Magyar Közlöny, Rendeletek Tára (Official Journal of Hungary, Collection of Decrees), Budapest.

Magyar Nemszet (Hungarian Nation), Budapest.

Magyar Statisztikai Szemle (Hungarian Statistical Review), Budapest.

Manchester Guardian, London.

Mesični Přehled Zahraničniho Obchodu (Monthly Reports on Foreign Trade), Prague.

Mirovoe Khoziaistvo i Mirovaia Politika (World Economy and World Politics), Moscow.

Le Monde (The World), Paris.

Monitor Polski (Official Gazette), Warsaw.

Monitorul Oficial (Official Gazette), Bucharest.

Monitorul Petrolului Romănesc (Monitor of Romanian Petroleum), Bucharest.

Monthly Bulletin of the National Bank of Hungary, new series, Budapest.

Nepszava (The Voice of the People), Budapest.

New Hungary, Budapest.

New York Times, New York.

Les Nouvelles Yugoslaves, Agence Yugoslave d'Informations (Yugoslav News, Yugoslav Information Agency), Paris.

Novoe Vremia (New Times), or *New Times* (English edition), Moscow.

Nowe Drogi (New Ways), Warsaw.

Ost-Europa (Eastern Europe), Stuttgart.

Otechestven Front (Fatherland Front), Sofia.

People's China, Peking.

Planovane Hospodarstve (Planned Economy), Prague.

Planovo Stopanstvo (Planned Economy), Sofia.

Planovoe Khoziaistvo (Planned Economy), Moscow.

Polish Affairs, London.

Polish Facts and Figures, London.

Polish Foreign Trade, Warsaw.

Prague News Letter, Prague.

Pravda (Truth), Moscow.

Průmyslové Zprávy, Státniho Uřadu Statistického, Republika Československá (Industrial Reports of the State Statistical Office of the Czechoslovak Republic), Prague.

Przegląd Gorniczy (Mining Review), Warsaw.

Quarterly Review of the Bank Gospodarstwa Karjowego (National Economic Bank), Warsaw.

Reports of the Statistical Offices on Plan Fulfillment, all countries.

Review of Economics and Statistics, Cambridge.

Review of International Affairs, Belgrade.
Review of Polish Law, Warsaw.
Revue commerciale hongroise (Hungarian Business Review), Budapest.
Revue economique internationale (International Economic Review), Geneva.
Revue mensuelle de la chambre de l'industrie yugoslave (Monthly Review of the Yugoslav Chamber of Industry), Belgrade.
Roumanie nouvelle (New Romania), Bucharest.
Rzeczpospolita (The Republic), Warsaw.
Službeni List (Official Gazette), Belgrade.
Socialistička Polioprivreda (Socialist Agriculture), Belgrade.
Spisanie i Izvestiia, Glavnata Direktsiia Na Statistikata—Revue et Bulletin, Direction générale de la statistique (Review and Bulletin of the Central Bureau of Statistics), Sofia.
Sprawy Międzynarodowe (International Affairs), Warsaw.
Statistical Bulletin of Czechoslovakia, Prague.
Statistički Bilten (Statistical Bulletin), Belgrade.
Statiztikai Tájékoztató (Statistical Review), Budapest.
Tarsadalmi Szemle (Social Review), Budapest.
UN *Economic Bulletin for Europe,* Economic Commission for Europe, United Nations, Geneva.
UN *Monthly Bulletin of Statistics,* United Nations, New York.
UN *Quarterly Bulletin of Housing and Building Statistics for Europe,* Economic Commission for Europe, United Nations, Geneva.
UN *Quarterly Bulletin of Steel Statistics,* Economic Commission for Europe, United Nations, Geneva.
Viața Sindicală (Trade Union Life), Bucharest.
Voprosy Ekonomiki (Economic Problems), Moscow.
Weltwirstschaftliches Archiv (Archives of World Economy), Kiel.
Wissenschaftlicher Dienst Sudost-europas (Scientific News Service of Southeast Europe), Munich.
World Affairs, Washington, D. C.
World Petroleum, New York.
World Politics, Princeton, New Jersey.
Yugoslav Review, Belgrade.
Zadružni Vjesnik (The Cooperative Messenger), Zagreb.
Zemedelsko Zname (Peasants' Banner), Sofia.
Życie Gospodarcze (Economic Life), Warsaw.
Życie Warszawy (Warsaw Life), Warsaw.

Selected Publications [2]

**Adresář Československého Průmyslu 1949* (Directory of Czechoslovak Industry for 1949), Orbis, Prague, 1949.
Alekseev, A. "Finansy Stran Narodnoi Democratii na Sluzhbe Stroitel'stva Sotsialisma" (The Finances of the Countries of People's Democracy in the Service of the Construction of Socialism), *Bolshevik,* No. 13, Moscow, 1950.

[2] All major books, articles, or publications quoted, are translated here. I have eliminated from this list secondary articles which have appeared with an English title. Asterisked items are books or pamphlets.

*Alkhimov, V., and I. Dudinskii. *Raspad Edinogo Mirovogo Rynka* (Disintegration of the Single World Market), Gospolitizdat, Moscow, 1953.

Alster, Antoni. "Some Questions of Organizing Work in the Polish United Worker's Party," *FLP,* Oct. 9, 1953.

Ames, Edward. "The Exchange Rate in Soviet Type Economies," *Review of Economics and Statistics,* XXV, 4 (November 1953).

Annuaire statistique de la republique tchecoslovaque (Statistical Yearbook of the Czechoslovak Republic), State Statistical Office, Orbis, Prague, annually.

Annuaire statistique hongrois (Hungarian Statistical Yearbook), Office central royal hongrois de statisque (Royal Hungarian Central Office of Statistics), Budapest, annually.

Anuarul Statistic al României (Romanian Statistical Yearbook), Institutul Central de Statistică (Central Institute of Statistics), Bucharest, annually.

*Atlas, S. V. *Ukreplenie Denezhnykh Sistem SSSR, Stran Narodnoi Demokratii—Infliatsia v Stranakh Kapitalizma* (The Strengthening of the Monetary System of the USSR and People's Democracies—Inflation in the Capitalist Countries), Gosfinizdat, Moscow, 1951.

*Bakulin, S. N., and D. D. Mishustin. *Vneshniaia Torgovlia SSSR za 20 let 1918–1937* (Foreign Trade of the USSR for 20 years, 1918–1937), Statisticheskii Spravochnik (Statistical Manual), Moscow, 1939.

Balog, Dr. Nikola. "Neka pitanja u vezi reorganizacije saveznih i republickih privrednoupravnih organa" (Some Questions in Connection with the Reorganization of Federal and Republican Economic-Administrative Organs), *Ekonomist,* III, 3 (1950).

*Baykov, A. *Soviet Foreign Trade,* Princeton University Press, Princeton, N. J., 1946.

Bell, E. A. "Romania to Revise Exports," *World Petroleum,* Nov. 4, 1947.

Berceanu, Ion. "New Regime of Grain Collection in Romania," *RR,* III, 11 (September 1948).

*Bergmann, Milos Ivan. *Kreditbanken in der Tschechoslowakei* (Credit Banks in Czechoslovakia), thesis, Frankfurt-am-Main, 1932.

*Bergson, Abram, editor. *Soviet Economic Growth: Conditions and Perspectives,* Row Peterson and Co., Evanston, Ill., 1953.

*Bergson, Abram. *Soviet National Income and Product in 1937,* Columbia University Press, New York, 1953.

*Bergson, Abram, and Hans Heymann, Jr. *Soviet National Income and Product, 1940–48,* Columbia University Press, New York, 1954.

*Bettelheim, C. *La Planification soviétique* (Soviet Planning), 2nd ed., Rivière et cie, Paris, 1945.

Bierut, Boleslaw. "Report of the Central Committee to the Second Congress of the Polish United Workers' Party," *FLP,* Mar. 19, 1954.

Biji, Mircea. "Intreprinderile Industriale Particulare având peste 10 persoane ocupate sau forţa motrică peste 20 HP, pe ramuri şi grupe de personal" (Private Industrial Enterprises with More than 10 Employees or More than 20 HP, Classified by Branches of Industry and Number of Employees). Reprint from *PE,* No. 2–3, March–April 1948, Institutul Central de Statistică (Central Institute of Statistics), Bucharest, 1948.

**Breviarul Statistic al României* (Romanian Statistical Digest), Bucharest, 1940.

"Le Budget général de l'état" (The General State Budget), *Bulletin d'information et de documentation,* National Bank of Romania, No. 4–6 (June 1947).

"Ceny v černém obchodě v září 1948" (Black Market Prices in September 1948), *SZ,* XI, 12 (December 1948).

**Československý průmysl* (Czechoslovak Industry), Central Union of Czechoslovak Industry, Prague, 1948.

Chernokolev, T. "The Agrarian Policy of the Bulgarian Workers' Party," *FLP,* July 1948.

Chervenkov, Vălko. "Along Trying Road of Building Socialism," *FLP,* Sept. 11, 1953.

Chervenkov, Vălko. "Report of the Central Committee to the 6th Party Congress," *FLP,* Mar. 5, 1954.

Chistiakov, A. "Razvitie Economicheskogo Sotrudnichestva Stran Sotsialisticheskogo Lageria" (Development of Economic Cooperation between the Countries of the Socialist Camp), *Komunist,* XXXI, No. 15 (October 1954).

*Clark, Colin. *Conditions of Economic Progress,* Macmillan and Co., London, 1951.

Coliu, D. "Eve of Elections to Local People's Councils in Romania," *FLP,* Nov. 27, 1953.

*Colocotronis, Constantin V. *L'Organisation bancaire des pays balkaniques et les capitaux étrangers* (Banking Organization of the Balkan Countries and Foreign Capital), thesis, Recueil Sirey, Paris, 1934.

*Commission for the Promotion of International Trade. *International Economic Conference in Moscow,* publ. by the Commission, Moscow, 1952.

Concise Statistical Yearbook of Poland, Chief Bureau of Statistics, Warsaw, annually.

Concise Statistical Yearbook of Poland, September 1939–June 1941, Polish Ministry of Information, Glasgow, 1941.

*Conrad, G. J. *Die Wirtschaft Jugoslaviens* (The Economy of Yugoslavia), Deutsches Institut für Wirtschaftsforschung (German Institute for Economic Research), new series, No. 17, Duncker and Humblot, Berlin, 1952.

Constantinescu, G. G. "Considerations sur la production du petrole en Roumanie" (Considerations on Petroleum Production in Romania), *Monitorul Petrolului Românesc,* No. IX–X, 1947.

Constantinescu, Miron. "Exposé sur le Plan Quinquennal à la seance du 14 Decembre 1950 de la Grande Assemblée Nationale" (Speech on the Five Year Plan at the December 14, 1950 meeting of the Great National Assembly) in: *Le Plan Quinquennal Roumain* (The Romanian Five Year Plan).

Constantinescu, Miron. "On the Road of Building Socialism. Some Problems of Economic Development in Romania in the Light of the Economic Tasks of the People's Democracies," *FLP,* Sept. 9, 1955.

Cornăţeanu, Prof. E. "Cercetări asupra Rentabilităţii Agriculturei Româneşti" (Researches on the Profitability of Romanian Agriculture), *Economia Română,* XXVII (December 1945).

*Čurčin, Slobodan. *Penetration des capitaux étrangers en Yugoslavie* (Penetration of Foreign Capital in Yugoslavia), Pierre Bossuet, Paris, 1935.

Cyrankiewicz, J. "O założeniach planu 5-letniego na lata 1956–1960" (The Premises of the 5-Year Plan 1956–1960), *TL,* July 26, 1956.

**Czechoslovak Economic Five-Year Plan: Act and Government Memorandum,* Czechoslovak Ministry of Information and Public Culture, Orbis, Prague, 1949.

Damianov, Raiko. "Bulgarian Trade Unions Fight to Carry Out Five-Year Plan," *FLP,* Mar. 1, 1949.

*Dean, Vera Micheles. "Economic Trends in Eastern Europe, I, II," *Foreign Policy Reports,* April 1 and 15, 1948.

*Dedijer, Vladimir. *Tito,* Simon and Schuster, New York, 1953.

**Deutsches Vermögen im Ausland, Internationale Vereinbärungen und ausländische Gesetzgebung* (German Properties Abroad, International Agreements and Foreign Laws), Bundesministerium der Justiz, Verl., des Bundeseinzeiger (publ. by Federal Ministry of Justice), Köln, 1951.

"Le developpement economique de la Pologn en 1948" (Economic Development of Poland in 1948), *Bulletin du bureau d'informations Polonaises,* Jan. 25, 1949.

*Dewar, Margaret. *Soviet Trade with Eastern Europe 1945–1949,* Royal Institute of International Affairs, London and New York, 1951.

Dimitrov, Georgi. "1947 Balance Sheet," *Free Bulgaria,* III, 2 (January 15, 1948).

Djordjević, Jovan. "Two Federal Laws and Their Significance," *Review of International Affairs,* IV, 11 (June 1, 1953).

**Documents Concerning the Right Deviation in the Romanian Workers' Party,* Romanian Worker's Party Publishing House, Bucharest, 1952.

**Documents sur l'évolution recente de la Republique Populaire de Tchecoslovaquie* (Documents on the Recent Evolution of the Czechoslovak People's Republic), Notes et études documentaires (Notes and Documentary Studies), No. 1792, La Documentation Française (French Documentation), Paris, Oct. 14, 1953.

*Dolanský, Jaromir. *Three Years of Planning in the Czechoslovak People's Democracy,* Orbis, Prague, 1949.

Dolanský, Jaromir. "Towards Further Rise in Well-Being of Working People of Czechoslovakia," *FLP,* July 3, 1953.

*Douglas, Dorothy W. *Transitional Economic Systems: The Polish-Czech Example,* Routledge and Kegan Paul, London, 1953.

**Drugi Powszechny Spis Lúdności, Dec. 9, 1931* (Second General Census, 1931), Statystyka Polski (Statistics of Poland), Series C Z-62, Warsaw.

Dudinskii, I. "Ekonomicheskoe Sotrudnichestvo SSSR i Stran Narodnoi Demokratii" (Economic Cooperation between the USSR and the Countries of People's Democracy), *Bolshevik,* No. 6 (March 1950).

**Dunaiskaia Konferentsia—La Conférence Danubienne* (The Danube Conference), Russian-French official texts, Belgrade, 1949.

Dvořák, R. "Economic Co-Operation of Countries of Democratic Camp," *FLP,* Feb. 12, 1954.

**L'Economie polonaise au seuil du plan de six ans* (Polish Economy on the Threshold of the Six-Year Plan), Notes et études documentaires (Notes and Documentary Studies), No. 1070, La Documentation Française (French Documentation), Paris, February 1949.

**L'Evolution economique de la Tchecoslovaquie* (The Economic Evolution of Czechoslovakia), Notes et études documentaires (Notes and Documentary Studies), No. 1426, La Documentation Française (French Documentation), Paris, January 1951.

*Fabry, Dr. Valer. *Agricultural Laws of the Czechoslovak Republic, May 1945–March 1949,* Ministry of Agriculture, Library of the Czechoslovak Institute for

International Collaboration in Agriculture and Forestry, Vol. 17, Brazda, Prague, 1949.

Farkasfalvi, Alexander. "La Statistique de la petite industrie en Hongrie" (Statistics of Small Industry in Hungary), *Journal de la Société hongroise de statistique,* XIII, 3 (1935).

*Feierabend, Ladislav. *Agricultural Cooperatives in Czechoslovakia,* Mid-European Studies Center, New York, 1952.

**First Czechoslovak Economic Plan: Act and Memorandum,* 2nd ed., Orbis, Prague, 1948.

Fonar, Adam. "Nowa Organizacja Państwowego Przemysłu Terènowego" (New Organization of the State Local Industry), *Życie Gospodarcze,* Apr. 16, 1951.

"Fontosabb Mutatók a Kereskedelmi Statisztikában" (Some Important Indicators in Commercial Statistics), *SS,* II, 3–4 (March–April 1950).

"For Constantly Strengthening the Party," *SC,* June 3, 1952, reprinted in *Documents Concerning the Right Deviation in the Romanian Workers' Party.*

"Foreign Trade of Hungary since the Introduction of the Florin Currency," *Monthly Bulletin of the National Bank of Hungary,* new series, III, 3–4 (March–April 1947).

Franges, O. "L'Industrialisation des pays agricoles du sud-est de l'Europe" (Industrialization of the Agrarian Countries in South-East Europe), *Revue économique internationale,* XXX, 2 (July 1938).

Gălătescu, V. "Les Sociétés privées d'assurances de Roumanie et la régie autonome des assurances d'état—R.A.A.S." (The Private Insurance Companies and the State Autonomous Insurance Administration in Romania), *Bulletin d'information et de documentation,* National Bank of Romania, XVII, 7–9 (July–September 1945).

Gay, Laszlo. "Consolidating Economic Co-operation between Soviet Union and Countries of People's Democracy," *FLP,* Nov. 14, 1952.

Gerő, Ernő. "The Policy of Hungarian Workers' Party in Countryside," *FLP,* Dec. 1, 1948.

*Gerő, Ernő. *The Position of the Hungarian National Economy in 1952 and the Task in Its Development,* publ. by *HB,* Budapest, 1952.

Gheorghiu-Dej, Gh. "Carrying Out the Great Leninist Teaching on the Alliance between the Working Class and the Peasantry," *FLP,* Apr. 15, 1955.

Gheorghiu-Dej, Gh. "Report to the First Congress of the Romanian Workers' Party," *RN,* May 22, 1949.

*Gheorghiu-Dej, Gh. *Raportul de Activitate al Comitetului Central al Partidului Muncitoresc Romîn la Congresul al Il-lea al Partidului* (Report on the Activity of the Central Committee of the Romanian Workers' Party at the Second Party Congress), Editura de Stat pentru Literatura Politică (State Publishing House for Political Literature), Bucharest, 1955.

*Gheorghiu-Dej, Gh. *Speech to the National Conference of Miners,* State Publishing House, Bucharest, 1952.

*Gheorghiu-Dej, Gh. *Speech to the National Conference of Railwaymen,* Publishing House of the Romanian Institute for Cultural Relations with Foreign Countries, Bucharest, 1953.

Gheorghiu-Dej, Gh. "Towards Further Development of National Economy, Towards Further Rise in Well-Being of People!," *FLP,* Aug. 28, 1953.

*Glos, Dr. B. *The Mobilisation of Labour in Czechoslovakia,* Orbis, Prague, 1948.

*Goldberg, I. *Les Banques Polonaises dépendants de l'état* (The Polish Banks Dependent on the State), thesis, Nancy, 1935.

*Golopentia, Dr. A., and Georgescu, Dr. D. C. *Populația Republicii Populare Române la 25 Januarie 1948. Rezultatele Provizorii ale Recensământului* (The Population of the People's Republic of Romania on January 25, 1948. The Provisional Results of the Census), Institutul Central de Statistică (Central Institute of Statistics), Bucharest, 1948.

Golopenția, Dr. A., and P. Onică. "Recensământul Agricol din Republica Populară Română, Januarie 25, 1948, Rezultate Provizorii" (Agricultural Census of the Romanian People's Republic, January 25, 1948, Provisional Results), *PE,* No. 3 (March 1948).

Gorácz, Dr. Béla. "A Magyar Hároméves Terv Statisztikai Felépítése" (The Statistical Construction of the Hungarian Three-Year Plan), *Magyar Statisztikai Szemle,* XXVI, 16 (June 1948).

*Gottwald, Clement. *Statement of Policy of Mr. Gottwald's Government,* Orbis, Prague, 1946.

Gruzín, Dr. V. "Oběživo a Vklady" (Currency Circulation and Deposits), *SZ,* XII, 1 (January 1949).

Gryziewicz, Stanisław. "Rolnictwo" (Agriculture), in *Kultura,* Numer Krajowy (special issue on Poland), Vol. I, 1952.

*Grzegorzek, Casimir. *Le Rôle économique de la Banque de l'économie nationale en Pologne* (The Economic Role of the National Economic Bank in Poland), thesis, Paris, 1935.

Hegedűs, András. "Tasks of Raising Agricultural Production in Hungary," *FLP,* Jan. 8, 1954.

*Hoeffding, Oleg. *Soviet National Income and Product in 1928,* Columbia University Press, New York, 1954.

Hoffman, Dr. J. "Organisační Změny v čs. peněžnictví a pojišťovnictví v letech 1945–48" (Changes in the Organization of the Financial System and Insurance in 1945–48), *SZ,* XII, 1 (January 1949).

Horoviț, M. "Despre Decontările Internaționale şi Relațile de Credit dintre Țările Lagărului Socialist" (On the International Payments and the Credit Relations among the Countries of the Socialist Camp), *PE,* No. 7 (July 1954).

Hsu Hsuen-han (Vice Minister for Foreign Trade for China). "China's Trade with the European People's Democracies," *People's China,* XVII, Peking, 1953.

**The Hungarian Oil Industry,* Mid-European Studies Center, New York, 1954.

**Hungarian Three-Year Plan,* publ. by *HB* (mimeo.), Budapest, 1947.

*Ikonnikov, V. V., editor. *Denezhnoe Obrashchenie i Kredit SSSR* (Money, Circulation, and Credit in the USSR), Gosfinizdat, Moscow, 1954.

"L'Industrie hongroise depuis la fin de la guerre" (Hungarian Industry since the End of the War), *EC,* IV, 3 (May–June 1949)

"Insurance Reform in Poland," *Review of Polish Law,* III, 1 (April 1949).

**Intreprinderile Particulare Industriale, Comerciale, şi de Transport. Rezultatele Provizorii ale Inventarului din Octomvrie 1947* (Private Industrial, Commercial, and Transportation Enterprises. Provisional Results of Census of October 1947), Statistica Industrială (Census of Manufacturers), I, 1, Institutul Central de Statistică (Central Institute of Statistics), Bucharest.

"Investment Financing in Poland," *Quarterly Review of the Bank Gospodarstwa Krajowego,* XVII, 3 (September 1948).

"Irányelvek a magyar népgazdaság fejlesztésének második ötéves tervéhez" (Directives on the Development of the Second Five-Year Plan of Hungary), *SN*, April 27, 1956.

Ivan, Colonel (pseud.). "On the Development of the Armed Forces of Cominform Countries," *Review of International Affairs*, IV, 2, 4, 5, 6 (January–March 1953).

Ivanović, Milan. "Agriculture in Yugoslav Social Plan," *Review of International Affairs*, V, 16 (April 1954).

Ivanović, Milan. "Cooperatives and Agricultural Development," *Review of International Affairs*, IV, 13 (July 1953).

Ivanović, Milan. "The Development of Yugoslav Agriculture," *Review of International Affairs*, III, 18 and 20 (September 16 and October 16, 1952).

Jackson, E. F. "Social Accounting in Eastern Europe," *Income and Wealth*, Series IV, International Association for Research in Income and Wealth, London, 1955.

Jędrychowski, Stefan. "Concern for Well-Being of Working People in People's Democracies," *FLP*, Jan. 29, 1954.

Jędrychowski, Stefan. "Economic Development and Growth of National Income in Poland," *FLP*, May 1, 1953.

Jenő, Rédei. "Magyarország Népességének Osztályszerkezete az 1949. Évi Népszámlálás Adatai Alapján" (The Social Structure of the Population of Hungary. Based upon Data from the 1949 Census), *SS*, III, 6 (June 1951).

*Jordan, Constantin. *The Romanian Oil Industry*, Mid-European Studies Center, New York University Press, New York, 1955.

*Jordan, Constantin. *The Romanian Oil Industry in 1947* (mimeo.), Mid-European Studies Center, New York, March 29, 1954.

Jordan, Z. "Structure of Population," *Polish Affairs*, II, 7–9 (September 1953).

*Jurković, Dr. Božidar. *Das ausländische Kapital im ehemaligen Jugoslavien* (The Foreign Capital in Former Yugoslavia), W. Kohlhammer Verl., Stuttgart, Berlin, 1941.

*Kaliuzhnaia, G. P. *Pravovye Formy Monopolii Vneshnei Torgovli SSSR v ikh istoricheskom Rasvitii* (The Juridical Forms of the Monopoly of Foreign Trade in Their Historical Development), Izdatel'stvo Akademii Nauk SSSR (Published by the Academy of Science of the USSR), Moscow, 1951.

*Kardelj, Edward. *On People's Democracy in Yugoslavia*, Yugoslav Information Center, New York, 1949.

Kazantsev, N. D. "Zemelnye Reformy i Puti Preobrazovaniia Selskogo Khozvaistva v Stranakh Narodnoi Demokratsii Tsentralnoi i Iugovostochnoi Evropy" (The Land Reforms and the Road toward the Reorganization of Agriculture in the Countries of People's Democracy of Central and South-East Europe), *Izvestiia Akademii Nauk SSSR, Otdelenie Ekonomiki i Prava*, No. 4 (July–August 1950).

Kemény, George. "Eastern European Developments in Social Economic Structure," *World Politics*, VI, 1 (October 1953).

*Kemény, George. *Economic Planning in Hungary, 1947–49*, Royal Institute of International Affairs, London, 1952.

Kenessey, Zoltan. "A Mezőgazdaság Fejlődése Bulgáriában" (Development of Agriculture in Bulgaria), *Statisztikai Tájékoztató*, No. 4, 1953.

Khranova, O. "Party Control in Enterprise," *FLP*, July 24, 1953.

*Kidrič, Boris. *On the Construction of Socialist Economy in the FPRY*, Office of Information of the FPRY, Belgrade, 1948.

*Kiesewetter, Bruno. *Statistiken zur Wirtschaft Ost–und Südosteuropas* (Economic

Statistics of East and Southeast Europe), Deutsches Institut fur Wirtschaftsforschung (German Institute for Economic Research), new series, No. 33, Duncker and Humblot, Berlin, 1955.

Kiritzesco, Costin. "La Reforme monetaire roumaine de 1947" (The Romanian Monetary Reform of 1947), Bulletin d'Information et de Documentation, National Bank of Romania, XIX, 7–9 (July–September 1947).

Kiss, Árpád. "Ten Years' Progress of Hungary's Chemical Industry" in *Hungarian Review,* No. 5, May 1955.

Klochek, V., and K. Viriasov. "Ekonomicheskoe Sotrudnichestvo Stran Lageria Sotsializma" (Economic Cooperation of Countries of the Socialist Camp), *VT,* XXII (February 1952).

Klosiewicz, Wiktor. "New Attitudes towards Labour in People's Poland," *FLP,* May 22, 1953.

Koenig, E. "Collectivization in Czechoslovakia and Poland," Paper presented at a Seminar on Collectivization of Agriculture in Eastern Europe. University of Kentucky, April 1955 (mimeo.).

Konoplev, A. "O znachenii ekonomicheskoi chasti Sovetsko-Germanskogo Soglasheniia" (On the Significance of the Economic Part of the Soviet-German Agreement), *Novoe Vremia,* No. 36 (September 2, 1953).

*Konstantinov, F. T. *Bolgariia na puti k Sotsialismu* (Bulgaria on the Road to Socialism), 2nd ed., Gosudarstvennoe Izdatel'stvo Politicheskoi Literatury (State Publishing House of Political Literature), Moscow, 1953.

*Konstantinov, F. T., editor. *Vtoroi Piatiletnii Plan Razvitiia Narodnoi Respubliki Bolgarii* (Second Five Year Plan of Development of the Bulgarian People's Republic), Sbornik Materialov (Collection of Materials), Izdatel'stvo Inostrannoi Literatury (Publishing House of Foreign Literature), Moscow, 1954.

Kopecký, Václáv. "Fifth Anniversary of February Victory of Working People of Czechoslovakia," *FLP,* Feb. 20, 1953.

Korolenko, A. "Printsipi Ravenstva i Vzaimnoi Vygody v Torgovle SSSR s Evropeiskimi Stranami Narodnoi Demokratsii" (Principles of Equality and Mutual Benefit in the Trade of the USSR with the European Countries of People's Democracy), *Voprosy Ekonomiki,* March 3, 1952.

*Košak, Vladmir. *Die bankmässige Finanzierung der Jugoslawischen Industrie* (Financing by the Banks of Yugoslav Industry), Bechhold Ver., Frankfurt-am-Main, 1938.

Kostiukhin, D. "Pod'em Narodnogo Khoziaistva Bolgarii" (The Advance of the National Economy of Bulgaria), *VT,* XIII, 7 (July 1952).

*Kořátko, Dr. J. *Land Reform in Czechoslovakia,* Orbis, Prague, 1948.

*Kovrizhnykh, M. F., A. B. Frumkin, and V. C. Pozdniakov, editors, *Vneshniaia Torgovlia Stran Narodnoi Demokratsii* (Foreign Trade of the Countries of People's Democracy), Vneshtorgizdat, Moscow, 1955.

Kowalczyk, Władysław. "Handel Panstwowy" (State Trade), *Kultura,* Numer Krajowy (special issue on Poland), Vol. II, 1952.

Kowalczyk, Władysław. "Kadry Pracownikow" (Workers' Cadres), *Kultura,* Numer Krajowy (Special Issue on Poland), Vol. II, 1952.

Kowalczyk, Władysław. "Prywatny Przemysł, Handel i Rzemiosło" (Private Industry, Trade, and Crafts), *Kultura,* Numer Krajowy (Special Issue on Poland), Vol. II, 1952.

Kraus, Alfred. "La Nationalisation de l'industrie en Pologne" (Nationalization of Industry in Poland), *Droit social,* X, 3–4 (March–April 1947).

Kristóf, István. "Report to the 18th Trade Union Congress," *Népszava,* Feb. 28, and Mar. 3, 1953.

Kristóf, István. "Socialist Emulation in Hungarian People's Republic," *FLP,* Apr. 3, 1953.

Kriz, Miroslav A. "Central Banks and the State Today," *American Economic Review, XXXVIII,* 4 (September 1948).

Kuibyshev, A. "Ekonomicheskoe Razvitie Chekhoslovakii" (Economic Development of Czechoslovakia), *VN,* No. 3, 1952.

Kulischer, Eugene M. "Population Changes behind the Iron Curtain." *Annals of the American Academy of Political and Social Science,* CCLXXI (September 1950).

Lámer, Mirko. "Die Wandlungen de ausländischen Kapitalanlagen auf dem Balkan" (Change in Foreign Investments in the Balkans), *Weltwirtschaftliches Archiv,* XLVIII (November 1938).

Lange, O. "Rozpad Jednolitego Rynku Swiatowego i Ukształtowanie się Dwóch Równoległych Rynków w Gospodarce Światowej" (Disintegration of the Single World Market and the Formation of Two Parallel Markets in the World Economy), *Ekonomista,* I (1953).

*Laurat, Lucien. *L'Économie Soviétique—sa dynamique, son mécanisme* (Soviet Economy—Its Dynamics, Its Mechanism), Bibliothèque économique universelle (Universal Economic Library), No. V, Librairie Valois, Paris, 1931.

*Lavrukhin, J. S. *Narodno-Demokraticheskaia Chekhoslovakiia na Puti k Sotsializmu* (The Czechoslovak People's Democracy on the Road to Socialism), publ. by *Pravda,* Moscow, 1950.

**Law on the Five-Year Plan of the Federal People's Republic of Yugoslavia,* Jugoslovenska Knjiga (Yugoslav book), Belgrade, 1947.

**Law on the Two-Year Economic Plan 1947–1948,* Ministry of Information and Arts, Sofia, 1947.

*League of Nations. *Agricultural Recovery in Continental Europe during the 1914–1918 War and the Reconstruction Period,* Economic and Financial Series, 11/A/7, Geneva, 1943.

*League of Nations. *Annuaire-statistique international* (International Statistical Year Book), Geneva, annually.

*League of Nations. *Europe's Trade: A Study of the Trade of European Countries with Each Other and with the Rest of the World,* Geneva, 1941.

*League of Nations. *The Network of World Trade,* Geneva, 1942.

*League of Nations. *Raw Materials and Foodstuffs,* Geneva, 1939.

Lebedev, A. "Zakony Reguliruiushchie Vneshniuiu Torgovliu v Rumynii" (Laws Regulating Foreign Trade in Romania), *VT,* No. 11, 1948.

*Lénárd, Paul. *La Crise industrielle et l'intervention de l'état en Hongrie—Étude économique et juridique* (The Industrial Crisis and the Intervention of the State in Hungary—An Economic and Juridical Study), thesis, Lyons, 1935.

*Litwin, Janusz. *ABC Planu Sześcioletniego* (The ABC of the Six-Year Plan), Warsaw, 1949.

Luca, Vasile. "New Orientations in Romanian Finances," *RR,* II, 5–6 (May–June 1948).

*Madgearu, Virgil. *Rumania's New Economic Policy*, King and Son, Orchard House, London, 1930.

**Magyarország 1939 évi. Külkereskedelmi Forgalma* (Foreign Trade Volume of Hungary in 1939), Budapest, 1940.

**Magyar Statisztikai Zsebkőnyv* (Hungarian Statistical Handbook) for 1956 only. Kőzgazdasági eś Jagi Kőnyvkiadó (Economic and Legal Book Publishers), Budapest, 1956.

Major, Márton. "A kisipari és kereskedelmi adatfelvétel szervezési tapasztalatai" (Organizational Experiences in Collecting Data on Small Trade and Commerce), *SS*, III, 3 (March 1951).

Malenković, Vladislav. "O pitanju ekonomskih odnosa izmedju SSSR-a i njemu potčinjenih zemalja" (On the Question of Economic Relations between the USSR and the Countries Subjected to Her), *Ekonomist*, III, 3, 1950.

*Mandelbaum, K. *The Industrialization of Backward Areas*, Institute of Statistics Monograph 2, Basil Blackwell, Oxford, 1947.

Manoilescu, M. "Arbeitsproduktivität und Aussenhandel" (Labor Productivity and Foreign Trade), *Weltwirstschaftliches Archiv*, XLII, 1 (January 1935).

*Manoilescu, M. *A New Conception of Industrial Protectionism*, Regia Monitorului Official, Imprimeria Natională (Official Gazette, National Printing House), Bucharest, 1931.

*Manoilescu, M. *Theorie de protectionisme et de l'échange international* (Theory of Protectionism and of International Trade), Bibliothèque Internationale d'économie politique (International Library of Political Economy), Giard, Paris, 1929.

Marczewski, J. "Le Rôle des comptes nationaux dans les économies planifiées du type soviétique" (The Role of National Accounts in the Planned Economies of the Soviet Type), *Income and Wealth*, Series IV, International Association for Research in Income and Wealth, London, 1955.

*Margold, Stela K. *Let's Do Business with Russia*, Harper and Bros., New York, 1948.

*Markert, Werner, editor. *Jugoslawien* (Yugoslavia), Osteuropa Handbuch (East Europe Handbook), Bohlau Verl., Köln-Graz, 1954.

Matov, Ivan. "Rozwój Gospodarki Planowej w Bułgarii" (Development of Planned Economy in Bulgaria), *GP*, VI, 8 (August 1951).

Matov, Ivan. "Social and Economic Changes in Bulgaria," *Free Bulgaria*, VI, 12 (June 10, 1951).

*Melik, Dr. Anton. *Jugoslavija* (Yugoslavia), Državna Založba Slovenije (State Publishing House of Slovenia), Ljubljana, 1952.

Menaše, Bernard. "O novom sistemu poslovanja u spoljnoj trgovini" (On the New System of Management in Foreign Trade), *Ekonomist*, Nos. 3–4, 1951.

*Mid-European Studies Center, *East Europe under the Communists*, Handbook Series, publ. by F. A. Praeger, 1957: *Czechoslovakia*—N. Spulber and V. Bušek, editors; *Poland*—O. Halecki, editor; *Hungary*—E. Helmreich, editor; *Romania*—S. Fischer-Galati, editor; *Yugoslavia*—R. F. Byrnes, editor; *Bulgaria*—L.A.D. Dellin, editor.

*Mid-European Law Project, *Economic Treaties and Agreements of the Soviet Bloc in Eastern Europe, 1945–51* (mimeo.), Mid-European Studies Center, New York, 1952.

*Mikoyan, A. I. "The Camp of Socialism and the Camp of Capitalism," speech of March 10, 1950, Foreign Languages Publishing House, Moscow, 1952.

*Miljević, Djordje, Stevan Blagojević, and Miloje Nikolić, *Razvoj privrednog sistema FNRJ* (Development of the Economic System of Yugoslavia), Znanje (Knowledge), Belgrade, 1954.

*Milovanović Milorad. *Jugoslav Post-War Reconstruction Papers,* Office of Reconstruction and Economic Affairs, Government of Yugoslavia, New York, 1943.

Minc, Hilary. "Concerning the Basis of Planning in the People's Democracy," *FLP,* Nov. 18, 1949.

*Minc, Hilary. *Poland's Economy Present and Future,* Documents and Reports on Poland, No. 5, Polish Research and Information Service, New York, 1949.

*Minc, Hilary. The Polish Three-Year Plan, speech of Sept. 21, 1946, to the National Assembly, in *Changing Epoch Series,* No. 2, Birch Books, London, 1947.

*Minc, Hilary. "Sześcioletni Plan Rozwoju Gospodarczego i Budowy Podstaw Socjalizmu w Polsce" (The Six-Year Plan of Economic Development and the Construction of the Basis of Socialism in Poland), *Nowe Drogi,* IV, 22, 1950.

*Minc, Hilary. *Zadania Gospodarcze na 1951 Rok* (Economic Tasks for 1951), Książka i Wiedza (Book and Science), Warsaw, 1951.

Mishustin, D. D. "Kak Gitlerovskaia Germaniia grabit Okupirovannye Strany" (How Hitlerite Germany Plunders the Occupied Countries), *Bolshevik,* No. 18, (September 1941).

*Mishustin, D. D. *Vneshniaia Torgovlia SSSR* (The Foreign Trade of the USSR), Mezhdunarodnaia Kniga (International Book), Moscow, 1941.

Mládek, J. V., E. Šturc, and M. R. Wyczalkowski. "The Yugoslav Experiment in Decentralization," International Monetary Fund Staff Papers II, reprinted in C. Black, *Readings on Contemporary Eastern Europe,* Mid-European Studies Center, New York, 1953.

Mladenatz, G. "Reform of the National Bank of Romania," *RR,* No. 4–5 (August–September 1946).

Moghioroș, Alexandru. "Consolidation of Party of Working Class—Guarantee of Victory of Socialism in Romania," reprinted in *Documents Concerning the Right Deviation in the Romanian Workers' Party.*

*Moore, W. E. *Economic Demography of Eastern and Southeastern Europe,* League of Nations Study, publ. by Princeton University Press, Princeton, N. J., 1945.

*Morris, John. *Yugoslavia,* St. Botolph Publ. Co., London, 1948.

Nagy, Imre. "A kapitalizmusból a szocializmusba való átmenet néhány közgazdasági problémája a népi demokratikus országokban (Some Economic Problems of the Transition from Capitalism to Socialism in the People's Democratic Countries), *SS,* June 1953.

Nagy, Imre. "On Measures of Hungarian Working People's Party and Government Aimed at Raising the Standard of Living," *FLP,* July 17, 1953.

**Les Nationalisations en Europe orientale* (Nationalizations in Eastern Europe), Notes et études documentaires (Notes and Documentary Studies), No. 1592, La Documentation Française (French Documentation), Paris, March 1952.

**Nationalization of Industrial, Banking, Insurance, Mining and Transport Enterprises,* Ministry of Arts and Information, Bucharest, 1948.

"Návrh Směrnic Ustředního výboru KSČ pro sestavení druhého pětiletého planu rozvoje narodniho hospodářství ČSR na léta 1956–1960" (Draft directives of the CC of the Czechoslovak Communist Party for the Second Five Year Plan of Development of the Economy of Czechoslovakia), supplement to *RP,* May 4, 1956.

"Die neue Jugoslawische Agrargesetzgebung und Agrarpolitik" (The New Yugo-

slav Agrarian Law and Agrarian Policy), *Wissenschaftlicher Dienst Sudosteuropa,* July 31, 1953.
**Observations concernant le Projet de Traité de Paix avec le Roumanie* (Observations Concerning the Draft Peace Treaty with Romania), Ministère des Finances de Roumanie (Ministry of Finance of Romania), Paris, 1946.
**Occupied Europe,* Royal Institute of International Affairs, London, 1944.
Ohlin, B. "Protection and Non-Competing Groups," *Weltwirtschaftliches Archiv,* XXXIII, 1 (1931).
**On People's Democracy in Yugoslavia,* Yugoslav Information Center, New York, 1949.
"O Rozwoju rolnictwa v latach 1956–1960 i zadaniach partii na wsi. Uchwata V. Plenum Komitetu Centralnego *PZPR*" (On the Development of Agriculture during the years 1956–1960 and the tasks of the Party in the Countryside. Resolution of the Vth Plenum of the CC of the Polish United Workers' Party), *TL,* Feb. 11, 1956.
"O wynikach wykonania Planu Sześcioletniego i Podstowowych Założeniach Planu Piecioletniego v latach 1956–60. Uchwała VII Plenum Komitetu Centralnego Pzpr" (On the Results on the Fulfillment of the Six Year Plan and on the Basic Premises of the Five Year Plan 1956–1960. Resolution of the VII Plenum of the Central Committee of the Polish United Workers' Party), *TL,* Aug. 3, 1956.
Paliiski, Ivan. "Novi Sotsilisticheski Merki v Bankovata Sistema" (New Socialist Measures in the Banking System), *PK,* No. 5, 1950.
**The Penetration of German Capital in Europe,* Inter-Allied Information Committee, H. M. Stationery Office, London, 1943.
Perović, Marko. "Osnovni principi reorganizacije spoljne trgovine FNRJ," (The Basic Principles in the Reorganization of the Foreign Trade of the FPRY), *Ekonomist,* No. 5–6, 1950.
**Pervyi Piatiletnii Plan Razvitiia Narodnogo Khoziastva Chekhoslovakii* (First Five-Year Plan of Development of the Czechoslovak People's Republic), Izdátel'stvo Inostrannoi Literatury (Publishing House of Foreign Literature), Moscow, 1950.
Pešković, M., and M. Čečez. "Nacionalizacija u FNRJ i Istočno Evropskim zemljama" (Nationalization in Yugoslavia and in the East European Countries), *Ekonomist,* II, 5–6, 1950.
"Les Petroles roumains" (Romanian Petroleum), *EC,* II, 12 (May 1947).
**The Petroleum Data Book,* edited by H. J. Struth, publ. by Petroleum Engineer Publishing Co., Dallas, Texas, 1948.
**Petroleum Industry Record 1918–1948,* Oil Industry Information Committee, New York, 1949.
*Petrov, F. N., editor. *Balkanskie Strany* (The Balkan Countries), Gosudarstvennyi Nauchnyi Institut "Sovetskaia Entsiklopediia" (State Scientific Institute "The Soviet Encyclopedia"), Ogiz, Moscow, 1946.
Petrovski, D. "Economic Development in the Countries of Popular Democracy," *New Times,* No. 8, 1949.
Pizanty, Mihail. "Some Post-War Aspects of the Romanian Oil Industry," *RR,* No. 7 (November 1946).
**Planirovanie Narodnogo Khoziastvo Vengrii, Sbornik Materialov* (Planning of Hungarian People's Economy, Collection of Materials), Izdatel'stvo Inostrannoi Literatury (Publishing House of Foreign Literature), Moscow, 1950.
"Le Plan polonais" (The Polish Plan), *EC,* II, 14–15 (July–August 1947).

*_Le Plan quinquennal roumain_ (The Romanian Five Year Plan), Notes et études Documentaires (Notes and Documentary Studies), No. 1534, La Documentation Française (French Documentation), Paris, Sept. 28, 1951.

"Podaci o posleratnom privrednom razvitku SSSR i zemalja Istočne Evrope" (Data on the Postwar Economic Development of the USSR and of the East European Countries), _Dokumentacioni Bilten,_ No. 8–9, 1954.

Polanyi, Ilona. "The Issues in Hungary," _World Affairs,_ No. 2–3, 1948–1949.

*_Polish National Economic Plan of Economic Reconstruction for the Period of January 1, 1949–December 31, 1949,_ Warsaw, 1946.

Popov, Christo. "Natsionalniiat Dokhod i Kapitalovlozheniia (National Income and Investment), _PK,_ No. 4, 1949.

Popovic, Milentije. "O ekonomskim odnosima izmedju socijalističkih država" (On the Economic Relations among the Socialist States), _Communist,_ July 1949.

*Pounds, N. J. G., and N. Spulber, editors. _Resources and Planning in Eastern Europe,_ Slavic and East European Series, Vol. 4, Bloomington, Indiana University Publications, 1957.

*_Prijedlog drustvenog plana FNRJ 1954_ (Proposal of the Yugoslav Social Plan for 1954), Belgrade, 1954.

*_Privreda FNRJ u 1952 godini s osvrtom na posleratni razvoj_ (Yugoslav Economy in 1952 with Reference to Postwar Development), Ekonomski Institut FNRJ (Economic Institute FPRY), Belgrade, 1953.

*_Le problème agraire dans les democraties populaires_ (The Agrarian Problem in the Popular Democracies), Notes et études Documentaires (Notes and Documentary Studies), No. 1799, La Documentation Française (French Documentation), Paris (September 1953).

*_Le programme roumain de redressement_ (The Romanian Recovery Program), Notes et études Documentaires (Notes and Documentary Studies), No. 710, La Documentation Française (French Documentation), Paris, August 26, 1947.

*_Prvni Československý Plan_ (The First Czechoslovak Plan), Ministry of Information, Prague, 1946.

*Puczyński, Bohdan. _Geografia Gospodarcza Polski_ (Economic Geography of Poland), Nakladem Państwowego Wydawnictwa Naukowego (State Scientific Publishing House), Warsaw, 1953.

*_Le Puissant mouvement populaire pour le renversement de gouvernement Radescu_ (The Powerful Popular Movement for the Overthrow of the Radescu Government), Ministry of Foreign Affairs of the Romanian People's Republic, Bucharest, 1952.

Rákosi, Mátyás. "On the Political Situation and Tasks of the Party-Resolution of the Central Committee of the Hungarian Working Peoples' Party" (March 2–4, 1955), _FLP,_ March 11, 1955.

Rákosi, Mátyás. "Report at the Central Committee of the Hungarian Working People's Party, Plenum of October 31, 1953," _FLP,_ Nov. 20, 1953.

Ralchev, Lazar. "Activnosta na Bankite na Zemedelskite Svetovni Cooperativi" (The Activity of the Banking Agencies of the Agricultural Universal Cooperatives), _PK,_ 3, 1948.

*Ramzaitsev, A. F. _Pravovye Voprosy Vneshnei Torgovli SSSR_ (Legal Questions of the Foreign Trade of the USSR), Vneshtorgizdat, Moscow, 1954.

*_Rapports du Conseil d'administration et du Conseil des censeurs_ (Reports of the

Council of Administration and of the Council of Censors), Banque Nationale de Roumanie (National Bank of Romania), Bucharest, annually.

Rastovčan, Pavao. *Pravo Zemljoradničkih zadruga* (Law on Agricultural Producers' Cooperatives), Zagreb, 1950.

Les Récentes experiences monétaires a l'etranger (Recent Foreign Monetary Experiences), Notes et études Documentaires (Notes and Documentary Studies), No. 604, La Documentation Française (French Documentation), Paris (Sept. 15, 1946).

**La Reforme agraire en Roumanie* (The Land Reform in Romania), Ministry of Information, Office of Foreign Cultural Relations, Bucharest, November 1946.

"Les relations extérierures de la Pologne," *EC,* IV, 5.

"Reorganization of Czechoslovak Industry," *Bulletin of the National Bank of Czechoslovakia,* May 1949.

"Report of the Central Bureau of Statistics on Economic Progress and the Trends of Material and Cultural Standards of the Population during the first Five-Year Plan 1950–1954," *Hungarian Review,* No. 6, June 1955.

**Reports to the Annual Meetings of the General Assembly of the National Bank of Hungary,* National Bank of Hungary, Budapest.

*Riauzov, N. N., and N. P. Titel'baum. *Statistika Sovetskoi Torgovli* (Statistics of Soviet Trade), Gostorgizdat, Moscow, 1951.

*Ripka, H. *Czechoslavakia Enslaved: The Story of the Communist Coup d'État,* Victor Gollancz, London, 1950.

*Rochlin, R. P., *Die Wirtschaft Polens von 1945 bis 1952* (The Economy of Poland from 1945 to 1952), Deutsches Institut fur Wirtschaftsforschung (German Institute for Economic Research), new series, No. 20, Duncker and Humblot, Berlin, 1953.

Rocznik Statystyczny (Statistical Yearbook), for 1949 and 1955 only. Głowny Urzad Statystyczny Polskiej Rzeczypospolitej Ludowey (Central Statistical Office of the Polish People's Republic), Warsaw, 1950 and 1956.

Rona, Francis. "Hungary's Banks before Nationalization," *The Banker,* July 1947.

Rónai, Gabor. "A Kelet-és Nyugat-Európa Közötti Kereskedelmi Kapcsolatok" (Trade Relations among East European Countries), *SS,* IV, 4 (April 1952).

Rosenstein-Rodan, P. N. *Agricultural Surplus Population in Eastern and South-Eastern Europe* (mimeo.), Royal Institute of International Affairs, London, 1943–45.

Rosenstein-Rodan, P. N. "Problems of Industrialisation of Eastern and South-Eastern Europe," *Economic Journal,* LIII, 1943.

*Schmidt, Dana Adams. *Anatomy of a Satellite,* Little, Brown and Co., Boston, 1952.

Schönfeld, I. "Problema Petrolului Romanesc" (The Problem of Romanian Petroleum), *PE,* No. 1 (Feb. 1948).

*Schwartz, Harry. *Russia's Soviet Economy,* Prentice-Hall, New York, 1951.

Selenyi, Dr. József. "A belkereskedelmi statisztika időszerű kérdései" (Timely Problems of Domestic Commercial Statistics), *SS,* XXXI, 5 (May 1953).

Serafin, Juliusz K. "Pieniądz i Bankowość" (Money and Banking), *Kultura,* Numer Krajowy (special issue on Poland), Vol. I, 1952.

*Šimacek, Radovan. *Czechoslovak Economy in a Nutshell,* Press Dept. of Czechoslovak Ministry of Foreign Trade, Prague, 1948,

*Simon, Brian. *Education in the New Poland,* Lawrence and Wishart, London, 1955.

Široký, Viliam. "Currency Reform and Abolition of Rationing in Czechoslovakia," *FLP,* June 5, 1953.

Široký, Viliam. "For Steady Advance of National Economy, for Raising Well-Being of the People of Czechoslovakia," *FLP,* Sept. 18, 1953.

Široký, Viliam. "Ekonomicheskoe Sotrudnichestvo—na uroven vozrosschikh zadach Sotsialisticheskih Gosudarstv" (Economic Cooperation on the Level of the Growing Tasks of the Socialist States), *Pravda,* April 6, 1956.

**The Six-Year Plan of Building the Foundations of Socialism 1950–1955,* Pol-Gos, Warsaw, 1951.

Slánský, Rudolf. "Report at the Conference of Nine Communist Parties in Poland," *FLP,* Dec. 15, 1947.

Smorgorzewski, Casimir. "Au Service de Staline," series in *Le Monde,* May 1952.

Sobaru, Al. "Despre Metodologia Planificării Circulației Mărfurilor cu Amănuntul" (On the Methodology of Planning the Circulation of Retail Trade), *PE,* No. 5–6 (June 1153).

**South-Eastern Europe: A Political and Economic Survey,* Royal Institute of International Affairs, Oxford University Press, London, 1939.

Spis Zakładów Przemysłowych 1945 (List of Industrial Enterprises), Statystyka Polski (Statistics of Poland), Series *D,* issue No. 3, Central Statistical Office, Warsaw, 1947.

Spulber, N. "Economic Thinking and Its Application and Methodology in Eastern Europe Outside of Soviet Russia," *The American Economic Review,* Vol. XLVI, No. 2, May 1956.

Spulber, N. "Effects of the Embargo on Soviet Trade," *Harvard Business Review,* XXX, 6 (November–December 1952).

Spulber, N. "On Yugoslavia's Trade Relations with the Soviet Bloc," *Economia Internazionale,* Vol. IX, No. 2, May 1956.

Spulber, N. "Problems of East-West Trade and Economic Trends in the European Satellites of Soviet Russia," *Economia Internazionale,* Vol. VIII, No. 3, August 1955.

Stalin, J. *Economic Problems of Socialism in the U.S.S.R.,* International Publishers, New York, 1952.

**Statistical Digest of the Czechoslovak Republic 1948,* State Statistical Office, Prague, 1948.

Statistical Yearbook of Poland, Central Statistical Office, Warsaw, annually.

Statistical Yearbook of the World Power Conferences, publ. by the Central Office of the World Power Conference, London, annually.

Statistika Spoljne Trgovine za 1939 (Statistics of Foreign Trade in 1939), Belgrade, 1940.

Statisticheski Godishnik' Na Tzarstvo Bălgariia—Annuaire statistique du royaume de Bulgarie (Statistical Yearbook of the Bulgarian Kingdom), Central Statistical Office, Sofia, prewar, annually.

Statistički Godišnjak FNRJ (Statistical Yearbook of the FPRY), Federal Statistical Office, Belgrade.

Statistički Godišnjak Kraljevine Jugoslavije—Annuaire statistique (Statistical Yearbook of the Kingdom of Yugoslavia), Central Statistical Office, Belgrade, prewar, annually.

Statistikata Na Vănshnata Tărgoviia (Statistics of Foreign Trade), Sofia, annually.

Statystyka Zakładów Przemyslowch i Rzemiesluiczych 1946 (Statistics of Industry and Crafts 1946), Statystyka Polski (Statistics of Poland), Series *D*, Central Statistical Office, Warsaw, 1948.

Stejskal, Dr. L. "Program Sčítání Zemědělských v.r. 1950" (Program of the Census of Agricultural Holdings in 1950), *SZ*, XIII, 2 (February 1950).

"Stočarstvo 1952" (Livestock 1952), *Statistički Bilten*, Series B, IV, No. 16, June 1953.

Studenski, P. "Methods of Estimating National Income in Soviet Russia," *Studies in Income and Wealth*, Vol. 8, National Bureau of Economic Research, New York, 1946.

**Survey of Poland*, Supplement to *The Statist*, Vol. CLXIV, No. 4107 (November 24, 1956).

*Switgall, Alfred. *La Pologne industrielle* (Industrial Poland), thesis, Montpellier, 1934.

Tătărescu, G. "Speech at the Paris Peace Conference," *RR*, II, 3–4, 1947.

*Terpeshev, Dobri. *Doklad o Piatiletnem Plane, Piatyi S'ezd B. K. P.* (Report on the Five-Year Plan at the Fifth Congress of the BWP), Izdatel'stvo Direktsii Pechati (Published by Department of Printing), Sofia, 1947.

*Tito, Marshal J. B. *For Independence and Equality*, Jugoslovenska Knjiga (Yugoslav Book), Belgrade, 1950.

**Today and Yesterday*, publ. by *HB*, Budapest, 1949.

Tomasevich, Jozo. "Collectivization of Agriculture in Yugoslavia" (mimeo.), Paper presented at a Seminar on Collectivization of Agriculture in Eastern Europe, University of Kentucky, April, 1955.

Transactions of the First World Power Conference, 5 vols., London, 1924.

Trnec, M. Miloslav. "Le Probleme de la nationalisation de l'industrie en Tchecoslovaquie" (The Problem of Nationalization of Industry in Czechoslovakia), *Droit Social*, IX, 4 (April 1946).

Trnka, Dr. V. "Representativní Šetření v Maloobchodě" (A Sampling Inquiry into Retail Trade), *SZ*, X, 1949.

Tsonu Tsontchev. "Campaniata v polza na capitalizievaneto na Bankovite Depoziti" (The Campaign in Favor of Capitalizing on Bank Deposits), *PK*, No. 3, 1948.

United Nations. "Developments in Trade between Eastern and Western Europe from 1950 to Mid-1952," *Economic Bulletin for Europe*, IV, No. 3.

United Nations. "Les Échanges commerciaux entre L'Europe orientale et l'Europe occidentale de 1951 a 1952" (Trade between East and West Europe from 1951 to 1952), *Economic Bulletin for Europe*, V, 2.

*United Nations Department of Economic Affairs. *The European Coal Problem*, New York, 1952.

*United Nations Department of Economic Affairs. *European Steel Trends in the Setting of the World Market*, New York, 1952.

*United Nations Department of Economic Affairs. *Progress in Land Reform: An Analysis of Replies by Governments to a United Nations Questionnaire*, New York, 1954.

*United Nations Department of Economic Affairs. *World Energy Supplies in Selected Years, 1929–1950*, Statistical Papers, Series J, No. 1, New York, 1952.

*United Nations Department of Economic Affairs. *World Iron Ore Resources and their Utilization*, New York, 1950.

*United Nations Department of Economic and Social Affairs. *Processes and Problems of Industrialization in Under-Developed Countries*, New York, 1955.

*United Nations Economic Commission for Europe. *Étude générale des industries mecaniques en Europe* (Survey of European Engineering Industries) (mimeo.), Geneva, 1951.

*United Nations Economic Commission for Europe. *The European Steel Market in 1953* (mimeo.), Geneva, 1954: and in 1954 (mimeo.), Geneva, 1955.

*United Nations Economic Commission for Europe. *The European Tractor Industry in the Setting of the World Market* (mimeo.), Geneva, 1952.

*United Nations Economic Commission for Europe. *Prospects of Exporting Electric Power from Yugoslavia* (mimeo.), Geneva, 1955.

*United Nations Economic Commission for Europe. *Quelques Aspects techniques du transport de l'énergie électrique* (Some Technical Aspects of the Transport of Electric Power) (mimeo.), Geneva, 1952.

*United Nations Economic Commission for Europe. *Transfers of Electric Power Across European Frontiers* (mimeo.), Geneva, 1952.

*United Nations International Labor Office. *Ad-Hoc Committee on Forced Labor. Supplement No. 13 of the Official Records of the Sixteenth Session of the Council and No. 36 of the Studies and Reports (New Series) of the International Labor Office*, Geneva, 1953.

*United Nations Relief and Rehabilitation Association. *Industrial Rehabilitation in Poland*, Operational Analysis Paper No. 35, New York, 1947.

*United States Congress, Mutual Defense Assistance Control Act of 1951, Public Law 213–82d Congress: Act and Accompanying Documents and Reports to Congress:
I. *A Program for the Denial of Strategic Goods to the Soviet Bloc;* II. *Problems of Economic Defense;* III. *World-Wide Enforcement of Strategic Trade Controls;* IV. *East-West Trade Trends;* V. *The Revision of Strategic Trade Controls;* VI. *Soviet Bloc Economic Activities in the Free World.* US Govt. Printing Office, Washington, D. C., 1951–55.

*United States Congress, Legislative Reference Service of the Library of Congress. *Trends in Economic Growth, A comparison of the Western Powers and the Soviet Bloc.* A study prepared for the Joint Committee on the Economic Report, 83rd Congress, US Govt. Printing Office, Washington, D. C., 1955.

*United States Congress. Subcommittee on Foreign Economic Policy, Committee on Foreign Affairs of the House of Representatives. 83rd Congress, Second Session: *East-West Trade*, US Govt. Printing Office, Washington, D. C., February 16, 1954.

*United States Congress. Subcommittee on Technical Assistance Programs. *Soviet Technical Assistance in Non-Communist Area.* Printed for the Committee on Foreign Relations, 84th Congress.

*United States Department of Commerce. Bureau of the Census. *The Population of Yugoslavia*, by Paul F. Myers and Arthur A. Campbell. International Population Statistics Reports, Series P–90, No. 5, US Govt. Printing Office, Washington, D. C., 1954.

*United States Department of Commerce, Bureau of Foreign and Domestic Commerce, International Economic Analysis Division. *Chemical Developments Abroad, 1939: Effect of Munitions and Preparedness upon Chemical Production,*

Consumption and Foreign Trade, Trade Promotion Series No. 211, Washington, D. C., 1940.

United States Department of Commerce. Bureau of Foreign and Domestic Commerce, International Economic Analysis Division. *World Chemical Developments,* Washington, D. C., annually.

*United States Department of State. *Treaties and Other International Acts Series,* Washington, D. C., 1947.

*United States Department of War. *Organization of the Iron and Steel Industry of Enemy Europe,* No. 31–35, Washington, D. C., 1945.

*United States Military Government in Germany, Finance Division. *Dresdner and Deutsche Banks.* Special Report to the Military Governor (mimeo.). Frankfurt/Main, June 1947.

United States Military Government in Germany. High Commissioner for Germany. *Report on Germany,* Fifth Quarterly Report, Frankfort-am-Mein, October–December 1950.

*Vaganov, B. S. *Voprosy Organizatsii Vneshnei Torgovli Stran Narodnoi Democratsii* (Problems of the Organization of Foreign Trade of the Countries of People's Democracy), Vneshtorgizdat, Moscow, 1954.

*Valev, E. B. *Bolgariia: Ekonomiko-Geograficheskoe Opisanie* (Bulgaria: Economic-Geographic Survey), Gosudarstvennoe Izdatel'stvo Geograficheskoi Literatury (State Publishing House of Geographic Literature), Moscow, 1949.

*Valev, E. B. *Narodnaia Respublika Bolgariia* (The Bulgarian People's Republic), Voennoe Izdatel'stvo Voennogo Ministerstva Soiuza SSSR (Military Publishing House of the War Ministry of the USSR), Moscow, 1952.

Vanagas, Iu. "Reorganizatsia Vneshnei Torgovli Vengrii" (Reorganization of the Foreign Trade of Hungary), *VT,* No. 1, 1949.

Varga, E. "Kontsentratsiia i Tsentralizatsiia Proizvodstva i Kapitala vo Vremia Voiny" (Concentration and Centralization of Production and Capital during the War), *Mirovoe Khoziaistvo i Mirovaia Politika,* No. 7–8, 1944.

*Vas Zoltán: *A hároméves terv befejezése—népünk győzelme* (The Completion of the Three-Year Plan—A Victory of Our People), Budapest, 1950.

Vasiljević, Dr. Kosta. "Pitanje organizacije plaćanja u privredi" (The Question of the Organization of Payments in the Economy), *Ekonomist,* No. 3–4, 1951.

"Vătreshen Pregled, Bălgarskoto Stopanstvo ot Sept. 1947 do Sept. 1948" (Domestic Outlook of the Bulgarian Economy), *PK,* No. 2, 1948.

*Voicu, Ştefan. "The New Economic Romanian-Soviet Agreements," *RR,* No. 11–12 (April 1947).

*Voinea, Serban. *La Socialisation* (Socialization), Presses universitaires de France (University Presses of France), Paris, 1950.

*Vučković, Dr. Miloš. *Uloga i organizacija banaka i kredita u FNRJ* (The Role and Organization of Banking and Credit in the FPRY), Rad, Belgrade, 1953.

Vukmanovič-Tempo, S. "Principi društvenog plana za iduću godinu" (Principles of the Social Plan for the Next Year), *Borba,* Oct. 18, 1955.

Vukmanovič-Tempo, S. "Usklađjivanje privrednog razvitka i podizanje životnog standarda" (The Coordination of Economic Development and Raising of the Living Standard), *Borba,* Oct. 11, 1955.

*Wasowicz, Jozef. *Outline of Economic Geography,* Polonia, Warsaw, 1955.

**White Book on Aggressive Activities by the Governments of the USSR, Poland,*

Czechoslovakia, Hungary, Romania, Bulgaria and Albania towards Yugoslavia, Ministry of Foreign Affairs of the FPRY, Belgrade, 1951.

**Wieś w Liczbach w Polsce Burżuazyjno-obszarniczej i w Polsce Ludowej* (The Countryside in Figures in Bourgeois-Feudal Poland and in People's Poland), Książka i Wiedza (Book and Science), Warsaw, 1st ed. 1952, 3rd ed. 1954.

Wiktorowicz, S. "Przemysl Panstwowy" (State Industry), *Kultura,* Numer Krajowy (special issue on Poland), Vol. II, 1952.

*Wronski, Henri. *Le Rôle économique et social de la monnaie dans les democraties populaires. La reforme monnetaire polonaise 1950–1953* (The Economic and Social Role of Money in the People's Democracies. The Polish Monetary Reform 1950–1953), Riviere et cie., Paris, 1954.

*Wszelaki, Jan H. *Fuel and Power in Captive Middle Europe,* Mid-European Studies Center, New York, 1952.

**Yougoslavie: Articles et documents* (Yugoslavia: Articles and Documents). Notes et études documentaires (Notes and Documentary Studies), No. 670, La Documentation Française (French Documentation), Paris, 1946.

**La Yugoslavie économique* (The Economy of Yugoslavia), Bureau du Commerce Exterieur (Office of Foreign Trade), Belgrade, 1935.

Zahranični Obchod (Foreign Trade of the Czechoslovak Republic), Prague, annually.

*Zaleski, Eugène. *Les Courants commerciaux de l'Europe danubienne au cours de la première moitié du XXè siecle* (Commercial Currents in Danubian Europe during the First Half of the 20th Century), Librairie générale de droit et de jurisprudence (General Library of Law and Jurisprudence), Paris, 1952.

*Zaltsman, L. M., V. A. Babitskii, M. M. Broshchul, and M. I. Vesnik. *Organizatsiia Sotsialisticheskih Selsko-Khoziaistvennykh Predpriiatii* (The Organization of Socialist Agricultural Undertakings), Ogiz-Soc-Khogiz, Moscow, 1947.

Zambrowski, R. "Development of Agriculture in Poland," *FLP,* Sept. 14, 1951.

"Zaměstnanost v Průmyslu" (Employment in Industry), *SZ,* IX, 7, 8 (1946).

Zeigher, I. "La Collaboration roumano-sovietique" (Romanian-Soviet Collaboration), *PE,* No. 3, 1948.

*Zmrhal, Antonín. *Československý Vnitřní Obchod* (Czechoslovak Domestic Trade), USO, Prague, 1947.

Zólkiewski, Stefan. "Polish Science Serves the People," *FLP,* May 24, 1953.

INDEX

www.ingramcontent.com/pod-product-compliance
Ingram Content Group UK Ltd.
Pitfield, Milton Keynes, MK11 3LW, UK
UKHW020222290926
15470UKWH00001B/339

9 780837 186092